Economic Resilience During Overlapped Crises

Emil Dinga

Economic Resilience During Overlapped Crises

Antifragility, Sustainability and Autopoieticity

palgrave
macmillan

Emil Dinga
Centre for Financial and Monetary Research "Victor Slăvescu"
Romanian Academy
Bucharest, Romania

ISBN 978-3-031-80223-2 ISBN 978-3-031-80224-9 (eBook)
https://doi.org/10.1007/978-3-031-80224-9

This Palgrave Macmillan imprint is published by the registered company Springer Nature Switzerland AG.
The registered company address is: Gewerbestrasse 11, 6330 Cham, Switzerland

Preface

The Concept of the Economic

First of all, it must be clarified the concept of the economic—what is such a qualification of something as being economic, that is, *what the economic is it?*

The predicate economic[1] is quite ambiguous even in the literature—from the most academic approaches to the most empirical ones—and its use oscillates from the narrowest to the largest sphere, for example, from the activity that produces goods and services for biological consumption to the general praxeology (see here Austrian School, especially Ludwig von Mises).

So, there are two categories of definitions for the economic, as they are ventilated in the literature:

(a) *universal definitions* (which are applicable to any domain of human activity)
- denotate/referential: subjects (either cultural or non-cultural) who have the faculty to make choices (either consciously or unconsciously);
- logical ground: the concept of opportunity cost (cost of chance)—the maximum advantage that is given up when making a choice; we have here a *competition among resources*;
- vulnerability: any decision (including emotional—see Gary Becker's contributions—sporting, political, aesthetic, etc.) can be considered as being economic;

Nota bene: the definition does not exactly refer to the concept of *economic* but to that of *economizing/saving*, as a reflection of the principle of minimum action (Maupertuis's principle).

(b) *general definitions* (satisfying individual needs that condition biological existence)
- denotate/referential: individual subjects conditioned (either non-culturally or culturally) by biological survival (primitive component of Maslow's pyramid of needs);
- logical ground: survival instinct: subject competition; we have here a *competition among subjects*
- vulnerability: any subject (including a non-cultural one) is presumed to be an actional subject because it is conditioned by survival;
- *Nota bene*: aspects of socially conditioned survival needs are eliminated (e.g., budget expenditures would not represent an economic activity).

However, there is a character of economic that is held only by a certain kind of human action and that, therefore, can define non-ambiguously the concept of economic—this character is the entropic (in its standard Thermodynamic meaning) exchange between human being (as individual, group, society) and nature.[2]

In our opinion, the concept of economic must verify the following sufficiency predicates:

- *ontology* (e.g., Heisenberg's indeterminacy is not something economic, because it refers exclusively to knowledge and not to existence/ontology);
- *choice* (e.g., the movement of light on the space-time geodesic is not something economic, although it is an aspect of existence/ontology and, according to the above universal definitions, minimizes the required time on its trajectory);
- *purpose* (e.g., natural selection is not something economic, although it is also ontological status and involves choice as well);[3]
- *entropic exchange between human being and nature* (e.g., marriage is not something economic, although it has ontological status, involves a choice, and there is also a purpose).[4]

The "algorithm" to capture the economic in the most general way is illustrated in Fig. P.1.

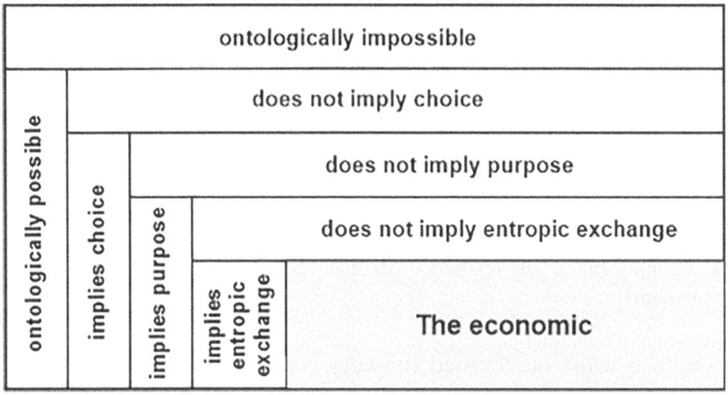

Fig. P.1 The logical separation of the economic. *Source*: Author

Elucidates:	*Relationship between:*		
	Object-object (O-O)	*Subject-object (S-O)*	*Subject-subject (S-S)*
The object	**Technical sciences** - Physics - Biology - Cosmology - Chemistry	**Artistical sciences** - Music - Painting - Sculpture - Literature - Architecture	**Practical sciences** - Critics - Politics - History - Metaphysics
The subject	**Logic sciences** - Logics - Accounting - Mathematics - Linguistics	**Praxeological sciences** - *Economics* - Sociology - Psychology - Theoretical philosophy	**Ethical sciences** - Religion - Morals Social philosophy

Fig. P.2 A general typology of sciences and the place of economics (a pure illustration). *Source*: (E. Dinga: *Social Time and the Economics of Science*, in Amfiteatru Economic, 24(16), Bucharest, Romania)

Nota bene: to establish the place of economics (or economic theory) it is useful to provide a general typology of sciences. We shall do that based on two criteria, which act simultaneously, in a matrix way: (a) relationship subject-object; (b) the entity elucidated by these relationships. Figure P.2 shows such a typology, from which we see that economics is a science regarding the relationships between subject and object, and it is aimed at elucidating the subject. We do not aspire to provide more than an illustrative/exemplificative picture, not an exhaustive one.

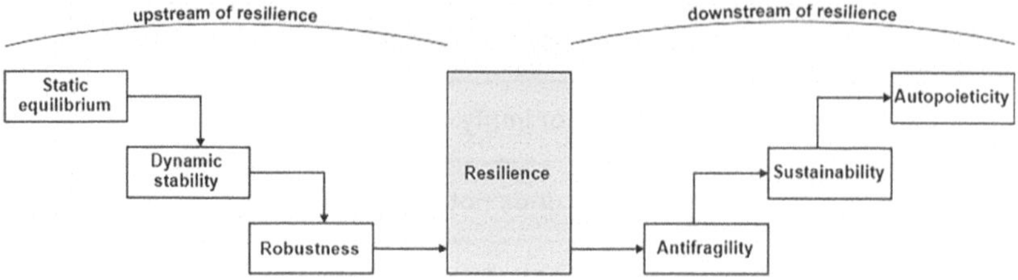

Fig. P.3 The place of resilience in the general movement of a system. *Source*: Author

Secondly, it must be clarified the very concept of resilience (especially, economic[5] resilience).

The kinematics and, especially, dynamics[6] of an economic/societal system are interlaced in a relatively inextricable network of processes, working both inside and outside that system. All these processes form a totality from which the system in the case is extracted only by the observer, according to his/her interest in knowledge and, after the case, action.[7] Consequently, to understand (better said, to explain) the system's kinematics/dynamics it is necessary to examine the basic, relevant and significant interactions between that system and the processes around it. In this book, the evoked processes are, based on an external logic, organized by considering the property and process of resilience (primarily economic resilience) of the system. So, according to this logic, there are some processes/properties[8] that work in the system's upstream, related to resilience, and some processes/properties that work in the system's downstream, related to resilience. The mentioned logical is called external since it is provided by the very definitions of those processes/properties and, as well-known, any *definiens* is external to the *definiendum*, although, of course, the definiens must capture, as specific as possible, the referential which objectifies the definiendum. The place of resilience in the network of processes in a generic system can be represented as in Fig. P.3.

The Properties Around the Property of Resilience

Processes/Properties in the Upstream of the System

In the upstream of the resilience stay the following processes/properties: (a) (*F2*) static equilibrium; (b) (*F3*) dynamic stability; (c) (*F4*) robustness. A short description of them is provided below.

(a) (*F2*) static equilibrium

Description: the entity must maintain its basic parameters in a reciprocal balance, from a causality and conditionality perspective.

An economic system is in static equilibrium if and when two or many causal interrelated variables or parameters are positioned as value or kinematics so that their changes are improbable in the short term. This improbability is an objective one (however, it is not of frequential Kolmogorov type); more exactly, it is a propensity probability (i.e., an objective probability of a singular event) as Popper has proposed. For an observer, to establish the static equilibrium it is always needed for an arbitrator (usually, a third) that is the causal result of at least two variables or parameters in the system—e.g., the equilibrium price, that is the third for the quantity demanded a good/service and the quantity supplied for the same good/service. The very condition for having a static equilibrium in that system is that the third is stable in the short term. Of course, in an economic system, there are many pairs (or, after the case, *n*-tuples) of variables or parameters that generate thirds; however, an attentive examination could lead to a small number of such pairs or *n*-tuples for which the thirds are stable on the short term. *Nota bene*: the stability is not exactly a stationarity; some (pre-established) gaps from the stationarity point are allowed, so the stability of the third, so, by extension, the static equilibrium, is always a pre-decision (a desirability) of the subject/observer/analyst.

(b) (*F3*) dynamic stability

Description: the entity must have its own resources to keep itself on the specific trajectory (chreode), according to its nature.

An economic system is in dynamic (or kinematic[9]) stability if its static equilibrium maintains itself inside an (also pre-established) tunnel of variation on medium and, especially, in the long term. It is to be mentioned that the assessment of the dynamic equilibrium is also based on the third, as defined for static equilibrium, which means that the third in the case must not exceed the established tunnel's borders. There are three main differences between dynamic equilibrium and static equilibrium: (a) it is (usually) possible that the variations or oscillations of the third are allowed in larger values than the variations or oscillations in the static equilibrium case; (b) dynamic equilibrium is relevant in long term only; (c) dynamic equilibrium is liable to be connected (see later) with the sustainability paradigm. In fact, dynamic equilibrium is a static equilibrium of static equilibrium. *Nota bene*: what about the medium term? From the perspective of equilibrium, the medium term is not too significant—both static equilibrium and dynamic equilibrium can "bite", from the medium term, one from a side, and the other from the other side, until this term is exhausted.

(c) (*F*4) robustness

Description: the entity must be capable of resisting perturbation (either from inside or from outside), of any nature, at least a period of time or, more exactly, to the threshold of break/capitulation.

An economic system is robust, as shown above, if it has internal principles (means, resources, know-how, etc.) to resist perturbations (either internal or external). To resist perturbations means to preserve its identity, that is, its structure, and, so, its functions.[10] Robustness is a grid property, that is its potential is limited by a ceiling threshold, upper which the quantity of perturbation (perturbation's intensity multiplied by the duration of perturbation exerting) certainty leads to infringement of the system. Since robustness constitutes one of the key factors/properties in providing economic soundness, more analytical considerations will be delivered below.

The general meaning of the concept of robustness is that of resistance to suffered action—shock, disturbance or any other impact, whether predictable or not. By resistance we will understand two alternative things: (a) preservation of the state of the system on which the action exerts; (b) preservation of the trajectory (kinematics) of the system on which the action exerts. It should be observed that the action exerted on the system can come both from outside the system and from within it.[11] An interesting and usually quite frequent case is when the internal action can trigger an external action (either convergent or divergent with the first) or, conversely, an external action can trigger an internal action (either convergent or divergent with the first). In the same vein, an action can trigger other actions with the same origin and so on. So, the issue of action, from the perspective of robustness (but also from the perspective of the other two mentioned phenomena, of course), is complicated[12]—one can talk here about a true "physiology" of action.[13]

First of all, we can only talk about robustness in relation to a given system, explicitly "extracted" from the environment in which it operates. In other words, robustness does not exist as such, but only as a property of an already established system, that is, it is a property *associated* (assigned) to a system, of whatever type it may be.

Secondly, it should be noted that robustness (more precisely, the property of robustness) is a passive property, in the sense that it is activated only when some action is taken (either from within the system or from outside it). Logically, then, robustness is a reaction, not an action. This characteristic is especially important, because a reaction (like an action, for that matter) must be foetal.[14]

Thirdly, as above mentioned, robustness (more precisely, its manifestation) is of a discrete type, that is, it takes response values (or reacts to action values) only when a threshold is reached (when the receptor system is affected) or at the value of a certain threshold (when the receptor system reacts). The fact that robustness is provided with thresholds should be considered because, generally, in economics, any phenomenon is of a discrete type (including the decision-making process, of course).[15]

Fourthly, robustness can act either discretionarily or automatically. Discretionary action refers to action that follows an explicit, current decision, while automatic action is the effect of a non-current explicit decision[16] that is "encapsulated" into a discretionarily implemented device.[17]

Fifthly, robustness, as a property of the system, is subject to both purely functional (technical) attrition and obsolescence as a result of its operation. Of course, together with technical attrition and the occurrence of obsolescence, the opposite phenomenon can occur (and usually does): improvement, so that, over time, the state and quality of the robustness property of a system is, in fact, a result *sui generis* of the kinematics (and inter-action) of obsolescence and improvement, including innovation.[18]

Processes/Properties in the Downstream of the System

In the downstream of the resilience stay the following processes/properties: (a) (*F*6) antifragility; (b) (*F*7) sustainability; (c) (*F*8) autopoiesis. A short description of them is provided below.

(a) (*F*6) antifragility

Description: the entity must have its own principles to fructify the new state or the new dynamic position on the trajectory (if the resilience is non-performative) so as to gain from the very actualized perturbation (Taleb, 2012).

The concept of antifragility with its basic denotations and connotations is introduced by Nassim Nicholas Taleb[19] (2012). The author does not intend to carry out a systematic treatment, possibly starting from the logical foundations of the concept and going to its institutional, ethical and civilizational aspects, although aspects regarding these (possible) dimensions of the concept of antifragility are, in some places, illuminated in the colloquial (though not superficial) style preferred by the author.

In this paragraph, where we shall present and analyse the concept of antifragility, the method applied will be far from that used by Taleb, more precisely, as we have done with the other two previous concepts, robustness and resilience (and as we shall do, of course, with the concept of sustainability, which follows), we shall use the logical and conceptual method.

Like robustness, antifragility is a property of systems. A working definition of antifragility, without too much pretensions to rigour, for now (but which will help us to formulate such a rigorous definition later), could be the following: a structural property of systems capable of generating advantages for the system (not it matters, for the time being, of what type or nature) from the disturbances suffered by that system. So, we have some concepts that intervene in this provisional formulation of the definition of antifragility and that need to be clarified as rigorously as possible: (a) ownership (but this concept has already been examined previously); (b) structural character (this concept was also previously examined); (c) advantage; (d) disruption. Therefore, we have to examine in detail the concepts of advantage and disruption, respectively.

The advantage (in the most general sense) means an excess of the effect over the effort associated with that effect.[20] Of course, there can also be a case where the effort is zero; for example, in economics, the so-called undue (windfall) profit is an advantage even though the effort to obtain it is zero, such as when prices fall and so the purchasing power of nominal income increases—this increase in purchasing power is an advantage. In a case where we have monetary measures of the effect, that is, the effort, the advantage can be formulated as an excess of income over cost, that is, what we call gain (or what is also called profit[21]).

Advantage has both an objective and a subjective dimension. The objective dimension of the advantage refers to the generally accepted community (or analyst) measure of that advantage—for example, an economic advantage is measured by money. The objective dimension is opposable to all interested individuals (or groups, as the case may be) and generally serves calculation and comparisons (e.g., accounting, either microeconomic[22]—at the level of the organization—or macroeconomic—at the level of the national economy[23]). The subjective dimension of the advantage refers to the perception that each individual has related to a certain objective value of the advantage. It is not necessary to develop, in this study, considerations regarding economic value (such considerations go far beyond the objectives we have set), but we shall examine some aspects of the concept of marginal utility, which, this time, is necessarily associated with the purpose of the present study.

As is known, (total) utility is a concept that refers to the potential/capacity of an entity (for the economic case it is a good or a service) to satisfy a fixed economic need.[24] Since, following the social division of labour, it is impossible for an individual or even a community, however large (including a state or nation) to have the material and energy resources, labour and technology capable of satisfying all economic needs of the individual, respectively of the community, economic exchange appeared. Economic exchange takes place, ultimately, between two products/services, each with its own utility (currency is only a technical intermediary, reducing the transaction cost[25] of economic exchange). In this exchange, the subjective dimension of the concept of advantage intervenes, which is called *marginal utility*.[26] More precisely, it is about the assessment that each individual participating in the act of economic exchange makes regarding the difference between the utility s/he gave up and the utility s/he received within that act of exchange. I was saying above that economic exchange takes place, in the last instance, between two goods/services, but in the first instance (at least in modern monetary economies), the exchange takes place between a good/service, on the one part, and money, on the other part. We shall do a specific analysis for this case.

- be a good/service (we shall call the genus incorporating these two species the syntagma real commodity), denoted by R, and another good or service which, in the first instance, as said before, is represented by money, denoted by M;
- the quantities exchanged between them will be denoted respectively by q_R and q_M;
- the reason an economic agent holding R wants to give up the quantity q_R in exchange for the quantity q_M consists in the fact that he has an excess of R and a deficit of M;[27]

- symmetrically, the reason an economic agent holding *M* wants to give up the quantity q_M in exchange for the quantity q_R consists in the fact that he has an excess of *M* and a deficit of *R*;
- suppose that the monetary (market) values of the two goods[28] are equal, i.e.: $V_{q_R} = V_{q_R}$, so we shall admit that will be exchanged (monetary) equivalents;
- *prima facie*, it seems that the two economic agents participating in the economic exchange neither win nor lose, since they exchange equivalents (e.g., the agent who sells therefore receives the quantity of money q_M and will be able to exchange it finally for a quantity of the desired good (R'), let's say, $q_{R'}$, so the exchange of equivalents is preserved);
- exchanging equivalents, from a monetary point of view, it would appear that neither of the two economic agents obtains any advantage (and, for that matter, does not register any loss). This conclusion is incorrect from at least two perspectives:
  - the perspective of *use* utility (value): each agent has obtained what s/he lacks (or what he wanted), giving up something s/he has in excess—so it can be said that each of them obtains a substantive advantage.[29] The use-value perspective is a background perspective, because economic agents pursue this use-value only in the last instance, while, in the first instance they pursue exchange value (price). But, as we have shown, even if the price of economic exchange (price, which, is unique) refers to exchange values that are equal for the two traders, since the use values (more precisely, the meanings of the use values) are different for the two partners of the economic exchange, it follows that each of them appreciates that s/he got more than s/he gave in exchange;
  - the perspective of *intensional*[30] utility (value): many times, the economic exchange, which has as its ultimate goal the obtaining of the use value in deficit (as shown previously), can have (and, in fact, has), in the first instance or in the first instances, a purpose that is limited to exchange value. As the exchange value is the same (since a certain transaction price is agreed upon at which the exchange takes place), it would follow that, from this perspective, no one gains any advantage. However, this time too, each of the participants in the economic exchange gains an advantage.[31] The advantage is also generated by deficits, but not from the perspective of use value, but from that of exchange value. (*Nota bene*: of

course, also in this case, evaluating the existence of the advantage and, in many cases, even its size is an effect of individual idiosyncrasy.) Let us resume the notations proposed above, to which we shall add others, in order to formalize a short reasoning.

(b) (*F7*) sustainability

Description: the entity has the capability to maintain itself inside a dynamic tunnel of parametrical variation. (*Nota bene*: sustainability is a long-term stability.[32])

Elsewhere, we have addressed the concept of sustainability (it is true, in rather general lines), but this time, the approach will be much more analytical and, as far as possible, formalized.

Sustainability is discussed (and, above all, written) a lot, often in a non-rigorous way,[33] which leads to an approximate, if not downright erroneous, understanding of it. In our opinion, a correct understanding of this concept can only be obtained by discussing it within the entire conceptual family that contains it. Our position is that sustainability is a property (in fact, a structural property) of a system/entity/process.

As it is known, there are three real entities and only three, from an abstract point of view: things, properties and relations. Choosing the property as the one that ultimately qualifies the concept of sustainability is based on the following considerations:

- sustainability can be associated with any of the three entities: for example, associated with things, it is called *durability*,[34] while associated with relationships, it is called *viability*;
- considering sustainability as a property is intended to ensure a predicate of sufficiency (which will be discussed below), namely its persistence (especially over time but, with strict precautions, also in space). Generally, the greatest persistence should be given to things, then to properties and finally to relationships. Somehow, choosing property as the "headquarters" of sustainability is a middle ground;
- by granting to sustainability the status of property, we implicitly refer to the idea that sustainability must be inherent to the structure of the system—the only way to ensure the persistence and (the most important thing, as we will show later) the replicability of the system in question;

- although there are discussions, still unresolved, in the specialized literature, regarding the priority of either the property or, respectively, the relationship in the general processuality,[35] we incline towards the position that considers that the property is the generator of the relationship and not vice versa, precisely by virtue of the fact that the property is structural in nature, while the relationship is functional in nature and, as accepted in systems theory (and obviously in Darwinian evolutionary theory), structure generates function, not the other way around (as, e.g., Lamarckian evolutionary theory requires).

To give a definition of the sustainability property of a system, we will need to identify and justify the set of sufficiency predicates of this property. Before that (see Chap. 1), we will provide a brief framing of the problem.

As previously shown, sustainability is associated with property, which means that the sufficiency predicates of sustainability must in turn be of the nature of properties. To understand the concept of property, we will examine the essence of the three ontological entities. Thus, we consider the essence (eidos, as a phenomenologist would say, or quiddity) of the thing to be its structure, the essence of property to be its function and the essence of relationship to be the very process. We can say, in an attempt to make these correlations as intelligible as possible, the following: durability is a property of thing, sustainability is a property of property, viability is a property of the relationship between things, and autopoieticity is a property of the relationship between properties.

We give a synoptic graphical image of these ideas in Fig. P.4 (where $x(y)$ denotes the application of entity x to entity y, where $x, y \in \{L, P, R\}$: L means things, P means properties, R means relationships).

Short Comment

- $T(T)$: things of things—*supra-systems* (aggregated, integrated, etc.): aims at the formation of things from things, common phenomenon of nature, life and culture;
- $T(P)$: things of properties—(?): needs further thought (postponed in this study);
- $T(R)$: things of relationships—(?): needs further reflection (postponed in this study);

y x	things	properties	relationships
things	supra-systems $T(T)$	? $T(P)$	? $T(R)$
properties	durability $P(T)$	*sustainability* $P(P)$	viability $P(R)$
relationships	? $R(T)$	autopoieticity $R(P)$	? $R(R)$

Fig. P.4 The (logical) combination of the three ontological entities. *Source*: Author

- $P(T)$: properties of things—***durability***: property of things (in principle), although this property has quantitative degrees (e.g., stone is more durable than wood, although both are things);
- $P(P)$: properties of properties—***sustainability***: we therefore believe that sustainability is a property, namely a property of properties;[36]
- $P(R)$: properties of relationships—***viability***: viability (***nota bene***: this concept is almost absent from the more demanding economic literature, although it deserves, in our opinion, greater attention because it is closely related to life and (co-)evolution) involves, unlike all previous concepts, values, i.e., it has an axiological imprint;
- $R(T)$: relationships of things—(?): needs further reflection (ignored in this study);
- $R(P)$: relationships of properties—***autopoieticity***: it is, in our opinion, the most "evolved" form of processuality, both in nature (highlighted by Maturana and Varela, since 1980) and in society.[37] It is, of course, to discuss separately the positioning of autopoieticity in Figure 25, namely as a relationship of properties or, equivalently, as a relationship between properties. We make a few comments on this:
  - in general, the previous forms of processuality (durability, sustainability, viability) were defined as being of the nature of property (all are positioned on the second line, which is the property line, in Figure 4);
  - autopoieticity, which is also a species of processuality, is positioned on the third line in Figure 25, that is, on the line that is under the "responsibility" of the relationship. It follows, *prima facie*, that autopoieticity is not of the nature of property, but of the nature of relationship;

- concretely, autopoieticity represents a relationship between properties. We will comment on this aspect:
    - the relationship property-relationship is a relationship, so to speak, without beginning or end, because a variation of the property (or of the properties put in the relationship) leads to a variation of the relationship (or relationships, as the case may be) between the properties and, reciprocally, a change in the relationship between the properties may lead to a change in the property (or related properties, as the case may be);[38]
    - so, at least from the point of view of dynamics, it is quite difficult to distinguish between property of relationship and relationship of property. As a result, since we nevertheless notice a (causal) dominance of the relationship compared to the property in terms of the essence of autopoieticity, we have considered the latter to be a *sui generis* property, namely a property of ... the relationship between properties. As the objective of the present study is sustainability, we leave the necessary reflections on the nature of autopoieticity to the discretion of the reader.
- *R*(*R*): relationships of relationships—(?): requires further reflection (deferred in this study).

(c) (*F*8) autopoiesis

Description: the entity has its own principles and resources for self-organizing, self-repairing and evolving, based on a general cognition about the environment and on getting its niches in that environment. The considerations of below are synthesized from Dinga et al. (2023).

The hypothesis we want to build regarding the functioning of the financial market is the hypothesis of autopoieticity or, in other words, the hypothesis of the autopoietic market. To this end, next, we will make an overview of the concept of autopoiesis which will later be customized to the financial market.

The concept of *autopoiesis* consists of the Greek terms αὐτο (self) and ποίησις (poiesis) and means a property of a system of self-perpetuation in many ways: conservation, repair, organization, reproduction and so on, all based on their own principles (structural and functional), although in the context of interactions with the environment. As we will see, the interplay between system and environment is seen at the most general and abstract level, namely through the concept of cognition as a simple sensory-reactive capacity, according to the proposal of the Santiago school of this concept).

Short History

The theme of autopoieticity was, as is well known, triggered by the inspired book of Chilean biologists Humberto Maturana and Francisco Varela. The new idea, which brings an ingenious explanation of the (functioning of the) living entities, then generated, as expected, many other takeovers. The concept of autopoiesis seeks to bring together the basic elements of continuous life ensuring, based on the internal principles of systems (in this case, living systems) and in the interactions with the environment. All the intellectual efforts made in the matter are meant to provide the foundations of the living fact. A brief introduction to the issue of autopoiesis is presented below.[39]

(i) the concept of autopoiesis has its origin in living biological entities (organisms), namely at their basic level (cell). Not only did the two Chilean biologists not extend the concept of autopoieticity beyond biological life, but they rejected the very idea of such an extension (e.g., to social entities);[40]

(ii) the concept of autopoiesis and the concept of knowledge (cognition) are put together and, in fact, are considered logically equivalent. But such an equivalence needs some clarification:
   - knowledge is no longer attributed to consciousness, but to any way of perceiving/recording what needs to be done for an entity that, only on the basis of that knowledge (perceptions), could repeat the experience of knowledge (i.e., could survive as a result of the cognitive action in question);
   - the very idea of reproducing the entity, based only on internal principles and mechanisms (operations) is seen as the essence of autopoieticity; all the sufficient conditions that ensure such reproduction by internal principles constitute the basis of the autopoietic property;
   - although knowledge is attributed to the observer of biological life as autopoieticity, such an attribution does not change anything in the idea that autopoieticity is conditioned by knowledge (of course, in the general, non-anthropomorphic sense mentioned);

- survival in the process of reproduction means that the interactions of the system involved with its environment are "chosen" by that system so that those interactions are appropriate for survival and reproduction; in fact, the main body of knowledge is to "know" which interactions are allowed and which are forbidden; it should be noted that Maturana calls such a set of allowed (or appropriate) interactions as forming a *niche* in the wider environment;[41]
- whereas, however, knowledge, understood as associated with consciousness, is not denied, then the extension of autopoieticity to non-biological entities of life (as is the case with our concept of *LLS*, or *logically living system*) is open, despite the scepticism of the two creative biologists;

(iii) the fundamental ideas, examined or suggested by the two scientists, even if they were taken up by other scientists interested in the topic of autopoieticity, remained quasi-invariant:

- the operational closure (through the membrane) of the system and the interactional (or relational,[42] as we prefer to say) openness of the system to its environment (in fact, to its niche);
- an evolutionary behaviour of the autopoietic system, i.e., a cognitively based selection of appropriate interactions with the environment, capable of ensuring the identitary invariance of the system and, at the same time, its reproduction within such an identity;
- a (somewhat) structural determinism of the autopoietic system, i.e., the Darwinian idea that functions arise from the structure and never the other way around.

The generality of Maturana and Varela's approach has encouraged other scientists to examine the concept of autopoieticity. One of the most original was the German sociologist, Niklas Luhmann. He tried to abstract and further extend the results obtained for living systems to apply them to social systems (note that those systems are human social ones). As in the case of Maturana, we do not examine the whole social theory of Luhmann, but only those elements that interfere with our intention to clarify the concept of autopoieticity in the financial market. Luhmann's main goals were:

(a) the identification and definition of the phenotype of social systems, i.e., the entity that has three predicates of sufficiency: (a) is self-replicable; (b) is reflective; (c) retains its specific identity when reproduced;
   - solution provided: ***communication*** (with some specifications that distinguish it from information or statement, or customize it for different subsystems in the social system—either organizations or interactions); it should be noted that Luhmann considers the event as a unit of reproduction (more precisely, he argues that a communication is an event), which eliminates the duration of the "equation" of reproduction—that is, a communication is reproduced exactly when it is produced.[43] The similarity of this treatment with our specification that, in the matter of *LLS*, we do not have growth/development of the phenotype is obvious;

(b) identifying and defining the genotype of social systems, i.e., the entity that can change (over time or even through its own functioning) and thus influence the reproduction of the phenotype;
   - solution provided: *existing social programmes* that include the "list" from which only the communications to be made must be selected; as programmes change, so do communications;[44]

(c) the identification and definition of the environment, i.e., the system with which the system involved (the system of interest) interacts in order to reproduce/replicate;
   - solution provided: Luhmann does not accept that the social system can have its (social) environment, because any environment of the social system is (in his conception) also of the nature of the social system, so it cannot be outside the social system involved, i.e., it cannot be an environment for the social system; consequently, he is obliged to introduce an internal environment, which is considered to be, in fact, widespread within that social system.[45] He called this medium an *understanding of communication*; such an understanding is, of course, different for different individuals and can mean either accepting or rejecting a particular communication. More precisely, the environment of the social system is considered the *psychic system*, which belongs to individuals understood as external sensors of communications.[46]

The Conceptual Family of Autopoieticity

Conceptually, autopoieticity is a property of systems. The concept of autopoieticity is integrated into a true conceptual family regarding the organization and functioning of systems (of any kind, not only of logical/symbolic systems, which we are mainly interested in here). In our opinion, this conceptual family includes the following individuals:

- *stationarity*: it is the property of the system which, in terms of its state vector, is absolutely invariant. A stationary system therefore replicates its structure, *punctually*[47] and for an indefinite period of time. For example, stationary economic systems existed in the human communities that preceded the technological civilization—those systems did not produce more than necessary consumption (there were no stocks of products, no production for sale/exchange) and they were rather characterized through autarchy; the principle of behaviour in stationary systems is *current survival*;
- *stability*: it is the property of the system which, in terms of its state vector, is relatively invariant. A stable system therefore replicates its structure in an *interval* mode[48]—the system remains stable if the variation of its state vector falls within a pre-accepted range. For example, stable economic systems can exist at any stage of human society's development. However, the interdependencies of economic systems, which today have reached a global dimension (networks), make stability vulnerable, as we will show in the following; the principle of behaviour in stable systems is *anticipated survival*;
- *optimality*: it is the property of the system that, in terms of its state vector, extremizes the potential of the system in question. Extremization that takes place under a set of restrictions/constraints of any kind (material, normative, behavioural, etc.) is called optimization; the principle of behaviour in optimal systems is to obtain the *first best* solution;
- *sustainability*: it is the property of the system which, in terms of its state vector, perpetuates the potential of the system in question, more precisely ensures the replication of its structure, provided that this replication contains sufficient attributes to continue replication (theoretically) indefinitely; the principle of behaviour in sustainable systems is *continued survival*;

- *viability*: can be considered a stage that will continue that of sustainability, namely by introducing values (axiological grid) in the design of the structure of the system involved (*nota bene*: as noted above, sustainability is axiologically "blind", if we do not consider survival as a value[49]); the principle of behaviour in viable systems, which can also be called logically living systems, (Dinga, 2021) is *adequate survival*;
- *autopoieticity*: can be considered a stage that will continue that of viability, namely by ensuring the regulatory principles exclusively from within.[50] The concept of autopoiesis (Maturana & Varela, 1980) makes a *sine qua non* connection between the self-organizing capacity of a system and its cognitive capacity—cognition means, in the broadest sense, the perception of actions/reactions that come from the environment to the system in question and on the basis of which the system either reacts to the environment (based on reaction norms) or changes its structure (and therefore its functions) in accordance with those actions/reactions. Of course, self-organizing actions/reactions can also come from within the system. The principle of behaviour in autopoietic systems is *self-survival*.[51]

Figure P.5 shows a synoptic systematization of the conceptual family of autopoieticity.

We mention that, from the point of view of the actional paradigms in the history of humanity, they have "settled" quite accurately, exactly on the properties discussed—for example, nowadays, the capitalist paradigm based on the property of optimality predominates, being emerging the paradigm (which does not yet have a name) that will be grafted onto the sustainability property.[52]

Nota bene: the features above mentioned are not necessarily distinct among them—there are some semantic overlapping—so, their additivity is not guaranteed as valid. This means that it is not true that the more many features verified, the more soundness has that entity. Some features are relevant and required in some conditions, so it is possible that a small number of features provide a high level of soundness and vice versa.

There are, however, some logical peculiarities of these attributes of soundness:

- (*F*3) is depending on (*F*2), and (*F*2) is depending on (*F*1)—perhaps not in a causal way but on conditional one;

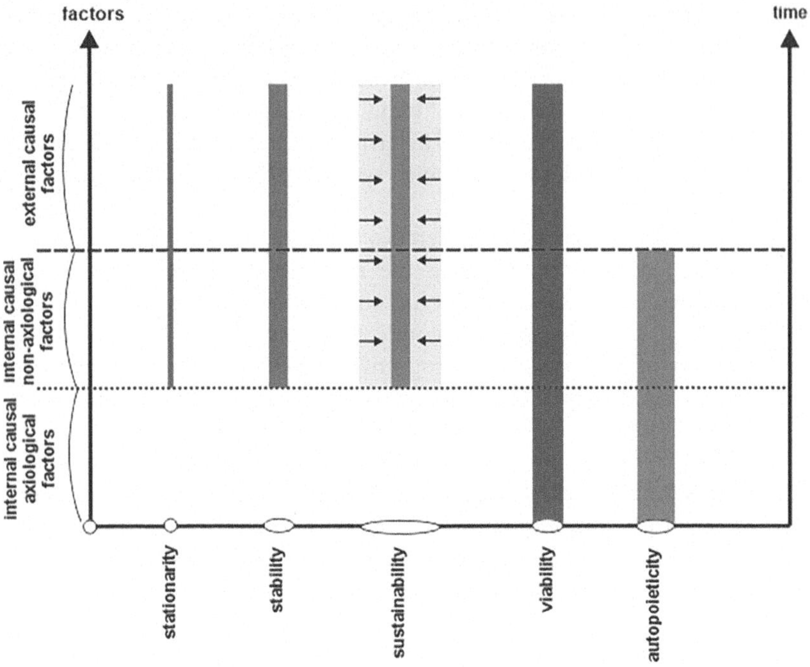

Fig. P.5 Causal factors of master-properties of systems. *Source*: Author

- (*F*6) acts if (*F*5) fails, and (*F*5) acts if (*F*4) fails;
- (*F*7) and (*F*8) are strongly interdependent (perhaps they develop a co-evolutive rapport).

A Possible Embedder of Resilience: The Soundness

The concept of soundness (*ES*) must also be understood in its abstract and general way. We consider that the economic soundness is composed of: (a) (*F*1) structural completeness; (b) (*F*2) static equilibrium capability; (c) (*F*3) dynamic stability potential; (d) (*F*4) robustness; (e) (*F*5) resilience; (f) (*F*6) antifragility; (g) (*F*7) sustainability; (h) (*F*8) autopoieticity. So, it requires all the eight properties already presented above, to which is added a new property, namely (F1) structural completeness. Indeed, an economic (or social/societal) system, no matter its size, gains the soundness attribute if its structure is complete, that is, its functions can be performed at their desired level based on its own structure. For example, for a national economic system, such a completeness can be viewed as in Fig. P.6.

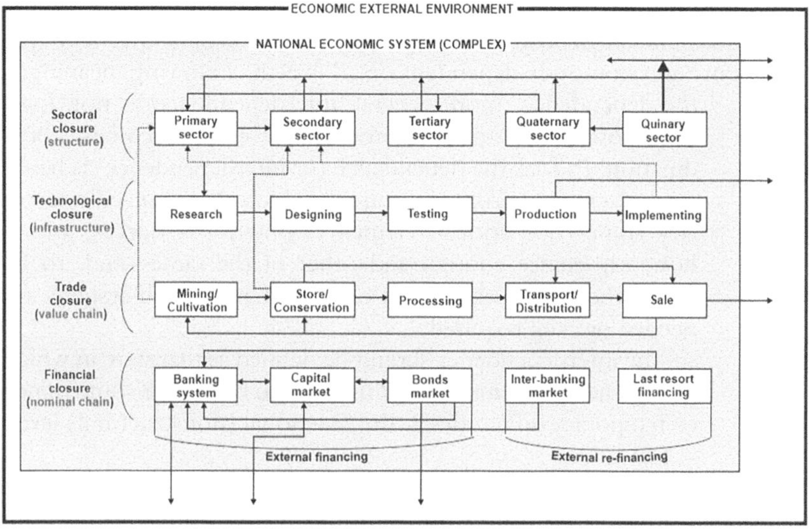

Fig. P.6 The completeness of a generic national economic system. *Source*: Emil Dinga: *Economic models for managing the COVID-19 pandemic shock. Strategic outline*. Economica Publishing House (in Romanian), 2021

Discussion

(i) the most important feature of the structural completeness of an economic system is its self-sustaining (what we name also as self-sustainabilizing). This means both the economic circulation among the four basic sectoral closures and the economic circulation among the five economic sectors.[53] (*Nota bene*: as we see next, these two closures give exactly the two sufficient predicates that deliver the sustainability);

(ii) the four sectoral closures ensure a double autonomy of the given economic system, related to the environment (presumed to be populated itself with other economic systems): (a) an autonomy at the level of each of the five economic sectors; (b) an autonomy at the level of the four sectoral closures. More than that, if one of the two autonomies fails, the general autonomy of the economic system in the case is altered and becomes non-genuine;

(iii) the mentioned autonomy (in its double meaning) is not absolutely… autonomous. More exactly, each economic sector is autonomously dependent on the other four sectors, and each sectoral closure is autonomously dependent on the other three closures. The very syntagm "autonomously dependent on…" has the following meaning:

- the dependence (more general, interdependence) is not, logically, possible outside the autonomy, or else it becomes subordination. In fact, the dependence (or interdependence) is based on and emerges from the state in which the involved systems lack some (non-critical) elements—physical resources, know-how, experience enough and other of the same—and, to fix them, the relationships with other systems or sub-systems are needed or even required;
- so, the interdependency should be defined as that state in which autonomous systems interact in order to overcome some minor or temporary difficulties at the functional (not structural) level.

All in all, structural completeness is the most subjacent ground of soundness—we hold the basic assumption that the structure generates the function. (*Nota bene*: we shall see, however, that, in the economic/social field, Lamarckism is very present, namely the cases in which the function generates the structure are numerous enough.)

Bucharest, Romania
September 16, 2024

Emil Dinga

Notes

1. We do not discuss here the nature or the statute of the economic theory/science/discipline, but only the predicate of economic, considered *per se*.
2. A human being (and the society) is considered to belong to culture. Any reality that is not belonging to culture is considered to belong to nature. There are, however, natural systems/entities which maintain entropic exchange relationships with nature.
3. Do not confuse the purpose/goal with the finality. While the purpose/goal is accessible to cultural subjects only (a cultural subject is a subject that is capable of representations), the finality is accessible to both cultural and non-cultural subjects (a non-cultural subject is capable only of perceptions).

4. Without this sufficiency predicate, economics is not else than a methodology of optimizing or of getting the equilibrium (similar to Walras's General Equilibrium Theory, so praised by Schumpeter).
5. In the literature it is accepted for granted the idea that the economic order is a special social order constituted around the market. However, in our opinion, the market is not a primitive attribute (much less a sufficiency predicate), but an institution, more or less formalized/codified, as a historical hypostases of objectifying the economic as such—other possible, different institutions could objectify the economic life.
6. The system's kinematics refers to the change in any way of that system without identifying the cause of change, while the system's dynamics considers the implied cause. However, such a pedantic distinction will be not strictly followed, except in the cases in which it is relevant—in such cases the necessary mentions will be provided.
7. Although our research is not put under the insignia of the phenomenology (such a demarch is "planned" for future work), it is clear enough that such an extraction is the result of the observer's intentionality, so function under the epoche (more exactly, under the naturalistic attitude, as proposed Husserl).
8. As we shall see later, some processes of interest can be considered (structural) properties of the systems, while the very processes are manifestations (regularly, objectifications) of those properties.
9. There is a difference between dynamics and kinematics: dynamics take into consideration the cause of the change, while kinematics is interested only in the change *per se*.
10. We adhere to the standard (in fact, Darwinian) assumption that the structure (causally and conditionally) generates functions and not vice versa (Lamarckian view). Obviously, functions imply both functionality (functions of the system inside that system) and behaviour (functions of the system outside that system). *Nota bene*: however, later we must accept a mix between Darwinism and Lamarckism in the economic (larger, social) field.
11. Of course, the treatment applied (or applicable) to external actions may differ, possibly considerably, from that applied (applicable) to internal actions. Likewise, the impact (as intensity, duration, point of exercise, etc.) differs or may differ depending on the origin of the action.
12. We avoid the term *complex* (preferred by the overwhelming majority of analysts) and prefer *complicated*, for reasons we will refer to later.
13. We remind you that *action* is an integrated concept of praxeology (for those interested, we refer to: (a) Tadeusz Kotarbiński, *A Treatise on Good Works*, Political Publishing House, 1976; (b) Georg Henrik von Wright, *Norm and Action*, Scientific and Encyclopaedic Publishing House, 1982;

(c) Cornel Popa, *Theory of Action and Formal Logic*, Scientific and Encyclopedic Publishing House, 1984). *Nota bene*: the referred works are in the Romanian language.

14. For an action/reaction to be foetal, it must fulfil, cumulatively, three conditions: (a) be in the set of actions/reactions accessible to the recipient system (*nota bene*: for a given system, its environment is also a system)—accessibility is understood here in its widest possible sense: spatial, temporal, in terms of intensity, nature, etc.; (b) be proportional to the action/reaction to which it is constituted as a response; (c) to have the meaning of the impact reversed compared to that of the impact for which it is constituted as a response.
15. It is known that economic phenomena obey, from the point of view of kinematics, rather a logistic curve $\left(y = \frac{C}{a + b \cdot e^{-kx}}, \text{cu } k > 0, C \neq 0\right)$. Although the logistic function is of a continuous type, one should, from a methodological point of view, construct a discrete function—the technical solution is probably a "scaled" logistic function based on successive thresholds (especially regarding the threshold at the inflexion point of the function in question).
16. Non-current decision means a decision taken previously, usually having a potential character, i.e., having the particularity that it is triggered when certain predetermined conditions are met, without the need for a current decision for this. (*Nota bene*: as we will show, this is the mode of operation of automatic stabilizers, of any type.)
17. Automatic stabilizers that work (or should work) in the *RRA* device will be examined in detail in the appropriate place in the economy of the study.
18. In other words, a learning process is produced from the very operation of robustness. (*Nota bene*: this learning process will also be encountered in the other two concepts that will be examined in this chapter.)
19. In the work *Antifragile: Things That Gain from Disorder*, published in 2012 by Random House (USA) and Penguin (UK).
20. For example, this is the abstract meaning of the concept of efficiency.
21. More precisely, it is about the gross profit, subject to profit taxation, since what remains after tax deduction is called net profit.
22. Managerial accounting (intended for the economic calculation necessary for the organization's management), respectively financial accounting (intended for the economic calculation necessary for the record of the organization's financial relations with the state).
23. The so-called national accounting is based on the system of national accounts.
24. In classical (more precisely, Marxist) economic theory, this type of utility is called use value.

25. We recall the concept of transaction cost: the costs associated with economic exchange, other than the price (either paid—when buying or collected—when selling)—for example, the cost of information.
26. There are three categories of utility, as standard economic theory holds: (a) economic utility (or substantive utility); (b) symbolic utility); (c) evidential utility. In the economy of the present study, we consider economic utility exclusively.
27. The excess and the deficit are calculated (often on the basis of mental accounting—see, in relation to the concept of mental accounting, the work of Richard Thaler, *Misbehaving: The Making of Behavioral Economics*, Allen Lane Publishing House, 2015) as an excess, respectively a deficit compared to a benchmark considered either sufficient, or adequate, or desirable.
28. Obviously, the monetary value of good M will be exactly the nominal value expressed by q_M, while the monetary value of quantity q_R will use the market price to get the related monetary expression.
29. There are four categories of economic value (the standard economic theory considers only the first two; the third is very little addressed in the specialized literature, and the fourth is a personal proposal that will be formulated in a future study): (a) *use value* (*UV*)—the potential of an economic object (either good or service) to satisfy an economic need (*nota bene*: an economic need is that need which concerns, ultimately, biological survival). *UV* is inextricably linked to every economic object as it is; (b) *exchange value* (*TV*)—the degree (rate) in which a certain economic object is effectively traded (exchanged) for (any) other economic object, regardless of whether the exchange is carried out directly (through barter) or indirectly (through currency), in both cases, one of two economic objects being, in fact, the price of the other. It is noticeable that, while *UV* has a potential character, *TV* has a real one, that is, *TV* cannot be established from the office, but only on the market in the process of actual exchange; (c) *entropic value* (*EV*)—this (possible) species of economic value is not treated in the specialized literature, although, starting with the works of Georgescu-Roegen, the entropy of the economic process is examined sufficiently intensively. In principle, *EV* means the low-entropy content (or, equivalently, the bound energy content as opposed to free energy content) that an economic object possesses, whether this content is naturally or artificially/anthropogenically caused.
30. The concept of intensional size is a size that I myself introduce into this reasoning, defined as a size of intensity of the variation of a size over the initial (basic) size—conceptually it has the meaning of a... rhythm. Thus, let the initial quantity x, and let it be a dimensional variation of it, Δx. Then the associated intentional quantity is $\frac{\Delta x}{x}$.

31. As in the use value perspective, where the advantages obtained by the two economic agents are different (for obvious reasons, since each of them pursues a different use value, otherwise the exchange would not take place), and this time each of partners get an advantage, but there is no longer certainty that it is different, although, most of the time, it is different for the two partners.
32. Sustainability is a concept inspired, for the economic/social sciences, from nature— nature is always sustainable based on two predicates (to which we shall come back analytically in the next chapters): (a) self-replicability; (b) recovering the inputs by own outputs.
33. Like many other concepts in the economic and social field, the concept of sustainability is demonetized both by its excessive use and, above all, by its improper use, often as a simple label, for the most diverse phenomena and processes, some of them without a connection with this property. (*Nota bene*: a similar case is that of the demonetization of the concept of globalization, on the same "recipe".)
34. Needless to draw attention to the confusions that are made (by article writers) between durability and sustainability, as if they were, semantically, interchangeable. In this sense, we insist on drawing the reader's attention to the way in which we propose, here, the three concepts associated with the three ontological entities: things—*durability*; properties—*sustainability*; relationships—*viability*. *Autopoieticity* could be defined, in this context, as a relation between properties.
35. Of course, under the impact of the Quantum theory, the ontological priority of the thing, in relation to the property, respectively to the relationship, is called into question. Thus, thing-type quantum entities are, in fact, mathematical operators, not ontological existences in the proper sense accepted at the macro level, so it can be accepted, at least as a hypothesis, that the property or relation, and not the thing, is a priority in ontologically terms. This is, however, obviously a problem that goes far beyond the ambitions of the present study.
36. This is the logical motivation for which we distinguish clearly and sharply between durability (see, e.g., the expression, indispensable in any study, *durable development*, as if development were a thing) and sustainability (which, by the way, is most of the time used just as carelessly, i.e., without a logical foundation).
37. We recall here Niklas Luhmann's ingenious (though somewhat forced, in our opinion) enterprise of an autopoietic theory of society.
38. Although we will not develop this subtlety here, we must note that there can be reflexive relations, that is, relations of the property to itself. This case is not at all rare, but for the moment, we do not analyse this aspect further.

39. This paragraph represents partly a takeover and partly a development of the article of the author dedicated to the abstract concept of autopoiesis as a generative "machine" of *LLS (logically living system).*
40. This rejection is, of course, strange, given the intellectual and creative openness shown by the two biologists. In our opinion, the form of behavioural entropy, which we introduced above (in order to replace thermodynamic entropy and, in part, informational entropy) is even more suitable for the use of the concept of autopoiesis—which we will continue to do, by the way.
41. As we have already shown, the interactional niche of a system with its environment is simply formed by the totality of foetal reaction norms (which "enter" and respectively "exit" from the system concerned).
42. From a logical point of view, the relationship is more extensive than the inter-action, because it can also refer to unidirectional actions/reactions that are obviously not of the nature of the inter-action (the latter implies bi-directionality).
43. The influence of Shannon entropy, which is of the communication type, is not difficult to observe here.
44. Here Luhmann makes an obvious analogy with Lakatos's concept of research programmes, trying to sketch a paradigmatic version of social evolution.
45. Again, the analogy between Luhmann's solution and our solution of the identity between the social genotype and the social selector (i.e., the idea that the environment is... inside the phenotype) is obvious.
46. The fact that the psychic environment is considered outside the social system is somewhat curious, though not too much, because it can be correlated with the distinction between Popper's three worlds: the psychic world is the second world, while society, as an objectification of inter-subjectivity, is the third world.
47. Punctuality accepts accidents of non-punctuality if the system has the potential to return to the point (resilience of point or punctual resilience).
48. Stability accepts instability accidents if the system has the potential to return in the interval (resilience of interval).
49. We consider that survival, as a goal, is not grafted on a value, precisely due to the fact that survival is the existential condition of any value. (*Nota bene*: this argument follows, somewhat, the way in which Kant rejected existence as a property/attribute, in the attempt to overturn the conclusion of Anselm of Canterbury's famous argument about the existence of God—a failed attempt, just like Descartes's attempt in the same matter.)
50. That is, as is the case with systems known as second-order cyber systems (those cyber systems in which the observer/controller is itself a component of the system concerned, as opposed to first-order cyber systems, where the observer/controller is outside the system concerned).

51. An equivalent expression, which we will use mainly in the following, is adaptive replicability (or replication).
52. The concepts of "green economy", "circular economy" and the like are, in fact, terms that refer to the concept of sustainability.
53. The significations of the five economic sectors are the following: *primary* sector—extraction/cultivation of economic resources/primary economic goods; *secondary* sector—processing of primary resources/goods; *tertiary* sector—services (production and consumption); *quaternary* sector—information, science, knowledge, education, art; *quinary* sector—values, visions/societal, moral, political models.

References

Dinga, E. (2021). *Logically Living System: A Generative "Machine" for Autopoietic Systems* (pp. 73–97). IGI Global.

Dinga, E., Oprean-Stan, C., Tănăsescu, C. R., Băriam, V., & Ionescu, G.-M. (2023). *Co-Evolution of Symbolic Species in the Financial Market. A Framework for Economic and Political Decision-Making*. Palgrave Macmillan - Springer Nature.

Maturana, H., & Varela, F. (1980). *Autopoiesis and Cognition*. Living. D. Reidel Publishing Company.

Taleb, N. N. (2012). *Antifragile: Things that gain from Disorder*. Random House.

Contents

List of Figures

List of Tables

CHAPTER 1

Some Formal Developments

1.1 Robustness

(i) Some formalizations

(i.a) Notations

- S_t: system at moment t
- E_t^S : S system's environment at moment t
- A_t^{int} : internal action on the system S at moment t
- A_t^{ext} : external (from environment) action on the system S at moment t
- F_t^S : space (set) of actions/reactions accessible to the system S at moment t
- $F_t^{M^S}$: space (set) of actions/reactions accessible to the environment of S at moment t
- N_t^S : reaction norm of system S at moment t
- $N_t^{E^S}$: reaction norm of environment of S at moment t
- p_t^S : minimal (floor) threshold to trigger an action/reaction of S at moment t
- P_t^S : maximal (ceiling) threshold to trigger an action/reaction of S at moment t
- DZ_t^S : dead zone of system S (the accumulation area of the pressure exerted on the system within which the system preserves its static identity—state—or kinematic identity—trajectory) at moment t

E. Dinga, *Economic Resilience During Overlapped Crises*,
https://doi.org/10.1007/978-3-031-80224-9_1

- i_t: intensity (appropriately measured) of the action/reaction (disturbance, shock) exerted on the system at moment t
- d_t: duration of exerting of the action/reaction (measured in an appropriate way) elapsed until the moment t
- Q_t: the amount of action/reaction (measured in an appropriate way) exerted on the system, accumulated at the time t

(i.b) Definitions

$$N_t^S \in F_t^{M^S}$$

$$N_t^{E^S} \in F_t^S$$

$$DZ_t^S = P_t^S - p_t^S$$

$$Q_t = i_t \cdot d_t$$

Nota bene: given the discrete character of both the action/reaction on the system and the system reaction (i.e., the manifestation of robustness or, rather, the exhaustion of the system's resilience), the function Q_t will have the generic form of Fig. 1.1.

(i.c) Kinematic/dynamic formulas

- Quantity of action/reaction

$$\Delta Q_t = 0 \rightarrow \Delta(i_t \cdot d_t) = 0$$

For the continue case,

$$dQ_t = 0 \rightarrow d(i_t \cdot d_t) = 0$$

namely,

$$(i_t)' \cdot di_t + (d_t)' \cdot dd_t = 0$$

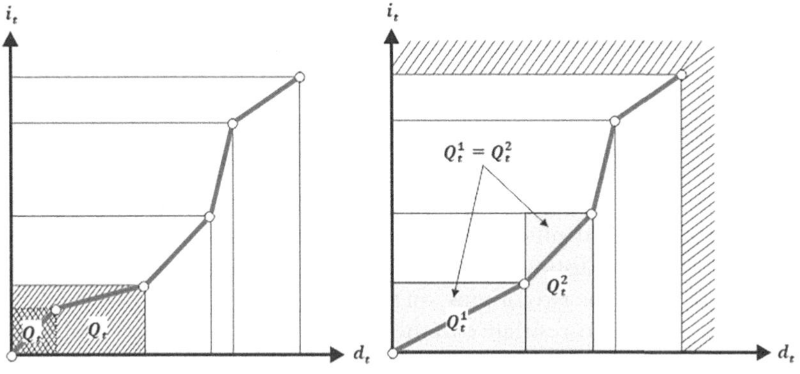

Fig. 1.1 "Scaling" function of the action/reaction quantity. (*Source*: Author)

from where the marginal rate of substitution ($rm_t^{i/d}$) is obtained between the intensity of the action/reaction and the duration of exerting of that action/reaction

$$rm_t^{i/d} = \frac{di_t}{dd_t} = -\frac{(d_t)'}{(i_t)'}$$

- functioning of the thresholds (of the dead zone)
- the system is insensitive to the action/reaction exerted on it as long as the amount of the action/reaction in question does not reach the minimum threshold (i.e., as long as the inequality: $Q_t < p_t^S$ is verified, whatever the ratio of intensity to duration in formation of the amount of action/reaction in question);
- once the minimum threshold is reached ($Q_t = p_t^S$), the robustness property of the system comes into operation and maintains the state, respectively the trajectory of the system in the initial positions as long as the inequality is verified: $Q_t < P_t^S$ (i.e., as long as it is not yet reached the maximum threshold—in other words, the system remains inert on its dead zone, as previously mentioned);
- once the maximum threshold is reached (i.e., $Q_t = P_t^S$), the system can no longer resist the change pressure exerted by the action/reaction in question and "allows" the change of state (or trajectory, as the case may be) of the system, in according to the direction and

sense in which that pressure for change is exerted. *Nota bene*: some formalizations of the operation of the robustness properties will be suggested below.

Discussion

We believe that distinguishing too strongly between actions/disturbances of internal origin and actions/disturbances of external origin to a given system does not add much value since, in principle, the affected system will not be able to distinguish (or will not always be able to distinguish), by itself, between the two origins, on the one hand, and if it could do that, the way it projects its resistance to the two categories of action should not differ (too much) according to these categories of action.[1]

The minimum threshold for triggering action/reaction on the part of system *S* refers to that threshold below which the system in question does not "observe" (register) the action exerted on it.

The interval between the minimum threshold and the maximum threshold is that interval in which the pressure build-up from the exerted action is kept under control, so to speak, by the system in question—for this purpose, the system activates (mobilizes), either discretionarily or automatically,[2] its conservative resources, which means that throughout this interval there is a dead zone (with the related dead time) of the system's reactivity to the action taken.

The maximum action/reaction trigger threshold on the part of system *S* refers to that threshold beyond which robustness of the system fails and its conservative action collapses. Above this threshold of changing pressure, the system loses either its static identity (state) or its kinematic identity (trajectory), or both.

The question arises whether, above the maximum threshold, the system in question still possesses the property of robustness. Our position on this matter is as follows:

- robustness is a feature generated, like any other feature, by the structure of the system, that is, by its state vector;
- therefore, whatever structure of a given system is (real or imaginary, objective, subjective or objectified) it possesses the property of robustness, at a potential level;
- once the state of a system is changed, as an effect of the action/reaction exerted on it (i.e., once the maximum threshold of conservabil-

ity has been reached), the system has, *eo ipso*, the property of robustness, of course, with the eventual change of the values for the minimum, respectively maximum thresholds (therefore with the eventual change of the dead zone sphere);[3]

- perhaps, it can be said that the robustness of a system is a genetic property. In any case, it can be said, at least, that this property of robustness is an inalienable property of any system.[4]

Nota bene: in relation to the property of robustness, the concept of *hormesis* must also be discussed. By hormesis is meant the acquisition, by a system, of an immunity to a disturbing factor by enduring, for a period of time, the action of that disturbing factor but in small "doses". Essentially, then, hormesis is a learning process (either at the structural level or at the purely functional level) that a system develops through familiarization (e.g., below the p^S level) with the change pressure in question. Similar to the dead zone, which we discussed above, in the case of hormesis there is a *hormetic zone* within which the action of the disturbing factor does not have a disturbing impact, but only a … training impact.

(ii) The sufficient predicates of robustness

Based on what was discussed above, we shall try to establish the sufficiency predicates of the concept of robustness, so that we can formulate a definition of it.

We believe that the following sufficiency predicates should be accepted:

1. (*RO*/1) *threshold sensitivity*: refers to that property of the system not to react (have no actions/reactions) at any level of the action/reaction experienced, but only upon the accumulation of an amount of change pressure that exceeds an upper threshold (P_t^S in the above notation). Also, this sufficiency predicate also refers to the insensitivity of the system to amounts of change pressure that are below a minimum threshold (p_t^S in the above notation). From a conceptual point of view, the two thresholds differ, however, from each other, so we make the clarifications below:
   I. the insensitivity of the system until the p_t^S level is reached is a *perceptual* insensitivity: the system simply does not perceive (in its specific way) the change pressure that has arisen and is exerted on it;

II. the insensitivity of the system during the dead zone (i.e., as long as the change pressure increases from p_t^S to P_t^S without reaching the value P_t^S) is a *resolutive* type insensitivity: the system decides[5] not to react. The reasons for such a decision can alternatively be the following:
   (a) the action/reaction is not likely to perturb the system, either in its state or in its trajectory—meaning, of course, that the system in question has a list of such harmless[6] actions/reactions and determines that the action/reaction it faces is entered in that list;
   (b) the action/reaction is of the "straw fire" type, that is, after an initial shock, it goes out by itself, not having enough persistence or reasons to continue; of course, also for this qualification the system needs either specialized lists or criteria based on which to establish, with an acceptable degree of certainty, the case at hand;
   (c) the action/reaction stabilizes at a certain level of change pressure (below the P_t^S level). Two additional problems arise here:
      - the first issue is one related to the predictive capacity of the system in question, which means that it needs specialized predictors to indicate that an action/reaction is becoming chronic without the risk of becoming acute (i.e., reaching threshold P_t^S). Depending on the internal structure of the system, the existence and usability of such predictors can be accepted;[7]
      - the second issue concerns the impact of a pressure that persists in the dead zone for a certain period of time. Here, in fact, three other issues should be discussed that together make up this second problem: (a) whether a chronic but non-acute pressure alters its potential to generate changes in the state or trajectory of the target system; (b) if the target system needs to consume resources (of any kind) to, perhaps, maintain the change pressure inside the dead zone; (c) if, as long as the change pressure is maintained as a level below P_t^S, the target system could reduce the pressure in question. We formulate our position, with a brief argumentation, on each of the three issues:

- our answer to this question is affirmative: maintaining, for a certain period, the change pressure in the dead zone (i.e., without reaching the P_t^S value) is likely to introduce a certain (let us call it) stress into the target system. Such a stress could, for example, lead to a weakening of the robustness of the system, which means that we have to accept, here, two aspects: (i) the robustness of the system undergoes fatigue processes (stress) against the background of maintaining the change pressure inside the dead zone; (ii) system's fatigue depends, directly proportionally, on both Q_t and d_t. As $Q_t = i_t \bullet d_t$, if we denote the robustness stress function by v_t, then: $v_t = Q_t \cdot d_t = i_t \cdot d_t^2$, which leads us to a 2nd order polynomial function (a parabola) of the stress function in relation to the duration of exerting the change pressure inside the dead zone[8] (Fig. 1.2 suggests this graphical form).
- our answer to this question is yes: the target-system will need to consume resources to maintain the change pressure inside the dead zone. First of all, this pressure must be measured (permanently) to see its dynamics and therefore to determine if and what measures should be taken to reduce or at least stabilize the level

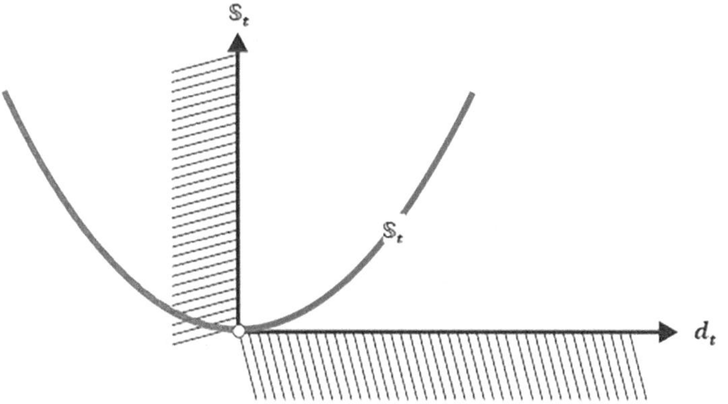

Fig. 1.2 The stress function of robustness. (*Source*: Author)

of change pressure so that it remains, further, below the threshold-ceiling level—and this measurement represents a first consumption of resources. Second, effective measures to reduce or maintain the pressure for change within the dead zone must be established and implemented—and this requires again consumption of specific resources, depending on the particular measures envisaged. In this sense, the question arises as to whether, by consuming resources for maintaining the pressure of change inside the dead zone, the robustness of the system in question is reduced. Our answer to this presumptive question is as follows:

- in general, the nature of the resources required/consumed to resist the change pressure (that resistance which operates during the—quantitatively and temporally—dead zone) is the same as the resources required/consumed either to reduce or at least to maintain the pressure of change within the dead zone;
- as a result, there seems to be an optimization problem here: between consuming resources to maintain change pressure inside the dead zone versus to conserve resources for the conservation of the robustness property itself;
- based on the above, we consider that the effort (respectively the consumption of resources) to reduce/maintain the change pressure inside the dead zone can have the necessary effect of the quantitative (thus, implicitly, temporal[9]) reduction of the dead zone itself. In other words, there is a trade-off here between avoiding reaching the P_t^S level of the change pressure and reducing the P_t^S level itself. Figure 1.3 shows, abstractly, the content of this possible trade-off (with t_c we denoted the time interval during which the change pressure is preserved/reduced, which means, implicitly, the amount of specific resources consumed by the system for this purpose, with $\overline{P}_t^S$ we denoted an in-compressible

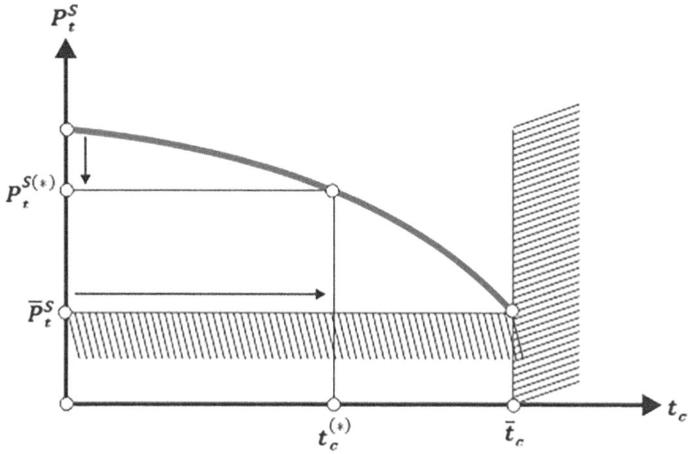

Fig. 1.3 The robustness threshold kinematic trade-off. (*Source*: Author)

value for the threshold-ceiling, and $\overline{t}_c$ denotes an in-extensible value for the duration of reduction/maintenance of the change pressure inside the dead zone). The concave shape of the function indicates that as the holding time of the change pressure extends, the rate of threshold-ceiling reduction increases, that is, the reduction in question is accelerated.

- the issue of reducing the change pressure that still remains in the dead zone is an important one because, in principle, it is likely to increase or at least prolong the robustness action of the system faced to the disruptive action/reaction. The possibility of such a phenomenon lies in the following:

  dissipating change pressure in system's components through intra-system communication. This means that those components of the system that are under the pressure of change (to which they resist, for now, by virtue of the fact that this pressure is below the level P_t^S) can learn from bearing the pressure in question—in other words, they can learn to work under stress. Once this learning is fed into the operating mechanisms of the components in question,[10] from the perspective of those components, the pressure to change can lessen;[11]

the question arises whether, through learning under stress, P_t^S changes itself. Our answer is affirmative, with the following condition: that learning must penetrate the structural level of the system, that is, it does not remain only at the functional (i.e., superficial, *ad hoc*) level;

there is also the question of whether it is necessary that ceiling thresholds, in switching under change pressure, should be set for each component of the system (as an alternative to the solution of maintaining a single threshold at the system level). Our answer is no, provided that the threshold of the system is set considering the "weakest link" component of stress—of course, this matter requires further conceptual and analytical developments.

In fact, the "fate" of the change pressure exerted on the target system, as long as it does not leave the dead zone, is a resultant of the impact of the three phenomena discussed above under the second problem. A synoptic picture of the combination of these three phenomena is given in Fig. 1.4.

2. (*RO/2*) *hormesis*: refers to that property[12] of the system to react by the logical negation of the expected action/reaction following an action/reaction (coming either from the system's environment or from within it). We shall develop this idea:
   I. hormesis (or hormetic behaviour) is a biphasic behaviour: (a) at relatively small values of the cause action/reaction, the response action/reaction is different (in fact, as we said above, exactly opposite) to the action/reaction response to relatively high values of action/reaction-cause;
   II. note that although, *prima facie*, it appears that hormesis is a species of threshold sensitivity (which is the *RO*/1 sufficiency predicate), there are some differences of this predicate from

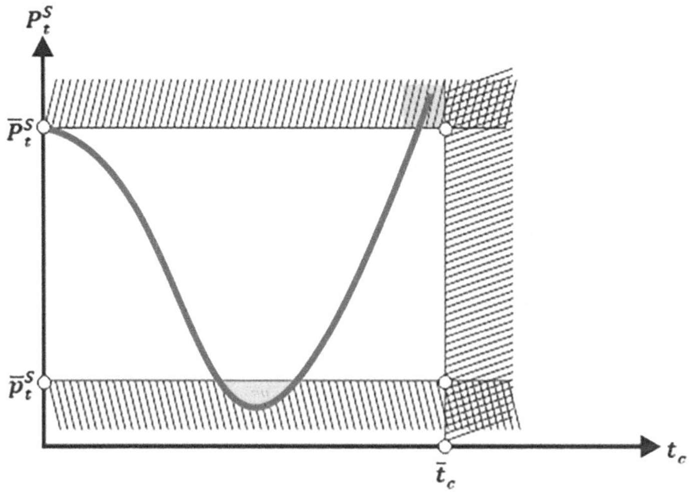

Fig. 1.4 Kinematics of change pressure in the dead zone of robustness. (*Source*: Author)

the previous one which it is useful to put into evidence (and which justifies the existence of this second sufficiency predicate precisely by the fact that it is neither redundant with *RO/1* nor inferable from it, i.e., it is not dependent on the latter):

(a) *RO/1* occurs at the same level of change pressure (disturbing factor), that is, as the amount of change pressure builds up to reach the threshold-ceiling, while *RO/2* only acts if the disruptor factor values are different: at some values (e.g., small) they act in one way, and at others (e.g., large) they act in the exact opposite way. In other words, while in the case of *RO/1* the reaction is different at the same intensity of the stimulus, in the case of *RO/2* the reaction is different only under the condition of varying the intensity of the stimulus;

(b) although in the case of *RO/2* there is no question of the accumulation of a pressure of change up to the level of a threshold-ceiling for triggering the negation type reaction (as it happens in the case of *RO/1*), however, in the case of *RO/2* as well, it must be posed a threshold problem: what exactly do we consider to be small values of the intensity of change and what exactly do we consider to be large values of this intensity? So, necessarily, a threshold must be established, which we propose to call the switch threshold[13] and which has the following meaning: up to the switch threshold, the target system's reaction to the switch impulse makes a certain sense (or sign), and after reaching the switch threshold, the respective reaction has the opposite meaning (or sign), so the switch threshold "objectifies", from a logical point of view, the biphasic character of the hormesis. The phenomenology of the hormesis can be suggested in Fig. 1.5 (with ST_k^S we denote the switch threshold of the disturbing factor *k* associated with the target system *S*—it should be noted that each disturbing factor has, on the one hand, its own switching factor and, on the other hand, the actual switch factor depends on the system on which that factor acts; with i_k^S we denoted the intensity—the qualitative level—with which the disturbing factor *k* acts on the system *S*; with HR_k^S we denoted the hormetic reaction—from the perspective of the meaning, not the intensity/quantity—of the system *S* to the action/reaction of the disruptive factor *k*).

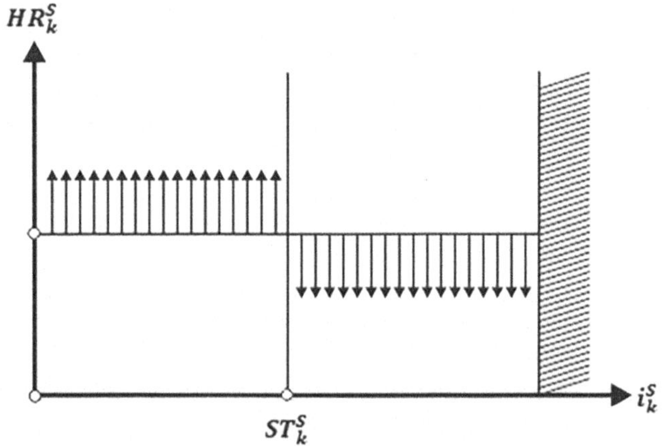

Fig. 1.5 Hormesis's phenomenology. (*Source*: Author)

3. (*RO/3*) *redundancy*: refers to that property of the system to have, from a structural point of view, "duplications"[14] of components/reaction devices (passive or active, depending on the context) to potentially destabilizing impulses coming either from outside the system or from inside of it. Two aspects are relevant in the issue of redundancy: (a) the cost of redundancy and (b) the mechanism of redundancy.

(a) The cost of redundancy

Redundancy has, of course, a cost, namely the very cost of implementing, in the system's structure, that redundancy, on the one hand, and the cost of scheduling the redundancy to come into operation, depending on the context, on the other hand. At the same time, the higher the number of duplicated structural components, the more the costs increase, although not linearly proportionally, because the critical infrastructure for the installation of these devices can be used as a common infrastructure (*Nota bene*: from an economic point of view, here we have in mind the concept of fixed cost).

- *prima facie*, the criterion for introducing redundancy is, of course, the cost-benefit analysis, more precisely, the positive value of the net utility. This means that substantive utilities[15] will have to be allocated, on the one hand, to maintain the identity of the system and, on the other hand, to the redundant component(s) to make the decision in question;
- in our opinion, there may also be criteria that exceed (or even are not related to) the substantive utility criterion—for example, if people's lives or their health are at stake—in which case the decision must be made on other bases than the cost-benefit analysis purely economic;
- if it is talking about a public system (e.g., a public institutional system), the problem of cost arises even less, because, in the matter of public goods and services, effectiveness[16] takes precedence over efficiency, but only efficiency is compatible with the cost-benefit analysis;

(b) The mechanism of redundancy

Regarding the mechanism of redundancy (for now, in its generic meaning) we shall use Fig. 1.6 to facilitate the examination and drawing of conclusions in the matter.

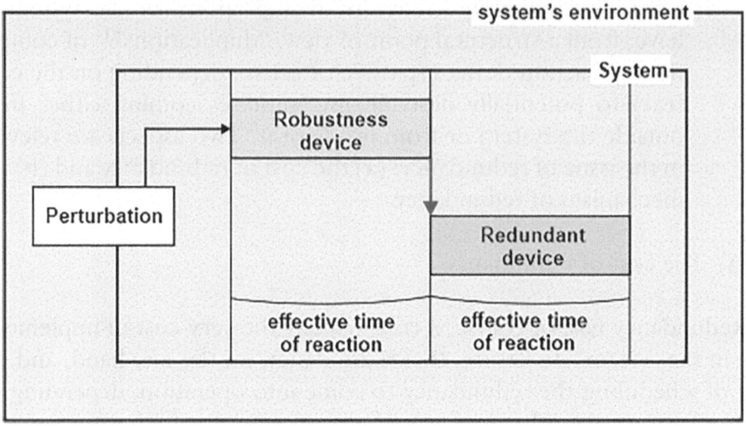

Fig. 1.6 Functioning of the redundancy in a robust system. (*Source*: Author)

- the system's first "line of defence" against disruption is its structural component that ensures its robustness;
- after the effective reaction capacity (i.e., the capacity to maintain the identity of the system) of the robustness device is exhausted, for example, it is exceeded in terms of the intensity of the disturbance or the duration of its exercise (namely, by the quantity of disturbance), the system automatically[17] switches to the robustness provided by the device redundancy of the robustness device;[18]
- after all the robustness devices (the "original" and the redundant ones) have been exhausted, the system will bear the impact of the disturbance and the resilience property of the system in question will start to act.

So, the logical definition of robustness has the following formalization:

$$RO \leftarrow (RO/1) \wedge (RO/2) \wedge (RO/3)$$

(c) A typology of robustness

Before proposing a typology of the robustness property, we shall examine two issues that need to be clarified: (a) is robustness a point property or a threshold property? (b) is robustness a singular or cyclical property?

(i) Punctual versus interval

In our opinion, given the first sufficiency predicate of the robustness property ($RO/1$), the robustness of a system is always an interval robustness, namely, as previously shown, a robustness that manifests itself exclusively in the dead zone (or, equivalently, the length of time during which the amount of change pressure builds up until it reaches the upper limit of the robustness property). It is true that at the point P_t^S the system in question suddenly switches, allowing the change pressure to take effect, such "delayed" until said point is reached, but that does not make robustness a point property. *Nota bene*: we recall that both P_t^S and p_t^S function as significance thresholds for the human subject involved in the decision of the system in question, although they have an objective component consisting of the amount of accumulated change pressure.

(ii) Singularity versus cyclicality

Some elements regarding the clarification of this (possible) dichotomy have already been presented, disparately, previously. We consider that the property of robustness is a cyclical one, in the sense that it is impossible for a system not to have this property, on the one hand, and that it, once "used", is not exhausted but starts from the beginning (of course, with new significance thresholds, both inferior and superior, and, respectively, of the manifestation of the dead zone related to other change pressures exerted on the system in question). In this sense, the property of robustness is inalienable to the system, although it is obviously not invariant as such. We shall see next that there are other properties of the generic system (such as resilience or antifragility) that are not inalienable to the generic system. In other words, the property of robustness is a necessary property, while other properties, such as the two mentioned, are contingent (i.e., non-necessary and possible) properties.[19]

After clarifying these two aspects (which otherwise could have led to artificial, logically contradictory typologies) of robustness, we propose a list of the main types of robustness that we consider relevant, at least from the perspective of economic systems, which we are mainly interested in the present research.

A. $(C1)$ by dead zone trend:

- (RO_{C1}^{1}) *narrowing* robustness: the size of the dead zone decreases, as a result of either the "climbing" of the minimum threshold, or the "falling" of the maximum threshold, or as a result of the simultaneous occurrences of the two mentioned movements of the thresholds;
- (RO_{C1}^{2}) *expanding* robustness: the size of the dead zone expands, as a result of either the "climbing" of the maximum threshold, or the "falling" of the minimum threshold, or as a result of the simultaneous occurrences of the two mentioned movements of the thresholds;
- (RO_{C1}^{0}) *conservative* robustness: both the maximum threshold and the minimum threshold are invariant (of course, during the analysis period, a condition also valid for the two previously mentioned types of robustness); obviously, conservative robustness can occur either "up"—the two thresholds rise in concert—or "down"—the two thresholds fall in concert.

B. $(C2)$ by trend of threshold levels:

- (RO_{C2}^{1}) *increasing* robustness: the maximum threshold "rises" (regardless of what happens to the minimum threshold), meaning that more amount of change pressure is needed to overcome the robustness of the system and produce a change, either of state or of kinematic position, as the case may be;
- (RO_{C2}^{2}) *decreasing* robustness: the maximum threshold "drops" (regardless of what happens to the minimum threshold), meaning that less amount of change pressure is needed to overcome the robustness of the system and produce a change, either of state or of kinematic position, as the case may be;
- (RO_{C2}^{0}) *stationary* robustness: the maximum threshold is stationary.

Nota bene: from the combination of the two previous criteria, $(C1)$ and $(C2)$, the following conclusions can also be drawn:

- (RO_{C1}^{0}) can be both of the type (RO_{C2}^{1}), if the minimum threshold "rises" by the same amount as the maximum threshold "rises", or of the type (RO_{C2}^{2}), if the minimum threshold "decreases" by the same amount that the maximum threshold "decreases";

- the variation of the minimum threshold does not matter for the evaluation of the robustness of the system, but for the evaluation of its sensitivity: the lower the minimum threshold, the higher the sensitivity[20] of the system (it requires a smaller amount of change pressure to start "accounting" for the exerting of that pressure) and vice versa, the higher the minimum threshold, the lower the sensitivity of the system (it requires a greater amount of change pressure to start "accounting" for the exerting of that pressure);
- (RO_{C2}^{0}) can be both of type (RO_{C1}^{1}), if the minimum threshold "falls", and of type (RO_{C1}^{2}), if the minimum threshold "rises".

C. (**C3**) according to the trend of the hormesis level:

- (RO_{C3}^{1}) *pro-sensitive* robustness: the minimum threshold "drops" (regardless of what happens to the maximum threshold), meaning that the change pressure doses that generate the system entering the dead zone decrease, making the system more sensitive to changing factors;[21]
- (RO_{C3}^{2}) *con-sensible* robustness: the minimum threshold "goes up" (regardless of what happens to the maximum threshold), which means that the change pressure doses that generate the system entering the dead zone increase, making system less sensitive to change factors;
- (RO_{C3}^{0}) *equi-sensitive* robustness: the minimum threshold is stationary.

Nota bene: it should be noted that the three classifications of the robustness property were established based on criteria that do not refer to a system's state, but to a system's kinematics/tendency. This means, conceptually, that robustness cannot be assessed as a level, but only as a trend. We remind you that many phenomena (but here we mainly consider economic phenomena) can only be measured as variation: the underground economy, tax evasion, economic preference (Kahneman, 2011) etc., and robustness falls under the category of these phenomena (we shall see that the same is not the case with the property of resilience, respectively with the property of antifragility, discussed later, which can also be measured in absolute size, not only in relative size, i.e., as a variation).

(d) The mechanism of robustness

We describe the essence of the robustness mechanism in Fig. 1.7.

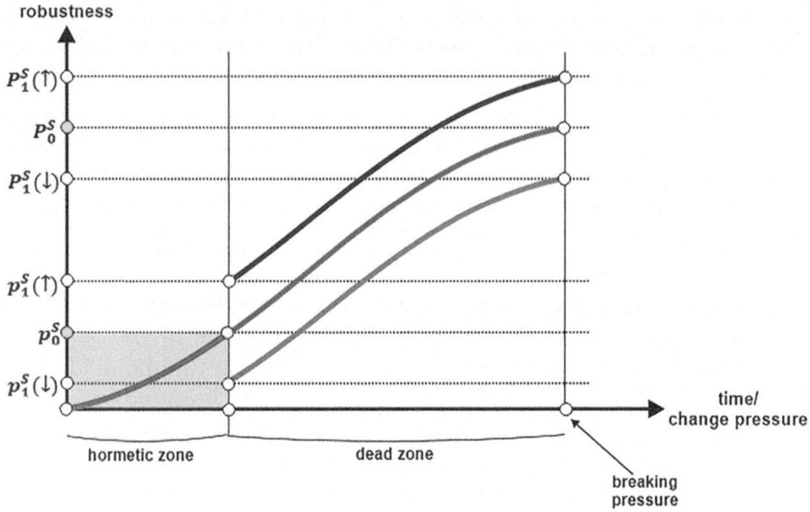

Fig. 1.7 Robustness's mechanism. (*Source*: Author)

1.2 Resilience

By resilience of a system is meant the ability of that system to return, by itself (i.e., through its own, internal principles and resources, usually of structural type) either to the state or to the trajectory from which it was disturbed (displaced) under the impact of actions/reactions internal or, as the case may be, external to that system. So, resilience is not in the nature of a resistance to change pressure (as is the case with robustness) but in the nature of an internal capacity to return to the state/trajectory held before the impact of the change pressure. This capacity is of the nature of a device that we call a ***resilient device*** (or, in a word, ***resilientor***) which, from a logical point of view, can be characterized as follows (we are dealing with a resilient device with three logical components[22]):

(1) (*RD*) a ***retrieval device*** (shortly, a current memory): it is a device, of any kind, of a structural nature, which records, with a predetermined frequency,[23] the state vector of the system in question, respectively the position on the trajectory[24] of that system. It should be noted that this memory device should have two addresses (*Nota bene*: here, the term address is used in the usual terminology of computer programming):

- an address at which the state (or kinematic position) of the system is recorded just before the start of the change pressure impact (at time *t*)—let us denote it *A*0, with two sub-addresses:
  - *A*0/1: related to memorizing the system's state vector;
  - *A*0/2: related to memorizing the kinematic position of the system;
- an address at which the state (or kinematic position) of the system is recorded at the moment considered as appropriate[25] for triggering of the resilience (i.e., at the moment $(t + \tau)$, therefore with the verification of the condition $\tau > t$)—let us denote it with *A*1, also with two sub-addresses:[26]
  - *A*1/1: related to memorizing the new (desired[27]) state vector of the system;
  - *A*1/2: related to memorizing the new (desired) kinematic position of the system.

(2) (*CD*) a *computing device*: it is a device capable of performing the comparison between the information recorded at the *A*0-type addresses, respectively between the information recorded at the *A*1-type addresses, and, so, determining the gaps in question, as follows:

- $G_{t+\tau}^{A/1} = S_{t+\tau}^{A1/1} - S_{t}^{A0/1}$, where t is the time at which the change pressure action/reaction on the system starts; τ is the time at which it is decided to trigger the resilient action (i.e., activating the resilient); *A*0/1 indicates the addresses in the retrieval device related to the state of the system; *A*1/1 indicates the addresses in the retrieval device related to the desired state of the system; $S_{t+\tau}^{A1/1}$ is the state vector[28] of the system at the time of the calculation; $S_{t}^{A0/1}$ is the state vector of the system at the time of the start of the action/reaction regarding the change pressure on the system; $G_{t+\tau}^{A/1}$ is the gap between the state vector at the time the resilientor is activated and the state vector at the time the action of the change pressure starts; this gap is calculated by the *CD*/1 sub-device;
- $G_{t+\tau}^{A/2} = P_{t+\tau}^{A1/2} - P_{t}^{A0/2}$, where: *A*0/2 indicates the addresses in the retrieval device related to the kinematic position of the system on its trajectory; $P_{t+Ä}^{A1/2}$ is the position vector[29] of the system at the time of the calculation; $P_{t}^{A0/1}$ is the position vector of the system at the time of the start of the action/reaction regarding the change pressure on the system; $G_{t+\tau}^{A/2}$ is the gap between the posi-

tion vector at the moment when the resilientor is activated and the position vector at the moment when the action of the change pressure starts; this gap is calculated by the *CD/2* sub-device;

(3) (*AD*) an ***adjustment device*** (an *elastic force*): it is a device, of any nature, also of a structural type, which provides "energy", usually as an institutional rule, but which also involves resources (substantial, energetic, informational) as sufficient to return the system to either the state or the position on the trajectory it had before the effect generated by the impact of the change pressure. As you can see below, the adjustment of each of the two mentioned gaps presents some differences in mechanism, therefore it is useful to "decree" the existence of two adjustment sub-devices: (a) *AD/1*—which is responsible for the resilience of the system from the perspective of its state vector; (b) *AD/2*—which is responsible for the resilience of the system from the perspective of its kinematic position. So, from a structural point of view, the resilience process is presented in Fig. 1.8.

Since this component of the resilientor is fundamental in its construction and operation, we give some additional details below, including a brief, minimal formalism. Before proposing this formalism, we shall review the rationale for designing such a device:

(i) according to the alternative name above (elastic force), this device will have to ensure the "recovery" of the system, either from a state or from a kinematic position perspective to the state/position it had before the change pressure had applied, as shown in *CD* description. The qualifier *elastic* suggests that resilience does not allow for plastic (i.e., permanent, irreversible) change in state or kinematic position because of the impact of change pressure (as, e.g., robustness would, after the amount of change pressure would exceed the upper threshold P_t^S);

(ii) similarly, to those discussed in the case of robustness, there is the question of the residual impact of change pressure. In other words, the question is as follows: is it possible to return "without rest" of the affected system to the previously held state or kinematic position? This is where the concept of *hysteresis* comes into play. By hysteresis is meant the property of a system to retain, following an impact received (either from the inside or from the outside), a

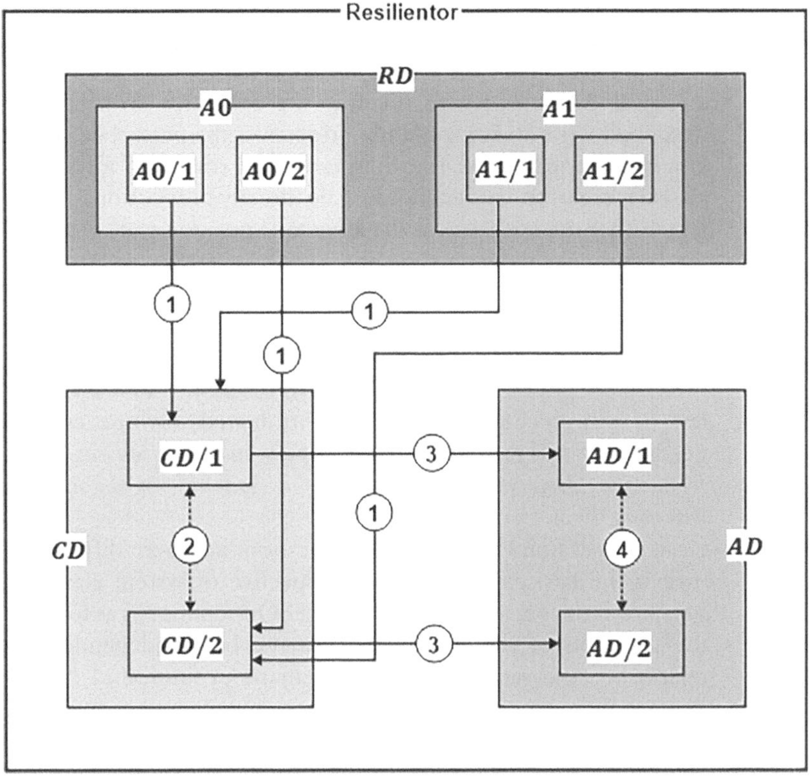

Fig. 1.8 Resilientor's structure. (*Source*: Author)

certain amount of the effect generated by that impact, after the action/reaction in question ceases. Elsewhere (Dinga, 2012) we have shown that after the action/reaction ceases, some quantity of tension is retained (see the concept of stress discussed under the concept of robustness which, in principle, weakens robustness for subsequent sessions of exerting change pressure). Adapted to the case of resilience, this concept of stress is transformed into the concept of resilience, in the sense that the recovery of the state/ kinematic position of the system is not done "without rest", that is, it is not done punctually, neither with respect to the state nor with respect to the kinematic position, but is actually done in their vicinity;[30]

(iii) the question arises whether the elastic force of the *AD* is affected by the size of the gap, as calculated by the *CD*. In relation to this matter, we make the following considerations:
- a logical consequence of the way the resilience property was described—the ability/potential to recover the perturbed state/kinematic position—is the following: the resilience force (the elastic force of the system) should be directly proportional to the gap (either the state gap or the kinematic position gap) recorded by the system following the impact of the change pressure. This consequence is analogous, with strict precautions, to the phenomenon of elasticity in mechanical physics;
- conceptually, resilience is also analogous to the third law of mechanical physics: the law of action/reaction (*Nota bene*: the law of action/reaction can be reformulated, for the current needs, thus: *the formation of the gap in one direction causes the formation, directly proportionally, of a resilience in the opposite direction*);[31]

(iv) we can also examine the following question: are there differences between the two gaps, from the perspective of system elasticity, that is, from the perspective of resilience? Our opinion is as follows:
- the variation of the state vector can be both independent in relation to the variation of the kinematic position and dependent on it;
  - in terms of the independent variation of the state vector:
    the state vector refers to the structure of the system and, respectively, its functionality (e.g., how the input-to-output operator works);
    if the change in the state vector is not caused (or significantly influenced) by the change in the kinematic position of the system, instead, its change will act as a cause (or as a significant influence factor) on the change in the kinematic position—for example, the rate of transformation of the input in the output can change, which changes the behaviour of the system, and the change of the behaviour has an impact on maintaining/changing the position of the system on its trajectory;[32]
    as a result, in general, Fig. 14 shows a mutual relationship of causality/influence (both at the *CD* level and at the

AD level), when the two gaps are calculated (of state, respectively of kinematic position);

- in terms of the dependent variation of the state vector:
  the state vector can undergo non-independent changes when the trajectory of the system (or its position on the trajectory) changes for whatever reason, and this change affects the state of the system. The justification for such an impact on the state vector consists of the following:
  (a) the new position on the trajectory requires either new functions (at least one) or significant changes to an already existing function(s). As the function is generated by the structure, it follows that the variation of the functions (either absolute—new functions—or relative—the adjustment of some existing functions) requires the variation of the structure, which constitutes exactly the content of the state (vector) change;
  (b) it must be specified that the change in the kinematic position of the system is not necessarily the effect of a disturbance—the simple evolution (or development, as the case may be) of the system changes this kinematic position,[33] generating, in turn, according to those already mentioned, state changes in the system;
  based on the above, we can now examine the question of the existence of differences between the resilient treatment of the gap regarding the state of the system and the resilient treatment of the gap regarding the kinematic position of the system. The following considerations contain our answer to this question:
  (a) there is an intrinsic way in which trajectory depends on state—trajectory is an objectification of behaviour, and behaviour represents relationships between the structural components of the system and its environment.[34] As a result, one of the factors (namely, among the fundamental factors) of the trajectory is the state of the system;
  (b) in this context, state resilience contains an ingredient that affects trajectory resilience. In other words,

within a well-developed analytical model, achieving state resilience can also result (at least partially) in kinematic position resilience;

(c) the inverse relationship (affecting the resilience of the state of achieving, totally or partially, the resilience of the trajectory) is not an intrinsic relationship, so it does not have a necessary character although it is not impossible, that is, it has a contingent character;[35]

- the mathematical operator of the resilience function
  - the mathematical operator of the resilience function must have as output (or value[36]) the state, respectively the kinematic position that the system had before the impact of the change pressure (which can often, although not always, be a disturbing factor);
  - this recovery of the previous state/kinematic position is logically done in accordance with the discussion above, but it must be modelled analytically. We propose, in the following, such an analytical operator of the resilience function:[37]

notations (taken from the above, respectively new)

(a) g_t: the gap at time t to the benchmark—we assume it is measured and stored[38] at time $(t - \tau)$;

(b) $\overline{b}_{t-\tau}$: the benchmark at time $(t - \tau)$ (*Nota bene*: usually or to simplify the reasoning, $\tau = 1$);

(c) b_t: the situation (either the state or the kinematic position, which we consider for now indiscernible) at time t;

(d) $\tilde{b}_{t+\varepsilon}$: the situation (either the state or the kinematic position) (re)established following the action of the resilientor[39] (*Nota bene*: usually or to simplify the reasoning, $\varepsilon = 1$);

(e) e: elasticity coefficient of the resilientor; it actually plays the role of the qualitative variable of the previously mentioned elastic force. *Nota bene*: the elasticity coefficient obviously expresses the "personality" of the considered system, each system (depending on its nature, size, history, operating context etc.) having different elasticity coefficients;

(f) F_t^e : elastic force of the resilientor, at time t;

definitions[40]

(a) $g_t = h\left(b_t, \bar{b}_{t-\tau}\right)$

(b) $F_t^e = f\left(g_t, e\right)$

(c) $e = \alpha + \beta \cdot g_t + \gamma \cdot g_t^2$, where α is a parameter that characterizes the "personality" of the system, $\gamma < 0$ (therefore, the function of the elasticity coefficient is—as we propose—a polynomial function of degree 2 of concave[41] type; the graphical form of the elasticity coefficient function is suggested in Fig. 1.9)

calculus

(a) $g_t = b_t - \bar{b}_{t-\tau}$

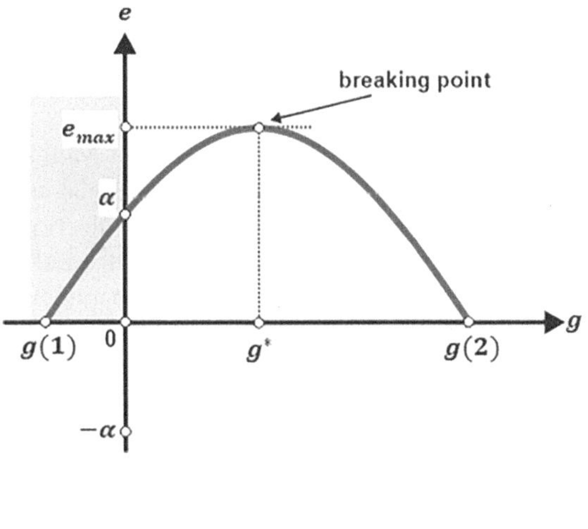

Fig. 1.9 Generic kinematics of the elastic coefficient of the resilientor. (*Source*: Author)

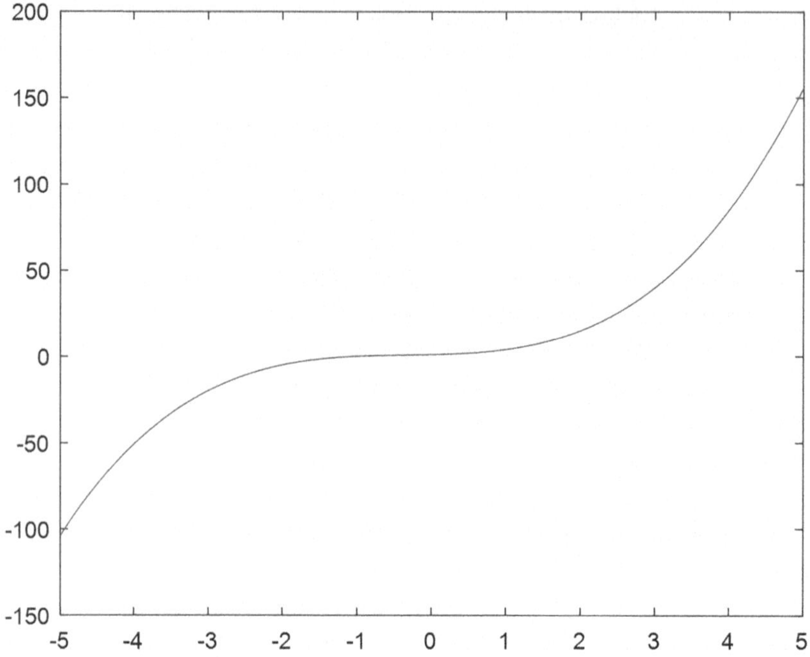

Fig. 1.10 Generic elastic force kinematics of the resilientor (case 1). (*Source*: Author)

(b) $F_t^e = e \cdot g_t = \alpha \cdot g_t + \beta \cdot g_t^2 + \gamma \cdot g_t^3$ (*Nota bene*: for the function of the elastic force, therefore, a polynomial analytical form of degree 3 is obtained—so that it admits an inflection point, because the second derivative is not a constant, but an affine function). The general shape of this function[42] (for all parameters taking positive values) is suggested in Fig. 1.10.[43]

- we must ensure that the operator (elastic force) achieves the purpose for which it is built:
- (case 1) for $\alpha > 0, \beta > 0, \gamma > 0$, F_t^e is permanently decelerated increasing, to the inflection point, then accelerated increasing;
- (case 2) for $\alpha > 0, \beta > 0, \gamma < 0$, F_t^e is permanently decreasing, decelerated to the inflection point, then accelerated—Fig. 1.11.
- (case 3) for $\alpha > 0, \beta < 0, \gamma > 0$, F_t^e behaves qualitatively as in (case 1);
- (case 4) for $\alpha < 0, \beta > 0, \gamma > 0$, F_t^e behaves qualitatively as in (case 1);

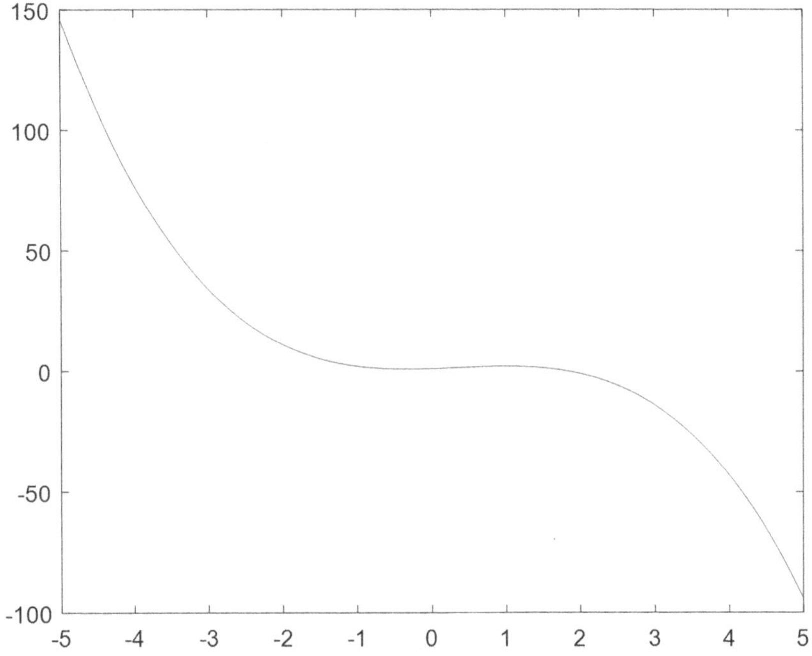

Fig. 1.11 Generic elastic force kinematics of the resilientor (case 2). (*Source*: Author)

- (case 5) for $\alpha > 0, \beta < 0, \gamma < 0$, F_t^e behaves qualitatively as in (case 2);
- (case 6) for $\alpha < 0, \beta < 0, \gamma > 0$, F_t^e behaves qualitatively as in (case 1);
- (case 7) for $\alpha < 0, \beta > 0, \gamma < 0$, F_t^e behaves qualitatively as in (case 2);
- (case 8) for $\alpha < 0, \beta < 0, \gamma < 0$, F_t^e behaves qualitatively as in (case 2);

Nota bene: it is observed that we have (case 1) when $\gamma > 0$ and (case 2) when $\gamma < 0$.

- to be noted that the gap (which constitutes the independent variable in the elastic function equation and also in the elasticity coefficient equation) is calculated with its "natural" algebraic sign (it is not taken in the module). We comment on the consequences of this method of calculation:

- first of all, it must be said that the difference $\left(b_t - \overline{b}_{t-\tau}\right)$ does not always have a relevant meaning. After all, what is the difference between two states, or between two state vectors, or even between two kinematic positions (although in the latter case things seem more comprehensible)? Assuming that (as a rule) by some computational artifice we can determine a difference between the initial state of a system and its resulting state following the impact of the change pressure (disturbing factor), then this difference can be either positive or negative. Without making value judgements[44] about the significance of the algebraic sign of this difference, we note only some methodological consequences in this matter:
  from a logical point of view, the algebraic form of the difference between the two situations (at time t respectively at time $(t - \tau)$) has only a symbolic meaning: since the two situations (either states or kinematic positions) are memorized, as such, in the *MD* device of the resilientor, the latter simply recovers the initial situation (in chronological order), comparing the two images in memory and considering the temporal distinction of the images in question;

Nota bene: of course, a better performing resilientor will have (either in "hard" or in "soft" components) information regarding the degree of recovery (or resilience). Here, we refer to the following aspect: considering the hysteresis (especially in the case of kinematic position changes), the recovery of the initial situation is not (theoretically) perfect/punctual but occurs only in the vicinity of that initial position. If this inherent deviation is predictable, it can obviously be introduced as a correction in the resilientor device (we shall return to this point below);

- second, by virtue of the fact that the resilience (therefore, the coefficient of elasticity) of the system is a structural property of it, it follows that any change of state or any change of kinematic position will, inherently, be "corrected" by the force elastic in question (F_t^e). It follows that, regardless of the cause of these changes, the system itself will restore, with certainty, the situation before the change. The question arises: if the changes are desirable (i.e., they are either discretionarily operated by the system itself—of course, through its leading subsystem—or, although generated by an external cause, they appear to be desirable) how should it be done so that the system be inhibited in its automatic action to restore the original situation which, in this case, becomes undesirable? This issue is especially important[45] (not only in the case of the "hard" nature of the resilience property but also in the case of the "soft" nature of this property). Our opinion on this is as follows:

- self-induced or desirable changes in situation, although induced by external, potentially disruptive[46] factors (state or kinematic position, as the case may be) must be marked as such. By marking the situation, we understand the association of a signal that is transmitted by the driving subsystem of the system to its resilientor device, namely only if the change in the situation is acceptable, desirable or deliberate. This signal—which we can call the desirability mark (*DM*)—will simply inhibit the resilience process;[47]
- in order to achieve the expected effect, the resilientor system must contain an internal, informational device that receives the desirability mark and stops the resilience process from being triggered;
- the programming of the operation of the desirability flag must be done with the utmost care so as to allow the resilientor device not to remain inhibited (i.e., stuck in the inhibited position) also for further, subsequent changes in the state of the system in question—in other words, the internal inhibition control must be of the nature of a single-action selector, unrepeatable under the same "order" of inhibition;[48]

• typology of the resilientor device: in principle, the resilient device is of two types: (a) *homeostatic* resilient device (*HSRD*); (b) *homeorhesic* resilient device (*HRRD*):
  - *HSRD*: refers to the restoration of the initial situation in a system that has undergone state changes (regardless of the cause and/or location of the cause of this change);
  - *HRRD*: refers to the restoration of the initial situation in a system that has undergone changes in kinematic position (regardless of the cause and/or location of the cause of this change).

Nota bene: of course, there is the question of the conjunction of the two types of resilience (or resilient processes). In this sense, based on what has already been mentioned above regarding the relationships between the change of state and the change of kinematic position in a system, we specify the following:

- the change in kinematic position of the system is more significant than the change in state, because the (recorded) change in kinematic position also implies a change in state,[49] while the reverse is not necessarily true—that is, the change in state can lead or not to the corresponding change in the kinematic position;
- symmetrically, a change of state can be in a kind of "dead zone" of the process of change, that is, of the change of kinematic position, which causes the change of state to remain without a correspondent in the change of kinematic position;[50]
- the mechanism (operation) of the resilientor device: based on the results (and conjectures) examined above, we propose a logical mechanism of the resilientor device. For this, we shall rely on Fig. 1.8 to which we shall add some results obtained after the development of this figure. The graphic expression of the working mechanism of the resilientor device is proposed in Fig. 1.12.

Since the components of the resilience device actually function as sufficiency predicates for the resilience property of the system in question, the logical formalization of resilience is as follows:

$$RE \leftarrow (MD) \wedge (CD) \wedge (CD)$$

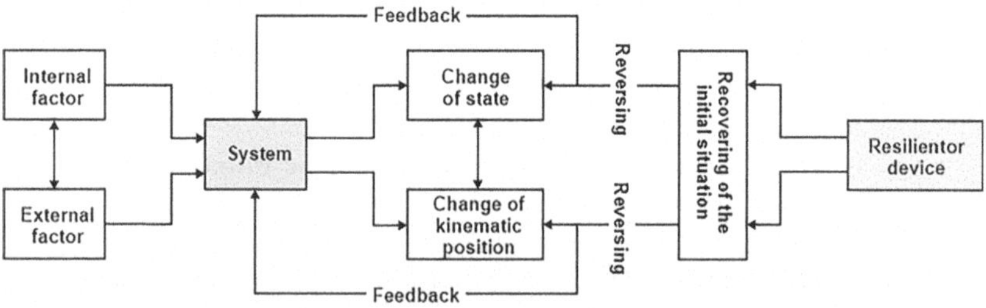

Fig. 1.12 Mechanism of the resilientor device. (*Source*: Author)

1.3 Antifragility

1.3.1 The Advantage

The most significant issue in the antifragility matter is the concept of advantage. Next, we shall provide some considerations in the context.

- denote by $\alpha_i^{(j)}$ a benchmark (a) quantity desired by economic agent j of good i, where $j \in \{1,2\}$, $i \in (M,R)$;
- we shall assume that an economic exchange takes place between economic agents 1 and 2, regarding goods M and R;
- then, necessarily, we have the following quantitative relations:

$$R > \alpha_R^{(1)}$$
$$M > \alpha_M^{(2)}$$
$$M < \alpha_M^{(1)}$$
$$R < \alpha_R^{(2)}$$

- suppose (a simplifying hypothesis, but which does not reduce the generality of the reasoning) that the two agents negotiate an exchange price at which agent 1 sells the entire surplus of R, against the entire surplus of M of agent 2;
- then, the following quantities of the two goods will be exchanged:

$$q_R^{(1)} = R^{(1)} - \alpha_R^{(1)} > 0, \text{of course}: q_R^{(1)} = q_R^{(2)}$$
$$q_M^{(2)} = M^{(2)} - \alpha_M^{(2)} > 0, \text{of course}: q_M^{(2)} = q_M^{(1)}$$

- to calculate the intentional values (denoted with the subscript i; the signs " – ", respectively " + ", written as superscripts), mean outputs from the good in question, (respectively inputs from the good in question) for each of the two agents, as well as in respect of the two goods traded, namely:

$$R_i^{(1)-} = \frac{q_R^{(1)}}{R^{(1)}} = \frac{R^{(1)} - \alpha_R^{(1)}}{R^{(1)}} = 1 - \frac{\alpha_R^{(1)}}{R^{(1)}}$$

$$M_i^{(1)+} = \frac{q_M^{(1)}}{M^{(1)}} = \frac{M^{(2)} - \alpha_M^{(2)}}{M^{(1)}}$$

$$R_i^{(2)+} = \frac{q_R^{(1)}}{R^{(2)}} = \frac{R^{(1)} - \alpha_R^{(1)}}{R^{(2)}}$$

$$M_i^{(2)-} = \frac{q_M^{(1)}}{M^{(2)}} = \frac{M^{(2)} - \alpha_M^{(2)}}{M^{(2)}} = 1 - \frac{\alpha_M^{(2)}}{M^{(2)}}$$

- let us determine the relations between the intentional values, as they are "recorded" (in fact, in a perfectly idiosyncratic way, perceived by the mental accounting of each of the two agents participating in the transaction) of the two economic agents:
  - for agent 1:

$$k^{(1)} = \frac{R_i^{(1)-}}{M_i^{(1)+}} = \frac{R^{(1)} - \alpha_R^{(1)}}{R^{(1)}} \cdot \frac{M^{(1)}}{M^{(2)} - \alpha_M^{(2)}} = \frac{M^{(1)}}{R^{(1)}} \cdot \frac{R^{(1)} - \alpha_R^{(1)}}{M^{(2)} - \alpha_M^{(2)}}$$

If we admit (which is perfectly reasonable) that $q_R^{(1)} = q_M^{(2)}$, that is, the transaction price objectifies the equivalence of the two goods exchanged, then $k^{(1)} = \frac{M^{(1)}}{R^{(1)}} < 1$, because, by hypothesis, economic agent 1 has a currency deficit ($M^{(1)}$), respectively a surplus of real goods ($R^{(1)}$).[51] So, we have the relation:

$$\frac{R_i^{(1)-}}{M_i^{(1)+}} < 1$$

So economic agent 1 will interpret the result of the economic transaction as having the following meaning: s/he gave $R_i^{(1)-}$, namely less than s/he received $M_i^{(1)+}$, so s/he obtained an economic advantage.[52]

  - for agent 2:

$$k^{(2)} = \frac{M_i^{(2)-}}{R_i^{(2)+}} = \frac{M^{(2)} - \alpha_M^{(2)}}{M^{(2)}} \cdot \frac{R^{(2)}}{R^{(1)} - \alpha_R^{(1)}} = \frac{R^{(2)}}{M^{(2)}} \cdot \frac{M^{(2)} - \alpha_M^{(2)}}{R^{(1)} - \alpha_R^{(1)}}$$

Putting the same condition as in the case of the first agent, that is, $q_R^{(1)} = q_M^{(2)}$, we obtain: $k^{(2)} = \frac{R^{(2)}}{M^{(2)}} < 1$, because, by hypothesis, agent 2 has a currency surplus ($M^{(2)}$), respectively a real good deficit ($R^{(2)}$). So, we have:

$$\frac{M_i^{(2)-}}{R_i^{(2)+}} < 1$$

Consequently, agent 2 will interpret the result of the economic transaction as having the following meaning: she/he gave ($M_i^{(2)-}$), namely less than she/he received ($R_i^{(2)+}$), so she/he obtained an economic advantage.

The bottom line is that by accepting mental accounting, that is, the perception that each of the two economic agents has of the transaction made, both wins.[53]

Additional discussion

- we discussed above the concept of advantage from a transactional perspective. Although this perspective is quite broad, it is not exhaustive, however, because it implies a certain activism of the economic agent (subject)—namely the running of a transaction, whether it is initiated by that economic agent or accepted by him/her;
- there is, however, also a perspective, so to speak, non-transactional, that is, a purely positional (or passive) perspective, in which an economic agent (subject) can "confront" the issue of advantage. In this perspective, the advantage no longer represents a net result (a resultant) of the comparison between effect and effort within an action, but appears as a singular (non-processual) benefit;[54] therefore, it could be called a *positional advantage*, towards different from the one discussed previously and which can be called a *transactional advantage*;
- the positional advantage is always an external effect—more precisely, an effect that has its source or effective causality in the environment of the agent (subject), being, therefore, independent of that subject;[55]
- we believe that there can be two categories (classes) of positional advantages:

(1) *Positive externality*: an advantage impersonally arising (e.g., as a result of natural changes) or generated non-intentionally[56] by economic agents located in the target agent's environment (including the perspective of the normative framework of society)—here falls a species discussed rather hotly in economic literature, especially from the perspective of taxation theory, but of course the scope of interest of the subject in question is much wider: the concept of undeserved advantage[57] (see the particular concept of windfall profit); to be specified, along with non-intentionality, another attribute of the externality (both positive and negative): the absence of consent of the recipient of the externality in question to receive that externality, otherwise, again, it falls into the category of transactional advantage;
(2) *Charity*: an advantage intentionally created by economic agents located in the target agent's environment (including, again, the perspective of the normative framework of society). The basic condition that must be respected in the matter of charity is that of the absence of considering any compensation from the beneficiary of the act of charity.

1.3.2 The Perturbation/Disturbance

In this paragraph we aim to examine the concept of perturbation, a concept that is central to the entire phenomenology of antifragility (as a property) or of antifragilizing (as a process of acquiring the property of antifragility).

(1) The concept of perturbance/disturbance

By perturbation, in general, is understood a deviation of a phenomenon or process (or, more generally, of a system), following a shock, either internal or external, from its state or from its trajectory. Of course, the idea of a threshold of significance is unavoidable here—beyond what size or speed of deviation[58] is a disturbance considered? In this context, we consider that there are two main classes of potential disturbances: (a) state disturbances (static disturbances); (b) process disturbances (kinematic disturbances). State disturbances refer to the deviation of the system from its structure and configuration above an accepted significance threshold, and process disturbances refer to the deviation of the system from the trajectory it is on at a given moment, obviously also above a given threshold of meaning. Each of the two classes of disturbances can have one of the following two specific situations: (a) increasing the predictability of the system, if the disturbance is above the threshold at which the change is irreversible;[59] (b) decreasing the predictability of the system if the disturbance is below the significance threshold at which the change is irreversible.

Here the following question can be raised: perturbations can, of course, be either systemic (when a perturbing cause has a high "energetic" potential to produce deviations, either from state or from trajectory[60]) or local (when a disruptive cause affects a relatively limited sphere—either spatially, temporally, or qualitatively). The issue is whether they are initialization disruptions/perturbations or corrective disruptions/perturbations. By initialization perturbations we mean those perturbations that initiate the deviations previously discussed, while corrective perturbations are those perturbations that act as negations (cancellations) of initialization perturbations. In our opinion, in both situations we are talking about disruptions, the distinction between them consisting, obviously, of their place along the whole process of disrupting/perturbing, on the one hand, and on the deliberative or non-deliberative character of the action implied, on the other hand—thus, initialization disruption stays (as a rule) are at the origin of perturbation and have (usually) a non-deliberative nature, while corrective disruptions stay at the effect of perturbation and have (usually) a deliberative nature.[61]

Disturbance must be considered a species of effect of a system, exerted on another system, and which verifies the following sufficiency predicates:

- (PS_1^P) *negative meaning* for the target system: the disturbance exists *qua* disturbance only if the target system (the system receiving the effect) evaluates it as such, by assigning that meaning. By negative meaning is meant a property of the disturbance to generate a disadvantage, either absolute or relative for the target system;[62]
- (PS_2^P) *significant level*: this is an "amount" of disturbance that exceeds the previously mentioned threshold of significance. Although, as mentioned, the assessment of the significance threshold is usually idiosyncratic, it is still possible to have automatic/automatized algorithms that calculate at each moment the accumulation of the amount of disturbance,[63] and, of course, provide decision-makers within the system in question information on the matter (or even, in more sophisticated cases, decisional alternatives). It should be noted that the *dead zone* and, implicitly (*Nota bene* 1, below), the *dead time*

to reach the significance threshold express exactly the robustness potential of the target system—the robustness of the system is exceeded only upon reaching the significance threshold. In this sense, from a theoretical point of view, we shall have to identify two components of the dead zone: (a) a *passive* component—which we call the *zone of insensitivity*; (b) an *active* component—which we call the *zone of opposition*:

- *Zone of insensitivity*: the zone of insensitivity is actually a zone of unobservability on the part of the target system, that is, it refers to an amount of change pressure that does not produce any relevant effect for this system (we denote this zone with DZ_t^*, and the observability threshold, i.e. the threshold at which the disturbance becomes observable, generating the action of the robustness property, we denote it by Π_t^*);
- *Zone of opposition*: the opposition zone is the actual zone in which the robustness property of the target system acts (opposing the production of the disturbance effect). So, the robustness property is activated only after an intermediate significance threshold is reached, namely the one that marks the beginning of the disturbance observability zone, we denote this zone by DZ_t^{**}, and the significance threshold, i.e., the threshold at which robustness gives way, possibly leaving the "place" for resilience, we denote it with Π_t^{**}; with Π_t^{***} we denote a threshold—in fact, a decision node—at which the target system can have one of the following options/decisions:
  - (*D*1) activation of the definitive structural change under the impact of the perturbation, with consequences either on the state, or on the kinematics, or on both characteristics;
  - (*D*2) activation of the resilience property, either homeostatic or homeorhesic;
  - (*D*3) activating the antifragility property.

Figure 1.13 schematically illustrates how the two sub-zones of the dead zone are "distributed".

Nota bene 1: the question (can) be asked: what phenomenon are we dealing with until the pressure of a shock reaches the significance threshold established for its qualification as a disturbance? Terminologically, we can call that phenomenon a pre-disturbance or a disturbance in the making (although the latter formulation contains the suggestion of the inherent nature of the disturbance, which is excessive, since it is possible to

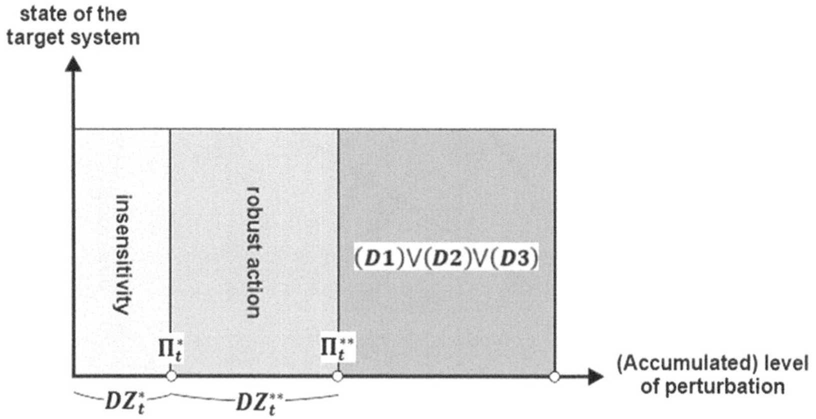

Fig. 1.13 The two sub-zones of the dead zone. (*Source*: Author)

produce fluctuations that resorb themselves, remaining permanently below the level of significance). We propose to have, here too, at any threshold of significance a ***dead zone***, that is, an interval of variation of the change pressure exerted on the target system that has not yet reached the threshold of significance. Obviously, any dead zone corresponds to a ***dead time*** (*or* ***dead duration***), which is precisely the time required for the change pressure to reach the level of the significance threshold. Of course, the association of dead time to dead zone is not linear but depends on the rate at which the amount of change accumulates towards the significance threshold level. The relationship between the dead zone and the dead time, by means of the rate of generation of stress/change pressure (which is the essence of disturbance), is suggested in Fig. 1.14 (v_i denoted the rate i of accumulation of stress or change pressure, and d_i denoted the dead time related to the speed v_i).

Nota bene 2: it is useful here to examine the concept of fluctuation in connection with that of disturbance. Fluctuation is a phenomenon characterized by the following:

a. represents a variation in the input of a system that does not compromise the output of that system,[64] that is, falls within the stability margin with which the black-box of the system in question generates its output;[65]

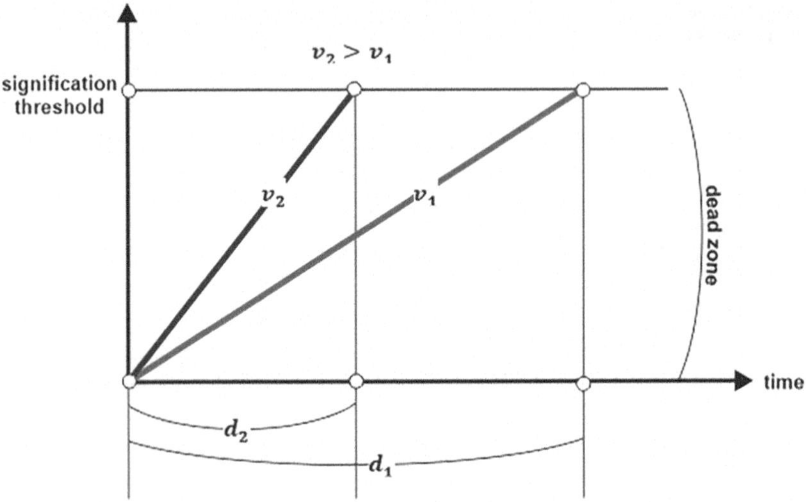

Fig. 1.14 The relationship "pressure build-up rate of change–dead time". (*Source*: Author)

b. represents an oscillating type variation (at the limit, sinusoidal)—this means that the variation in question of the input is followed by a variation in the opposite direction (usually of the same amplitude) of the input; moreover, the current meaning of the term fluctuation quite obviously suggests this oscillatory characteristic of the variation in question;[66]
c. it is internal—this characteristic of the fluctuation concept is especially important because, as we shall see, the disturbance can be both internal to a system and external to it. So, fluctuation is (exclusively from the perspective of this characteristic/specificity) a species of disturbance;
d. the fluctuation is exclusively structural, not functional[67]—this feature (attribute) of the fluctuation is especially important; therefore, we shall make more clarifications in the following:
    - the structural character of the fluctuation is compatible with its internal nature (see point (c))—more precisely, the internal nature results, by logical inference, from the structural character—and, in fact, represents the causal explanation of the oscillating character of the fluctuation. Indeed, if the fluctuation were not

"encoded" in the structure of the system, then the oscillating character would no longer have a necessary character, but a contingent one (either this contingent character would be ensured from the inside or it would have as its source the environment of the system concerned). The contingent (as opposed to the necessary) character of the fluctuation would no longer allow us to affirm its oscillating behaviour as a distinctive or defining feature of the fluctuation;

- the structural character of the fluctuation could be introduced[68] in any system exposed to disturbances, because the dead zone, which we talked about previously, represents the very area of manifestation of the fluctuation, as it is easy to ascertain from the argumentation produced up to this point;
- based on the above, it is immediate to conclude that fluctuation can represent not only an internal mechanism of any system subject to disturbances but also a predictor of the behaviour of the system in question in the face of disturbances.[69]
  - (PS_3^P) ***mutational role***: a disturbance must have a function/role of a mutational nature, that is it must tend to institute a change that is destined to perpetuate itself (*Nota bene*: it is easy to see that, if we did not also consider this sufficiency predicate of the perturbation, the latter could easily be considered a simple fluctuation).[70]

So, the logical definition of a disturbance ($\mathcal{P}$) is as follows:

$$\mathcal{P} \leftarrow \left(PS_1^P\right) \wedge \left(PS_2^P\right) \wedge \left(PS_3^P\right)$$

Any impulse exerted on a system that verifies the next logical condition is a non-disturbance.[71]

$$\bar{\mathcal{P}} = \left[\left(\overline{PS1}^P\right) \wedge \left(PS_2^P\right) \wedge \left(PS_3^P\right)\right] \vee \left[\left(PS_1^P\right) \wedge \left(\overline{PS2}^P\right) \wedge \left(PS_3^P\right)\right] \vee \left[\left(PS_1^P\right) \wedge \left(PS_2^P\right) \wedge \left(\overline{PS3}^P\right)\right] \vee$$
$$\vee \left[\left(\overline{PS1}^P\right) \vee \left(\overline{PS2}^P\right) \wedge \left(PS_3^P\right)\right] \vee \left[\left(\overline{PS1}^P\right) \wedge \left(PS_2^P\right) \wedge \left(\overline{PS3}^P\right)\right] \vee \left[\left(PS_1^P\right) \wedge \left(\overline{PS2}^P\right) \wedge \left(\overline{PS3}^P\right)\right] \vee$$
$$\vee \left[\left(\overline{PS_1}^P\right) \wedge \left(\overline{PS_2}^P\right) \wedge \left(\overline{PS_3}^P\right)\right]$$

(2) A typology of perturbation/disruption

A typology of disruption, however general, is logically required by examining the concept of antifragility, since antifragility is a property of a system to capitalize on disruption, in the sense of obtaining benefits/advantages for the system that is the target of that disruption. We propose the following typology of disruption:

a. By nature:
    - *Institutive perturbations*: perturbations that introduce a change, of any kind and magnitude, into the target system. As we have shown above, in most cases such disturbances are emergent (i.e., non-deliberative). Although then, deliberative institutional disruptions are not ruled out,[72] we "expect" institutive disruptions to occur emergently (obviously, emergence implies quasi-unpredictability);
    - *Corrective perturbations*: perturbations that are driven, in their design and implementation, by institutive disruptions. They have the role of annihilating institutive disturbances (totally or in part), usually, as previously shown, by means of the resilience property of the target system. Corrective perturbations have, in most cases, a deliberate, discretionary character.[73] Although emergent corrective disruptions are therefore not ruled out, we "expect" corrective disruptions to occur deliberately (obviously, deliberativeness implies predictability);
b. By amplitude:
    - *Hormetic perturbations*: perturbations which, by the amplitude and/or speed with which they affect the target system, are located in the dead zone of that system, that is, below the threshold of significance to trigger the first "line of defence", namely robustness. Obviously, the amount of hormetic perturbation is a multiplicative result of the intensity of the perturbation (which can be assimilated to its amplitude) and the duration of application of the perturbation in question. In fact, the problem is somewhat more complicated, because the duration of the disturbance impulse, on the one hand, increases the amount of disturbance and, on the other hand, decreases this amount, because it allows the dissipa-

tion of the impact in the system (*Nota bene*: this dissipation is, largely, moreover, "responsible" for the very hormetic character of the disturbance category discussed at this point). A graphic image of this interesting phenomenon (extremely present in the economy,[74] as it is known) is presented in Fig. 1.15 ($Q_t^{\mathcal{P}}$ expresses the amount of accumulated disturbance: $Q_t^{\mathcal{P}} = I_{\rightarrow t}^{\mathcal{P}} \cdot d_{\rightarrow t}^{\mathcal{P}}$, where $I_{\rightarrow t}^{\mathcal{P}}$ represents the intensity of the disturbance during its exercise, i.e., until the moment of analysis t, measured in some way, compatible with the research interest, and $d_{\rightarrow t}^{\mathcal{P}}$ represents the duration of the disturbance until the time of analysis t).

- *Supra-hormetic perturbations*: perturbations which, by the amplitude and/or the speed with which they affect the target system, are located above the dead zone of that system, that is, above the threshold of significance that triggers robustness. Although the threshold of significance for the action of robustness should generally be considered relatively constant, however, in accordance with what was exposed and argued in the category of hormetic disturbances, it is obvious that this threshold is increased (as a level) precisely by the action of hormetic disturbances.[75]

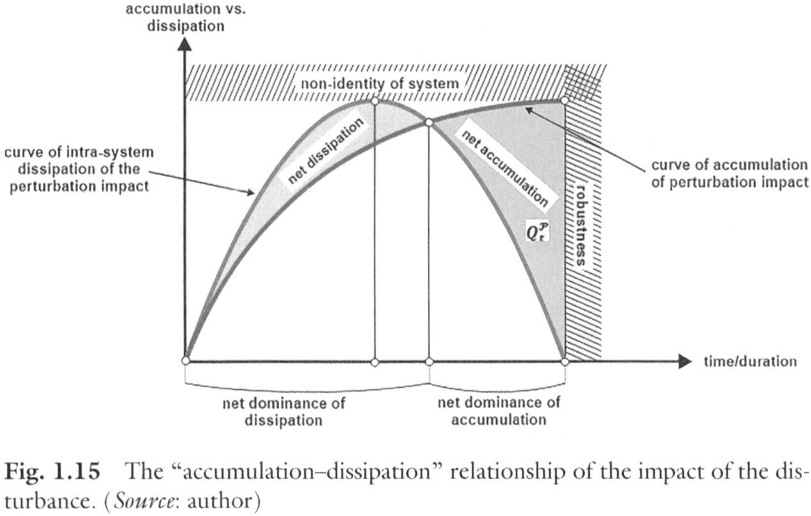

Fig. 1.15 The "accumulation–dissipation" relationship of the impact of the disturbance. (*Source*: author)

c. By mechanism:
   - *Repeatable perturbations*: perturbations that occur with a certain periodicity (having, therefore, a certain potential to be predictable[76]). The repeatability of this type of disturbances is based on their structural character at the level of the generating system;[77]
   - *Unrepeatable/singular perturbations*: singular perturbations, in terms of their causality and structure. They are generated by very unlikely, almost unpredictable[78] contexts. However, synergistic analysis could detect, on a purely functional basis, a measurable probability of such perturbations occurring;
d. By origin:
   - *Internal perturbations*: perturbations that originate[79] in the target system of the perturbation in question;
   - *External perturbations*: perturbations originating outside the target system of the perturbation in question;
e. By impact:
   - *Structural perturbations*: perturbations (of any of the types discussed above) that have the potential to affect the structure of the target system. This potential can refer to both quantitative aspects—for example, high intensity or long duration of manifestation—and qualitative aspects—for example, their "ability" to target certain structural components of the target system. Of course, structural perturbations are perturbations that must be given the greatest importance because, through changes to the structure of the target system, the very functions of this system are altered;
   - *Functional perturbations*: perturbations (of any of the types discussed above) that can only affect the operation (possibly only certain functions) of the target system, which, not affecting the structure, so, they have no potential to produce lasting or permanent changes;
f. By behaviour:[80]
   - *Spontaneous perturbations*: perturbations that are not triggered by other perturbations, but by causalities independent of the latter;
   - *Induced perturbations*: perturbations that are triggered by other perturbations,[81] not by causalities independent of the latter;

g. By affinity:
  - *Cumulative perturbations*: perturbations which, through certain qualitative and quantitative properties, become additive/summable among them (generally regarding perturbations of the same type and exerted on the same component of the target system) so that, over time, the final (cumulative) perturbation represents a multiple of the punctual perturbations of cumulative type. Since the cumulative perturbations have a significant role in the objective of the present study, we shall develop, in a discussion section, this topic;[82]
  - *Isolated perturbations*: perturbations that are "immiscible" with previous or next perturbations (of course, a total immiscibility is difficult to accept, therefore, in a deeper analysis, more specific properties will have to be identified in order to declare a perturbation as isolated), that is, perturbations that do not accumulate with previous perturbations, being either simply juxtaposed (which could eventually lead to synergy) or completely distinct causally, structurally and functionally from the perturbations already installed in the target system.

(3) Avatars of perturbation

A perturbation, once it has occurred[83] on the target system, can experience the following avatars:

- is dissolved/neutralized by the resilience device, in the sense that the system is brought (with the unavoidable approximation, generated by the hysteresis effect) to the state—through homeostasis—or to the trajectory—through homeorhesis—held before the occurrence of that disturbance. In this case, the disturbance disappears as such, leaving only its "traces" (some of which we refer to immediately below);
- it is put into conservation, through its causal isolation. This (less common but theoretically non-ignorable) process refers to a rapid solution of the target system which, prior to (or as an alternative to) finding a solution to dissolve/neutralize the perturbation, simply "wraps" the disturbance in a causal insulating cocoon. This operation is done, of course, in any way that the target system can develop, according to its structural properties;[84]

- it is directed to produce its specific effects on the structural periphery of the target system, so preserving the identity of the system;
- is susceptible to not being possible to be stopped or diverted from its path of attack on the target system, which is of a nature, as a rule, to affect the very identity of the target system (identity that refers to its basic structure).

Nota bene: of course, there is the question of the effect of a disturbance, under the conditions of the operation of resilience, on this very property of the target system. In relation to this aspect (which is part of the learning effects category), we make the following considerations:

- hormetic perturbations obviously improve the resilience capacity of the target system, which expands the scope—that is, raises the quantitative threshold—of perturbations that can be considered hormetic type. Somehow, a hormetic perturbation initiates positive feedback to support more hormetic perturbations, which improves resilience;
- corrective perturbations can also improve the resilience of the target system because they are, over time, assimilated, through learning, by the resilience device in question, so that when an institutive perturbation occurs, the resilience device mobilizes, almost automatically, the associated corrective disturbance.

1.3.3 Defining the Antifragility

(1) The duality of the concept of antifragility

The concept of antifragility is, at the same time, a new concept and an old one, having, for this reason, a dual structure.

(a) The old aspect of the concept of antifragility

Consists in the fact that any system (whether non-living or living and, in the latter case, either a non-cultural living system or a cultural one) tries to transform the disturbance or, more precisely, the impact of the disturbance, in a new state of its own, accommodated to that impact. In other words, the target system tries to survive the impact of the disturbance by a *passive reaction*. By passive reaction of the target system to a disturbance we mean that reaction[85] which has as its "goal" the identity survival of the target system, identity survival referring, of course, to the preservation of the basic structure of the system in question. Here we need to make some considerations regarding the concept of the ***basic structure*** of the target system.[86]

- the basic structure consists of those component elements that fulfil the *conditio sine qua non* in the functioning of that system (*Nota bene*: an analogue regarding the normative structure of society is the Constitution, which represents the basic structure of the normative framework);
- the basic structure has the significance of a hardcore of the target system structure, having a relatively low sensitivity to disturbances;
- preserving the basic structure means preserving the identity of the target system and vice versa;
- therefore, if the structural (therefore, implicitly functional) resettlement of the target system is done without affecting the basic structure (i.e., the hardcore), then what we called above identity survival of the system in question occurs;
- from a logical point of view, it follows that, under the conditions of preserving the basic structure, the resettlement of the target system as an effect of the disturbance allows structural changes, let us say peripheral. Here we have the equivalent of what Lakatos called the protective belt (to keep the analogy with the normative structure of society, the protective belt represents the set of ordinary legislation—primary, secondary, tertiary—elaborated on the basis of and consistently with the Constitution);[87]
- therefore, the structure of the target system consists of two components: (a) hardcore or the basic structure or, still, the central structure; (b) protective belt or peripheral structure. While modification—including destruction or irreversible alteration—of the protective belt preserves the identity survival of the target system, modification[88] of the core structure signifies either (i) non-identitary[89] survival of the target system or (ii) non-survival of the very target system;
- the old aspect of the meaning of the concept of antifragility consists, therefore, in the passive reaction of the target system that seeks to preserve its basic structure, with the acceptance of the changes induced by the disturbance on the protective belt of its structure.

(b) The new aspect of the concept of antifragility

Consists, especially following the recent emphasis by Taleb (2014), in what we want to call the ***active reaction*** of the target system. By active reaction of the target system, we mean that reaction whose objective is to capitalize on the disturbance (more precisely, on the impact of the disturbance) to the advantage of the target system in question. So, this time, the target system is no longer "satisfied" with identitary survival but aspires to gain an advantage[90] from bearing the impact of the perturbation. Before continuing the discussion on this matter, it is necessary to make some considerations about the "goal" of antifragility, from the perspective of what we have called active reaction:

- the first problem is the following: what does the term advantage or gain from perturbation refer to:
  - in our opinion, we have to consider, here, the concept of utility. We refer to the concept of integral utility (Dinga et al., 2022), not only to that of substantive utility (generally considered in economic analyses). (*Nota bene*: integral utility contains three interdependent components: (a) substantive/economic utility; (b) evidential/evidential utility; (c) symbolic/positional utility). So, the target system aims to obtain, following the impact of the disturbance, a net (integral) utility increase;[91]
  - of course, the concrete manifestation of this increase in net integral utility depends on the nature of the target system, as well as the nature of the disturbance in question. It should be noted that there is an inter-conditioning between the nature of the target system and the nature of the perturbation: a target system is not sensitive to (cannot be affected by) any perturbation, just as a perturbation cannot affect any target system. In fact, there are what we can call *bright cones* that allow (only) compatible interactions between perturbations and target systems. A synoptic view of this idea is shown in Fig. 1.16.
- the second problem concerns the "fate" of the identity of the target system following the occurrence of the disturbance. In this sense, we make the following brief considerations:
  - the target system maintains its identity as long as the basic structure (the previously mentioned hardcore component) is not affected as a result of the disturbance. Of course, this is an identity

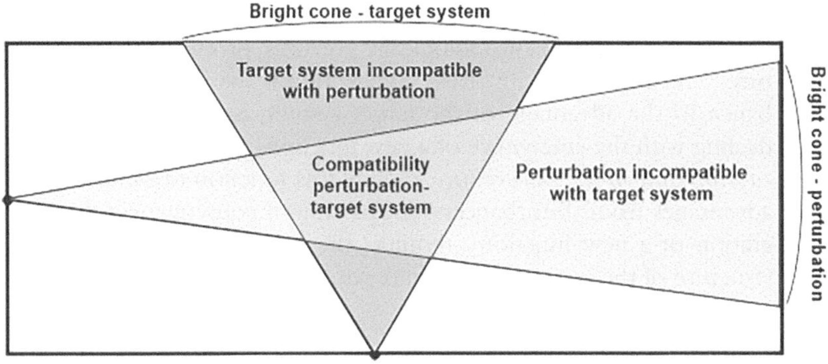

Fig. 1.16 Superposition of the light cones of the perturbation and the target system. (*Source*: Author)

which, in turn, is somewhat of a core identity, since the modification of the peripheral component of the target system's structure cannot ensure a complete or a punctual preservation of the identity in question;[92]

- if, instead, the impact of the disturbance affects the considerably basic structure of the target system, then its identity is no longer preserved; it simply becomes another system. It is obvious that the antifragility property is compatible only with the preservation of the identity of the target system.

(2) The sufficiency predicates of the concept of antifragility

In this paragraph we shall examine the logical bases of the definition of antifragility, that is, we shall identify the attributes/predicates which, as being met, confer, *eo ipso*, the property of antifragility to a given system. In our opinion, the sufficiency predicates of the antifragility property[93] are as follows:

- (***AF1***) *peripheral plastic capacity*: as known, the function(s) of a system is/are the effect of its structure.[94] This means that, given the fact that the stability of the system, both within its membrane (what we call functionality) and in relation to its environment (what we call behaviour), depends on its functions and these, in turn, (causally) depend on its structure, a modification of the function/functions implies a change, logically and chronologically previous, produced in the structure.[95] As antifragility involves capitalizing on the impact of a disturbance to the advantage of the target system, it follows that we are dealing with the emergence of a new function, namely the *function of capitalizing on the disturbance*: exactly this function of obtaining net advantages from disturbances—so, by way of consequence, the generation of a new function—requires the possibility of changing the structure of the system, a possibility we call structural plasticity.[96]

1.4 Discussion:

(i) as we have shown several times before, structural plasticity must somehow lie outside the structural hardcore of the target system, because changes to last component led to the loss of the identity of the target system. This is the reason the sufficiency predicate *AF*1 was not called structural plasticity, but peripheral structural plasticity (*Nota bene*: from an evolutionary point of view, the peripheral aspect of structural plasticity would shift the focus from genetic evolution to epigenetic evolution);

(ii) of course, the question of accepting the loss of the identity of the target system (and, as a result, the appearance of another system, different from the previous one) can be raised but, in this case, some clarifications must be made and certain "insurances" must be taken:

- any system has its role and place in an ensemble of interconnected systems (either in system mode or in network[97] mode), which boils down to saying that it is expected to have a certain functionality, that is a certain behaviour such that, if this expectation is violated, disturbances will occur both in the system and in the supersystem that contains it;
- therefore, among the functions and behaviours that are generated by the hardcore of the system, those functions and behaviours that do not alter the identity of the supersystem in question must be selected;
- in conclusion, some change in system identity is acceptable as a result of changes made in the hardcore of the structure, provided that some kind of hardcore of the hardcore continues to deliver those functions and behaviours that preserve the iden-

tity of the supersystem, although it sacrifices preserving the identity of the target system.

- (***AF2***) ***inability to discriminate the perturbation***: this sufficiency predicate of the antifragility property is "suspicious" from several points of view, so we shall develop, below, some clarifications:
- although a sufficiency predicate is usually asserted positively (an existence—i.e., a cataphatic assertion), this time the sufficiency predicate is asserted negatively (an absence—i.e., an apophatic assertion). The explanation is as follows:
- a given system obviously has a certain cognitive capacity,[98] which inherently has a certain discriminative capacity in relation to the variations in the environment of that system. Such a discriminatory capacity also refers to disturbances (nature, intensity, duration, origin etc.)—well, precisely this last discriminatory capacity is prohibited by the sufficiency predicate under discussion, because otherwise we can no longer speak of the property of antifragility. So, this predicate of sufficiency ensures a function precisely through the absence of the structure that would prevent the formation of the discriminative function in question;[99]
- it should not be understood from this that, for a system to have (or acquire, as the case may be) the property of antifragility, an existing capacity to discriminate against disturbances must be prevented (or annihilated, as the case may be), but that only those systems that lack the respective discriminatory capacity qualify as antifragile systems;[100]
- we emphasize the fact that the target system is not devoid of any discriminatory capacity in general, but only the discriminatory capacity regarding disturbances (either internal or external—as they were specified, from a conceptual point of view, previously). So, the target system is able to sense/record any disturbance as a general disturbance (thus as a genus) and not as a species of disturbance and even less as a particular disturbance. The explanation of the assertion of this predicate of sufficiency consists in the fact that, with regard to special disturbances (i.e., of the type of species) or that of particular disturbances, any system can develop actions or even structural-functional devices of prevention (robustness), counteraction (resilience) or capital-

ization (antifragility), but only a *general* ability of the target system to capitalize on any perturbation that might impact that system genuinely constitutes the property of antifragility. Through a deliberately paradoxical expression, we could state that an antifragile system does not target any specific disturbance in the conditions in which it targets any disturbance;
- (***AF3***) *inability to predict the perturbations*: this sufficiency predicate, while not dependent on *AF2*, is somehow logically "required" by the latter, in the sense that if a certain perturbation were predictable, then the target system would constitute its capitalization devices according to the predicted perturbation—or, this turns the perturbation in question from generic perturbation to special (i.e., species-type) perturbation or even particular perturbation, which would be contradictory to *AF2*.[101] *Nota bene*: we therefore have a second negatively asserted[102] sufficiency predicate. Of course, there is a risk that this sufficiency predicate is relatively "strange": what is the rationale for disallowing the predictive ability of some system with respect to perturbations? The risk can only come from not noticing that predictive incapacity is only stipulated for perturbations, otherwise the target system in question keeping intact both its existing predictive capabilities and the potential to develop new predictive capabilities.

Brief discussion

The "requirement" that the target system has no predictive capability regarding the disturbances (either internal or external), which was justified on logical grounds above, is also suggested—of course in the much more … *friendly*, characteristic style—even by Taleb, when he implies that an antifragile system no longer needs to account for or take into account the occurrence of risks (*Nota bene*: that is, in our terminology here, it no longer needs to predict nor to cover the risks; or, the risks are, in an inherent way, associated with disruptions; therefore, we have only made explicit, in a more firm expression, Taleb's suggestion, with which we obviously agree) or the uncertainty. The idea that an antifragile system acquires, so to speak, a "blind spot" with respect to risks and uncertainty (i.e., disruptions) has especially important consequences, both at the purely theoretical level and at the level of public policy, which we are interested in particularly in this research study.

- (***AF4***) *capacity of fructifying the impact of the disturbance*: this predicate of sufficiency refers to the potential of the target system to integrate, in one way or another, the impact of the disturbance, maintaining its structural identity, that is, the previously evoked hardcore. The fructifying capacity can have different instantiations, depending both on the nature and characteristics of the disturbance and on the nature and characteristics of the target system. Essentially, this sufficiency predicate ensures the completion of the acquisition of net advantages for the target system by harnessing the disruption. From a structural point of view, the respective predicate implies the following:
  - the target system has—namely, in its permanent structure, called hardcore—a component that we shall call the *antifragilizing component*, characterized by the following:
    represents a structural device for "*translating*" the impact of the disturbance:[103] the impact of the disturbance, regardless of its nature, size, intensity, duration etc., must be converted into effects that avoid both the negative[104] meaning and the neutral[105] meaning of that impact for the target system—obviously, only the positive meaning remains, that is, exactly what represents an advantage that the target system obtains (or can get) from disturbance;
    it is completely *non-specific*: in an especially important sense, this feature of the antifragilizing structural component constitutes the essence (the eidos, the quiddity) of the antifragility property of a system.[106] It has the following relatively important connotations:

(a) the antifragility property lacks the ability to distinguish between perturbations, as shown above (see *AF2*). However, for antifragilit y/antifragilizing to work, this discriminatory inability must also be extended to the antifragilizing component (*AF4*), instead not relative to the disruption, but to harnessing the impact of the disruption. This means that harnessing disruption is a general effect, applicable to any disruption (more precisely, to any impact of any disruption);[107]

(b) the non-specificity of the antifragilizing component has an extremely important consequence, this time from an epistemological perspective. We can formulate this consequence in the following way: ***the structural introduction of the second-best solution to the problem of capitalizing (transforming into an advantage) the impact of the disturbance.*** The justification for this assertion consists of the following:

there seems to be an equivalence[108] between the first-best choice from a small number of alternatives and the second-best choice from a large number of alternatives. In other words, the more "ensured" a number of alternatives from which to choose, the more desirable (i.e., brings greater utility) a second-best choice, and vice versa, as the number of alternatives decreases, the more desirable a first-best choice becomes (for a visualization of the indifference curve in question, see Fig. 1.17).

the non-specificity of the antifragilizing component that operationalizes the *AF*4 sufficiency predicate has exactly this effect: the (theoretically, indefinite) increase in the number of alternatives for capitalizing on the impact of the disturbance, which justifies (as we said, from an epistemological point of view) the fact that we are in the situation of an accentuated propensity towards a second-best choice;

has an ***evolutionary*** character: the evolutionary character of the antifragilizing component results, of course, first of all, from the fact that it has an "appetite" for ***second-best*** type solutions in the fructification of the impact of disturbances, this being an indirect argument in this regard. However, we will also bring some direct arguments for this particularity:

(a) the non-specificity of the antifragilizing component means that, strictly speaking, any impact of a disturbance represents a surprise for this device.[109] As a surprise, the response of the antifragilizing component will be designed, except for some general functionality, exclusively according to the "look and like" of the impact in question. In other words, the reaction of the target system, from the perspective of the sufficiency predicate *AF*4, is generated, so to speak, by the action itself (i.e.,, by the impulse generated by the impact of the disturbance);

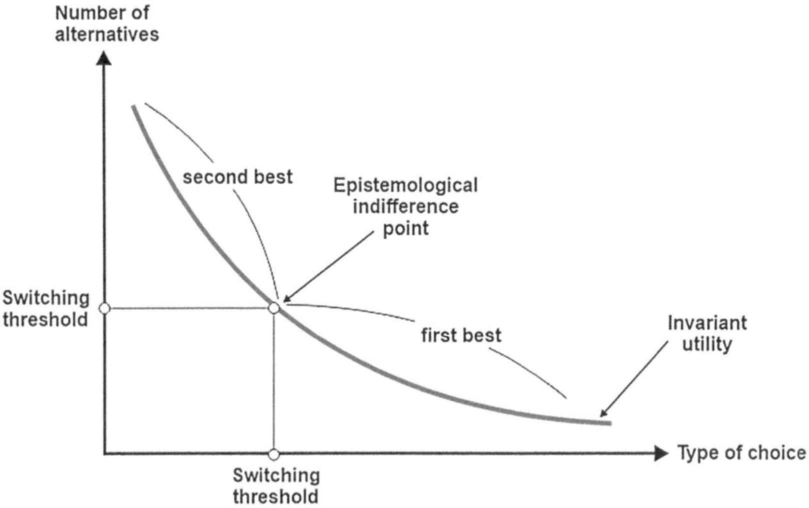

Fig. 1.17 First-best–second-best indifference curve. (*Source*: Author)

(b) based on the above, it can be asserted that we are dealing with a co-evolution process in which the co-evolutionary species are, respectively, the disturbance, more precisely, the impact of the disturbance,[110] on the one hand, and the component of antifragilizing, on the other hand. Thus, this component develops its capabilities (*Nota bene*: up to the threshold of the predictability of the disturbance or its impact) as the disturbances occur, respectively their impacts, from which it must extract advantages for the target system;[111]

- *Nota bene*: the fructifying capacity of the target system is not confused or intersected with either robustness or resilience, since these last two properties are not aimed at obtaining any advantage from the impact it that treats, each in its specific way, so as shown above.

From a theoretical point of view, the fruition of the impact of a disturbance can be achieved in the following four ways:

(a) (AF4.1) *increasing of the robustness* of the target system: this mode of fructification is a species of hormesis, but it refers to the structural aspect of the system in question. More precisely, it is about the learning process—the exposure of the target system to the perturbation (actually, the impact of it) usually has or can have the effect of increasing the resistance of the target system to the perturbations. From a quantitative point of view, this effect manifests itself by increasing the threshold value up to which the system resists disturbances;[112]

(b) (AF4.2) *increasing of the resilience* of the target system: this mode of fruition is also an advantage for the target system, as it manifests itself through an increase in its elasticity to the dislocations suffered from disturbances (either state disturbances or trajectory disturbances). Increasing the elasticity of the target system (i.e., increasing its resilience) can manifest itself in the most diverse ways:
   - increasing the "distance" from which the system is returned to its original position—either as a state, through homeostasis, or as a trajectory/process, through homeorhesis. Obviously, increasing this "distance" means an improvement in resilience, which is an advantage gained by the target system;[113]
   - increasing the speed (or, equivalently, reducing the time) with which/in which the system is restored to the initial kinematic state/position;
   - reducing the margin of hysteresis with which the target system is returned to its initial position. Hysteresis logically represents a mix between structural elasticity and structural plasticity of the target system. Zero hysteresis means maximum elasticity, and maximum hysteresis represents (by symmetry) maximum plasticity, or, in other words, identitary switching of the target system (conservation of its identity). Reducing the margin of hysteresis has the meaning of improving the resilience of the target system;[114]

(c) (AF4.3) extending the functionality[115] of the target system: what needs to be argued about this type of fruition or advantage obtained from the disruption is to show why the extension of functionality is beneficial to the target system. We present the following considerations in this matter:

- an expansion of functionality means, according to the concept of functionality, an increase in the number of inter-actions inside the system;
- the increase in the number of internal inter-actions means, among other things, the increase in the degree of intra-system communication;
- increasing the degree of intra-system communication means increasing the possibility (and probability) that the distortions, either internal or external, affecting the system in question will be dissipated, neutralized or, at the limit, fructified by the system. This kind of fructification obviously represents the autopoietic component of the property of antifragility: antifragility reproduces itself, *qua* antifragility, through its very operation. This self-reflexive function of antifragility has not been identified and thus not discussed in literature dedicated to antifragility concept, so in what follows we will develop it in a more analytical way:
  - intra-system communication represents an essential structural device for dealing with disturbances, whether internal or external, because, through communication, the impulse generated by the disturbance is dissipated in the system, leading to the reduction of the pressure/tension of change induced by that impact (Dinga, 2001, 2012);
  - the dissipation of the disruptive impulse has the effect of preserving the identity of the system which, thus, in its operation and behaviour reproduces/replicates this identity, which is exactly the content of the concept of autopoiesis/autopoieticity.

A suggestive visualization of the autopoietic effect of antifragility is given in Fig. 1.18.

(d) (AF4.4) *extending the behaviour*[116] of the target system: similarly, to AF4.3, this type of fructification of the impact of the disturbance refers to the extension of the relations between the target system and its environment system, that is, those relations that transit membrane of the target system. We indicate the most important aspects of this expansion that have positive meaning/connotation:

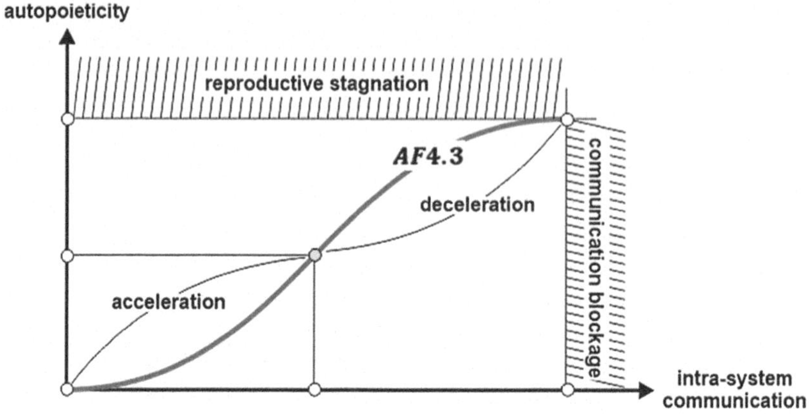

Fig. 1.18 The autopoietic effect of antifragility. (*Source*: Author)

- as is known (see Maturana & Varela, 1980) the totality of trans-membrane relations of a system constitutes its so-called *niche*[117] (of course, the niche represents an actual subset of the set of possible/potential relations between the target system and its environment);
- the extending of the niche (which is exactly equivalent to the expansion of the behaviour) means, therefore, the increase of the chances of (evolutionary) survival of the target system;
- increasing the chances of survival (possibly, increasing the chances of general improvement) of the respective system is, of course, of a positive, favourable nature, so it constitutes an advantage that antifragility extracts/procures for the target system through a specific fruition of the impact of the disturbance.

(3) A general definition of the property of antifragility

Based on the sufficiency predicates of antifragility, we can formulate now a general-abstract definition of the antifragility property of the generic system: ***antifragility is that structural property of a system capable of extracting evolutionary advantages for the system from the impact of perturbations exerted, either from the inside or from the outside, on the system in question.***

(4) Antifragility and antifragilizing

The property of antifragility is, as its definition states, an evolutionary one. This means that it is built and reconstructed through a permanent and continuous relationship of the system with its environment. This co-evolution is also related—causally and functionally—to the autopoietic feature (see AF4.3, above) of antifragility.

In this context, the relationship between the concept of antifragility (as a property) and that of antifragilizing (as a process) is immediately intelligible: antifragilizing is the phenomenon of creating (either institutionally or spontaneously) the property of antifragility. As, by virtue of the co-evolutionary (and autopoietic) character, the property of antifragility is dynamic, it follows that the phenomenon of antifragilizing also occurs in a permanent and continuous way.

(5) Reversibility and irreversibility in antifragility matter

In natural systems, antifragility is a spontaneous phenomenon, being driven by the survival needs of the species, so on the path of "random mutation–cumulative selection" (the selection criterion being the fitness, i.e., the degree of compatibility of the system in question with the constraints of its environment). In this type of systems, the property of antifragility is reversible, depending on the dynamics of environmental constraints: if these constraints decrease, then the need for antifragility (as a property) decreases accordingly, the mechanism of decrease being even a phenomenon of dis-antifragilizing (or, equivalently, of fragilizing[118]). In most cases, dis-antifragilizing is not perceptible as such, because the change in the selective pressure of the environment will usually manifest itself in structural changes in the target system, and the antifragility property will accommodate these structural changes.

Instead, in cultural systems, it must be admitted that antifragility is irreversible. The property to take advantage from disturbances, once established—discretionary, this time—will continue to be maintained, either by discretionary means or by automatic stabilizers,[119] as it means added value from the perspective of the target system's performance. Of course, this irreversibility should not be seen in absolute terms, but in relative ones, namely in terms that correlate with the goals/objectives of the target system and sometimes even with the means available to that system.

(6) Antifragility and entropy

In general, both robustness and resilience exhibit the anti-entropic properties of the system, or, more precisely, properties that have, among their outputs, the reduction (or, at least, maintaining) of the entropy of that system. If we consider the order-related meaning of entropy in the social domain (Dinga et al., 2020), then the reduction (or stagnation) of entropy generated by the property of antifragility refers to the maintenance of order precisely through the gains/advantages obtained by fructifying the impact of disturbances.[120]

However, what can be said if, precisely through the fruition of the impact of the disturbance, a system changes its internal order (e.g., the core structure[121])? In our opinion, the answer to this question could be the following:

- the core structure of a system can change either as a result of the impact of the disturbance or as a result of the very fruition (positive capitalization) of that impact. So, from a logical point of view, it does not matter whether the core structure changes as a result of the first cause or as a result of the second;
- the modification of the core structure of the target system as a result of the fruition of the impact of the disturbance through the antifragility property is not contradictory to the purpose of this property—antifragility does not aim to preserve the identity of the target system (i.e., the identity preservation which involves the preservation of the core structure) but to obtain advantages after bearing the impact of the disruption—obtaining advantages may have, among its (usually, unintended) consequences, the identitary transition of the target system;
- an interesting issue, here, is the following: if antifragility has an anti-entropic role, can this role "endangers" the identity of the target system, that is, the core structure? The answer seems to be a positive one:
  - reducing entropy below a certain threshold[122] has (or can have, with a significant probability) impact on the modification of the core structure, symmetrically with the effect that an increasing entropy above a certain threshold would also have;
  - in other words, a certain variation of entropy (in this case, by reducing it) necessarily leads to the modification of the order of

> the target system—but the modification of the internal order is equivalent, from a logical point of view, to the modification of the core structure that is, in turn, equivalent to the identitary modification of the system in question.

A synoptic representation of considerations regarding the causal relationship between target system identitary persistence, entropy and antifragility is shown in Fig. 1.19.

From the combination of the four functions mentioned in Fig. 21, the endogenous variables of interest can be extracted:[123]

$E = f(A)$, respectively $A = f^{-1}(E)$
$A = g(Q)$, respectively $Q = g^{-1}(A)$
$P = r(E)$, respectively $E = r^{-1}(P)$

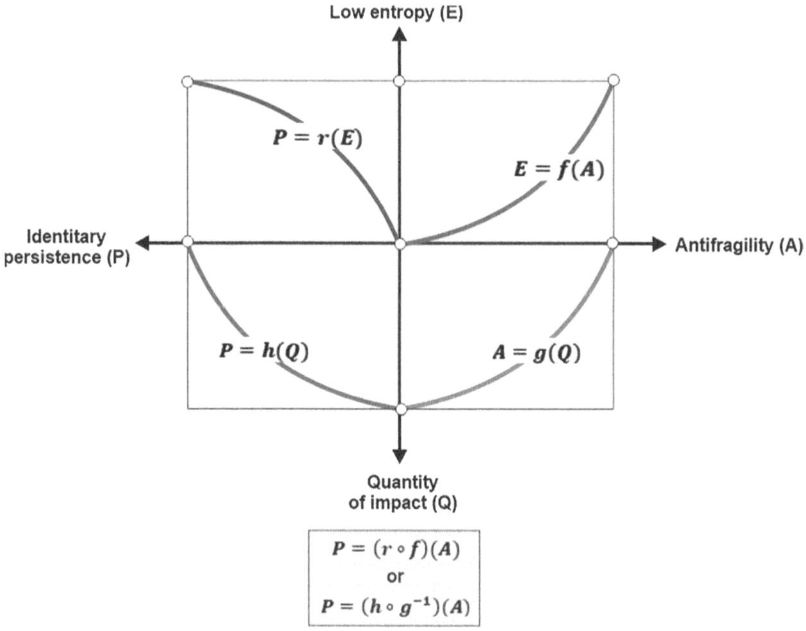

Fig. 1.19 Identitary persistence, entropy and antifragility . (*Source*: Author)

$P = h(Q)$, respectively $Q = h^{-1}(P)$whence, in terms of the analytical construction of the functions in question, we have:

$$f(A) = r^{-1}(P)$$
$$g(Q) = f^{-1}(E)$$
$$g^{-1}(A) = h^{-1}(P)$$
$$r(E) = h(Q)$$

(7) Antifragility and redundancy

If, in the case of robustness or resilience, redundancy is one of the solutions to achieve the respective properties,[124] in the case of the antifragility property, the need for redundancy is not obvious or natural enough. In this context, we make the following considerations regarding the relationship between antifragility and redundancy:[125]

- in its essence, redundancy refers to the multiplication of a device[126] (usually structural, but often simply functional), provided that the duplicate in question performs exactly the same function as the original device;
- logically, the duplicate is a clone of the original device;
- the duplicate remains unused as long as the original device is working and is not yet exceeded by the task it must perform, and comes into operation at the moment when the original device can no longer cope with the task in question;
- in this context, depending on the *objective pursued*, redundant duplicates can be of two types:
  - *Augmentation* (G) duplicates: they are duplicates that intervene in the performance of the function for which they were designed while the original device is still working, thus increasing its capacity to cope with the assigned task;
  - *Substitution* (S) duplicates: they are duplicates that intervene to perform the function for which they were designed at the moment the original device stopped working or exhausted its operating capacity, fully taking over the performance of the task in question;

Nota bene: in practice, it is of course possible to design mixed-type redundant duplicates according to this criterion, so that the duplicate (i.e., redundancy) entering the process occurs in a way analogous to that in which the races are carried out in relay sports.

- According to the *mode of activation*, redundant duplicates can also be of two types:
  - *Discretionarily* (*D*) activated duplicates: these duplicates come into action following a deliberative decision taken by the human agent (respectively, institutionally, as the case may be). The decision-maker monitors how the original device fructifies the impact of the disturbance and, when it detects either a diminution or a cessation of this fructification, triggers the redundant duplicate in the matter;
  - *Automatically* (*A*) activated duplicates: these duplicates are introduced into the structure of the target system in a deliberate/discretionary way, setting the activity threshold of the originary device at which the redundant duplicate comes into operation. This activation is no longer the effect of an ad hoc decision by the human/institutional decision-maker, but occurs automatically, simply by reaching the threshold in question. Obviously, the two criteria for classifying redundant duplicates in the case of antifragility work simultaneously, so we will have four categories of redundant duplicates (Table 1.1).

where:

- R_{AF}^{DG} : redundant duplicate of the antifragility triggered discretionarily and intended to improve the operation of the original antifragility device;

Table 1.1 The four redundant duplicate classes of antifragility

	Purpose	
Activation	*Augmentation (G)*	*Substitution (S)*
Discretionarily (D)	R_{AF}^{DG}	R_{AF}^{DS}
Automatically (A)	R_{AF}^{AG}	R_{AF}^{AS}

Source: Author

- R_{AF}^{DS} : redundant duplicate of the antifragility triggered discretionarily and intended to replace the original antifragility device;
- R_{AF}^{AG} : redundant duplicate of the antifragility triggered automatically and intended to improve the operation of the original antifragility device;
- R_{AF}^{AS} : redundant duplicate of the antifragility triggered automatically and intended to replace the original antifragility device.

(8) Costs of antifragility/antifragilizing

The costs of antifragilizing, that is, of implementing the property of antifragility, are analogous to any costs of structuring a system—since the fructification devices (previously called antifragility components), both the original components and the redundant duplicates, must be introduced into the structure. Of course, limiting ourselves to examining the costs related exclusively to the antifragilizing component, we can say the following:

- the cost of antifragilizing is of a *fixed cost* nature—indeed, the antifragilizing component "serves" any structural component of the target system that is affected by the impact of a disturbance. Furthermore, the antifragilizing capability does not vary directly proportionally (linearly or non-linearly) to the "amount" of perturbations or perturbations' impact exerted on the target system;
- instead, the cost of antifragilizing depends *directly proportional*, probably in a concave polynomial fashion—see Fig. 1.20—on the number of redundant devices (duplicates, triplicates etc.). The concave shape, which indicates a deceleration of the variation of the endogenous variable in relation to the variation of the exogenous variable, is explained by the fact that, already, by implementing the original antifragilizing component, an antifragile "infrastructure" is created, which means that the replicas of this original component will benefit from this structural basis, thus saving resources for implementing redundancy.

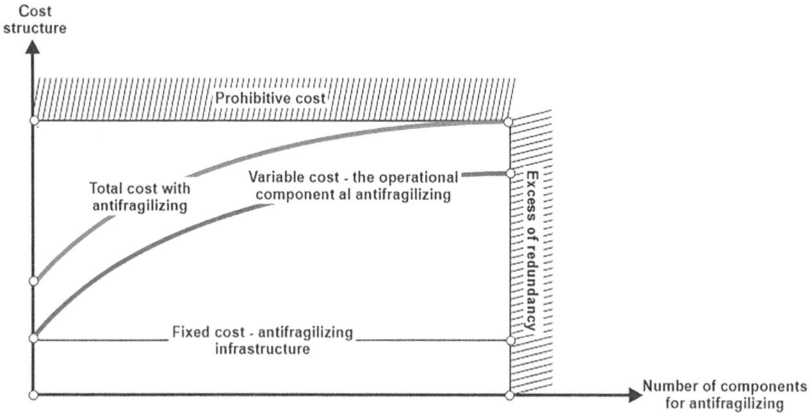

Fig. 1.20 Antifragilizing cost. (*Source*: Author)

(9) A general typology of antifragility

I have presented, above, the four classes of fructification of the impact of disruption, as they fall under the impact of antifragility. These classes can, in fact, also constitute a classification of antifragility, according to the mode of fructification of the disturbance, the latter being the very criterion for identifying the respective classes of antifragility. In this paragraph, however, we will examine the possibility of a general typology of the antifragility of a system, establishing other classification criteria. In this sense, we propose the following criteria for classifying antifragility (as a property) and, based on them, the theoretically possible antifragility classes.

- (*CAF.* 1) according to the mode of fructification of the impact of the disturbance (antifragility mode):[127]
  - (*CAF.* 1.1) increasing of robustness;
  - (*CAF.* 1.2) increasing of resilience;
  - (*CAF.* 1.3) extension of functionality;
  - (*CAF.* 1.4) extension of behaviour.

- (*CAF.* 2) according to the ratio implementation/activation of the fruition from the disruption impact:
  - (*CAF.* 2.1) ***discretionary/discretionary ratio***: the implementation of the antifragilizing component is done by the human factor (or institutional,[128] as the case may be), formally explicitly (i.e. discretionarily), and its activation, of course, according to an algorithm (a procedure) pre-set—usually upon reaching a critical point or critical mass, as discussed above—it is also done in a discretionary manner;
  - (*CAF.* 2.2) ***discretionary/automatic ratio***: the implementation of the antifragilizing component is done by the human factor (or institutional, as the case may be), in a formal-explicit way (i.e., discretionarily), and its activation is done by a structural non-human factor/device, also according to a predetermined algorithm (procedure), that is automatically. This time, therefore (although the algorithm is designed and implemented in the system structure by the human/institutional factor), this algorithm becomes independent of the implementation factor;
  - (*CAF.* 2.3) ***automatic/discretionary*** ratio: this is a case with a lower probability than the first two. It implies that the operation of an antifragilizing component that has been implemented in a discretionary manner[129] has the ability to design/implement another antifragilizing component (redundant or not with the original component) within the same system. Although, as we said, this case is only a theoretical one, it should not be neglected, especially in contemporary conditions, where artificial intelligence[130] is able to make decisions following the self-learning process (*Nota bene*: see here the concept "trendy" machine learning). The specific difference is, in this case, that the auto-generated antifragilizing component will be enabled on a discretionary basis;
  - (*CAF.* 2.4) ***automatic/automatic*** ratio is analogous to automatic/discretionary ratio, with the specific difference being that the activation of the new antifragilizing device is activated, this time, automatically.
- (*CAF.* 3) according to the method of networking[131] the antifragilizing devices:
  - (*CAF.* 3.1) ***series networks***—antifragilizing devices/components connected in *series*. The case in which these devices (of any of the classes identified according to the *CAF.* 2 criterion) are connected

to each other in series, that is, the output of one constitutes (in whole or in part) the input of the next device, in causal order—which can coincide with the temporal/chronological order in which their activation is desired;

- (*CAF.* 3.2) *parallel networks*—antifragilizing devices/components connected in *parallel*. The case in which these devices (of any of the classes identified according to the *CAF.* 2 criterion) are connected to each other in parallel, that is, the output of one is constituted (in whole or in part) as a simultaneous input of some number, predetermined by structural criteria—functional, of other devices;
- (*CAF.* 3.3) *closed networks* of antifragilizing components. The case where the initial antifragilizing component (the initial node) coincides with the final antifragilizing component (the final node);
- (*CAF.* 3.4) *open networks* of antifragilizing components. The case where the initial antifragilizing component (the initial node) does not coincide with the final antifragilizing component (the final node);

Nota bene: here comes the critical issue of self-regulation (negative feedback) of the antifragilizing network.

- (*CAF.* 4) according to the evolution of the antifragilizing devices:
  - (*CAF.* 4.1) *static/stationary* antifragilizing devices: are those antifragilizing devices that maintain, indefinitely (more precisely, as long as they are part of the structure of the system in question) their identity, that is, their structure and functions. Of course, this class of antifragilizing devices has rather a theoretical-logical meaning, because in reality they are not exactly the most … productive devices in the matter;
  - (*CAF.* 4.2) *evolutionary* antifragilizing devices: they are those antifragilizing devices that can adapt their identity (structure and functions) both to the environment from which the disturbances originate and to the system itself of which they are a part;
  - (*CAF.* 4.3) antifragilizing devices with *autonomous learning*: they are those antifragilizing devices which, through their very operation, as a reaction to the challenges generated by disturbances (of course from the perspective of the fruition of their impact), develop new capabilities in the matter of this fruition, on the one

hand, or related to one's own evolution, on the other hand—it can also be said that we are dealing, in this case, with automatic learning;
- (*CAF.* 4.4) antifragilizing devices with *assisted learning*: they are those antifragilizing devices that react to challenges also by developing new capabilities for fruition or by increasing their own performance but, this time, assisted by the human factor (or institutional, as the case may be)—it can also be said that we are dealing, in this case, with discretionary learning.

(10) Structure of the antifragility device

In this paragraph we propose to examine the issue of the structure of the antifragility device or, in semantically equivalent terminology, the antifragilizing device/component. The main logical premise for such an analysis is, of course, the assumption of functionalism (in Parsons's sense), namely that structure generates function and not the other way around. In this context, some considerations regarding the features of antifragilizing in society[132] may be useful:

- in the social field, feedforward works, which make the desired or necessary function to be designed before the existence (or deliberate implementation) of the structural element capable of objectifying that function. In this context, some analysts (especially sociologists) have reversed the relationship between structure and function, saying that it is function that generates/requires structure.[133] Obviously, simplifying things quite a bit, this means that, in the case of human social systems, Lamarckism prevails over Darwinism;
- however (i.e., although the identification of the function is done, by feedforward, in general, but not only, before the corresponding structural component), the operationalization or objectification of the function in question cannot take place until the corresponding structural component is introduced into the overall structure of the system considered;
- furthermore, as we have shown, the antifragility property is (or rather must be) "blind" to the class of perturbations, and even more so to a particular perturbation. As a result, in principle, nothing or almost nothing essential can be known about the function that the antifragi lity/antifragilizing component is supposed to objectify;

- based on the above, we believe that the structure of the antifragilizing device/component should be developed in the general, abstract and non-directed sense, as previously shown in relation to the antifr agility/antifragilizing issue.

Accordingly, our opinion regarding the structure of the antifragility device/component of a human social domain system can be described as follows:

(a) ($\mathcal{M}$) *memorizing cell*: is a component of the antifragilizing device that stores the situation (*statu quo*) of the target system. By the situation (*statu quo*) is meant the following set of information that is memorized:
   - the *state* of the target system ($\mathcal{M}_t^S$), which is stored in the form of its state vector—the state vector contains the values, usually numerical, of the defining coordinates regarding the identity of the target system; denote by $\bar{\mathcal{M}}_\tau^S$ the perturbed (i.e., current) state of the target system, respectively by $G_{(t,\tau)}^S$ the state gap following the perturbation, where $G_{(t,\tau)}^S = \left|\bar{\mathcal{M}}_\tau^S - \mathcal{M}_t^S\right|$;
   - the *position* of the target system ($\mathcal{M}_t^P$) on the trajectory on which it is engaged. *Nota bene*: with *t* was noted the time at which the memorization[134] operation is performed; denote by $\bar{\mathcal{M}}_\tau^P$ the disturbed (current) state of the target system, respectively by $G_{(t,\tau)}^P$ the position gap following the disturbance, where $G_{(t,\tau)}^P = \left|\bar{\mathcal{M}}_\tau^P - \mathcal{M}_t^P\right|$;
   - *Robustness capacity* of target system ($\mathcal{M}^{R^1}$): refers to the maximum amount of impact developed by the involved disturbance that the target system still withstands while preserving its identity (i.e., its structure and associated functions); denote by $\bar{\mathcal{M}}_\tau^{R^1}$ the effective amount of change pressure developed by the disturbance on the target system, respectively by $G_{(t,\tau)}^{R^1}$ the change pressure gap following the disturbance, where $G_{(t,\tau)}^{R^1} = \left|\bar{\mathcal{M}}_\tau^{R^1} - \mathcal{M}_t^{R^1}\right|$. Of course, we will actually have two such gaps: (1) a gap that concerns the state— $G_{(t,\tau)}^{R^1(S)} = \left|\bar{\mathcal{M}}_\tau^{R^1(S)} - \mathcal{M}_t^{R^1(S)}\right|$; (2) a gap regarding the position on the trajectory—$G_{(t,\tau)}^{R^1(P)} = \left|\bar{\mathcal{M}}_\tau^{R^1(P)} - \mathcal{M}_t^{R^1(P)}\right|$;

- *Resilience capacity* of target system ($\mathcal{M}^{R^2}$): refers to the maximum "distance" the target system is moved away following the disturbance, the distance from which resilience can return the target system to its initial state (either as state or as position);[135] denote by $\bar{\mathcal{M}}_{\tau}^{R^2}$ the effective "distance" that the perturbation displaced the target system, respectively by $G_{(t,\tau)}^{R^2}$ the state gap following the perturbation, where $G_{(t,\tau)}^{R^2} = \left| \bar{\mathcal{M}}_{\tau}^{R^2} - \mathcal{M}_{t}^{R^2} \right|$. Again, here we will have, in fact, two such gaps: (1) a gap that concerns the state— $G_{(t,\tau)}^{R^2(S)} = \left| \bar{\mathcal{M}}_{\tau}^{R^2(S)} - \mathcal{M}_{t}^{R^2(S)} \right|$; (2) a gap regarding the position on the trajectory— $G_{(t,\tau)}^{R^2(P)} = \left| \bar{\mathcal{M}}_{\tau}^{R^2(P)} - \mathcal{M}_{t}^{R^2(P)} \right|$;

(b) ($\mathcal{A}$) the *activation cell*: it is a component of the antifragilizing device that performs measurements[136] on the gap produced between the situation of the target system as it is memorized and its situation at a moment after the memorization (let's denote this last moment by τ, where $\tau > t$) and, when the gap between the benchmark and the current situation is reached, triggers (activates) the antifragilizing component. However, given the considerations already made previously regarding the (temporal, especially) relationship between robustness, resilience and antifragility, some methodological clarifications are necessary, which we present below:
- the activation cell ($\mathcal{A}$) consists of two components, serially connected:
  - ($\mathcal{A}_{\tau_1}^{R}$) *resiliency activation cell*: this component performs measurements on reaching the robustness operating gap. By the robustness operating gap is meant the difference (usually expressed numerically, with a conveniently chosen unit of measure) between the resistance capacity (robustness) of the target system and the amount of change impact developed by the disturbance involved. When this gap is crossed, the target system is "thrown" from the initial state or position into a state or position called perturbed. At the same time, the resilience of the system is activated so, according to the established protocol (procedure), will bring the target system to the state or position it had before the impact of the disturbance to have produced its effect;

- ($\mathcal{A}_{\tau_2}^{A}$) *antifragility activation cell*: this component performs measurements regarding the achievement of the resiliency functioning gap. By the resilience operating gap is meant the difference (usually expressed numerically, with a conveniently chosen unit of measurement) between the recovery distance (i.e., in the "territory" of resilience) of the target system and the distance that the target system has been disturbed. If the effective distance that the system has been disturbed exceeds the distance included in the resilience capacity of the system, given that the elasticity of the target system has been exceeded (so, its plasticity comes into play), the operation of antifragility is activated, that is, the possibility that in the new situation (state, respectively position) of the target system, which, this time, remains rigid to obtain specific advantages for the system.

(c) ($\mathcal{F}$) *fructification cell*: is a component of the antifragilizing device that transforms the impact of the disruption into an advantage of some kind for the target system. This component is of the nature of a "translator", having to choose, among the four types of fruiting, the one that, so to speak, has the highest yield. The fruiting cell is the most complicated[137] component of the antifragilizing device. We argue this assertion as follows:

- since, like the entire antifragilizing device, the fruiting cell must be "blind" relative to nature, type, intensity, origin, duration etc. of the disturbance in question, it must, in compensation, have the ability to examine, from all these perspectives, that disturbance, in order to choose the best form of fructification of the impact of the disturbance. Such a capability is possible only on the basis of an overly complicated and obviously exceptionally reliable filter-decision structure;
- the fruiting cell goes into action as soon as antifragility is activated, so it must contain specialized "sensors" to pick up the antifragility activation signal. This function also requires a rather elaborate (complicated) structure;
- the fructification cell is activated by the activation cell but, after activation, this component of the antifragility device must also perform some internal operations in order to "design" and implement the fructification of the impact of the disturbance. So, this component must contain the following structural sub-component:

- ($\mathcal{F}_{\tau_2}^{\alpha}$) *disturbance identification filter*: the purpose of this filter's actions is to fit the actual disturbance into a certain category. Here it must be specified that this filter has a framework-list of possible disturbances (the list- α), more precisely a list of possible classes of disturbances, each class being characterized by a set of predicates or characteristics: origin, nature, intensity, mode of affectation etc. This list is pre-existing, and although it is supposed to be somehow exhaustive, it will be updated as disturbances arise which do not fit into any of the classes already nominated in the list;
- ($\mathcal{F}_{\tau_2}^{\beta}$) filter to establish the *primary consequence* of the perturbation: the purpose of the actions of this filter is to establish the potential consequences that an effective perturbation, once it has exceeded both the robustness and the resilience of the target system, can have on that system. Of course, such a verdict can only be based on a list of potential consequences (the β-list), which is managed by this filter and which, like the previous list of perturbation classes, is updated under the influence of experience. In principle, each disturbance class will be associated with a specific list of potential consequences; therefore, the result of applying the filter $\mathcal{F}_{\tau_2}^{\alpha}$ leads to obtaining, inferentially (automatically), also the result of applying the filter $\mathcal{F}_{\tau_2}^{\beta}$. *Nota bene*: establishing the identity of the disturbance, in the context of the antifragility properties operation, is done only for two types of disturbance: (1) classified by *impact*: disturbances with structural consequences versus disturbances with functional consequences; (2) classified by *affinity*: cumulative perturbations versus isolated disturbances;
- ($\mathcal{F}_{\tau_2}^{\gamma}$) filter to establish the *maximum fruition* of perturbation: the purpose of the actions of this filter is to identify and operationalize the fruition of plastic perturbation impact to the advantage/benefit of the target system. As can be seen in Fig. 23, the input to the $\mathcal{F}_{\tau_2}^{\gamma}$ filter is the output of the $\mathcal{F}_{\tau_2}^{\beta}$ filter. As a result, we will have to "endow" the filter $\mathcal{F}_{\tau_2}^{\gamma}$ with its own list (the γ-list) of ways of fruition, based on the four categories/classes of possible advantages for the target system, as mentioned before;

– ($\mathcal{F}^{\delta}_{\tau_2}$) *operational* device of fructification: the purpose of the action of this device is to implement (designing, introduction into structure—or only in function, as the case may be—materializing, initiating, modifying and controlling maintenance and kinematic replication) identified by the filter $\mathcal{F}^{\gamma}_{\tau_2}$.

Figure 1.21 shows a scheme of the serial working of the filters in the disturbance fruiting cell.

(11) Functioning of the antifragility device

To analyse the functioning of the antifragility device we will use Fig. 1.22.

Discussion

- Stage "0"
  - the disturbance occurs, whether internal or external; as shown above, the antifragility device is blind to any predicate (any feature) of (a) the perturbation;
  - the impact of the perturbation occurs either on the state of the target system ($\mathcal{M}^{S}_{t}$) or on the kinematic position (the position on the trajectory or, with a more general term, on the chreode) of the target system ($\mathcal{M}^{P}_{t}$); either the state or the position, or, more often, both are disturbed, that is displaced (quantitatively or qualitatively) from the initial situation;

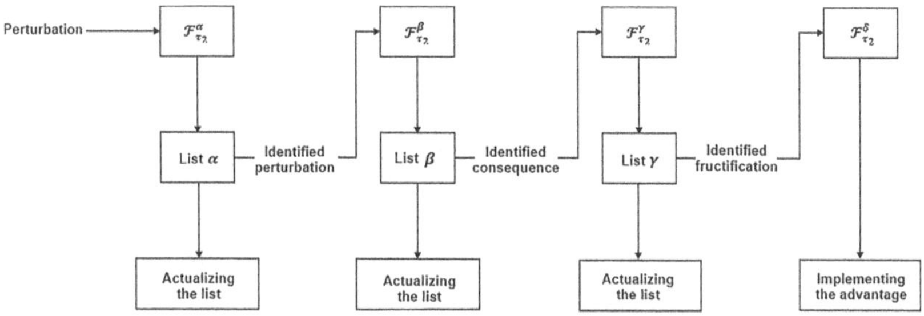

Fig. 1.21 The fruition cell functioning. (*Source*: Author)

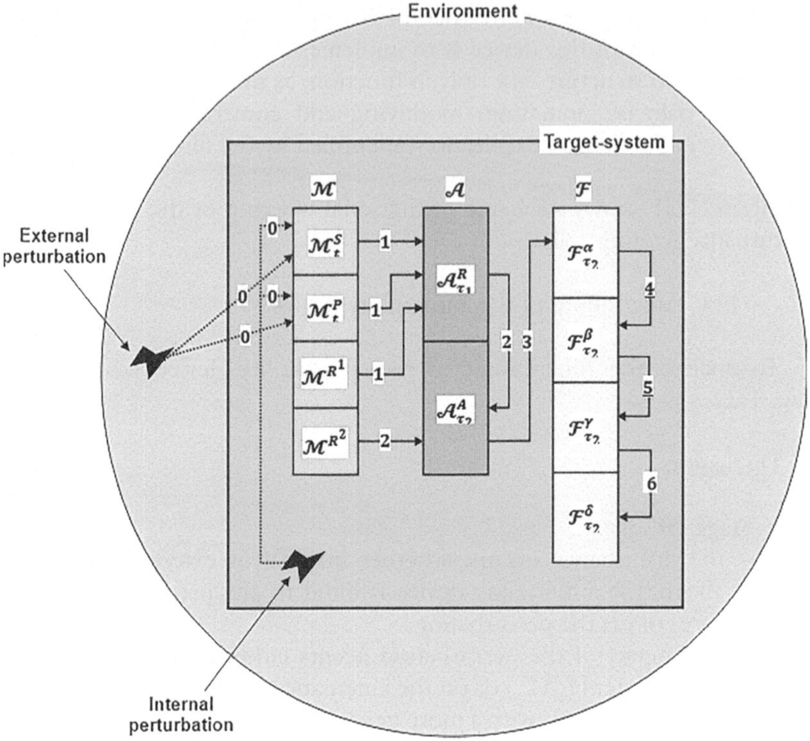

Fig. 1.22 The abstract structure of the antifragility device. (*Source*: Author)

- Stage "1"
  - any of the perturbations actually produced on the target system is compared to the stored value ($\mathcal{M}^{R^1}$) for the maximum robustness capacity; the robustness of the target system works until that maximum value is exceeded;
  - upon reaching the maximum value of robustness, the resilience activation cell ($\mathcal{A}^{R}_{\tau_1}$) is triggered and the target system returns to the situation (either the state or the position or both) to the initial level, obviously provided that the elasticity threshold is not exceeded in the inside of which the resilience property works;

- Stage "2"
  - when resilience is overcome (i.e., the target system goes from elasticity to plasticity, either structural or functional), the cell that controls antifragility ($\mathcal{A}_{\tau_2}^{A}$) is activated;
- Stage "3"
  - the entry into operation of the fructification cell of the antifragility device is done at the level of the disturbance identity establishment filter ($\mathcal{F}_{\tau_2}^{\alpha}$); this filter identifies[138] all aspects that can help classify the disturbance as stated above;
- Stage "4"
  - performing the task of the filter $\mathcal{F}_{\tau_2}^{\alpha}$ automatically transfers the action to the filter $\mathcal{F}_{\tau_2}^{\beta}$, which determines the potential consequence (or consequences) of the disturbance in question, according to the methodology already specified;
- Stage "5"
  - performing the task of the filter $\mathcal{F}_{\tau_2}^{\beta}$ automatically transfers the action to the filter $\mathcal{F}_{\tau_2}^{\gamma}$, which determines which of the possible advantages contained *in nuce* inside any disturbance can be operationalized at the level of the target system;
- Step "6"
  - performing the task of the $\mathcal{F}_{\tau_2}^{\gamma}$ filter automatically transfers the action to the $\mathcal{F}_{\tau_2}^{\delta}$ filter, which effectively incorporates the selected advantage into the structure, respectively into the functioning of the target system.

1.5 Sustainability

Based on the above logical framework, we consider that the following sufficiency predicates regarding the property/the concept of sustainability should be accepted (*Nota bene*: we always consider a given system, so both the sufficiency predicates to be identified, respectively the sustainability property as such, generated by the conjunction of sufficiency predicates, concerns a given system):

(1) (S_1) ***robustness***: this predicate has already been discussed previously;
(2) (S_2) ***resilience***: this predicate has already been discussed previously;
(3) (S_3) ***output inputation***: this sufficiency predicate means ensuring that the output of the system is transformed into a new input, either in the same system or—the most frequent case—in other systems.

Brief discussion:

A first problem concerns the typology of this sufficiency predicate. In this sense, inputation of the output can be of several types:

a. by the number of links in the input-output relationship:

a1) *self-inputation* (or homo-inputation)—when the output of a system is constituted, in its entirety, as the input of the same system in the next cycle of its functioning;[139]

a2) *hetero-inputation* (or *k*-instance inputation)—when the output of system 1, O_1, is constituted as an input in the system *k*, I_k;

b. according to the input-output concatenation mode of the systems:

b1) *Serial inputation*—when the output of a system is constituted as an input in another system which, in relation to the first system, is located downstream of the process in question (whether scientific, or technological, or economic, or financial); in other words, the two concatenated systems (or more, as the case may be) are ordered, logically and chronologically, vertically, for example, an economic system transforms the raw material into an intermediate (semi-finished) product and passes it to another system that transforms the semi-finished product in the finished product;

b2) *Parallel inputation*—when the output of a system is constituted as an input in at least two other systems at the same time, either from a quantitative point of view or (the most representative case) from a qualitative point of view. For example, if a system has, as output, a semi-finished product and specific waste, the semi-finished product is the input of a system that transforms it into a finished product, and the waste is the input of a system that treats it specifically (either to return it to the economic circuit or to neutralize it from an ecological point of view). The most frequent and representative case for parallel inputation is that of an energy-producing system—its output is constituted as a simultaneous input in several systems that need that energy;

b3) *Mixed inputation*—when, in one way or another, the serial inputation is combined with a parallel inputation.

A graphic image of the operation of this sufficiency predicate for the property of sustainability is shown in Figs. 1.23 and 1.24, respectively (i_t^k denotes the input at time *t* in the system *k*; o_t^k denotes the output at time *t* from system *k*; τ_k denotes the lag between output of the origin-system and the input of the destination-system, referring to system *k*).

Nota bene: we no longer graph the mixed input, as this is either a series "connection" of two (or more) parallel inputs or a parallel "connection" of two (or more) serial inputs—we leave this graphical exercise at the discretion of the interested reader.

A second problem relates to the regionality of the output inputation. Thus, it is possible that, from the perspective of this sufficiency predicate,

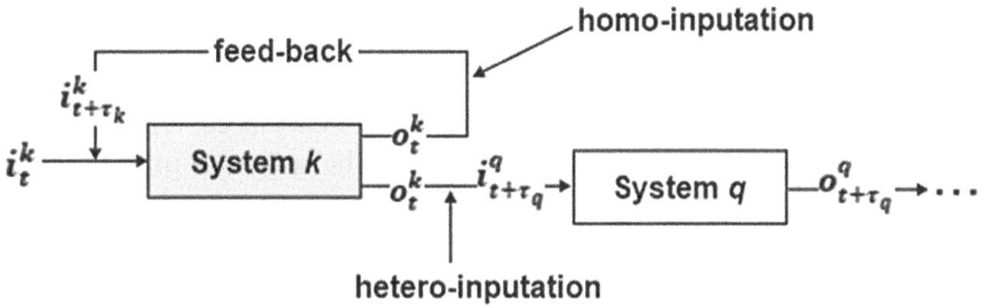

Fig. 1.23 Functioning of the sufficiency predicate S_3 of the property of sustainability (I). (*Source*: Author)

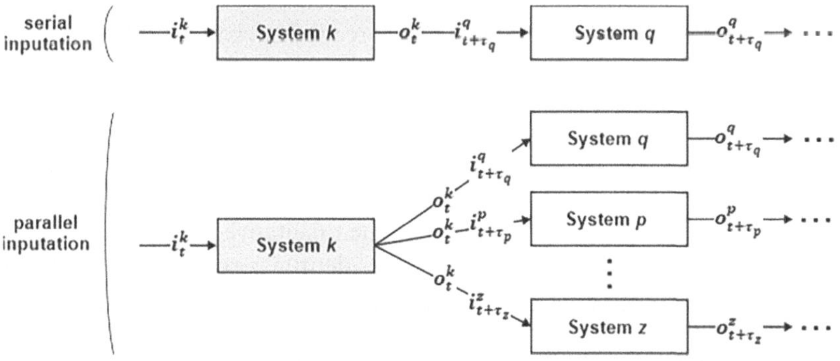

Fig. 1.24 Functioning of the sufficiency predicate S_3 of the property of sustainability (II). (*Source*: author)

a system has subsystems that are sustainable, respectively subsystems that are not sustainable. What can be said, in this case, about the sustainability of that system? We believe that the problem can be dealt with as follows:

(i) if the output inputation is not verified in a certain region of the system in question, obviously in that region we do not have sustainability,[140] although where it is verified, the sustainability property will exist;
(ii) therefore, in our opinion, although we can talk about sustainable regions and unsustainable regions of a system, it is meaningless to talk about degrees of sustainability, because we consider that the property of sustainability is, from a qualitative point of view, exclusively dichotomous—a system is sustainable or not sustainable; however, on regions of the system—that is, on subsystems or aggregations of subsystems, as the case may be—we can talk about sustainable regions, respectively unsustainable regions;[141]
(iii) sustainability (of a dichotomous type, as we accepted above) is always judged regarding the output of the system of interest. This means that, in principle, we can say about a system that it is sustainable if all its subsystems are sustainable, but we cannot say about a system that it is not sustainable if one (or more subsystems) is unsustainable: in the latter case, the system can be either sustainable or unsustainable, depending on how its unsustainable subsystems integrate their inputs and outputs so that, at the system level, sustainability (or unsustainability, as the case may be) can be demonstrated. In Annex 2, several theorems/lemmas in the matter of sustainability are put to the reader's debate.

Nota bene: it should be noted that the sufficiency predicate called inputation of the output has (apparently) the same meaning as a possible sufficiency predicate (with which it seems, *prima facie*, to be semantically equivalent) which would be called (capacity for) *identitary replicability* of the system in question. As the identity (the qualitative "personality") of a system lies in its structure, it follows that identitary replicability refers to the ability of a system to replicate its structure. We will analyse the two options (between which we have already made a choice, which, on this occasion, we will justify it):

- firstly, it must be shown that ensuring the identitary replication of a system (or ensuring the identitary replicability property of the system) is, however, different from the point of view of the final effect (result) of the inputation of the output. The differences consist, at least, in the fact that it is possible (although the probability is not extremely high) that a preservation of the structure (i.e., an identitary replication of the system) does not guarantee the inputation of the output. There could be many causes/reasons for this:
  a. from a normative point of view, there could be changes regarding the output flows (depending on their qualitative nature as well as their quantitative dimension)—which means that, although the structure is the same (at least from a formal point of view, which is the fundamental aspect in the structural preservation of a system), however, the sustainability can be vulnerable or even blocked;
  b. although the structure of the system may change (i.e., identitary replication of that system does not occur), the output flows are not affected—either these flows change as a result of the change in structure or they do not change under the impact of the change in structure, which guarantees the sustainability property even if identitary replication is violated;
  c. the risk of dis-sustainabilization[142] can occur at any time (e.g., an input that valorises an output is abolished); therefore, non-identitary replication can, in fact, represent a solution precisely to preserve or recover, as the case may be, the property of sustainability;
     - therefore, from a logical point of view, the output inputation is of the nature of result, while identitary replicability is, rather, of the nature of the means for obtaining this result;
     - in other words, the highest degree of assurance of the sustainability property (of course, from the perspective of this sufficiency predicate) belongs to the output inputation, this being the reason this sufficiency predicate was "preferred" from the beginning;

(4) (S_4) ***input replication***: this predicate of sufficiency means that, at the level of the considered system, the input "spent" in a cycle of system operation is remade/reproduced, in quantity, quality, structure and rate required by the input to output transformation operator (the

black-box of the system). A few aspects need to be discussed in more detail here:

- preservation of the four predicates of input replication (quantity, quality, structure and rate) is desirable only as long as the input-to-output transformation operator is invariant (i.e., the rate of this transformation is invariant, discussed earlier). The variation of the parameters of the transformation operator, for any reason, must have a (viable) correspondent in the modification of the predicates of the replicated input; only in this way can sustainability be preserved. So, a more appropriate expression in relation to this aspect of input replication seems to be the following: *input replication, with its four predicates, appropriate to the state of the transformation operator at the time the system cycle resumes*;
- now the relevance of the first two sufficiency predicates of the sustainability property (robustness, respectively resilience) emerges more meaningfully, namely by the fact that the two sufficiency predicates ensure, in tandem, a certain invariance of the transformation operator, so that the sufficiency predicates of input replication can be preserved for as long as robustness and resilience are not overcome by disruptive factors (internal or external);
- the question arises: why is the input replication sufficiency predicate needed, since the inputation of the output (S_3) seems to ensure exactly the replication of the input? We will answer this question in the following:
  - logically, inputation of the output is not equivalent to replicating the input:

    inputation of the output refers to the “obligation” that any output of a system (or of a supersystem, as the case may be) constitutes an input;

    this input, however, can refer both to the same system that produced the output in question and to another system. So, the sufficiency predicate *inputation of the output* only ensures that no output will remain unimputed (i.e., it will not remain untaken by the input of a system, whatever it may be). This meaning is (as we have already shown) very important, because it ensures that, for example, there will be no outputs that will pollute the environment or there will be no outputs that will constitute dangers for people;[143]

on the other hand, input replication refers to the need for an input of a system, once consumed in the cycle of obtaining the output, to be remade so that the system in question can resume its cycle of operation (i.e., to be, in fact, sustainable). This means that we can have situations where any output is input but the input of a given system (fixed, chosen for examination) is not restored by checking the four proper predicates of sufficiency; the conclusion being that the system in question cannot by itself replicate the operation, so it is not sustainable;

- considering what was discussed about the sufficiency predicate imputation of the output, it follows that there is no need for any input-replication condition—this replication can occur after a wide "circulation" of the output which is input from one system to another until it gets to restore the input for the first system, but that is enough to ensure the sustainability of the latter. Figure 1.25 shows in a synoptic way the difference between S_3 and S_4.

• in conclusion, predicate S_4 is neither superfluous nor logically dependent on any of the other three sufficiency predicates of the sustainability property.

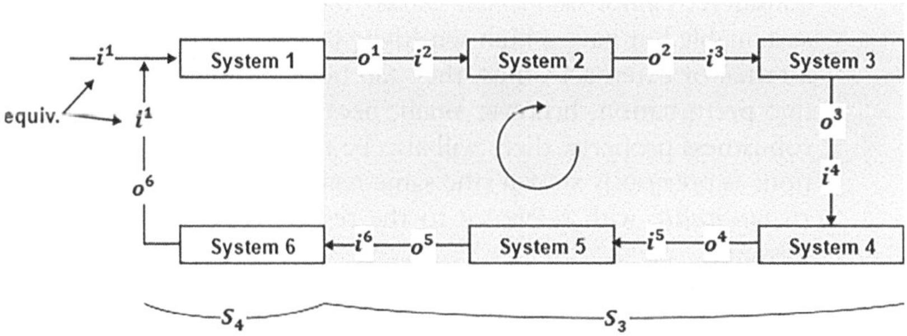

Fig. 1.25 The distinction between predicates of sufficiency S_3 and S_4. (*Source*: Author)

Additional comment (the *quasi-sustainable systems*)

The sufficiency predicates S_1 and S_2 can be called predicates of existence (or existential predicates), while the predicates S_3 and S_4 can be called predicates of functioning (or functional predicates). This typology is not superfluous, because:

- there can be systems that are robust or resilient or robust and resilient but that violate at least one of the functional predicates, thus not falling into the class of sustainable systems;
- symmetrically, there can be systems that verify both functional predicates but violate either predicate S_1 or predicate S_2, or both of these last two predicates, thus not falling too into the class of sustainable systems;
- our opinion in this matter is the following:
  - existential sufficiency predicates are "weaker" relative to functional sufficiency predicates, in the sense that the former predicates can be easier designed for and implemented in the systems of interest than the latter predicates. So, the distinction we make between the two categories of sufficiency predicates is useful (or relevant) especially from the perspective of the construction (or re-construction) of sustainable systems—especially in the economic and/or social field;
  - theoretically, systems that check S_3 and S_4 could be called (and considered) *quasi-sustainable systems*, that is, systems that manifest sustainably but have a high sensitivity to disruptive factors (either internal or external)—thus, they can behave sustainably until the first perturbation, however small, because in the absence of the robustness property, there will also be no dead zone of perturbation, as previously shown (the same reasoning is applicable *mutatis mutandis*, with reference to the resilience property, which is missing);
  - there may be situations where a quasi-sustainable system[144] is desirable, rather than a sustainable one—for example in the case of early warning systems/mechanisms: in this case, robustness (or excessive robustness) or resilience is inappropriate, as it delays (possibly, catastrophically) signalling the occurrence of a disturbance.

(b.3) Definition

(i) Meaning of predicates of sufficiency—resuming
- *Robustness*: refers to the resistance that the system opposes to disruptive factors, either internal or external, or both categories (including the synergy effect generated by the combination of internal and external disruptive factors). The exhaustion of this first line of defence of the system occurs at reaching a threshold-ceiling for the accumulation of change pressure;
- *Resilience*: after the robustness of the system is exhausted, the system is "moved" either from the state or from the kinematic position on its trajectory. From this moment on, the property of resilience comes into action, which consists in returning the system to its initial state (homeostasis) or to the initial kinematic position on its trajectory (homeorhesis);
- *Inputation of the output*: it refers to ensuring that each output of a system constitutes an input, either in the same system or in another system in a supra-system;[145]
- *Replicating of the input*: refers to ensuring that any input is ultimately retrieved from the perspective of the four predicates: quantity, quality, structure[146] and rhythm or tempo;

(ii) The logical definition

The logical definition refers to the verification of the truth condition of the conjunction of the four sufficiency predicates ($S_1 - S_4$) (the sustainability property of a given system was denoted by S):

$$S \leftarrow (S_1) \wedge (S_2) \wedge (S_3) \wedge (S_4)$$

(iii) The verbal definition

Sustainability is a property of a generic system that completely ensures the use of the output and the replication of the input, over a given time horizon. In relation to the definition of sustainability, the following additional comments can be made:

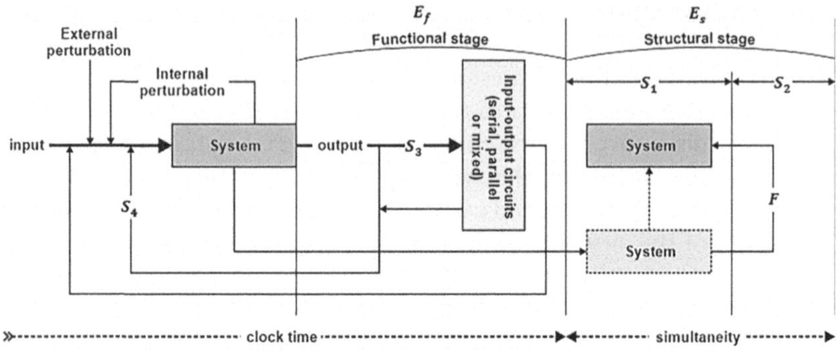

Fig. 1.26 The logical phenomenology of the sustainability. (*Source*: Author)

- it is not a property with *sine die* significance, but one that is strictly associated with a given time horizon. In this sense, the preservation of sustainability after the exhaustion of that time horizon requires further analysis;
- during the maintenance of the property of sustainability according to the verbal definition, the first two predicates of sufficiency (robustness, respectively resilience) act permanently and continuously; in other words, these predicates are considered present and functional during the entire period in which predicates S_3 and S_4 act;
- thus, the verbal definition of sustainability can be formulated as follows: ***a system is sustainable, during the action of robustness and resilience, if and only if both output inputation and input replication occur.***

The way in which the four sufficiency predicates of sustainability property work in Fig. 1.26.

1.6 Autopoieticity

In order to obtain a logical definition of autopoieticity, it is necessary to establish/choose the predicates of sufficiency which, through their conjunction, provide the content of that definition. To do this, we will first identify the predicates of sufficiency of sustainability—the actional paradigm closest, in essence, to that of autopoieticity. In our opinion, a system is autopoietic if and only if it contains the following properties/attributes, which we call sufficiency predicates:

- (S_1): *structural replicability*: identity preservation through structure reproduction;[147]
- (S_2): *operational openness*: regulating of structural replicability involves both internal and external (environmental) principles;
- (S_3): *relational openness*: the system is open in relation to its environment, that is, there is an exchange of substance, energy and information between the system and its environment;
- (S_4): *processual closure*:[148] the system can ensure substantial and energetic recovery of the input based on its own output.[149]

Therefore, as a logical formalization, the sustainable system (SS) can be described as follows:

$$SS \leftarrow (S_1) \wedge (S_2) \wedge (S_3) \wedge (S_4)$$

While an unsustainable system can be described as follows:

$$\begin{aligned}\overline{SS} \leftarrow & \left[(\overline{S_1}) \wedge (S_2) \wedge (S_3) \wedge (S_4)\right] \vee \left[(S_1) \wedge (\overline{S_2}) \wedge (S_3) \wedge (S_4)\right] \vee \left[(S_1) \wedge (S_2) \wedge (\overline{S_3}) \wedge (S_4)\right] \\ & \vee \left[(S_1) \wedge (S_2) \wedge (S_3) \wedge (\overline{S_4})\right] \wedge \left[(\overline{S_1}) \wedge (\overline{S_2}) \wedge (S_3) \wedge (S_4)\right] \vee \cdots \vee \left[(\overline{S_1}) \wedge (\overline{S_2}) \wedge (\overline{S_3}) \wedge (\overline{S_4})\right]\end{aligned}$$

1.6.1 The Logical Conditions of Autopoieticity

Before we establish the logical conditions (more precisely, the predicates of sufficiency) of autopoiesis, we must distinguish between autopoiesis and autopoieticity. Autopoieticity is a property of a system, while autopoiesis is a process that is made possible by autopoieticity and that results in autopoieticity—(re) confirmation and strengthening of autopoieticity.[150] On the basis of this conceptual dissociation, it becomes obvious that, firstly, the predicates of sufficiency for property, that is, for autopoieticity, must be established.

(a) The predicates of sufficiency for autopoieticity

The sufficiency predicates of autopoieticity are a list of attributes that, if a system has cumulatively verified, then it possesses the property of autopoieticity. Some preliminaries are useful in this context:

- the existence of a system, either real or ideal, is presumed;
- the observability of that system is presumed;

Nota bene: in the case of logical/symbolic systems, the system contains, as an internal component, the human individual (or human group or human society).

In our opinion, autopoieticity is a sustainability that is operationally closed. Therefore, if we note an autopoietic system with *APS*, then the predicates of sufficiency for autopoieticity are as follows:

- (AP_1): structural replicability
- (AP_2): operational closure
- (AP_3): relational openness
- (AP_4): procedural closure

Consequently, compared to a sustainable system, the autopoietic system shows a change at the level of the second predicate of sufficiency: the replacement of the operational opening with the operational closure—(AP_2).

The logical construction of an autopoietic system (*APS*) is therefore:

$$APS \leftarrow (AP_1) \wedge (AP_2) \wedge (AP_3) \wedge (AP_4)$$

While a non-autopoietic system can be described by the following conjunction disjunction:

$$\overline{SAP} = \left[(\overline{AP_1}) \wedge (AP_2) \wedge (AP_3) \wedge (AP_4) \right] \vee \ldots \vee \left[(\overline{AP_1}) \wedge (\overline{AP_2}) \wedge (\overline{AP_3}) \wedge (\overline{AP_4}) \right]$$

Nota bene: obviously, $S_1 \equiv AP_1$, $S_3 \equiv AP_3$, $S_4 \equiv AP_4$.

We will examine in more detail the sufficiency predicates of the autopoietic system, given that the purpose of this study is to develop an autopoietic model of the financial market.

- (AP_1): *structural replicability*: identitary preservation by reproducing one's own structure

The identity of a system (more precisely, the preservation of the identity of a system, in time and space) is a rather delicate issue, as it must be indicated on the basis of which criterion/measure can be made the statement that the structure of the system in question has been replicated in such a way we are dealing with the same system after the replication in question. In our opinion, the structural replication (and replicability) of a system must be aimed at its *formal structure*. It is therefore necessary to define or at least describe the meaning of the phrase formal structure. We consider that the formal structure of a system is replicated (or, equivalently, preserved by replication) if the following two conditionalities are verified:

- (C_1) preservation of the number of internal components—by replication, the system must neither lose nor gain structural components;
- (C_2) preserving the hierarchy of internal components—by replication, command relationships versus reporting relationships (i.e., relationships between leading components vs. executing components) must be maintained;

Nota bene: we did not say anything about the nature of the internal components of the system. Is structural replicability hermeneutically indifferent to the changing nature of these components? Our answer is, in this respect, affirmative: the change in the nature of the internal components following structural replication preserves the identity of the system—of course, if the conditionality (C_2) is further verified. The justification of this answer is provided by the very phrase that is analysed here: formal structure—a formal structure allows "filling" each structural component/form with any type of "substance"; this can be: material, ideal/logical, energetic, equational etc.

- (AP_2): *operational closure*: the regulation of structural replicability involves only internal principles

This predicate of sufficiency is the one that casually distinguishes the autopoietic system from the sustainable one and which (as we will show immediately) generates the property of self-organization. It can be said that this predicate of sufficiency is the very mark of autopoieticity. Of course, the very mechanism of self-organization is to be described and explained (which we will do in the following). Operational closure generally means that the autopoietic process takes place without the need for environmental intervention (which, therefore, should pass through the membrane). These external interventions can refer to resources (substantial, energetic, informational), principles, actions/forces etc. Of course, all these potential external interventions (which are forbidden by the predicate of sufficiency discussed here) interact with the given system, but only in the form and with the finality of their own input-output relations.[151] The problem of distinguishing between a simple input-output relationship output (I/O) and an external intervention on the kinematics of the system in question (K) is also difficult, because in both cases the transit of the system membrane is allowed, so we suggest, below, some criteria to help their differentiation:

- an I/O flow depletes its potential for influence after a single operating cycle[152] of the penetrated system, while K lasts, in principle, for the duration of the system itself;
- a logical consequence of the characteristic of a K-type flow is, although it came from the system's environment, the fact that it later remains in the system makes this flow to be considered internal[153] in nature or, more precisely, internalized in nature;
- however, the consequence inferred above is of the nature of Achilles's heel: indeed, at any moment, the membrane of a system can be penetrated by a K-type flow (later it is internalized) but, given this repeatable possibility, can we still talk about operational closure of the system? In this regard, we make the following considerations:
  - the K-type flow must not have a causal nature/function, but only a conditional one. Thus, it must "dictate" only the margin within which the action/reaction of the system must be framed to the action/reaction of the environment, in such a way that the action/reaction of the system is foetal in relation to the environment;
  - this restriction on K-type flow is general and permanent;
  - the possibility that K-type flows (of an exclusively conditional nature regarding the foetality of the norms of action/reaction, as we mentioned) exist permanently, does not violate, therefore, the predicate of sufficiency regarding the operational closure of the autopoietic system;

- (AP_3): ***relational openness***: the system is open in relation to its environment, that is, there is an exchange of substance, energy and information between the system and its environment
  - there are no controversial or delicate issues regarding this predicate of sufficiency, as it is required by the quality of the system to be dissipative;
  - relational openness to the environment ensures that the system can maintain or reduce its internal entropy (inside the membrane) by extracting negative entropy (neg-entropy, or low entropy) from the environment and spilling high entropy (or positive entropy) into the environment;[154]
- (AP_4): ***processual closure***: can ensure substantial and energetic recovery of its input based on own output
  - this predicate of sufficiency also defines sustainable systems;[155]
  - processual closure is not implied by operational closure, so the two predicates of sufficiency are not redundant with each other;
  - procedural closure is, in our view, a dimensional mark of systems, whether sustainable or autopoietic, in the sense that the membrane of the system in question extends to cover the entire minimum space in which the processual closure occurs;[156]
  - processual closure can be thought of both serially—concatenated subsystems in such a way that the output of the system (k) is the input of the subsystem ($k + 1$), provided (called final condition or closure condition) that the output of the subsystem (n) to be the input of the subsystem (1)—and parallel, based on the same relationship between outputs and inputs.

The most important logical consequence of the property of autopoeticity is that of self-organization. It results from the predicate of sufficiency (AP_2)—operational closure—which prohibits processes within the autopoietic system from being caused/conditioned by principles external to that system (i.e., principles within the system's environment), as permitted, from the point of view of logical view, in the case of sustainable systems. For example, a tax system may be sustainable but not autopoietic, because it must be constantly updated from outside (by the Government, which is not structurally part of the tax system).

A problem that arises at this point is that of cognition associated with autopoietic systems. As mentioned above, Maturana and Varela (1980) build autopoieticity/autopoiesis bundled with the concept of cognition, understood in its broadest sense (known today as the position of the Santiago school). But in its broadest sense, cognition includes the most mechanical sensitivity, that is, a property that is common to every system imaginable, not only autopoietic systems (and not only, even, living systems[157]). This is why, in the list of predicates of sufficiency for the conceptual definition/delimitation of autopoieticity, there is no predicate that claims the cognitive capacity of the system.[158]

1.6.2 Theorems on Autopoieticity

We will examine now the possibility of the functioning of some theorems regarding autopoietic systems (from the perspective of the property of autopoieticity). In this sense, we propose the following theorems:

(a) *The behaviour of an autopoietic system is a function of its functionality*

Proof: the functionality of a system consists of the relationships (either potential or actual) between its components. These relationships generate the functions (and, by their interpretation, i.e., more precisely, by giving them meaning, generate the roles) that the system is able to perform or actually perform. The behaviour of a system consists of the relationships (either potential or actual) between the components of that system and its environment. If the functionality remains inside the system membrane, the behaviour can only be actualized by transiting this membrane. So, of the functions generated by functionality, some will pass through the membrane and interact with the environment (in the form of actions/reactions)—this is the meaning in which the statement in this "theorem" must be understood. *Nota bene*: of course, the entry from the environment, through the transit of the membrane, of some actions/reactions also enters the behaviour of the system, from the perspective of the fact that some functions ensure precisely this penetration of the actions/reactions from the environment. More generally, it can be said that behaviour should be discussed only in the plural: system behaviour is a reflective projection of the interference between one's own behaviour and environmental behaviour, just as environmental behaviour is a reflective projection of this interference, this time on the environment. Q.E.D.

Reciprocal: the functionality of a system cannot be said to be an effect of its behaviour. However, an influence of behaviour on functionality (i.e., actualizing the set of functions, especially on those intended to generate the behaviour) must be accepted, at least from the perspective of adaptation.[159]

(b) *Any autopoietic system is a sustainable system*

Proof: given that the operational closure, specific to autopoietic systems, is of the nature of restricting the operational sphere, and not of its extension,[160] it follows that sustainability is not affected (denied) by the elimination of the open operational part. Q.E.D.

Reciprocal: any sustainable system is an autopoietic system is obviously *false* because the part of the operationality of the system that has an open character (as allowed by the definition of sustainability) violates the predicate of sufficiency (AP_2).

Lemma: any autopoietic system contains at least one sustainable subsystem. The proof is immediate if we consider, for example, the subsystem as the system itself.[161]

(c) *A set of autopoietic systems always form an autopoietic supersystem*

Proof: if all systems are autopoietic, so, if each of them verifies the four predicates of sufficiency for autopoieticity, then the (logical) sum of those systems cannot violate any of these predicates, which means that they will form an autopoietic supersystem.

Reciprocal: an autopoietic supersystem contains only autopoietic systems; it is *not true*, because inside the supersystem there may be two systems that are not autopoietic, each separately, but their cooperation to generate, at the level of the membrane that comprises them, an autopoietic system.[162]

1.7 Soundness

In our opinion, the concept of soundness is, by far, the most integrative and synthetic concept regarding desirability in the economic field and, of course, for the societal system as a whole. We sketch below some considerations in this matter.

We think soundness is instituted in the "world" if concomitantly verifies eight properties:

- (*F*1) structural *completeness*
- (*F*2) static *equilibrium*
- (*F*3) dynamic *stability*
- (*F*4) *robustness*
- (*F*5) *resilience*
- (*F*6) *antifragility*
- (*F*7) *sustainability*
- (*F*8) *autopoiesis*

A logical examination of the eight properties which the macro-property of economic soundness must verify, in total or in part, is useful for the next developments of the research. The main points of such examination are the following:

(a) There are some internal relationships between the properties:
  - (F3) is depending on (F2), and (F2) is depending on (F1)—perhaps not in a causal way but on a conditional one;
  - (F6) acts if and only if (F5) fails, and (F5) acts if and only if (F4) fails;
  - (F7) and (F8) are strongly inter-dependent (perhaps they develop a co-evolutive rapport);

(b) (*F*1) seems to be the general (logical and institutional) ground of all the other properties;

(c) in fact, we can form three composed properties which will be called sufficiency predicates of the financial soundness (*FS*), as follows:
  - (*ES*1): which is the (*F*1), that is, the *completeness causal/conditional* ($ES1 \equiv F1$). The role of *ES*1 is to close the output to input, so that to ensure the replicability of the system;
  - (*ES*2): *statu quo causal/conditional*, that is, $ES2 \equiv (F2) \wedge (F3) \wedge (F4) \wedge (F5)$. The role of *ES*2 is to ensure the conservation/preservation of the system face to (internal or external) perturbations from its state or from its kinematic position on own path (chreode);
  - (*ES*3): *evolving causal/conditional*, that is, $ES3 \equiv (F6) \wedge (F7) \wedge (F8)$. The role of *ES*3 is to ensure that the replicability unfolds in the evolutionary pattern.

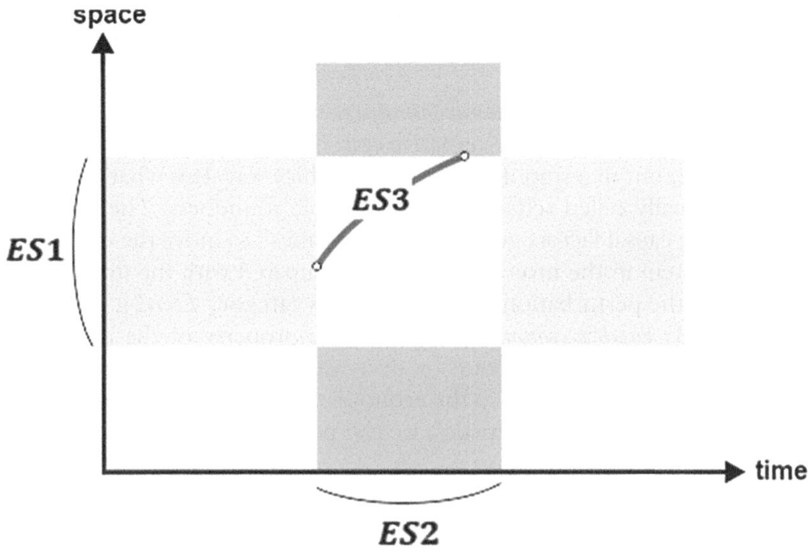

Fig. 1.27 Causal/conditional determinants of the economic soundness. (*Source*: Author)

The causal/conditional determinants of the economic soundness can be represented as in Fig. 1.27.

1.7.1 On a Typology of Economic Soundness

Based on the general properties of the economic soundness as well as on the three sufficiency predicates of it, it could be of usefulness to identify the adequate criteria to classify the economic soundness as macro-property of the economic system/process.[163] In our opinion, two criteria can be of scientific interest in the matter of the economic soundness: (a) the stability of the property of economic soundness; (b) the structure of the property of economic soundness.

(a) According to the stability of the economic soundness—criterion α
  - (α1) *inertial economic soundness*: the property of the economic soundness is very conservative, so it does neither reduce nor increase, but maintains in an indefinite time horizon; we can note

this category $ES(\alpha 1)$. If no perturbing causal factor acts on the economic system in question, the state of its soundness is kept as such;

- ($\alpha 2$) *oscillating economic soundness*: the property of the economic soundness exhibits alternative episodes of increasing and decreasing, but in a smooth (non-catastrophic) way. It is what could be equally called self-sustained economic soundness. The perturbing causal factors generate the "enzymes" to move the economic system in the inverted direction, compared with the first impact of the perturbation; we can note this category $ES(\alpha 2)$;
- ($\alpha 3$) *ratchet economic soundness*: the property of the economic soundness can increase or decrease but the new level of it is instantly ratcheted, so the economic system in question is acquiring inertial characteristics; we can note this category $ES(\alpha 3)$.

Table 1.2 focuses on the logical correlations among the analytical properties or the economic soundness and the classes of the economic soundness according to the criterion α.

(b) According to the structure of the economic soundness—criterion β

- ($\beta 1$) *conservative economic soundness*: the property of the economic soundness objectifies through maintaining the current course of the economic system; we can note this category $ES(\beta 1)$;
- ($\beta 2$) *replicative economic soundness*: the property of the economic soundness objectifies through reproducing, in essence, the current course of the economic system; we can note this category $ES(\beta 2)$;
- ($\beta 3$) *evolutive economic soundness*: the property of the economic soundness objectifies through integrating the environment reac-

Table 1.2 How the properties of *ES* ground the classes α of *ES*

	F1	*F2*	*F3*	*F4*	*F5*	*F6*	*F7*	*F8*
$ES(\alpha 1)$	x			x				x
$ES(\alpha 2)$		x	x		x			
$ES(\alpha 3)$	x					x	x	

Source: Author

tion, so providing either the conservation/preservation or the evolving of the economic system; we can note this category $ES(\beta 3)$.

Table 1.3 focuses on the logical correlations among the analytical properties or the economic soundness and the classes of the economic soundness according to the criterion α.

By combining the information of Tables 1.2 and 1.3, the logical/conceptual relationships between the α-typology and β-typology can be obtained (Fig. 1.28).

Discussion

- generally, there is a causal relationship from the α-typology to the β-typology of the economic soundness, $ES(\alpha i) \rightarrow ES(\beta i)$, with $i = 1, 2, 3$;
  - *meaning*: inertiality generates conservativeness; oscillation generates replicativity; ratchetness generates evolution;[164]
- $ES(\alpha 1)$ conditionalizes $ES(\beta 2)$, and $ES(\beta 1)$ conditionalizes $ES(\alpha 2)$;
  - *meaning*:
    replicative economic soundness is possible if and only if there is a property of inertiality in the economic system;
    oscillating economic soundness is possible if and only if there is a property of conservativeness in the economic system;
- $ES(\alpha 2)$ and $ES(\beta 3)$ are linked by functional relationships;
  - *meaning*: oscillating economic soundness objectifies the evolutive feature of the economic system, and, reciprocally, the evolutive economic soundness allows the oscillations of that economic system.

Table 1.3 How the properties of *ES* ground the classes β of *ES*

	F1	*F2*	*F3*	*F4*	*F5*	*F6*	*F7*	*F8*
$ES(\beta 1)$	x	x	x	x				
$ES(\beta 2)$					x	x	x	
$ES(\beta 3)$	x					x	x	x

Source: Author

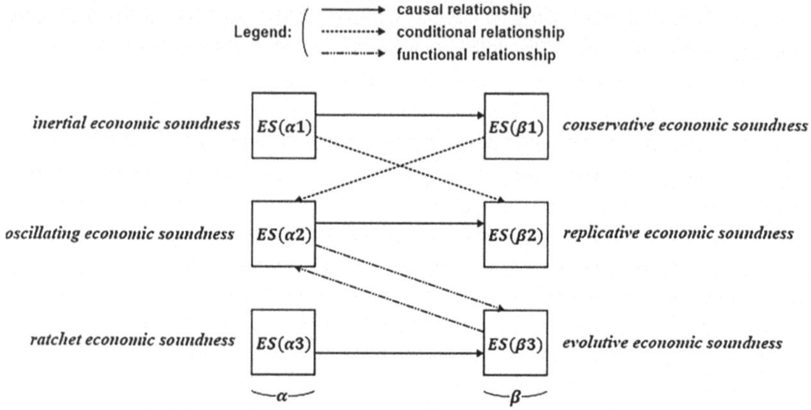

Fig. 1.28 Conceptual relationships between α-typology and β-typology of *ES*. (*Source*: Author)

1.7.2 Mechanism of Economic Soundness

It is interesting to examine the very mechanism by which the economic soundness (ES), of any type, emerges and maintains. Although different types of the ES exhibit different particularities of such a mechanism of economic soundness ($M_{ES}^{(\cdot)}$), a hard core of the last can be extracted from a logical point of view. To describe this hard core of the mechanism, we shall identify its logical components.

(i) (M_{ES}^{1}) *institutive* component
- Definition: it is that component which generates the structure of the mechanism in question (see, e.g., the *F*1 feature of the ES, which addresses the structural completeness of the economic system);
- Structure:
  - general (theoretical) rationality at the societal level (more exactly, the general axiology, and the dominant beliefs);
  - normative framework in force;
- Role: to introduce the (generally) formal conditionalities—for example, normative framework—regarding the economic soundness in the economic system;

- Emergence: predominantly of deliberative type but it is not impossible that the "invisible" hand to introduce informal norms (of customary nature) in the functioning of economic system;

(ii) (M_{ES}^{2}) *operative* component
- Definition: it is that component which generates and maintains the functionality and the behaviour[165] of the economic system in question;
- Structure:
  - necessary operations—that is, those operations which are required for the survival of the economic system;
  - contingent operations—that is, those operations which lead to the dynamics of the economic system, from any point of view;
- Role: to put into working the structure (institutive component);
- Emergence: like in the case of the institutive component (see above);

(iii) (M_{ES}^{3}) *regulative* component
- Definition: it is that component which ensures the path of the economic system such a way so to keep the economic soundness;
- Structure:
  - monitoring procedures;
  - protocols of designing the proposals of required mutations (generally of normative nature);
- Role: to keep the path of the operative component and, if the case, to change (through the intermediation of mutations) the institutive component;
- Emergence: only deliberatively, although some "suggestions" provided by the market (i.e., by the free functioning part of the economic system) and be taken into consideration to be introduced normatively.

1.7.3 Measuring of the Economic Soundness

One of the most important questions linked to the economic soundness is how to measure it. Of course, to measure an economic property needs adequate indicators. Consequently, in this last paragraph of the chapter, we shall focus on this topic. We shall discuss four main issues: (a) criteria to identify the indicators of economic soundness; (b) classes of indicators for economic soundness; (c) qualitative analysis of the classes of economic soundness; (d) relevant indicators of economic soundness.

(a) Classification criteria of economic soundness

Regarding the set of criteria aimed at finding the classes of indicators which are presumed to provide measures of the economic soundness, we propose the following four criteria:

- (O) *origin*—the source of economic soundness: this criterion addresses the bases on which the economic soundness is implemented or/and works inside the economic system;
- (D) *degree*—the depth of economic soundness: this criterion addresses the degree in which the economic soundness is supported by the structure, by the simple functioning or by both;
- (T) *trend*—the propensity of economic soundness: this criterion addresses the propensity (both in time and in space) of the economic soundness;
- (C) *connectivity*—the potential economic soundness to evolve (or, rather, to co-evolve): this criterion addresses the links between the kinematics of economic soundness, on the one part, and the evolution features of that kinematics, on the other hand.

Classes of Economic Soundness

(1) According to O-criterion

Based on the O-criterion, we propose three classes of economic soundness:

- (O^1) *law-based* economic soundness—that is, that economic soundness which is instituted, monitored and adjusted by intermediation of the law (norms of large applicability) or by the "visible hand" of the society; note it $ES(O^1)$;
- (O^2) *market-based* economic soundness—that is, that economic soundness which is emerged through the very working of the economic market; note it $ES(O^2)$;
- (O^3) *mix-based* economic soundness—that is, that economic soundness which is the result of both normative framework and free market working; note it $ES(O^3)$;

(2) According to *D*-criterion

Based on the *D*-criterion, we propose three classes of economic soundness:

- (D^1) *deep economic soundness*—that is, that economic soundness which is set in the institutive component of economic soundness mechanism (see point 1.5 above); note it $ES(D^1)$;
- (D^2) *peripheral economic soundness*—that is, that economic soundness which is not set in the very structure of the economic system, but it manifests at the functional level only; note it $ES(D^2)$;
- (D^3) *medium economic soundness*—that is, that economic soundness which combines a small structural depth with a small functional conditioning; note it $ES(D^3)$;

(3) According to *T*-criterion

Based on the *T*-criterion, we propose three classes of economic soundness:

- (T^1) *deepening economic soundness*—that is, a deepening of economic soundness is possible by structural improvements only, so it is talking about positive change in the institutive component of the mechanism of ES;
- (T^2) *superficializing economic soundness*—that is, it is the opposite process related to the deepening, namely, it is talking about negative change in the institutive component of the mechanism of ES;
- (T^3) *stationary economic soundness*—that is, the situation in which economic soundness relatively keeps its degree (or its rapport between depth and periphery);

(4) According to *C*-criterion

Based on the *C*-criterion, we propose three classes of economic soundness:

- (C^1) *self-sustainable economic soundness*—that is, that economic soundness, which is closed enough, under the structural and causal perspectives, so that it can self-replicate sine die, without interfere too much with its environment;

- (C^2) ***dissipative soundness***—that is, that economic soundness which is open enough so that it can maintain its low entropy far for equilibrium exactly by entropic change with its environment;
- (C^3) ***co-evolving economic soundness***—that is, that economic soundness which upholds necessary and permanent relationships of co-evolution with its environment. Such a class is possible since economic soundness is a symbolic species, as are the components of its environment (*Nota bene*: Annex 1 provides a short presentation of the concept of symbolic species, which will be operationalized especially in Chap. 10).

(b) Some logical correlations

Between the typology of economic soundness based on a pure logical determination and the typology of economic soundness based on methodological considerations, some significant relationships can be put into evidence, so as to suggest directions of analysis and modelling in the matter of economic soundness. To this end, a matrix of compatibility between the two categories of classes regarding the economic soundness could be useful (Table 1.4). *Nota bene*: the meaning of notations are

Table 1.4 Compatibility between the two typologies of economic soundness

To:			*α*			*β*	
From:		*α1*	*α2*	*α3*	*β1*	*β2*	*β3*
O	O^1	*MC*	*SRA*	*MRA*	*SRA*	*MC*	*LI*
	O^2	*WC*	*SC*	*MRA*	*WRA*	*MC*	*MRA*
	O^3	*MC*	*MRA*	*WRA*	*MC*	*WC*	*MC*
D	D^1	*SC*	*MRA*	*WC*	*SC*	*SRA*	*LI*
	D^2	*LI*	*WRA*	*LI*	*LC*	*LI*	*LC*
	D^3	*LI*	*MRA*	*WRA*	*WRA*	*LI*	*LI*
T	T^1	*SC*	*SRA*	*LI*	*MC*	*MRA*	*MRA*
	T^2	*LC*	*LI*	*LI*	*LC*	*LI*	*LI*
	T^3	*WC*	*MRA*	*WRA*	*WC*	*SRA*	*LC*
C	C^1	*SC*	*SRA*	*MRA*	*MC*	*SRA*	*SRA*
	C^2	*SC*	*SC*	*LC*	*MC*	*SRA*	*WRA*
	C^3	*LI*	*WRA*	*SRA*	*LC*	*SRA*	*SC*

Source: Author

as follows: *SC*—strong causation; *MC*—medium causation; *WC*—weak causation; *SRA*—strong reciprocal adequation; *MRA*—medium reciprocal adequation; *WRA*—weak reciprocal adequation; *LC*—logical contradiction/incompatibility; *LI*— logical indifference/co-existence.

Notes

1. The following question could be asked: do internal disturbances have a greater degree of predictability than external ones? Our answer to this question is negative: the system's ability to anticipate is based on models of rationality that can be applied, *mutatis mutandis*, to both internal and external environment, so that the predictability of disturbances does not fundamentally differ (too much) depending on their origin.
2. We will analytically develop these distinctions below.
3. Obviously, changing the thresholds or/and changing the extent of the dead zone are contingent effects, not necessary, once the robustness of a system is defeated.
4. We will see below that resilience (like antifragility) are not inalienable properties of systems, but alienable ones. Or, in other words, while robustness is a necessary property, resilience and antifragility are contingent properties. The similarity between the three concepts (properties), however, is that they all have a structural location (origin); they are not purely functional—*Nota bene*: by pure functionalism we mean a superficial functionalism, that is, a functionalism that is not generated by the structure (we come back to this matter).
5. Of course, through its structure, as designed for this purpose.
6. Such a list can be constructed either deliberatively, based on models of rationality, or emergently (in the case of natural or non-human living systems), through learning or, in some cases, memetic imitation.
7. We will return to this issue in the economy of the study because it is also relevant for the other two concepts discussed: resilience, respectively antifragility and, obviously, for the *RRA* trinomial .
8. In fact, only the ascending branch of the parabola (which is convex, since $i_t > 0$) is of interest, provided the fact that ($d_t > 0$).
9. The transformation of quantitative reduction into temporal reduction obviously requires the introduction of a rate of variation of the change pressure inside the dead zone, an aspect we will refer to later.
10. A "complication" that would be useful to discuss here is the following: different components are expected to have different learning rates (and/or learning limits), so that reducing change pressure through stress adaptation should be differentiated to different components of the system—

we will return to this idea when we discuss the institutional design of the *RRA* device.

11. The switching of the system will be done, therefore, when the threshold P_t^S will be reached by the first component in the system—here we find the idea of the weak link of the system. It is therefore important to note that it is not necessary for all components to simultaneously reach the system's change threshold, but it is sufficient for one component to reach that threshold (as we said, the most vulnerable component).
12. The concept (and term) of hormesis comes from the Greek *ormao* (to stimulate).
13. This is no longer an accumulation threshold, as in the case of RO/1, but a jump threshold. In a psychological terminology, RO/1 is a repression threshold and RO/2 is a counter-repression threshold.
14. Or even tripling and quadrupling, after the case.
15. We recall that substantive utility is the utility generally considered by economists, who call it economic utility (and even by other social science researchers, such as social justice lawyers, behavioural sociologists or libertarian state theorists).
16. Effectiveness, efficient and economical are praxeological terms for concepts very different: effectiveness (or efficacy) means target reaching, economical means reducing the costs, efficient means to optimize the relationship between economical and effectiveness.
17. This automation must, of course, be introduced into the hardware or software of the system in question.
18. Obviously, the consideration of several redundant devices (which can be connected either in series or in parallel) does not fundamentally change the scheme shown in Fig. 6.
19. Obviously, anything necessary is also possible (here with reference to the robustness property).
20. This aspect is analysed in the C3 robustness classification criterion.
21. We avoid using the syntagm perturbing factors instead of change factors because change factors can have positive connotations, unlike perturbing factors which are credited with negative connotations.
22. The components of a system constitute the structure of that system. The components must be indiscernible by at least one predicate (to be able to form a set) and, at the same time, be distinguishable by at least one predicate (to be countable, i.e., to form the cardinality of the set). From a logical point of view, the two mentioned conditions represent sufficiency predicates of a set (*Nota bene*: in addition to them, the system also implies the existence of a membrane that separates it from its environment).
23. The method of saving (or updating the memory) is analogous to the way in which, on ordinary PCs, the well-known save function is used, which

means exactly that: saving the last state of the system (or, in the case discussed here, of the last position of the system on the trajectory).

24. The trajectory equation must obviously also be memorized, but this memorization should probably be more of a hardware type, while the mnemonic device should be more of a software type (these distinctions are not, however, of too much relevance in the general, purely logical discussion we are developing here).
25. If the exact moment at which the pressure to change ceases can be known, then the moment when resilience is triggered will be this moment of cessation of change action/reaction on the system. If, however, this moment is not known (or its prediction, with an acceptable probability, is not possible), then the decision-maker of the system (its leading subsystem) can choose any other moment for triggering resilience, including during the continuation of the pressure to change, in conditions that must be well-specified.
26. It should be noted that, in principle, the value $(\tau - t)$ could express the duration for which the dead zone of the robustness "acts".
27. Of course, the desirability must meet the possibility—the possible desirability is, in a word, feasibility.
28. Which can, obviously, have a number of coordinates or parameters of this state, that's why the term vector is used, but in its algebraic sense, that is, without directional orientation (like in Physics).
29. Obviously, the position vector also contains several coordinates (several parameters) depending on the parameters considered when describing the trajectory—the number of parameters/coordinates represents the size of the space considered in that case. For example, if we consider a simple movement in space, the usual number of spatial dimensions is three but, at least in the economic domain, we can have spaces with a different number of dimensions (either higher or lower than three).
30. Of course, this problem can be handled by making predictions, based on analytical models, so that a feed-forward is considered to possibly (if desirable) correct the recovery of the previous kinematic state/position "with no rest".
31. We have used the term *sense* and not that of *direction*, because (despite their quite frequent confusion in quite pretentious studies) they have different meanings: we will only say that a given direction always has two senses, namely opposites (right-left, up down). Incidentally, the reaction in the third law of mechanics is a force (i.e., a vector) that has the same direction as the action, only in the opposite sense, which means that to say that action and reaction occur in opposite directions is, of course, simply wrong. An alternative is to say, instead of "action and reaction are of opposite sign", "action and reaction are of opposite (algebraic) sign".

32. Indeed, if the functionality of the system is "closed" inside the membrane of the system, the behaviour involves the transit of this membrane, therefore the interference with the environment (in other words, the behaviour is immersed in the environment of the system).
33. Of course, the modification of the trajectory as such is not excluded either (*Nota bene*: here the concept of trajectory must be understood in its broad sense, namely as chreode). However, changing the trajectory, which means changing the law of motion of the system, is all the more likely to generate changes in the state vector.
34. According to the cybernetic theory.
35. We remind the reader that, logically, the contingent is a non-necessary possible.
36. A function, denoted f, is a binary relation defined on a domain/set, called the domain/set of definition (X), and transports this set to a domain/set called the domain/set of values (Y). We write this transformation $f: X \rightarrow Y$. Thus, if $x \in X$, then $f(x) = y$, where $y \in Y$ and is called the value corresponding to x by the function f.
37. For now, for the generic case, we do not dissociate between state resilience and kinematic position resilience, but later such customizations are easy to introduce.
38. According to the previous notations, the measurement is done by *DC* and the memorization by *DM*.
39. According to the previous notations, this situation is achieved by *DA*.
40. Even assuming that the elasticity coefficient is a "hard" property of the system, the elastic force will depend on what happens in the system, so on the moment t at which the gap appears (regarding either state or position).
41. The rationale for such a proposal seems quite obvious, qualitatively: as the gap (of either state or kinematic position) increases, the system will generate an increased (but decreasing) tendency to recover the initial situation. However, after a certain level of the gap, this tendency begins to decrease (namely, with an increasing decrease) because, in another hypothesis, it would mean that any evolution would be forbidden, in the sense that the opposition of the system would be all the greater as the change pressure increases (or, which is quantitatively equivalent, increases its exercise duration). The maximum point of the concave parabola of the elasticity coefficient represents a "breaking point" beyond which the system will "want" less and less to return to the initial state. The decrease in the elasticity coefficient signifies precisely the idea that, after the breaking point, the system increases its eagerness to adopt the new posture (either as a state or as a kinematic posture, as the case may be).
42. For the purely didactic (and symmetrical) case, the program sequence in Matlab was used: x = [−5:0.001:5]; y = 1 + x + x.^2 + x.^3; plot(x, y).

43. Some illustrative calculations: (a) the abscissa of the breaking point in the elasticity coefficient curve is as follows: $\frac{\partial e}{\partial g_t} = 0 \rightarrow g_t^* = -\frac{\beta}{2\gamma}$, deci $e(g_t^*) = \frac{4\alpha - \beta^2}{4\gamma}$; (b) the abscissa of the inflection point in the elastic force curve is as follows: $\frac{\partial^2}{\partial (g_t)^2} = 0 \rightarrow g_t^{**} = -\frac{\beta}{3\gamma}$, deci $F_e(g_t^{**}) = \frac{-9\alpha\beta\gamma + 3\beta^2 - \beta^3}{27\gamma^2}$.
44. Refraining (as much as possible, because it is not always possible) from issuing value judgements on some results or levels of variables (e.g., on inflation, unemployment and GDP pace) constitutes one of the minimum conditions of a scientific research of positive type (*Nota bene*: of course, not all scientific research is positive type).
45. The issue is, conceptually, comparable with the biological case in which the cells of the immune system must be instructed to make difference between cancer cells and healthy cells.
46. The idea that a change in the situation of the system, induced by a disturbing factor (which can be both internal and external), can generate a desirable situation is not rejectable *ab ovo*; it refers to a possible fact and, apparently, such in fact it is not even that rare (just think of the "maxim" that any constraint causes innovation).
47. This inhibition is analogous to the inhibition that occurs in the case of the biological system, with the difference that, in the latter case, the inhibition mechanism is chemical, while in the case discussed in the present study, the inhibition mechanism is informational. Obviously, the inhibition mechanism can no longer be of the "hard" type; it must be of the "soft" type.
48. The question of whether this selector should (or could) learn, in the sense of reaching the ability to automatically recognize itself which situations are desirable and which are not, is extremely complicated (technically, it concerns the so-called artificial intelligence, but logically presents some difficulties)—we will not, however, discuss this extension of the problem in the present study.
49. Of course, identifying the state change responsible for the (recorded) change in kinematic position is a problem of the inverse problem type—that is, the answer to the question "what state change could have led to the (recorded) change in kinematic position?" must be found. Unfortunately, in a problem of this type, there is no single answer, since the same effect can be produced (depending on the actual conditionalities involved) by different causes.
50. It is worth noting that, in our opinion, there is no "dead zone" regarding the change in kinematic position leading to a change in the state of the system, in the sense that the change in kinematic position has a necessary (almost punctual) counterpart in the change in state.

51. Obviously, it is not about a direct comparison between $M^{(1)}$ and $R^{(1)}$, because the two goods are incommensurable (possibly the establishment of the deficit, respectively the surplus could be done on the basis of benchmarks for each of the two goods, and in the case of each of the two economic agents), but about an evaluation (or rather, about a ... feeling) that the economic agent in question has—as we said above, here we simply have mental accounting.
52. If it were not for this subjective interpretation, no economic transaction would have any ... economic reasons for taking place (although, of course, there may be other reasons why the exchange in question does take place).
53. What was obtained (from a different perspective, but on the same logic) is exactly the content of the standard comparative economic advantage (*Nota bene*: we recall the difference between the two types of economic advantage from classical economic theory: (a) *absolute* advantage (Smith), resulting from the comparison between two economic agents regarding the same good; (b) *comparative*/relative advantage (Ricardo), resulting from the comparison between two goods regarding the same economic agent).
54. Of course, the concept of benefit must itself be defined or at least associated with a somewhat operational description. In this sense, we say that by benefit must be understood the effect of a change in the state of an economic agent (subject), a change that has signification (which, of course, must be given by that agent, so it will have a strong subjective, idiosyncratic character, which makes it incommensurable with the appreciation of the effect of the same change issued by another economic agent) of an increase in the well-being of that agent. *Nota bene*: the concept of well-being must be understood in all its generality, that is, it refers to any increase in the well-being (at the level of subjective perception) of the person in question.
55. Here arises the important (and difficult) ethical problem regarding the merit of the positional advantage (we remember that it is about the case of a complete passivity of the agent and even more than that of a complete absence of his intentionality; otherwise we would be dealing with one form or another of consuming an effort in the direction of obtaining the expected effect, so we would return to the case of the transactional advantage).
56. The non-intentional aspect is fundamental in defining the externality; otherwise it would fall under the category of transactional advantage. As a consequence, the (rather wide) view that public goods are of the nature of a positive externality is obviously wrong, because the provider of public goods (the state) does so deliberately, hence intentionally. Moreover, the

transactional aspect is quite obvious in this case: the production and distribution of public goods is financed through the price paid by the beneficiaries of these goods, the taxpayers, to the public budget (the price paid is called tax).

57. By *windfall profit* is meant a positional advantage (*Nota bene*: the specialized literature does not make such a categorical classification of the concept of advantage from which the class of advantage that was called here positional advantage can result) that is not deserved by the one who benefits from it and, as a result, it is considered that it should be returned, in whole or in part, to the agent (personal or institutional) that generated it. This problem faces some difficulties that are not clarified, however: (a) establishing the fact that the economic agent beneficiary of this advantage does not deserve it implies, from a logical point of view, the non-existence of the effort (however small) to obtain that advantage—but this assumption already shifts the discussion from positional advantage to transactional advantage; (b) the return of the benefit represented by the positional advantage implies the existence (and precise, punctual identification) of the agent (personal or institutional) who caused/generated/created that advantage—but, this identification is not always possible (e.g., if an individual cured himself of an illness by sitting in the sun, who is "responsible" for creating this positional advantage? Of course, for all cases where such a "responsible" cannot be identified, a generic "responsible" can be substituted for him (which seems unwilling to take such a position also in the case of negative externalities without an "author"): the state—but here also arises the problem of… the merit of the state. We do not continue the discussion of this interesting problem, because it goes beyond the (narrower) objectives of the present research.
58. The problem of the threshold of significance is important in two aspects: (a) not every deviation is something negative—all balances in the economy and society are of a dynamic type, that is, they record small oscillations (periodically or not) that ensure precisely this balance (which is also called, by the way, dynamic balance); (b) the threshold of significance does not always coincide with the threshold of "breaking" the dynamic equilibrium (although it may, of course, coincide), because the significance differs from individual to individual (because of the individual idiosyncrasy) or from group to group.
59. Using a paraphrase of a phrase used in the field of cosmology, but which fits, from the semantic point of view (of meaning), even the problem discussed here, we could call this threshold (or this limit) with the phrase the *horizon of predictability* (*Nota bene*: the phrase "plagiarized" is the *events horizon*, or Schwarzschild limit, in relation to the distance beyond which no real entity can escape the attraction of a black hole).

60. As is the case with the two (non-economic) disruptions that are still ongoing (overlapping, to a large extent) at the time of this research: (1) the COVID-19 pandemic; (2) the war initiated by Russia against Ukraine. Previously, the financial (and partly economic) crisis triggered in 2007 in the United States and in 2008 in Europe also acted as a systemic disruption.
61. With one notable exception: automatic stabilizers that represent a mix between deliberativeness (discretionary) and automatism (non-discretionary).
62. By relative disadvantage is meant a partial reduction of a pre-existing advantage, without completely cancelling that advantage. By absolute disadvantage is meant either a disadvantage not associated with any existing advantage or a disadvantage that completely reduces (cancels) or even "over-cancels" a pre-existing advantage (see, at point (2), the typology of disruption).
63. This includes the well-known *early warning* systems that measure not only the reaching of the significance threshold but also some values prior to reaching it—either as a level or as a trend (speed/acceleration), or, as a rule, below both aspects.
64. Here we have a peculiar illustration of the Latin saying *fluctuat nec mergitur*.
65. Logically, there is no need to mention anything about the variation of the output of the system, because unless the output in question constitutes the input to another system (which is theoretically possible), the variation of that output has no meaning. We remind here, for those interested, that the concept of fluctuation is a central concept in Prigogine's theory of dissipative systems, more precisely in the economics of his concept of order: thus, macroscopic order is assumed to be generated precisely by microscopic "disorder"—the slow phrase is *order from/through fluctuations*.
66. The most appropriate metaphor for the concept of fluctuation is the *wave*.
67. As structure generates function, to be structural but not functional means to be placed, as impact on the structure, under a threshold which is presumed to effectively change that structure (so, we remain here ... Darwinist).
68. We believe that a normative obligation should even be imposed here.
69. Of course, the fact that perturbation cannot be a predictor of the system's behaviour (or, by mirroring, of that system's environment) is a self-evident conclusion.
70. Moreover, this predicate of sufficiency will be able to serve to substantiate some evolutionary claims that will be made in the continuation of the research.

71. Of course, interested analysts will be able to identify, from this condition, different species of non-disturbance, including the fluctuation one, but this direction of research will not be developed in the present study.
72. For example, the current establishment of economic sanctions by the European Union (and, more generally, the West) against the Russian Federation, as a result of the latter's launching of unprovoked, illegal and unjustified armed aggression against Ukraine.
73. Even in the cases in which the corrective disruptions act automatically (through automatic stabilizers), at their origin, they are, in fact, deliberative (discretionary).
74. For example, a relatively small increase in inflation is dissipated in the system if it is not followed too quickly by a too large increase in it, so that the next "round" of increasing inflation "takes it from zero", that is, exhibits the same hormetic character as in the first cycle (the issue of whether the hormetic threshold is influenced, in the form of learning, by this repetition of the phenomenon is, of course, very important, both theoretically and from a public policy perspective).
75. That is why, for example, stress tests carried out on different organizations/institutions are not neutral from the perspective of the ability to withstand the exact stress tested, that is, they can raise the level of stress to which the organization/institution in question becomes resistant. The phenomenon is similar to some physical phenomena, such as, for example, measuring body temperature with a thermometer—locally, the thermometer does not actually measure the temperature of the body, but the joint temperature of the body and the thermometer, after the two temperatures are equalized according to the principle of the second law of Thermodynamics.
76. A distinction must be made between the predictability of corrective disturbances (see above) which is an internal, deliberative predictability from the perspective of the target system, and the predictability of repeatable disturbances, which is an external, non-deliberative predictability from the perspective of the target system.
77. This idea is based, for example, on the typology of economic cycles (some authors even refer to the typology of economic crises from this perspective).
78. We are referring, here, to an objective probability of the singular event, a probability which is called, as is known (according to Karl Popper's proposal), *propensity*, so not to the objective probability of a statistical type, based on an archive of events (the latter are also known as objective frequency probabilities or Kolmogorov probabilities).
79. The localization of the origin needs not necessarily coincide with the location of the cause (or causality), although most of the time this coincidence is likely to occur.

80. We specify that this criterion does not overlap with the criterion of nature, as it seems *prima facie*: both types of disturbances according to the criterion of behaviour are institutional disturbances, just as both disturbances according to the criterion of behaviour can be corrective disturbances, but never a trained disturbance can be of otherwise type, according to the criterion of behaviour, except that of the initiating disturbance of training.
81. We can speak here about perturbation chain or (in some contexts) about perturbation network.
82. Thus, we will probably also have to accept the mirror image (or, more precisely, the logical negation) of cumulative perturbation, namely what we might call de-cumulative perturbation.
83. The impact of a disturbance on the target system occurs only after the robustness threshold of this system is exceeded, as shown previously.
84. This phenomenon of "causally neutralized cocooning" is encountered, above all, in the case of living systems: for example, in the case of organisms, the skin surrounds an open wound with a biological crust, in order to avoid its infection from the environment; similarly, the production of economic inequality in society is neutralized by the (discretionary or, as the case may be, automatic) application of the principle of difference (see John Rawls's theory of social justice).
85. Modellable by the concept of *reaction norm* and by the procedural rules that characterize the mechanism of reaction norms.
86. We will proceed in an analogous way to that in which Imre Lakatos proceeded when he introduced the concept of research program in his epistemological attempt to combine Popper's logical theory with Kuhn's historical theory in the matter of the theory of knowledge.
87. It is obvious that a basic structure is compatible (not simultaneously, but alternatively, or rather, successively) with several peripheral structures, just as a peripheral structure is compatible with different basic structures.
88. Obviously, a certain quantitative threshold must be accepted here too, above which the impact exerted by the disturbance on the basic structure manages to produce changes in it.
89. Non-identitary survival is a nominal survival, because the target system, in its personality, disappears, being replaced by another system, with another identity, given by a new basic structure, different from the previous one. *Nota bene*: we will see, immediately, that antifragility (according to the new semantic aspect, introduced by Taleb) is compatible, above all, with the non-identitary survival of the target system.
90. For now, the nature of this advantage does not matter, but in general, it can be reduced to the (common) concept of utility (not only substantive utility, but also including symbolic utility).

91. By net utility we obviously mean the difference between the increase in utility from the exploitation of the disruption and the increase in disutility generated by the impact of the disruption.
92. The same assessment is also valid for the human organism (or any living entity)—at a certain time interval, all the cells of the organism are replaced by other cells, having identical functions, namely on the same structural-genetic basis of the respective organism, this one from the latter being considered identical to itself despite this complete anatomical replacement.
93. Since the sufficiency predicate is, in fact, a property, it means that the sufficiency predicates of antifragility are properties of properties, that is, properties of order 2, given that antifragility, in turn, is considered a property of the systems—in the sense that there are antifragile systems, respectively non-antifragile systems.
94. From the "doctrinal" point of view, this assumption is a logical consequence of the acceptance of the system concept as a relationship between parts and the whole (including the synergy effect), which is considered by some analysts to be ... outdated. We invite you to notice that none of the three proposed alternatives to this understanding (*Nota bene*: which we consider to be the fundamental understanding) is contradictory to it, representing, rather, logical derivations from it: (a) the functionalist proposal (Talcott Parsons); (b) the cybernetic proposal (Norbert Wiener); (c) the autopoietic proposal (Niklas Luhmann).
95. It is easy to see that we have here a complete logical picture of ... Darwinism. This is probably the greatest vulnerability of the acceptance of the system concept as a part-whole relationship, because, in the social domain (more precisely, in the cultural domain), most of the time the function creates the structure (*Nota bene*: what we call, usually, Lamarckism).
96. We make an important clarification here: structural plasticity, in this case, of the peripheral type, is initiated after resilience has exhausted its "defence" capacity, just as resilience itself comes into operation after robustness has exhausted itself, in turn its "defence" capacity, each of these properties—robustness and resilience, respectively—acting in their own specific way, as described and examined above.
97. The difference between system and network lies in the fact that the system is organized hierarchically (some components have greater relevance in relation to others, e.g., the driving subsystem in relation to the operational subsystems), while the network is organized in a matrix (there are no privileged components, from any point of view, in relation to other components).
98. We specify that, here, we have in mind the concept of cognition (or cognitive capacity) introduced by Maturana and Varela (1980) and which

refers to a generic capacity of the system to react to variations in its environment. More precisely, the concept of cognition considered here (and known, in the specialized literature, as the Santiago School concept of cognition) refers to the generic adaptability capacity of the system to its environment.

99. An important complication arises here, of the nature of a logical consequence (which will, however, be ignored, leaving it for examination by researchers interested in the subject of our research): will not, through learning, the antifragile system acquire capabilities/dexterities/skills to perturbation discrimination? What can we say, in this case, about the property of antifragility?
100. However, when it comes to artefacts, the deliberate design of those systems implies that the design of this capability is ignored. From a cost perspective (both design, and implementation, and operation of the respective systems), it is much more "economical" to design antifragile systems than to design standard, that is, non-antifragile, systems.
101. We recall that, from a logical point of view, the set of sufficiency predicates must be consistent, that is, all sufficiency predicates must be non-contradictory with each other, considered two by two.
102. From an epistemological perspective, negative assertion (like negative definition) is also called *apophatic* assertion.
103. Translation "variants" will be discussed later.
104. The negative meaning is represented, for example, by the loss of the identity of the target system.
105. The neutral meaning is represented, for example, by the manifestation of resilience.
106. It is immediately noticeable that this non-specificity (or, in other words, generality) is logically required by the sufficiency predicates *AF*2 and *AF*3, respectively.
107. It is easy to see that "imposing" this particularity on the antifragility component is equivalent to minimizing the implementation cost of this component—the alternative being the design of one component for each possible impact (possibly from a minimal list of potential impacts), which would mean an enormous multiplication of the cost involved in antifragility.
108. For details on this matter, we recommend Robert Nozick, *The Nature of Rationality*, Princeton University Press, 1993.
109. Logically, an unpredictable event (such as disruptions, from the perspective of the antifragility component) is equivalent to a surprise.
110. Not disruption as such, since a disruption, depending on the target system (i.e., depending on its particularities), can exhibit a relatively rich spectrum of impacts.

111. Of course, the target system itself is in co-evolutionary relations with the environment (both internal and external) but it can be said that, at the level of the target system, the most dynamic part from the evolutionary perspective is the component of antifragilizing.
112. We recall that, unlike antifragility, robustness (like resilience, for that matter) is specific, in the sense that the target system possesses structures or resistance devices for a given list of perturbations, a list that is updated as the respective system has fended off several "attacks" from disruptions.
113. One may, however, question the "stretch" of this benefit/advantage. Resilience is a property that ensures the *statu quo* (i.e., it is a conservative/preservative property), which constitutes, above a certain threshold, an evolutionary disadvantage—that is, in other words, there must be a dynamic balance between structural elasticity (resilience content) and structural plasticity (evolutionary content). This means that the benefit of disruption from a resilience perspective (as, of course, from a robustness perspective) has limits beyond which it turns into a disadvantage.
114. As in the case of reducing the "distance" of resilience, also in the case of reducing the margin of hysteresis, the question arises: how beneficial is this reduction or, in another expression, above what threshold of reduction of this margin risks arise (if they arise) for the target system. Our opinion on this matter is: here, also there is a threshold beyond which reducing the hysteresis margin is no longer beneficial. Indeed, the existence of hysteresis has the meaning (from an evolutionary perspective) of the installation of a mutation selected by the environment of the target system. Of course, a mutation can be beneficial or harmful—in the case discussed here the environment does not select only beneficial mutations (as in the biological case) but any mutation, the environment being "blind" as to the character (positive or negative) of the mutation in question. Annex 4 indicates what could be called the *hysteretic evolutionary tunnel.*
115. We recall that *functionality* means the set of relationships between the component elements of a system (i.e., relationships within the system membrane). Functionality is an intra-system property.
116. We recall that by *behaviour* we mean the set of relations between the component elements of a system, on the one hand, and the environment of that system, on the other hand (i.e., relations that involve the transit of the system's membrane, in both directions). Behaviour is an inter-system property, given that the environment of a system can itself be considered a system.
117. We remind you that the *niche* represents that set of relationships between the system and its environment that are consistent and convergent with the survival of the system in question—something analogous also indi-

cates the so-called *constructal law*, a concept introduced in the literature by the Romanian-American researcher Adrian Bejan (Dinga et al., 2022).

118. The term fragilizing, used here, has nothing to do with the homonymous term used by economists eager for labels that save from explanations; it simply means the negation of antifragilizing.
119. The relationship between discretionary interventions and automated interventions will be examined later.
120. The anti-entropic impact of antifragility should not be confused with the anti-entropic impact of robustness (robustness prevents the increase of entropy through "brutal" opposition) or resilience (resilience prevents the increase of entropy through elasticity). The anti-entropic effect of antifragility consists in "fueling" the maintenance or even the decrease of entropy precisely by reaping the impact of disturbances, these being neither avoided (the case of robustness) nor neutralized (the case of resilience), but accepted and capitalized according to the pre-existing purpose/objectives of target system. On the other hand, of course, one cannot accept the idea that antifragility is one of the aims/objectives of the target system although (at least in the financial domain) such aims/objectives can be encountered—for example, hedge funds.
121. Because, as we have shown, antifragility nevertheless accepts structural changes of a peripheral type, which do not affect the identity of the system in question.
122. Which cannot have a theoretical and general nature, but an empirical and local one.
123. We assume that all four evoked functions are invertible, that is, they are bijective (injective and surjective).
124. This is, obviously, a solution of last resort or, in a militaristic expression, a "last line of defence" from the perspective of the two properties, because until the redundant devices are triggered, many other actions, programmed structurally or just functionally, will have already contributed either for the resistance to or for the restoration from disturbed positions.
125. Of course, the concept (and the term) of redundancy does not have, here, the relatively pejorative meaning in common ("civilian") language—unnecessary, excessive, gratuitous etc.—but a completely respectable meaning.
126. In most cases, it is a duplication of the device of interest but, obviously, there can also be a tripling or quadrupling of it. As we will show below, the costs involved in redundancy are directly proportional (though not linearly) to the number of also multiplied (duplicated, triplicated etc.).
127. We do not further develop the analysis on this criterion, since it has already been presented previously (in the discussion of the *AF*4 sufficiency predicate of antifragility).

128. It is easy to see that, ultimately, the institutional factor is confused with the human factor—institutions are made up of and operate through human individuals formally affiliated with the institution/organization in question.
129. We specify that, ultimately, any antifragilizing component is implemented in a discretionary manner, even if it, as is the case just discussed here, is capable (being, of course, programmed to do so) of "implementing" another component(s) of antifragilizing.
130. See, in this context, the concept of *machine learning*.
131. Networking means the formation of links (as structural relations) between the components of a system (or, as the case may be, of an already established network). We will not go into the details of the conceptual distinctions between system and network here (we have presented these distinctions in many other places), but will only say that the matter discussed in this research study is an intra-system network. *Nota bene*: one can, of course, ask the question whether other structural relationships/ratios are possible between the antifragilizing components of a system (intra-network system, intra-network network, intra-system system) but such an analysis does not bring much added value to the topic discussed here.
132. Antifragility, as a property, respectively antifragilizing, as a process, exists, of course, in natural systems, either living or non-living, as a collateral effect of adaptation (either mechanical, as in the case of non-living systems, or final, as in non-human living systems—*Nota bene*: in the case of human systems or "endowed" with human individuals, finality is replaced by purpose, i.e., by an aware finality and acting *ex ante*).
133. Most notable in illustrating this line of research in general systems theory is, of course, the original German sociologist Niklas Luhmann, whose theory is, however, not without controversies (which began during his lifetime—see here the controversy, sometimes leaving the sphere of academicism, between Luhmann and another outstanding German sociologist and political scientist, Jürgen Habermas).
134. The memorizing cell has the role of constituting a benchmark against which both robustness and resilience are compared, respectively antifragility in order to fulfil its specific functions, although we mention it, for methodological reasons, to the concept of antifragility.
135. Of course, recovering with the "price" hysteresis, which we discussed when we examined the concept and mechanism of resilience.
136. Although these measurements can be made both discretionally and automatically, we believe that the automatic mode of measurement should predominate. *Nota bene*: obviously, here we do not have an *ex ante* (or *early warning*) signal, but an *ex post* (*just in time warning*).

137. Or, as it is said in almost all approaches, the most *complex*—we have shown, elsewhere, that by *complex* is meant the characteristic of a system to contain subjects capable of free will (not necessarily cultural subjects, such as human beings), that is, having the potential to introduce unpredictability into the system. Complex means unpredictable, not *complicated*, while complicated simply implies the difficulty of being described in its causal structure and operation. In this sense, the complicated is historical in nature, while the complex is logical in nature.
138. Due to the aforementioned "blinding" property, the identity of the disturbance cannot be established in advance, that is, there is no *early warning* regarding this identity, otherwise, the entire issue of antifragility is reduced to other aspects: predictability, observability, controllability etc.
139. This case is rarer (in fact, it verges on autarky), although, depending on the internal structure of the system in question, it is not entirely impossible to have self-inputation—even if this case is theoretical, it should be mentioned, from a methodological point of view.
140. Even if the other sufficiency predicates of sustainability (which we present next) are verified, the sustainability property does not exist until we have the conjunction of all sufficiency predicates.
141. Depending on the context, one can also talk about sustainable networks, respectively unsustainable networks, within a given system.
142. We generally treat sustainability as a property but it should not be forgotten that a property emerges through a process (*Nota bene*: the idea of "innate" properties is not superfluous, but for the moment it will not be the subject of our analyses in this study); therefore, in addition to the concept of sustainability as a property, two processes must also be taken into account: (1) the sustainability process—through which an unsustainable system acquires the property of sustainability; (2) de-sustainability—whereby a sustainable system loses the property of sustainability.
143. Here we give an extreme but, we think, suggestive example: anti-personnel mines or sea mines, planted by the belligerents of a military confrontation and which remain unexploded (cynically, from a logical point of view, their explosion verifies the sufficiency predicate called output inputation), are placed in the situation where the output is not inputed.
144. The concept of a quasi-sustainable system will be used in the following, because the behaviour often involves alerting/signalling systems regarding the modification of some connected variables.
145. This sufficiency predicate covers the meaning of the *circular economy* concept. The "related" concept of *green economy* is, in our opinion, somewhat ambiguous and, in any case, more limited in its denotative scope than the referential of this predicate of sufficiency.

146. The predicate *structure* refers to the fact that the input of a system is, as a rule, a vector that includes several categories of inputs: substance (e.g., raw material), labour, energy, information etc.
147. Obviously, we refer to the formal, logical structure, regardless of the substantive/material nature of the components that "fill" that formal structure.
148. We did not call this predicate of sufficiency as functional replicability because, as we know, structure generates function. However, since the system replicates structurally, it turns out that it also replicates its functions, which is why the predicate was called operational replicability.
149. Thus, a sustainable system can contain either sustainable subsystems (in the sense defined here), unsustainable subsystems (systems that violate at least one of the sufficiency predicates of sustainability), or, as the case may be, both sustainable subsystems and unsustainable ones.
150. Autopoiesis can also be understood in a different sense (analogously to the understanding of semiosis in relation to semiotics or, more precisely, to the sign): as the process that produces the property of autopoieticity.
151. It is easy to see that operational closure (AP_2) is not contradictory to relational opening (AP_3)—in fact, no system can be dissipative unless it is relational open (substantially, energetically, informationally) in relation to its environment.
152. The identification of an operating cycle is made on the basis of establishing the resumption of the need for input—thus, an operating cycle (which is, of course, different as depending on the nature of the analysed system) has a duration that stretches between two consecutive inputs (immediately successive).
153. This external origin which is internalized will become even more evident when the issue of automatic stabilizer is discussed, below, in the context of autopoietic systems.
154. The literature shows that the balance sheet of such an entropic exchange is always in favour of the dissipative system: global entropy (i.e., at the level of the Universe, which is the only system that can be considered genuinely closed) is accelerated by the dissipation of component systems.
155. However, we cannot say that the autopoietic system is a self-sustaining system, because autopoieticity contains, in addition to the exclusivity of the internal principles of kinematics/dynamics, the potential for self-organization, which cannot be imposed on simple sustainable systems.
156. Here, we have a peremptory illustration of the implicit concept of economic space (a concept in the mirror of economic time): the economic space of a system is the physical space in which that system develops interactions with the environment, that is, manifests itself behaviourally.

157. We will find, below, that the so-called *constructal law* (proposed by the Romanian-American researcher Adrian Bejan) also targets the whole world, not just living systems.
158. It is obvious that between mechanical sensitivity and more efficient types of cognition there is only a difference of degree, not of quality. However, a qualitative leap seems to occur in the case of conscious cognition or, in other words, in the case of the humans and, consequently, in the case of logical/symbolic species. We will take this matter back to the right place. We will perhaps have to introduce, on that occasion, the concept of reflexive cognition, which is not present (as far as we know, in biology studies) in the case of non-human living entities.
159. Moreover, it is obvious, for example, that selection is not possible without behaviour, that is, without an environmental reaction to the externally manifestation of the functions of the system.
160. It is clear that operational opening includes operational closure, while operational closure does not include operational opening: in other words, in any operational opening we have operational closure, but in no operational closure do we have operational opening.
161. According to set theory, any set is a component of the set of its parts.
162. Obviously, a very important logical problem arises here, namely the problem of the degree of analyticity of a system from the perspective of its subsystems. A system can be made up of subsystems which, in turn, are made up of subsystems and so on. When judging autopoieticity (or sustainability, as the case may be), we need to determine the level of subsystems we go to, because (although not always) it is possible that by packing two non-autopoietic systems we obtain an autopoietic system—in this case, for example, we continue packing until we get the operational closure. Therefore, when discussing or applying this theorem it is necessary to establish in advance the degree of analyticity of the subsystems of a system—this degree usually depends on the research interest or, in some cases, on the praxeological or practical interest, being therefore, either a methodological problem or an empirical one, but by no means a theoretical question.
163. We shall ignore here the (logical) problem of the regression ad infinitum—that is, to find the criteria for identifying criteria for economic soundness typology and so on.
164. As known the evolution does not imply a progress arrow, so the regression ratchet generates evolution as well as the progression ratchet does.
165. See notes 115 and 116.

References

Dinga, E. (2001). *Inertial Phenomenon in the Economic Process.* Economica Publishing House.

Dinga, E. (2012). *Rebuilding Economics: A Logical, Epistemological, and Methodological Approach.* Lambert Academic Publishing.

Dinga, E., Oprean-Stan, C., Tănăsescu, C. R., Brătian, V., & Ionescu, G.-M. (2022). *Financial Market. Studies in Theory and General Methodology. Phenomenology of the Autopoietic Market.* Palgrave Macmillan—Springer Nature.

Dinga, E., Tănăsescu, C. R., & Ionescu, G.-M. (2020). *Social Entropy and Normative Network. Entropy, 22*(9).

Kahneman, D. (2011). *Thinking, Fast and Slow.* Farrar, Starus, and Giroux.

Maturana, H. R., & Varela, F. J. (1980). *Autopoiesis and Cognition. The Realization of Living.* D. Reidel Publishing Company.

Taleb, N. N. (2014). *Antifragile: Things That Gain from Disorder.* Penguin.

CHAPTER 2

What a Crisis Is It?

2.1 Preamble

Any phenomenon, either natural, psychological or social (i.e., belonging to any of the three Popperian worlds), must be examined under two perspectives: (a) the ontological view; (b) the epistemological view. Of course, the ontological view is previously, both logically and chronologically, related to the epistemological view.

The ontological view (hence, ω-perspective) addresses the causation[1] of that phenomenon, either necessary or contingent. The ω-perspective should provide a *rationality model* (RM) of the phenomenon, and it does not depend on the observer, although the causal bearer can be a human being who is sharply different from the observer.

The epistemological view (hence, ε-perspective) addresses the comprehension of that phenomenon. The ε-perspective should provide a *comprehension model* (CM) of the phenomenon.

There is a difference between the rationality model and the comprehension model (Biebricher et al., 2022), from the following points of view:

- the RM provides explanations, that is, syllogisms, based on covering laws and (especially) the two logical modes: modus ponens and modus tollens,[2] while CM provides understandings;
- explanations are logical, while understandings are intuitive;

E. Dinga, *Economic Resilience During Overlapped Crises*,
https://doi.org/10.1007/978-3-031-80224-9_2

- there is not a deductive relationship between RM and CM, so the two perspectives (ω-perspective and ε-perspective) are, somehow, independent from one another;
- generally, the RM comes into attention (or into intentionality, as Husserl would have said) before the CM enter that attention, although the per-locutionary statements could reverse this order.[3]

So, the state of crisis is a *sui generis* combination of ω-perspective and ε-perspective. The concrete way in which that combination occurs seems to be not a theoretical issue, but an empirical one and, even, a practical issue.[4]

2.2 The Concept of Crisis

2.2.1 Narrative Issues

The word crisis is, generally, used to denominate an unfavourable or undesirable situation (either as state or kinematics) regarding a system or process, no matter its nature (objective, subjective, or objectified as an artefact). It results, of course, that, behind the label *crisis*, must resides a value (i.e., an axiological matrix) that is considered to be or to have had been, or that imminently follows to be violated by facts, events, trends, and so on, in relevant ways, degrees or significance. Such a primary characterization of the (abstract) concept of crisis needs some extra analytical considerations:

- a crisis situation must be "decreed" by the votes of the scientific or/and political community, because it represents a *sui generis* combination between expectations and facts, that is, between teleology and ontology—this combination is facilitated by the CM;
- crisis is, like any social phenomenon, an artefact. Such an artefact is, generally, generated unintentionally, although the case of an intentional, i.e., deliberative causation of a crisis must not be excluded, especially in the political field;
- although a crisis is always a social phenomenon, it can have its roots in the natural field or in the subjectivity of the individuals or groups; these roots are, however, activated by the social actions (either as acts or as abstentions);

- a crisis is a process, not a simple event,[5] consequently it has a duration and develops its own chreode;[6] however, generally, a concrete event can be identified to trigger the crisis process, without representing the crisis itself. As we shall see next, such an event will be, usually, considered a causation switcher, but not the cause as such;
- as it will be shown below (see point 2.6), the crisis is not at all a component (or phase, or stage, etc.) of a cycle, no matter the nature of such a cycle. However, for example, especially in the economic field, but also in historical analyses, the crisis is, generally, accepted by many analysts as a turning point of a cycle.

In a civil terminology, a crisis should be considered a kind of functional blockage in a mechanism of a given process/system (*Nota bene*: the structural causes of the functional blockage must be, of course, elucidated). The idea that the crisis is not of structural nature, but a functional one only, is so fundamental that we shall provide some extra considerations here.

(i) We consider that the causal arrow *structure–function*, namely that structure generates function, must be kept in the phenomenology of crisis at a societal level. Such basic assumption (which is of Darwinian methodology) is not compromised by the fact that, in the societal field, the structure itself is built starting from the desired/anticipated/expected function (which is of Lamarckian methodology), since that function, which is, until now, virtual only, cannot be actualized than by the intermediation of the (modified) structure;

(ii) This means that the possibility of the crisis, in its generic meaning, must be searched and can be found in the very structure involved. From a public policy point of view, the structural *locus* of the functional bottleneck constitutes exactly the site of control variables[7] for the crisis phenomenology,[8] both as prevention and as therapy;

(iii) As already suggested above, we must operate a clear distinction between meaning and signification. The meaning of a crisis refers to the (causal) explanation of it (namely, based on the ω-perspective), while the signification of a crisis refers to the valuation made by the subject either as observer or actor upon the involved crisis (namely, based on the ε-perspective). Again, the crisis "exists" if and only if

the phenomenon in the case signifies a crisis from ε-perspective. This is as if the crisis is "initiated" from the subject's head;
(iv) So, in fact, the crisis has three kind of causality: (a) an *efficient* causality (which includes also the material one), related to the ω-perspective; (b) a *formal* causality, related to the structure of the system in the case, namely also related to the ω-perspective; (c) a *significant* causality;[9] related to the ε-perspective, namely to the epistemological/axiological view.[10] The relevance of the significant causality is, generally, ignored in the literature (Dinga, 2022), although all the phenomenological qualifications (and, consequently, the actions) in the economic/societal world have a constitutive function, i.e., only such qualifications (based on the significant causality) bring into the objectified world, i.e., into Popper's third world, namely the artefacts;

We shall discuss such potential functional (or functionalist) blockages from the two mentioned perspectives (see point 2.1.).

(a) The Crisis from the ω-Perspective

From the ω-perspective, a crisis resides in a blockage inside the RM, that is, in the objective causality of the system. So, we must examine the ways in which such an ontological blockage can occur. We think there are the following classes of ontological blockage in a generic process/system. Description: actualization of the objective causes (or casual mechanism).

- (class $\omega 1$) one (or more) new cause comes into existence and acts

No matter its/their origin in a process/system can occur a new cause (or more). This will change the RM based on which the causality acts. Logically, this comes to the idea that a structural change occurs and, consequently, leads to a functional change, when the change manifests as a blockage of the previous functioning.

- (class $\omega 2$) one (or more) current cause disappears and ceases to act

Symmetrically with the previous case, the disappearing of a cause (or of more) changes the structure of causality and, this way, changes the functionality of the process/system, that is, in fact, changes the RM.

- (class $\omega 3$) one (or more) current cause changes

The change of a current cause (or of more, after the case) is logically equivalent to either the appearance or disappearance of causes, although the scale at which the alteration of the current state occurs is smaller.

(b) The Crisis from the ε-Perspective

From the ε-perspective, a crisis resides in alteration of one (or more) of the three pillars of the CM (the three "C"): (i) completeness; (ii) consistency; (iii) convergence.

- (class $\varepsilon 1$) alteration of the completeness

The phenomenology unfolded under the given RM escapes, usually in part but, in some cases, totally, from the CM capacity/ability to provide intelligibility and/or justification of that phenomenology. In other words, some facts (objective, subjective, or objectified) can no longer be understood from the intuition perspective which grounds the CM;

- (class $\varepsilon 2$) alteration of consistency

Although the CM can still provide intelligibility/justification for the causalities involved by the RM, some of the facts seem inconsistent among them. This alteration of the consistency, which is required for each and for all the facts exhibited by the RM constitutes, probably, the most important class of crises from the ε-perspective. To be mentioned, that the consistency addresses also the compatibility between the facts and the expectations/anticipations/needs/desires, i.e., signification;

- (class $\varepsilon 3$) alteration of convergence

This class addresses the situations in which, although each understanding (intelligibility/justification) is sufficient in its own right, the combination of them fails to indicate a macro-understanding, namely fails to be convergent to such a macro-understanding.[11]

2.2.2 *Sufficiency Predicates*

The very substance of an (any) concept resides in its sufficiency predicates. In fact, the definition of a concept is simply the verbal (or formal, after the case) expression of the totality of the sufficiency predicates. So, after the general "deciphering" of the crisis from a narrative point of view, it is time to find and analyse the sufficiency predicates that, once verified, logically deliver the very concept of the crisis.

(i) The Criteria to Select the Sufficiency Predicates

First of all, we must establish the criteria set based on which the sufficiency predicates of the concept of crisis will be selected. We think these criteria must verify, in turn, five sufficiency predicates of… sufficiency predicates:

- *Causality nature*: the sufficiency predicates must be of causal type, of any of the five categories of causes—material, effective, formal, final, and significant. This proto-criterion is required by the fact that a crisis is a phenomenon or event[12] that brings a change, either in the RM or in the CM, but a change always implies a cause;
- *Observational nature*: although it can exist hidden (or latent) factors that can generate a crisis (according to the narrative allegations above), the sufficiency predicates must be observational, i.e., they must allow formulation of observational statements/propositions. This means, *inter alia*, that it can be detected proximal factors (usually, causes), no matter the hidden (or latent) unobservable causes founding the proximal ones;[13]
- *Consistency*: the sufficiency predicates must not be contradictory among them, taken two by two;
- *Independency*: the sufficiency predicates must not be redundancy among them, taken two by two;[14]
- *Completeness*: the set of sufficiency predicates must provide certainty (i.e., non-ambiguity) regarding the qualification of a phenomenon under examination to be a crisis. We have, here, an expression of Leibniz's principle.

(ii) The List of Sufficiency Predicates

Based on the point (i), now, a set of sufficiency predicates of the concept of crisis, in its abstract view, will be proposed. We think there are four such crisis's sufficiency predicates (*CSP*).

- (*CSP*1) *structurally generated*: a crisis is (and "must" be) always caused by the structure of the system involved, that is, it is always a structural caused phenomenon. As it is known, a system is an intellectual cutting up in the world, so we talk here about that system which are of interest either from gnoseological or praxeological perspective. Consequently, this sufficiency predicate is, generally, "negotiable" i.e., it is subjectively established regarding the system's borders. To be mentioned that the structural generativity is not equivalent with the structural generation or structurally generated—something which is structural generativity can be not actually generated. Any structure holds a repertoire of the generativity (i.e., a list of functions possible to be objectified), but not all individuals of the repertoire is always actualized. To have to deal with a crisis means that such a function belonging to that repertoire be observationally actualized;
- (*CSP*2) *functionally under-explained*: the phenomenon cannot be grasped under an explanation which maintains itself inside the functional path of that phenomenon. Let us presuppose that an increase of a certain good's price occurs. Examining the demand and the supply of that increase we shall come to observe that the demand for the good in the case increased or the supply decreased, or the demand increased and the supply decreased related to the previous period. Consequently, according to standard "law" of demand and supply in a free market, the price "had" to go up, which is a complete (covering) explanation from the functional perspective, so that we do not have to deal with a crisis. To be mentioned that a crisis is not under-explainable, but under-explained only. From this, a conclusion is very important: the explainability of the crisis has a historical character—for example, a crisis which was under-explained (at limit unexplained) at a moment can become completely explainable (or even completely explained) at a subsequent moment;

- (*CSP3*) *inferentially unpredicted*: the phenomenon occurring in a time horizon cannot be deduced (inferred) from its known structure. If we could predict the phenomenon based on the structure that underpins it, then we could control the occurrence of that phenomenon and, so, either the phenomenon would have been blocked, or it would have been no longer functionally under-explained.[15] This issue convoke the question of the rationality model. A rationality model (or model of rationality) is a logical device that models a structure of something—event, phenomenon, process—so that the functions belonging to the respective structure's repertoire can be inferred from the structure following the inference rules valid within the rationality model in the case. Consequently, the inferentiality from a given structure is depending on that rationality model. Since to any structure can be associated to whatsoever models of rationality, again, the crisis (following the sufficiency predicate examined here) is credited with strong local and temporal coordinates. The locality and the temporality of a crisis is, besides, since a logical … inference from the structure-based reasoning—a real structure is always a local and temporal one;

Nota bene: Why, however, it is "forbidden" to call as crisis a phenomenon which is perfectly predicted (or, at least, predictable)? To answer this question, it must be reminded that the prediction is of two kinds: (1) anticipations – predictions are inferential results of a rationality model; (2) expectations – predictions are non-inferential desires.[16] So, our answer is based on two reasons: (a) if the phenomenon concerned is rationally predicted, this means we assume the structure based on which the rational prediction was formulated—an assumed effect of the structure designing cannot be, … rationally, considered as a crisis; (b) if the phenomenon concerned is intuitively predicted (i.e., it is an expectation), *a fortiori* it cannot be considered to be a crisis, since it is our very desire or purpose.[17]

- (*CSP4*) *axiologically signified*: as in any artefact, a problem arises (or exists) if and only if that problem exhibits some relevance for the human subject, as either individual or group. In fact, the significance (which is not confused with the knowledge, explanation and so on) is a kind of flashlight which allows to identify and (axiologically) evaluate the *qua* problem.[18] Practically (and, then, praxeologically) just the significance, once perceived, will trigger the human being preoccupations, of any sort, to handle the problem concerned.

To be observed that all the sufficiency predicates of the generic crisis are formulated in actual (not potential) terms, which means that to qualify a generic occurrence (event/phenomenon/process) as crisis requires that the occurring concerned be actualized.

So, as logical formalization, a crisis (C) is the conjunction of the four sufficiency predicates:

$$C \leftarrow (CSP1) \wedge (CSP2) \wedge (CSP3) \wedge (CSP4)$$

(iii) A Qualitative Analysis of the Sufficiency Predicates

In fact, to examine if the four sufficiency predicates of a generic crisis, we must verify the four sufficiency predicates which qualify them as crisis's sufficiency predicates.

(iii.1) *Causality nature*

Causality nature of the four sufficiency predicates is quite obvious. *CSP*1 is of efficient cause, *CSP*2 is of formal cause, *CSP*3 is also of formal cause, and *CSP*4 is of significant cause, as proposed before (a fifth cause alongside the four Aristotle-ian classical causes).

(iii.2) *Observational nature*

Observational nature of the sufficiency predicates is obvious as well. Firstly, the structure of the involved system is known for the observer, so the *CSP*1 impact is observed too. Secondly, both *CSP*2 and *CSP*3 are observable since explanations and predictions are both experiencing by the observer. Thirdly, the significance (*CSP*4) is, by definition, an observational predicate.

(iii.3) *Consistency*

- *CSP*1 vs. *CSP*2: these sufficiency predicates are not contradictory one with another, since it is possible that not all the functions of a given structure be known (or even knowable, at a given time—*Nota bene*: for this reason, we have talked above about the historical character of *CSP*2;

- *CSP*1 vs. *CSP*3: the argument is similar to that presented for the previous pair of sufficiency predicates;
- *CSP*1 vs. *CSP*4: the significance of a function/effect is not contradictory with the structure that generated that function/effect;
- *CSP*2 vs. *CSP*3: these two sufficiency predicates are, in fact, at the limit of mutual inferability (but, of course, they are not mutually inferable), so they cannot be mutually contradictory;
- *CSP*3 vs. *CSP*4: the significance of an occurrence cannot be contradictory with the unpredictability of that occurrence, since whatever is the way of an occurrence, it will mandatorily have a signification for the observer (or actor).

(iii.4) *Independency*

- *CSP*1 vs. *CSP*2: as shown, the under-explanation (or under-explainability) is not inferable from structural generation; much less the inversely process is likely;
- *CSP*1 vs. *CSP*3: since *CSP*1 and *CSP*2 are independent one in relation to another, *CSP*1 and *CSP*3 are mutually independent too, since the explanation and prediction are logically equivalent by simply the time arrow inversion;
- *CSP*1 vs. *CSP*4: it is obvious that the two sufficiency predicates cannot be inferred one from another, so they are mutually independent;
- *CSP*2 vs. *CSP*3: these two sufficiency predicates have some degree of semantic overlapping, that is, they are liable to be a little bit dependent on each other. However, such redundancy occurs if and only if the logical equivalence is accepted between explanation and prediction (see note 235). Not all scientists agree with such an equivalence, since it requires a condition hard to accomplish, namely that the explanation be of such a level of generality and abstraction that constitute a model of rationality which, in turn, will deliver the prediction in the case. Obviously, not all explanations are also models of rationality, so the logical equivalence between explanation and prediction remains a possibility but not a certainty. Based on this reasoning, we consider that the possible redundancy between *CSP*2 and *CSP*3 is not at all problematic;
- *CSP*2 vs. *CSP*4: between under-explainability and significance does not subsist inferentiality, so we have not here dependence relationships;[19]

- *CSP3* vs. *CSP4*: as in the previous case, it does not subsist inferentiality between unpredictability and significance.

(iii.5) *Completeness*

The completeness of the list of sufficiency predicates is the most disputable... sufficiency macro-predicate. If the four analytical sufficiency predicates belong to a logical judgment, their completeness belongs to belief. More exactly, by the very choice of the sufficiency predicates in the list, we "establish" the completeness of it. The discussion is analogous to the case of choosing the list of axioms in an axiomatic science. In other words, the completeness is assumed in the *as if* (germ. *Als Ob*) horizon.

(iv) The new necessary predicates

Once a crisis get its ontological being, it necessarily exhibit two new predicates. Since these new predicates come into existence as result of the very crisis existence, they have a necessary character. Since any sufficient predicate is also a necessary one, it results that the new predicates must be called new necessary predicates, to avoid any theoretical confusion.

We think two new necessary predicates (*CNNP*) of a generic crisis should be considered, namely:

- (*CNNP1*) *discontinuity*: the issue of discontinuity can be examined, in a large sense, from the perspective of the history and historicity (for example, along the line of Nietzsche and Foucault, especially regarding the replacing of the rationality with relationship/structure or regarding the replacing of the causality with the genealogy), or in a narrow sense, from the perspective of chreode, i.e., of the expected dynamic trajectory of a process. Of course, we shall make some considerations only in the latter sense. A crisis, according to the sufficiency predicates, must exhibit a significance for either the observer or actor (including the state as both observer and actor in the economic/societal system). Such significance cannot arise than as a discontinuity with the past (else it cannot be perceived at all). The discontinuity at the comprehensive level is the counterpart of a real (ontological) discontinuity in the economic or societal system. Then the following question can arise: why this predicate is not of sufficiency type? The answer is that, on the one hand, in the economic/

societal system can occur many discontinuities, i.e., lack of resemblances between events, phenomena, processes, but not any such a discontinuity is a crisis and, on the other hand, no crisis can lack the feature of discontinuity. The formal generation of the new necessary predicate of ***discontinuity*** is:

$$CNNP1 \leftarrow CSP4$$

- ($CNNP2$) ***non-singularity***: a crisis is a periodical phenomenon/process. This new necessary predicate is grounded on the fact that it is the effect of the very structure in the system considered. As the structure is an invariant (at least on a given time horizon) of the system, it results that the cause (s) of the crisis can act again and again, so the crisis cannot be a singular event/phenomenon/process. Of course, the periodicity of such a re-occurring is a separate issue (*Nota bene*: we shall retake this aspect below). The non-singularity of the crisis is the ontological underpinning of the possibility to control it. More exactly, just the structure constitutes a potential control variable of the crisis.[20] The formal generation of the new necessary predicate *of non-singularity* is:

$$CNNP2 \leftarrow CSP1$$

Nota bene: a question can be put here, namely, if the structure is (or can be) the (unique) control variable about the crisis, it results from this that there is the possibility to eradicate the crisis? Our answer is affirmative—the crisis is a necessary effect of the structure, but the crisis is a contingent (not necessary) phenomenon as such. Instead, the cycle is a necessary phenomenon as such, or, equivalently, the cyclicality is an immanent property of the artefactual objects (as the society, economy, etc., are). In Annex 1, we discuss the relationships between necessity and contingency. The essence of those discussions, which is useful for the new necessary predicates of the crisis, can be synoptically represented as in Fig. 2.1.

Discussion

(a) With $\mathcal{N}$ -Necessity has been described the necessity that functions in the Nature. This is, so, a natural necessity, outside the human being control, governed by the natural laws as the natural sciences

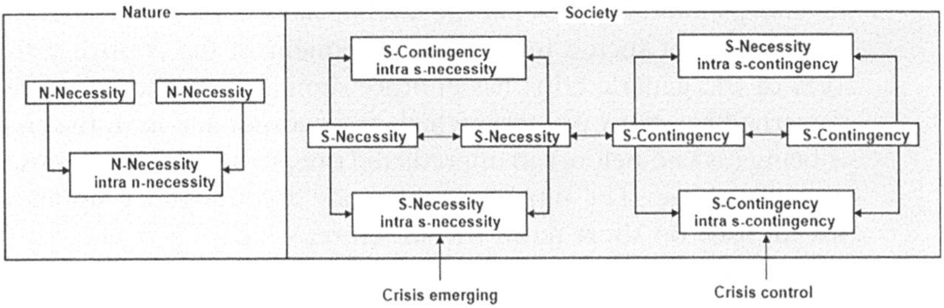

Fig. 2.1 Ontological concatenation between necessity and contingency. *Source*: author

put into evidence. It is an absolute necessity and has an ontological character. With $\mathcal{S}$ -Necessity has been described the necessity that functions in the Society. This is, so, a social necessity, under the human being control.[21] When we talk about freedom as a manifestation of the human being's free will, the free will is understood as the potential of human being to oppose to $\mathcal{S}$ -Necessity, not to $\mathcal{N}$ -Necessity, since to $\mathcal{N}$ -Necessity no one can oppose (for example, the opposition to the death);

(b) A crisis emerges as an s-necessity intra s-necessity, just since the efficient, material and formal causes are hosted by the structure of the system in the case. Once that structure contains the germs of the crisis (*Nota bene*: about such germs will shall discuss further), somewhat, the crisis is a $\mathscr{s}$-necessary phenomenon—this automatism is analogous to the $\mathscr{n}$-necessity belonging to Nature;

(c) Since the crisis triggering is an s-necessity (not a $\mathscr{n}$-necessity one), the free will could intervene to handle the phenomenon in case. Such an action is, obviously, a $\mathscr{s}$-contingent one and, in our opinion, the $\mathscr{s}$-contingency is of intra $\mathscr{s}$-contingency type;

(d) The different places in which crisis emerging and crisis control occur have the following meanings: (i) crisis emerges/occurs in a $\mathscr{s}$-necessary way, since it is causal originated in the structure. The structure is an intra $\mathscr{s}$-contingency $\mathscr{s}$-contingency although, after its entering into existence, i.e., after its ontologizing as objectified world (Popper's third world), it becomes $\mathscr{n}$-necessary; (ii) it seems "natural" that the control variables to be exactly the structure of the entity concerned, based on the common-sense principle that the effect should be off-set at the level of causes, not of the level of symptoms. But such a topological placement of the control variables of the generic crisis has another signification: the structure concerned has many purposes which are incorporated in it, the crisis being (as said before) an unpredicted one, so an adverse purpose or anti-purpose. The intra *s*-contingency *s*-contingency signifies that, at least on short term, the structure, which is a *n*-necessity, will be not changed, in order to not compromise the other purposes embedded, while the occurred crisis will be (or should be) handled at the very functional layer of the crisis concerned. Perhaps, after extinguishing the crisis, the structure in the case will enter an examination to avoid (if it is possible and to the extent to which it is possible) the re-occurring of the crisis. Consequently, we have, in fact, two stages which work at two levels (layers) of the crisis handling phenomenology: (a) the functional level/layer, by handling the symptoms/effects, as an intra *s*-contingency *s*-contingent action—just during the crisis unfolding; (b) the structural level/layer of the entity in the case, by handling the causes, as an intra *n*-necessity *s*-contingent action.

- (*CNNP3*) ***manageability***: once triggered, the crisis "signals" its signification to the individual or group (including the society as a whole and, possible, the humankind). If signification is of type and size (including anticipated consequences) which violates the values and interests of human subjects, then the crisis enters a process of treating. As shown above, this possibility is provided by the fact that a crisis is a *s*-necessary phenomenon, so it can be handled by an intra *s*-contingency *s*-contingency action or set of actions (in Chap. 8, the crisis handling will be examined in detailed). The formal generation of the new necessary predicate of ***manageability*** is:

$$CNNP3 \leftarrow (CSP1) \wedge (CSP2)$$

Nota bene: we would insist on the issue of preventing the crisis emergence, evoked above, at the sufficiency predicate CSP2. Indeed, the question can be put: why to treat an occurred crisis instead of preventing its occurring? In other words, would it not be cheaper to avoid a crisis than to "repair" its consequences?

Formally, we have:

$$C \rightarrow (CNNP1) \wedge (CNNP2) \wedge (CNNP3)$$

2.2.3 A Definition of the Crisis

An authentic definition of a concept must be always provided based on the sufficiency predicates chosen. Consequently, in our opinion, a crisis is an *observational phenomenon, structurally generated, under-explained, unpredicted, and bearer of significance*. Obviously, any phenomenon which does violates at least one of the sufficiency predicates is not a crisis. It is understood that this definition is of the largest scope and hence has the most general meaning. The economic crisis is that crisis which is associated to an economic process, as such a process was defined before, especially from the perspective of the entropic exchange between human beings and nature.[22]

2.3 On the Typology of Crisis

It is of strong usefulness to establish a (general) typology of the crisis, for epistemological, methodological and policy reasons.

2.3.1 Criteria for Typology

- (T_1) the *cause* of crisis: this criterion does address the proximal efficient cause that triggers the crisis. By proximal (efficient) cause, it must be understood the cause that is most likely to trigger the crisis under examination—the property of proximity must be taken in all possible meanings—as nature, force, immediacy in time, and so on. The concept of proximal cause is aimed at avoiding the recursive searching of the ultimate cause (or the cause of last resort) for two reasons: (a) in fact, the variable of control, either for the current occurrence of crisis or for future such occurrences is exactly the proximal (efficient) cause, although, of course, the ultimate cause can provide a more general explanation in a theoretical tentative of larger scope; (b) searching the ultimate (efficient) cause could engage the analyst in a very long causal analysis which can have adverse effects, especially on the public policy for handling the crisis in the case;

- (T_2) the *origin* of crisis: this criterion does not address the causality (or causes as such) of the crisis but the *locus* from which the spark of crisis erupts. Indeed, the society is composed of many distinct (although, more or less, overlapped between) fields of distinct nature: economy, politics, religion, culture, etc. Each of them can be the starting point of a crisis. This criterion is important since depending on the field in which the crisis erupts, the analysis, explanation and policy needed will be specified accordingly;
- (T_3) the *chreode* of crisis: this criterion does address the unfolding way of the crisis. By chreode of crisis, we understand the time-space trajectory of a crisis, including its ramification and overlapping, its self-feeding or external feeding and so on, any of these with their own mechanisms. In fact, the concept of chreode will ground the phenomenology of crises overlapping, which is the red thread of the present study;
- (T_4) the *impact* of crisis: this criterion does address the effects (in the short, medium and long term) that a crisis can introduce in the directly affected system as well as at the societal level as a whole. The effects will be qualitatively identified, so they constitute, together with the outcomes of the other four criteria, a distinctive mark of the crisis;
- (T_5) the *significance* of crisis: this criterion is, in fact, the "decisional" criterion to establish if there is or is not a crisis. It must be mentioned that this criterion has the smallest degree of observationality, although it cannot lack observationality as such. The significance depends on the general *statu quo* of the society (especially the values matrix or the axiology), as well as on the system of interests mapped on different time horizons.

2.3.2 Classes of Crises

The classes of crises will be established based on the five criteria identified above. We speak about classes of crises, not of crises as such, since each of the classes contains however many particular crises, in the sense that a particular crisis is a historical (i.e., spatio-temporal) hypostasis of its class. A class of crises can also be named as a species of crises (*Nota bene*: here we again give a suggestion for an evolutionary assessment of the phenomenology of the societal crisis).

- (Based on T_1) According to this criterion, the species of crisis will follow the distinct causes that are presumed to trigger a crisis. We shall consider the following five types of crisis species from the perspective of the cause:[23]
  - (T_1^1) *insularization*: some phenomena that, usually, are functionally (if not even structurally) connected among them, arrive, at a given time, in a state of self-catalysing. As a result, those phenomena break the connection with other phenomena with which they were, until then, in a mutual balancing relationship, and continue to unfold independently. Such independence, augmented by the self-catalysing process, leads to an insularly functioning and, consequently, without a balancing control, triggering crisis. The most obvious example is the financial crisis (the only genuine type of crisis in the economic field, as shown later), which is triggered by the excessive autonomization (insularization) of the financial (better said, nominal) flows which, thus, are broken from the economic real flows (the latter should be the counter-part which balances the financial/nominal flows for an economic soundness);
  - (T_1^2) *friction*: refers to those phenomena or processes which meet some operational difficulties by the simple game of functioning of a system. Such difficulties, that increase the "friction" within that system are products of the very functioning (again, of a unpredictable nature) of the system concerned. To take an example from economy, when there are job vacancies, on the one hand, and, concomitantly, unemployment, on the other hand, but neither number of vacant jobs nor unemployment do not decrease. The explanation is that the requirements for the vacant jobs do not fit the actual qualifications of the unemployed, or the vacant jobs are in geographic regions for which the unemployed must cover high transaction costs (transport, accommodations, cultural environment, etc.);
  - (T_1^3) *insemination*: refers to the case in which some (formal but, especially, informal) behavioural institutions are introduced, usually in a memetic way, in the functioning of processes within a given system of interest. It is not mandatory that such inseminations to come from the exterior (although, the probability of an external insemination seems to be higher than that of an internal one) but is mandatory that it be, to some extent, inconsistent or

non-convergent with the existent rules of functioning (based on the existent structure) of the system concerned. Such a cause could be metaphorized as a grain of sand that enters a mechanism and blocks or tends to block it. *Nota bene*: of course, insemination can be not only a memetic taking over but a deliberative action as well, either from the interior or exterior, for example, in war cases. It seems, however, that, effectively, the insemination should act by the intermediation of other of the four cases, not directly by itself (such an allegation should, of course, be developed in a more analytical way);

- (T_1^4) *exhaustion*: refers to the case in which a system or a process becomes "tired" either as a result of its own functioning or by becoming obsolete. The exhaustion brings a (relative) decrease of performance (for example, productivity), of quality, of security (of any kinds, depending on the system concerned—for example a military defence system), of confidence, etc. Such cause acts in all societal regions and layers and can have both quantitative and qualitative connotations.
- (T_1^5) *futurization*: refers to the case (somewhat) opposed to the exhaustion, namely acts in those cases in which radical innovations (in any fields and of any kinds) bring rupture with the past—the so-called disruptive innovations. Schumpeter[24] already spoke about the destructive creation in the economic field in his book *Capitalism, Socialism, and Democracy* (Harper Perennial Modern Classics, 2008). Such phenomena bring the future today, usually suddenly or massively, so generating breaking, discontinuance, re-organization and re-construction in the today system concerned. For example, the current course of digital transformations, especially based on the AI (artificial intelligence), has the potential to produce such perturbations that could generate crises—for example, on the labour market. After all, the novelty is (by definition) completely unpredictable, so it can find the current days quite unprepared for assimilation of the new challenges without tremors.

• (Based on T_2) according to this criterion, the source or region (meaning the *locus*) where a crisis is triggered generally follows the (significant) societal regions that can be established. We will consider the following *loci* (*Nota bene*: some overlaps among the fields cannot be avoided but, as we think, it is neither necessary nor useful to avoid them completely):

- (T_2^1) *theoretical* field: refers to the *object–object* relationships (of course, as these relationships are perceived and internalized by the human being). It addresses the abstract intellectual positioning of the society related to the knowledge model assumed at a given moment (science, philosophy/metaphysics, epistemology and other of the same). For example, the passing from pre-modernism to modernism or from modernism to post-modernism came with new philosophies, epistemologies and methodologies of knowledge, including new models of rationality (either ontological or gnoseological);
- (T_2^2) *praxeological* field: refers to the *subject–object* relationships. Basically, this field contains the economic life of the society, i.e., it addresses the impersonal mechanisms embedding market freedom, on the one part, and governmental regulation, on the other part, aimed at producing, distributing, redistributing and consumption of the economic product. As it will be shown later, there is a more punctual locus in the economic field for the emergence of crises, namely the financial sub-field, in the sense that any economic crisis is, in fact, and always, a financial one, i.e., a nominal crisis, that can (or cannot) transfer into the real economy;
- (T_2^3) *practical* field: refers to the *subject–subject* relationships. It addresses the social interactions in the society that considers individuals or groups of individuals *per se*, with their motivations, interests, models of rationality and ways of life. This field includes, *inter alia*: education, religion, social justice, arts and other of the same;
- (T_2^4) *political* field: although politics means subject–subject relationships, so it should be included in the practical field, we have decided to nominate it separately by considering its very high power of influencing the societal path, including crisis triggering. The political factor in society is the most agile one, as both speed of action/reaction and depth of the impact. Distinctly, we include in the political field the *military* one as well. In fact, the military field is an example of interference among more fields (praxeological, practical, political). At least in recent times, the relevance of military field becomes more and more stronger (for example, in Europe and in the Middle East);

- (T_2^5) *natural* field: the natural (of Nature) field becomes more and more significant from the perspective of crises triggering. Partially as a consequence of human activity (especially in the praxeological field), and partially as the effect of the geological natural cycles, from Nature come more and more persistent dis-equilibria which, beyond a threshold (either of intensity, of impact, or duration) transform into crises—so-called natural crises.

- (Based on T_3) according to this criterion, any crisis will be given a mark regarding its modality, i.e., the chreode according to which that crisis unfolds, once initiated. We shall consider the following five classes of crises from this perspective:
  - (T_3^1) *self-extinguishing* crisis: this type of crisis is characterized by dominant negative feedbacks,[25] so its chreode is closed, at least as duration. The mechanism of such type of crisis is based on an exhaustible "fuel" that feed the crisis, so when the fuel disappears, the crisis ceases. Generally, this type of crises is rather local and they do not trigger other crises (of the same type or of other ones). Metaphorically, the self-extinguishing crisis is a "straw fire". Generally, the self-extinguishing crises are non-periodical (i.e., are singular). However, an analytical examination is required in order to identify the possible periodicity of appearing the "fuel" in the case; this type of crisis moves in circle;
  - (T_3^2) *self-maintaining* crisis: this type of crisis is characterized by dominant positive feedbacks, so the chreode is open, as least as duration. The mechanism of such type of crisis is based on the fact that among the outcomes of the crisis is also the cause of it. A crisis that reproduce its own cause (the "fuel") is a very interesting one, since from it we can learn how to reproduce the crisis's own inhibitor. Anyway, the self-maintaining crisis is the species of crisis that is perfectly placed to be examined under the perspective of evolutionism (see Chap. 10); this type of crisis moves in spiral;
  - (T_3^3) *trans-field* crisis: this type of crisis passes from the region of its origin to other fields/regions, without ceasing to manifest in the initial region. Such a propensity is sustained by some outcomes in the initial origin that can act as triggers of crises in other regions. So, somewhat, this type of crisis generates causes that are specific for other regions. We shall give an example for the region Nature—a crisis generated by climate exchange (no matter if it is

due to geological cycles or/and human actions) will affect the availability of natural resources, so it will pass into the praxeological/economical region, maintaining its presence in the natural region. Only when the crisis ceases in the natural field/region,[26] its manifestations in the praxeological/economical will cease, of course, with a lag (of an empirical only signification, however); this type of crisis moves vertically;

- (T_3^4) ***migratory*** crisis: this type of crisis passes from the field of its origin, in other fields, ceasing to manifest in the initial region, or can pass from a geographical region (a country, for example) to other geographical region (other country). Such cases generally occur when between the two areas (either as fields or as geographical regions) there are functional connections—for example, inside some networks—so that the "fuel" of the initial field or geographical region there is as well in other fields or geographical regions. In contrast to T_3^3 , a migratory crisis, once migrated to other field or region, ceases (with an empirical lag) to manifest in the initial field or region. For example, the recent financial crisis occurred in USA beginning with august 2007 (the so-called subprime crisis), passed into Europe around the end of 2008, so we have here an inter-regional migration; this type of crisis moves horizontally;
- (T_3^5) *synergetic* crisis: this type of crisis is specific for the phenomenon of crises overlapping, that constitutes, alongside of resilience, another red thread of our study. When two crises inter-act in one way or another, some crisical effects can emerge, that is, a new crisis can arise. Of course, synergetic process can act either positively, namely constructively, when a new crisis appears as a result of two (or many) crises, or negatively, namely deconstructively, when an old (or many) crises disappear as a result of their interaction. Annex 4 provides some analytical developments of the concept of synergy (Dinga et al., 2023); this type of crisis moves obliquely.

• (Based on T_4) according to this criterion, any crisis has a set of impacts at the societal level. Some impacts come alone, others come packaged—more different impacts, either independently among them, or compatible, or incompatible. Of course, this criterion is co-related with the criterion T_3, since a given chreode "secrets" a certain impact (*Nota bene*: this statement will be of useful while discussing the issue of crises overlapping). We think the following classes of crises can occur based on this criterion (*Nota bene*: inevitably, some possible intersections between the five classes of crises could occur—for example, between the impact on the structure and the impact on the political regime):[27]

- (T_4^1) impact on ***structure***: Although the structure of a system does not imply the predictions inference regarding crises (although it allows predictions as anticipations), an occurred crisis can suggest some changes in the structure to prevent or mitigate the risk for new crises, at least of the type/class that already occurred. The logic to operate such structural changes starts, of course, from the periphery, namely from the system functioning where the crisis found the ground to emerge and, in a Lamarckian way, continues until the structure. A model of rationality is, obviously, needed in this procedure, to avoid, as much as possible, the way of trial and error.[28] So, by identifying the function(s) or the functionality that seems to trigger or create sufficiency conditions for triggering the crisis, the structure could be modified in such a way that will prevent/avoid generating those conditions;
- (T_4^2) impact on ***rationality model***: A crisis can highlight and put under discussion some assumptions regarding the rationality model (either of ω-perspective, namely ontological, or of ε-perspective, namely comprehensive) of the society concerned. For example, the current functioning of the consumerist capitalism model (or logic), which can be called the optimality model, will necessarily lead to a new model of rationality (both ontological and comprehensive), namely the sustainable model. Another example refers to the collapse of the so-called socialist/communist economy, which, as manifested as a crisis, led to the replacement of that economically centralized rationality model with one based on free market (*Nota bene*: increasingly more, it seems that the market failure, as well as the social justice requirements, will lead to something as a new Ordoliberalism, at least in the economic field;[29]
- (T_4^3) impact on ***values matrix***: the impact on the values matrix of the society is distinct from the impact on the rationality model of that society, although, as said above, some interferences or intersections between them are unavoidable. The values matrix refers to the set of fundamental values dominantly shared by the society members, which could be put under question or at least prob-

lematized as a result of crisis occurring. For example, the traditions could be contested or leaved in a penumbra by the so-called post-modernity, or the consumerism could be perceived as a harmful positive feedback, or the egoism (as an exacerbated individualism) could be valued as being counter-productive, by contesting the self-regulation function of the invisible hand, etc. In fact, it must be mentioned that this type of crisis impact is the most important, relevant, and active among the five ones, since it can ground all the other four categories of impact. We can say that an impact on the values matrix has the potential of producing effects on the other manifestations of the crisis impact, more or less, in one way or another;

- (T_4^4) impact on *political regime*: this type of crisis impact is a rare one, since the crisis involved must be particularly strong. A change in the political regime can be produced either as a reform (gradual, small, convergent, compatible, additive changes, caught in a pre-established logic chain or strategic program—based on values—that is, it is speaking rather of an evolution) or as a revolution (sudden, radical and contradictory with the *statu quo*). An impact on political regime does not necessarily have to lead to a revolution, of course, especially if the intensity of the crisis concerned is relatively low, but can initiate some changes, even critical. In our opinion, it is likely that only an overlapped crisis can have as impact a radical change in the political regime, including a political revolution;
- (T_4^5) impact on *meta-narrative*: this impact is of the largest scope and, correlatively, of the lowest specification. Principled, it focuses on the metaphysics of the society concerned—including religion, art, language, urbanization, technologizing, relationships society-nature and other of the same—that provides/delivers the main meta-narratives. The meta-narratives are indispensable to the society as a way of living. Again, it is possible that such an impact be performed only by a "package" of crises but, in our opinion, it cannot be ignored as impact of "large wave" sort. From observational point of view, the meta-narrative impact is a long-term phenomenon and its lags are considerably large.

• (Based on T_5) according to this criterion, a crisis can bring effects that have signification (*Nota bene*: we remind that there must be made a distinction between meaning and signification—while meaning refers to the explanation, commonly rational (for example, based on causes), of the effect, signification is relevant from an a-rational perspective of the individuals, groups and society as a whole. Signification is, briefly said, the meaning *for* humans, not the meaning in itself (*per se*, as such). *Nota bene*: of course, the signification is "coloured", especially, by the values matrix and by the meta-narrative at the societal level.

- (T_5^1) signification related to ***survival***: it is the most primitive significance for individuals, groups or societies. Being so primitive, it is shared by all living entities, more or less in an instinctive way. Essentially, such a significance puts into brackets (in an inverse Husserlian epochē) all values and reasons for action and "commands" the only action (or abstention, after the case) which can lead to biological survival. For example, a natural crisis or a military one is most likely to generate such significance;
- (T_5^2) signification related to ***opportunities***: this significance addresses opportunities of any kind, not only economic or social, spreading out from the subjective relevance to the communitarian or even global one. Opportunities are understood as, those capabilities[30] that the societal system provides to individuals or groups in order to be used for their accomplishment. Of course, this signification is equally related to those opportunities which are at the individual's or group's latitude to be created and used, so to the societal conditions aimed at favouring such direct findings or building up of opportunities.
- (T_5^3) signification related to ***way of life***: way of life is the largest scope of the person's flourishing (*Nota bene*: in an ascendant line, there are standard of living, quality of life, way of life, life style—the last do not extend the scope but particularize the way of life according to individual's idiosyncrasy). Consequently, this signification combines the instinctual assessing of the crisis's impact with the cultural evaluation, in a *sui generis* mixt;
- (T_5^4) signification related to ***freedom***: this signification increases the weight of the cultural evaluation of the crisis's impact, by relating it to the most relevant value of the individuals, groups and society as a whole, namely the freedom (*Nota bene*: by freedom, here is understood the absence of private constraints on the for-

mation of the private purposes.[31]) After survival, freedom is the most sensible signification which faces individuals and groups, as well as the societies;[32]

- (T_5^5) signification related to *self-esteem*: this significance is the most ineffable one since it is extremely subjective and idiosyncratic. To become active, it must reach many individuals at the same time and in the same societal area. To this end, the axiological matrix of the society in the case must be sufficiently crystallized and shared, to produce a perceptual "wave" of lack or decrease of the self-esteem generated by the impact of the crisis concerned.

2.3.3 A Qualitative Remark

- Formally, a crisis can be identified by a pentad-based notation, by the formal particularization of each criterion discussed above;[33]
- All the species of crisis, as identified above, can be systematized in a matrix (we note the set of the crisis species with $\mathcal{M}$):

$$\mathcal{M} = \begin{pmatrix} T_1 & T_2 & T_3 & T_4 & T_5 \end{pmatrix} = \begin{pmatrix} T_1^1 & T_2^1 & T_3^1 & T_4^1 & T_5^1 \\ T_1^2 & T_2^2 & T_3^2 & T_4^2 & T_5^2 \\ T_1^3 & T_2^3 & T_3^3 & T_4^3 & T_5^3 \\ T_1^4 & T_2^4 & T_3^4 & T_4^4 & T_5^4 \\ T_1^5 & T_2^5 & T_3^5 & T_4^5 & T_5^5 \end{pmatrix}$$

So, a concrete/particular crisis will be written as $C_{12345}^{\alpha\beta\gamma\delta\varepsilon}$, where the lower index refers to the species, and the upper index refers to the class within the respective species (with α, β, γ, δ, $\varepsilon \in \{1,2,3,4,5\}$), since a concrete/particular crisis can belong to more species and classes. When a crisis does not belong to any species, then the lower locus of that species will be given the value 0, and the same for the correspondingly upper locus. For example, a particular crisis that is written as C_{02045}^{04012}, must be "read" as follows: a crisis of class 4 of species 2, class 1 of species 4, and class 2 of species 5. By "decoding" we get a crisis from the *political* region, that has impact on the *structure* of the system, and focuses on the *way of life*;

- Such a notation is useful not only for the case of overlapping crises but even in the case of non-overlapped crises, since this way we get the necessary information to design and implement the public policy in the most appropriate form for the particular crisis in the case. Of course, the hardest work must be done to correctly identify the five species and the class within each species. To this end, an (even automatic) procedure/algorithm could be designed, so that based on a set of empirical characteristics that are introduced into the procedure, the species and the classes of belonging in the given case can be delivered.

2.4 A General Logical Scheme of Crisis's Movement

In this paragraph, we shall try to describe a very general way in which a generic crisis runs its course. By the general and abstract character, this (logical) scheme of the crisis to objectify its chreod is applicable, ***mutatis mutandis***, to any current empirical crisis—and, of course, also for past crises or for anticipated ones. To decipher the class of future crisis based on current (and/or past) signals would be a great achievement and would be of great signification, as well as a decisive commitment of the society/government in handling that crisis.

2.4.1 Generalities

As shown before, a crisis, of any species and class, is anchored to two pillars: (a) a rationality model—a crisis does exist if and only if the rationality model in the case "says" it does; (b) a signification for the individuals, groups or society involved. If these two anchors do not work, the phenomenon in the case is not considered a crisis, so the reaction to that phenomenon will be not circumscribed to the treatment recipe in hand.

The awareness of a coming or an acting crisis is critical for the success of handling it and, consequently, for either avoiding/mitigating the negative impact of the crisis or benefitting from that negative impact (by antifragility) from that crisis. Obviously, the awareness of the crisis is simply its anchoring to the two mentioned pillars. The proceduralization of such an awareness is at least so important as the formal construction of the generic crisis at point 2.3.3. We shall come back in this matter in Chap. 8.

2.4.2 An Abstract (Stylized) Crisis Chreode

As proved at the point 2.5, there is no causal or structural relationship between crisis and cycle, not only in the economic field, but generally. Of course, there could exist functional relationships, especially on the line of synergy (either positive/constructive or negative/destructive). The cyclicalness and the crisisness are causally autonomous properties of a generic system, so causally autonomous phenomena link to that system.

In our opinion, and ignoring the particularities of the 25 classes of crisis, an abstract chreode (four-stages model) of the crisis can be designed as in Fig. 2.2.

Discussion

- In the area of *triggering*, the crisis is triggered as an autonomous phenomenon, although, as shown by the typology of crisis, the government itself can trigger a crisis (usually, a political one). In the area of triggering from the phenomenon in the case, there is an area of surprise from the government's perspective. Indeed, as shown before, the crisis is unpredictable,[34] so it cannot be blocked before arising (if something like this happens, then it is not speaking about a crisis). Together with the surprise of crisis occurring, the government triggers in turn a specific mobilization of its strategies and procedures regarding the handling of the crisis;
- In the area of *unfolding*, the crisis phenomenon can go on linearly or can spread into many other directions, regions, etc., according to "fuel" identified on its basic route. Of course, such spreading can be,

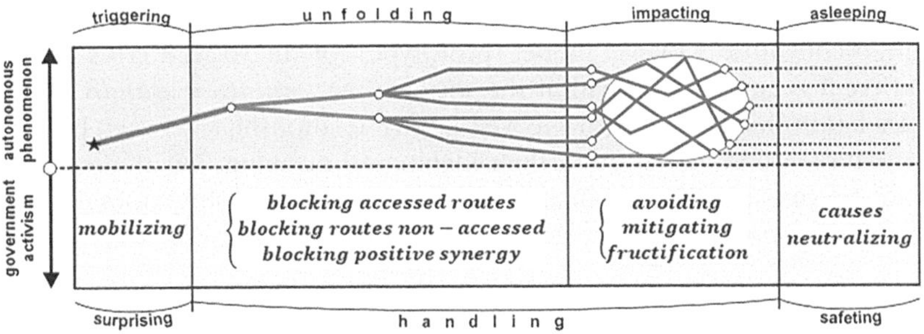

Fig. 2.2 The abstract chreode of the crisis. *Source*: author

at least to some degree, predictable as anticipations, based on the marks held by the crisis in the case. Consequently, the government can act in three ways: by blocking the routes on which the crisis advances, by blocking the routes still not accessed by the crisis but in danger of being accessed (such accessibility can be predicted to some degree based also on the marks of the crisis), or by blocking the positive synergy that is possible to be activated by the crisis, either with other contemporary crises or with other phenomena so that causing the strengthening of it or of other ones (*Nota bene*: of course, the negative synergy will be encouraged or, if it is possible, generated by the government itself);

- In the area of *impacting*, the crisis (either as it was initially or by an augmenting based on overlapping) delivers its impacts, of the types above mentioned. To decipher the set of these impacts is of the most importance since the government action is guided by this outcome. In this phase, the government acts in three directions: avoiding the impacts, mitigating the impacts, or fructification (by intermediation of the antifragility devices) of the impacts;
- In the area of *asleeping*, the crisis exhausts its potential of impact and enters a period of "hibernation". More exactly, the crisis waits for the resuscitation of its specific cause to resurrect itself. This is the reason why the government has to work hard in this area in order to neutralize, as much as possible, the cause (of the same nature or of compatible nature) to minimize the probability of a resurrection of that crisis. Of course, a crisis always leaves traces, some of them even of a causal nature (as we shall see in Chap. 10—the co-evolutionary crisis), so this governmental action is of great importance.

From now on, our study will be focused on the economic field. In our opinion, the economic phenomenology of crisis (and of cycle as well) could constitute a logical model (prototype) for the societal crisis or for different regional crises within the societal one, *mutatis mutandis*. Such idea has nothing to do with the well-known relationships between base—structure—supra-structure in their ideological meaning, but the logic of such relationships (by eliminating the univocal directionality) does not fail from being useful.

2.4.3 *Considerations on the Generic Economic Cycle*

First of all, it must be mentioned that the cyclicality of a process is a property, namely a property caused by relationships.[35] Of course, we consider the relationships at the level of structure, so the cyclicality is a property generated structurally. As we shall see below, the structural genesis of the cyclicality, on the one part, and of the crisis (as shown above), on the other part, does not imply at all that it is talking about the same structure although, logically, such a case it is not forbidden.

The economic cycle represents the macroscopic way (observable paradigmatically) in which the individual economic processes take place. It is, on the one hand, about an aggregation mechanism and, on the other hand, about a self-development mechanism. In the present study we will deal only with some aspects, which we consider fundamental, regarding the self-development mechanism of the economic cycle.

In general, by the economic cycle we will understand a complex process, of an economic nature, triple conditioned: natural, institutional and psychological. Each of these conditionalities has its own development pattern, especially from the perspective of the two essential categories of the processualism: (a) time; (b) space. Thus, the time specific to natural conditionality is clock time, mechanical time that does not depend on the measured/quantified process. It is a Laplacian time, absolutely independent of the process. The time specific to institutional conditionality is as autonomous from the process as the time specific to natural conditionality, with the difference that the former is a discretionary time (or, rather, a temporary interval), while the latter is a non-discretionary time. The time specific to psychological conditionality is a time assigned to the process, so a time that has a beat dependent on the measured/quantified process. We suggest that, if we are dealing with an economic process,[36] the result of overlapping the three categories of time associated with the economic process should be called economic time. Analogous considerations can be made about space, arriving at the concept of economic space.

The question that arises here is the following: why is there a need to introduce a time specific to the economic process? The answer is simple but fundamental: that specific time is necessary because the economic process's beat of depends on the economic process itself. In other words, in an economic process we will have accelerations or decelerations of the economic beat relative to the self-equal, absolute and autonomous beat of clock time. These accelerations or decelerations of the economic beat in relation to the clock beat explain, in our opinion, in the most profound ways, both the temporal geometry of the economic cycle and its real causalities. We will even say that, perhaps, the reason why the discipline or science of economics is so ill-equipped to predict the economic process is precisely the wrong use of the clock beat instead of a proper economic beat. The proper time of the economic process must have the same "right" to exist as so many other types of proper time that are used both in the natural sciences (e.g., quantum mechanics or general relativity) and in the human sciences (e.g., in psychology, sociology, history).

The methodological solution for the introduction of economic time in the measurement/quantification of the economic process is the following: the reintegration of the economic subject into the economic process, by renouncing the principle of objectivity, specific to the natural sciences, and by preserving the second principle of scientific knowledge: the principle of intelligibility (comprehensibility). The reintegration of the economic subject into the economic process (at the limit, the acceptance of the logical subject-object indiscernibility in the economic process) implies, however, a new paradigm of the economic process: the paradigm of the logically living system. So, the economic system will have to be considered a living system in a logical sense. The living system in the logical sense assumes that the economic system considered contains two additional sufficiency predicates: (a) dissipativeness, i.e., the ability to maintain or decrease the intra-system entropy; (b) functional redundancy (which implies structural redundancy). These two predicates of sufficiency for an economic system to be considered a logically living system represent the premises on which the next epistemological level is built, namely the sustainable system. So, finally, the introduction of the economic time and space into the description of economic processuality implies the description of the economic system as a sustainable system. We will see that a logically living system becomes a sustainable system if two other sufficiency predicates are added: (a) microscopic hyper-cycles; (b) dominance of negative feedback.

In this conceptual context, we will further develop some considerations regarding the need to review the epistemological and methodological bases of understanding, explaining, describing and modelling the economic cycle.

2.4.4 *The Conceptual Framework of Orthodox Models Regarding the Economic cycle*

The orthodox theories (models) that currently describe the economic cycle are mainly characterized by three conceptual-methodological features (Dinga, 2016):

(1) They accept the dominance of one of the two classical components of the economic "metabolism" as a criterion for identifying the formation of an economic cycle: demand and supply.[37] The abstract scheme considered here can be rendered as in Fig. 2.3:

Thus, for example, if, for some reason, the demand for a certain good or service increases in relation to the supply of that good or service, there is a pressure in the direction of the increase in the price of that good, which encourages producers (according to the demand curve on the coordinates price—quantity demanded) to expand their specific business, including through investments. As investments can exceed the need to increase the supply required by the increase in demand, a gap of the

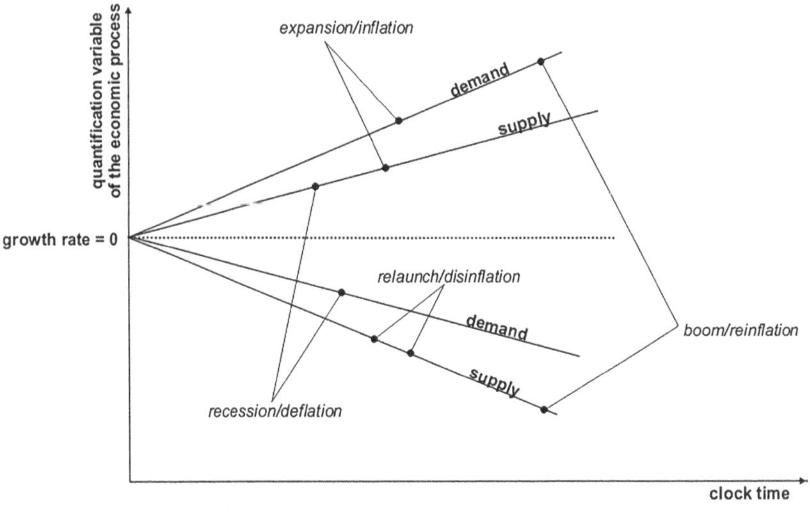

Fig. 2.3 Abstract design showing the formation of the cyclic elements within the orthodox economic process. *Source:* author

opposite direction is produced between demand and supply, etc. This scheme can be quite complicated, considering more complex aspects such as population dynamics, technological innovation, product/service life cycle, financial innovation, etc. but, essentially, it is about the dynamic gap between demand and supply in a given economic market.

(2) They consider the clock time (calendar time), i.e., an external time, which is not influenced by the measured process, as the "counter" of the economic process, therefore implicitly of the economic cycle. In this sense, there are "typologies" of the economic cycle based, also, on the clock time: annual or sub-annual cycles, decennial cycles, secular cycles, etc.

(3) Considers the goods and services market as the fundamental (primary) economic market, while the money and labour markets are considered derived (secondary) markets. Thus, it is implicitly assumed that both monetary-financial and labour flows closely follow, perhaps with a certain lag or lead, the real flows. In the best case, it is accepted that it is possible that the monetary-financial flows, at least, become autonomous in relation to the real flows and thus imbalances appear which, however, are also considered at the level of the demand-supply gap on the market of goods and services. In this sense, although the economic crises of the last eight decades indicate something completely different about the causality of the economic cycle, the orthodox theory has not yet overcome this pattern of analysis and description. An example here is the establishment of the internal economic balance with the help of the IS-LM (investment-saving–liquidity-money) model, precisely based on the direct "communication" between the market of the real economy and the market of the nominal economy.

A graphical representation of how economic cyclicality is understood in the traditional (orthodox) sense is given in Fig. 2.4:

2.4.5 The Current State of the Rapport Between Economic Cycle and Economic Crisis

In our opinion, the orthodox models regarding the economic cycle can be criticized, mainly, for the following:

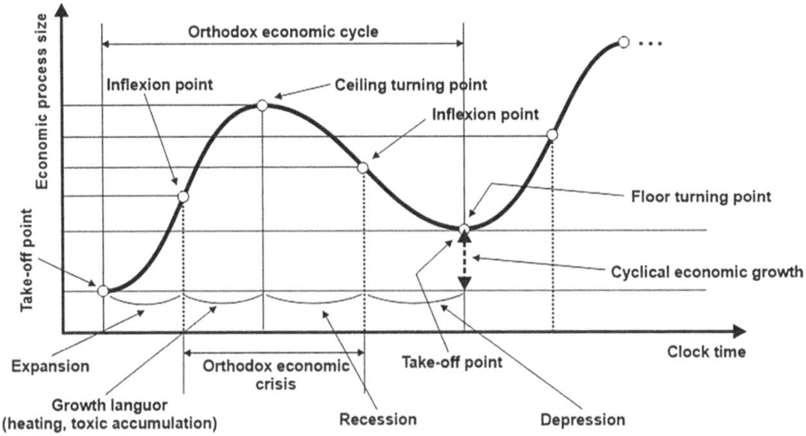

Fig. 2.4 Abstract design showing the orthodox economic cyclicality. *Source:* author

- Regarding the Structure of the Economic Cycle

The most important issue of economic cyclicality concerns its structure. We will say, from the very beginning, that the orthodox modelling of the business cycle considers the economic crisis is a component part (covering some temporary interval) of the business cycle (see Figure 35). Well, in our opinion, the economic crisis has no such status. In other words, the economic crisis is not part of the structure of the economic cycle but is, in reality, a break, a discontinuity in this cycle. Moreover, the economic crisis cannot even signify or chronologically separate two successive cycles. Accepting such a "role", namely of chronologically inter-cycle separating, would mean giving the economic crisis a cyclical character as well. Or, based on what was already exposed previously, the economic crisis does not have a regulated frequency even after the clock time, that is, the economic crisis is not cyclical. This statement has a particularly important consequence from a conceptual point of view: the economic cycle is the rule in the economic process, while the economic crisis is an exception, an accident. We will even state that the economic crisis has nothing to do with the economic cycle, its etiology being outside of the economic cyclicality, as we will show below.

This means that an economic crisis can appear at any time in the economy, at any point on the "trajectory"[38] of the economic cycle (to mention only the orthodox syntagma "economic crisis of overproduction", where the crisis occurs on the upward component of the economic cycle; "economic crisis of underproduction", where the crisis occurs on the downward component of the economic cycle). Therefore, the economic crisis will no longer have to play any role in the description (or, even worse, in the causal explanation) of the business cycle. And even less in the business cycle management. The occurrence of an economic crisis means disaster for the economic cycle, which is disrupted, distorted, "turned",[39] etc. The effect of the formation of a crisis in the economic space is analogous to that produced in physical space in the form of an enormous black hole (the analogy can go as far as finding an enormous consumption of economic resources, especially financial, just as the black hole consumes an enormous amount of cosmic matter).

Once we have removed the economic crisis from the phenomenology of economic cyclicality, the economic cycle should have the following form (Fig. 2.5):

- Regarding the Causality in the Economic Cycle

If we accept an economic cycle with no economic crises (let us call such an economic cycle, an "adjusted economic cycle"—AEC), and if we take the economic cycle to be a "natural"[40] phenomenon, then AEC is the form of movement of the economic phenomenon (as macroscopic manifestation of the economic process). Therefore, AEC causality lies in the

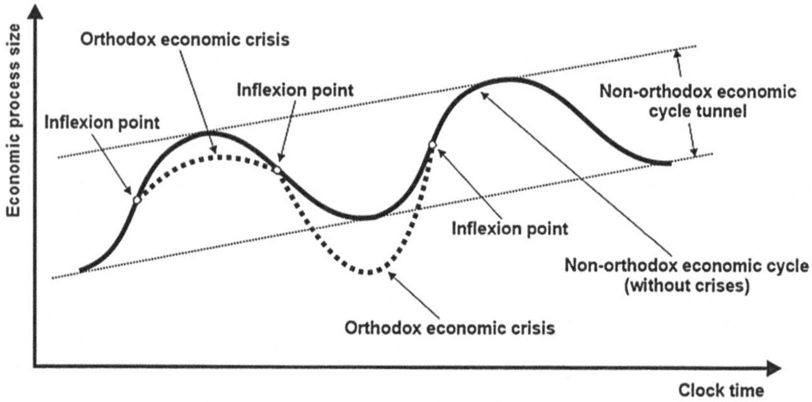

Fig. 2.5 Abstract design showing the orthodox economic cyclicity vs. the non-orthodox economic cyclicality. *Source:* author

permanent, oscillating differences that may appear between the basic determinants of the economic cycle. Which are these basic determinants? In our opinion, they are: (1) the anticipated financial flows; (2) the current real flows (of goods and services); (3) the anticipated demand for workforce; (4) the current demand for direct investments. Figure 4 shows a graphical description of our proposed understanding of the origin of the economic cyclicity (causality), of the economic crisis. Here are some comments:

(v) The main economic transaction is accomplished via the relation between the real flows (goods and services created by the real economy) and the financial flows (exact monetary equivalent value of the real flows). The exchange rate of these transactions is the average transaction price. The average transaction price also includes the cost of the transaction generated by the search, by the information asymmetry and by the adverse selection. We will call this category of economic transactions: ***primary economic transactions (PET)***. Figure 2.6 shows the causality relation of TEP.

(vi) The causality of both the economic cycle and the economic crisis lies within the general relation between the real economy and the symbolic (or nominal) economy.[41] The essential difference between the two categories of causalities (which justified our proposition to remove the economic crisis from the structure of the economic cycle) is that, while the economic cycle is generated by a mechanism of sway, of oscillation of the sign of the gap existing between the real flows and the financial flows, the economic crisis is generated

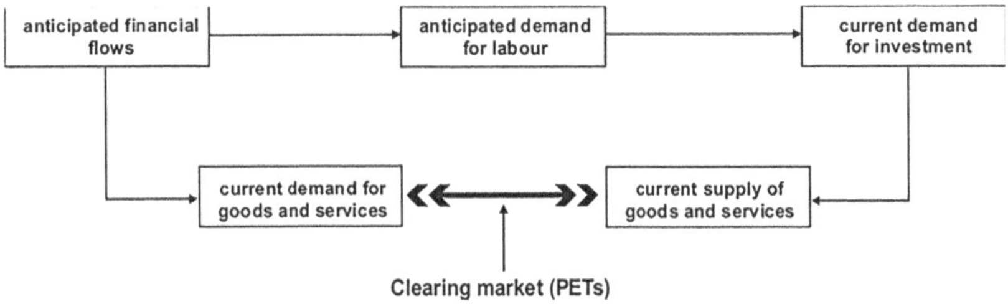

Fig. 2.6 Abstract design of primary economic transactions (PET) generation. *Source:* author

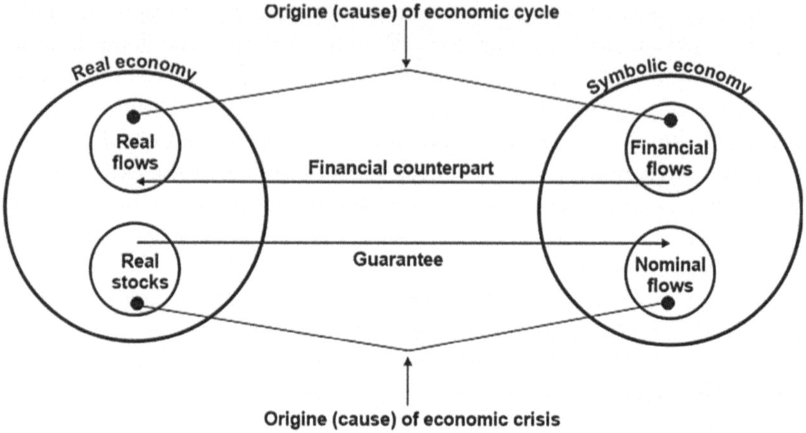

Fig. 2.7 Origin (cause) of the economic cycle and of the economic crisis. *Source:* author

by a mechanism of asymmetric accumulation, i.e., by a strong increase of the nominal flows in relation with the real stocks.[42] Figure 2.7 shows the distinction between the two types of causality.

- Regarding the Causality in the Economic Cycle

We will develop briefly what we mentioned above regarding the causality of the economic crisis.

(i) As already shown, an economic crisis can develop, most times, independently of the phenomenology of the economic crisis. This statement relies on two arguments: (1) a *theoretical* argument—the nominal flows are not intended to directly cover a demand for goods and services; rather, they are intended to do it in an indirect manner (for instance, by starting a business or by direct investments of portfolio which supply the financial flows used as equivalent value for the real flows). Even if, in some cases (for instance, the credit for consumption) the nominal flows can be used as direct equivalent values for real flows, these are isolated cases, not significant as proportion. Therefore, this argument says that, in principle, the nominal flows are autonomous (as amplitude or dynamics) in relation with the real flows; (2) an *empirical* argument—the economic crisis of 1929–1933 and that of 2007–2010 have shown that the main generative cause of these crises has been the huge and fast multiplication of the nominal flows in relation with the real stocks in support;

(ii) Therefore, the economic crisis can start and develop in parallel with the development of the economic cycle. There is interference between the phenomenology of the economic cycle and that of the economic crisis. In this matter we propose the following evaluations: (1) *structurally*, the two phenomena are independent between them, as already mentioned before: the economic crisis is not a component (stage, phase) of the economic cycle; (2) strictly *causally*, there may be the following interference: the anticipation of the financial flows variation, which is also reflected in the variation of the demand for labour force (see Figure 4) and which leads eventually to the variation of the current demand for investments, generates the variation of the nominal flows (for instance, higher demand for bank credits, but there can also be influences in the current variation of the inflation, of the interest rate, or of the exchange rate). Therefore, we don't exclude a possible causal interface between the phenomenology of the economic cycle and that of the economic crisis, but, most times, it is not decisive, rather complementary to the autonomous dynamics of the nominal flows; (3) *functionally*, we will accept, nevertheless, a massive interference between the two phenomena. The onset of the economic crisis, which refers to the start of the accelerated multiplication of the volume of the nominal flows in relation with the volume of the real stocks, will affect both currently and by the formation of anticipations, the form and speed of the economic system on the path of the economic cycle. Actually, the outbreak of an economic crisis can change rather radically the phenomenology of the economic cycle.[43]

- Regarding the Measuring of the Economic Cycle

At this point we will introduce our second suggestion to review the theory of the economic cyclicity (the first one was the causal and structural separation of the economic crisis from the economic cycle). In our

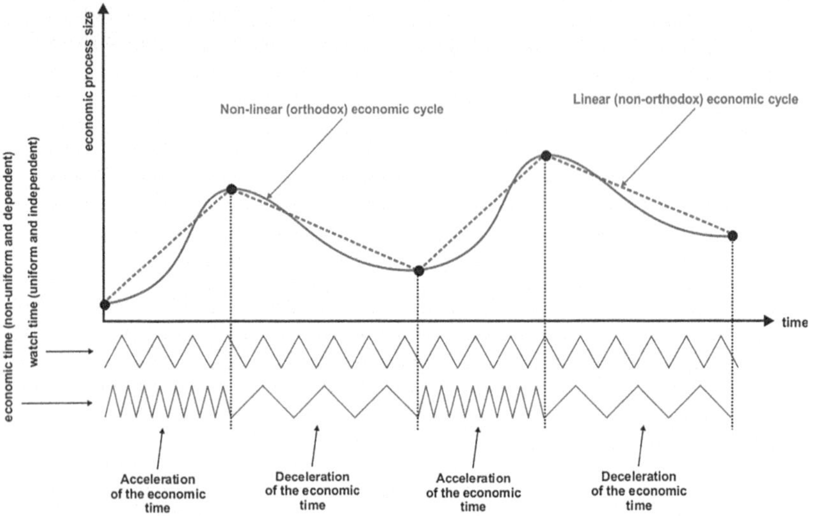

Fig. 2.8 Linearization of the economic cycle when using the economic time instead of the clock time. *Source*: author

opinion, the measurement calculating the economic cycle via the clock time is incorrect. The economic process develops its own pace of progress of the economic action. We suggest that actually only from the perspective of the clock time there is an economic cycle, while from the perspective of the economic time[44] the dynamics of the economic system is linear.[45] Figure 2.8 shows the appearance of the economic cyclicity by operating the clock time instead of the economic time:

2.4.6 Other Developments

The next theoretical step is to define the quantum of economic action (QEA) and to associate such a quantum to each unit of economic time (UET). On this basis we can introduce the accelerations of economic time in relation with the clock time simply by accepting the fact that several QEA occur within the same unit of clock time. As this is impossible once that we defined the QEA as the amount of economic action which can be produced in the UET, it results that the only way in which we can accept the occurrence of several QEA within the same unit of clock time is to accept the occurrence of several UET within the same unit of clock time, that is to say, to accept accelerations of the economic time in relation with the clock time (in terms of the beat or pace). On this basis we can introduce the following conjecture: the pace of the economic time is directly proportional to the intensity of the economic process which, in turn, is directly proportional to the density of the economic space. The distinction between the physical space (associated to the clock time) and the economic space (associated to the economic time) can lead to the idea of a *continuum of the economic space-time* (CEST). Both the space and the time of a CEST depend on the economic process, therefore they are no longer autonomous in relation with it. On this basis we can construct the economic "geodesics", i.e., the minimal "routes" of the economic action (production, distribution, consumption, saving, etc.) on the basis of the principle of minimal action in nature (Maupertuis' principle).

All the above allow us to make a synthesis of our proposed new vision on the theory and methodology of the economic cycle and on the theory and methodology of the economic crisis. Essentially, our proposition is as follows:

First, the economic crisis must be considered distinctly from the economic cycle, having its own causality, although there are some causal interferences (particularly of functional type) with the economic cycle. The economic crisis is not a periodical phenomenon; it doesn't have an inherent cyclicity. The cause of the economic crisis is the autonomous increase of the nominal flows in relation with the real stocks, due to multipliers much higher than the unit, working at high speed. The economic crisis can, however, disturb seriously the economic cycle when it bursts out, but economic cycles with no financial crisis are also (and generally) possible.

Second, the adjusted economic cycle (AEC), i.e., the economic cycle where the economic crisis is not a structural part, is a rather symmetric oscillation from a trend which, according to the currently dominating economic culture, has an increasing course. This structural trend or path is given by the succession of the inflexion points of the curve which describes, bidimensionally, the economic cycle (see Fig. 2.5).[46]

Third, we consider that there might be a second order cyclicality (by developing Kuznets's suggestion on the secondary economic cycle), which results from the trend of the first order economic cycle (the primary economic cycle). Following are some notes on the second order cyclicity:

(a) The shape of the second order cyclicity is described by the curve joining the inflexion points of the first order cyclicity; if no economic crises occur within a first order cyclicity, the clock time distribution of the inflexion points is "smooth", meaning that it follows closely the rate of increase of the particular economic activity (for instance, of the GDP);
(b) Unlike the first order cyclicity, this cyclicity includes, as component part, the economic crisis; therefore, the second order cyclicity will influence the first order cyclicity, meaning that the disturbances which the economic crisis has on the location of the inflexion points of the first order cyclicity determines the new coordinates, in the clock time of the latter cyclicity—Fig. 2.9 shows a synoptic image of the interference between the first order cyclicity and the second order cyclicity. The mechanism shown in the figure describes the way in which the secondary economic cycle plays a role of pilot[47] for the primary economic cycle.

Fourth, both the adjusted economic cycle (AEC) and the economic crisis must be quantified/measured and evaluated in the specific, proper time introduced above: the economic time. Based on the impossibility of a quantum of economic action to "take" more than one unit of economic time, we can draw the conclusion that the economic cycle measured in the clock time shows stages of growth or decrease, as the economic time is accelerated or decelerated in relation with the clock time. Actually,

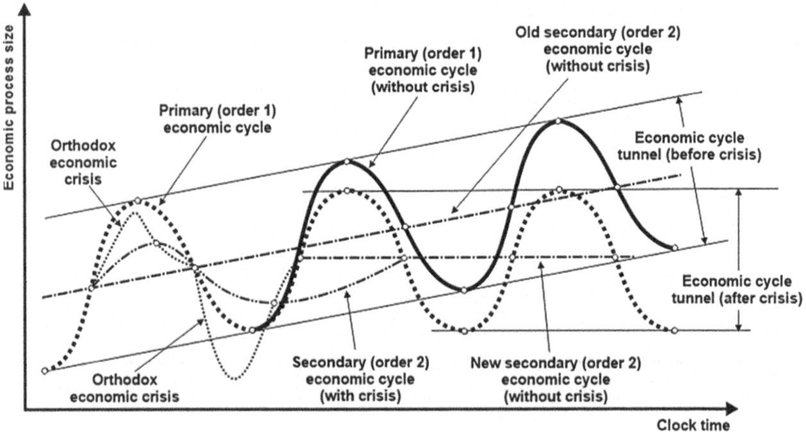

Fig. 2.9 Interference between the primary economic cycle and the secondary economic cycle. *Source*: author

according to the economic time there are neither stages of growth, nor stages of decrease; the economic activity merely intensifies or moderates. Analogously, we will consider that an intensified economic activity generates a denser economic space, while a moderated economic activity generates a more rarefied economic space. Therefore, the variation of the economic space density is equivalent with the acceleration of the economic time and vice versa. Within the context, we consider that we should talk of a continuum economic space-time (CEST), and all the trajectories which we associate to the economic cycles must be actually considered as geodesics of this CEST. On the basis of the economic rationality, we will therefore admit that the economic activity describes economic cycles (measured by the dimension of the economic activity) which simply follow these economic geodesics.[48] The utility, both conceptual and methodological, of introducing CEST in the description of the economic process is even more important when we discuss about the economic crisis. The autonomy of the nominal flows formation in relation with the economic stocks makes the acceleration of the economic time within the phenomenology of the nominal flows to be huge in relation with the clock time.[49]

Fifth, as seen before, the continuum of the economic space-time is generated by the presence of the economic subject within the economic process, which introduces the third time within the equation, the psychological time, next to the clock time and the institutional time. The removal of the economic subject in the modelling of the economic process (inheritance of the wrong analogy of the economic science with the physics[50]) has been one of the major epistemological errors in the development of the economic science. The presence of the subject within the economic process turns the economic system into what we can call a logically vivid system. In relation with the standard system, the logically vivid system has two additional attributes: (a) dissipativity (the capacity to preserve or reduce the entropy) and (b) the structural and functional redundancy (replication principles for the structures/functions which "decay"). Both attributes are generated by the presence of the subject. Therefore, the economic cycle should be studied within the paradigm of the logically vivid system. Within this paradigm, the economic time will link to the two mentioned attributes of sufficiency, and the resulting model of the economic cycle will be utterly different from the orthodox one. The living, non-human nature also has logically vivid systems, but this kind of systems manifest with predilection within the systems where man is present as individual or as social group. Furthermore, if we add another two supplementary attributes to the logically vivid system: (a) the exclusive existence of the hyper-cycles (any output of a subsystem is an integrated input of another subsystem or of a system within the environment of the particular system); (b) dominance of the anti-cyclicity (any positive feedback is wrapped by a negative feed-back), then we will get an extremely important "institutional device": the sustainable system. Therefore, in the broadest paradigmatic framework (the most adequate, in our opinion), the economic cycle should be evaluated (described, explained, forecast, etc.) within the context of the sustainable economic system. The proposition to remove the economic crisis from the structure of the economic cycle aims to bestow properties of sustainability to the economic cycle. Within this context, the economic crisis is an extraordinary, non-periodical, event which takes the economic cycle out of its tunnel of oscillation, out of its tunnel of sustainability (Fig. 2.9). Actually, the intervention of an economic crisis disturbs the economic cycle, relocates its points of inflexion (as well as the points of cycle minimum and maximum) and yield, as shown, a secondary order economic cycle.

2.4.7 *Some Concluding Remarks*

The CEST model of the economic cycle involves the following basic logic consequences:

(a) The separation of the generative causality of the economic cycle from the generative causality of the economic crisis. The economic cycle and the economic crisis are two distinct "institutional animals", despite some superficial resemblance. While the economic cycle is generated by gradients (quantitative gaps of dynamics) between the real economic flows and the counterpart financial flows to the real economic flows, the economic crisis is generated by gradients (quantitative gaps of between the real stocks and the nominal flows.

(b) The mechanisms (regarding the economic cycle or the economic crisis) driven by gradients of amplitude (quantitative gaps) differ, both in terms of "anatomy" and in terms of "physiology" from the mechanisms drive by speed gradients (gaps of dynamics);

(c) The clock time is not fitted for the quantification/measurement of the economic process in general thus of the economic cycle or of the economic crisis; the proper time for this quantification/measurement is the economic time, which is a resultant of the three categories of counters associated to the economic process: the clock time, the institutional time and the psychological time;
(d) "Decreeing" the content of economic activity of a unit of economic time as always representing a quantum of economic action[51] allows drawing a basic conclusion for our endeavour: the economic time actually is linear. Its non-linearity, which is conveyed to the shape of the economic cycle, is generated by the acceleration of the economic time in relation with the clock time. The same considerations are valid for the evaluation of the economic crisis phenomenology; analogously, the economic space is "deformed" in relation with the physical space: it is more dense than the associated physical space when the economic time is accelerated in relation with the clock time, and it is more rarefied than the associated physical space when the economic time is decelerated in relation with the clock time; this continuum of the economic space-time generates the geodesics on which the economic process "moves" (actually we only have economic cycles if we measure the economic process with the clock time; if we would measure it with the economic time, we would see that the path of the economic process simply follows the economic geodesic);
(e) The reintroduction of the economic subject within the economic process, in the economic cycle too, sets the epistemological conditions to use the paradigm of the logically vivid systems (or, broader, of the sustainable systems) to describe, explain and forecast the economic cycle, the economic crisis. The four ingredients which we propose for a new vision on the economic cycle (removal of the economic crisis from the structure of the economic cycle, the use of the continuum of the economic space-time, the introduction of the secondary economic cycle, the introduction of the paradigm of the logically vivid systems and of the sustainable systems) might bring, in our opinion, useful contributions to the new bases of the economic cycle theory within the current conditions of globalization and de-globalization.

Notes

1. Including the conditionalities which in our view are included in what can be named the causal vector (formed by the direct cause—material, effective, formal, or final, after the case—and the causal conditionalities).
2. The mode modus ponens is formalized as (M) $A \rightarrow B$; (m) A; (C) B, where: M is the major premise, m is the minor premise, C is the conclusion. The mode modus tollens is formalized as: (M) $A \rightarrow B$; (m) $\overline{B}$; (C) $\overline{A}$. *Nota bene*: from logical point of view, the Popperian falsificationism is a modus tollens mode of syllogism.
3. For example, the general theory of relativity (that belongs to CM) "creates" the curved space (that belongs to RM). On the other part, Heidegger (2009) that primarily we get the understanding and secondarily we get knowledge, the last through explanation.
4. The term practical has, here, the Kantian sense, i.e., addresses the subject-subject relationships.
5. By event we understand a contextual hypostasing of a phenomenon, while a phenomenon must be understood as a contextual hypostasing of a process.
6. A chreode is a family of trajectories —so, if a phenomenon has a trajectory, all phenomena which compose a process put together their trajectories to form a chreode, i.e., a family of trajectories.
7. The concept of control variable has the meaning discussed by Skinner (2005), that is, that variable which can influence the response (re-action) of a system to the environment actions.
8. There are essays to identify the structural conditions which necessarily "germinates" the crises—see, for example, the most notable of them: (Minsky, 2008).
9. Such a causality will be of a great importance and productivity when we shall discuss the new logic required by the economic (more general, societal) phenomenology, applicable to the crisis examination as well.
10. As can be observed, the final causality (from Aristotle's causal quadrilateral) disappears, while a new cause appears: the significant cause (or causality), which must not be confused with the teleological cause (or causality). In fact, it can be considered that Aristotle's causal quadrilateral becomes a causal pentagon: (a) *efficient* cause; (b) *material* cause; (c) *formal* cause; (d) *final* cause; (e) *significant* cause. The logic of causes action is different between quadrilateral and pentagon, namely (1) in quadrilateral causality: final cause – formal cause – material cause – efficient cause; (2) in pentagon causality: significant cause – final cause – formal cause – material cause –

efficient cause. The fact that the significant causality acts as primordial cause (before the final causality) is methodologically and empirically acknowledged, for example, by elaborating ex ante studies of impact.

11. To be reminded that we do not discuss here about an explicative convergence (this is in the "court" of the RM) but about an understanding convergence.
12. An event is a concrete/particular manifestation/objectification of a phenomenon.
13. Tireless econometricians already developed statistical techniques to identify (or just to suspect) so-called latent variables in the system's dynamic. In fact, it is no needed to identify more than proximal causal factors. More than that, as we shall try to show, even the predictions could be "replaced" with the control variables of those predictions.
14. The independency is logically equivalent with the non-redundancy.
15. We accept the assumption that a prediction is an ex ante explanation, while an explanation is an ex post prediction.
16. Principled, the expectations should be placed outside any rationality model, unless we would wish to give citizenship to a sort of intuitive (non-rational) model of "rationality". The current behaviourism (which is connected rather to psychology than to logic) seems to accept, in a sort of hidden background, the possibility of such intuitive model of "rationality". The issue is interesting but we do not stay more onto it in the present study.
17. If the predictions are not deterministic but of stochastic type (*Nota bene*: no prediction can be of random type, by definition), to rational predictions it can be given frequential (Kolmogorov), i.e., objective, probabilities, while to expectations it can be given Bayesian, i.e., subjective, probabilities.
18. It is to be mentioned that any theory (hypothesis/assumption, etc.) works similarly—the world is exactly what our theory about the world says the world is.
19. From a metaphysical perspective, any explanation contains (or even consists in) significations, as Heidegger claims in his allegations about the concepts of being and time.
20. Of course, the possibility of the control upon the crisis does not mean the possibility of the control upon the cycle. As we shall try to explain below (see point 2.6) between crisis and cycle does not exist a necessary connection, although a contingent one can arise.
21. S-Necessity is created by the very creating of the artefacts, for example, the social contract or the normative framework of the society as a whole or the economic system or the religious system or the political system.
22. Obviously, the animals (and even plants) perform entropic exchanges with Nature, but these facts are not of economic type, since the facts in the case

violate at least one of the other sufficiency predicates of the concept of economic—mandatorily they violate the purpose.

23. We remind that the emergence of the causes must not be the result (at least not an inferable one) of the structure put in place, else we cannot at all speak about crisis, as argued before, but it must be a result just provided by the very functioning of the system concerned.
24. The concept (although not the term as such) there was in Marx and Sombart's works.
25. Of course, in any phenomenon/process, there are both negative and positive feedbacks, the condition is that the negative feedback be dominant, not exclusive.
26. Generally, we shall keep using the term field when we refer to the five classes of T_2 criterion, and the term region when we are talking about geographical areas.
27. As known, not even Aristotle himself was able to find a zoological typology so overlapping among the classes do not exist in the case.
28. The modality called trial and error is common in the Darwinian processes, but, within the society, where the Lamarckian processes are dominant, it has not anymore too much usefulness (beside, the learning through trial and error, introduced by Thorndike was still rejected by Skinner—see his book *Science and Human Behaviour*, The B.F. Skinner Foundation, 2005).
29. Do not be forgotten that European Union is based (at least according to its two treaties (TEU and TFEU, respectively) on the market social economy, which is the philosophical background of Ordoliberalism (Dinga, 2024).
30. The concept of capability is that used in the social justice theory (see, for example, Amartya Sen or Martha C. Nussbaum), that is, the set of conditions of any kind aimed at flourishing the individual as person.
31. So, there is not limitations of freedom in the following cases: (a) public constraints of the formation of private purposes; (b) private or public constraints on the allocation of means to get the private purposes.
32. Generally, it is considered that individual freedom (or the freedom of the individual) is really relevant. However, post-modernity has a tendency to couple individuals into communities so that it seems that group freedom or, more exactly, the individual freedom inside the groups becomes more and more relevant.
33. We can anticipate here that, finally, a generic crisis can be non-ambiguously identified by intermediation of a heptad (seven marks) – at the mentioned pentad it will be added other two marks: of entropic, respectively of fractal.
34. As shown in Chap. 1, if the system in the case is antifragile, or has some degree of antifragility, the predictions on the crisis, even if would be possible (but it is not) become useless, since the crisis will bring rather benefits.

35. We remind that there are only three logically distinct entities in the world: (a) things; (b) properties; (c) relationships. In such a framework, we discuss about the cyclicality as a property caused by relationships.
36. The economic is that attribute of an act that involves the intervention of the human being in nature, in order to achieve the material exchange between the actional subject and nature, by means of an artefactual membrane.
37. We have in mind here the three fundamental economic markets, each with its own supply-demand pair: (1) the market of goods and services; (2) the money market; (3) the labour market.
38. Here the term trajectory must be understood in a non-mechanistic sense (for example, it has no reversibility, and if it has, it is characterized by hysteresis), rather as a metaphor that we cannot escape when we want to describe a dynamic economic system.
39. See below for considerations of turning points that arise in the problem of critical thresholds between the real economy and the nominal economy.
40. We will show, subsequently, that the economic system is a logically vivid system, so the attribute of natural must be understood here with the meaning of logically necessary. So, neither the common meaning of non-vivid system nor the more sophisticated meaning of phenomenon of equilibrium (present, for instance, in syntagms such as "natural interest rate", "natural unemployment rate", "natural price", etc.) are acceptable within the context.
41. We maintain the hypothesis that the labour force market derived from the market for goods and services.
42. Of course, there is a possibility that a nominal flow is not guaranteed by a real stock, rather by a future financial flow (for instance, a bank credit is guaranteed by the wage). In this case, the part of the total financial flow which forms the collateral for the reimbursement of the loan must be considered, conceptually, as a stock, not a real one, rather a financial one because, in principle, that part cannot be used as equivalent value for the real flows, rather as source to reimburse the bank loan. However, in most cases, the collateral for the nominal flows is in the nature of the real stocks.
43. We will refer in detail to this aspect at the time when we will propose a set of critical thresholds at which the economic crisis can interfere in the economic cycle.
44. As it hopefully resulted from the introduction to this study, the economic time is the result of three categories of time (counters) of the economic process: the *clock time* (the natural time), the *institutional time* (introduced by the norms regulating the economic action), the *psychological time* (introduced by the presence of the subject within the economic process, which generates anticipations and interests).

45. This conclusion might prove particularly important in terms of the necessity to ensure the *epistemological simplicity* not just for the theory of the economic cyclicity, but also for the methodology and technology to deal with this phenomenon—the epistemological simplicity means getting the simpliciter in comprehension.
46. According to the sustainability criteria, we may also accept, in our opinion, decreasing trends, as humanity will pass from the paradigm of the optimality (currently dominant and causal generator of the process of financial and economic globalization) to the paradigm of sustainability. Within this context, it becomes perfectly possible (or maybe even necessary) to have a theory of the sustainable economic ... decrease.
47. Practically, the secondary economic cycle builds permanently (by integrating the effects of the economic crises occurring at different moments in time) the configuration pattern of the next first order economic cycle.
48. Of course, this is a mere suggestion (largely relying on intuition). The formal part is yet to be constructed. The main problem at this point is: do we still need models of economic optimization, if the path of the economic process is "forced" to follow the economic geodesic? Our answer is negative: the economic modelling will have to give up optimization and this is equivalent with the transition from the paradigm of optimality (current today, together with its methodological corollary: the *homo œconomicus* model) to the paradigm of sustainability. This study makes only brief mentions about these more general aspects of the economic epistemology and methodology.
49. An example at hand is the very empirical analysis of the economic crisis of 2007–2010. Both the explosion of the financial derivatives, on the one hand, and the insurances/reinsurances succession of the bank credits (with the resulting huge moral hazard) multiplied enormously the value of the nominal flows in relation with the value of the real stocks, which is equivalent, as shown above, with a staggering acceleration of the economic time in relation with clock time and a corresponding increase of the density of the nominal economic space.
50. Also see the current development of a very epistemologically dangerous hybrid: the Econophysics.
51. The definition of the quantum of economic action remains one of the basic issues (actually the key-problem) of the CEST model of the economic cycle, of the economic crisis.

References

Biebricher, T., Bonefeld, W., & Nedergaard, P. (2022). *The Oxford Handbook of Ordoliberalism*. Oxford University Press.

Dinga, E. (2016). *Economic Cyclicity* (in Romanian). Romanian Academy Publishing House.

Dinga, E. (2022). Proference: Behavioural Mix Between Propensity and Preference on Financial Market, European. *Journal of Interdisciplinary Studies*, (7).

Dinga, E. (2024). Ordoliberalism as Theory of Smart Governance. *International Journal of Social Sciences and Management Review*, 7.

Dinga, E., Oprean-Stan, C., Tănăsescu, C.R., Brătian, V., & Ionescu, G.-M. (2023). *Economic and Financial Market Behaviour. The Autopoietic Market Hypothesis*. Palgrave Macmillan-Springer Nature.

Heidegger, M. (2009). *History of the Concept of Time: Prolegomena*. Indiana University.

Minsky, H. P. (2008). *Stabilizing an Unstable Economy*. McGraw-Hill Education.

Skinner, B. F. (2005). *Science and Human Behaviour*. The B.F. Skinner Foundation.

CHAPTER 3

Crisis as a Societal Entropic Mark

3.1 Preamble

In this chapter, we try to discuss the possibility that the concept (and, of course, the objectified reality) of crisis, as it was considered earlier, be associated with the concept or mark of entropy so that any class of generic crisis to be given such an entropic mark. This allocation is not only of a theoretical (somewhat abstract) significance but, also, can be of considerable usefulness for the crises overlapping, on the one hand, and for designing the governmental policy aimed at handling the crisis phenomenology, on the other hand. These two potential benefits provided by the association of the crisis and entropy will be analytically discussed and assessed at the appropriate points in the economy of the book.

3.1.1 The Natural Entropy

The concept of entropy originates, as it is well known, from (the so-called phenomenological) thermodynamics, as a macro-label of the state of a closed system to its environment.[1] There is already an extremely rich literature on the primary concept of entropy (originated in Thermodynamics), and consequently, it is well-known to everyone, and *a fortiori*, to the constant readers of the dedicated publications, so our task is considerably eased in introducing the concept concerned. Thus, we shall do this by

E. Dinga, *Economic Resilience During Overlapped Crises*,
https://doi.org/10.1007/978-3-031-80224-9_3

briefly pointing out the main attributes that usually are associated with the primary concept of entropy:

- it is a concept of maximum generality, being equally applicable (in its essence) to any of the three Popper-ian worlds, as well as to combinations of them, as the social system is, in fact;
- it has three basic meanings:
  - *ontological*: as parameter of a real existential entity (objective or subjective);
  - *epistemological*: as cognitive significance for the subject (it indicates the level of order the concerned entity experiences);[2]
  - *methodological*: as selector of the procedure for "querying" the object;
- its referent (denoted) is a state of an existential entity (system, process);[3] so, the entropy could be formalized as a state-variable, or state-function or state-vector;
  - the size of the entropy variation does not depend on the intermediate stages (that is, on the "road" pursued), but only on the initial and final points;

Nota bene: dependence on intermediate stages leads to processual quantities (functions).[4]

- the state referred to by the concept of entropy is embedded in the concept of order;[5]
  - entropy is a parameter that "moves" inversely in relation to the order associated;
    - more precisely: the size of the entropy is inversely proportional to the degree of ordering;
- entropy is non-static: in a closed system (e.g., our Universe) the entropy necessarily and permanently increases;[6]
  - so, the global entropy (i.e., inside a closed system) is irreversible;[7]
- it is a macroscopic variable, obtained by modelling the integration of the microscopic states;
  - more precisely, it signifies a macroscopic irreversibility derived from a microscopic reversibility (see, here, also, the problem of Maxwell's demon);

- it is a statistical quantity (based on the statistical formulation of thermodynamics, in line with Boltzmann's works);
  - this justifies the appearance of probability in the analytical formula of entropy in statistical thermodynamics (because probabilities can only model the average of a population);
- it is an additive variable.

3.1.2 Some Basic Ways of Currently Using the Concept of Entropy in Social Sciences

In fact, with the concept of entropy, whose origin is claimed by thermodynamics in its trying to escape from micro states (imposed by mechanical statistics) and coming up to macro ones, things similarly happened like with most of the basic concepts (and, often, principles) of the social sciences (primarily, of economics): an uncritical and *tale quale* import from the natural sciences. Such an appetite, not too difficult to understand, of social sciences for foreign quantitative and a-contextual conceptual constructions has not tired yet. In the present chapter, we shall try to depart as much as possible from such an undesirable epistemological account.

It seems there are three strands of importing (not of own constructing) the concept of entropy into social sciences: (a) a strand based on *similarity*—by a Procust-ian gathering of the concepts concerned in order to isomorphically find the thermodynamical design of the entropy: temperature, energy, exergy and so on (Tribus & Evans, 1963);[8] such an approach stays at intersection between physics and economics; (b) a strand based on *analogy*—the originary concept of entropy is only a starting point, instead an analogous model of functioning in spirit but not in a letter way being built in order to attain an entropic understanding of the social (in fact, of the economic) process functioning (Georgescu-Roegen, 1971); such an approach is located deeply in the economic/social process although, however, with a too little appeal, in our opinion, to the sociality and to the specific third Pooper-ian world which subsists inside the social system;[9] (c) a strand based on *operational sociality*—an own model of the society's structural functioning which constitutes, in our opinion, a promising way to build, not to import as such, a genuine concept of social entropy (Bailey, 1990); this time, five variables, which typically are social, are identified and embedded in a logical structural model known as PISTOL/PILOTS (population, information, space, technology, organization, living), and it is obvious why we would name such an approach as operational sociality and not, for example, pure or full sociality approach. What we propose in this chapter is, in fact, if it could be so said, a fourth strand of approaching the concept of social entropy, which could be appropriately named *social justice-based social entropy*.

An exciting issue regarding the concept of social entropy debated in the literature is that focuses on the logical relationship between order and entropy. Generally, in such debates, the order is thought through a too-closed link to thermodynamics, as heterogeneity, while the disorder is thought as opposed: homogeneity. Such a mechanical approach is wrong. If it is right, this means that a dictatorship, which is very "ordered" has a very low social entropy, which would be a desirable state, although freedom is almost inexistent there, while the natural state, where the order is very low means having a high social entropy, although the people has a large freedom.[10]

3.2 On the Concept of Order

3.2.1 The Order in the Common Language

Common (natural or "civil") language has, of course, a definition of the concept of order—this is considered a configuration, either spatial or temporal or (most often) a combination of the two which characterizes a phenomenon and which is detectable as such a configuration, that is, it is intelligible to the empirical observer without s/he to possess special powers for this observation. In other words, the "common" order is simply a pattern, static or cinematic, that the average observer "throws" over a real phenomenon (either objective, subjective or objectified) and that pattern "fits" on the reality in question. Two aspects seem important at this point: (a) what is the "method" by which the pattern in question is detected, and (b) what is the potential of truth (more concretely, of true prediction) of that pattern?

(a) it is quite obvious that, in the common sense of the term, the order observed at the unspecialized empirical level is of an inductive type. The observer notices regularities, periodicities and other replicability characteristics of a phenomenon and, by inductive inference, that is, by generalization, constructs the order in question. Of course, inductive inference is falsifiable, so the common concept of order is a vulnerable concept;

(b) in terms of its potential to enable the formulation of true predictions, the common concept of order is extremely deficient. Of course, predictions can be made, but they are true (i.e., the previous predictive statement coincides with the subsequent descriptive statement) only by chance. The explanation lies in the fact that the generalization has an enormous probability to be local (both temporally and spatially), while the truth of a prediction is "governed" (especially) by the universal character of the major premise, not by its (only) general character.

So, the common understanding of the concept of order consists in considering reality as it appears to the non-specialized observer and infers the causality associated with the pattern of order by generalization, that is, by induction.

3.2.2 The Order in the Logical Language

It is obvious that, from a scientific perspective (primarily, from an epistemological one), we need a different examination of the concept of order. This consists in identifying the sufficiency attributes (or predicates) that the concept of order must verify in order to qualify as such. We propose that the list of these sufficiency predicates be as follows:

- (*PSO*1) *sensorial perception*: the phenomenon that will be the basis of the finding (or non-finding) of an ordered configuration must be observable at the sensorial level, even if, of course, after the sensorial detection, the perception, conceptualization and judgement (reasoning) occur which they ultimately lead to the formulation, through universalization, of the order in question;
- (*PSO*2) *intellectual reasoning*: if *PSO*1 involves the natural senses of the cognitive subject, *PSO*2 involves the intellect of that subject. As is known, perception represents the form that consciousness gives to sensation. The formation of concepts and the preparation of judgements require the subject's intellect, which transforms perception into concept. Conceptualization is the crucial step in the deductive identification of order;
- (*PSO*3) *psychological intuition*: the order is a binary construction, that is, it comes from two directions: one based on the perception and reasoning (which could be called *substantial emerging*), and one

based on the individual idiosyncrasy (which could be called *emotional emerging*). In fact, we think that all decisions taken by individuals are based, *prima facie*, on the perception of order, more precisely, of the social (or, narrower, economic) order. All the other factors or conditionalities are secondary (or tertiary, after the case[11]) and rather shape irrelevant features of those decisions/actions;

- (*PSO4*) *catalogue registration*: applying the first two sufficiency predicates only leads to the possibility of notifying an order. The effective establishing of the order occurs only if the result of the application of *PSO2* is found in the already existing catalogue[12] of possible orders, a catalogue which is, of course, accessible to the cognitive subject in question.

We can write that the order (O) is given by the logical conjunctions of the three sufficiency predicates:

$$O \leftarrow (PSO1) \wedge (PSO2) \wedge (PSO3) \wedge (PSO4)$$

A brief discussion may be helpful here:

(a) how does the cognitive subject come into possession of the catalogue containing the list of already known orders (with the basic, defining characteristics to ensure the recognizability of each one separately)? Obviously, only as a result of previous experience, so it will have to be accepted that this catalogue is an *a posteriori* one;

(b) how is the comparison of the concept sketch of the possible new order with the catalogue entries actually done? One could ask, here, for the postulation of a fourth sufficiency predicate to guarantee this operational capacity. We consider, however, that this predicate would be redundant; therefore we will assume that the cognitive subject has the intellectual capacity on the simple basis of its quality as a cultural subject;

(c) if the cognitive subject does not find, in the catalogue, the order that seems to him/her to be identifiable based on the first two predicates of sufficiency, what does s/he do? Two alternative options should be mentioned here:

- (c.1) "decrees" that there is no order in the phenomenon in question; here there is a type 1 error—the rejection of a true hypothesis;

- (c.2) completes the catalogue with the new presumed order, with distinguishing characteristics from those already existing in the catalogue; here there is a type 2 error—admitting a false hypothesis. From a logical point of view, if we do not accept an *a priori* nature of the catalogue of orders, the catalogue is formed, over time, and for each individual cognitive subject, excluding the practice of type 2 errors;

(d) are there also order catalogues that are supra-subjective (supra-individual)? The answer is obviously affirmative: in society, a common (social, community) catalogue of orders works (and is accepted at the level of all individuals). Their inclusion in the common catalogue is done by a democratic "vote";

(e) both the catalogues of orders of individuals and those at the community (social) level are, in turn, on fields of interest or on typological fields: ontological orders, epistemological orders, axiological orders, praxeological orders, etc.

A logical definition of the concept of order can be, now, provided: an order is a configuration, either spatial or temporal, or (most often) a combination of the two, which characterizes a phenomenon and is detectable as such a configuration, that is, it is intelligible to the cognitively and performatively competent empirical observer. A synthesis of all considerations regarding the concept of order from a logical perspective is provided, synoptically, by Fig. 3.1.

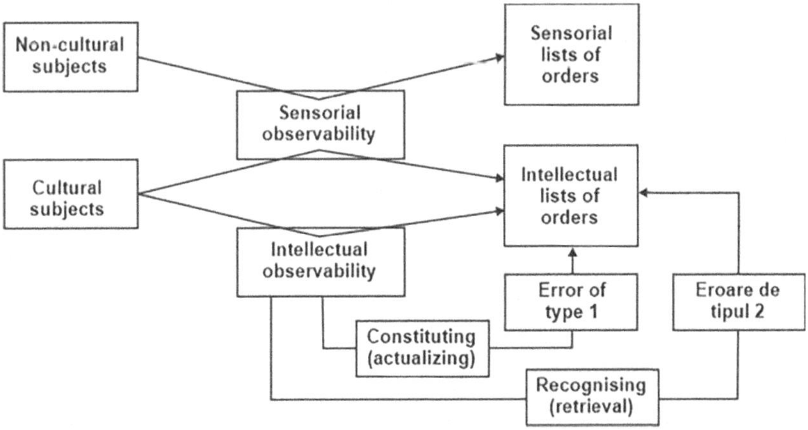

Fig. 3.1 The mechanism for establishing the list of orders. *Source*: Author

3.3 What the Societal Entropy Is It?

In our opinion, the social/societal entropy must be viewed as a measure (or a metric) of the social/societal order. About the order we have discussed earlier (see point 3.2). The order of a system is a qualitative mark of that system, not a quantitative one. However, by assigning to it an entropic degree, it gains a quantitative mark. In fact, as will result below, we have to put into a logical relationship three concepts: order, entropy and crisicity (for the last concept, see point 3.4)—we call such a model *OEC*.

3.3.1 About the Social/Societal Order

The social/societal order is the result of a mix between meaning and signification of a state of affairs of the society as a whole. So, the social/societal order is both an explanation and a sentiment, and the social action is simultaneously caused by the two factors. We can call the explanatory factor the rational factor, and the sentiment factor the propensive[13] factor. Starting with the behaviourism initiated by Skinner, the mix between rationality and emotion is quite present in approaching economic process (Lo, 2019; Dinga et al., 2022), without considering the recent ambitious tendency to build up a phenomenological economic theory (Düppe, 2009).[14] The "shares" of rationality and emotion in forging the final decision for action (either as an act or as an abstention) is, of course, not a theoretical question, but an empirical one.

In this context, the social/societal order is a (macro) state of affairs, according to which the "things" unfold in line with the anticipations permitted by or inferred from the rationality model in force, on the one part, and with the expectations of the society members as the majority,[15] on the other part. Some punctual considerations are of usefulness here:

- the social/societal order is, in the last instance, an intellectual perception, based on the above-mentioned mix between explanation and emotion;
- the mix of rationality—emotion is, however, quite problematic. Let us presuppose that the anticipation inferred from the rationality model indicates that the anticipation is (logically) valid, but the signification of that anticipation for the individuals (perhaps, for the society as a whole) is negative. In such a case (which is not of a too-small probability), we must establish a prioritization between the

rational factor and the emotional one. We think that the signification must be considered more important than the meaning, that is, the quality of life (including the values, first of all, the self-esteem) must have priority, related to the rationally assumed consequences of the societal model of rationality.[16] So, in the case described above, the individuals/the society will perceive a decrease in the order (*nota bene*: the quantitative issue, in this case, is, at least by now, irrelevant);

- so, the order is perceived as order if and only if the state of affairs indicated by the rationality model (the meaning) is semantically equivalent to the state of affairs indicated by the emotion, that is, by the belief/preferences (the signification);
- for example, be a society with a coherent and strong normative framework, which, in fact, grounds and legalizes an authoritarian state. Any practical[17] consequence is a valid inference from the rational model provided by that normative framework. Although the probability of a consequence (or anticipation) with a negative signification for individuals and/or groups is high, because of the authoritarian character of the state[18] (e.g., the freedom could be reduced or blocked), the social/societal order will be perceived, in fact, as... a disorder.

Nota bene: one could develop, starting from this semantic equivalence, an ingenious "theory" of the (possibly named) *teleological-truth*, symmetrically with the concept of the correspondence-truth. So, the proposition which plays the role of prediction inferred from the rationality model (i.e., predictive statement) will be compared with the proposition describing the individual's feeling associated with the anticipation in the case (i.e., the descriptive statement)—if the semantic coincidence occurs between the two statements, then the prediction is true, else, it is false. Of course, the discussion maintains within the bivalent (Aristotle-ian) logic, that is, there are two truth values: (a) teleologically true and (b) teleologically false.

- is there a symmetrical case, when the anticipation indicated by the rationality model has a negative meaning while the expectations have a positive signification? We think yes, and the discussion in this case is as follows:
  - first, it must be clarified what is the "negative meaning" of the event that occurred as anticipation inferred from the rationality model—it is simply an invalid inference, that is, an event/phe-

nomenon/process occurred by logically fraud. Is it possible such a case? We think yes, since the normative framework, which materializes the rationality model in its objectivity, can be unproperly used, either intentioned or non-intentioned (e.g., power abuse or, respectively, negligence in power managing);
- that such a negative meaning can be consistent with a positive signification is, also, possible, which, in fact, denotes that the rationality model has to be improved so that the invalid inference happened to become a valid one in the future—it is the classical case when the violation of a rule means that that rule is wrong;
- the question is: what is the perception of individuals regarding the mix between a negative meaning and a positive signification?

3.3.2 *Social/Societal Order and Social/Societal Entropy*

We come now to the following problem: how to assign a (social/societal) entropic measure for the (social/societal) order.

(a) Preliminaries

While in the natural domain, the entropic measure can be relatively easily assigned to a system or process, based on measuring the degree of order in that system/process, in the social field, the issue of significance, as it has been introduced in the present study, implies some difficulties related to the subjective (idiosyncratic) perception of the significance of an event/phenomenon occurred, from the order perspective. So, although, we think that the social/societal entropy also must refer to the order (social/societal order), the order as such is not easy to be established. We think that, essentially, the social order perception must be discussed within the pair objective-subjective, that is within the pair meaning-signification, as the two concepts have been introduced before. Moreover, the measure of the social/societal entropy should be of ordinal nature, not of cardinal one, as the latter case happens in the natural field. In other words, we can say if the social/societal entropy has increased, or has decreased, or has maintained, but not with how much these variables have changed. From a conceptual point of view, the things are analogous with the preferences ordering of an individual—the preferences are related to each other only from an ordinal, not cardinal, perspective.

(b) Assignment Protocol

The assignment protocol can be described as in Fig. 3.2 (with *SO* is noted the social order; ↑ means increases, ↓ means decreases, ↔ means maintains).

Discussion

- the strongest increasing of order is that when both meaning and signification are positive, i.e., $(PM) \bigwedge (PS) \rightarrow (SO\uparrow)$, we have here a positive synergy of the two factors—rational, respectively emotional;
- when one of the two factors is of indifferent type, the order also increases, with the condition that the alternative factor be positive, i.e., $[(IM) \bigwedge (PS)] \bigvee [(PM) \bigwedge (IS)] \rightarrow (SO\uparrow)$;
- instead, a negative factor conjunctively associated with an indifferent one generates a decreasing of the order, i.e., $[(IM) \bigwedge (NS)] \bigvee [(NM) \bigwedge (IS)] \rightarrow (SO\downarrow)$;
- an interesting case is when one of the factors is positive while the other is negative. This time, there is no longer a symmetric formal relationship, as in the cases when one of the two factors is indifferent, i.e., $[(NM) \bigwedge (PS)] \rightarrow (SO\leftrightarrow)$, but $[(PM) \bigwedge (NS)] \rightarrow (SO\downarrow)$. This asymmetry is, of course, explainable by the fact, introduced previously as a ground supposition, namely, that the significance is decisively related to the meaning;
- when both factors are indifferent, the order is perceived as being stationary, i.e., $[(IM) \bigwedge (IS)] \rightarrow (SO\leftrightarrow)$.

(c) The Dilemma Cardinal-Ordinal

In the economic and social field, the cardinal marks/labels of the variables (e.g., the numbers) are much less important (more precise,

		Positive meaning	Indifferent meaning	Negative meaning
		PM	*IM*	*NM*
Positive signification	*PS*	*SO* ↑	*SO* ↑	*SO* ↔
Indifferent signification	*IS*	*SO* ↑	*SO* ↔	*SO* ↓
Negative signification	*NS*	*SO* ↓	*SO* ↓	*SO* ↓

Fig. 3.2 Social order as a function of pair meaning-signification. *Source*: Author

much less significant) than the ordinal marks/labels. There are two reasons for this statement: (1) a *methodological*/technological reason—the economic/social variables are rather ideal than objective, so the measurement used in the natural field is not working at all in the social field; (2) an *ontological* reason—the economic/social variables are oscillating ones, based on the (relatively) unpredictable actions (acts and abstentions) of individuals.[19] Consequently, the decision is taken based on the trends (tendencies, propensities) of those variables rather than on the size of them (as such or as gaps to benchmarks). In our opinion, the change in the size of a variable (related to itself or to a pre-established benchmark) generates a more inertial behaviour than a change in the tendency (or propensity) of that variable, which simply means that, in the economic/social field, the driving change is the qualitative, not the quantitative one. However, as said many times, both in philosophy and in political pragmatics, quantity has its quality, which means that there is a threshold in the quantitative change above which the significance of the quantitative change is equivalent to the significance of a qualitative change. These allegations can be synoptically represented, in a stylized form, in Fig. 3.3.

Discussion

- it can be presumed that the quantitative change occurs in a logistical manner (an increasing curve, starting in a convex form and continuing, after the quantitative threshold, concavely);
- the quantitative change, however, has no influence on the significance after the second (concave) increases—this point can be called the start of the meaning inertia;
- till the quantitative threshold, significance is stationary (i.e., insensible to the quantity change) but, after this point, it increases convexly, without an asymptotic limit, even after the quantitative change enters the interval of meaning inertia. This state of affairs is explained by the fact that the significance is, generally, an inertial phenomenon, so its inertia works not only to the quantitative threshold but also after this point. Once the significance increase has started, it maintains even if the meaning enters, in its turn, the inertia.

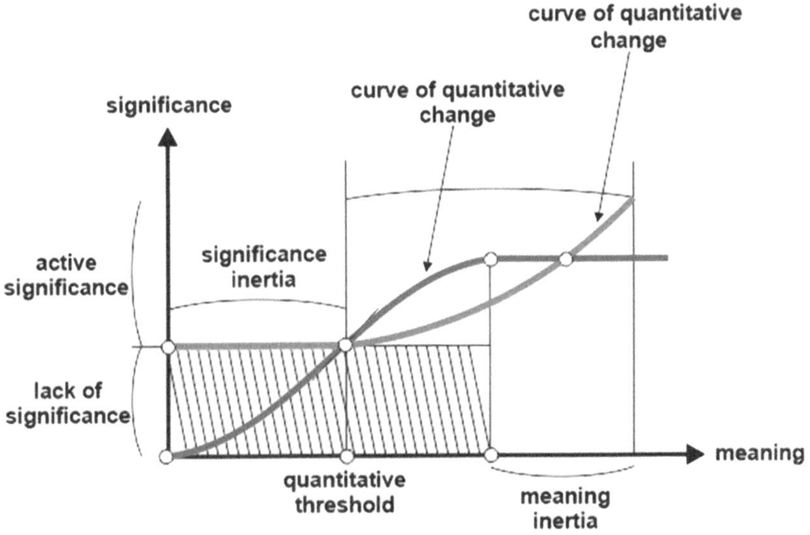

Fig. 3.3 The quantitative accumulation and qualitative jump in the perception of order. *Source*: Author

Nota bene: the quantitative threshold in Fig. 3.3 has just a metaphorical sense because, as said before, in the economic/social field, there is a strong dominance of the ordinal order, if we can so say.

(d) Assignation of the Social Entropy to the Social Order

The assignation of the social entropy mark (M_t^{SE}) to the social order state (S_t^{SO}) will follow the suggestions provided in Fig. 3.3 and will be based on the logical relationships proposed in the assignment protocol. Formally, there is a function $f : S_t^{SO} \rightarrow M_t^{SE}$ (where *t* denotes the time), with the following mathematical features:

- the independent variable is the social order, which is perceived, continuously and ordinally, by the individuals (or groups); such perception is "measured" by a qualitative mark noted S_t^{SO} (social order state);

- the dependent variable is the social entropy (M_t^{SE}), which is associated, in a non-perceiving intuitive way, with the social order state;
- the dependence between S_t^{SO} and M_t^{SE} must be bijective, so there is $f^{-1}: M_t^{SE} \rightarrow S_t^{SO}$;
- although we do not develop more of the idea, we think that the independent variable must be not of punctual nature but of interval one. So the spectrum of the social order must be shared in intervals[20] (perhaps equal among them), noted $I_{t/k}^{SO}$, where $k = \overline{1,n}$, so to each such interval be assigned, by the function *f*, a single value for the social entropy;
- the values of the independent variable (perhaps, assigned to intervals) must be cardinally ordered, either increasing or decreasing, and the reverse for the values of the dependent variable, to ensure the inverse proportionality between the two variables. Considering the presuppositions contained in Fig. 3.3, such a concomitant ordering can be represented as in Fig. 3.4.

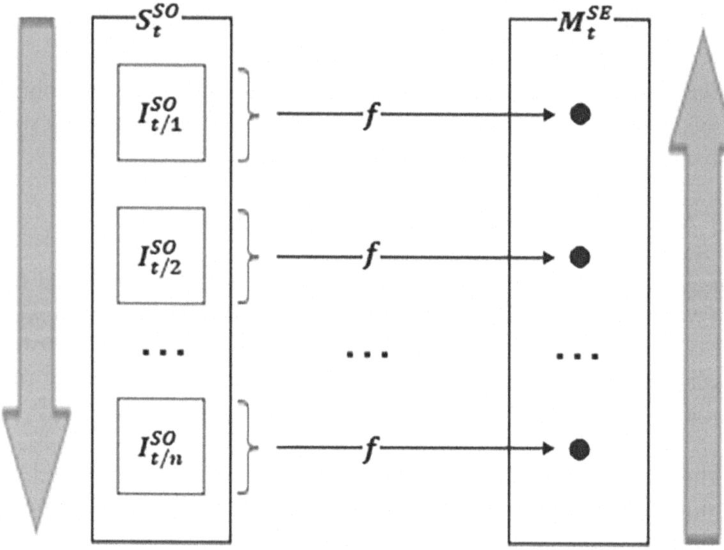

Fig. 3.4 The function *f*. *Source*: Author

3.4 The Crisicity

We shall try, now, to associate entropy with crisis, so the crisis (or, more exactly, the crisicity) can be used as an entropic mark of society. We shall do that in two stages: (1) assigning a mark of social order to a special state of the society which we call crisicity; (2) assigning a mark of social entropy to the crisicity, that is, in fact, to the crisis.

3.4.1 The Concept of Crisicity

While the crisis is a phenomenon (or an event within a phenomenon), the crisicity should be considered a property. The question is: to what entity (thing, property or relationship) such a property should be associated/assigned? In our opinion, the crisicity must be assigned to the social/societal system, that is, to a thing. The crisicity is, so, a property of the society as a whole, that is, it is a macro-property. We shall analytically discuss further the following issues: (a) What must we understand, more precisely, by crisicity? (b) Why the crisicity cannot be a regional (either sectoral or geographical) property? (c) What is the relationship between meaning and significance related to the concept of crisicity? (d) What is the relationship between crisicity and crisis? (e) Why do we need the concept of crisicity?

(a) The Referential of the Crisicity
 (a1) Generalities

The crisicity is a property of the social/societal system which announces an imminent crisis, or a crisis imminence within the society. The announcement and the imminence have the following contents.

- About Announcing
  - it is a result of a presumptive inference from the *statu quo* of the society as a whole, no matter if that inference is actually made or not by someone. In other words, the announcement is, basically, rather an inferentiality than an effective inference. More exactly, it is speaking about the fact that, if such an inference would be made, then it will necessarily deliver a non-ambiguous result of dichotomic nature: either there is a crisis imminence or there is not a crisis imminence;

- semiotically, an announcement is formed by a representamen (the result of inference) that evokes an object (society), aimed at generating an interpretant.[21] The interpretant has a special constitution in the present study, considering the distinction made between meaning and signification:
    - we shall call, from here on, the (relatively odd) mix of meaning and signification with the term *meanfication*, obtained from *mean*ing concatenated with signi*fication*;
    - as suggested in Fig. 3.2, the meanfication can be "calculated" on a logical basis, so in rather a qualitative way and, then, interpreted;

- About Imminence
    - the announcement can be interpreted as either an imminence of crisis or a non-imminence of crisis;
    - the interpretation is, essentially, based on the intuition of the decision-maker (no matter who or what is he/she/it[22]), so no analytical calculus can be or is made;[23]
    - this content of the imminence of a crisis is in line with the observation made a long time ago according to which not the reality is relevant for the decision-making but the perception of that reality, which results in the crucial role played by the meanfication.[24]

(a2) The Interpretation

Since it is not possible to (rigorously) extract an "exact" announcement about the crisicity, it is necessary to describe, however vague, the performative way to decide in this matter. We provide the following considerations.

- we recall that the crisicity property, if and as it is established through the announcement, is an early warning signal about the imminence of a crisis;
- the (qualitative) way in which the crisicity is inferred from the announcement could be of the following "rationality"—Fig. 3.5. (*Nota bene*: we shall use the results obtained in Chap. 2 regarding the content of the concept of crisis.)

Discussion

- the logic of Fig. 3.5 is based on the crisis causality and on the sufficiency predicates identified for the concept of crisis, as these issues were established in Chap. 2;
- *A*, *B*, ..., *F*: can be called crisicity marks;
- the "definitions" of the crisicity marks are as follows: $A = (\omega 1) \bigwedge (\varepsilon 2)$; $B = (\omega 2) \bigwedge (\varepsilon 1)$; $C = (\omega 3) \bigwedge (\varepsilon 2)$; $D = (\omega 1) \bigwedge (\varepsilon 3)$; $E = (\omega 2) \bigwedge (\varepsilon 3)$; $F = (\omega 3) \bigwedge (\varepsilon 3)$;

Nota bene: if note with "$\succ$" the logical constant called "more relevant than", then we assume the following: $(\omega 1) \succ (\varepsilon 1) \succ (\omega 2) \succ (\varepsilon 2) \succ (\omega 3) \succ (\varepsilon 3)$. So $[(\omega i) \bigwedge (\varepsilon j)] \succ [(\omega k) \bigwedge (\varepsilon q)]$, where $i, j, k, q \in \{1,2,3\}$, if either (a) $(i > k)$ or (b) $(i = k) \bigwedge (j > q)$.

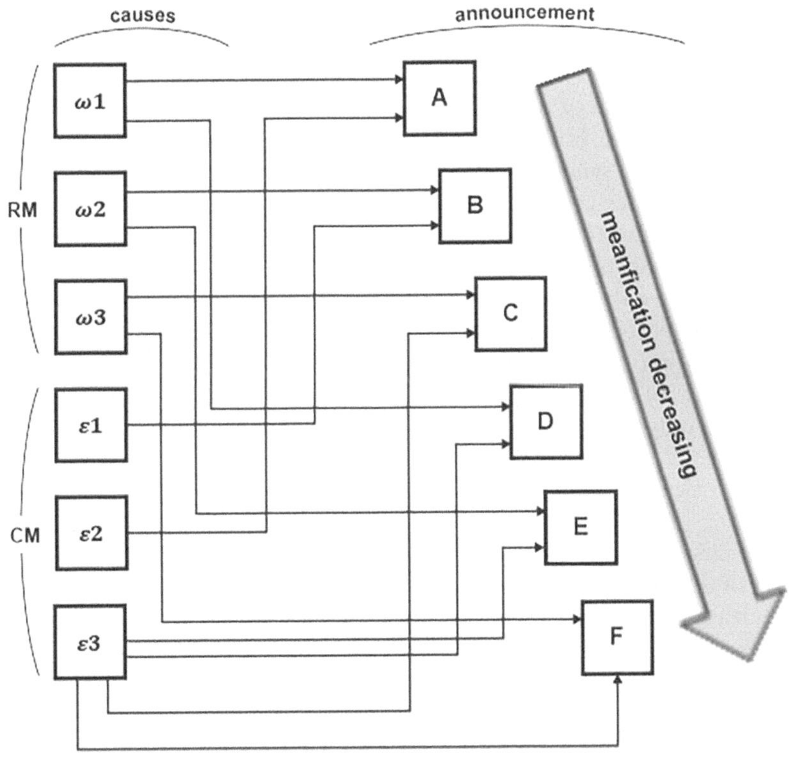

Fig. 3.5 The "rationality" of deciphering the announcement *meanfication*. *Source*: Author

- consequently, the relevance order among the crisicity marks identified in Fig. 3.5 are shown in Table 3.1—we note with "⋊" the logical constant "more relevant than", with "⋉" the logical constant "less relevant than" and with "⋈" the logical constant "equally relevant as"; the comparison is made thus: the lines are the left members and the columns are the right members. *Nota bene*: the more relevant the crisicity is, the more disorder it indicates.

(b) Crisicity as an (Only) Macro-property

The crisicity cannot be then a macro-property, that is, a property which manifests at the societal level. The reasons to assert this consist in, at least, the following:

- inside the societal system there is a network of relationships not only among geographical regions, but also among markets, activities, etc., so a crisicity occurred in a region or in a market quickly migrates to other regions or/and markets;
- the circulation of the crisicity's "buds" among regions and/or markets can have both positive and negative synergetic effects—while the negative synergetic effects can "dry" some crisicity's "buds", the positive ones can exacerbate and, primarily, extend them to those regions and/or markets, so, quite quickly, a punctual crisicity property is spread at the societal level;
- in fact, we shall adopt the assumption that the crisicity property is a macro-property, which means that we shall wait for a punctual crisicity (either of a region or of a market) spread into the society as a whole. In other words, we shall observe and recognize a crisicity as such only if it is observed/recognized at the societal level.

(c) Crisicity and the Pair Meaning-Signification

The crisicity as societal property (both as state and as kinematics) is the result of the meanfication, as the last is formed for the individuals, groups, organizations and government in a given society. We think that combination (in fact, a quite inextricable mix) of meaning and signification is the only way by which the crisicity can be observed. Our positioning seems to pay some tribute to phenomenology (*nota bene*: namely, the reality is exactly that on which the subject focuses its conscience—the so-called intentionality—and the reality is exactly as it is observed/registered by the

Table 3.1 The relevance relationships of the crisicity marks

		A	*B*	*C*	*D*	*E*	*F*
		$(\omega 1) \wedge (\varepsilon 2)$	$(\omega 2) \wedge (\varepsilon 1)$	$(\omega 3) \wedge (\varepsilon 2)$	$(\omega 1) \wedge (\varepsilon 3)$	$(\omega 2) \wedge (\varepsilon 3)$	$(\omega 3) \wedge (\varepsilon 3)$
A	$(\omega 1) \wedge (\varepsilon 2)$	$\bowtie$	$\rtimes$	$\rtimes$	$\rtimes$	$\rtimes$	$\rtimes$
B	$(\omega 2) \wedge (\varepsilon 1)$	$\ltimes$	$\bowtie$	$\rtimes$	$\ltimes$	$\rtimes$	$\rtimes$
C	$(\omega 3) \wedge (\varepsilon 2)$	$\ltimes$	$\ltimes$	$\bowtie$	$\ltimes$	$\ltimes$	$\rtimes$
D	$(\omega 1) \wedge (\varepsilon 3)$	$\ltimes$	$\rtimes$	$\rtimes$	$\bowtie$	$\rtimes$	$\rtimes$
E	$(\omega 2) \wedge (\varepsilon 3)$	$\ltimes$	$\ltimes$	$\rtimes$	$\ltimes$	$\bowtie$	$\rtimes$
F	$(\omega 3) \wedge (\varepsilon 3)$	$\ltimes$	$\ltimes$	$\ltimes$	$\ltimes$	$\ltimes$	$\bowtie$

Source: Author

subject in the case, i.e., the phenomenon perceived is exactly the reality as such, without the Kantian distinction between phenomenon and *Das Ding an Sich*[25]) which seems to "attack" more and more insistent the neoclassical edifice of the economic theory, and even some of the new establishments as behavioural, institutional, (post)structuralist, autopoietic or evolutionary models of the economic process (Benzecry et al., 2017). We strongly believe that the crisicity and meanfication are inherently bound.

(d) Crisis and Crisicity

Once the concept of crisicity is clarified, it is necessary to examine the relationship between crisicity and the crisis. The following considerations can be useful.

- the crisicity is a state, i.e., a property liable to trigger a crisis, while the crisis is a process (at the limit, an event)—so the crisicity is static, while the crisis is kinematic;
- the crisicity is a dichotomic state—it either does exist or does not exist; if crisicity does exist, then the societal system enters a propensity to crisis (such propensity is not, however, irreversible, see below), i.e., the imminence of a crisis arises; instead if crisicity does not exist, the propensity to the crisis does not occur;
- so, in fact, the crisicity is a result of the combination of the causes (above examined) and, thus, it is a causal complex or a causal architecture. The equivalence between the causality and propensity in the crisicity phenomenology is justified by the fact that, as Popper proposed (1959) the propensity is, simply, a very cause of a singular event—the propensity is understood as a kind of probability, of course, neither a frequential probability nor a subjective one, but a combination between a property of the system under analysis and the signification for the observer, that is, exactly as the content of the concept of meanfication;
- somewhat, the crisicity is the bearer of the crisis or, metaphorically, is the soil inside which the crisis sprouts. This means something extremely important, as follows:
  - the societal[26] structure contains *in nuce*, in a potential state, the crisicity; such assumption is very important because it tells us that the crisis constitutes a permanent and immanent Damocles sword over our heads;

- the potential character of the crisis, caused by the structural possibility of the crisicity, is perfectly approachable through the logical theory of Lupasco (1987), a sort of trivalent logic;[27] thus, if the crisicity is "approved" by the signification (in the meanfication concept), the actualization of the crisis increases, while its potentiality decreases and vice versa (*nota bene*: here, the pair of concepts actual and potential have the meaning of Aristotle's theory);
- the crisis is, somewhat, a quasi (or semi)structural phenomenon/event, because its actualization is intermediated by the crisicity which, as explained above, is the result of meanfication, which puts together the meaning (ontology) and the signification (comprehension);

(e) Utility of the Concept of Crisicity

Firstly, the concept of crisicity allows us to construct a logical (partially, psychological) mechanism of crisis arising at the societal level. Indeed, the passing from the pure ontology (objectivity) to the pure epistemology (subjectivity) is facilitated by this intermediate state called crisicity. As it is easy to observe, the crisicity is of objectified nature, because it must be recognized (or "decreed") by the community involved, for example, by the government. So, the crisicity has a role that can be denominated "ripening".

Secondly, the concept of crisicity constitutes, for observers, an early warning signal regarding the imminence of a crisis. Indeed, even if we know the potential causes of a generic crisis, the crisis triggering does not occur if the combination of those causes does not generate the crisicity state at the societal level. In fact, the crisicity state acts similarly to a dashboard of the crisis phenomenology. Although there are, of course, other proposals in this matter (e.g., that of Minsky, regarding the financing structure in the economy) they are regional and too particular, while our proposal tries to reach as large as possible such a criterion.

Thirdly, the concept of crisicity puts into evidence the fact that the crisis could be a "natural" phenomenon of the society. By "natural" character we mean that the economic (larger, the societal) system always keeps the crisis potential, but this is actualized if and only if the crisicity occurs. We think that the ideological examinations of such a "naturalness" are not relevant although some particularities could be of interest, especially from the perspective of public policy.

Fourthly, it is interesting to discuss the type of utility brought by the concept of crisicity. As known, there are three classes of utility: (a) substantive (economic) utility; (b) evidential utility; and (c) symbolic utility (Nozick, 1993). We think the evidential utility and symbolic one are activated by the state of crisicity, while the substantive utility has no relevance at all. More precisely, the evidential utility addresses the explanation (meaning), and the symbolic utility addresses the comprehension (signification). Here we find again the concept of meanfication.[28]

3.4.2 Relationship Between Crisicity and Order

The crisicity is, metaphorically,[29] a "fever" of the societal system. Until the fever is installed, no danger is in place. But which is the (generic) societal danger? As discussed above, this danger is the order compromising, so the relationship between crisicity and (societal) order is to be mandatorily elucidated to go further.

Generally, the crisicity indicates a deterioration of the order just by its simple occurring. Therefore, when we observe/register the crisicity's presence, we must be sure that we have a problem with the societal order. This qualitative inference must, however, be completed with a quantitative one. In this matter we make the following considerations (*nota bene*: the quantitativism is reduced, for the moment, to getting a functional relationship between the variation of crisicity and the variation of the order).

- we have seen before that, based on the two categories of causes affecting the order (ω-perspective and ε-perspective, respectively), six states of the order can be logically extracted (Fig. 3.5), corresponding to the six evaluations of the meanfication ($A \ldots F$);
- in fact, the six labels of the order (or meanfication) should be related just to the "levels" of crisicity. In this intention, let us note with ($a \ldots f$) exactly six intensities of the crisicity, in a decreasing sense of that intensity;
  - be a bijective function, $g : M \rightarrow n$, where $M = \{A, B, C, D, E, F\}$, and $m = \{a, b, c, d, e, f\}$; of course, there is $g^{-1} : m \rightarrow M$;
  - such a way, we can represent punctually the function g, analogously with the function f above, as in Fig. 3.6.

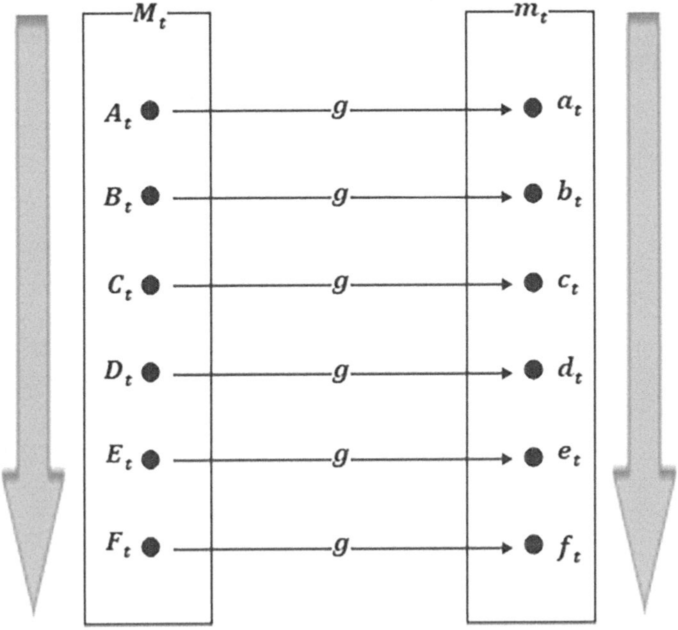

Fig. 3.6 The function *g*. *Source*: Author

- in contrast to the function *f*, which is monotonically decreasing: $\left(S_1^{SO} > S_2^{SO}\right) \to \left(M_1^{SE} < M_2^{SE}\right)$, function *g* is monotonically increasing: $\left(M_t^1 > M_t^2\right) \to \left(m_t^1 > m_t^2\right)$;
- in contrast to the function *f*, which bears an interval to a point, the function *g* bears a point to a point.

3.4.3 *Relationship Between Crisicity and Societal Entropy*

Now, we shall pass from the relationships between order and crisicity to the relationships between order and entropy.

(a) Some Preliminaries

To assign the (societal) entropy mark to the (societal) order, we must use the logical intermediation of the crisicity. In fact, we shall build up a sort of a *modus ponens* syllogism. If we note the societal order with O, the crisicity with C and the entropy with E, we can write ($\overline{x}$ means the logical negation of x, $(\uparrow)x$ means increasing of x, $(\downarrow)x$ means decreasing of x):

$$(\uparrow)C \rightarrow (\downarrow)O$$

$$(\uparrow)C$$

$$\therefore (\downarrow)O$$

respectively,

$$(\uparrow)C \rightarrow (\uparrow)E$$

$$(\uparrow)C$$

$$\therefore (\uparrow)E$$

The two syllogisms obey Popper's criterion of falsifiability, that is, to *modus tollens* syllogism:

$$(\uparrow)O \rightarrow (\downarrow)C$$

$$(\uparrow)C$$

$$\therefore (\downarrow)O$$

respectively,

$$(\uparrow)E \rightarrow (\uparrow)C$$

$$(\downarrow)C$$

$$\therefore (\downarrow)E$$

Nota bene: the syllogisms can, of course, be written also for the (symmetrical) case of decreasing, *mutatis mutandis* within the logic assumed.

In a sense, the order is an unobservable or latent variable, which is observed by (directly) observing the crisicity. In its turn, the entropy should also be considered an unobservable, because it is rather an ideal mark thrown by the intellect onto the objective reality, to make it more intelligible. So, we have an observable, namely, the crisicity which is associated, both upstream and downstream, with some unobservables. Those unobservables are "observed" just by the intermediation of the functions f and g, as they have been introduced above.

Regarding the proportionality between C and O, C and E, and O and E, respectively, we think the following:

- it seems to us that these relationships must be non-linear, so it is important if the phenomenon starts from low values or from high ones (*nota bene*: the term values has here rather a qualitative sense, based on the concept of meanfication);
- as shown before the $O(C)$ curve is decreasing, and the $E(C)$ curve is increasing;
- both $O(C)$ and $E(C)$ are convex.

(b) The $E(O)$ Curve

Procedurally, the $E(O)$ curve will be obtained in the following way (Fig. 3.7).

Discussion

- the graph in Fig. 3.7 aims to derive, synoptically, the curve $E(O)$, based on the curves $O(C)$ and $E(C)$. More exactly, in the four-coordinate framework (i.e., $C - O$, $C - E$, $O - O$, and $O - E$), two different points belonging to $E(O)$ curve are identified, based on the equilibrium condition drawn in the graph ($O - O$);
- the order 2 form of the $E(O)$ can be only established by external (and qualitative) assumptions, as follows:
  - the entropy mark (likewise the order mark) is rather a perception[30] than a calculus, since even the inference from crisicity is an intuitive one, not quite a rational one. Being intuitive, the perception obeys the magnitude of variable involved—thus, if the order decreases from high levels (e.g., from O_1 in Fig. 3.7), the entropy mark will increase less than in the case in which the order decreases from low levels (e.g., from O_2 in Fig. 3.7);

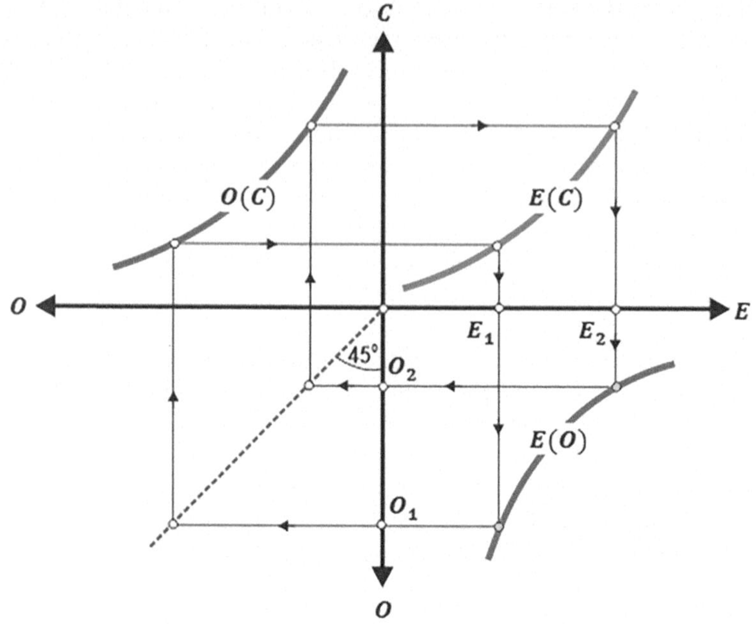

Fig. 3.7 The graphical derivation of $E(O)$ curve. *Source*: Author

- to be observed that if $E(O)$ would be concave, then an order decreasing from high values will cause a bigger increase than in the case of a convex curve of $E(O)$;
- consequently, the form of $E(O)$ curve—convex or concave—constitutes, as said before, an external assumption, which we, of course, corroborate, so we presume a convex form;
- a last comment: why is it more "credible" that for the order decrease from high values, the entropy mark assigned to the new order degree is less than when the order decreases from low levels? We provide the following (both logical and psychological) arguments:

  firstly, at high levels, the two different levels of order (*nota bene*: we do not at all forget that, always, the order level is intuitively inferred from the observed/registered level of the crisicity) are less discernible between them than two symmetric levels perceived at low levels. Somewhat, the intuition "says" to us that there are still reserves to bear declines, so we should not problematize too much the case;[31]

secondly, when the order decreases from high levels, it seems that it can easier reverse the trend,[32] while, at low levels, such a probability of recovering substantially reduces. Somewhat, our (intuitive) observer behaves as if in an aeroplane case which losses from altitude (e.g., caused by air gaps)—if the cruise altitude is big, the plane still keeps the chance of redressing, while if the cruise altitude is small, such a chance disappears.[33]

(c) Assigning Entropy to Order

Based on the above, now we can proceed to an effective allocation/ assignment of the entropy mark to the order. To get a general form of such an assignment, we will re-note some variables as follows:

$$(A,B,C,D,E,F) \rightarrow (M_1,M_2,M_3,M_4,M_5,M_6)$$

$(a, b, c, d, e, f) \rightarrow (m_1, m_2, m_3, m_4, m_5, m_6)$, with $m_i > m_{i-1}$, for $i = \overline{2,6}$

$\left(I_{/1}^{SO}, I_{/2}^{SO}, I_{/3}^{SO}, I_{/4}^{SO}, I_{/5}^{SO}, I_{/6}^{SO}\right) \rightarrow (\alpha_1,\alpha_2,\alpha_3,\alpha_4,\alpha_5,\alpha_6)$, with $\alpha_i < \alpha_{i-1}$, for $i = \overline{2,6}$

$\left(M_1^{SE}, M_2^{SE}, M_3^{SE}, M_4^{SE}, M_5^{SE}, M_6^{SE}\right) \rightarrow (e_1,e_2,e_3,e_4,e_5,e_6)$, with $e_i < e_{i-1}$, for $i = \overline{2,6}$

$$M \rightarrow m \rightarrow \alpha \rightarrow e$$

where M is the causality (or causal complex or causal architecture), m is the crisicity (or crisicity intensity), α is the social order and e is the entropy.

So, we have the relations:

$$m_i = g(M_i), \text{ with } \frac{\partial g}{\partial M} > 0$$

$$\alpha_i = h(m_i), \text{ with } \frac{\partial h}{\partial m} < 0$$

$$e_i = f(\alpha_i), \text{ with } \frac{\partial f}{\partial \alpha} > 0$$

The crisicity as middle term in our syllogisms can be synoptically represented as in Fig. 3.8.

We need $e_i = \xi(m_i)$, so:

$e_i = \xi[g(M_i)]$, or, alternatively, $e_i = \xi[h^{-1}(\alpha_i)]$

As said before, the analytical forms of the functions f, g, h, ξ are rather of empirical origin.

(d) An Empirical Typology of Assignment

Since, according to the causes (and their most probable combinations—see point 3.4.1, a2) of crisicity, there are six distinct and relevant cases, it is possible to provide a proposal regarding the typology of causality of societal crisis, societal crisicity, societal order and societal entropy, as they are correlated among them (*nota bene*: the classes are ordered decreasingly from the point of view of relevance and are labelled by a three-letter mark).

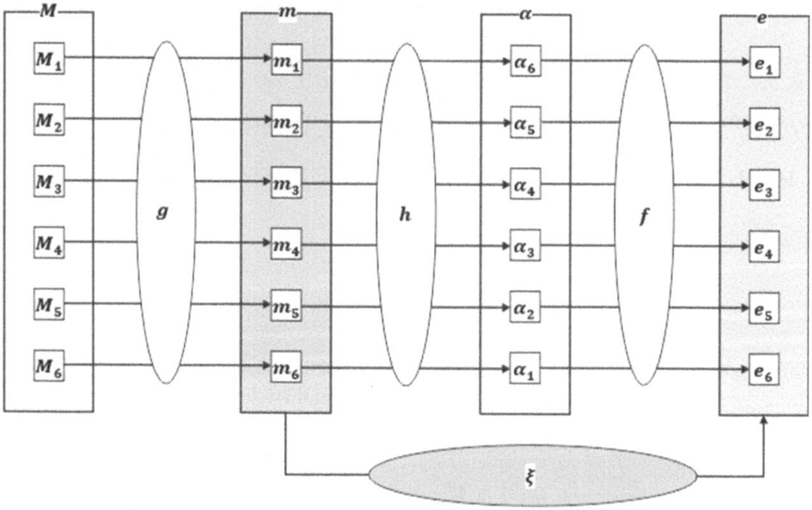

Fig. 3.8 Assigning the entropic mark to crisicity. *Source*: Author

(d1) Causality Typology (Based on the Statements of Point 2.2.1, in Chap. 2)

- (M_1) ontologically constructively inconsistency (*OCI*)
- (M_2) ontologically distructively inconsistency (*ODI*)
- (M_3) ontologically adjusting inconsistency (*OAI*)
- (M_4) ontologically constructively divergence (*OCD*)
- (M_5) ontologically distructively divergence (*ODD*)
- (M_6) ontologically adjusting divergence (*OAD*)

(d2) Crisicity Typology

- (m_1) acute, urgent and hidden (*AUH*)
- (m_2) acute, urgent and noticeable (*AUN*)
- (m_3) severe, optional and hidden (*SOH*)
- (m_4) severe, optional and noticeable (*SON*)
- (m_5) temperate, optional and hidden (*TOH*)
- (m_6) temperate, optional and noticeable (*TON*)

(d3) Order Typology

- (α_6) fractured, structural and dangerous (*FSD*)
- (α_5) fractured, structural and intolerable (*FSI*)
- (α_4) blocked, structural and intolerable (*BSI*)
- (α_3) blocked, dysfunctional and intolerable (*BDI*)
- (α_2) inertial, dysfunctional and intolerable (*IDI*)
- (α_1) inertial, dysfunctional and tolerable (*IDT*)

(d4) Entropy Typology

- (e_1) high, persistent and increasingly (*HPI*)
- (e_2) high, persistent and stationary (*HPS*)
- (e_3) medium, persistent and increasingly (*MPI*)
- (e_4) medium, irresolute and stationary (*MIS*)
- (e_5) low, irresolute and increasingly (*LII*)
- (e_6) low, irresolute and stationary (*LIS*)

3.4.4 Some Additional Remarks About the Social Entropy and Crisicity

The social entropy has rather an epistemological statute, not an undisputable ontological one. In fact, the degree of social order and the degree of social entropy are substitutable between them, as a bijective and inverse proportional relationship. The ontological relevance is "borrowed" from the relevance of the social order, so to operate with the concept of social entropy seems handier and expeditiously. The social (societal) entropy is a quite complicated concept (Dinga et al., 2020), but in the present study, we only refer to it in relation to the concept of (societal) crisis, so it can provide to observer and actor (including the government) a "map" of the statu quo of the society.

As far as the concept of crisicity, we think that it introduces a necessary (perhaps, sufficient) and useful "litmus paper" that provides a picture of the statu quo of society from the perspective of a good and desirable functioning. Although this proposal is very general and abstract, this was our exact intention, aimed at delivering a device that can be particularized anytime and anywhere. In such a way, by passing from M to m, it is possible to identify the crisicity state of the society and, from this, infer about the social order and social entropy (*nota bene*: later in the book, when the concept of autopoieticity and that of fractality in the crisis topic will be approached, the usefulness of the crisicity will appear more obvious). Moreover, the concept of crisicity allows the integration, with the required precautions, of other interesting and ingenious proposals to find early warning signals for the crisis imminence, as Minsky's structure of financing the economy, for example, being, so, a background for any such essays.

3.4.5 The Entropy-Based Positional State of Society Relative to the Crisis

It is interesting and relevant to associate the crisis typology with societal entropy. Remember the general typology of the crisis, as established in Chap. 2.

A generic crisis is identified by the label, $C_{12345}^{\alpha\beta\gamma\delta\varepsilon}$, where the inferior index indicates the five species of crisis, and the corresponding superior index indicates the class of crisis within the species in the case—when a position of the inferior index is null, this means the crisis does not belong to that species, accepted being the fact that a crisis can belong to more species simultaneously. So, we have:

- species 1 (T_1): crises according to their cause/s;
- species 2 (T_2): crises according to their origin;
- species 3 (T_3): crises according to their chreode (trajectory)
- species 4 (T_4): crises according to their impact/s;
- species 5 (T_5): crises according to their significance.

Each of the species can contain five classes of crisis, so there are 25 classes of crisis, of course, each of them being particularly hypostasized in time and space. One who is passionate about economic history could inventorize the crises that happened and classify them according to our proposed typology.

Here, we shall try to assign the three marks identified before to the 25 classes of crisis. Such an assignation has, obviously, only a didactical meaning, it is aimed to suggest to other scientists a way in which they could picture a map of the theoretical assumptions regarding the phenomenology of crisis.

We shall perform this in Table 3.2.

Short Comments

- the distribution of the α, m and e marks on the species and classes of crises is, of course, pure illustrative, since different evaluations of the crisis classes can lead to different such distributions; consequently, the proposed distribution is one of the possible such distributions;
- however, from the public policy perspective, a largely accepted distribution is desirable so that distribution could be obtained by a dedicated committee;
- at the same time, it is also obvious that different national features of the society (from cultural, historical, geopolitical and governmental perspectives) will introduce specific "attractors" for the marks distribution in the case.

Table 3.2 Assigning of the degree of order, crisicity and entropy to the classes of crisis

Species of crisis $(T_{(.)})$	*Class of crisis* $(T_{(\cdot)}^{(\cdot)})$	*Order degree/ mark* (α)	*Crisicity degree/ mark* (m)	*Entropy degree/ mark* (e)
T_1	T_1^1	α_1 or α_2	m_6 or m_5	e_6 or e_5
	T_1^2	α_3	m_4	e_4
	T_1^3	α_4	m_3	e_3
	T_1^4	α_5	m_2	e_2
	T_1^5	α_6	m_1	e_1
T_2	T_2^1	α_1	m_6	e_6
	T_2^2	α_2	m_5	e_5
	T_2^3	α_3	m_4	e_4
	T_2^4	α_4	m_3	e_3
	T_2^5	α_5 or α_6	m_2 or m_1	e_2 or e_1
T_3	T_3^1	α_1	m_6	e_6
	T_3^2	α_2	m_5	e_5
	T_3^3	α_3 or α_4	m_4 or m_3	e_4 or e_3
	T_3^4	α_5	m_2	e_2
	T_3^5	α_6	m_1	e_1
T_4	T_4^1	α_5 or α_6	m_2 or m_1	e_2 or e_1
	T_4^2	α_4	m_3	e_3
	T_4^3	α_3	m_4	e_4
	T_4^4	α_2	m_5	e_5
	T_4^5	α_1	m_6	e_6
T_5	T_5^1	α_1	m_6	e_6
	T_5^2	α_2	m_5	e_5
	T_5^3	α_3	m_4	e_4
	T_5^4	α_4 or α_5	m_3 or m_2	e_3 or e_2
	T_5^5	α_6	m_1	e_1

Source: Author

Notes

1. The considerations of this paragraph are taken over from Dinga et al. (2020).
2. See Chap. 2 for the sharp distinction between meaning and significance.
3. But not event, which is understood as spatial-temporal (i.e., contextualized) hypostasis of a phenomenon.
4. Dependence on intermediate stages leads to processual variables (of functions), not to state ones. The confusion between the process-based variables and state-based variables is not under scarcity in the scientific literature.
5. The concept of order is understood, for now, in its most abstract way.
6. The continuous versus quantum way of entropy variation is not yet fully elucidated. At the right time we'll provide our position on the matter in more detail. Here we can say that, since the variation of order in a system is perceived/measured quantum, we can infer a quantum variation of entropy (in the hypothesis of an entropy-order bijectivity).
7. This feature seems in the nature of a vitalism, a kind of like the Bergson-ian *élan vital*. (*Nota bene*: Boltzmann tried to introduce a reversibility of entropy in closed systems, based on statistic probabilities, but the issue is still unresolved. In fact, Boltzmann does not consider probabilities in their usual sense, i.e., inductively derived, as is the case, for example, of objective probabilities, but rather as possibilities: by possibilities we mean states or events, necessary or contingent, without any connection to a previous archive of states, somewhat like the propensive probabilities of Popper.)
8. Especially from an economic perspective (Tribus is granted with coining the term of thermoeconomics).
9. A very productive concept, we believe is, here, that of the fund, which is a stock having only outputs but no inputs (the pure example is the Sun). The opposition between the stock and the fund is an interesting dissociation to understand the entropical functioning of the society as a whole.
10. Such a question arise also in cosmology: if the global entropy of the Universe (as closed system) is permanently and irreversibly increasing, this means at the big-bang time, the entropy was at its minimum level, which entails a maximum degree of heterogeneity, although the singular point can be easily thought being fully homogenous.
11. Probably, the coming in cascade of the causes/conditionalities in generating the decisions and actions could not be reasonably rejected.
12. Basically, such a catalogue is formed into the individual memory but, of course, it can be also externally (so, publicly) organized, in one way or another.
13. The propensity is, generally, a manifestation of belief or, equivalent, of preferences. However, the belief is stronger and more conservative than

the preference—somewhat, the belief is the hard core, while the preference is the peripheric belt (by paraphrasing Imre Lakatos's epistemological construction).

14. For example, Düppe considers that the economic language (or the language of the economy) is or must be the language of markets. We think that, probably, such a language should be searched around the (economic/social/societal) entropy.
15. We presume we are inside a democratic and free society. If the society in the case is either non-democratic or authoritarian/totalitarian, or both, the judgements must be adjusted by introducing some normative-political constraints.
16. By societal model of rationality we understand, generally, the normative framework (both formal and non-formal) of the society, based, essentially, on the social contract as this concept is clarified by the theory of justice.
17. Of course, the term practical has here the Kantian meaning, that is, subject-subject relationship.
18. Russian Federation, China and Iran are suggestive examples for such situations.
19. Do not forget here the "law" of the announcement effect.
20. Of course, the intervals (I_j) must represent a cover of the spectrum (S), that is: (a) $\bigcup_{j=1}^{n} I_j = S$; (b) $I_i \bigcap I_j = \varnothing$, for $i \neq j$ and $i, j = \overline{1,n}$.
21. Here, we adhere to the triadic semiotic model of Peirce (firstness, secondness, thirdness).
22. The "it" evokes here an organization: government, parliament, political parties, etc.
23. The intuition can have many sources: (a) experience; (b) qualitative reasoning; (c) flair; (d) interest (especially political interest), etc.
24. Or, meanficance, or meanfying.
25. The thing in itself or, in Kant's terminology, the noumenon.
26. This allegation is valid for any kind of structure, so, for any system that can be epistemologically selected from the world (Lebenswelt), but we discuss the topic especially from the social/societal perspective.
27. Stéphane Lupasco is a Romanian-French philosopher who developed an innovative logic, starting from the natural sciences (especially from Relativity Theory and Quantum Theory) but equally applicable to Physics, Biology, and Psychic. Lupasco's logic accepts three truth values, being, in fact, a logic of the middle included: (a) *actual* (true); (b) *potential* (false); (c) *resolutional* (undetermined). *(Nota bene*: it provides a resolution of the duality between actual and potential, on a higher level of reality, but not in a Hegelian manner, since the duality is not destroyed.)

28. Of course, we can take the terminological construction further, namely, from *expla*nation and compre*hension* we can form the term (and concept, besides) of *explahension*, which has the same referential (denotate) as the term (and concept) meanfication.
29. By paraphrasing Bertrand Russell, an appropriate metaphor can suggest the very result/conclusion (*nota bene*: Russell referred to notations in logic and mathematics).
30. We remember that the perception implies, logically (usually, chronologically, too): (a) a sensation—received through one or more (in the last case, by the synaesthesia) of the six natural senses; (b) an intellectual processing of the sensation, which generates the perception. *Nota bene*: as known, besides the five "ordinary" senses, there is a sixth one, named the proprioceptive sense, i.e., the sense of the own body positioning in space—phenomenology is particularly interested in elucidation of such a sense, see, for example, the works of Maurice Merleau-Ponty.
31. *Mutatis mutandis*, the same is the case with the decreasing law of the marginal utility in the standard economics.
32. Of course, by "paying" the inherent price of the hysteresis.
33. It is hard to not observe here an issue that could generate interesting results, both logical and (perhaps) psychological, namely, the change in the perceptual behaviour (to say so) of the individual, depending on the values s/he faces or, better, depending on the assurance s/he think can count on. It seems to us we have here an issue comparable to the problem of the moral hazard but, probably, much more theoretically interesting and methodologically productive than in the case of asymmetric information or market incompleteness.

References

Bailey, K. D. (1990). *Social Entropy Theory*. SUNY Press.

Benzecry, C. E., Krause, M., & Reed, I. A. (2017). *Social Theory Now*. The University of Chicago Press.

Dinga, E., Oprean-Stan, C., Tănăsescu, C.-R., Brătian, V., & Ionescu, G.-M. (2022). *Financial Market Analysis and Behaviour. The Adaptive Preference Hypothesis*. Routledge – Group Taylor & Francis.

Dinga, E., Tănăsescu, C. R., & Ionescu, G.-M. (2020). Social Entropy and Normative Network. *Entropy, 22*(9).

Düppe, T. (2009). *The Phenomenology of Economics Life-World, Formalism, and the Invisible Hand*. Haveka BV.

Georgescu-Roegen, N. (1971). *The Law of Entropy and the Economic Process*. Harvard University Press.

Lo, A. W. (2019). *Adaptive Markets: Financial Evolution at the Speed of Thought*. Princeton University Press.
Lupasco, S. (1987). *Le principe d'antagonisme et la logique de l'énergie*. Éditions du Rocher.
Nozick, R. (1993). *The Nature of Rationality*. Princeton University Press.
Popper, K. R. (1959). A Propensity Interpretation of Probability. *British Journal for the Philosophy of Science, 10*.
Tribus, M., & Evans, R. (1963). *The Thermo-Economics of Sea-Water Conversion*, Report No.: 62–63. UCLA.

CHAPTER 4

Crisis Singularity and Crisis Periodicity

4.1 On the Singular Event in the Society

4.1.1 About the Concept of Economic

To get this, we would distinguish among three abstract ontological spaces: (a) the natural space (NS); (b) the social space (SS); (c) the economic space (ES). Although the three spaces can be viewed and analysed separately, they are, in fact, like the Russian Matryoshka, that is, the social space is included in the natural space and the economic space is included in the social spaces.[1]

To put the basic differences among the three ontological spaces, we want to establish some predicates of any of them (we will not examine here, however, the sufficiency character of such lists).

(1) In the natural space (NS): there exists *absolute necessity*
  (a) the *predictability* must be considered available at a 100% level for any natural phenomenon, i.e., that phenomenon which is under the natural laws only. Really, the natural laws require always and only the necessity. But, the necessity, by its definition, is completely predictable, once the natural law involved is known;[2]

E. Dinga, *Economic Resilience During Overlapped Crises*,
https://doi.org/10.1007/978-3-031-80224-9_4

   (b) the absence of *goals* (*nota bene*: by goal we understand that finality which is projected by the consciousness). It is not sufficient to say "which is accessible to the consciousness", because any known finality is, through that knowledge, accessible to the consciousness, but the finality could be associated with other entity than the subject in case). So, the natural space has finalities, but not goals;
   (c) the absence of *choice*. The logical combination between the complete predictability and the absence of goals requires the absence of choice. The phenomena will follow, without exceptions, the "algorithm" imposed by the natural laws; they cannot oppose them. But, any such "algorithm" excludes the choice.

(2) In the social space (SS): there exists the *necessity as objectification*
   (a) the *predictability* does not exist, because of the presence of free will; by free will we understand the capacity of a subject (either of cultural[3] type or of non-cultural type) to oppose the social necessity—generally the social necessity is expressed by institutions, formal or informal;
   (b) the presence of the *goals*, concomitantly with the *finalities*—while the goals are caused by the individuals' free will, the finality is the result of the inter-actions at individual or group level;
   (c) the presence of choice.

(3) In the economic space (ES): there exists the *contingency*
   (a) the *predictability* does not exist;
   (b) the presence of the *goals*;
   (c) the absence of *finalities*;
   (d) the presence of *choice*;
   (e) the *entropic change*.[4]

So, in the most abstract signification, the *economic* means that in ontological field where are absent the predictability, and the finality, are present the goal, and the choice, and, especially, happens the entropic change. The last sufficiency predicate—the entropic change—finely distinguishes the economic acts from all other human acts.[5]

4.1.2 About a Grammar of the Economic Event

By grammar of something must be understood the internal logic of emerging, developing, changing and disappearing of that something. By an economic event we understand a contextual (historical, social, institutional,

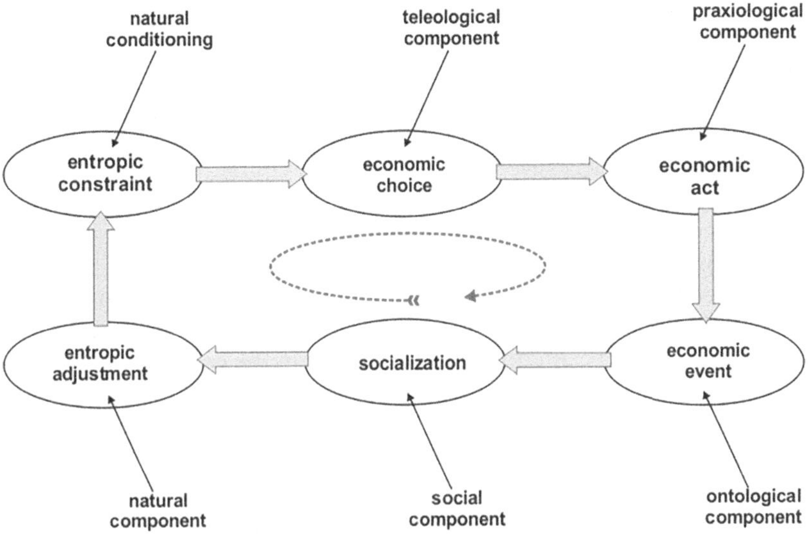

Fig. 4.1 A possible grammar of the economic event. *Source*: Author

etc.) hypostasis of an economic phenomenon. Of course, the economic phenomenon must verify the above-mentioned conditions for the economic as such. In Fig. 4.1 we try to synoptically represent a possible (stylized) grammar of the economic event.

Discussion

So, always, the entropic constraint (i.e., the necessity of the entropic change between humans and the non-anthropic environment) triggers/provides the economic. Once the entropic constraint works, the teleological component (i.e., the goal) comes and, as a result, an economic act is performed. Only that economic act, i.e., the praxeological component of the economic grammar, creates the economic "animal" named economic event, as an ontological component. The next step is the socialization of the economic event created, that is, a kind of social recognition/acceptation of such an event. This is exactly the sense in which, above, we have talked about the necessity as objectification in the social field, which—in the form of contingency—is held also in the economic field.[6] After all these, the initial entropic constraint is solved (through the entropic adjustment) and the cycle is resumed (or not, after the case[7]).

4.2 Identity, Alterity and Repeatability in the Economic Event

By identity of an event, we understand the coincidence (under an acceptable gap) between the state vectors of parameters essentially describing that event at two successive time moments. Of course, the alterity of that event is the logical negation of the identity. However, the question must be differently put regarding the dissipative systems compared with the non-dissipative systems. Considering the above mentions about the concept of economic, as well as the simple grammar of the economic event, we think Fig. 4.2 could be credited to offer a general view of the relationships among identity, alterity and repeatability in the economic territory.

So, since the economic event is conditioned from both non-dissipative and dissipative systems (blocks), both invariances and non-invariances of the initial conditions will happen in the economic causality. For example, in the case of the non-invariance of the initial conditions, which are specific for the dissipative systems, the identity is compromised (i.e., the replication will be replaced by recreation of the next state vector of describing parameters). The combination between identity and alterity, as well as between replication and recreation in the economic phenomenology, leads to the result that the economic event cannot be considered, purely, a

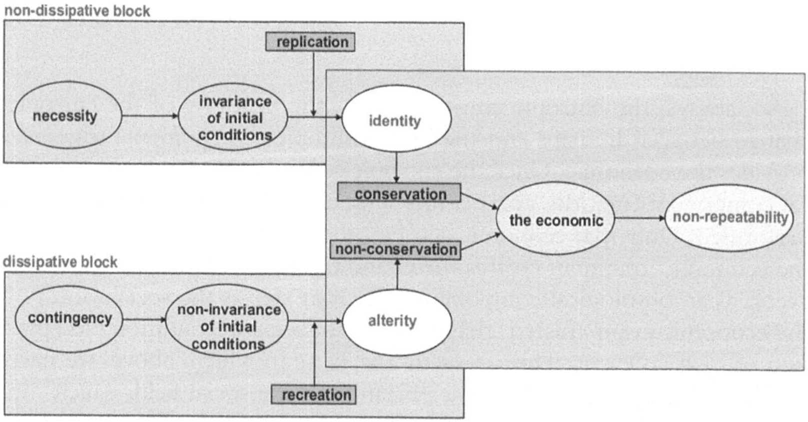

Fig. 4.2 Relationships among identity, alterity and repeatability in the economic phenomenon. *Source*: Author

repeatable event. We will name the economic non-repeatable event just an economic singular event.

In principle, the non-singular economic event (or phenomenon, as general case) is impossible, if taken into consideration the above-mentioned arguments.

4.2.1 *The Concept of Singular Economic Event*

To get the concept of singular economic event (SEE), some preliminary considerations must be done:

- as said before, an event is a particular hypostasis of a phenomenon. So, an economic event is a particular hypostasis of an economic phenomenon (the particular hypostasis is done by the historical—social, cultural, political, etc.—context);
- logically, we never meet economic phenomena, but only economic events; it is the same with the fact that, in general knowledge, we never meet the genus or the species of a concept, but only their individuals;[8]
- so, an economic event is always contextualized not only historically, but also temporally, i.e., an economic event is produced (never it happens from itself!—here resides the basic argument for a possible phenomenological economic theory in Husserlian philosophical tradition (Duppe, 2009)) by the cultural subject at a given moment of time and in a given space;
- if such an event replicates, between two successive moments of time, the state vector of describing parameters (within a pre-accepted gap) assigned to the economic phenomenon (as its genus) changes, we will talk about an economic process. In other words, an economic process is the alterity of an economic event between two successive moments of time, if the identity of the economic phenomenon concerned is maintained.

Now, a singular economic event (SEE) should be that economic event that never enters an economic process. In other words, a singular economic event is produced once and only once, that is, its genus—the corresponding economic phenomenon—has a single component as individuals or species. If, somehow, a given singular economic event is produced again, we necessarily will record an alterity of it, that is, an unacceptable

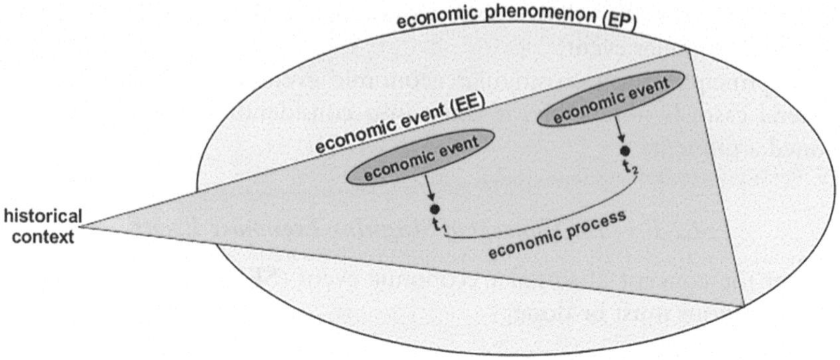

Fig. 4.3 The concept of economic event, from which the concept of singular economic event can be drawn. *Source*: Author

gap between the state vectors describing the parameters of the economic event in a case between the two moments of time considered; this means we have not to do with the same economic event, but with very different economic events only. Figure 4.3 tries to synoptically show these considerations.

4.2.2 *Economic Explanation and Prediction: The Orthodox View*

For the non-singular economic events, the standard theory accepts the logical equivalence (and chronological mirror reversal) between the explanation and prediction. More exactly, the prediction is viewed as an *ex ante* explanation, while the explanation is viewed as an *ex post* prediction (or, as used, as a post-diction). This equivalence is possible (although with some cautions, of course) only because of the non-singularity of the "classical" economic events. The most important reason for which the standard economic theory always fails in both explaining and predicting economic events consists of just considering that economic events are non-singular (i.e., repeatable). Figure 4.4 visualizes such equivalence between explanation and prediction.

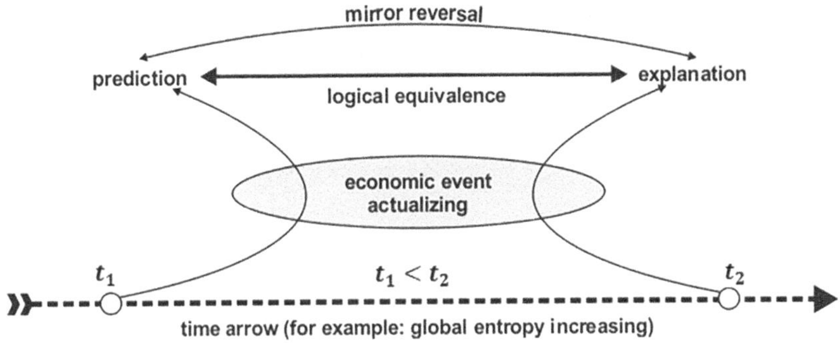

Fig. 4.4 Explanation and prediction of the economic event in the orthodox theory. *Source*: Author

As the result of logical equivalence of explanation and prediction, as well as of mirror reversibility of the two concepts, it is possible (in fact, we would say, it is logically necessary), in formulating the prediction, to take into consideration the last (or the lasts) handy explanations, and vice versa, in formulating the explanation, to take into consideration the last (or the lasts) handy predictions. But, in the economic field, as we have already seen before, the goal is present. The goal presence means some normative targets are included in our predictions, not only the phenomenological kinematics assigned to natural phenomena or events. So, our predictions, and, necessarily, our explanations, will contain a lot of such normative ingredients. Figure 4.5 shows this.

In a logical transcription, the relationships between explanation and prediction in the non-singular economic event case can be expressed as below (*E*: explanation, *P*: prediction, *N*: norm).

$$E_1 \rightarrow \left[P_1 = P_1\left(E_1\right)\right] \rightarrow \left[E_2 = E_2\left(P_1\left(E_1\right)\right)\right] \rightarrow \left[P_2 = P_2\left(E_2\left(P_1\left(E_{11}\right)\right)\right)\right] \rightarrow \cdots$$

$$E_1\left(N_1\right) \rightarrow \left[P_1\left(E_1\left(N_1\right)\right)\right] \rightarrow \left[E_2\left(P_1\left(E_1\left(N_1\right)\right), N_2\right)\right] \rightarrow$$
$$\left[P_2\left(E_2\left(P_1\left(E_1\left(N_1\right)\right), N_2\right)\right)\right] \rightarrow\rightarrow \left[E_3\left(P_2\left(E_2\left(P_1\left(E_1\left(N_1\right)\right), N_2\right)\right), N_3\right)\right] \rightarrow \cdots$$

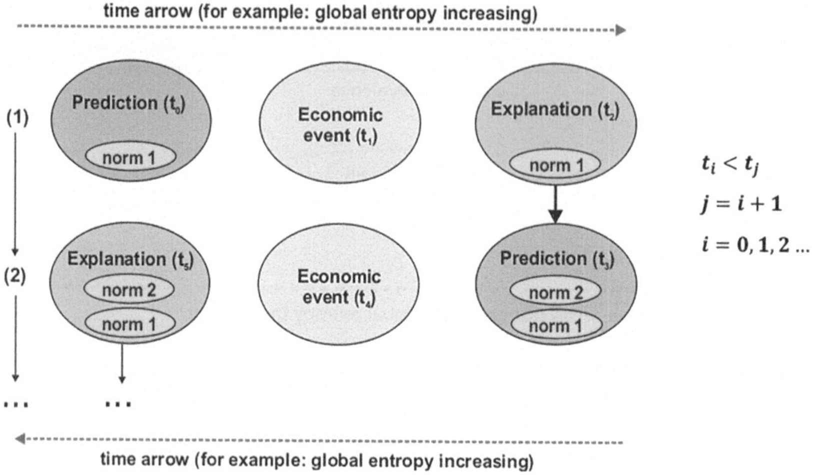

Fig. 4.5 Including the norms in the economic prediction and explanation respectively. *Source*: Author

4.2.3 *Explaining the Singular Economic Event: The Desiderative Explanation*

In the case of the singular (i.e., non-repeatable) economic event, an explanation as a description of causality is not possible anymore, because the contiguity and the constant association between cause and effect cannot be anymore observed. In such a case, we propose the concept of *desiderative explanation*. The desiderative explanation does not connect the objective cause with the objective effect, as the standard explanation does, but it connects the teleological cause (for example, the target, or norm) to the teleological effect (i.e., the expected effect related to the target or norm). To explain…the desiderative explanation, we need now to introduce a distinction between human nature and the human condition. We will say the human condition is the human nature "altered" by the culture. So, human nature requires an economic goal, while the human condition rather requires economic desirability. The combination between the two targets or norms will form just the economic event. All these considerations can be put synoptically as in Fig. 4.6. *Nota bene*: of course, symmetrically we can talk about a desiderative prediction—in Annex 4.1, an

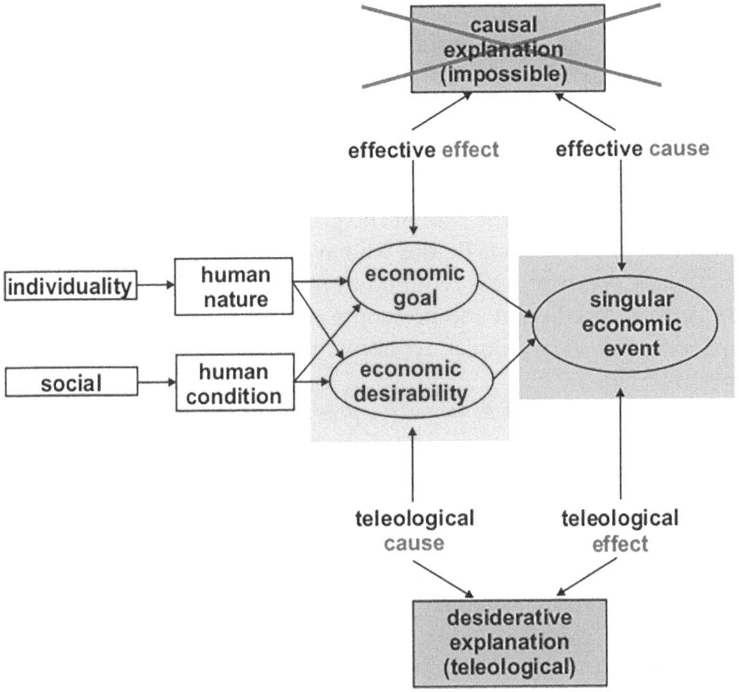

Fig. 4.6 The concept of desiderative explanation in the singular economic event. *Source*: Author

extra detailed presentation of the ***desiderative prediction*** will be provided by the intermediation of the tetravalent logic in the economic process.

In a logical transcription, the desiderative explanation could be expressed as below (*G*: goal, *DE*: desiderative explanation, *NL*: natural laws, *M*: praxeological mean, *R*: model of rationality, i.e., the justification of assigning means to the goal, *MG*: mean assigned to the goal, according to a model of rationality).

$$D_E = D_E\left(G, M_G\right)$$

$$R = R\left(G, N_L\right)$$

$$M_G = M_G\left(G, R\right)$$

$$D_E = D_E\left(G, N_L, R\right)$$

4.2.4 *Predicting the Singular Economic Event: The Desiderative Prediction*

As understood by now, in the case of a singular economic event, the prediction contains both the necessary requirements of the natural laws, and the targets/norms of the cultural subject implied. If, regarding the natural laws consequences, we can talk about the standard prediction (like in the pure natural events), in the case of the goals we must talk about prescription instead of prediction. Before we have seen that, alternatively, either prediction or prescription is required to make a "prediction". We will call a mix between prediction and prescription with the term *pres-diction*. So, the pres-diction of a singular economic event could be described completely as in Fig. 4.7.

So, a pres-diction is a *desiderative prediction*. More than that, because we do not have anymore a pure prediction in the case of the singular economic event, Popper's falsifiability testing cannot be applied here.[9] We propose four truth values (instead two, like in the classical bivalent logic: true, and false, respectively) which should be considered when testing the pres-diction in the case of a singular economic event: (a) getting the goal—which could be assimilated with the classical truth value: true; (b) failing the goal—which could be assimilated with the classical truth value: false; (c) getting the goal accompanied by negative spillovers; (d) failing the goal accompanied by positive spillovers. Consequently, the classical concept of truth values must be replaced with these four softer kinds

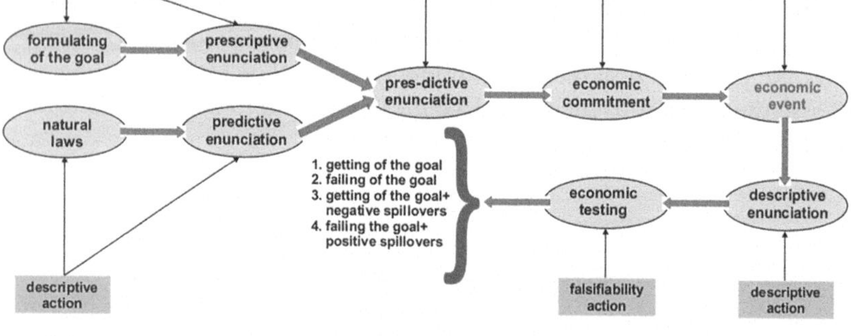

Fig. 4.7 The pres-diction in the singular economic event, and Popper's falsifiability. *Source*: Author

regarding the coincidence or not, the more or less coincidence between the expectations based on the pres-dictions and the factuals.

In a logical transcription, the desiderative prediction could be expressed as below (*G*: goal, *EP*: predictive enunciation; *EN*: normative or prescriptive enunciation; *EPN*: pres-dictiv enunciation; *ED*: descriptive enunciation; *SEE*: singular economic event).

$$E_N = E_N(G)$$

$$E_{PN} = E_{PN}(G, N_L)$$

$$E_D = E_D(S_{EE})$$

$$E_{PN} \equiv R$$

4.2.5 Predicting the Singular Economic Event: The Propensive Prediction

We want to propose, now, another type of prediction that could work in the field of the singular economic event. Such a prediction must be based on the well-known concept of the propensive probability, introduced by Karl Popper, regarding not the sets (like the classical Kolmogorov probability) but the judgements (or enunciations, in the term here used). In essence, the propensive probabilities are structural probabilities, that is, they are emerging from the structure itself of the event in case. Such probabilities never need archives of the past individuals of the event in case (so, they are adequate to the singular economic event), and in addition, they are of the same nature as Bayesian probabilities (i.e., subjective probabilities[10] which can be improved by experience/experiment). So, the propensive probabilities are not connected at all with the cognitive capacity of the subject, like the standard probabilities, but they are directly focused on the ontology of the object (singular economic event). The object itself does not exhibit uncertainties to the subject; on the contrary, it is perfectly known in advance (because of the prescription component of the pres-diction) by the subject. But, how is it possible to perfectly know a factual (an economic event) that is singular, that is, unrepeatable? Just because the economic event, including the singular economic event, doesn't happen *per se*, but it is produced, created, established even through the

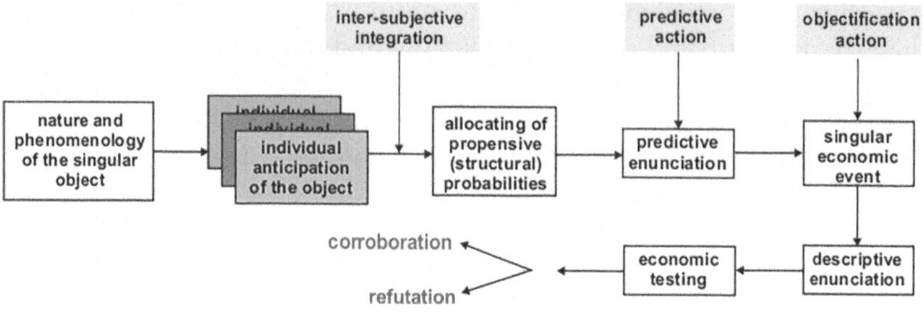

Fig. 4.8 The propensive prediction of the singular economic event. *Source*: Author

subject's action. Figure 4.8 indicates the general way of working regarding the *propensive prediction* in the singular economic event case.

In a logical transcription, the propensive prediction could be expressed as below (*CI*: individual conviction/anticipation; *CS*: inter-subjective conviction/anticipation, as result of social integration of the individual convictions/anticipations, *IS*: the process of inter-subjective integration of the individual convictions/anticipations, $\oplus$: logical constant meaning "logical sum").

$$I_S = \otimes\left(C_I\left(S_{EE}\right)\right)$$
$$C_S = C_S\left(I_S\right)$$
$$E_P = E_P\left(C_S\right)$$
$$E_D = E_D\left(S_{EE}\right)$$

4.2.6 *About the Testability of the Singular Economic Event*

To give some opinions about the testability of the singular economic event, we would say firstly that it is useful to put in the mirror the situation of the testability in the natural world and in the economic world, respectively. Figure 4.9 suggests some relevant conclusions in this matter.

So, in the economic world, where there are pres-dictions, the factual falsification in Popper's sense is not possible anymore. Consequently, we could have a procedural (i.e., confirmationalist) mechanism of testing the

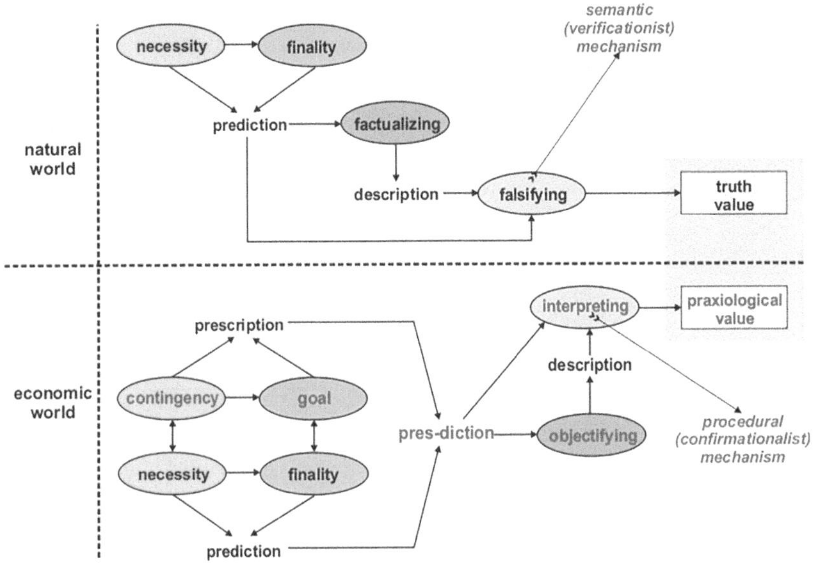

Fig. 4.9 The procedural mechanism of testing in the singular economic event world. *Source*: Author

singular economic event, while in the natural world, we can still maintain the semantic (i.e., verificationist) mechanism of testing. As a result, in the economic world we are speaking about praxeological value in testing the pres-dictions, while, in the natural world, we can still maintain the truth value of testing the predictions. Finally, in the economic world we are speaking about interpreting the comparison between the pres-diction enunciation and the descriptive enunciation, while in the natural world we can still maintain the concept of falsifying, that is, of comparing the predictive enunciation with the descriptive one.

4.2.7 *Structural Probabilities and the Singular Economic Event*

Since we have introduced above the concept of propensive probabilities in order to speak about the testability of the singular economic event, it seems to be necessary to give some details on the concept of structural probabilities in the context of a comparison between the natural world and

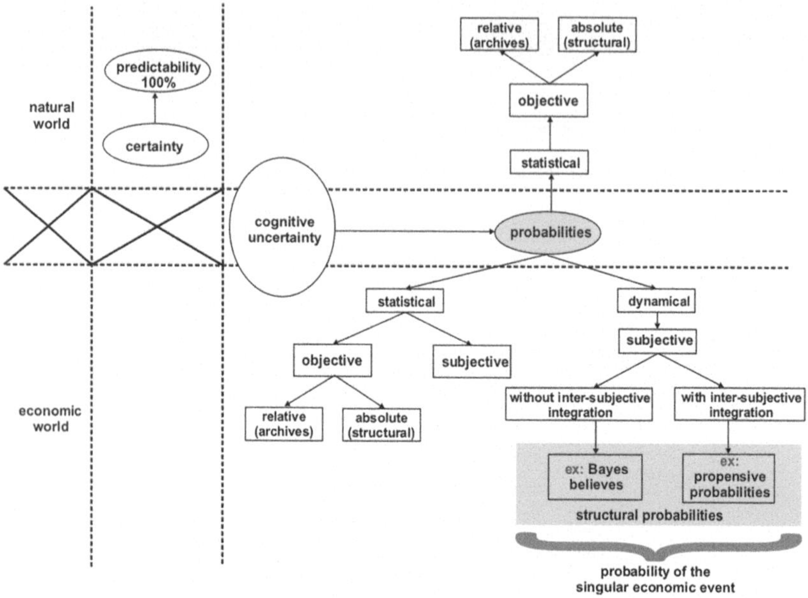

Fig. 4.10 The probability and the singular economic event. *Source*: Author

the economic world, like above. In fact, we would say that there are two kinds of probabilities which could be seriously assigned to the singular economic event: (a) the Bayes probabilities and (b) the propensive probabilities. While the Bayes probabilities are adequate rather for objects (events, processes and so on), the propensive probabilities are adequate rather for judgements, sentences, statements, enunciations, propositions and so on. In any case, the two species of probabilities can be integrated under the denomination: ***structural probabilities***. Figure 4.10 tries to systematize these short considerations.

4.3 Singularity and Periodicity in the Crisis Phenomenology

4.3.1 About the Crisis Singularity

The predicate of the singularity of an event addresses the case in which that event is not repeatable as such, i.e., it has not a repeatable invariance, if we can so say. In other words, a (societal) crisis will not happen again and again within the same parameters—cause/origin, intensity, directions of actions/effects, etc. The singularity of an event (in our case, of a crisis) is different from unicity of that event. The main semantic (referential) distinctions that must be made are as follows:

(i) Singularity Characteristics

- (*C*) *contextuality*: a singular crisis must be the outcome of its (societal) context. So, it is not conceivable a crisis which comes from "ether" with its profile and then unfolds within the society. The (societal) context, through all its conditionalities, must configure the profile and the phenomenology of the crisis. As we have seen previously, contextuality engages the interdependences between the economic crisis and the economic cycle, without the crisis being a phase or a structural component of the cycle, as considered usually both in theory and in policy;
- (*M*) *markability*: a singular crisis leaves a mark on society (structures, functions and so on). In fact, the markability of the crisis is the symmetrical effect of its contextuality: contextuality means the impact of society on the profile of the crisis (somewhat before the crisis triggering[11]), while the markability means the impact of the crisis on society.

Nota bene: to be observed the co-evolutionary suggestion of this paired impact. Society will be never the same as it was before the crisis impact and, in turn, the new crises will be never the same as the crises before. As we shall see later, we have here a so-called co-evolution of symbolic species (Dinga et al., 2023).

Therefore, generally, by crisis singularity it must be understood that the basic characteristic of the crisis is to be the "fruit" of the society functioning (so, of the society's structure) and, at the same time, to mark the society with its impact.

(ii) Unicity Characteristics

- (*nC*) *non-contextuality*: a unique crisis is not conditioned by the societal context at all. The reason is quite simple: if such a crisis would be conditioned by the societal statu quo, then it would have the potentiality to occur again, in new societal contexts. As, by definition, it is unique, and its repeatability is excluded.[12]

Nota bene 1: a question arises here: why could not we consider that a crisis is, in fact, always a... unique one, exactly because its profile is so dependent on the societal context? Although, from a logical point of view such a question can arise, it must, however, keep the possibility for crises that are completely independent from the societal context, for example, a societal crisis caused by a natural event. Therefore, we consider that the concept of a unique crisis does not lack real individuals.

Nota bene 2: another question arises, namely linked to the predictability of the unique crisis. If the singular crisis is (theoretically) predictable, based on the societal context, which acts as a causal complex, the unique crisis seems to be unpredictable (at least from the societal context perspective). Of course, it can exist in other (non-societal) contexts from whose perspective such a predictability could be found, for example, for nature-originated crises.

- (*M*) *markability*: the markability of the unique crisis is obvious since an event that occurred inside the societal system cannot affect that system. In fact, the markability of a singular crisis and the markability of a unique crisis do not exhibit notable differences. To be as scrupulous as it is necessary, it must be said, however, the following:
  - the heterogeneity between a singular crisis and society is much less than the heterogeneity between a unique crisis and society, just for the singular crisis has its causes in the society in the case;
  - consequently, the mark that a unique crisis leaves on the society is, somewhat, more heterogeneous with society than in the case of the singular crisis. Such "more heterogeneity" can objectify more radical changes caused in the structure and functioning of society.

(iii) Similarities Between Singularity and Unicity

The basic similarity between a singular crisis and a unique one is met regarding markability—both types of crisis leave traces in the structure and functioning of society inside which they occur. The changes caused upon society will have consequences for the next singular crises since the causal complex of society becomes different.

(iv) Differences Between Singularity and Unicity

The main difference between the singular crisis and the unique crisis consists in the attribute of contextuality, that is, in the connection between the society's general configuration and the cause and effect of the crisis—while the singular crisis is completely societally contextualized, the unique one is (almost) societally non-contextualized. Other differences can be noticed regarding (a) the mark the crisis leaves on the society—the singular crisis leaves marks that "resemble" the structure and functioning of the society, while the unique one leaves marks that could be strange for the current structure and functioning of the society; (b) the crisis predictability—the singular crisis is, to a large extent and with great accuracy, predictable based on the society features, while the unique crisis is, principled, unpredictable from the society profile perspective.

In conclusion, it can be said that, from the present study perspective, is of interest the singular crisis, that is the crisis that can occur repeatably, caused by the society profile itself, although in societal contexts which are changed, *inter alia*, exactly by those singular crises.

4.3.2 Singularity and Repeatability

As suggested above, the singularity of the crisis is not incompatible with its repeatability. Since the distinction between repeatability and periodicity or cyclicality will be examined later (see point 4.4.3), in this paragraph we shall try to explain why should be accepted that a (singular) crisis can come back again and again.

(a) Arguments for the Crisis Repeatability

A singular crisis, as it was been described before, is caused by the very functioning of the society.[13] In other words, the society, with its structural profile, potentially constitutes the source of the causal complex which can (and necessarily will) trigger a particular crisis, according to the "codification" provided in Chap. 3, point 3.4.5. Although the crisis occurring changes (more or less) the societal profile, the potential for new triggering of crises is kept. Remember that exactly such keeping of the potentiality of the society to generate crises, despite the impact of the past occurred crises, "guarantees" that the singular crisis is repeatable, which, in fact, justifies the compatibility of singularity with repeatability in the phenomenology of the crisis. Logically, it is impossible for two successive crises to be identical, since the first crisis has already modified the societal profile, so the new societal conditionalities will change the identity of the new crisis.[14] It results that exactly the singularity of the crisis requires its repeatability.

From a semantical point of view, there is a problem here: generally, repeatability is understood as an event that occurs again and again in its very identity, that is, it is speaking about the same event that occurs many times. From our perspective, repeatability does not imply the same event (namely, the same crisis) but a crisis that is triggered by the same cause (or causal complex). This time is, indeed, necessary to say something about the thresholds implied. Our comments are as follows:

- an effect is always the result of two factors: (a) the cause (or causal complex) and (b) the conditionalities around the cause. Consequently, the identity of an effect must be described as shown below:
  - we have said that any crisis changes the societal profile, i.e., it changes the conditionalities that will constrain the future crisis occurring;
  - the degree of such changes of conditionalities is important; if they are of such extent or/and intensity that have an impact on the causes of societal crises, then such extent or/and intensity constitute a threshold in the societal conditionalities;
  - reaching the mentioned threshold of societal conditionalities leads to the change of the cause triggering the next crisis, so changes the identity of that crisis, which means that the singular crisis repeatability is broken. (*Nota bene*: a new series of repeatability begins with the new singular crisis, generated by the new cause);
  - if, by the contrary, that threshold is not reached, the singular crisis repeatability is kept;
- it results that the chreode of a singular crisis is always interrupted when the threshold in changing the societal conditionalities is reached.

A synoptical view of the issue of singular crisis repeatability is presented in Fig. 4.11.

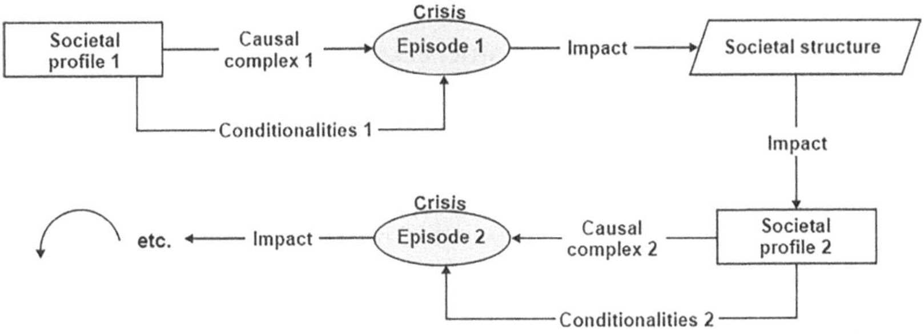

Fig. 4.11 Repeatability and threshold in the singular crisis phenomenology. *Source*: Author

Discussion

- the own structure of the society hosts the potential cause of the crisis. When the conditionalities reach their maturity, convergently with the cause (or the causal complex), the crisis is triggered. We remember that the singularity of the crisis is justified just by this ontological convergence between the cause and the conditionalities;
- the crisis unfolding impact (more or less) upon the societal structure, so the mark (the trace) of the crisis on the societal (general) profile is inevitable, in other words, has a necessary character;
- that impact changes the societal profile (at least from an economic perspective);
- recurrently, the new societal profile hosts a new causal complex targeting the crisis, concomitantly with the convergent action of new conditionalities;
- this ontological new state of affairs will trigger a new (singular) crisis (or a new episode of the singular crisis) and so on.

(b) The Meaning of the Crisis Repeatability

The repeatability of the singular crisis seems perfectly possible, under the nuances provided for the concept of singular crisis. The main significance of this repeatability is the following: the society, in its general and abstract meaning, inherently holds the potential cause and conditionalities for crisis triggering. As we shall see later, the necessary nature of the singular crisis constitutes, in fact, a self-regulating mechanism of any society whenever some functional bottlenecks happen. Simply, the society cleans up in its own yard and, of course, such a cleaning up happens repeatedly. A question could arise here: if the society's functioning can necessarily secret the conjunction between causal complex and triggering conditionalities for crises, could we not predict the crisis happening and, so, could we not prevent some possible negative impact of the crisis's occurring? We develop the following answer:

- *firstly*, it must be said that the prediction of the crisis is possible, based on the fact that the cause of crisis triggering is of structural nature. Of course, this possibility depends on the degree (and accuracy) with which the (ontological) rationality model—RM (see Chap. 2, point 2.1) identifies the real mechanism through which the potential of society to feed and trigger the crisis. Consequently, the prediction possibility has a historic character and is closely related to the scientific level of social science and economic science, respectively;
- *secondly*, we cannot be at all sure that a societal crisis should be avoided, perturbed, re-directed or limited and so on. Being the result of the actual societal profile, a crisis signals the dysfunctionalities inside the social/economic structures. To force a little bit of the language, it can be said that the crisis should be searched and expected (Taleb, 2012), especially if the society is endowed with the antifragility potential (see Chap. 1, point 1.3, for the concept of antifragility);
- *thirdly*, and against common sense, the repeatability of the singular crisis should constitute itself even as an intellectual project aimed at provoking the occurrence of crisis exactly for solving some dysfunctionalities in the societal system of interest;
- *fourthly*, it can be tried to draw a long-term "map" regarding the "eternal recurrence" (see Nietzsche's doctrine) of the singular crisis. This way, society could draw also the so-called second curve (Handy, 2016) for the most important phenomena staying under the crisis aegis.

4.3.3 *Repeatability, Periodicity and Cyclicality*

Now we shall discuss the relationships between the repeatability and the periodicity of the singular crisis. Periodicity of a repeatable phenomenon is understood as an attribute of that phenomenon to objectify itself again and again. Of course, some variability (i.e., under an established threshold) inside a pre-accepted interval size conserves the periodicity. The problem is: has the singular crisis repeatability such a periodicity? Our answer is negative and the main arguments for this are as follows:

- the impact of a given crisis on the societal profile, and, so, on the causal complex and, respectively, the conditionalities involved in a new crisis triggering, is depending on that very structure and those conditionalities. Considering that the previous impacts were cumulative,[15] it is uncertain that the new cause will be "baked" at the same time as in the past. Consequently, the maturation, so to say, of all causes and conditionalities to trigger a new singular crisis requires different intervals of time for different episodes of the crisis recurrence;
- based on the definition above provided for the singular crisis, no crisis episode is identical with the previous ones, so its chreode is strongly particularized, both as impact and as the time interval of unfolding and going out;
- maintaining the interval of two successive episodes of crisis is purely accidental, so a singular crisis is inherently repeatable but, generally, non-periodical;

Regarding the relationships between periodicity and cyclicality, we think the following considerations are of usefulness:

- the cyclicity is a periodicity with fixed time intervals of episodes occurring (of course, this time too, the thresholds inside which the cyclicality is still conserved are accepted); as the singular crisis is not periodical, *a fortiori* it is not cyclical;
- since the singular crisis is not cyclical, it cannot be a structural part (component, stage, phase) of the economic cycle, as this state of affairs has already been explained in the previous chapters.

4.4 The Economic Hypostasis of the Societal Crisis: The Financial Crisis

In this chapter, we shall try to show that any economic crisis (which our study will especially focus on) is, at least as origin, a financial crisis.

4.4.1 About Economic Identity

(i) A Conceptual Distinction

Accounting identity means a quantitative relationship between quantitative variables, a relationship that assumes quantitative equivalence between the left member and the right member of that relationship. A distinction must be made between identity and equality—while identity is definitionally justified, equality is equationally justified. (*Nota bene*: the term identity comes from the Latin *idem-identitas*, which means to be the same, and the term equation comes from the Latin *aequare*, which means to make be the same.) Specifically, identity is a *positive* quantitative equivalence (in the sense of positivism, i.e., it *is* a quantitative equivalence), while equality is a *normative* quantitative equivalence (i.e., it *must be* a quantitative equivalence). An observation: once the definitions of the variables in question are given, the identity is necessary (here the necessity has its logical meaning, i.e., the mandatory, inherent one), and therefore, in the case of the identity, there is no freedom of its construction—it is unique. On the contrary, in the case of equality, the latter is not necessary; the researcher has all the freedom to propose quantitative associations between variables, according to his research interest (freedom limited, however, by considerations of logic, obviously). It is therefore worth noting that, in the case of identity, we are dealing with a pure inference from the model of rationality proposed precisely by the accepted definitions, while in the case of equality, we are somehow dealing with a prediction—we propose the existence of a quantitative equivalence relation and then we test (logically or factually) the existence of that equivalence. As shown above, identity (which we call accounting identity) exists by virtue of the definitions given to the variables entering the identity relation, which means that identity is definitionally closed. Consequently, different definitions of the variables being worked with will generate different identities—each of which is incommensurable with any other, due to definitional closure. It is obvious the error that would be made if one were to construct an identity based on quantitative variables that come from different definitional systems. However, such an error is extremely unlikely, because when a researcher constructs identities, s/he is surely working within a single established definitional system.

Nota bene: In the present research we do not consider the concept of identity used in rather theoretical-philosophical contexts, where it has the meaning of uniqueness/personality/distinctiveness. For example, the identity of a system is given by its structure, so in this case, establishing the identity is reduced to establishing the invariance of the structure in question. In other cases, which transcend economic analysis, by identity it meant a specific, recognized mark that... identifies an individual in a population, for example, that individual's name or Social Insurance Number (SIN). All these meanings that go beyond a simple quantitative equivalence of some quantitative variables are not of interest here.

(ii) The Economic Identity

According to the distinctions made above, economic identity (or identity in economy, whether at the micro or macro level) concerns economic variables as they are defined in the pre-accepted definitional system. Economic identity has a predominantly methodological role, not a conceptual one, because conceptual identity was already given through definitions. However, economic identity is not completely superfluous, although, as has been shown, it is necessarily derivable from definitions. In other words, it must be said that identity brings an informational addition to the simple evaluation of definitions. This informational advantage (or informational added value) brought by the economic identity can be described as follows:

- it makes a logical correlation of the definitions of the economic variables involved; in fact, by constructing the identities, a *sui generis* verification of the consistency of the system of definitions in question is carried out;
- it concentrates, in a single formal relationship, a large amount of information that, otherwise, is dissipated in the definitions of the respective economic variables;
- it allows the construction of integrated (molecular) economic variables from separate economic variables (elementary, atomic), which is very useful in constructing economic judgements and reasoning;

- it allows the formulation, as such, of judgements and reasonings, by building *sui generis* syllogisms involving elementary (atomic) economic variables;
- it allows the elaboration of logical molecular sentences from the meaningful concatenation of atomic sentences.

Of course, a system of economic identities is specific to each research in the economic field and even to each researcher in that field. The versatility of the economic identity has as many degrees of freedom as the researcher who uses it has him(her)self, and it depends both on the purpose of the research and, above all, on the personality of the researcher in question—imagination, ingenuity, methodological non-orthodoxy, etc. Some problems that can be raised in connection with the construction of the economic identity, respectively with its use, are highlighted in the following:

- *tautology*: according to the definition of identity, what is written in the left member of the identity is identical (semantically) to what is written in its right member. This is, in fact, the definition of tautology. So, it must be accepted, from the beginning, that writing (formalizing) an identity means writing (formalizing) a logical tautology. Obviously, this feature of the identity does not reduce its usefulness, but it should not be ignored. Ignoring the tautological character of identity (here, of economic identity) has the serious consequence of confusing identity with equality, that is, confusing what is with what must (or expected) to be;
- *consistency*: from a logical (more general, scientific) point of view, consistency means non-contradiction, i.e., the verification of one of the principles of bi-valent (Aristotelian) logic, called the principle of non-contradiction. This means that the economic variables introduced into the quantitative identity relation must be logically compatible with each other—compatibility is checked by taking the variables in question two by two;
- *completeness*: this represents a problem of closing the identity relationship, that is, it involves the use of all the economic variables that, precisely through their totality, ensure the coherence of the respective identity. If tautology, namely consistency, is relatively easy to verify and therefore to ensure, the question of completeness in the identity relation is somewhat more difficult, and the "sentence" regarding this completeness is more problematic.

However, it is an important issue that must be satisfactorily resolved whenever an economic identity is formalized;
- *signification*: the signification[16] of economic identity is an essential "guide" in the structuring and formalization of economic identity, because, ultimately, any quantitative formalism must represent a signification (i.e., an understanding of the role or function of the identity in question) for the individual or group considered. As previously stated, the construction/formalization of an economic identity is, for the most part, a combination of pre-accepted definitions of the quantitative variables involved and the ingenuity of the researcher constructing that identity. But this ingenuity is, in turn, situated in the research interest, that is, in the signification that the future economic identity will have (or may have) for that researcher. Herein lies the source of creativity in research—the different possible significations for different researchers.

(iii) Basic Conditions of an Economic Identity

An economic identity must verify a coherent (and, as far as possible, complete) set of conditions (*nota bene*: in fact, it is about the four conditions mentioned above) which, on the one hand, ensure identity content and, on the other hand, avoid its transformation into equality (equation). Starting from the four conditions above, an economic identity will have to be characterized, in addition, by the following:

- to have a *static* character: the economic identity must refer to a given moment in the movement of the economic phenomenon in question, that is, in other words, to represent a state vector;
- to be focused on *balance*: consistently with its static character, economic identity aims at the balance of the economic phenomenon or process under consideration. The balance of an economic phenomenon/process means the identity between the variables (or sets of variables, as the case may be) that are defining for that phenomenon/process. For example, if the phenomenon/process is the market, then, as "textbook" economic theory tells us, the defining variables of the market are supply and demand—so, the deepest identity that can be written in this context is the identity between demand and supply (of course, with reference to a good or service or, at the macroeconomic level, between aggregate demand and

aggregate supply, both variables expressed, this last time, in monetary terms);

Nota bene: the simultaneous verification of the above two attributes (the static character and aiming for balance obviously leads to the concept of static balance—therefore, an economic identity always has in mind the static balance of the phenomenon, process, event considered).

- be *discrete*: in our opinion, the economic identity must be discrete. This means that if functions are used that express the economic variables entering the identity in question, these functions must be of discrete type. Discreteness seems quite natural, given that economic decisions are made discretely, economic actions are also discrete, and the recording of economic variables in state vectors or time series is discrete too;
- to be *non-causal*: this condition (or characteristic) is particularly important in the formalization of an economic identity. It is consistent and convergent with the static character of the economic identity, respectively with the fact that it aims at balance. The economic identity must express variables that are "passive" within the identity, regardless of their role and functionality in the overall dynamics of the phenomenon/process under consideration. Indeed, if economic identity is to represent a state vector, then any causation within it is inadmissible;
- contain functionally *homogeneous* variables, either only causes or only effects. This condition, in turn, is consistent and convergent with the immediately preceding one. It requires that the identity must contain either only variables representing causes or only variables representing effects, but not both variables representing causes and variables representing effects.

Nota bene: a characteristic of the set of conditions evoked above for economic identity is observed, namely that they are not independent of each other (two by two), that is, in other words, that there are semantic and logical overlaps (i.e., redundancies) among them. This is why these conditions were not "decreed" as sufficiency predicates of the concept of economic identity, but simply conditions or features of economic identity.

(iv) A Typology of Economic Identities

There are the following classes of economic identities:

(iv.1) *aggregation* identities: they are those identities that generate sum-variables from term-variables (variables are usually expressed monetarily to ensure comparability, therefore methodological summability), by indicating the sum-variable in the right-hand member of the identity, respectively the variable-terms in the left member of the identity. Of course, inverting the left member with the right member (which are, by definition, identical in value) yields identities that can be called disaggregation or analyticization. An example is GDP formation (Dinga et al., 2023);

(iv.2) *equilibrium* identities: they are those identities that reflect the state of equilibrium in an economic system or process (it is, of course, a static equilibrium, as it was pre-defined). As a rule, the equilibrium identity is not unique (while the aggregation identity is unique, at least at some level of synthesis of variable-terms), because equivalences can be found between the variables involved in the equilibrium identity in question. Equilibrium identities usually refer to markets, so we can have a master equilibrium identity (which therefore accepts variations on the possible levels of synthesis, as mentioned above) for each of the relevant economic markets in a particular analysis or research. Some synthetic examples:

- *market for goods and services*: in the aggregate market (at the value level, that is, of the sum of prices) the fundamental identity is that which "identifies" aggregate demand for goods and services with aggregate supply of goods and services

$$AD_{\Delta i} = AS_{\Delta i}$$

where: AD is aggregate demand, AS is aggregate supply and Δi is interval i (usually a fiscal year)

- *money market*: in the money market (i.e., the short-term loan market), the fundamental identity is that which "identifies" the demand for money with the supply of money.[17]

$$L_{\Delta i} = M_{\Delta i}$$

where: L is the demand for money and M is the supply of money

- *capital market*: in the capital market (i.e., the long-term loan market), the fundamental identity is that which "identifies" the total demand for financial assets with the total supply of financial assets

$$D_{\Delta i} = S_{\Delta i}$$

where: D is the demand for financial assets and S is the supply of financial assets

- *labour market*: in the labour market the fundamental identity is the one that "identifies" the labour demand with the labour supply

$$D_{\Delta i}^{L} = S_{\Delta i}^{L}$$

where: $D_{\Delta i}^{L}$ is the labour demand and $S_{\Delta i}^{L}$ is the labour supply

- *foreign exchange market*: in the foreign exchange market the fundamental identity is that which "identifies" the demand for currency with the supply of currency

$$D_{\Delta i}^{V} = S_{\Delta i}^{V}$$

where: $D_{\Delta i}^{V}$ is the currency demand and $S_{\Delta i}^{V}$ is the currency supply
Nota bene: it is easy to observe (or analytically examine) the fact that the particular identities mentioned above verify all the conditionalities proposed for the definition of the concept of economic identity.

(iv.3) *equivalence identities*: are those identities which (also based on the definition, like any identity, as shown previously) indicate the equivalence between two (or more, as the case may be) variables. It must be said that this is not a quantitative equivalence (this is covered by either the aggregation or equilibrium identities), but an equivalence of meaning, or semantic equivalence. Equivalence identities can be formulated either at the level of markets or at the level of phenomena, processes or even events, as appropriate. Examples:

- at the level of the labour market:
  - the demand for labour is equivalent to the supply of jobs

$$D_{\Delta i}^{L} = S_{\Delta i}^{J}$$

where: $S_{\Delta i}^{J}$ is the job offer

- the supply of labour is equivalent to the demand for jobs

$$S_{\Delta i}^{L} = D_{\Delta i}^{J}$$

where: $D_{\Delta i}^{J}$ is the demand for jobs

- at the level of the foreign exchange market:
  - the demand for currency is equivalent to the supply of currency

$$D_{\Delta i}^{V} = S_{\Delta i}^{M}$$

where: $S_{\Delta i}^{M}$ is the money supply

- the supply of currency is equivalent to the demand for currency

$$S_{\Delta i}^{V} = D_{\Delta i}^{M}$$

where: $D_{\Delta i}^{M}$ is the money demand.

4.4.2 *Any Economic Crisis Is a Financial One*

The statement in the sub-title requires, of course, to be proved. In Chap. 2, point 2.4.5, we have brought up some arguments regarding the distinction among the economic flows, showing that exactly that (conceptual) distinction grounds the idea that the crisis is not (cannot be) a component or phase or stage of the economic cycle. Here we shall develop those reasonings in order to reach the conclusion that, in the economic field, any crisis, as this concept has been developed by now, is, at least initially, a financial crisis only.

(a) Remembering of the Economic Flows

There are three distinct economic flows: (i) real flows; (ii) financial flows; (iii) nominal flows.

(i) *real* flows are those economic flows, either substantial or immaterial, which are susceptible to enter the consumption, either current or future consumption, as such—for example, bread, aeroplanes and wealth services. The real flows must be considered the "individuals" of the real economy. The most significant attribute of the real flows is the following: they are *non-autonomous*, obeying themselves demand and supply of goods and services;

(ii) *financial* flows are those economic flows, in a monetary form, which are constituted as value counterparts of the real flows. Since the real flows circulate within an economy by intermediation of the prices, in fact, those prices are the very financial flows. Therefore, the financial flows occur if and only if the real flows require a monetary counterpart to pass from sellers to buyers. This means the financial flows are *not* at all *autonomous* but completely depend on the real flows. The financial flows must be considered the "individuals" of the financial economy;

(iii) *nominal* flows are those economic flows, in a monetary form too, which are not directly linked either to the real or to the financial flows, although, indirectly, they have, in a last instance, such a destination. So, the nominal flows are, in fact, completely autonomous, since the mentioned last instance is, regularly, far in time from the current moment and, often, also far in space. For example, the banking loan, the interest rate, the exchange rate, the bonds and so on are nominal flows. The nominal flows must be considered the "individuals" of the nominal economy.

Figure 4.12 indicates the relationships among the three economic flows, as well as among the three economic areas.

(b) The Economic "Circuit" of the Crisis

Firstly, we shall try to demonstrate that a crisis (in fact, a species of it, namely, an economic crisis) cannot arise (or cannot be initiated) either in the real economy or in the financial economy.

(i) Real Economy Cannot, in Itself, Initiate a Crisis

The real economy, as it has been described above, balances itself, based on the following logical mechanism:

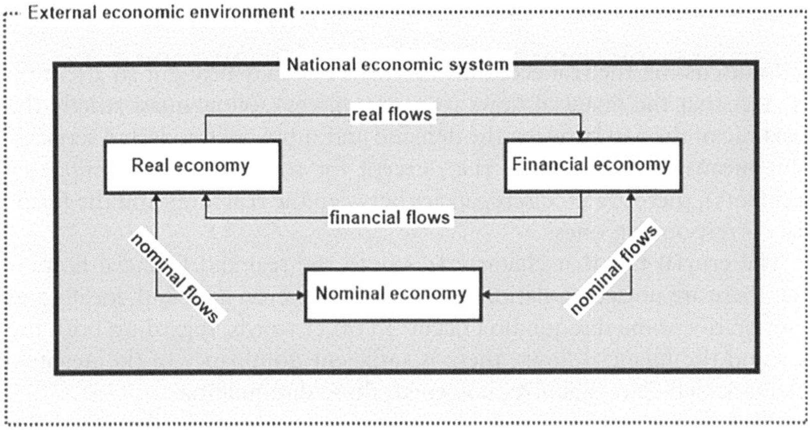

Fig. 4.12 Economic flows and economic areas. *Source*: Author

- the demand for goods and services generates investments to ensure a corresponding response from the part of the supply of goods and services;
- the gap positive between the variation of demand and the compatible variation of supply (caused by the lag between the moment of required investment and the moment of expected variation of supply) generates a variation in the general price (inflation or, more exactly, the GDP deflator), so to accommodate the new demand with the current supply;
- to put else, the demand and the supply accommodate each other, by intermediation of the price variation, ensuring, in monetary expression, the fundamental identity in the area of real economy;
- in conclusion, except accidental (and regional, for example, on certain markets) imbalances between demand and supply, the real economy does not exhibit persistent and large imbalances regarding its identity;
- as a result, we think that in the area of the real economy, there is no possibility to arise an economic crisis (of either under-production or supra-production).

(ii) Financial Economy Cannot, in Itself, Initiate a Crisis

In discussing the real economy above, we already brought to attention the fact that the financial flows (e.g., the prices) follow quasi-strictly the dynamic of the gap between the demand and supply of goods and services. This means that, essentially (i.e., except for some local and temporary accidents), there are no discrepancies between the real flows and the financial corresponding ones.

The crucial fact that characterizes both the real and financial flows is that there are no accumulations of disequilibria, even if, as said, locally and temporarily, some disequilibria occur. In other words, regarding both the real and the financial flows, there is sufficient dominancy of the negative feedbacks which re-stabilize, if needed, those disequilibria.

What it is worth noting is the following fact: the real flows and the financial flows are reciprocally led to the (dynamic) equilibrium, exactly because of the (total) dependence of the financial flows on the real ones. Metaphorically, it can be said that the financial flows are the (inherently) shadow of the real flows, since they vary in size, direction and rhythm (i.e., synchronically and diachronically) with the last.

(iii) Nominal Economy Necessarily Initiates a Crisis

We shall (try) now to show that an (economic) crisis cannot be else than a nominal crisis, namely that it mandatorily is initiated inside the nominal economy, as the (necessary, i.e., logical) result of the nominal flows mechanism.

The nominal flows have two "reasons of existence": (a) to finance the changes in demand and supply in the real economy (e.g., the banking loans, the shares selling, etc.), or the changes in the financial flows (e.g., prices increase, either of goods and services or of the labour force); (b) to speculate the money market, the currency market, the capital market and the insurance market (see the point iv.1). The first component of the nominal flows is relatively linked to the real flows (*nota bene*: in fact, by this mechanism, the lags or leads occur in the investment variation needed as a result of the variation of the demand for goods and services), and their accumulation is not viable on medium or long term, of economic reasons. Instead, the second component has another "physiology". We shall shortly describe this.

- by virtue of their autonomy from both real and financial flows, the nominal flows take that size and dynamics which are optimal for the implied economic agents;
- in contemporary economies, the phenomenology of the nominal economy is quasi-decoupled from the real economy (and, as a consequence, from the financial economy);
- in fact, excepting the initial moment in which the real flows (and stocks) trigger the nominal economy functioning (and values), rather the nominal economy "dictates" the values in the real economy than inversely;
- since the nominal economy has the potential to establish the basic values for the real economy (implicitly, for the financial economy), and, still, since the nominal economy finds in itself the reasons to function, without negative feedbacks or stabilization, this component of the economic system has, also, the potential to accumulate its own results. In other words, inside the nominal economy, there is a dominance of the positive feedbacks (and, of course, of positive feed forwards), so the nominal economy has no limit in its own exuberance;
- this way, in the economic system arises the false,[18] namely, the nominal flows cease to express the economic value of the current real flows which, based on their initial values, have initiated the forming of the nominal flows;
- this gap between the market value, delivered by the nominal flows, and the intrinsic[19] value of the real flows (and stocks) work under the market logic which, inside the nominal economy has no own pawls;
- since the economic agents operating inside the nominal economy are tempted rather to exploit the positive (for their profit) trends, they will remain on the trend of the momentum[20] and, thus, will trigger and conserve the positive feedback;[21]
- the above-mentioned behaviour will stimulate and nourish the accumulation of the evoked gap. Such an accumulation is exactly the logical content of the so-called financial bubble (the correct denomination, according to the terminology used in the present study, is, of course, nominal bubble—financial bubble is, logically, impossible as such);
- so, no matter what the cause is, and by what channels that cause acts (e.g., as Minsky shows, the structure of microeconomic level financing), the accumulation of the gap above mentioned and, conse-

quently, the nominal bubble forming are necessary phenomena, that is, they have an immanent causality which cannot be either avoided or repressed, at any rate. The only solution is (as our study will show) to accept the reality and to try to benefit from the given phenomenon;
- based on the described mechanism of the inherency of the crisis arising (only) inside the nominal economy, we shall extract the periodicity (not the cyclicality) of that singular economic event called economic crisis (*nota bene*: which is, properly said, a nominal crisis).

(iv) About Avatars of the Nominal Crisis

As we have tried to show above, an (economic) crisis can arise, namely in a necessary way, only inside the nominal economy. The problem that can be put is that of the (possible) avatars of such a nominal crisis. Does it remain inside the nominal economy and, in one way or another, it goes out on its own? Does it transgress borders and affects the other two components of the economic system, that is, real economy and financial economy, respectively? And, fundamentally, how does a nominal crisis finish itself? We shall comment, briefly, on the three questions.

(iv.1) The "Internal Circulation" of the Nominal Crisis

Inside the nominal economy, the nominal crisis has a single direction: to swell more and more, since, as said before, there is a propensity to decide and act in line with the actual momentum. There are four basic nominal markets that are working inside the nominal economy: (a) money market;[22] (b) capital market; (c) currency market; (d) insurance and reinsurance market.

Phenomenologically, the nominal crisis is the result of the quadrilateral "money-capital-currency-insurance" (MCCI), namely it is both triggered and nourished by the reciprocal augmentation of the gaps between the nominal "prices" compared with the financial ones, as those gaps emerge through the singular functioning of the MCCI components as well as through the relationships among the MCCI components. Any empirical economic crisis that occurred in recent or less recent times, at the global level, can be formalized in a mechanism that integrates the four components evoked. *Nota bene*: It is not our target here to develop the very (presumptive) general mechanism of any nominal crisis emerging and holding.

(iv.2) Nominal Crisis's "Steps over Borders"

As shown above, the nominal crisis circulates among the MCCI's components, with the inherent result of the expansion of the gap between nominal values and real/financial values (the so-called bubbling). Based on some considerations, which we shall refer to next, the nominal crisis will pass beyond MCCI's territory and will enter the real, respectively, financial economy. The problem that, from a theoretical (including epistemological) point of view, must be posed is the following: is the passing of the nominal crisis beyond MCCI a necessary or a contingent process? Our answer is organized below:

- the nominal flows are, as already shown, autonomous as related to the real/financial flows. However, this autonomy is, somewhat, only an autonomy of the "middle". We mean by the syntagma ***autonomy of the middle*** the following characteristics:
  - the nominal values (for any of the four structural components of MCCI) start based on the current values of real/financial entities (quantities, prices and so on);
  - once the real/financial values become nominal values, i.e., the nominal markets take over those values, these markets start to work independently from the real/financial economy; more exactly, the respective markets work based on relationships among them only;
  - this way, the nominal economy enters its logic (preponderantly based, as shown above, on positive feedback which is based, in turn, on the propensity to decide in line with the momenta of the four nominal markets;
  - this mechanism is specific to the middle of the nominal crisis chreode, for which we have said that the nominal economy keeps the autonomy of the middle;
- at a (given) moment of time, however, the nominal crisis reaches a breaking point, but this moment of time is no longer independent from the real/financial economy, exactly like the starting point was not independent from the real/financial economy. In other words, the edges of the nominal crisis are linked to the real/financial economy—both the emerging and the breaking of the nominal crisis imply the real/financial economy.

(iv.3) The Going out of the Nominal Crisis

(iv.3a) Some Preliminaries

Any system, no matter its nature (objective, subjective or objectified), has either a turning point or a breaking point. The system endowed with one (or many, after the case) turning point(s) possesses a relative predominance of the negative feedback, so, after a threshold of accumulation of the changes, the system works counter-cyclically (also, no matter whether this turning is caused by the human factor within that system or it is incorporated into the very structure of the system, for example, through automatic stabilizers). The system endowed with one (or many, after the case) breaking point(s) possesses a relative predominance of the positive feedback, so, after a threshold of accumulation of the changes, that system explodes or implodes its structure and, as a result, destroys its (standard) functioning. We can call the systems/processes endowed with turning point(s) sustainable systems/processes (SS/P), and the systems/processes endowed with breaking point(s) catastrophic systems/processes (CS/P).

It is required now to show what kind of system/process is the nominal crisis. In our opinion, the nominal crisis, as it was described and characterized above, is a system/process of CS/P type. The arguments brought in defending such a position are the following:

- the nominal crisis takes the "colour" of the nominal economy (which is its institutional framework); as the nominal economy is almost completely autonomous as related to the real or financial economy, it results that the nominal crisis has, in turn, an almost complete autonomy within the economic system;
- such an autonomy favours the pro-cyclical behaviour, no matter if the momentum of the nominal market is increasingly or decreasingly;
- necessarily, a pro-cyclical behaviour (nourished by the predominance of positive feedbacks) is not compatible with turning points but, on the contrary, builds up breaking points;
- consequently, the nominal crisis is a system/process of CS/P type.

Nota bene: we recall that the CS/P nature of the nominal crisis does not depend on a particular normative framework, a particular political or governmental regime, and other of the same kind, although it depends, of course, on a sufficient degree of market freedom and, also, on a sufficient degree of development of the (four categories of) nominal markets. In other words, it is needed a complete system of markets (real, financial and nominal) and a robust and sufficiently predictive normative framework.

(iv.3b) The Mechanism

The final edge (deadly finality) of the nominal crisis consists in its throwing upon the real/financial economy. To describe the mechanism through which the nominal crisis reaches its breaking point and, so, (which is logically equivalent) it spills over into the real/financial economy, we use the synoptic representation in Fig. 4.13.

Discussion

(1) Qualitative Generalities
   (a) based on the structural (inherent) positive feedback, the nominal crisis unfolds by a chain of its own cycles, so at each such cycle its "distance" from the eventual breaking point narrows—in Fig. 4.13, this path is represented by more and more areas of the nominal crisis in the case;

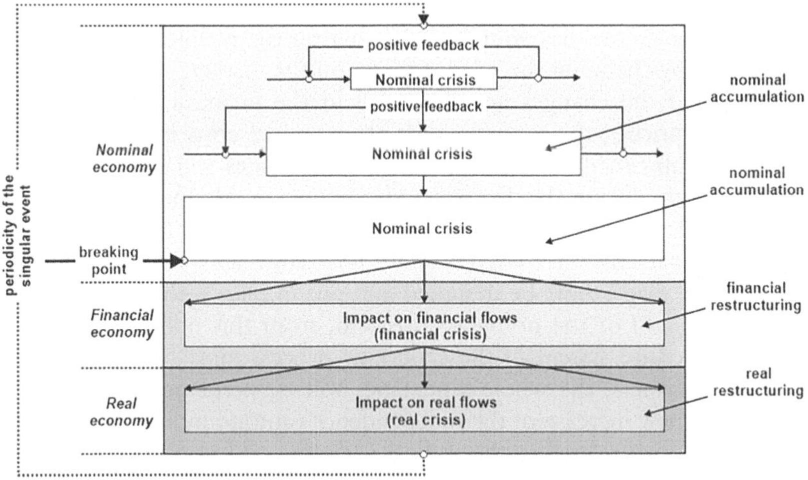

Fig. 4.13 The mechanism of nominal crisis's breaking point. *Source*: Author

(b) each cycle of functioning of the nominal crisis leads this crisis in a single direction, namely towards the breaking point, through the accumulation of nominal tension in the economic system—by nominal tension we understand exactly the increase of the independence of the nominal flows from the initial (and of substrate) real flows.[23] This self-catalysing phenomenon is named, in the economists' jargon, financial (*nota bene*: correctly, nominal) bubble and, indeed, the meaning is exactly like a balloon/bubble that is continuously inflated. In fact, we have, here, a kind of… nominal flow inflation;[24]
(c) at the breaking point, the nominal crisis (flows) impact the financial ones—we can say that the nominal crisis passes into a financial crisis. As a financial crisis, the former nominal crisis changes the financial counterparts of the real flows—for example, the prices—in an attempt to reduce the accumulated tension related to the independence of the nominal flows from the real ones. These (general) changes introduced into the financial economy could be sufficient to de-tension the nominal bubble until a point of stability—this point could constitute a starting point for a new cycle of the nominal crisis, without it entering the real economy (real economic flows). Here we have an *incomplete overspill* of the nominal risk into the real economy—we can say that since by modifying the prices, nominal crisis has an indirect impact on the real economy, exactly by changing the relative prices on the market;
(d) if the changes are generated in the financial flows (relative prices), the tension inside the nominal crisis is not integrally absorbed, and the relative price changes will pass further in modifying the demand and supply of goods and services, so in modifying the real economy (real flows). This time, the nominal crisis has arrived at its final edge and a new economic "map" must be designed and put in place—this is a *complete flood* of the nominal crisis and, from this point further, the entire system of the economic process must be changed. Of course, the whole kinematics will be perpetually resumed: a new increase of the independence (autonomy) of the nominal flows related to the real ones begins and so on.

Annex 4.1: The Tetravalent Logic of the Economic Process (an Illustrative Sketch)

The bivalent logic usually performed in the economic discipline and thinking seems to be unsatisfactory because, in the social field, almost all the actions are based on teleology, i.e., on the goals. Consequently, Annex 4.1 discusses a proposal to introduce tetravalent logics in the social field (so, in the economic one) that exhibits four truth values. In this context, the chapter develops some considerations regarding the conceptual and methodological issues associated with such a tetravalent logics proposal.[25]

1. *General Framework*

We consider that the following coordinates should underlie a possible solution to clarify the matter of truth in the economy (broader, within the social field):

- in the economy (broader, within the social field), due to the presence of the cultural subject within the structure of the economic phenomenon/process, the purpose is the dominant cause of any such phenomenon/process. For the moment, we are not interested in whether this purpose is individual or not, whether it is decided at the individual level or not. As shown, the economic phenomenon/process doesn't exist per se; rather it is generated by the decision and/or the action of the subject (all the economic phenomena/processes are, so, artefacts);[26]
- the immediate consequence of the previous trait is that the prescriptive statements (enunciations) are dominant in the economy. By prescriptive statement we understand a statement or assertion which indicates goals or procedures/means to reach the goals.[27] The prescriptive statements are, like the predictive ones, prior to the relevant factual, but they don't refer just to the factual itself, like the predictive statements, but rather concomitantly the factual, the subject and its action to generate the factual. The formal presentation of the two categories of statements (predictive and prescriptive) might look like this:
  - *F*: concerned factual
  - t_{-1}: moment of time when the prescriptive or predictive statement about the concerned factual is formulated

- t_0: moment of time when the factual concerned by the prescriptive or predictive statement occurs
- t_1: moment of time when the descriptive statement is formulated
- $t_{-1} < t_0 < t_1$: time arrow condition
- F_0: actual factual
- $\dot{F}_{-1}$: factual concerned by the predictive statement
- $\ddot{F}_{-1}$: factual concerned by the prescriptive statement
- $\dddot{F}_1$: factual concerned by the descriptive statement
- P_{-1}: predictive statement
- N_{-1}: prescriptive statement
- D_1: descriptive statement

We might then have the following formal presentations (which we will subsequently use):

$$P_{-1}(F) = P(t_{-1}, \dot{F}_{-1})$$

$$N_{-1}(F) = N(t_{-1}, \ddot{F}_{-1})$$

$$D_1(F) = D(t_1, \dddot{F}_1)$$

- based on the first two explanations, we can now make the third one: in the economic field (broadly, in the social field), the correspondence-truth is not relevant because the economic factual is not described by predictive statements, but rather by prescriptive ones. Within this context, the descriptive statement doesn't inform about the factual only, but about three elements: (a) the factual itself; (b) the subject which has issued the prescriptive statement which, most times, at the individual, collective or representative level is the same with the subject which generates the focused factual; (c) the action which led to the appearance of the factual;[28] on this basis, the formal description above concerning the prescriptive statements and the descriptive statements associated to them, will change as follows:

$$\mathcal{N}_{-1}(F) = \mathcal{N}\left(t_{-1}, \ddot{F}_{-1}, NS_{-1}, SA^{N}_{[-1,0]}, AN_{[-1,0]}\right), \text{ where:}$$

NS_{-1}: deciding subject (or normative subject); $AS^{N}_{[-1,0]}$: actional subject as it is set by the normative subject; $NA_{[-1,0]}$: the action required (normed) to perform the factual F_{-1} .

$\mathcal{D}_1(F) = \mathcal{D}\left(t_1, \dddot{F}_1, AS^A_{[-1,0]}, ES_1, PA_{[-1,0]}\right)$, where:

$SA^A_{[-1,0]}$: actual actional subject (or praxeological subject); SE_1: evaluating subject (or observing subject); $PA_{[-1,0]}$: action accomplished (implemented) which produced the factual F_0.

- therefore, in the economic field, testing the "truth" is done by comparing the prescriptive and descriptive statements, as they were described above:

$\mathcal{N}_{-1}(F) \backslash \mathcal{D}_1(F)$, or

$\mathcal{N}\left(t_{-1}, \ddot{F}_{-1}, NS_{-1}, AS^N_{-1}, NA_{[-1,0]}\right) \backslash \mathcal{D}\left(t_1, \dddot{F}_1, AS^A_{[-1,0]}, ES_1, PA_{[-1,0]}\right)$, where:

"\": our choice of noting the logic constant *is compared with*.

- due to the complex character of the economic system/process (generated by the structural presence of the subject), any prescriptive statement will have two components: an eutaxiological one, aimed to capture, within the economic process, the necessary type of causality,[29] and a teleological one, aimed to capture the contingent type of causality (in our case, the causality based on purpose). We may accept[30] that we have a linear overlapping of these two types of causality. If we describe a prescription based on this linear overlapping as $\mathcal{N}_{-1}(F) = \alpha \cdot E + \beta \cdot T$, where E is the eutaxiological component and T is the teleological component, while α and β are weighting coefficients ($\alpha << \beta$ and $\alpha + \beta = 1$), then a prescriptive statement can be represented as in Fig. 4.14

The prescriptive statement will thus have the following formulation:

$$\mathcal{N}\left(t_{-1}, \dot{F}_{-1}, \ddot{F}_{-1}, NS_{-1}, AS^N_{-1}, NA_{[-1,0]}\right)$$
$$= \alpha_{-1} \cdot E\left(t_{-1}, \dot{F}_{-1}, NS_{-1}, AS^N_{-1}, NA_{[-1,0]}\right) + \beta_{-1} \cdot T\left(t_{-1}, \ddot{F}_{-1}, NS_{-1}, AS^N_{-1}, NA_{[-1,0]}\right)$$

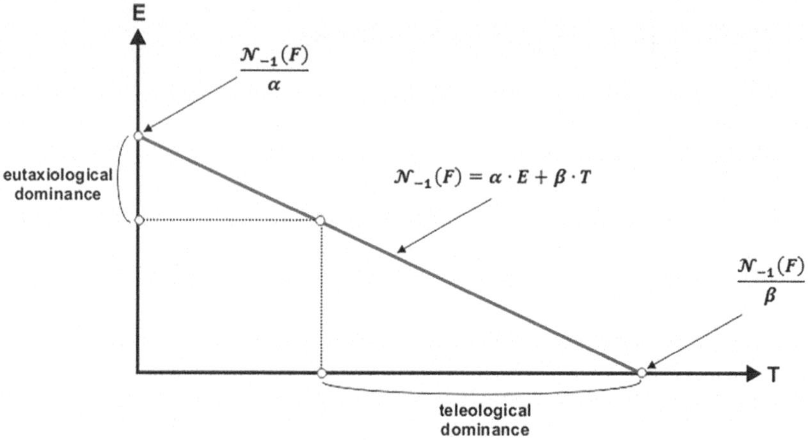

Fig. 4.14 Linear overlapping within the structure of the prescriptive statement. *Source*: Author

The descriptive statement will thus have the following formulation:

$$\mathcal{D}\left(t_1, \dddot{F}_1, AS^A_{[-1,0]}, ES_1, PA_{[-1,0]}\right) = \\ = \alpha_1 \cdot E\left(t_1, \dddot{F}_1, AS^A_{[-1,0]}, ES_1, PA_{[-1,0]}\right) + \beta_1 \cdot T\left(t_1, \dddot{F}_1, AS^A_{[-1,0]}, ES_1, PA_{[-1,0]}\right)$$

As α_1 depends on β_{-1} (the proportion "allocated" to normativity in developing the prescriptive statement introduces restrictions for the accomplishment of eutaxiology when the factual occurs, therefore within the linear structure of the descriptive statement), we may write:

$$\mathcal{D}\left(t_1, \dddot{F}_1, AS^A_{[-1,0]}, PA_{[-1,0]}\right) = \\ = f(\beta_{-1}) \cdot E\left(t_1, \dddot{F}_1, AS^A_{[-1,0]}, ES_1, PA_{[-1,0]}\right) + \beta_1 \cdot T\left(t_1, \dddot{F}_1, AS^A_{[-1,0]}, ES_1, PA_{[-1,0]}\right)$$

Purely theoretically, and simplifying the algebraic formulations just with an illustrative role, we may have the following cases of the prescriptive statement, depending on the values taken by coefficients α and β (Table 4.1):

Table 4.1 The prescriptive statements cases

	α	β_{-1}	β_1	β_1 vs. β_{-1}	β	$\mathcal{N}\left(t_{-1}, \ddot{F}_{-1}, SN_{-1}, AN_{[-1,0]}\right)$
Case 1	$\alpha \neq 0$	$\beta_{-1} = 0$	$\beta_1 = 0$	$\beta_1 = \beta_{-1}$	$\beta = 0$	Exclusive eutaxiology
Case 2			$\beta_1 \neq 0$	$\beta_1 \neq \beta_{-1}$	$\beta \neq 0$	Linear superposition between eutaxiology and teleology
Case 3		$\beta_{-1} \neq 0$	$\beta_1 = 0$	$\beta_1 \neq \beta_{-1}$	$\beta \neq 0$	
Case 4			$\beta_1 \neq 0$	$\beta_1 = \beta_{-1}$	$\beta = 0$	Exclusive eutaxiology
Case 5				$\beta_1 \neq \beta_{-1}$	$\beta \neq 0$	Linear superposition between eutaxiology and teleology
Case 6	$\alpha = 0$	$\beta_{-1} = 0$	$\beta_1 = 0$	$\beta_1 = \beta_{-1}$	$\beta = 0$	Doesn't formulate prescriptive propositions
Case 7			$\beta_1 \neq 0$	$\beta_1 \neq \nu_{-1}$	$\beta \neq 0$	Exclusive teleology
Case 8		$\beta_{-1} \neq 0$	$\beta_1 = 0$	$\beta_1 \neq \beta_{-1}$	$\beta \neq 0$	
Case 9			$\beta_1 \neq 0$	$\beta_1 = \beta_{-1}$	$\beta = 0$	Doesn't formulate prescriptive propositions
Case 10				$\beta_1 \neq \beta_{-1}$	$\beta \neq 0$	Exclusive teleology

Source: Author

- *Cases 1 and 4*: pure phenomenological predictive statements (exclusively eutaxiological)
  - for instance: predictions regarding the evolution of fossil fuel reserves
- *Cases 7, 8 and 10*: pure normative prescriptive statements (exclusively teleological)
  - for instance: prescribing (norming) the maximal public budget deficit
- *Cases 6 and 9*: impossibility (or uselessness) of formulating prescriptive statements in economy
- *Cases 2, 3 and 5*: standard prescriptive statements, relying on the linear overlapping between eutaxiological and teleological
  - for instance: prescribing the annual inflation (average or at the end of the year) or prescribing the nominal exchange rate.

2. *Concept of Truth in Economy*
   2.1. Four Values of Occurrence[31] in the Economic Field

Let us see how the comparison between the prescriptive and the descriptive statements must be done and how to decide on the "truth" of the prescriptive statement.

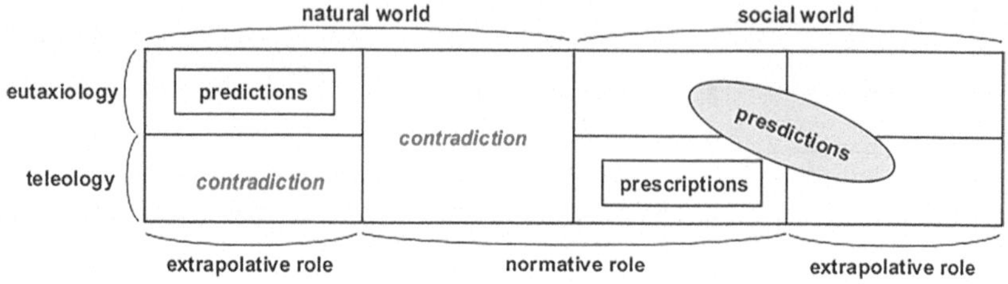

Fig. 4.15 Cases of predictions, prescriptions and presdictions. *Source*: Author

First, we set, within the new framework of the discussion, the differences between the predictive and the prescriptive statements. These are shown in Fig. 4.15.

Nota bene: the term invented by us for the present needs—*presdictions*—signifies the linear overlapping of predictions and prescriptions, when both eutaxiological and teleological causalities appear concomitantly.

Second, remember that we have to compare three entities which can be found, at particular moments of time, both in the prescriptive statement and in the descriptive statement:[32] (a) the factual itself; (b) the subject which issued the prescriptive statement; (c) the action which caused the appearance of the factual.

- for the factual: $\ddot{F}_{-1} \setminus \dddot{F}_{1}$;
- for the decision-making subject: $NS_{-1} \setminus AS^{N}_{[-1,0]}$; $NS_{-1} \setminus AS^{A}_{[-1,0]}$; $NS_{-1} \setminus ES_{1}$; $AS^{N}_{[-1,0]} \setminus AS^{A}_{[-1,0]}$; $AS^{N}_{[-1,0]} \setminus ES_{1}$; $AS^{A}_{[-1,0]} \setminus ES_{1}$;
- for the action: $NA_{[-1,0]} \setminus PA_{[-1,0]}$.

Therefore, unlike the standard case (for instance, that of the correspondence-truth), this time we don't just compare semantically the content of the prescriptive and descriptive statements (in terms of the coincidence of denotations signified by each of the two statements); instead we have to check other two "coincidences": between the involved subjects and between the involved actions.

Third, we consider, relying on what we have already shown, that in the economic field (broadly, in the social field) it is necessary that the bivalent logics, with the two truth values—true (A) and false (F)—which is compatible with the correspondence-truth (inadequate, irrelevant and impossible to verify because, in this field, we almost don't have predictive statements)—must be replaced by a tetravalent logics,[33] with four "truth" values:

1. A: nominal accomplishment, "with no rest", of the prescribed purpose;
2. $\bar{A}_+$: nominal missing of the purpose,[34] however, accompanied by unintentional[35] consequences, convenient to the subject;
3. A_-: nominal accomplishment of the purpose, but accompanied by unintentional consequences, non-convenient to the subject;
4. $\bar{A}$: nominal missing, "with no rest", of the purpose.

We have to notice the following issues regarding this proposal:

(a) we don't put the issue of the discrete levels of accomplishing the purpose, because that would lead to logics with an infinite, even countable, set of truth values (polyvalent logics); we also don't raise the issue of the continuous levels of purpose accomplishment, because it would lead to logics with an infinite and uncountable set of truth values (fuzzy logics); therefore, the purpose is either accomplished or unaccomplished, and for each of these cases, we introduce the possibility that the accomplishment or unaccomplishment is accompanied by unintended consequences with opposite significance: non-convenient to the subject (nominal accomplishment, "with rest", of the purpose), or convenient to the subject (nominal missing, "with rest", of the purpose);

(b) the nominal missing, "with rest", of the purpose is not equivalent with the partial accomplishment (therefore with a partial level of accomplishment of the purpose) because the convenient unintentional consequences, by definition, are not part of the purpose; similarly, the nominal accomplishment, "with rest", of the purpose is not equivalent with the full (more precise, accurate) unaccomplishment of the purpose, because the non-convenient unintentional consequences, by definition, are not part of the purpose;

(c) applying Karl Popper's suggestion to make predictions about the unintended consequences of our decisions leads, in terms of logics, in our opinion, to the classical prediction: indeed, an unintended consequence, not being part of a purpose (case in which it would become intended), can't have a contingent character, rather a necessary one; therefore, it will not submit to the teleological causality, rather to an eutaxiological causality. However, as seen in Figure 68, such a situation can only be dealt with using predictions;

(d) we will also notice that we have no less than six comparative situations regarding the subject involved in the matter of the economic truth, while in the case of predictions (the correspondence-truth) the subject appears neither in the predictive statement nor in the descriptive statement, because we only have eutaxiological causality generated by necessity;

(e) the two values of truth in the cases "with rest" are generated by the fact that, in the economic field, the normative subject (*NS*) can differ from the actional subject (*AS*) and from the evaluating subject (*ES*). Here there are the following possible situations:

(1) $NS \equiv AS \equiv ES \equiv S^{NAE} \rightarrow \mathcal{N}\left(t_{-1}, \ddot{F}_{-1}, S_{-1}^{NAE}, NA_{[-1,0]}\right) \setminus \mathcal{D}\left(t_{1}, \ddot{F}_{1}, S_{1}^{NAE}, PA_{[-1,0]}\right)$

(*Nota bene*: the sign "≡" has the significance of ***identical*** or ***equivalent***): therefore, in this case we have only two elements to compare: (a) $\ddot{F}_{-1} \setminus \ddot{F}_{1}$; (b) $NA_{[-1,0]} \setminus PA_{[-1,0]}$. We may formulate this comparison as follows: the prescribed factual is compared to the produced factual under the conditions in which the prescribed action is compatible with the actual action. But what does it actually mean that the prescribed action is compatible with the actual action? Here there are some considerations:

- *first*, what does it mean that all the three involved subjects are identical (or equivalent, more generally)? It means, of course, that all subjects aim for the same purpose, which means that we have the following expectation: $\ddot{F}_{-1} \equiv F_{0} \equiv \ddot{F}_{1} \equiv F$. Of course, the equivalence of the subjects doesn't involve their ontological identity: this means that the three subjects may be ontologically different[36] (each of them is a different person) but praxeologically equivalent (have the same purpose, each in terms of their "role": prescribing the purpose, accomplishing the purpose, evaluating the accomplished purpose). In order to suggest in a formal manner this difference between the ontological equivalence and the praxeological equivalence, we will adjust the above notation as follows:

  ontological equivalence: $x \overset{\leftarrow}{\equiv} y$
  praxeological equivalence: $x \overset{\rightarrow}{\equiv} y$

On the other hand, the subjects can be ontologically identical, but praxeologically different. This situation occurs when the initial conditions of the subjects change either in the temporal interval $[-1,0]$, i.e., between the time of formulating the prescription and the time of accomplishing the action, or in the temporal interval $[0,1]$, between the time of accomplishing the action and the moment of evaluating its result. In terms of our scientific interest, the praxeological equivalence of the subjects is important, not their ontological equivalence;[37]

- *second*, it is obvious that the prescribed factual is the very purpose; therefore comparison $\ddot{F}_{-1} \setminus \dddot{F}_1$ tells us whether the purpose has been accomplished or not;
- *third*, from comparison $NA_{[-1,0]} \setminus PA_{[-1,0]}$ we should find out whether unintended consequences appeared after $PA_{[-1,0]}$; in our opinion, if the three involved subjects are praxeologically equivalent, the prescribed action will be identical (or equivalent, in terms of significance) with the accomplished action, namely $NA_{[-1,0]} \equiv PA_{[-1,0]}$;
- *fourth*, therefore, the compatibility between the prescribed action and the accomplished action (actual action) means that the two stances of the action (prescribed and actual) have the same significance for the subject who makes the evaluation;

(2) $\overrightarrow{NS} \equiv \overrightarrow{AS} \equiv S^{NA} \cdot \overrightarrow{ES} \rightarrow \mathcal{N}\left(t_{-1}, \ddot{F}_{-1}, S_{-1}^{NA}, NA_{[-1,0]}\right) \setminus \mathcal{D}\left(t_1, \dddot{F}_1, ES_1, PA_{[-1,0]}\right)$: in this case we have a praxeological equivalence between the normative subject and the actional subject, but the evaluating subject is different from the two subjects. The comparison between the prescriptive statement and the descriptive statement is also done for two components of the two statements, (a) $\ddot{F}_{-1} \setminus \dddot{F}_1$ and (b) ,$NA_{[-1,0]} \setminus PA_{[-1,0]}$, but there is the possibility that $\ddot{F}_{-1} \equiv \dddot{F}_1$ because of the different evaluation of $NA_{[-1,0]}$, or of $PA_{[-1,0]}$. Therefore, we may have here the following sub-cases:

- $\ddot{F}_{-1} \hat{\equiv} \dddot{F}_1$ (where $\hat{x}$ denotes the situation "with rest", convenient, which accompanies the logical constant x), showing that the prescribed (normed) purpose was not accomplished, but unintended consequences, convenient for the evaluating subject[38] appear; formally, we have a situation of the type $\overline{A}_+$;
- $\ddot{F}_{-1} \check{\equiv} \dddot{F}_1$ (where $\check{x}$ denotes the situation "with rest", non-convenient, which accompanies the logical constant x), showing that the prescribed (normed) purpose was accomplished, but unin-

tended consequences, non-convenient for the evaluating subject appear; formally, we have a situation of the type A_{-};

- $\ddot{F}_{-1} \equiv \dddot{F}_{1}$: the prescribed (normed) purpose is accomplished, "with no rest"; although the normative subject is different praxeologically (but possibly equivalent ontologically[39]) from (with) the evaluating subject, we cannot exclude the situation in which the two subjects have the same evaluation about the accomplishment of the prescribed purpose; formally, we have a situation of the type A;
- $\ddot{F}_{-1} \equiv \dddot{F}_{1}$: the prescribed (normed) purpose is not accomplished, "with no rest"; formally, we have a situation of the type $\bar{A}$;

(3) $\overrightarrow{NS} \equiv \overrightarrow{ES} \equiv S^{NE} \not\equiv \overrightarrow{AS} \rightarrow \mathcal{N}\left(t_{-1}, \ddot{F}_{-1}, S_{-1}^{NE}, NA_{[-1,0]}\right) \setminus \mathcal{D}\left(t_{1}, \dddot{F}_{1}, S_{1}^{NE}, PA_{[-1,0]}\right)$: in this case we have a praxeological equivalence between the normative subject and the evaluating subject and a difference between them in relation to the actional subject. Similarly to the above situation, the differences in accomplishing the purpose (leading to the same four situations as those described at pct. (2)) are generated by the fact that the actional subject, being different both from the normative subject and from the evaluating one, can implement an action which deviates from the normed action, namely $NA_{[-1,0]} \setminus PA_{[-1,0]}$;

(4) $\overrightarrow{AS} \equiv \overrightarrow{ES} \equiv S^{AE} \not\equiv \overrightarrow{NS} \rightarrow \mathcal{N}\left(t_{-1}, \ddot{F}_{-1}, NS_{-1}, NA_{[-1,0]}\right) \setminus \mathcal{D}\left(t_{1}, \dddot{F}_{1}, S_{1}^{AE}, PA_{[-1,0]}\right)$: in this case we have a praxeological equivalence between the actional subject and the evaluating one, as well as a difference between the two subjects, on the one hand, and the normative subject, on the other hand. The possible consequences are, again, the four situations which we already analysed, because, although the evaluating subject and the actional subject can "agree" on the implemented action, therefore about the accomplishment of the purpose, and on the unintentional consequences that occurred by the implementation of that particular action, the normative subject may have a different "opinion".

Based on types of occurrence we may now state the types of statements.

We have seen that in the economic (more generally, social) field, almost all statements fall into two categories: (a) prescriptive statements,[40] $\mathcal{N}(.)$, and (b) descriptive statements, $\mathcal{D}(.)$. In terms of their form, these statements are functions of five variables: moment of formulation, involved subjects (two in each case), purpose and action. We may strike out the time variable, because it is decided that the prescriptive statement will be formulated before the accomplishment of the action associated to the prescribed purpose, while the descriptive statement will be formulated after the accomplishment of that action. We may also remove the variable referring to the action because we may presume that the differences between the prescribed action and the actually accomplished action are preserved in the differences between the prescribed purpose and the actually accomplished one (of course, only nominally, because the differences between the prescribed purpose and the actually accomplished one are of a different nature than the differences between the prescribed action and the accomplished one). We may also remove the variable referring to the actional subject, because the differences between the prescribed actional subject and the actual actional one can also be found (nominally, too) within the differences between the prescribed purpose and the accomplished one. Therefore, according to the previous notations, the two types of statements have the following form:

- prescriptive statement: $\mathcal{N} = \mathcal{N}\left(NS, \ddot{F}\right)$
- descriptive statement: $\mathcal{D} = \mathcal{D}\left(ES, \ddot{F}\right)$

All the four occurrence values proposed earlier (A, $\bar{A}_+$, A_-, $\bar{A}$) are possible because of the differences between F and $\ddot{F}$, correlated with (forcing the language we might also say: generated by) the praxeological differences between *NS* and *ES*.[41]

We will now give names to the statements of $4\mathcal{A}$ logics, as they verify the occurrence values (Table 4.2).

Table 4.2 Typology of statements within $\underline{4}\mathcal{A}$ logics

Value of occurrence	*Type of statement (This typology of the statements refers, of course, to the prescriptive statements, after they were tested by comparing them with the associated descriptive statements (the same procedure as for the values of truth from the classical bivalent logics, where the typology of the statements made reference to the predictive statements, after they were tested by comparison with the associated descriptive statements))*
A	Performative statement ($\mathcal{N}_{[p]}$)
A_-	Non-convenient performative statement ($\mathcal{N}_{[p\bar{c}]}$)
$\bar{A}_+$	Convenient, non-performative statement ($\mathcal{N}_{[\bar{p}c]}$)
$\bar{A}$	Non-performative statement ($\mathcal{N}_{[\bar{p}]}$)

Source: author

Table 4.3 The truth table within $\underline{4}\,\mathcal{A}$ logics

«∧»	A	A_-	$\bar{A}_+$	$\bar{A}$
A	A	A_-	$\bar{A}_+$	$\bar{A}$
A_-	A_-	A_-	$\bar{A}$	$\bar{A}$
$\bar{A}_+$	$\bar{A}_+$	$\bar{A}$	$\bar{A}_+$	$\bar{A}$
$\bar{A}$	$\bar{A}$	$\bar{A}$	$\bar{A}$	$\bar{A}$
«∨»	A	A_-	$\bar{A}_+$	$\bar{A}$
A	A	A	A	A
A_-	A	A_-	A_-	A_-
$\bar{A}_+$	A	A_-	$\bar{A}_+$	$\bar{A}_+$
$\bar{A}$	A	A_-	$\bar{A}_+$	$\bar{A}$
«¬»	A	A_-	$\bar{A}_+$	$\bar{A}$
A	$\bar{A}$			
A_-		$\bar{A}_+$		
$\bar{A}_+$			A_-	
$\bar{A}$				A

Source: Author

The basic logic constants could be exposed as below (Table 4.3):

2.2. Significance of the Values of Occurrence

It is obvious that the significance of the occurrence values proposed in $4\ \mathcal{A}$ logics, which we find adequate to the economic field (otherwise, broadly, to the social field) is no longer related to the correspondence-truth concept, specific to the natural field. In conclusion of this chapter we would like to make some comments on the significance of the prescriptive statements[42] associated to the values of occurrence.

- *Performative statement* ($\mathcal{N}_{[p]}$). The value of occurrence of this prescriptive statement is noted with A. A performative statement signifies that the purpose prescribed within has been accomplished through the action associated to that purpose. Furthermore, this statement "specifies" that no unintended consequences[43] appeared while accomplishing the purpose, therefore this was done "with no rest". Purely analogically, this type of statement corresponds to the type of true statements from the bivalent logics;

- *Convenient, non-performative statement* ($\mathcal{N}_{[\bar{p}c]}$). The value of occurrence of this prescriptive statement is noted with $\bar{A}_+$. A convenient, non-performative statement signifies (by the term *non-performative*) that the prescribed purpose has not been accomplished; however, some consequences unintended by the normative subject were produced, which are convenient to the evaluating subject (by the term *convenient*). We have two things to notice here: (a) the unintended consequences must also be convenient for the normative subject, because the attribute of *convenient* also bears on the prescriptive statement, which has been formulated by the normative subject; (b) the unintended convenient consequences don't mean a partial accomplishment of the purpose, but they merely and unavoidably accompany the unfulfilment of the purpose. The suggestion of benefit associated to a failure cannot be circumvented here.[44] Purely analogically, this type of statement corresponds to the types of statements from the bivalent logics;
- *Non-convenient performative statement* ($\mathcal{N}_{[p\bar{c}]}$). The value of occurrence of this prescriptive statement a is noted with A_-. A non-convenient performative statement signifies (by the term *performative*) that the prescribed purpose has been accomplished and that consequences unintended by the normative subject were produced during the process and are non-convenient to the evaluating subject (shown by the term *non-convenient*). Same as before, there are two things to notice: (a) the unintended consequences must be non-convenient to the normative subject too, because the attribute of *non-convenient* bears on the prescriptive statement formulated by the normative subject; (b) the unintended non-convenient consequences don't mean a partial failure of the purpose, but they merely and unavoidably accompany the accomplishment of the purpose. The suggestion of transaction cost associated to a performance cannot be circumvented here.[45] Purely analogically, this type of statement does not correspond to the types of statements from the bivalent logics;
- *Non-performative statement* ($\mathcal{N}_{[\bar{p}]}$). The value of occurrence of this prescriptive statement is noted with $\bar{A}$. A non-performative statement signifies that the prescribed purpose has not been accom-

plished through the action associated to that purpose. Furthermore, this statement "specifies" that no unintended consequences appeared while trying to accomplish that purpose; therefore this was done "with no rest". Purely analogically, this type of statement corresponds to the type of false statements from the bivalent logics.

Annex 4.2: On the Intrinsic Economic Value

Firstly, it must be said that the term *value* as related to the economic phenomenon has no connotation linked to the axiology, but it is a general term aimed at representing the genus for different species of prices, costs or other monetary marks used in describing the economic phenomenology (production, exchange, distribution, redistribution, consumption, investment, saving, etc.).

Secondly, the term (or concept) *value* constitutes a secondary anchor to which all the "regional" terms relate like to a benchmark. If it is a secondary anchor, this means it is, in turn, anchored to a primary anchor.

(1) On the Primary Anchor of the Value

The primary anchor of the concept of value cannot be outside of the economic process, since it must measure something economic (see Chap. 1 for the concept of the economic). The basic predicates of the primary anchor for the concept of value are, in our opinion, the following:

- (predicate α) direct (at limit, unique) relationship with the leading economic factor of the economic process/activity;
- (predicate β) the leading economic factor of the economic process is that factor[46] to which any other economic factors can be reduced, in the last instance; this reduction must be made (in a logical way) based on the very mechanism of the economic process/activity;
- (predicate γ) the leading economic factor of the economic process must be mandatorily present in any economic process/activity, no matter its peculiarities in space and time, namely, it must be irreducible to other economic factors.[47]

(2) The Main Existing Proposals for the Intrinsic Economic Value

(2.1) The Theory of Labour-Value

The theory of labour-value is developed by Karl Marx, following the suggestions of the so-called classical political economy. Essentially, the (intrinsic) economic value is considered the quantity of abstract labour incorporated into the good or service in the case. Abstract labour (a concept coined by Marx, in the first volume of his opus *Das Kapital*, in 1867) is understood as a qualitatively homogenous quantity of labour, unspecified to a certain good, service or activity, so being differentiated only from the quantitative point of view. Indeed, this proposal verifies the three sufficiency predicates mentioned at point (1):

- (predicate α): the relationship with the leading economic factor of the economic process is direct (in fact, unique);
- (predicate β): according to the logic of the economic process/activity, in which three production factors are involved—labour, physical capital and natural resources—it is obvious that the physical capital and the natural resources can be reduced to the labour, based on the following reasonings: (i) the physical capital is the result of previous economic activity, so it is obtained using the labour—in last instance, we do not find in the current physical capital anything else than labour; (ii) the natural resources are, in turn, the result of previous economic activity, so they are obtained using the labour—in last instance, we do not find in the current natural resources anything else than labour, too. It is to be mentioned that the current labour itself is obtained, from the perspective of its qualification and competence, based on previous labour performed on the workers (e.g., in education activity);
- (predicate γ): it is obvious that there is no economic activity which can lack labour (*nota bene*: even an activity which uses only AI—artificial intelligence—is only possible based on the fact that the labour constructed, previously, that AI, both as hard and soft).

So, labour as the primary anchor for the (intrinsic) economic value verifies the three sufficiency predicates required, which shows that Marx's intuition is correct and productive (Dinga, 2022).

(2.2) The Utility Theory of Value

The utility theory of value is not anymore anchored to the labour as such but to the perception of the individual involved in the economic activity (in fact, in any of the stages of the economic activity, from production to final consumption) regarding the economic object: good or service. That perception overwhelmingly depends on the individual idiosyncrasy, on the one part, and on the economic positioning (social statute, economic needs spectrum, wealth and so on), on the other part. Consequently, the theory of the utility of value does not associate the same price with a given good or service, as the theory of labour-value did[48] (*nota bene*: the price is the second anchor of the economic value) but different prices based on the different perception of different individuals, occurred regarding the same good or service.

(2.3) The Administrative Theory of Value

This kind of theory of value is not, in fact, approached in the speciality literature, although, for example, the public goods are not subject to the market so, principled, they are not anchored either to the theory of labour-value or to the utility theory of value. More exactly, public goods are not considered useful goods but required ones, so they do not contain utility but requireness. In this case, the value of the good or service is coincident with its price, called administrative price (or, equivalent, administrative value). The prices of public goods and services are objectified by the mandatory and legal collecting of the money from individuals (i.e., the taxes, direct and indirect). These values/prices—the tax rates and the tax base—are determined based, generically, on the provisions of the social contract (particularly, of the Constitution) and depend on the political regime, the degree of the society's freedom and the degree of the democracy (either social or liberal).

Notes

1. This is the reason according to which the economic analysis must be concomitantly modelled in the natural *and* the social ways (not only in the natural ways—for which many Nobel prizes were been awarded—*and* not only in the social way or even in the psychological one—for which the Nobel prizes already have begun to be awarded).
2. We discuss here the ideal case, of course. The fact that, *hic et nunc*, we cannot perfectly measure the initial conditions is an issue outside the main road of the current discussion.

3. Remember that the subject of cultural type is that subject which is capable to have representations (i.e., perceptions without the physical appearance of the object perceived). The non-cultural subject is capable to have perceptions only (i.e., only in the physical appearance—*in actu*—of the object perceived).
4. See Introduction for a detailed examination of the concept *economic*.
5. As we will see below, no economic fact (event, process, action) happens without the human action. More exactly, the economic is only the result of the human subject—as individual or as social group.
6. It is easy to remember that objectification gives components of the famous Popper's Third World.
7. As it will be shown, in the case of the singular economic event, the cycle described by such a grammar is unique in its turn. The degree to which the term grammar could be still maintained regarding the singular economic event is an issue of the same nature as the degree to which the explanation or the prediction could be maintained regarding the singular economic event.
8. Here is the origin of the endless debates between the nominalists and realists regarding the relationships between the particulars and the generals (or universals).
9. Popper's falsifiability test works by comparing a predictive enunciation (or proposition) with a descriptive one, referring, of course, to the same factual (*ex ante* as prediction, and ex post as explanation). In the singular economic event case, we have to compare a descriptive proposition (explanation) with a pres-dictive one (or, in some cases, in which the natural laws are not implied at all, with pure prescriptive one).
10. Here we have a problem: as known, Popper considered the propensity (or the propensive probability) as an objective feature of an event (or phenomenon or process), in part because he thought his proposal for the quantum events. However, in the economic field, the economic events are neither purely objective nor purely subjective—they are, as discussed before, objectified events, that is, they belong to the Popper's third world. Consequently, we would put together the objectivity with the subjectivity of the economic event and, in such a context, it can be associated, from a functional point of view, with the propensity (or the propensive probability) with the Bayes probability. In fact, in the economic field, the uncertainty will be treated like in the natural field, namely based on Laplace's principle of insufficient reason.
11. An interesting idea is here, in our opinion, the fact that any current society allows (or, in fact, causes) the crisis that suits it, or, better said, the crisis it "deserves".
12. We have here a reasoning of *modus tollens* type: $A \rightarrow B$; but $\bar{B}$; so, $\bar{A}$.

13. The "signs" of the crisis imminence will be examined later in the economy of the study.
14. The problem of the thresholds that act in establishing the "personality" of the crises is important; therefore it will be approached below.
15. To be observed, here, a suggestion for the (co)evolution in the matter of crisis phenomenology, on which we shall return at the appropriate place.
16. We recall the distinction between meaning (closer to the explanation) and signification (closer to the sense).
17. The demand for money is, in turn, composed of the demand for money for income (e.g., paying wages) and the demand for money for speculation. As we will see below, the first component of the demand for money is a function of income (more precisely, of national income, at the limit, of GDP), and the second component is a function of the bank lending rate or (as the case may be) of the bank interest rate spread, i.e., the difference between the active bank interest rate and the passive bank interest rate).
18. It is difficult to discern between falsity and lying, since most of the economic players inside the nominal economy, even if know the truth, will prefer to ignore it (so to lie), to move with at least a step forward on the profitable trajectory. Of course, enough players purely believe that the nominal economy goes correctly and without problems.
19. The concept of intrinsic (economic) value is, almost certainly, the most difficult (and important, as well) issue of economics (more exactly, of political economics). In Annex 4.2, we provide, briefly, a point of view on this matter.
20. The term momentum has, here, the following meaning: the time interval (duration) within which a tendency of a nominal variable maintains (desirably, without… jerks) its course (azimuth).
21. Of course, it is possible to exist a few economic players in the nominal economy who play based on the contrarian strategy (i.e., against the current momentum) but, preponderantly, the economic agents will play in line with the momentum, because of the dominance of the prudential behaviour and, at the same time, because of the memetism (memetic behaviour) provided by the implicit information. (*Nota bene*: see the concept of implicit information in our book *Financial Market Analysis and Behaviour. The Adaptive Preference Hypothesis*, Routledge—Group Taylor & Francis, 2022.)
22. Both the primary money market (e.g., banking loans) and the secondary money market (e.g., inter-banking loans). Also, in the money market, we include the loan of last resort granted by the central bank to the commercial banking system, inside a national economic system.
23. The nominal crisis develops a sui generis *amnesia* regarding the real economic flows so that, once triggered, the nominal crisis is guided by what,

perhaps, should be called a nominal arrow, i.e., an arrow directed to the logically necessary breaking point.

24. The term inflation is "arrested" to signify the general increase of the prices (more exactly, of the average price in the economy) but, for example, cosmologists (who, probably, did not hear about the price increase) use the term to describe the Universe's expansion after an infinitesimal time from Big Bang.
25. Of course, this idea must be separately and in itself developed, following all art rules.
26. Hence, in the economic (social) field, the future doesn't come, rather it is built; it is not emergent, but rather planned.
27. In terms of semiotics, such statements are of the same type as Austin's *perlocutionary statements* (statements which change the situation within the context of their formulation; for instance, Habermas's concept of *communicative action* is a species of perlocutionary statement, because it aspires to change the polemic stance of the interlocutor).
28. Here, the expression *appearance of the factual* must not be taken *ad litteram*, because in the economic field, as mentioned before several times, the factuals don't emerge, but rather they are objectified through the decision and, subsequently, by the action of the subject.
29. Although the proportion of the eutaxiological causality is still very small within the economy (broadly, within the social field), there is, however, what we called above an intra-contingent necessity, which overlaps this type of causality (for instance, the exhaustion of the fossil resources is a necessity within a process decided within a contingent manner).
30. We are using here an analogy with the situation from the quantum mechanics of the linear overlapping of the potential states of a quantum object before proceeding to an experiment with that object. The result of the experiment collapses the wave function which describes the state of the quantum object, so that the observer (the scientist) notices a unique state. Although the collapsing method used to explain the transition from the quantum state to its macroscopic description is rather unsatisfactory, it remains, nevertheless, an explicative alternative until new suppositions emerge.
31. We prefer to replace the term of *truth* with the term of *occurrence*. The justification for this preference lies in the higher possibility to persist, in our memory, the significance of the correspondence-truth when we are discussing the concept of truth as such. As it resulted from several arguments presented so far, the correspondence-truth has no relevance for the economic field. Therefore, when we approach the matter of the *tables of truth*, we will call them *tables of occurrence*.

32. We are ignoring here the fact that the prescriptive statement contains, many times, eutaxiological causality too (i.e., cases when $\alpha \neq 0$, using the notation formalized above). This disregarding doesn't compromise the generality of our considerations, although technically, in this disregarded case we will have two "modules" to analyse: (a) the eutaxiological module, for which the eutaxiological component plays a role of predictive statement; (b) the teleological module, for which the teleological component plays the role of normative statement.
33. For instrumental reasons, we propose to call this possible logics: $4\mathcal{A}$ *logics* .
34. The negation sign $(\bar{A})$ has the same significance as in the classical logics, which allows the formulation of the principle of identity ($A = A$), the principle of non-contradiction ($\overline{A \wedge \bar{A}}$) and the principle of the excluded third ($A \vee \bar{A}$).
35. The concept of unintended consequence has been highly theorized by Karl Popper, who said that the most important task of the social sciences is to make predictions about the unintended consequences of the taken decisions.
36. The expression *ontological difference* involved by the reasoning of this study has, of course, nothing to do with the complicated concept of *ontological difference* (distinction between being and Being) discussed by Heidegger. We hope we didn't confuse our scrupulous readers.
37. Nevertheless, from other perspectives (social, political, etc.) the ontological identity (equivalence) of the subjects is also relevant.
38. Which, of course, may have not the same significance for the prescriptive (normative) subject or may even not exist for it (which means that the purpose is accomplished "with no rest").
39. The praxeological non-equivalence concomitant with the ontological equivalence can be also explained by the Oedipus effect.
40. In some cases, they will be of a mixed type: predictive-prescriptive, that is, what we earlier named *presdictive* (or *presdictions*).
41. The reader has already learned that the differences between the two categories of subjects are praxeological differences, namely differences in design and evaluation of the purpose. Although it is not impossible that the two subjects also are ontologically different (i.e., different natural persons), we are only interested in the praxeological differences.
42. Actually, prescriptive statements can also be found in the natural domain, but they are *conditional* prescriptive statements, while in the economic field, the prescriptive statements are *unconditional.* A prescriptive statement is conditional if the involved norm depends on (i.e., it is function of) the occurrence of some random condition(s) stipulated by that specific norm, and is unconditional if no such conditions are stipulated. Usually, the conditional prescriptions are called *instructions* of procedures (they are

of the following general form: "if condition x occurs, then act in manner y", "if you aim x result, then act in manner y", etc.). On the contrary, the unconditional prescriptions are of the following general form: "you have to act in manner x", "you have to do this or that", etc. Grammatically, we may also have formulations such as "this or that objective is to be accomplished" or "this or that action is to be carried out", or even more vaguely "this or that phenomenon will have the following evolution...". Although no imperatives appear explicitly in the latter three types of formulations (e.g., "must to", "have to", etc.), these imperatives are implicit because, as mentioned several times before, they cannot take existence unless being accomplished by the subject.

43. The problem of evaluating the unintended consequences while accomplishing a purpose is not too simple. Logically, the assessment of the appearance or not of consequences beyond the purpose cannot be done unless there is a benchmark. But the prescriptive statement expresses no such consequences. Would they have been expressed, they would no longer be unintended, thus being part of the purpose. We revert thus to the initial problem, not having a benchmark to evaluate the unintended consequences. The situation "worsens" further when praxeologically $NS\_1 \not\equiv ES1$.
44. This is an idea to be developed subsequently, because it seems to us that it has a great explanative potential for the process of evaluating the human action in general.
45. The concept of cost of transaction is well known to economists: that cost (not necessarily monetary) which accompanies any transaction (here, the term of transaction is taken in its most general meaning, of voluntary, inter-subjects, interaction), and it adds to the price of the transaction. Therefore, we have a price of transaction (*pt*), we have a cost of transaction (*ct*) and we have a transactional price (*pT*) so that $pT = pt + ct$. *Nota bene*: *ct* must be recalculated in units equivalent to those used to measure *pt* (for instance, in monetary units).
46. An economic factor is an economic resource that was attracted in the actual economic process/activity.
47. It is to be observed that (β) and (γ) are not redundant or contradictory with each other, but they close the logical circle inside which the primary anchor of the value must be found.
48. It is to be mentioned that, even from the perspective of the theory of labour-value, the price, i.e., the second anchor of the value, is established on the market, by comparing, in a specific way (e.g., by the rapport between demand and supply), so a unique occur just in the last instance (at the clearing market).

References

Dinga, E. (2022). Social Time and the Economics of Science. *Amfiteatru Economic, 24*(16).

Dinga, E., Oprean-Stan, C., Tănăsescu, C. R., Brătian, V., & Ionescu, G.-M. (2023). *Co-Evolution of Symbolic Species in the Financial Market. A Framework for Economic and Political Decision-Making*. Palgrave Macmillan – Springer Nature.

Duppe, T. (2009). *The Phenomenology of Economics. Life-World, Formalism, and the Invisible Hand*. Haveka BV.

Handy, C. (2016). *The Second Curve. Thoughts on Reinventing Society*. Cornerstone.

Taleb, N. N. (2012). *Antifragile: Things That Gain from Disorder*. Random House.

CHAPTER 5

Crises Overlapping: Crises Between System and Network

5.1 Preamble

The crises overlapping is a phenomenon of contingent nature, that is, it is not (logically) necessary, but is, at the same time, (logically) possible. As our book is a theoretical one, and the grounding method of approaching is the logic, this chapter will discuss the basic issues that can be associated with the overlapping phenomenon in the crisis question, exclusively from a logical view.

The *first* interest is, of course, to learn about the very concept of overlapping the crises—the main determinants, the presumed impact and the form/configuration given to the resulting set of the overlapped crises.[1] *Secondly*, it must be clarified the nude mechanism through which the crises overlaps—we shall call such a mechanism as an interleaving process. *Thirdly*, it must be examined something like an affinity among different crises so that they attract with each other and go towards the overlapping (or not), *inter alia*, of course, the factors leading to such an attraction. *Fourthly*, it must be studied the context (its structure, configuration and functions) in which the crises overlap—here the concept of system vs. network will be examined. *Fifthly*, the concept and the physiology of the chreode born from the crises overlapping will be introduced and qualitatively analysed. And, *finally*, the chapter will try to build a system-network pair of crises overlapping and the chreode associated with it.

E. Dinga, *Economic Resilience During Overlapped Crises*,
https://doi.org/10.1007/978-3-031-80224-9_5

5.2 What Means Crises Overlapping?

Conceptually, the overlapping of something (things, properties, relationships) means a temporal and spatial co-existence.[2] It can be, perhaps, three meanings of the overlapping: (a) overlapping without causal or conditional interference among the entities overlapped—let us called it *immiscible* overlapping (*IO*); (b) overlapping with interference among the entities involved, causally and conditionally but, somehow, keeping the entities that overlap as distinct and recognizable phenomena/processes—let us call it *conservative* overlapping (*CO*); (c) overlapping implying the transition in a common (supra)phenomenon/(supra)process, by dissolving the entities involved in each other so resulting (through synergy effect) a new entity of crisis, inside which no one of the initial entities can be identified anymore as such—let us call it *transformative* overlapping (*TO*).

Some examples for the three classes of crises overlapping could be as follows:

- for the *IO* class: a technological crisis overlapped with a moral one—although, based on the universal principle of entanglement, any entity is correlated with any other entity, in the deepest substrate it is possible to find non-autonomy between the two concrete crises, but, in the proximate instance, they are of immiscible category;
- for the *CO* class: an educational crisis overlapped with a political one—the two concrete crises interfere between them both as causality, conditionality and reciprocal impact but, essentially, they remain distinct as crises, keeping their logic and functionality;
- for the *TO* class: an ecological crisis overlapped with a technological one—the two crises are so strong interfering under almost all aspects (both structural and functional) so, finally, they become a single crisis that could be called an economic model crisis. The initial crises are inextricably interleaved and, consequently, the "parents" are no anymore recognizable as such (*Nota bene*: the evolutionist suggestion—parents/offsprings—is, obviously, irresistible here).

5.3 Crisis Affinity

The most important and relevant issue in the crises overlapping phenomenology is that of the affinity that lead the crises to overlap among them. The affinity is a concept (and term) arisen in Biology, regarding the substrate-limited microbial growth[3] (Monod, 1942), but its meaning extensively transited into many others fields of research, although the life sciences and humanities sciences remain the most populated areas with this term.

5.3.1 What Affinity Is It?

First of all, it must be said that the affinity is a property of a relationship, not of a thing, nor of a property. Consequently, the affinity is induced by a relationship, i.e., the relationship is primordially related to the affinity, being, so to say, the substrate of the affinity, to make a parallel with the biological meaning of the affinity. Although the concept of affinity seems rather mysterious (especially when it is introduced as a constant parameter in different processes), it is not at all so. In fact, in the issue of the crisis case, we think it is, even, calculable (point 5.3.3).

As in the common language enough, the affinity acts as a kind of sympathy, apparently unexplainable but, as we shall see soon, not so strange at all, however. In the first "civil" instance in the beginning, the affinity could be understood as an attraction between things, properties or relationships, while it remains, essentially, a property of a relationship. So, if no relationship exists, no affinity occurs. Of course, a sophisticated reader could ask: is it not possible that, inversely, an affinity to cause a relationship? Our position in this matter is the following:

- as being, essentially, an attraction between two (or more) entities, the affinity must identify the two (or more) entities as such. Such an identification is logically equivalent with occurring a relationship;
- consequently, it seems that, somewhat, the affinity and the relationship arise simultaneously. If, however, we are "pressed" to choose a causal priority between the two—affinity and relationship—we think it is more plausible that the relationship occur prior to the affinity;
- the above conclusion can be extra-supported by the following reasoning: presuppose a relationship occurs between two (or more) given entities. This relationship could be characterized by many attributes,[4] one of them being exactly the affinity as attribute (or predicate) of that relationship;

- so, we think that the most plausible causal (or temporal[5]) choice of the priority between relationship and affinity is that the relationship is before the affinity.

5.3.2 *Rapport Between Affinity and Propensity*

The relationship between affinity and propensity is exactly based on the fact that the propensity is a property of a thing (no matter its nature), while the affinity is a property of a relationship. As said before, the primordial entity for the propensity is the thing, while the primordial entity for the affinity is the relationship. So, the propensity can subsist as long as the thing involved subsists, while the affinity subsists as long as the relationship involved subsists. As the relationships can occur both between things, between properties and even between relationships (*Nota bene*: something of relationships of second order), and because in previous chapters (especially point 4.2 in Chap. 4) we have discussed about propensity in the context of the singular event, as the generic (economic) crisis is, the logical relationship between propensity and affinity is of a great importance and significance. Next, we shall discuss the most relevant, as we think, issues regarding such a correlation.

(i) propensity is a property of a thing (*PT*), so it can exist including the case of the singular event, while affinity is a property of a relationship (*PR*), so it can exist if and only if there exists a relationship (no matter its nature) between at least two entities, either things, or properties, or relationships;
(ii) propensity has a necessary character (it cannot/do not exist once a thing exists), while affinity can or cannot come into existence although the required relationship exists; here resides the justification of the contingent nature associated, previously, with the affinity;
(iii) as a relationship can occur in three hypostases (between things, between properties and between relationships), it results that, in the case of relationship between things, we can state the following:
    - between the two things there are two propensities, each of them belonging to each of the two things that inter-relate;
    - the two propensities could act convergently (i.e., one in harmony with another) or divergently (i.e., one in dis-harmony with another);

- concomitantly, the relationship generates the possibility (not the necessity, as said carefully before) for an affinity between the two things that entered into a relationship based on their propensities;

(iv) of course, if the relationship occurs between properties, or between relationships, the question of the rapport between propensity and affinity is without object;

(v) a question arises now: if propensity (always in two "copies"—one for a thing, that is, a singular event, and one for the other thing, as a singular event too) and affinity are contemporary, i.e., concomitantly in space and time, in a given relationship, what happens with the rapport between them? Our considerations in this matter are as follows:
- if the affinity is not triggered (see point 5.3.3), then the two propensities work specifically, according to their parameters;
- if the affinity is triggered, we think the following phenomena occur:
  - based on the assumption[6] that relationship is dominant compared with contemporary properties or things, it seems that the affinity will "lead the hostilities". This means that propensities will align themselves to the direction in which affinity works;
  - an effect of this state of affairs is that the affinity will be augmented by the pressures exerted by the two propensities;[7]

(vi) a last question can be put now: if we have the propensities, why is it required to introduce another concept—i.e., affinity—in the phenomenology of crisis and of crises overlapping? The basic reasons to do that are the following:
- *firstly*, even if between two entities, of thing nature, a relationship occurs, it is possible that the two propensities of the two things be antagonist as direction. In such a case, the interaction between the two things is unintelligible enough in the absence of the affinity;[8]
- *secondly*, a more analytical examination could lead to the conclusion that the affinity is a synergic effect of the interaction of the two propensities. To be honest, this is exactly the hypothesis we want to advance and, consequently, develop in the paragraph at point 5.3.3.

5.3.3 The Calculability of the Crises Affinity

To handle the provocative issue of the affinity calculability, it is useful to come back to the formalization of a generic crisis, as it has been provided in Chaps. 2 and 3, respectively. Let us remind the basic considerations to this end.

Preamble

- a generic crisis can be labelled as $C_{12345}^{\alpha\beta\gamma\delta\varepsilon}$. The bottom indexes mean (1) the cause of crisis; (2) the origin of crisis; (3) the chreode of crisis; (4) the impact of crisis; (5) the significance[9] of crisis. The up indexes mean (α) species of class T_1 of crisis—cause; (β) species of class T_2 of crisis—origin; (γ) species of class T_3 of crisis—chreode; (δ) species of class T_4 of crisis—impact; (ε) species of class T_5 of crisis—significance;
- we remind, synoptically, the classes and species of the generic crisis (Table 5.1.) from Chap. 2, point 2.3.2.

About Calculability of Affinity

We must say that the calculability of affinity regarding the crises overlapping issue addresses the qualitative dimension of that affinity, not the quantitative one or, in other words, the ordinality not the cardinality in the affinity matter. This positioning is based on at least two reasons: (a) the reason of necessity—it is not necessary to establish the cardinality of an affinity, perhaps, for example, to compare it with another cardinality itself or with another affinity. It is sufficient to "know" about the order of the set of possible (or presumable) affinities to operate the adequate judgements in the matter; (b) the reason of possibility: it is not, as we think, to quantitatively estimate the affinity of a given relationship because we do not have a reference for such a cardinality.[10] Consequently, all we can do is draw a hierarchy of the affinities in the set of possible affinities, stipulating, at the same time, that the order of affinity force ... overlaps with the order of nominal affinity in the case. Of course, a problem, that could be called the problem of *affinity dominance*, arises here (*Nota bene*: it will be examined at point 5.4).

Table 5.1 General (abstract) typology of a generic crisis

			Species of crisis				
			α—cause	*β—origin*	*γ—chreode*	*δ—impact*	*ε—significance*
Classes of crisis	1	1	by insularization				
		2	by friction				
		3	by insemination				
		4	by exhaustion				
		5	by futurization				
	2	1		theoretical			
		2		Praxeological			
		3		practical			
		4		political			
		5		natural			
	3	1			self-extinguishing		
		2			self-maintaining		
		3			trans-field		
		4			migratory		
		5			synergic		
	4	1				on structure	
		2				on rationality	
		3				on values	
		4				on political regime	
		5				on meta-narrative	
	5	1					to survival
		2					to opportunities
		3					to way of life
		4					to freedom
		5					to self-esteem

Source: author

5.4 How the Crises Overlap?

The crises overlap based on their affinity. Conceptually, any crisis is thing and is endowed with a propensity. Such propensity addresses may development possibilities of the crises: extending/narrowing, intensifying/diluting, combining/isolating and so on. All these propensities interact between them and produce effects of many nature. We are interested here by one of these possible effects, namely the overlapping under the aegis of affinity.

5.4.1 *The General Order of Affinity*

We have seen in Table 5.1 the marks assigned to any possible crisis, not only economic ones. This means that when two (or more, after the case) crises are contemporary, the inherent relationships, by the intermediation of the associated propensities, are liable to generate affinities between them. Here we meet the above-mentioned problem of ***affinity dominance***. To elucidate this problem, the following issues must be (briefly) examined: (a) the lexicographic order of the classes of crises; (b) the lexicographic order of species within each class of crises; (c) the general lexicographic order of a generic crisis; (d) some extra algebraic considerations on the dominance relationship based on affinity.

(a) the lexicographic order of the classes of crises

A lexicographic order of a "population" of any nature means a hierarchy based not on a logical criterion but on an implicit axiom of dominance from the significance perspective. Again, we find the importance and relevance of the significance (not of meaning!), since, as generally said, the human being could be defined, ***inter alia***, as a significance allocator for the world.

Principled, we assume that the order of the classes of generic crises is that of their "natural" enumeration in Table 5.1. We note with the logical constant $\rtimes$ the dominance relation, so the constant must be read "…is dominant over…". So, we propose that the lexicographic order of the classes of crises be:

$$T_5 \rtimes T_1 \rtimes T_4 \rtimes T_2 \rtimes T_3$$

or, with the same meaning of the dominance order,

$$T_{51423}$$

Nota bene: so, the inferior composed index of any crises will be exactly the "number" 51423, that is:

$$C_{51423}^{\varepsilon\alpha\delta\beta\gamma}$$

To memorization!: on keyboard: 5, then 1, to the left of 5, i.e., 4, then to the right of 1, i.e., 2, then to the left of 4, i.e., 3.

(b) the lexicographic order of species within each class of crises

Inside each class of generic crisis must be established a hierarchy, according to the same "axiom", namely the signification/significance for the human individual (and, by extension, for the society as a whole). Our proposal is the following:

(b1) for the class "1" (i.e., for values of *α—cause*), the hierarchy of species is:

- species 3: by insemination
- species 4: by exhaustion
- species 2: by friction
- species 5: by futurization
- species 1: by insularization

(b2) for the class "2" (i.e., for values of *β—origin*), the hierarchy of species is:

- species 2: praxeological
- species 3: practical
- species 4: political
- species 5: natural
- species 1: theoretical

(b3) for the class "3" (i.e., for values of γ—*chreode*) the hierarchy of species is:

- species 1: self-extinguishing
- species 2: self-maintaining
- species 3: trans-field
- species 5: synergic
- species 4: migratory

(b4) for the class "4" (i.e., for values of δ—*impact*) the hierarchy of species is:

- species 1: on structure
- species 3: on values
- species 2: on rationality
- species 4: on political regime
- species 5: on meta-narrative

(b5) for the class "5" (i.e., for values of ε—*significance*) the hierarchy of species is:

- species 1: about survival
- species 4: about freedom
- species 2: about opportunities
- species 5: about self-esteem
- species 3: way of life

Nota bene: for example, if someone shows us a crisis mark as: C_{51423}^{35142}, we know that it is speaking about a crisis which is about opportunities (e.g., the advance of AI), which addresses the future impacts on the structure of the society, is originated in the political field and tends to maintain itself (by positive feedback).

(c) the general lexicographic order of a generic crisis

Now, we should combine (a) and (b) to see if it is possible to construct a general lexicographic order of crisis marks, based both on the dominance of classes (the order marked by the inferior indexes of the crisis symbol, i.e., 51423) and the numerical values of the species of each class, as proposed at point (b) above. Let us take the above example, $C_1 = C_{51423}^{35142}$, and let us take another one, $C_2 = C_{51423}^{31425}$. *Nota bene*: the inferior indexes always maintain the class order. We can write the following:

- according to class "5": $C_1(\varepsilon) = 3$, and $C_2(\varepsilon) = 3$, so $C_1 \bowtie C_2$ (the logical constant $\bowtie$ must be read "... equally dominates and are dominated by ...", that is, there is equilibrium or equivalence regarding the dominance, while the logical constant $\ltimes$ must be read "... is dominated by ...");
- according to class "1": $C_1(\alpha) = 5$, and $C_2(\alpha) = 1$, so $C_1 \ltimes C_2$;
- according to class "4": $C_1(\delta) = 1$, and $C_2(\delta) = 4$, so $C_1 \rtimes C_2$;
- according to class "2": $C_1(\beta) = 4$, and $C_2(\beta) = 2$, so $C_1 \ltimes C_2$;
- according to class "3": $C_1(\gamma) = 2$, and $C_2(\gamma) = 5$, so $C_1 \rtimes C_2$;

To be observed that, between the species that mark the two crises subsists all the dominance rapports: to dominate, to be dominated and to equally relating from the dominance perspective. A question arises: is it possible (and plausible) to calculate a global dominance rapport between given marked crises? We shall deliver a proposal in this matter based on the following logical reasons:

- since the inferior indexes of the crisis were placed in a decreasing order from left to right, and this ordering is invariant, it results that the further to the left the dominance is between two crises the more the dominance gap between those two crises;
- regarding the superior indexes of the compared crises, the greater the absolute gap between the numerical values of the species in question, the more pronounced the dominance;
- in the last case, the direction of the dominance is given by the positive algebraic sign of the absolute gap.

The next question is this: how to combine the numerical values of gaps in the superior indexes and the positioning from left to right of those gaps?

To resume the above example of $C_1 = C_{51423}^{35142}$ and $C_2 = C_{51423}^{31425}$, the gaps calculated are thus: according to class "5": $g_5 = 3 - 3 = 0$; according to class "1": $g_1 = 5 - 1 = 4$; according to class "4": $g_4 = 1 - 4 = -3$; according to class "2": $g_2 = 4 - 2 = 2$; according to class "3": $g_3 = 2 - 5 = -3$.

The "distance" for any class in the inferior indexes is as follows: for class "5": $d_5 = (5 - 1) + 1 = 5$; for class "1": $d_1 = (5 - 2) + 1 = 4$; for class "4": $d_4 = (5 - 3) + 1 = 3$; for class "2": $d_2 = (5 - 4) + 1 = 2$; for class "3": $d_3 = (5 - 5) + 1 = 1$. *Nota bene*: 1 is added everywhere to avoid the value 0.

The values of gaps must be weighted by the positioning of that values, that is, by the "distance", namely (with $\tilde{g}_i$ is noted the weighted gap assigned to the class *i* of crisis):

$$\tilde{g}_i = g_i \bullet d_i$$

So, we have the following results for the weighted gaps of dominance between C_1 and C_2 (in this ordering):

- according to class "5": $\tilde{g}_5 = g_5 \bullet d_5 = 0 \bullet 5 = 0$
- according to class "1": $\tilde{g}_1 = g_1 \bullet d_1 = 4 \bullet 4 = 16$
- according to class "4": $\tilde{g}_4 = g_4 \bullet d_4 = -3 \bullet 3 = -9$
- according to class "2": $\tilde{g}_2 = g_2 \bullet d_2 = 2 \bullet 2 = 4$
- according to class "3": $\tilde{g}_3 = g_3 \bullet d_3 - 3 \bullet 1 = -3$

The dominance between C_1 and C_2 ($G_{(12)} = \sum_{i=1}^{5} \tilde{g}_i$) is calculated as follows:

$$G_{(12)} = 0 + 16 - 9 + 4 - 3 = 8$$

Nota bene: to be observed that $G_{(kk)} = 0$, i.e., any crisis neither dominates itself nor is dominated by itself, it is in a perpetual equilibrium with itself from the perspective of the relationship based on affinity.

Discussion

- the absolute value of *G* has only one significance: it indicates an intensity of the dominance without any other use except the comparison between two (or more) pairs of crises. So, as said previously, the numerical value of the dominance rapport can only establish an ordering between two dominance rapports based exactly on the absolute values ordering of *Gs* but not more than that—its value as such has no significance for, for example, the level of affinity; besides, the level of affinity is not of interest to us but only the dominance arrow, which *G* provides is and must be of interest;

- the algebraic sign of G indicates the dominance arrow: if it is positive, then the first crisis (in our example, C_1) dominates, from the perspective of affinity, the second one (in our example, C_2) in the pair, in this ordering, (C_1, C_2), that is: $C_1 \rtimes C_2$;
- if G^{12} had been negative, then the result would have been: $C_1 \ltimes C_2$.

(d) some extra algebraic considerations on the dominance relationship based on affinity

Be three crises, C_1, C_2, and C_3, and the binary relation of dominance based on affinity, defined on the set of crises (noted $\mathcal{C}$), and noted with $\rtimes$ ("is dominant over…") or $\ltimes$ ("is dominated by…"), or $\bowtie$ ("are mutually dominated"). Then, on this set, we have the following valid relationships:

- (R) *reflexivity*: $(\forall)k$, $C_k \in \mathcal{C}$ can be compared with itself from the perspective of dominance relationship based on affinity: $C_k \bowtie C_k$;
  comment: indeed, a crisis $C_k = C_{51423}^{\varepsilon_k \alpha_k \delta_k \beta_k \gamma_k}$ can be compared with itself by calculating $G_{(kk)}$ (of course, always $G_{(kk)} = 0$);
- (A) *antisymmetry*: $(\forall)k$, q, for $C_k \in \mathcal{C}$, and $C_q \in \mathcal{C}$, if $(C_k \rtimes C_q)$, and $(C_q \rtimes C_k)$, then $(C_k \bowtie C_q)$;
  comment: since the absolute values of the species of crises (the superior indexes) are the same but with the opposite algebraic sign;
- (T) *transitivity*: $(\forall)k$, q, p, for $C_k \in \mathcal{C}$, $C_p \in \mathcal{C}$, $C_q \in \mathcal{C}$, if $(C_k \rtimes C_p)$ and $(C_p \rtimes C_q)$, then $(C_k \rtimes C_q)$.

A binary relation that verifies RAT is called a partial order relation. Since, in addition, it obvious that any two crisis can be compared between them under the property of dominance based on affinity, it results that the binary relation $\rtimes$ on the set $\mathcal{C}$ generates a total *order relation* on the set $\mathcal{C}$.

5.4.2 *Comparability of the Crises Under the Dominance Relation Based on Affinity*

In fact, now we shall proceed to identify, on a logical basis, the incompatibilities among all the possible crises (all $C_\cdot$), by analysing the possibility of co-existence of different species of the classes of crisis. The analysis is made taking two by two all the possible combinations between the crisis's "individuals", so this analysis will be organized in Table 5.2. To indicate the

Table 5.2 Analysis of logical compatibility of co-existence of crises

			α—cause				
			1. By insularization	*2. By friction*	*3. By insemination*	*4. By exhaustion*	*5. By futurization*
α—cause	1.	by insularization	5	2	0	4	1
	2.	by friction	2	5	3	0	1
	3.	by insemination	0	3	5	2	4
	4.	by exhaustion	4	0	2	5	3
	5.	by futurization	1	1	4	3	5
β—origin	1.	theoretical	1	2	0	3	4
	2.	praxeological	2	2	3	3	0
	3.	practical	1	3	2	2	3
	4.	political	1	2	0	2	4
	5.	natural	3	0	0	3	2
γ—chreode	1.	self-extinguishing	4	3	0	5	1
	2.	self-maintaining	3	2	1	0	4
	3.	trans-field	0	2	5	3	4
	4.	migratory	0	1	3	4	2
	5.	synergic	0	2	3	1	4
δ—impact	1.	on structure	0	2	0	4	0
	2.	on rationality	2	1	0	2	0
	3.	on values	2	1	0	3	4
	4.	on political regime	3	2	2	3	4
	5.	on meta-narrative	1	1	2	2	3
ε—significance	1.	to survival	3	3	2	4	5
	2.	to opportunities	0	2	4	3	4
	3.	to way of life	0	3	2	4	5
	4.	to freedom	0	1	2	3	0
	5.	to self-esteem	2	2	2	2	0

			β—origin				
			1. Theoretical	*2. Praxeological*	*3. Practical*	*4. Political*	*5. Natural*
α—cause	1.	by insularization	1	2	0	1	3
	2.	by friction	2	2	3	2	0
	3.	by insemination	0	3	2	0	0
	4.	by exhaustion	3	3	2	2	3
	5.	by futurization	4	4	3	4	2
β—origin	1.	theoretical	5	3	4	0	0
	2.	praxeological	3	5	4	3	4
	3.	practical	4	4	5	3	0
	4.	political	0	3	3	5	0
	5.	natural	0	4	0	0	5
γ—chreode	1.	self-extinguishing	0	3	2	0	0
	2.	self-maintaining	1	0	0	2	3
	3.	trans-field	2	4	3	3	3
	4.	migratory	3	4	3	2	1
	5.	synergic	2	2	2	2	2
δ—impact	1.	on structure	0	3	2	3	0
	2.	on rationality	5	4	3	0	2
	3.	on values	0	0	5	0	2
	4.	on political regime	0	0	4	5	0
	5.	on meta-narrative	4	3	3	2	0
ε—significance	1.	to survival	0	3	4	2	1
	2.	to opportunities	1	4	3	2	1
	3.	to way of life	0	2	4	0	1
	4.	to freedom	0	2	4	5	0
	5.	to self-esteem	0	0	3	0	0

(*continued*)

Table 5.2 (continued)

			γ—*chreode*				
			1. Self-extinguishing	*2. Self-maintaining*	*3. Trans-field*	*4. Migratory*	*5. Synergic*
α—cause	1.	by insularization	4	3	0	0	0
	2.	by friction	3	2	2	1	2
	3.	by insemination	0	1	5	3	3
	4.	by exhaustion	5	0	3	4	1
	5.	by futurization	0	4	4	2	4
β—origin	1.	theoretical	1	1	2	3	2
	2.	praxeological	3	0	4	4	2
	3.	practical	2	0	3	3	2
	4.	political	0	2	3	2	2
	5.	natural	0	3	3	1	2
γ—chreode	1.	self-extinguishing	5	0	0	0	3
	2.	self-maintaining	0	5	4	2	2
	3.	trans-field	0	4	5	0	2
	4.	migratory	0	2	0	5	3
	5.	synergic	3	2	2	3	5
δ—impact	1.	on structure	3	1	2	0	3
	2.	on rationality	3	0	2	2	2
	3.	on values	2	0	0	3	0
	4.	on political regime	0	0	0	2	3
	5.	on meta-narrative	3	3	3	3	4
ε—significance	1.	to survival	5	5	4	3	0
	2.	to opportunities	5	4	4	3	3
	3.	to way of life	4	5	3	3	0
	4.	to freedom	0	0	3	0	2
	5.	to self-esteem	0	0	0	0	0

			δ—*impact*				
			1. On structure	*2. On rationality*	*3. On value*	*4. On political regime*	*5. On meta-narrative*
α—cause	1.	by insularization	0	2	2	3	1
	2.	by friction	2	1	1	2	1
	3.	by insemination	0	0	0	2	2
	4.	by exhaustion	4	2	3	3	2
	5.	by futurization	0	0	4	4	3
β—origin	1.	theoretical	0	5	0	0	4
	2.	praxeological	3	4	0	0	3
	3.	practical	2	3	5	4	3
	4.	political	3	0	0	5	2
	5.	natural	0	2	2	0	0
γ—chreode	1.	self-extinguishing	0	3	2	4	3
	2.	self-maintaining	1	0	0	0	3
	3.	trans-field	2	2	0	0	3
	4.	migratory	0	2	3	2	3
	5.	synergic	3	2	0	3	4
δ—impact	1.	on structure	5	4	0	3	0
	2.	on rationality	4	5	0	3	2
	3.	on values	0	0	5	0	2
	4.	on political regime	3	3		5	2
	5.	on meta-narrative	0	2	2	2	5
ε—significance	1.	to survival	3	3	0	1	0
	2.	to opportunities	3	3	0	2	0
	3.	to way of life	0	3	3	0	2
	4.	to freedom	4	0	4	5	3
	5.	to self-esteem	0	0	5	0	3

(*continued*)

Table 5.2 (continued)

			ε—significance				
			1. To survival	*2. To opportunities*	*3. To way of life*	*4. To freedom*	*5. To self-esteem*
α—cause	1.	by insularization	3	0	0	0	2
	2.	by friction	3	2	3	1	2
	3.	by insemination	2	4	2	2	2
	4.	by exhaustion	4	3	4	3	2
	5.	by futurization	5	4	5	0	0
β—origin	1.	theoretical	0	1	0	0	0
	2.	praxeological	3	4	2	2	0
	3.	practical	4	3	4	4	3
	4.	political	2	2	0	5	0
	5.	natural	1	1	1	0	0
γ—chreode	1.	self-extinguishing	5	5	4	0	0
	2.	self-maintaining	5	4	5	0	0
	3.	trans-field	4	4	3	3	0
	4.	migratory	3	3	3	0	0
	5.	synergic	0	3	0	2	0
δ—impact	1.	on structure	3	3	2	4	0
	2.	on rationality	3	3	3	0	0
	3.	on values	0	0	3	4	5
	4.	on political regime	1	2	0	5	0
	5.	on meta-narrative	0	0	2	3	3
ε—significance	1.	to survival	5	5	2	0	0
	2.	to opportunities	5	5	3	3	0
	3.	to way of life	2	3	5	3	4
	4.	to freedom	0	3	3	5	4
	5.	to self-esteem	0	0	4	4	5

Source: author

incompatibility between species of crisis, we use the number "0". Obviously, what is not incompatible is compatible. Also, we indicate something like a "degree of compatibility", namely with "5" is noted the maximum of compatibility and with "4", "3", "2" and "1", the corresponding decreasing compatibility.

Nota bene: of course, the notations in Table 5.2 constitute an expert opinion only, and has a didactical point of view, only—it is not at all a result of a dedicated deep research; they just show "how we could proceed with". Consequently, the numbers filled in can be completely substituted with other numbers by other experts in that matter.

The cases of incompatibility are listed in Annex 5.1.[11]

The conclusion is that there are crises that cannot be compared between them since they are incompatible, so set C is not a total order relation, regarding the affinity-based dominance, but just an order relation.

5.4.3 The Generic Mechanism of Crises Overlapping

Some Generalities

The incompatibilities identified above (we remind: exclusively with an illustrative, i.e., from a methodological general perspective) show us the cases in which some crises or "combinations" of crises are … forbidden. Now, we must pass further, namely, to clarify the operational way in which the affinity works in the process of crises overlapping.

We have seen above (point 5.4.1) that, between crises, there are relationships of dominance, based on the affinity parameter. Although the dominance number, as previously calculated, is an ordinal, not cardinal, parameter, it allows us, however, to provide a primary highlighting on the phenomenon of crises overlapping, as follows:

- no matter what (marks of) crisis contemporarily meet, they automatically enter a process of comparison and identifying of the reciprocal positioning leading to the final result of the meeting;
- the comparison addresses all the five identifiers of the mark (i.e., the numerical values of the categorial five classes of the generic crisis), and "calculate" the dominance number between two (or more) crises that happened to meet within a societal system;

- if the dominance number is positive, the affinity-based dominance exerts from the left-side crisis over the right-side crisis; if it is negative, the affinity-based dominance is exerted in the opposite direction;
- the affinity-based dominance is important since its direction indicates, of course, just broadly, the tendency of incorporating a crisis by another—more exactly, the incorporating of the crisis towards which is oriented the dominance arrow by the crisis from which is oriented the dominance arrow; this is very important for both the general social behaviour and the state intervention (if the case);
- if more than two different crises are in place, then the establishment of the affinity-based dominance must be subject to the following "rules":
  - the dominance numbers (*DNs*) are calculated for each pair of the contemporary crises involved in the crisis phenomenology;
  - the *DNs* are decreasingly ordered;
  - the dominance (including incorporating or transforming the crises—see the point 5.2.) is exerted from the higher to the smaller *DN*;
  - this way, any dominance is exerted by the result of the proximate interfering with the upstream of the crises;
  - the relationships between the different "waves" of interferences take time, so, in fact, we have, in such a situation, a temporal causality besides the dominance and spatial causality;[12]

The (More Analytical) Consequences of the Dominance Direction
It could be useful to examine the following issue: is there a logical rapport between the dominance number (*DN*) and the typology of the crisis interference/overlapping? Although some speculative features cannot be completely eradicated in possibly answering this question, we wish to remind the readers that theoretical (logical) speculation is, sometimes, the chance to highlight something particularly relevant that, otherwise, would remain hidden.[13]

We remind the three types of results when two (or more) crises overlap or, the same, the three categories of overlapping process (see point 5.2): (a) overlapping without causal or conditional interference among the entities overlapped—let us called it *immiscible* overlapping (*IO*); (b) overlapping with interference among the entities involved, both causally and conditionally but, somehow, keeping the entities that overlap as distinct and recognizable phenomena/processes—let us call it *conservative* overlapping (*CO*); (c) overlapping implying the transition in a common (supra)phenomenon/(supra)process, by dissolving the entities involved in each other so resulting (through synergy effect) a new entity of crisis, inside which no one of the initial entities can be identified anymore as such—let us call it *transformative* overlapping (*TO*).

It is obvious that a decreasing order of *DNs* of two entities (crises) interacting or overlapping must be associated with the order of overlapping types: $TO - CO - IO$: the higher the *DN*, the more likely is that the result of overlapping be nearer *TO* than nearer *IO*. In a (somewhat) speculative but suggestive way, we can think like this:

- the maximum value of the *DN* is, theoretically, done by the interaction between $C(1)_{51423}^{55555}$ and $C(2)_{51423}^{11111}$, namely:

$$DN_{\max} = 4 \cdot 5 + 4 \cdot 4 + 4 \cdot 3 + 4 \cdot 2 + 4 \cdot 1 = 4 \cdot 15 = 60$$

- the minimum value of the *DN* is, theoretically, $DN_{min} = 0$, since if it is negative, simply the relationship can be examined inversely and, so, it becomes positive as previously;
- we can, now, to reconfigure the interval $[0, 60] \subset N$ into the interval $I_{dn} = [0, 1] \subset R$ by the technique called normalization:

$$dn = \frac{DN_k - DN_{\min}}{DN_{\max} - DN_{\min}} = \frac{DN_k}{60}$$

where ***dn*** is the dominance number framed within I_{dn}, that is, $dn \in I_{dn}$.

- let us break the real interval $[0, 1]$ into three real intervals, namely: $I_{dn}^1 = [0, 0.5)$, $I_{dn}^2 = [0.5, 0.8)$, and $I_{dn}^3 = [0.8, 1]$, so that: $I_{dn} = \bigcup_k^3 I_{dn}^k$.

  Nota bene: so, the three sub-intervals constitute, by the operation of union, a cover of the set I_{dn};

- our (somewhat speculative) proposal is the following:
  - a pair of crises, $C(i)$ and $C(j)$, whose $dn_{(i,j)} \in I_{dn}^1$ to be considered as forming an *IO* (***immiscible*** overlapping);
  - a pair of crises, $C(i)$ and $C(j)$, whose $dn_{(i,j)} \in I_{dn}^2$ to be considered as forming a *CO* (***conservative*** overlapping);
  - a pair of crises, $C(i)$ and $C(j)$, whose $dn_{(i,j)} \in I_{dn}^3$ to be considered as forming a *TO* (***transformative*** overlapping).

Nota bene: framing the *DN* absolute values in positive, relative and sub-unitary values, ***dn***, means that our natural values associated with the classes of crises have no arbitrary impact on determining the size and direction of the affinity-based dominance.

However, this is a linear relation between exogenous variable (***dn***) and endogenous variable (type of crises-pair). It seems that the higher ***dn***, the higher speed of approaching from *IO* to *TO* of those pairs,[14] so we think a more "realistic" membership could be the following:

$I_{dn}^{1} = [0, 0.5)$, so 50% of the field
$I_{dn}^{2} = [0.5, 0.8)$, so, 30% of the field
$I_{dn}^{3} = [0.8, 1]$, so 20% of the field

Some Theoretical Illustrations

(1) $C(1)_{51423}^{\varepsilon\alpha\delta\beta\gamma} \equiv C(1)_{51423}^{43452}$, and $C(2)_{51423}^{\varepsilon\alpha\delta\beta\gamma} \equiv C(2)_{51423}^{13322}$

$$DN = 5\cdot(4-1)+4\cdot(3-3)+3\cdot(4-3)+2\cdot(5-2)+1\cdot(2-2)=27$$

$$dn = \frac{27}{60} = 0.45 \in I_{dn}^{1}$$

So, the crises overlapping is of *IO* type.

(2) $C(1)_{51423}^{\varepsilon\alpha\delta\beta\gamma} \equiv C(1)_{51423}^{43454}$, and $C(2)_{51423}^{\varepsilon\alpha\delta\beta\gamma} \equiv C(2)_{51423}^{21122}$

$$DN = 5\cdot(4-2)+4\cdot(3-1)+3\cdot(4-1)+2\cdot(5-2)+1\cdot(4-2)=35$$

$$dn = \frac{35}{60} = 0.58 \in I_{dn}^{2}$$

So, the crises overlapping is of *CO* type.

(3) $C(1)_{51423}^{\varepsilon\alpha\delta\beta\gamma} \equiv C(1)_{51423}^{55453}$, and $C(2)_{51423}^{\varepsilon\alpha\delta\beta\gamma} \equiv C(2)_{51423}^{12113}$

$$DN = 5\cdot(5-1)+4\cdot(5-2)+3\cdot(4-1)+2\cdot(5-1)+1\cdot(3-3)=49$$

$$dn = \frac{49}{60} = 0.82 \in I_{dn}^{3}$$

So, the crises overlapping is of *TO* type.

Of course, an empirical analysis of the crises (of any type) that happened across the world in the last, let us say, 150 years could calibrate these theoretical proposals (a little bit speculative, but based on logic), including the I_{dn}^{k} intervals. Such an examination exceeds, however, the objectives of the present study; consequently, we invite interested scientists to try to verify the plausibility of our suppositions.

5.5 Aggregations as Artefacts

It is useful to examine the general (societal) context in which the crisis phenomenology unfolds, since this context is, in fact, the "host" of causal and conditional factors in such a phenomenology.

5.5.1 *A Typology of Aggregations*

The Individual (Atom)

The reality, either objective, subjective, or objectivated, is composed of individuals (atoms) that develop relationships, of different natures, among them. The limits under which an individual (atom[15]) cannot be divided are, regularly, based on the stability criterion, that is, if a new dividing of an entity makes that entity unstable, then, the state of the entity in the case is considered to be its atomic state. The criterion of stability—which is specific to the natural sciences, like Chemistry or Physics—must be replaced in other fields of reality with other criteria. For example, in Biology, such a criterion of atomization could be the structural replicability (as is the cell level), in Psychology it could be the unity of signification (signifier), in humanistic sciences it could also be the units of signification—phoneme, morpheme, sememe, etc. In the social (societal) field, probably, the most appropriate criterion for such a limit in the atomizing (cognitive) process should be the replicability of functionality. In other words, we have a social (societal) individual or atom where a new dividing operation on the entity in the case leads to the loss of existing (or desired) functionality—of course, the functionality is a property that is externally defined and is depending on the cognitive or praxeological interest. For example, a firm can be divided into workplaces, which are formed by a unit of the human labour force and a unit of physical capital (equipment); if we want to disaggregate further the workplace, i.e., to separate the human labour force from the physical equipment, we shall observe that the workplace does not function anymore, so the individual (the atom) of the firm is the workplace.[16] Of course, these general considerations should be particularized—and this particularization will be delivered below—to the very phenomenon of crisis.

Ways and Finalities of Individuals' Interactions

Beginning with this paragraph, our attention will be focused exclusively on the social (societal) entity. The interactions (relationships) among the individuals are, generally, of two kinds: (a) relationships of cooperation; (b) relationships of competition. Of course, mixes between the two "pure" relationships are possible and, in fact, are predominantly within the society. Based on the constellations of the interactions, three categories of aggregations are possible to arise: (i) conglomerates; (ii) systems; (iii) networks (*Nota bene*: from a logical point of view, the aggregate is the genus, while the conglomerate, system, network are the species).

(i) the conglomerate

The conglomerate (noted C) is a set of those components[17] that share among them at least one property. The sharing of at least one property is required as the reason for which the components in the case justify their gathering together.[18] A problem arises regarding the case in which all the components share among them all their properties. They are, so, indiscernible among them but, as they are not identical among them, they remain countable and, so, can provide the cardinal of the set to which they belong. A set-conglomerate has the following sufficiency predicates:

- (SP_1^C) commonly shared properties[19] (at least one);
- (SP_2^C) a membrane which differentiate (either physically or logically) the conglomerate from the rest of the world;

So, we could write:

$$C \leftarrow \left(SP_1^C\right) \wedge \left(SP_2^C\right)$$

A conglomerate, once born, develops a necessary new[20] predicates (NNP_1^C),[21] called relationships between conglomerate and the rest of the world, so:

$$C \to NNP_1^C$$

(ii) the network

The network (N) is a conglomerate that exhibits a new sufficiency predicate, addressing the relationships among the components of the conglomerate, inside the membrane, noted SP_1^N . Exactly such (internal) relationships transform, logically, the conglomerate into network. Consequently, in a network there are no dominant components; all the components are equal from the perspective of dominance of any nature. So, we can write:

$$N \leftarrow C \wedge \left(SP_1^N\right)$$

or

$$N \leftarrow \left(SP_1^C\right) \wedge \left(SP_2^C\right) \wedge \left(NNP_1^C\right) \wedge \left(SP_1^N\right)$$

A network does not need to develop a necessary new predicate regarding the relationships between its components and the environment, since it inherits such a predicate from the conglomerate. Instead, the network develop a specific necessary new necessary predicate, called self-catalysing attractor of internal relationships, and noted NNP_1^N , i.e.:

$$N \to NNP_1^N$$

This necessary new predicate has the following content: by chance or not, one of the components of the network develops more relationships with the rest of the components than do the other components. In some conditions, this relational ascendant can work as a catalyser, so the number of relationships of that component continues to increase more quickly than the number of relationships of the other components. We speak, in this case, about the forming of a hub, and the process of arising and continuing increasing of the hub can be called hubbing process—in fact, the hubbing process is a process of agglomeration or densification. Regarding the reversibility of the hubbing process, we think this process is impossible, except in the case in which the hub is eliminated, in one way or another, from the network. In fact, there is, at the final, the spectrum of the implosion of the hub, which, above a threshold of the relationships, cannot function correctly anymore. *Nota bene*: the self-catalysis of the nominal flows, which we talked about in this study, is a hubbing process and its finality is exactly the implosion that leads to the nominal crisis (see Chap. 4).

(iii) the system

A system (S) is a network in which there is a dominant component, called leading component (*Nota bene*: it could be, of course, more than one such a dominant component), and driven components, constituted by the rest of the components. The specific sufficiency predicates of the system are:

- (SP_1^S) one or more (but not all) components own a dominant position towards the rest of the components. This dominance can be of any nature: size, power, energy, cognition, credibility, etc.

So, the dominant component (or components) forms the leading components, while the rest of the components form the driven components. From the leading components are transmitted to the driven components orders/commands, and from the driven components are transmitted to the leading components reports on the orders'/commands' achievement.

So, we could write:

$$S \leftarrow N \wedge \left(SP_1^S\right)$$

or

$$S \leftarrow \left(SP_1^C\right) \wedge \left(SP_2^C\right) \wedge \left(NNP_1^C\right) \wedge \left(SP_1^N\right) \wedge \left(NNP_1^N\right) \wedge \left(SP_1^S\right)$$

A system does not develop necessary new predicates (*NNPs*).

Nota bene: one could ask why the necessary new predicate in the case of network does not introduce a rapport of dominance inside that network, so transforming the network into a system. We provide the following argument to support that the hub rapport is not a dominance rapport: the hub rapport generation of relationships is of the same nature, no matter if the direction of the relationship is from the hub to the other components or vice-versa, while the dominance rapport generates relationships of different nature—orders/commands from the leading component/s to the driven components, and reports on executions of orders/commands from the driven component/s to the leading component/s. Consequently, if the hub rapport is of quantitative nature, the dominance rapport is of qualitative nature.

Based on the above definitions, that, in turn, are based on the sufficiency predicates, it can be inferred the spontaneous "logic" that governs the constitution of the three aggregates, namely firstly occur the conglomerates, secondly, inside the conglomerates arise the internal relationships among components—i.e., the networks are formed—and thirdly, inside the networks arise the internal dominance among the components—i.e., the systems are formed.

An important question can be put here: is possible the reversibility in the three processes, and how is it working? Our position is the following.

- all the three aggregates are reversible—by losing one or more sufficiency predicates, they transform either into individuals (atoms) or in other aggregates which, in the new state, verify the logical conditions based on the sufficiency predicates (the logical constant "$\setminus$" means "by losing", and with *Is* are noted the individuals/atoms);

$$C \setminus \left\{ \left(SP_1^C\right) \vee \left(SP_2^C\right) \vee \left[\left(SP_1^C\right) \wedge \left(SP_2^C\right) \right] \right\} \rightarrow Is$$

$$N \setminus \left(SP_1^N\right) \rightarrow C$$

$$S \setminus \left(SP_1^S\right) \rightarrow N$$

- the reversibility follows the inversely order of constituting the aggregates: constituting order is $Is \rightarrow C \rightarrow N \rightarrow S$, and reversibility order is $S \rightarrow N \rightarrow C \rightarrow Is$.

Figure 5.1 indicates the logical relationships among conglomerate, system and network.

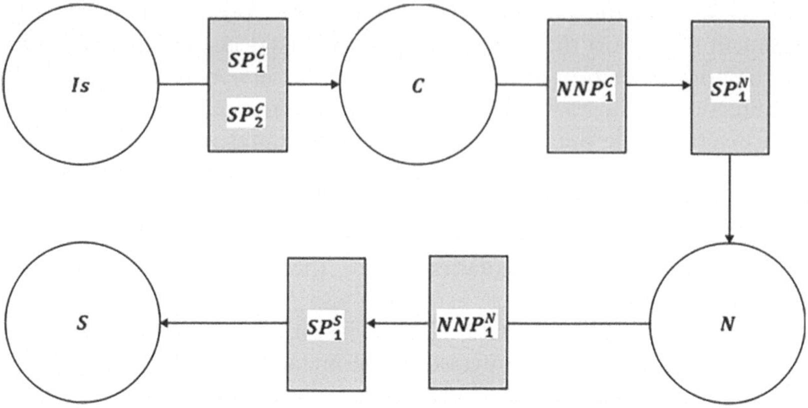

Fig. 5.1 Logical rapports among conglomerate, network and system. *Source*: author

Discussion

- the three species of the aggregates are linked among them in a sui generis evolutionary way:
  - the individuals gain, either necessarily or contingently, common attributes that gathered them into conglomerates;
  - the conglomerates develop, either necessarily or contingently, relationships among the individuals, so generating the networks;
  - the networks develop, either necessarily or contingently, hubs; at a moment of time, one of these hubs becomes the biggest[22] and, so, changes the hubbing process into a domination process, so generating the systems;
- it is remarkable that the germs of an aggregation species are "born" always inside the aggregation species which is in its logical antecedent—the common attributes in conglomerate arise in the set of individuals, the relationships among the components of the network arise inside the conglomerate, the hubbing process which leads to dominance inside the system arises in the network.

Four Extra Comments

(1) there are two concepts that are very important in relation with the aggregates as they were discussed above: (a) the functionality; (b) the behaviour. We clarify these two concepts.

(a) the functionality addresses the relationships among the components of an aggregate, so the relationships inside the membrane (see the sufficiency predicate SP_1^C). The functionality is born when the network arises and, of course, it is maintained in the system. The functionality is the effect of the structure and, consequently, it connects the conglomerate with the network;

(b) the behaviour addresses the relationships between the components of the aggregate and the environment (the components of the rest of the world). Of course, the components of the rest of the world, in turn, are structured into (the three) aggregates, so we can speak about the relationships between the aggregate in the case and the other aggregates from the environment. *Nota bene*: in fact, the behaviour is the "headquarter" of the (co)evolution of symbolic species, including the (co)evolution in the case of nominal crisis.

(2) the sub-aggregates "allowed" in any of the three aggregates

For a unitary terminology, we could consider the three categories of aggregates, as well as the logical combinations among them, as sets of different order, like this: (a) individuals (atoms)—sets of order "0"; (b) conglomerates—sets of order "1"; (c) networks—sets of order "2"; (d) systems—sets of order "3"; (e) networks of systems—sets of order "4"; (f) systems of networks—sets of order "5".

Of course, the ordering of systems of networks after the networks of systems requires an explanation.

- as shown, logically, the network occurs before the system, since the system needs to "wait" the hub process to generate the dominance, to create the leading components;
- as the process of passing from the hub component to the leading component can occur anywhere inside the network, it is presumable that, inside a given network many sub-aggregates of the system type will arise;
- as a consequence, a network of systems (or, at least, a network that contains systems) is more likely to arise before a system of networks;
- to configure a system of networks, it is required that at least one of the already formed networks becomes, by a process of hubbing of order 2 (i.e., by arising of a network-hub, while the order 1 hubbing

means arising of a component-hub inside a network). Although, from a logical point of view, such a phenomenon is not forbidden, it is obvious that it, generally, can occur, with a great probability, only after the network of systems has already occurred.

So, about the sub-aggregates of each of the five (possible and proper[23]) aggregates, we think the following:

(a) inside a conglomerate can exist all four categories of aggregates (for terminological unity, we consider, however, the individuals/atoms as some sets of degree 0); however, it is possible to be coagulated, based on more analytical attributes, many sub-conglomerates, so a conglomerate can contain both individuals and sub-conglomerates but the sub-conglomerates behave exactly as the individuals (somewhat as … composed individuals). The same, some networks or systems can subsist inside the conglomerate, with the "condition" do not develop relationships among them, although they can develop relationships internally. So, any sub-aggregates arise inside the conglomerate, they behave as composed individuals, i.e., without developing relationships among them;
(b) inside a network can exist, too, the four types of aggregates but, this time, the sub-aggregates can develop relationships among them (including relationships with themselves[24]) and, as shown previously, can constitute hubs;

Nota bene: it is to be mentioned that, for both networks and systems, the components are named vertices/nodes, and the relationships among components are named arcs/edges. Sometimes (especially in mathematics), the networks are called graphs.

(c) inside a system can exist, of course, the five types of aggregates, where (at least) one of them institutes itself as the leading component, while the rest of the components "fall" under the label of driven components;
(d) inside the networks of systems, as well as inside the systems of networks, as a logical consequence of the above mentioned, can subsist the five types of aggregates.

(3) the membrane/border of the network

If the concept of the membrane of the conglomerate does not put questions (it separates the set of individuals that share a given property from the individuals that do not share that property), in the case of a network things are not as clear anymore, so we shall provide some considerations in that matter:

- in a given set of individuals (including composed individuals) there are many relationships of different natures, exactly as the things happen inside a network. So, from the point of view of existing nominal relationships between components, a network seems to be indiscernible from its environment (including from other networks);
- here, we need another criterion of discernibility, very different from that quantitative/nominal only, namely a qualitative one. We propose, as a qualitative criterion to extract the network from its environment, the stability of the relationships developed among the components of a set. Let us develop, a little bit, this suggestion:
  - the stability is, it seems, difficult to measure or quantify, since it would require the marking of each interaction and, then, the monitoring of maintaining the marked interaction; so, as a proxy for the stability, could be considered the frequency[25] of the relationships in the case;
  - in turn, the frequency is a relative concept but, since it is uniformly applied to both the "searched" network and the environment of that network, the criterion is working and its result is significant;
  - however, a threshold (which might be called the threshold of rank "0"), as the minimum value of the frequency of relationships, must be established; such a threshold could be very different for different interests of knowledge or of praxeology but, at any rate, it provides a feasible criterion to cognitively isolate a network;
  - consequently, regarding the membrane/border of the network, it is traced to include all the nodes (and associated arcs), which ensures that the arcs in the case occur with a frequency that is situated above the established threshold.

Nota bene: the same criterion could be applied to identify (isolate) the hub/s in a network. We think the following "points" should be considered:

- obviously, a new threshold must be established to quantify the point above which a node of the network could (or must) be considered as a hub;
- we think that such a threshold (which might be called the threshold of rank "1") should be established at the value where the number of interactions "hosted" by the given node reaches the weight of a third of all the interactions in the network. Of course, the proposal "a third" is an expert opinion, so it could be improved by using some empirical observations or experimental findings.

(4) the membrane/border of the system

Regarding the tracing of the system's membrane/border, we propose the following reasoning:

- since we are, already, in a network "endowed" with (at least) a hub, we must, this time, observe if and how many of the interactions hosted by the hub are of orders/commands type;[26]
- we think that the threshold (which might be called the threshold of rank "2") above which the number of order/commands interactions starting from the hub qualifies that hub as a leading component of the (so born) system must be 80% of all the interactions among the network's components;
- based on the above proposals, the membrane/border of the system will "convoke" all the nodes in the network which receive at least an order/command from the hub in question;
- we would mention that, in a system, cannot subsist components which are bypassed by the arcs of orders/commands nature starting from the hub considered. Here arise a question regarding the societal organization (or the political regime in the society)—about this issue we provide some considerations below:
  - an authoritarian society is associated, regularly, with a strong leading component (generically called state), the rest of the society constituting the driven components, while the democracy is associated, regularly, with a less strong state, although not a weak state, (the leading sub-system) and a relatively strong part of the so-called civil society, i.e., the driven sub-systems, somehow organized in a diffuse network of non-governmental organizations (NGOs);

- although some analysts oppose the state to the civil society, in fact, the civil society is organized and function based on the rules established by the leading component (the state), and the degree of democracy is not proportionally increasing with the state power decreasing—all is depending on the normative framework introduced by the state (of course, in cooperation with civil society);
- even the so-called free market (in the economic field of the society) is functioning based on the normative framework enacted by the state (the leading component) and, in fact, in a deep democracy and free society, the state has as crucial role/function exactly to ensure individual freedom and democratic taking of public decisions.

(5) complexity vs. complicatedness

The term (and the concept signified) of complexity is, like other terms, used in the most unexpected contexts and with the most bizarre connotations, whether it is or is not the case. That is why we will make some clarifications on the matter.

- something is considered complicated if that something (thing, property, or relationship) has a high degree of difficulty in describing and/or explaining it—for example, because too many components and interactions among the components, or even because some lack of knowledge about the object that requires the description or explanation;
- it is clear that the complicatedness depends on our state of knowledge, so it has a historical mark—what we call today as complicated could become describable and/or explainable tomorrow, so that the complicatedness could disappear;
- instead, the complexity is referring to the unpredictability of the kinematics/dynamics of an object (thing, property or relationship). Accordingly to this definition, some consideration are required:
  - about the complicatedness we can speak no matter from what perspective we see at the object involved, while about complexity what we can speak is only we see at the object from the perspective of its predictability;
  - consequently, the complexity (as property of an object) is associable only to the kinematics/dynamics of that object—an object

that does not change in time is not liable to be discussed under the mark of complexity;

- one can say, in this point, that the unpredictability is, also, an effect of our lack of sufficient knowledge and, so, the complexity has a historical mark like the complicatedness, from which it results that the complicatedness and the complexity seem to be, in fact, indiscernible; we will dispel this presumptive objection in the following:
  - we refer to a principled unpredictability, not to a performative one (that has, indeed, a historical character);
  - a principled unpredictability is only provided by the presence of the free will;
  - the free will is only provided by the presence of the cultural beings (by now, we know, at least on Earth, a single cultural being, namely the human being);
  - so, the presence of the human being, in any object, necessarily induces, by the intermediation of the free will, the unpredictability of that object, no matter the degree of complicatedness of the object—for example, even the simplest dynamic object (so, easy to be described and explained *per se*), by the presence of the human being, becomes unpredictable;
  - consequently, the complexity has no historical character,[27] while the complicatedness does.

5.5.2 *Other Mentions*

Our proposal and suggestions regarding the aggregates (and aggregation process) at the societal level keep an abstract and general character. We need them for examining the "destiny" of the crisis, in its entire theoretical unfolding provided by now, and, especially, under the possibility of crises overlapping, the red thread of our book.

The four "pure" aggregates (in fact, three, since the individuals/atoms can be ignored here) can address both the societal framework as such and the crisis as such—for example, a crisis can manifest in a societal aggregate of network type, or the crisis itself can exhibit a networked profile or both. The same for the societal aggregate called the system. Therefore, the analysis, however general and abstract it may be, should consider this "distribution" of the aggregation profile, not to mention the much more complicated (*Nota bene*: this time, complex, too) cases of the network of systems or the system of networks, as discussed above.

5.6 Crises and Societal Context

We have seen above that the chreode of the (societal) crisis—the class γ—can, generally, of five species: $\gamma = 1$: self-extinguishing crisis; $\gamma = 2$: self-maintaining crisis; $\gamma = 3$: trans-field crisis; $\gamma = 4$: migratory crisis; $\gamma = 5$: synergic crisis. It is relevant to discuss, in such a context, the behaviour of crisis, in each of the five hypostases and in the three societal contexts: (a) conglomerate societal context, (b) network societal context and (c) system societal context.

Nota bene: taking into consideration the definition of conglomerate, since inside such an aggregate are not relationships among the components, the crisis simply does not exist.[28] The reason is that the mechanism of initiating, and developing a crisis need relationships both among nominal flows and between nominal flows, on the one part, and the financial and real flows, on the other part. Consequently, the conglomerate will be ignored in the next analyses.

5.6.1 *Networked Chreode (NC) of Crises Overlapping*

By a networked chreode of crisis overlapping is understood that situation in which more crises, having temporal intervals of contemporaneity among them, occur in the same societal system and are not directed by a dominant crisis. Somewhat, all the involved crises are positioned to each other approximatively from "equal" positions. *Nota bene*: of course, the dominance based on affinity, as discussed above, maintains, but there is not, so to say, non-affinity-based dominance. So, we have a network of crises, which will overlap among them exclusively from the perspective of affinity-based dominance.

(a) network societal context

This is the case in which there are networks of both crises and the societal context. In other words, society is organized as a network[29] (which is a kind of societal aggregates) and, in this networked context, a network of crises occurs.

It is happened that a network (of crises) interacts with other network (of the societal organization). An inter-network collision is rather a spontaneous interaction, since there is not a "coordinator", neither from the society, nor from the crises.[30] The main features of crisis chreode, when that chreode is of network profile and arises in a networked society, seems to be the following:

- the initiation of the crises is random,[31] i.e., it could happen in any node of the network in the case;
- as the randomness implies the causality (except for the causa finalis, which is compatible with deliberativeness only), it is interesting to search for the efficient cause that could develop a network of crises;
- in fact, the (generic) cause of the crisis initiation has been advanced in Chap. 4, namely the autonomization of the nominal flows related to the real flows;
- now, it is important to identify/establish the efficient cause of arising a network of crises which are liable to overlap among them in a networked way of society organizing. To this end, we advance the following mechanism:
  - the (financial) crisis is triggered when the (generally quantitative) gap between the nominal economic flows and the real economic flows reaches a given threshold; let us presume, what is realistic enough, that a crisis arises in a single node of the societal network;
  - once triggered, the crisis will naturally "search" the weak points in the societal network when it could extend; but what means "weak points" in this context? A weak point is a point (better said, a node of the societal network) where the "distance" between the autonomization degree of the initiated node and the other autonomization degrees of the other societal nodes is smallest;
  - the crisis will penetrate that nodes with which the mentioned "distance" is the smallest—we can say that the criterion of expanding the crisis to a networked profile is the minimal gradient of autonomization (*MGA*);[32]
  - after a new node is "colonized", the searching of the MGA will be resumed, since the "map" of such gradients is changed for every new expansion of the crisis, and the process continues until, possibly, the entire network of the society is contaminated; this process happens simultaneously with the forming of the crisis network itself;

(b) system societal context

This is the case in which there is a network of crises, and the societal context is of a system type. In other words, society is organized as a system (which is also a kind of societal aggregates) and, in this systemed context, a network of crises occurs.

It is happened that a network (of crises) interacts with a contextual system (of the societal organization). An interaction between a network and a system is, in a great measure, under the action of the leading component of the societal context. The main features of crisis chreode, when that chreode is of network profile and arises in a systemed society, seem to be the following:

- the initiation of the crises is random too, i.e., it could happen in any node of the societal system, either in the leading node or the driven nodes;
- if the crisis is initiated in the leading node of the society, the mechanism of networking (extending) the crisis is the same as in the case 5.6.1, point (a), i.e., based on the *MGA*;
- instead, if the crisis is initiated in one of the driven nodes of the society, the leading node can intervene to manage the crisis expansion—regularly by two (separated or mixed) institutional tools:
  - by blocking/interrupting the connections between the contaminated node and the other driven nodes, which has the logical signification of turning the nodes with a high degree of autonomization to a quasi-conglomerate, of course, artificially maintained for the required interval of time (*Nota bene*: obviously, such a blockage/interruption can be operated regarding the leading node itself, too);
  - by reducing the degrees of autonomization, for the driven nodes of the society where is the case, the crisis does not "find" the opportunity points where can expand to create a networked crisis;[33]
- consequently, in the case of initiating a path to a networked crisis in the context of a systemed society, the networked crisis development is liable to be controlled by the intervention.

5.6.2 *Systemed Chreode (SC) of Crises Overlapping*

By a systemed chreode of crisis overlapping is understood that situation in which more crises, having temporal intervals of contemporaneity among them, occur in the same societal system being directed by a dominant crisis. Somewhat, all the involved crises, except one, are positioned to each other approximatively from "equal" positions, but, at the same time, they are positioned under the dominance of exactly the crisis excepted. *Nota bene*: of course, the dominance based on affinity, as discussed above, maintains, and, concomitantly, there is, so to say, one non-affinity-based dominance. So, we have a system of crises, which will overlap among them directed by the leading crisis from the perspective of affinity-based dominance.

(a) network societal context

This case is less likely to happen since a system (in this case, of the crises) that arises in a network (in this case, of the society) seems to have not an … ontological base—once the society is a network, this means there are not privileged nodes when occurring a leading crisis or, at least, a leading germ of crisis. Rather, maybe we have here an inverse situation: a contingent crisis, with a strong power of "leadership" could transform a node of the society network into a privileged one, so coming back to the case 5.6.1., point (b), i.e., to the case of a systemed society.

(b) system societal context

The case of a systemed (structured) crisis occurring in a systemed society is, by far, the most important and significant one. Two distinct cases can happen: (b1) the crisis germ is triggered exactly in the leading node of the societal system; (b2) the crisis germ is triggered in a driven node of that societal system.

(b1) crisis leading node is coincident with the societal leading node

This case means, most likely, that the germs of crisis are generated by the structure (and functions) of the state (Government, Parliament, Judicial Power or the private domain of the state[34]). For example, the corruption[35] can arise in any of the mentioned leading components of the society, generating a crisis in the matter. Being "hosted" in a leading component of the society, the crisis will be easily extended by intermediation of the relationships between the leading component and the driven components, namely by the relationships of orders/commands type. Thus, the crisis will invade the driven nodes, to such an extent that it can lead to a systemed chreode of crisis since the hypostases of the crisis as manifested at the level of the driven nodes are somewhat "coordinated" by the central core of the crisis in question. It seems that, when the origin and/or cause of the crisis is located in the leading node of the societal system, the crisis acquires, *eo ipso* (i.e., in a necessary way), the configuration of a systemed chreode.

(b2) crisis leading node is "hosted" by a driven node of the societal system

This time, the germs of crisis arise in a driven component of the societal system, and these germs immediately gain the leading role in the future crisis extending. At the same time, the leading component of the societal system monitors the crisis by initiating and self-structuring it as a systemed crisis. Consequently, while in (b1) case, the systemed crisis is mapped on the systemed society, this time the systemed crisis could be built up by the systemed society. As being externally related to the leading component of the crisis, the leading component of the society has the latitude for two alternative options, based on different purposes: (i) to "help" the crisis to become a systemed crisis; (ii) to manage the crisis inside the form of a networked one. Principled, a systemed crisis is easier to control than a networked crisis, when the society is organized as a system.[36]

Annex 5.1: The List of Cases of Incompatibility of Crisis Marks, Taken Two by Two

- $\alpha_1\alpha_3$: (and vice-versa, i.e., $\alpha_3\alpha_1$);
- $\alpha_2\alpha_4$: (and vice-versa, i.e., $\alpha_4\alpha_2$);
- $\beta_1\alpha_3$: (and vice-versa, i.e., $\alpha_3\beta_1$);
- $\beta_2\alpha_3$: (and vice-versa, i.e., $\alpha_3\beta_2$);
- $\beta_2\alpha_5$: (and vice-versa, i.e., $\alpha_5\beta_2$);
- $\beta_4\alpha_3$: (and vice-versa, i.e., $\alpha_3\beta_4$);
- $\beta_5\alpha_2$: (and vice-versa, i.e., $\alpha_2\beta_5$);
- $\gamma_1\alpha_3$: (and vice-versa, i.e., $\alpha_3\gamma_1$);
- $\gamma_2\alpha_4$: (and vice-versa, i.e., $\alpha_4\gamma_2$);

- $\gamma_3\alpha_1$: (and vice-versa, i.e., $\alpha_1\gamma_3$);
- $\gamma_4\alpha_1$: (and vice-versa, i.e., $\alpha_1\gamma_4$);
- $\gamma_5\alpha_1$: (and vice-versa, i.e., $\alpha_1\gamma_5$);
- $\delta_1\alpha_1$: (and vice-versa, i.e., $\alpha_1\delta_1$);
- $\delta_1\alpha_3$: (and vice-versa, i.e., $\alpha_3\delta_1$);
- $\delta_1\alpha_5$: (and vice-versa, i.e., $\alpha_5\delta_1$);
- $\delta_2\alpha_3$: (and vice-versa, i.e., $\alpha_3\delta_2$);
- $\delta_2\alpha_5$: (and vice-versa, i.e., $\alpha_5\delta_2$);
- $\delta_3\alpha_3$: (and vice-versa, i.e., $\alpha_3\delta_3$);
- $\varepsilon_2\alpha_1$: (and vice-versa, i.e., $\alpha_1\varepsilon_2$);
- $\varepsilon_3\alpha_1$: (and vice-versa, i.e., $\alpha_1\varepsilon_3$);
- $\varepsilon_4\alpha_1$: (and vice-versa, i.e., $\alpha_1\varepsilon_4$);
- $\varepsilon_4\alpha_5$: (and vice-versa, i.e., $\alpha_5\varepsilon_4$);
- $\varepsilon_5\alpha_5$: (and vice-versa, i.e., $\alpha_5\varepsilon_5$);
- $\beta_1\beta_4$: (and vice-versa, i.e., $\beta_4\beta_1$);
- $\beta_1\beta_5$: (and vice-versa, i.e., $\beta_5\beta_1$);
- $\beta_3\beta_5$: (and vice-versa, i.e., $\beta_5\beta_3$);
- $\beta_4\beta_5$: (and vice-versa, i.e., $\beta_5\beta_4$);
- $\gamma_1\beta_1$: (and vice-versa, i.e., $\beta_1\gamma_1$);
- $\gamma_1\beta_4$: (and vice-versa, i.e., $\beta_4\gamma_1$);
- $\gamma_1\beta_5$: (and vice-versa, i.e., $\beta_5\gamma_1$);
- $\gamma_1\beta_5$: (and vice-versa, i.e., $\beta_5\gamma_1$);
- $\delta_1\beta_1$: (and vice-versa, i.e., $\beta_1\delta_1$);
- $\delta_3\beta_1$: (and vice-versa, i.e., $\beta_1\delta_3$);
- $\delta_4\beta_1$: (and vice-versa, i.e., $\beta_1\delta_4$);
- $\delta_3\beta_2$: (and vice-versa, i.e., $\beta_2\delta_3$);
- $\delta_4\beta_2$: (and vice-versa, i.e., $\beta_2\delta_4$);
- $\delta_2\beta_4$: (and vice-versa, i.e., $\beta_4\delta_2$);
- $\delta_3\beta_4$: (and vice-versa, i.e., $\beta_4\delta_3$);
- $\delta_1\beta_5$: (and vice-versa, i.e., $\beta_5\delta_1$);
- $\delta_4\beta_5$: (and vice-versa, i.e., $\beta_5\delta_4$);
- $\delta_5\beta_5$: (and vice-versa, i.e., $\beta_5\delta_5$);
- $\alpha_1\gamma_3$: (and vice-versa, i.e., $\gamma_3\alpha_1$);
- $\alpha_1\gamma_4$: (and vice-versa, i.e., $\gamma_4\alpha_1$);
- $\alpha_1\gamma_5$: (and vice-versa, i.e., $\gamma_5\alpha_1$);
- $\alpha_3\gamma_1$: (and vice-versa, i.e., $\gamma_1\alpha_3$);
- $\alpha_4\gamma_2$: (and vice-versa, i.e., $\gamma_2\alpha_4$);
- $\alpha_5\gamma_1$: (and vice-versa, i.e., $\gamma_1\alpha_5$);
- $\beta_2\gamma_2$: (and vice-versa, i.e., $\gamma_2\beta_2$);

- $\beta_3\gamma_2$: (and vice-versa, i.e., $\gamma_2\beta_3$);
- $\gamma_1\gamma_2$: (and vice-versa, i.e., $\gamma_2\gamma_1$);
- $\gamma_1\gamma_3$: (and vice-versa, i.e., $\gamma_3\gamma_1$);
- $\gamma_1\gamma_4$: (and vice-versa, i.e., $\gamma_4\gamma_1$);
- $\delta_1\gamma_4$: (and vice-versa, i.e., $\gamma_4\delta_1$);
- $\delta_2\gamma_2$: (and vice-versa, i.e., $\gamma_2\delta_2$);
- $\delta_3\gamma_2$: (and vice-versa, i.e., $\gamma_2\delta_3$);
- $\delta_3\gamma_3$: (and vice-versa, i.e., $\gamma_3\delta_3$);
- $\delta_3\gamma_5$: (and vice-versa, i.e., $\gamma_5\delta_3$);
- $\delta_4\gamma_1$: (and vice-versa, i.e., $\gamma_1\delta_4$);
- $\delta_4\gamma_2$: (and vice-versa, i.e., $\gamma_2\delta_4$);
- $\delta_4\gamma_3$: (and vice-versa, i.e., $\gamma_3\delta_4$);
- $\varepsilon_1\gamma_5$: (and vice-versa, i.e., $\gamma_5\varepsilon_1$);
- $\varepsilon_3\gamma_5$: (and vice-versa, i.e., $\gamma_5\varepsilon_3$);
- $\varepsilon_4\gamma_1$: (and vice-versa, i.e., $\gamma_1\varepsilon_4$);
- $\varepsilon_4\gamma_2$: (and vice-versa, i.e., $\gamma_2\varepsilon_4$);
- $\varepsilon_4\gamma_4$: (and vice-versa, i.e., $\gamma_4\varepsilon_4$);
- $\varepsilon_5\gamma_1$: (and vice-versa, i.e., $\gamma_1\varepsilon_5$);
- $\varepsilon_5\gamma_1$: (and vice-versa, i.e., $\gamma_1\varepsilon_5$);
- $\varepsilon_5\gamma_2$: (and vice-versa, i.e., $\gamma_2\varepsilon_5$);
- $\varepsilon_5\gamma_3$: (and vice-versa, i.e., $\gamma_3\varepsilon_5$);
- $\varepsilon_5\gamma_4$: (and vice-versa, i.e., $\gamma_4\varepsilon_5$);
- $\varepsilon_5\gamma_5$: (and vice-versa, i.e., $\gamma_5\varepsilon_5$);
- $\alpha_1\delta_1$: (and vice-versa, i.e., $\delta_1\alpha_1$);
- $\alpha_3\delta_1$: (and vice-versa, i.e., $\delta_1\alpha_3$);
- $\alpha_3\delta_2$: (and vice-versa, i.e., $\delta_2\alpha_3$);
- $\alpha_3\delta_3$: (and vice-versa, i.e., $\delta_3\alpha_3$);
- $\alpha_5\delta_1$: (and vice-versa, i.e., $\delta_1\alpha_5$);
- $\alpha_5\delta_2$: (and vice-versa, i.e., $\delta_2\alpha_5$);
- $\beta_1\delta_1$: (and vice-versa, i.e., $\delta_1\beta_1$);
- $\beta_1\delta_3$: (and vice-versa, i.e., $\delta_3\beta_1$);
- $\beta_1\delta_4$: (and vice-versa, i.e., $\delta_4\beta_1$);
- $\beta_2\delta_3$: (and vice-versa, i.e., $\delta_3\beta_2$);
- $\beta_2\delta_4$: (and vice-versa, i.e., $\delta_4\beta_2$);
- $\beta_4\delta_2$: (and vice-versa, i.e., $\delta_2\beta_4$);
- $\beta_4\delta_3$: (and vice-versa, i.e., $\delta_3\beta_4$);
- $\beta_5\delta_1$: (and vice-versa, i.e., $\delta_1\beta_5$);
- $\beta_5\delta_4$: (and vice-versa, i.e., $\delta_4\beta_5$);
- $\beta_5\delta_5$: (and vice-versa, i.e., $\delta_5\beta_5$);

- $\gamma_1\delta_1$: (and vice-versa, i.e., $\delta_1\gamma_1$);
- $\gamma_2\delta_2$: (and vice-versa, i.e., $\delta_2\gamma_2$);
- $\gamma_2\delta_3$: (and vice-versa, i.e., $\delta_3\gamma_2$);
- $\gamma_2\delta_4$: (and vice-versa, i.e., $\delta_4\gamma_2$);
- $\gamma_3\delta_3$: (and vice-versa, i.e., $\delta_3\gamma_3$);
- $\gamma_3\delta_4$: (and vice-versa, i.e., $\delta_4\gamma_3$);
- $\gamma_4\delta_1$: (and vice-versa, i.e., $\delta_1\gamma_4$);
- $\gamma_5\delta_3$: (and vice-versa, i.e., $\delta_3\gamma_5$);
- $\alpha_1\varepsilon_2$: (and vice-versa, i.e., $\varepsilon_2\alpha_1$);
- $\alpha_1\varepsilon_3$: (and vice-versa, i.e., $\varepsilon_3\alpha_1$);
- $\alpha_1\varepsilon_4$: (and vice-versa, i.e., $\varepsilon_4\alpha_1$);
- $\alpha_5\varepsilon_4$: (and vice-versa, i.e., $\varepsilon_4\alpha_5$);
- $\alpha_5\varepsilon_5$: (and vice-versa, i.e., $\varepsilon_5\alpha_5$);
- $\beta_1\varepsilon_1$: (and vice-versa, i.e., $\varepsilon_1\beta_1$);
- $\beta_1\varepsilon_3$: (and vice-versa, i.e., $\varepsilon_3\beta_1$);
- $\beta_1\varepsilon_4$: (and vice-versa, i.e., $\varepsilon_4\beta_1$);
- $\beta_1\varepsilon_5$: (and vice-versa, i.e., $\varepsilon_5\beta_1$);
- $\beta_2\varepsilon_5$: (and vice-versa, i.e., $\varepsilon_5\beta_2$);
- $\beta_4\varepsilon_3$: (and vice-versa, i.e., $\varepsilon_3\beta_4$);
- $\beta_4\varepsilon_5$: (and vice-versa, i.e., $\varepsilon_5\beta_4$);
- $\beta_5\varepsilon_4$: (and vice-versa, i.e., $\varepsilon_4\beta_5$);
- $\beta_5\varepsilon_5$: (and vice-versa, i.e., $\varepsilon_5\beta_5$);
- $\gamma_1\varepsilon_4$: (and vice-versa, i.e., $\varepsilon_4\gamma_1$);
- $\gamma_1\varepsilon_5$: (and vice-versa, i.e., $\varepsilon_5\gamma_1$);
- $\gamma_2\varepsilon_4$: (and vice-versa, i.e., $\varepsilon_4\gamma_2$);
- $\gamma_2\varepsilon_5$: (and vice-versa, i.e., $\varepsilon_5\gamma_2$);
- $\gamma_3\varepsilon_5$: (and vice-versa, i.e., $\varepsilon_5\gamma_3$);
- $\gamma_4\varepsilon_4$: (and vice-versa, i.e., $\varepsilon_4\gamma_4$);
- $\gamma_4\varepsilon_5$: (and vice-versa, i.e., $\varepsilon_5\gamma_4$);
- $\gamma_5\varepsilon_1$: (and vice-versa, i.e., $\varepsilon_1\gamma_5$);
- $\gamma_5\varepsilon_3$: (and vice-versa, i.e., $\varepsilon_3\gamma_5$);
- $\gamma_5\varepsilon_5$: (and vice-versa, i.e., $\varepsilon_5\gamma_5$);
- $\delta_1\varepsilon_5$: (and vice-versa, i.e., $\varepsilon_5\delta_1$);
- $\delta_2\varepsilon_4$: (and vice-versa, i.e., $\varepsilon_4\delta_2$);
- $\delta_2\varepsilon_5$: (and vice-versa, i.e., $\varepsilon_5\delta_2$);
- $\delta_3\varepsilon_1$: (and vice-versa, i.e., $\varepsilon_1\delta_3$);
- $\delta_3\varepsilon_2$: (and vice-versa, i.e., $\varepsilon_2\delta_3$);
- $\delta_4\varepsilon_3$: (and vice-versa, i.e., $\varepsilon_3\delta_4$);
- $\delta_4\varepsilon_5$: (and vice-versa, i.e., $\varepsilon_5\delta_4$);

- $\delta_5\varepsilon_1$: (and vice-versa, i.e., $\varepsilon_1\delta_5$);
- $\delta_5\varepsilon_2$: (and vice-versa, i.e., $\varepsilon_2\delta_5$);
- $\varepsilon_1\varepsilon_4$: (and vice-versa, i.e., $\varepsilon_4\varepsilon_1$);
- $\varepsilon_1\varepsilon_5$: (and vice-versa, i.e., $\varepsilon_5\varepsilon_1$);
- $\varepsilon_2\varepsilon_5$: (and vice-versa, i.e., $\varepsilon_5\varepsilon_2$);
- $\varepsilon_4\varepsilon_1$: (and vice-versa, i.e., $\varepsilon_1\varepsilon_4$);
- $\varepsilon_5\varepsilon_1$: (and vice-versa, i.e., $\varepsilon_1\varepsilon_5$);
- $\varepsilon_5\varepsilon_2$: (and vice-versa, i.e., $\varepsilon_2\varepsilon_5$);

Notes

1. We shall provide some own considerations on the so-called *constructal theory* (or constructal law), which is vehiculated in the literature, especially among physicians/mathematicians but liable to be examined from an economic or social perspective too.
2. The limits of the time interval or of space areal are not of importance here.
3. More exactly, the affinity is introduced as a constant in the equation regarding the substrate-limited microbial growth. This substrate-based limitation of the growth (or, in other words, the growth limitation by the substrate) will constitute an important suggestion for us in describing (and explaining) the phenomenon/process of crises overlapping.
4. Such a path of analysis—i.e., to establish which are, logically, the attributes a generic relationship could develop—is, obviously, interesting enough but, in developing it, we would go too far from the targeted objective of the chapter.
5. Of course, we are positioned in the "standard" view of causality, in which the cause is temporally situated before the effect generated by that cause. As known, quantum mechanics also asserts the possibility of an inverse temporal ordering between cause and effect.
6. This assumption is, of course, simply a belief. In fact, in a lexicographical order, we think there is the following ranking of the primordiality among the three primitive entities in the world: (1) relationship; (2) property; (3) thing. This means that the dominance in a given context is adjudged by relationship, then (if the relationship does not occur) by the property, then (if the property does not occur) by the thing.
7. An image borrowed from Physics is here the following: affinity acts as an electric tension that directs the propensities (the … "electrons") to the same direction, namely the direction in which the affinity acts itself, so generating the "electric current".

8. Of course, as we established before, even in the presence of a relationship it is possible that the affinity does not occur. In such a case, the unintelligibility of the phenomenon conserves itself.
9. See, here, the semantic crisp difference we made before between meaning and signification.
10. The state is not too different from the case of entropy, underground economy or economic preferences—in all cases we can only establish at most an order between the "individuals" of the species in the case, not cardinal differences.
11. The incompatibility is, of course, symmetric: $x(i) - y(j)$ is equivalent with $x(j) - y(i)$, for $x, y, i, j \in \{1,2,3,4,5\}$.
12. This temporal causality will be implied in the crisis fractality issue (see Chap. 6).
13. Is, somewhat, a parallel discussion with the assertion of Bertrand Russell according to which an inspired notation (of, e.g., a variable) has the potential to illuminate on exactly the … solution.
14. It is easy to observe an analogy with fractality (*Nota bene*: Chap. 6 will approach the issue of fractality in the matter of societal crisis), namely, the neighbourhood to a border leads to a similar behaviour with that of the "resident"' located beyond that border.
15. The concept (and term) atom is a Greek word meaning indivisible, namely ἄτομος (átomos), or ἄτομον (átomon).
16. The neoclassic economic theory advanced the hypothesis that the human individual is the "atom" of the economic process and developed, around it the standard homo œconomicus logical model. But, it seems that the individual thinks and actions within the households, which means that the economic individual is not the individual as person but the households (*Nota bene*: Economics comes from the Greek οἰκονόμος (*oikonomos*)—οἰκο (*oikos*) and νόμος (*nómos*)). So, economy refers to the households as unit of economic signification. The problem is that, in a household we have cooperation only, not competition, so, a societal system where the competition arises must be otherwise called—in fact, Hayek proposed, in such a direction, the term catallaxy (or catallactics), from the Greek katallattein, meaning both "to exchange" and "to turn from enemy to friend".
17. One could ask why is used the term component instead of the term individual (atom). The reason is that any aggregate (so, including the conglomerate) can contain both individuals (atoms) and other aggregates—in this case, other conglomerates. So, the term components addresses both the individuals (atoms) and the aggregates that belong to the discussed aggregate. *Nota bene*: some analysts use the term element instead of the term component, but we disagree with them since the term element gener-

ally connotes the individual as an atom—it is obvious that is not always the case when the component is an element.

18. Of course, based on other commune properties, other aggregates can be formed.
19. The property can be any that exhibits an interest, either cognitive or praxeological. Consequently, depending on that interest, different aggregates can be "extracted" from the same reality (*Nota bene*: as we shall see, the same is valid for systems and networks).
20. We must explain the qualifier "new". The sufficiency predicates, i.e., the set of cumulative attributes that qualify an entity are, concomitantly, necessary predicates, since, once an entity is qualified as such, it does not lose its sufficiency predicates. As a result, since, after qualifying as such, the entity endows itself with a necessary predicate that is not also a sufficient one, that necessary predicate must be called as being a necessary new predicate, given that the other necessary predicates (i.e., the sufficiency predicates themselves) are ... old necessary predicates.
21. We remind you that once an entity is qualified as an aggregate, of any species, that entity can gain one or more new predicates. These new predicates are necessary; therefore, they must be named necessary new predicates (*NNP*).
22. It is easy to observe here the same logical "pattern" which is proposed by Robert Nozick in the matter of arising the state as the "best" association of the human individuals (1993).
23. The individual (atom) is improperly called as being an aggregate.
24. For instance, self-catalysis is the effect of a loop—a relationship (arc) from a node to itself.
25. It is easy to observe that the frequency can well enough quantify the stability, although many relationships are not maintained *per se*, but are maintained statistically.
26. The establishment of the criterion to discern between arcs of orders/commands nature and the arcs of simple functional interactions is at the very disposal of the observer/researcher/praxeologist.
27. Of course, if we do not consider the hypothesis of the disappearance of free will, therefore of cultural beings (human being) from our planet. Obviously, artificial intelligence will not have the property of quiddity of free will.
28. In this reasoning consists, for example, the "solution" of blocking the propagation of a crisis by blocking the relationships among the components of the aggregate in case (either network or system)—logically, by such a blocking, the respective area is transformed into a ... conglomerate, in which the crisis will suffocate on its own.
29. The idea of a (human) society to be organized as a network, as this concept is defined in the present study, is somewhat non-realistic. Indeed, however

simple a society could be, it has, however vaguely, a leading component, so it is systemed organized, i.e., organized as system. The case of a networked organized society is, consequently, discussed only from a logical perspective (as a possible world).

30. It is, of course, incomprehensible the carelessness with which some call several crises that are contemporary with each other or even overlap among them as a … system of crises, when it is only speaking about a network of crises.
31. We remind you that it is difficult (although, of course, it is not impossible) to associate a stochastic pattern to a networked crisis/crises. *Nota bene*: obviously, the randomness obeys causality as any conceivable event.
32. The formalization of this process is simple enough, so we do not proceed to such a formalization.
33. An example, here, is the institutional mechanism, usually driven by the central bank in an economic system, by which the nominal flows in the economy are mutually compensated so the amount of the nominal flows over the amount of the real flows drastically decreases—in fact, as a result of the mutual compensation, what remains are just the net nominal liabilities or credits.
34. The central bank is a state institution with public capital and private patrimony, so, probably, its "place" is in the private domain of the state. On the other hand, the monetary/currency policy produces public goods; consequently, the central bank could be integrated into the public sector. At any rate (even when it is a private institution), the central bank enters the leading component of the societal organization.
35. By corruption must be understood that behaviour of public servants, related to the public money, by which they gain personal illegal advantages, of any nature, for the performance of the duties that they are obliged to perform, for the performance of the duties that they are obliged not to perform, for the non-performance of the duties that they are obliged to perform or for the non-performance of the duties that they are obliged not to perform (Dinga, 2012).
36. You control a pack of dogs if you target the pack leader.

References

Dinga, E. (2012). *Rebuilding Economics: A Logical, Epistemological, and Methodological Approach*. Lambert Academic Publishing. especially Chapter 10 "On the Dual (Informal) Economy".

Monod, J. (1942). *Recherches sur la croissance des cultures bactériennes*. Hermann and Cie.

Nozick, R. (1993). *The Nature of Rationality*. Princeton University Press.

CHAPTER 6

On a Possible Crisis Fractality

6.1 Preamble

All the concepts are artefacts; they are, more precisely, "labels" that people stick to reality (either objective, subjective or objectified). In the social field, which is, essentially, an objectified world,[1] although objective and subjective "ingredients" are indispensable, the artefactual character of the concepts, including the properties and relationships, is all the more obvious. In fact, our "labels" are hypotheses that we throw over the world and, then, we try to see if they are or not corroborated by the factuals involved. In other words, not only the sophisticated theories constitute hypotheses on the reality (Popper, 2002, 2005) but, also, our definitions, the properties associated with the things and relationships and so on, with which we try to decipher the world for our understanding and action. As said countless times, the world is exactly what our language says it is.[2]

In this epistemological context, it is not without interest and relevance to examine one of the most spectacular (not yet totally corroborated, however) scientific labels, namely the fractality. More precisely, it is about the possibility that the crisis phenomenon and, especially, the overlapping of crises, to exhibit the property of fractality.

Of course, the exam of such a possibility will be conducted from the same logical perspective used previously, i.e. we do not provide empirical (or historical) research on the matter. We are especially interested, as said

E. Dinga, *Economic Resilience During Overlapped Crises*,
https://doi.org/10.1007/978-3-031-80224-9_6

above, in the very possibility that the crisis and the phenomena associated with them have, among their attributes, the property of fractality. Below, we shall develop such an examination.

6.2 What Fractality Is It?

6.2.1 General Issues on Fractality

Fractality is a property of a network, system, phenomenon, process and so on. It can characterize both the things, the properties (as a property of order 2) and the relationships. In essence, the fractality is that property which ensures a self-similarity of either structuring or replication of an entity in the world. So, by now, it results the following predicates of the fractality.

(1) fractality is a *property*—we shall see, further, that this property is caused (generated) by a relationship;[3]
   - a question must be asked here: the property of fractality is *contingent*, or *necessary*? Our position in that matter is as follows:
   - as any property, fractality has a necessary character, namely once a relationship is born and works, any properties that are associated to the given relationship will occur, no matter they are or not are observed;[4]
   - this statement should, however, be amended for the social field, where there are, preponderantly, artefacts, and, in addition, based on the presence of human individuals, free will is in force—the free will could oppose the (social) necessity,[5] including the fractality property, so the property of fractality in the social field can have (or, more drastically, have) a contingent character;
   - consequently, in the social field, fractality should be considered either an intra-necessity contingency or an intra-contingency necessity, after the case (see our detailed considerations in the matter in Chap. 2, point 2.2.2, (iv)); the concrete cases will be examined further when the fractality of crisis will be analytically approached;

(2) fractality is definable as a *self-similarity* at different scales.[6] Since this attribute/predicate is, in our opinion, exactly the specific difference (in Aristotle's terminology), applied to the proximal genus called property, some extra considerations are needed, as follows:

- *firstly*, what is a similarity, and when the question of *similarity* must be posed:

• similarity is a double-paired concept;

the first conceptual pair consists in the fact that similarity cannot be invoked without indicating the criterion (or criteria, after the case) based on which the similarity must be judged; in other words, there is not a similarity *per se*, but only related to a criterion pre-established; some examples of such criteria: the topological form, the structure, the role, etc.

the second conceptual pair consists in the fact that similarity cannot be invoked than by bringing face to face two entities of the same nature: things, properties, relationships, between which the property of the similarity be examined, based on the above-mentioned criterion (or criteria);[7]

• similarity is a genus with different species: (a) if no criterion can be applied to identify the similarity, then the two (or more) entities compared are simply different between them; (b) if a criterion (or more) can be applied to identify the similarity, then the entities compared are similar between them, according to this and that criterion (criteria); (c) if all the criteria convoked to examine the similarity are verified, then the two entities are identical with each other from the perspective of the convoked criteria;[8]

• so, the similarity is a double-paired property, based on a given criterion,[9] which establish the membership, to an adequate set of entities, of the two (or more) entities taken into consideration:

- *secondly*, it must be clarified the composed concept of *self-similarity*:

• the self-similarity is, obviously, a reflexive property, that is, the similarity is judged by comparing an entity with itself, again from the perspective of a given criterion (or criteria set);

• but the reflexive relation is a tautology, since any the criterion for the similarity examination would be, it will be automatically verified.[10] The conclusion is at hand: the self-similarity analysis implies the displacement of the entity in the case. This displacement can be of four relevant categories: (i) displacement in space; (ii) displacement in time; (iii) displacement in both space and time; (iv) displacement in signification. We will examine each one separately:

(i) self-similarity within the displacement in space

The self-similarity within a displacement in space constitutes a self-invariance of a given criterion at a spatial scale variation or different spatial scales. In this case, a version of an entity located in a place/space is compared, under a given criterion, with another version of the same entity located in another place/space. Such operation implies:

- the co-existence (i.e., the contemporaneity) of the two versions of that entity; somewhat, the entity "throws" two versions of itself in two different places/spaces, at the same time;
- the two contemporary versions of the same entity cannot occur by replication, since replication implies some non-contemporaneity—at a moment, in a place/space, does exist the parent/s, and, at a different moment, in another place/space, does exist the offspring/s; although the separation of places/spaces is verified, the non-separation of times is violated;[11]
- if replication cannot be the way in which the self-similarity is examined in the displacement in space case, then which is such a way? In this matter, we provide the following considerations:
  - the case of networks: the simultaneity of occurring and maintaining of some events or phenomena in more than a node. The causality for a given event/phenomenon could be the same in many places within a network, so the effects generated will be liable to obey similarity, under some criteria; of course, such a simultaneity can be either spontaneous or deliberative—i.e., can be the effect of either the invisible hand or the visible hand, or both;
  - the case of systems: to some extent, this case is ... similar to that of networks, except that, this time, the simultaneity of spatially separated versions of the entity involved is caused by the leading component;

Nota bene: as shown before, in analysing the relationships between crisis and society, in the case of systems, the causality of simultaneity can reside in either the crisis's leading node pressure or the society's leading component pressure, or both pressures.

- the self-similarity in space, i.e. maintained within the displacement in space, rather belongs to the topological "discourse" and can even be examined with topological tools. For example, the famous Mandelbrot's fractals fit this perspective.[12] Also, the so-called decentralized or deconcentrated governmental authorities, institutions and agencies must resemble each other across the national territory as, for example, structure or/and functions;
- the self-similarity in space can cover the following basic typology:
  - self-similarity of geometric form—geometry's self-similarity;
  - self-similarity of structure—structure's self-similarity;
  - self-similarity of function—function's self-similarity.[13]

However, the self-similarity in space is rather a theoretical construct, since the same entity cannot be, at the same time, in two different places/spaces, without to have clones in those places/spaces. The question is, now, a clone of an entity means "the same entity"? We shall provide some thoughts in this matter:

- principled, a clone is not "the same entity" as the entity cloned;[14] at the same time, the original and the clone are spatially displaced;
- if the original and the clone are not "the same entity", they are outside the issue of self-similarity within the displacement in space;
- if the only way to have "pure" self-similarity is the cloned version of a given entity, and if the two obtained versions are not "the same entity", it results that, probably, the case of self-similarity within the displacement in space remain a theoretical (or logical) possibility, not a realistic one.

In the same line of discussion, it must be clarified (or suggested a reasonable clarification) regarding the relationship between the syntagma "the same entity" and the syntagma "different scales", the last being used in describing, above, the concept of fractality. We think that:

- rigorously, the two syntagmata are inconsistent between them, since the sameness implies the same scale, too; however, the fractals require different scales and, concomitantly, it is talked about ... self-similarity as the mark of fractals;
- consequently, the self-similarity within the displacement in space makes sense only if every time the criterion behind the self-similarity examination is displayed. For example, based on the proposed (rather illustrative not exhaustive) typology of the self-similarity in space, the criteria that must be always announced are even the form, or the structure, or the function, etc.;
- this means that the syntagma "the same entity" must be understood only under the announced criterion—indeed, for example, if the criterion is the form, can exist self-similarity at different scales because the form is ... the same. In other words, under the criterion of form, two spatial versions of an entity, although at different scales, represent "the same entity".

(ii) self-similarity within the displacement in time

The self-similarity within a displacement in time constitutes a self-invariance of a given criterion at a time scale variation or different time scales. This case is, to some extent, more interesting (and more frequent in reality) than the previous one. It implies that two versions of the same entity are compared regarding the similarity between them, under a given criterion, based on the non-separateness of space and separateness of time. If in case (i) we had an invariability of time and a variability of space, now we have a non-variability of space and a variability of time.

The basic logical features of the similarity within the displacement in time are the following:

- the replication of the entity is necessary[15]—cannot exist two versions, in different moments, of the same entity, without the entity being replicated; therefore, if in the case of displacement in space the replication was prohibited, now the replication is mandatory;
  - the replication of an entity does not necessarily mean self-replication[16] (or homo-replication); it can be, also, a hetero-replication, including a deliberative one—such an alternative is preponderant, besides, in the case of artefacts, namely in the social field;

- like in case (i) above, the replication conserves the entity, i.e. ensures "the same entity", only under a precise criterion for performing the analysis of similarity;
- however, in case (ii), the probability that the two versions—one at the initial moment, and the other at a different next moment—be exactly "the same" from the perspective of almost all possible criteria regarding the similarity is very high, so the precautions needed in this topic do not matter too much;

• what about the case in which no replication of an entity occurs but, simply, that entity conserves itself or is invariant in its own? We think that:
  - the path through which a new version of an entity comes into existence is not relevant at all. In fact, the observer/analyst freely chooses another place/space and another moment to make the similarity exam from the perspective of a given criterion. So, it is sufficient that in those other places and moments, s/he will find a version of the entity in the case;
  - this statement could be called the *principle of non-dependency on the path*;
  - generally, the self-replication is rather a rare event in the social field (field of artefacts); the majority of the entity versions are hetero-replicated or are sustainable, i.e. conserve their identity;
• the self-similarity in time can cover the following basic typology:
  - self-similarity of duration—lifespan's self-similarity;[17]
  - self-similarity of rhythm—rhythmicity's self-similarity;[18]
  - self-similarity of finality—finality's self-similarity.[19]

(iii) self-similarity within the displacement in both space and time

The self-similarity within a displacement in both space and time constitutes a self-invariance of a given criterion at a concomitant variation of space scale and time scale. In reality, case (iii) is the most "populated", since it avoids both "purity" of spatial separation with temporal coincidence and "purity" of temporal separation with spatial coincidence.[20] This time, the dominant situations are characterized by the concomitancy of space separation and time separation. Before analysing the main features of self-similarity in this case, it is useful to try to clarify the very concept of the entity's versions and, implicitly, the syntagma "the same entity".

- we have seen previously that the clone does not mean "the same entity", so it should be considered a replication of the original entity; consequently, the clone can make the object of the similarity analysis, considering that the clone simultaneously verified the space separation and the time separation between the two versions—original and clone;
- what is discussed in the literature as fractals is always frameable into case (iii); even the mathematical (in fact, topological) illustrations of forming the self-similarity (of geometric nature) at different scales for the concept of fractals imply the time separation—since the computer needs a duration to calculate and display the scale modification in line with the similarity of forms—and the space separation—since the new self-similar versions of the entity are drawn alongside not over the original entity or an entity at a different scale, but is drawn in other place/space.

The self-similarity within the displacement in both space and time is, besides, the standard case which is of interest for the present research, since the concept of chreode (applicable to the crisis—either as network or system) implies both space and time separation. Consequently, the next allegations on the fractality of the crisis will be framed into case (iii).

Before discussing case (iv) of this issue, we would wish to provide some comments on the concept of inertia, as it can be related to self-similarity and, next, to the fractals and, more punctually, to the crisis fractality.

- inertia[21] is a conservative property, inherent to any entity; inertia keeps, on its own, the current state of an entity, whatever would be that state, until some external principle changes the state in the case;
- so, inertia can ground including the replication of an entity, by keeping its state—structure, function, place, etc.—and, this way, providing the entity's self-similarity;[22]
- it seems, however, that the inertia is adequate rather to the case of self-similarity within the displacement in time.

(iv) self-similarity within the displacement in signification

The attentive reader will have already noticed the importance and relevance we give to the concept of signification in the entire research. This time we introduce the significance into the very issue of self-similarity and, further, of fractality and crisis's fractality. The self-similarity within a displacement in signification constitutes a self-invariance of a given criterion at a significance scale variation or different significance scales. Since the syntagma "significance scale variation" seems somehow odd, we shall provide some considerations in the matter:

- as shown previously, significance is the result of the association, in consciousness, of an interpretation (something as an axiological colour) to any observation—date, information, cognizance;
- signification constitutes the third filter of "viewing" the world, after the first filter—the sensation—and the second one—the perception;
- this third filter is the most drastic, as the power of discrimination, and is the most relevant, as the basis of understanding and, then, of action;
- so, what is to be discussed addresses the very way in which significance constitutes (or can constitute) the "source" of different versions of a given entity and, consequently, allows analyses from the perspective of self-similarity. In this matter, our opinion is the following:
  - this case does not imply the effective replication of the entity, as required in the previous three cases;
  - in fact, the "new version" of a given entity is the same (i.e., the "original") but is associated, instead, with a new signification, no matter what considerations ground the signification change;
  - it is to be observed that the displacement of signification is of a property nature, not of a relationship nature since that displacement (changing) of the significance does not presuppose the comparison of two versions of the entity involved;
  - if the previous three displacements (in space, in time and both) had an inter-personal (i.e., objectified) character—since they were favourably "voted" by a large community—in the case of displacement of signification, the subjective character of evaluation comes into relevance: each individual can assign a personal signification to an entity, although some coagulation (i.e., communitization) of the signification changing is not … forbidden;
  - of course, the signification displacement regarding a given entity obeys the fundamental condition of judging the self-similarity only based on a chosen criterion, as in the other three hypostases discussed previously;

- the self-similarity in signification can cover the following basic typology:
  - self-similarity of self-esteem—individual life plenitude's self-similarity;
  - self-similarity of freedom—personal freedom's self-similarity;
  - self-similarity of controlling—situation mastering's self-similarity;
  - self-similarity of impact/consequences—existential pressure's self-similarity;

Case (iv) is heterogeneous compared with the previous cases, since it refers to the subjectivity, while the others bear an objective (or, at least, an objectified) character, as shown above. This fundamental feature, by the way, will reject the fractality (see point (3) below) from case (iv) of self-similarity.

It is interesting to examine the algebraic relation that is instituted by the similarity property or, the same, the relation called similarity.

Be three entities, E_1, E_2 and E_3, and the binary relation of similarity based on a criterion α. The binary relation is defined on the set of entities $\mathcal{E}$, and noted with $\rhd^{\alpha}$ ("is similar, according to α, with …"). Then, on this set, we have the following valid relationships:

- (R) *reflexivity*: $(\forall)k$, $E_k \in \mathcal{E}$ can be compared with itself from the perspective of similarity relationship: $E_k \rhd^{\alpha} E_k$; indeed, an entity $E_k \in \mathcal{E}$ can be compared with itself based on the criterion $\rhd^{\alpha}$;
- (S) *symmetry*: $(\forall)k, q$, for $E_k \in \mathcal{E}$, and $E_q \in \mathcal{E}$, if $(E_k \rhd^{\alpha} E_q)$; it results that $(E_q \rhd^{\alpha} E_k)$;
- (T) *transitivity*: $(\forall)k, q, p$, for $E_k \in \mathcal{E}$, $E_p \in \mathcal{E}$, $E_q \in \mathcal{E}$, if $(E_k \rhd^{\alpha} E_p)$ and $(E_p \rhd^{\alpha} E_q)$, then $(E_k \rhd^{\alpha} E_q)$.

A binary relation that verifies RST is called a (binary) *equivalence relation* on the set $\mathcal{E}$.[23] Obviously, every criterion based on which the similarity is examined will generate classes of equivalence on $\mathcal{E}$.

(3) it must be examined the issue: how the concept of similarity, as it has been introduced above, can be applied to the fractality property:
   - as (partially) suggested above, fractality is, like similarity, a relational concept, namely it constitutes a property of a relationship;

– logically, fractality is a species of similarity and more analytically, a species of self-similarity; the specific differences of the fractality from the genus self-similarity seems to be the following;

- fractality belongs to the self-similarity cases (iii) and (iv), i.e. addresses the simultaneous displacement in space and time of the entity involved—case (iii)—the displacement of the signification—case (iv);
- as known, generally, fractality is considered (rather implicitly, because the literature does not approach the similarity as a genus for fractality as a species) as belonging to case (iii) only, i.e. as addressing only the objective/objectivated character of generating new versions of a given entity;[24]
- however, in the social field, where artefacts are predominant and actions are purpose based (i.e., are teleological), the subjectivity is much more important and relevant than in Popper's first world, so case (iv) cannot be ignored.

A synoptic view of the rapport between similarity, self-similarity and fractality is provided in Fig. 6.1.

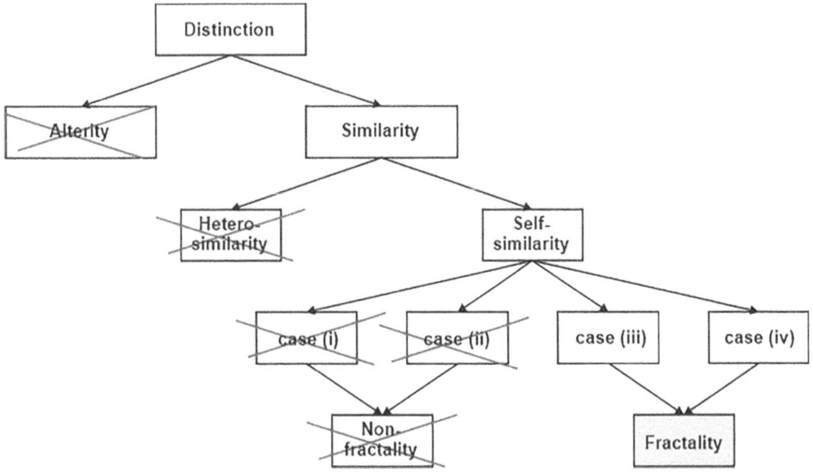

Fig. 6.1 The speciation of fractality from the genus self-similarity. *Source*: author

6.2.2 *Particular Issues on Fractality Applied/Applicable to Crisis*

After concluding on the general aspects of the fractality as a property of a relationship (in this case, the relationship is that of a comparison), it is time to particularize the fractality (better said, its possibility of being) applied to the entity which we are interested about: the crisis.

It is fruitfully, we think, to examine the property of fractality in connection with the concept of crisis, once again based on our abstract typology of crisis's predicates, by classes and, within the classes, by species of those predicates. Let us resume, therefore, the general mark (notation) of a generic crisis—a systematization of the general mark of crisis is done in Table 6.1 (*Nota bene*: the classes are ordered from left to right in the decreasing order of the dominance potential; also, for each class, the species are listed, from top to bottom, in the decreasing order of dominance within the class, as they have been established in Chap. 5).

From the five classes of crisis's predicates, according to the findings regarding the concept of fractality, it seems that only two "qualify" for applying that concept on them, namely class "3" γ—chreode; and class "1": ε—signification. Consequently, the next analysis will focus on these two classes of crisis.

(a) fractality in class "3": γ—chreode
  (a1) γ = 5—synergic chreode

Table 6.1 The "map" of the generic crisis

Class "5": ε—signification	*Class "1": α—cause*	*Class "4": δ—impact*	*Class "2": β—origin*	*Class "3": γ—chreode*
5. about self-esteem	5. by futurization	5. on meta-narrative	5. natural	5. synergic
4. about freedom	4. by exhaustion	4. on political regime	4. political	4. migratory
3. way of life	3. by insemination	3. on values	3. practical	3. trans-field
2. about opportunities	2. by friction	2. on rationality	2. praxeological	2. self-maintaining
1. about survival	1. by insularization	1. on structure	1. theoretical	1. self-extinguishing

Source: author

This species of the crisis's predicate of class "3" focuses rather on the time displacement (the space displacement is insignificant). It, principally, means that the synergic potential of the crisis involved is reproduced identically. Identical reproducing of the synergic potential/capacity of the crisis means that the chreode of that crisis has acquired a *sui generis* "DNA" to perpetuate its synergic potential. Such cases are rare enough and their measurability is debatable. So, the crisis keeps a fractality in reproducing its synergic resource.

(a2) $\gamma = 4$—migratory chreode

The migratory chreode of a crisis is relatively easy to observe and measure since the spatial displacement is included in the mark "migratory". It is to be mentioned that, in this case, the combination of displacement in space and the displacement in time is particularly put into evidence. The case focuses on the replication of the migratory propensity of the crisis, in space-time coordinates, for a relevant while (theoretically ... perpetually), with the strict condition of keeping the societal sector—for example, a crisis in the moral "region" is forbidden from migrating into the economic one. Crisis migration can be of two kinds: (i) endomorphic migration; (ii) metamorphic migration.

(i) the *endomorphic* migration addresses the crisis migration without change its nature—for example, a nominal crisis migrates in other regions (other spatiotemporal territories) as a nominal crisis;
(ii) the *metamorphic* migration addresses the crisis migration accompanied by a changing of its nature—for example, a nominal crisis passes into a financial crisis, or a financial crisis passes into a real one (see Fig. 4.13, in Chap. 4).

So, the fractality is manifested exactly by reproducing the migratory propensity of the crisis involved.

(a3) $\gamma = 3$—trans-field chreode

The trans-field chreode is crisply different from the migratory chreode. While the last cannot pass from one region to another, the former exactly does so: transgresses different regions. For example, an economic crisis—as a severe poverty—can pass into a political crisis, or a moral crisis—as a consumerism fundamentalism—can pass into an economic crisis, and so on. The fractality occurs by the very reproducing, in space and time, in a self-similarity way, of the “destiny” of the crisis to transgress the regions across society.

(a4) $\gamma = 2$—self-maintaining chreode

As can be observed, the previous three cases ($\gamma = 5, 4, 3$) view the fractality as, somewhat, external manifestations of the crisis involved (for $\gamma = 5$, by keeping the synergism; for $\gamma = 4$, by keeping the propensity to migrating; for $\gamma = 3$, by keeping the propensity to transgressing). This time, it is about an internal principle of the crisis, namely an auto-feeding with resources to perpetuate itself. Of course, the concept of resources for auto-feeding needs some extra specifications.

- by self-perpetuation resource of crisis must be understood a self-similar replication (i.e., a fractal phenomenon) of the principles/causes that triggered the crisis in the case. For example, let us consider a political crisis triggered by the corrupt (and corruptible) officials in the legislative structure of the society (Parliament): at the next political elections, on the list of candidates for the legislative fore will be registered the former parliamentarians or other candidates by face and likeness of the formers, that is, the political crisis of corruption in the legislative institution will be fed by an internal resource;
- from a logical point of view, the self-perpetuation resource of crisis implies a dominance of the positive feedback.

Nota bene: it is important to note that the positive feedback must act inside a “tunnel” delimitated by thresholds, so that the crisis replicates, in a self-similarity way (i.e., by fractality) without reaching a triggering threshold of escalating. Beyond that threshold, the crisis phenomenology convokes either the migration chreode or the trans-field chreode. Somehow, the self-maintaining chreode of the crisis is a bifurcation point[25]—from which the crisis can go either to the migration chreode or the trans-field chreode, but it does not go either in one direction or another, keeping its self-maintaining phenomenology.

(a5) $\gamma = 1$—self-extinguishing chreode

This case is of particular interest from the fractality perspective since it evokes the path of the crisis towards its extinction by its own internal phenomenology. More exactly, the crisis unfolding exhausts exactly the resources feeding that crisis. Of course, the question is this: how such a process is linked to the concept/property of fractality of crisis? We provide some explanatory assertions:

- indeed, the "visual" fractality is hard to put into evidence in the phenomenon of self-extinguishing of the crisis, since the crisis "must" self-extinguish, so its versions cannot be self-similar, *eo ipso*, cannot be fractal;
- however, something is similar here: exactly the propensity to the self-extinction—such propensity is replicated, at each version, so the path towards the self-extinction is irreversible;
- so, the fractality of crisis is regularly applicable also in the case of self-extinguishing chreode.

(b) fractality in class "5": ε—signification[26]

The occurrence of a crisis, no matter its nature, character, origin, cause, impact or chreode unfolded, troubles the respective spatiotemporal region. However little is modified as a result of that crisis, things do not remain the same after a crisis occurring. The most relevant perspective from which a change arises following a crisis (and, obviously, even during the crisis unfolding) is the significance of that crisis, which constitutes the mark "5" of the generic crisis.

(b1) $\varepsilon = 5$—about self-esteem signification

Self-esteem is, by far, the crucial value for the generic person, namely for the human condition (Dinga et al., 2020). A crisis, whatever it would be, is firstly judged by individuals from this perspective. In this case, the fractality of the crisis means, therefore, that the versions of that crisis conserve (i.e., does not affect, of course, above an accepted threshold, which has a strong enough idiosyncratic feature) the self-esteem.[27]

(b2) $\varepsilon = 4$—about freedom signification

On the second "place" from the perspective of significance of a crisis phenomenology is the freedom.[28] As observed the self-esteem is more important for the generic human being than the freedom, and the historical examples in this context are abundant enough. In this case, the fractality of crisis addresses the conservation, for the given individual, of his/her freedom, within the society (generally, a societal system). In other words, the phenomenology of crisis "must" be such that the feeling of freedom is not deteriorated—as a result, we can say, if so, that the crisis is fractal under the freedom signification;

(b3) $\varepsilon = 3$—about way of life signification

The way of life addresses all the conditions and habits under which a person or community lives and develops activities within the society. The occurrence of a crisis could disturb the way of life by changing (again, above a pre-accepted threshold) those conditions and habits.[29] The property of fractality in this case consists in the fact that different versions of the crisis (e.g., by its replications, migrations, and so on) conserve the significance of the way of life. In other words, the individual will appreciate that his/her way of life is not disturbed by those different versions of the crisis involved. Of course, the fractality maintains as long as the mentioned non-distortion effect maintains.

(b4) $\varepsilon = 2$—about opportunities signification

One of the most common/ordinary significances of a crisis addresses the modification in the structure and quality of opportunities for life—labour/jobs, education, environment, health, taxation, etc. It is to be mentioned that such a significance can have both positive and negative connotations. Indeed, a crisis not only disables some opportunities (either quantitatively or qualitatively) but can create new opportunities or positively change the existing ones. Therefore, the fractality of the crisis means that its different versions do not worsen the *statu quo* of the disposable opportunities. A question can arise here, based on the ambivalence of the signification regarding the opportunities, namely what about an improvement of the issue of opportunities as a result of the crisis? Some considerations in the matter are provided below:

- principled, any change in the opportunities with which the individual is accustomed could change the signification regarding the opportunities. From our logical perspective, even an improvement in the state of affairs about opportunities has the potential to change the significance in the case; as the conservation of the signification is the key to the fractality of crisis, it results that, even in the case of the opportunity set improvement the fractality of crisis will be "destroyed"—for example, AI (artificial intelligence) has the potential of creating new jobs, let us say, in computer programming, but, at the same time, some existent jobs could disappear;
- the issue is difficult enough since it implies a qualitative comparison, not only a quantitative one. Consequently, the best solution is to leave to the individual this assessment of conserving or not the significance of the opportunities and, as a result, accepting or not of the fractality of crisis.[30]

(b5) $\varepsilon = 1$—about survival signification

The case of survival signification in a crisis occurring is, as shown before, at least in contemporary developed societies a rare enough one, based on two conditionalities: (a) the high potential of the societies to find and operate alternatives when the survival is threatened, and (b) the refined axiological matrix in which the survival *per se* is not a prevalent value. In this context, almost any crisis is fractal, since its versions have a very little probability of really threatening the survival.

6.3 The Periodicity of Crisis and Its Fractal Dimension

6.3.1 *Crisis Periodicity*

As shown in point 4.4 of Chap. 4, the generic (singular) crisis can be periodical, although not cyclical as well. To be singularly periodical means to be singularly repeatable without keeping the same period of recurrence. The explanation of this feature consists in the fact that any crisis is generated by the societal context (what we call causal complex, which contains both the causes and the conditionalities) and, concomitantly, mandatorily impresses that societal context which although will necessarily generate crises again, i.e. periodically, this periodicity does not cover a cyclicality.

Based on how the non-cyclical periodicity of crisis has been explained, three of the five marks identified for the generic crisis (α—cause, β—origin and δ—impact) are excluded from the self-similarity possibility, since all three are necessarily affected by the very occurrence of a crisis, although the other two marks (γ—chreode and ε—signification) are affected too, but only contingently. We remember that, logically, the non-cyclicality of the crisis led us to the idea of the impossibility that crisis enters as a phase/stage/component of the economic cycle.[31] A synoptic representation of these findings is done in Fig. 6.2.

6.3.2 Fractal/Fractional Dimension: The "Standard" Concept

The concepts of fractal and fractal dimension (or fractional dimension) were introduced in literature by Benoît Mandelbrot (1997),[32] from a purely mathematical (topological) point of view. "Philosophically", a fractal dimension establishes the ratio between the change in detail and change in scale (*Nota bene*: so, it is talking, by now, about the geometrical approach of the issue). In theory, whenever the number of the dimensions is not a natural number, we leave the topology (or topological dimensions) and enter into the fractal geometry (or fractal/fractional dimensions). In fact, the fractal geometry behaves quite similarly to the fuzzy set theory—between any two dimensions denoted by natural numbers is introduced, as possibility, an infinite number of dimensions, marked by real positive numbers. From a gravitational perspective, the closer a fractal dimension is to a topological dimension, the more likely that the entity in the case behaves as if it would have the respective topological dimension.[33]

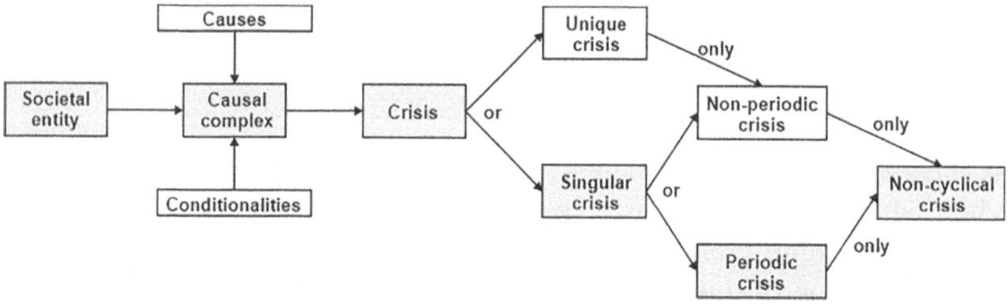

Fig. 6.2 The generic crisis liable of fractality is singular, periodical and non-cyclical. *Source*: author

6.3.3 A Possible Terminology

Obviously, the subject of this research—the (societal) crisis and its general phenomenology—is neither of topological geometry nor of fractal geometry nature but of a social (including economic) one. Consequently, although the issue of fractality, including fractal dimension, is an insightful perspective, a reason that has justified point 6.3.2., we shall try not to repeat a mistake too many times performed in the economic/social science, namely the *tale quale* taking over of concepts, mechanisms and even ... algebra from natural sciences or from the general cognitive methodology called mathematics—among the most known examples, entropy, probability and, you have guessed, fractality. Instead, we try to use the brilliant cognitive productivity of this ingenious concept, to build up something analogous (not ... similar) for social science, although limited, for now, to the topic of (societal) crisis.[34]

We have seen that the generic crisis is liable to self-similarity which, for cases (iii) and (iv), is assignable to the abstract concept of fractality. As, in the case of the (societal) crisis, the topological dimension (and, of course, the fractal dimension) lacks sense, since it is not well covered by reality, we are "obliged" to use the interesting suggestion of the fractality to build up something, as said above, analogous.

First of all, it must be observed that we have here to do with an analogy of formal type (Dinga et al., 2022). The basic elements of such an analogy can be systematized as follows:

- self-similarity must be maintained as the "logical anchor" for describing, analysing and evaluating the possible fractality in the crisis matter;
- the multiple versions of a crisis must be viewed from two perspectives (very different from those of the mathematical/topological approach), namely (a) from a space-time perspective—i.e. case (iii) of the crisis mark; (b) from the significance perspective—i.e. case (iv) of the crisis mark;
- a dimension label of a crisis, from the self-similarity perspective, could be of great usefulness, both theoretical and methodological. Although we would keep the denomination fractal dimension[35] but add "of crisis" so, *fractal dimension of crisis* (*FDC*), this dimension will be defined below very differently from the current literature;

- however, the relationship between the change in details and the change in scale, which is fundamental in defining and calculating the fractal dimension in its purely mathematical approach, will be replaced by something specific to the crisis phenomenology.

6.3.4 *Fractal/Fractional Dimension of a Crisis*

We wish now to discuss the issue: to what is applicable the fractal dimension of crisis? There are two possible answers: (a) to any individual crisis (of course, from the fractal "area" of self-similarity only—see Fig. 6.1) and (b) to crises overlapping. The two possibilities will be examined next. For both alternatives will be considered the singular periodic non-cyclical (*SPnC*) generic crisis:

(a) fractal dimension of an individual crisis

As shown above, from the perspective of fractality, a generic crisis of type *SPnC* must be written as $C_{5---3}^{\varepsilon---\gamma}$ or, even simpler, $C_{53}^{\varepsilon\gamma}$. Therefore, we must examine the possibility of assigning an *FDC* number to such a generic form of crisis. We provide the following considerations in that matter:

- first of all, we must describe the logical content of an *FDC* number. We think that:
  - self-similarity should be judged by analogy to the "standard" fractality (as we engaged above), so, as a ratio between changes in the "γ" species (numbered from 1 to 5), and changes in the "ε" species (numbered too from 1 to 5);
  - regarding all the possibilities, we must see the compatibility of the species for the classes "5" and "3" of the crisis marks. As Table 5.2 of Chap. 5 shows, 15 combinations between the species involved are compatible (60% from total) and 10 combinations are incompatible (40%);
  - let us resume the affinity-based of the dominance values when only ε and γ matter (we made notations: ε values and γ values; N^{ε} the numerical value of ε; N^{γ} the numerical value of γ; $D^{\varepsilon\gamma}$ the numerical value of compatibility between ε and γ;[36] $FDC^{\varepsilon\gamma}$ the fractal dimension of crisis for the ε and γ numerical values);

– we propose that:

$$FDC^{\varepsilon\gamma} = \frac{\Delta N^{\varepsilon}}{\Delta N^{\gamma}} \cdot C^{\varepsilon\gamma}$$

where: $\Delta N^{(\cdot)} = N_i^{(\cdot)} - N_{i-1}^{(\cdot)}$, where with i is noted the time, and $(\cdot) \in \{\varepsilon,\gamma\}$.[37]

For any pair (ε,γ), so that N^{ε}, $N^{\gamma} \in \{1,2,3,4,5\}$, and ΔN^{ε}, $\Delta N^{\gamma} \in \{-4,-3,-2,-1,0,1,2,3,4\}$, the *FDC* numbers will be those of Table 6.2 (I–V). *Nota bene*: the cases of incompatibility have been omitted.

Discussion

- the largest *FDC* is ±20, while the smallest *FDC* is ±0.5, so the largest difference between the maximum and minimum *FDC* is ±20.5;
- a negative $N_i^{(\cdot)}$, where $(\cdot) \in \{\varepsilon,\gamma\}$, means that the version of the $(\cdot)$ mark passes from a value "stronger"/more dominant to one "weaker"/less dominant, while a positive value means the opposite; so, the algebraic sign, either plus or minus indicates the direction of changing;
- the absolute value of $N_i^{(\cdot)}$ gives an account of the steps "jumped" at a time: "k" means k steps, where $k \in \{1,2,3,4,5\}$; so, the absolute value indicates the amplitude/size of changing;
- so, the *FDC* say something about the crisis behaviour (analogously to the meaning of the topological fractal) but linked to a *sui generis* concept of dimension, which is specific for the societal field—about such a concept we provide some extra considerations:
  - *firstly*, the societal dimension is not a physical/spatial dimension but one of significance—the higher the *FDC*, the more significant the *FDC*;
  - *secondly*, the absolute size of *FDC* gives a measure of the shock suffered by the observer or practitioner when s/he integrates the information about that *FDC*; so, the societal dimension has rather an informational character;
  - *thirdly*, by contrast with the topological dimension, the societal dimension can be either positive or negative or zero, with the following significations:

    a negative dimension means that the new version of *SPnC* has a smaller relevance than before, either from ε perspective or γ perspective;

Table 6.2 *FDC* numbers in the internal interactions between ε and γ in an *SPnC* crisis (I)

		γ = 1—*self-extinguishing*									
		$\Delta N^{\gamma} = -4$	$\Delta N^{\gamma} = -3$	$\Delta N^{\gamma} = -2$	$\Delta N^{\gamma} = -1$	$\Delta N^{\gamma} = 0$	$\Delta N^{\gamma} = 1$	$\Delta N^{\gamma} = 2$	$\Delta N^{\gamma} = 3$	$\Delta N^{\gamma} = 4$	$C^{\varepsilon\gamma}$
ε = 1—about survival	$\Delta N^{\varepsilon} = -4$	5.000	6.667	10.000	20.000	0.000	−20.000	−10.000	−6.667	−5.000	5
	$\Delta N^{\varepsilon} = -3$	3.750	5.000	7.500	15.000	0.000	−15.000	−7.500	−5.000	−3.750	5
	$\Delta N^{\varepsilon} = -2$	2.500	3.333	5.000	10.000	0.000	−10.000	−5.000	−3.333	−2.500	5
	$\Delta N^{\varepsilon} = -1$	1.250	1.667	2.500	5.000	0.000	−5.000	−2.500	−1.667	−1.250	5
	$\Delta N^{\varepsilon} = 0$	0.000	0.000	0.000	0.000	0.000	0.000	0.000	0.000	0.000	5
	$\Delta N^{\varepsilon} = 1$	−1.250	−1.667	−2.500	−5.000	0.000	5.000	2.500	1.667	1.250	5
	$\Delta N^{\varepsilon} = 2$	−2.500	−3.333	−5.000	−10.000	0.000	10.000	5.000	3.333	2.500	5
	$\Delta N^{\varepsilon} = 3$	−3.750	−5.000	−7.500	−15.000	0.000	15.000	7.500	5.000	3.750	5
	$\Delta N^{\varepsilon} = 4$	−5.000	−6.667	−10.000	−20.000	0.000	20.000	10.000	6.667	5.000	5
ε = 2—about opportunities	$\Delta N^{\varepsilon} = -4$	5.000	6.667	10.000	20.000	0.000	−20.000	−10.000	−6.667	−5.000	5
	$\Delta N^{\varepsilon} = -3$	3.750	5.000	7.500	15.000	0.000	−15.000	−7.500	−5.000	−3.750	5
	$\Delta N^{\varepsilon} = -2$	2.500	3.333	5.000	10.000	0.000	−10.000	−5.000	−3.333	−2.500	5
	$\Delta N^{\varepsilon} = -1$	1.250	1.667	2.500	5.000	0.000	−5.000	−2.500	−1.667	−1.250	5
	$\Delta N^{\varepsilon} = 0$	0.000	0.000	0.000	0.000	0.000	0.000	0.000	0.000	0.000	5
	$\Delta N^{\varepsilon} = 1$	−1.250	−1.667	−2.500	−5.000	0.000	5.000	2.500	1.667	1.250	5
	$\Delta N^{\varepsilon} = 2$	−2.500	−3.333	−5.000	−10.000	0.000	10.000	5.000	3.333	2.500	5
	$\Delta N^{\varepsilon} = 3$	−3.750	−5.000	−7.500	−15.000	0.000	15.000	7.500	5.000	3.750	5
	$\Delta N^{\varepsilon} = 4$	−5.000	−6.667	−10.000	−20.000	0.000	20.000	10.000	6.667	5.000	5

$\varepsilon = 3$—about way of life	$\Delta N^{\varepsilon} = -4$	4.000	5.333	8.000	16.000	0.000	−16.000	−8.000	−5.333	−4.000	4
	$\Delta N^{\varepsilon} = -3$	3.000	4.000	6.000	12.000	0.000	−12.000	−6.000	−4.000	−3.000	4
	$\Delta N^{\varepsilon} = -2$	2.000	2.667	4.000	8.000	0.000	−8.000	−4.000	−2.667	−2.000	4
	$\Delta N^{\varepsilon} = -1$	1.000	1.333	2.000	4.000	0.000	−4.000	−2.000	−1.333	−1.000	4
	$\Delta N^{\varepsilon} = 0$	0.000	0.000	0.000	0.000	0.000	0.000	0.000	0.000	0.000	4
	$\Delta N^{\varepsilon} = 1$	−1.000	−1.333	−2.000	−4.000	0.000	4.000	2.000	1.333	1.000	4
	$\Delta N^{\varepsilon} = 2$	−2.000	−2.667	−4.000	−8.000	0.000	8.000	4.000	2.667	2.000	4
	$\Delta N^{\varepsilon} = 3$	−3.000	−4.000	−6.000	−12.000	0.000	12.000	6.000	4.000	3.000	4
	$\Delta N^{\varepsilon} = 4$	−4.000	−5.333	−8.000	−16.000	0.000	16.000	8.000	5.333	4.000	4

FDC numbers in the internal interactions between ε and γ in an SPnC crisis (II)

		$\gamma = 2$—*self-maintaining*									
		$\Delta N^{\gamma} = -4$	$\Delta N^{\gamma} = -3$	$\Delta N^{\gamma} = -2$	$\Delta N^{\gamma} = -1$	$\Delta N^{\gamma} = 0$	$\Delta N^{\gamma} = 1$	$\Delta N^{\gamma} = 2$	$\Delta N^{\gamma} = 3$	$\Delta N^{\gamma} = 4$	$C^{\varepsilon\gamma}$
$\varepsilon = 1$—about survival	$\Delta N^{\varepsilon} = -4$	5.000	6.667	10.000	20.000	0.000	−20.000	−10.000	−6.667	−5.000	5
	$\Delta N^{\varepsilon} = -3$	3.750	5.000	7.500	15.000	0.000	−15.000	−7.500	−5.000	−3.750	5
	$\Delta N^{\varepsilon} = -2$	2.500	3.333	5.000	10.000	0.000	−10.000	−5.000	−3.333	−2.500	5
	$\Delta N^{\varepsilon} = -1$	1.250	1.667	2.500	5.000	0.000	−5.000	−2.500	−1.667	−1.250	5
	$\Delta N^{\varepsilon} = 0$	0.000	0.000	0.000	0.000	0.000	0.000	0.000	0.000	0.000	5
	$\Delta N^{\varepsilon} = 1$	−1.250	−1.667	−2.500	−5.000	0.000	5.000	2.500	1.667	1.250	5
	$\Delta N^{\varepsilon} = 2$	−2.500	−3.333	−5.000	−10.000	0.000	10.000	5.000	3.333	2.500	5
	$\Delta N^{\varepsilon} = 3$	−3.750	−5.000	−7.500	−15.000	0.000	15.000	7.500	5.000	3.750	5
	$\Delta N^{\varepsilon} = 4$	−5.000	−6.667	−10.000	−20.000	0.000	20.000	10.000	6.667	5.000	5

(*continued*)

Table 6.2 (continued)

FDC numbers in the internal interactions between ε and γ in an SPnC crisis (II)

		γ = 2—self-maintaining									
		$\Delta N^{\gamma} = -4$	$\Delta N^{\gamma} = -3$	$\Delta N^{\gamma} = -2$	$\Delta N^{\gamma} = -1$	$\Delta N^{\gamma} = 0$	$\Delta N^{\gamma} = 1$	$\Delta N^{\gamma} = 2$	$\Delta N^{\gamma} = 3$	$\Delta N^{\gamma} = 4$	$C^{\varepsilon\gamma}$
ε = 2—about opportunities	$\Delta N^{\varepsilon} = -4$	4.000	5.333	8.000	16.000	0.000	−16.000	−8.000	−5.333	−4.000	4
	$\Delta N^{\varepsilon} = -3$	3.000	4.000	6.000	12.000	0.000	−12.000	−6.000	−4.000	−3.000	4
	$\Delta N^{\varepsilon} = -2$	2.000	2.667	4.000	8.000	0.000	−8.000	−4.000	−2.667	−2.000	4
	$\Delta N^{\varepsilon} = -1$	1.000	1.333	2.000	4.000	0.000	−4.000	−2.000	−1.333	−1.000	4
	$\Delta N^{\varepsilon} = 0$	0.000	0.000	0.000	0.000	0.000	0.000	0.000	0.000	0.000	4
	$\Delta N^{\varepsilon} = 1$	−1.000	−1.333	−2.000	−4.000	0.000	4.000	2.000	1.333	1.000	4
	$\Delta N^{\varepsilon} = 2$	−2.000	−2.667	−4.000	−8.000	0.000	8.000	4.000	2.667	2.000	4
	$\Delta N^{\varepsilon} = 3$	3.000	−3.600	−2.400	−1.200	0.000	1.200	2.400	3.600	4.800	4
	$\Delta N^{\varepsilon} = 4$	−4.267	−3.200	−2.133	−1.067	0.000	1.067	2.133	3.200	4.267	4
ε = 3—about way of life	$\Delta N^{\varepsilon} = -4$	5.000	6.667	10.000	20.000	0.000	−20.000	−10.000	−6.667	−5.000	5
	$\Delta N^{\varepsilon} = -3$	3.750	5.000	7.500	15.000	0.000	−15.000	−7.500	−5.000	−3.750	5
	$\Delta N^{\varepsilon} = -2$	2.500	3.333	5.000	10.000	0.000	−10.000	−5.000	−3.333	−2.500	5
	$\Delta N^{\varepsilon} = -1$	1.250	1.667	2.500	5.000	0.000	−5.000	−2.500	−1.667	−1.250	5
	$\Delta N^{\varepsilon} = 0$	0.000	0.000	0.000	0.000	0.000	0.000	0.000	0.000	0.000	5
	$\Delta N^{\varepsilon} = 1$	−1.250	−1.667	−2.500	−5.000	0.000	5.000	2.500	1.667	1.250	5
	$\Delta N^{\varepsilon} = 2$	−2.500	−3.333	−5.000	−10.000	0.000	10.000	5.000	3.333	2.500	5
	$\Delta N^{\varepsilon} = 3$	−3.750	−5.000	−7.500	−15.000	0.000	15.000	7.500	5.000	3.750	5
	$\Delta N^{\varepsilon} = 4$	−5.000	−6.667	−10.000	−20.000	0.000	20.000	10.000	6.667	5.000	5

FDC numbers in the internal interactions between ε and γ in an SPnC crisis (III)

		γ = 3—*trans-field*									
		$\Delta N^{\gamma} = -4$	$\Delta N^{\gamma} = -3$	$\Delta N^{\gamma} = -2$	$\Delta N^{\gamma} = -1$	$\Delta N^{\gamma} = 0$	$\Delta N^{\gamma} = 1$	$\Delta N^{\gamma} = 2$	$\Delta N^{\gamma} = 3$	$\Delta N^{\gamma} = 4$	$C^{\varepsilon\gamma}$
ε = 1—about survival	$\Delta N^{\varepsilon} = -4$	4.000	5.333	8.000	16.000	0.000	−16.000	−8.000	−5.333	−4.000	4
	$\Delta N^{\varepsilon} = -3$	3.000	4.000	6.000	12.000	0.000	−12.000	−6.000	−4.000	−3.000	4
	$\Delta N^{\varepsilon} = -2$	2.000	2.667	4.000	8.000	0.000	−8.000	−4.000	−2.667	−2.000	4
	$\Delta N^{\varepsilon} = -1$	1.000	1.333	2.000	4.000	0.000	−4.000	−2.000	−1.333	−1.000	4
	$\Delta N^{\varepsilon} = 0$	0.000	0.000	0.000	0.000	0.000	0.000	0.000	0.000	0.000	4
	$\Delta N^{\varepsilon} = 1$	−1.000	−1.333	−2.000	−4.000	0.000	4.000	2.000	1.333	1.000	4
	$\Delta N^{\varepsilon} = 2$	−2.000	−2.667	−4.000	−8.000	0.000	8.000	4.000	2.667	2.000	4
	$\Delta N^{\varepsilon} = 3$	−3.000	−4.000	−6.000	−12.000	0.000	12.000	6.000	4.000	3.000	4
	$\Delta N^{\varepsilon} = 4$	−4.000	−5.333	−8.000	−16.000	0.000	16.000	8.000	5.333	4.000	4
ε = 2—about opportunities	$\Delta N^{\varepsilon} = -4$	4.000	5.333	8.000	16.000	0.000	−16.000	−8.000	−5.333	−4.000	4
	$\Delta N^{\varepsilon} = -3$	3.000	4.000	6.000	12.000	0.000	−12.000	−6.000	−4.000	−3.000	4
	$\Delta N^{\varepsilon} = -2$	2.000	2.667	4.000	8.000	0.000	−8.000	−4.000	−2.667	−2.000	4
	$\Delta N^{\varepsilon} = -1$	1.000	1.333	2.000	4.000	0.000	−4.000	−2.000	−1.333	−1.000	4
	$\Delta N^{\varepsilon} = 0$	0.000	0.000	0.000	0.000	0.000	0.000	0.000	0.000	0.000	4
	$\Delta N^{\varepsilon} = 1$	−1.000	−1.333	−2.000	−4.000	0.000	4.000	2.000	1.333	1.000	4
	$\Delta N^{\varepsilon} = 2$	−2.000	−2.667	−4.000	−8.000	0.000	8.000	4.000	2.667	2.000	4
	$\Delta N^{\varepsilon} = 3$	−3.000	−4.000	−6.000	−12.000	0.000	12.000	6.000	4.000	3.000	4
	$\Delta N^{\varepsilon} = 4$	−4.000	−5.333	−8.000	−16.000	0.000	16.000	8.000	5.333	4.000	4
ε = 3—about way of life	$\Delta N^{\varepsilon} = -4$	3.000	4.000	6.000	12.000	0.000	−12.000	−6.000	−4.000	−3.000	3
	$\Delta N^{\varepsilon} = -3$	2.250	3.000	4.500	9.000	0.000	−9.000	−4.500	−3.000	−2.250	3
	$\Delta N^{\varepsilon} = -2$	1.500	2.000	3.000	6.000	0.000	−6.000	−3.000	−2.000	−1.500	3
	$\Delta N^{\varepsilon} = -1$	0.750	1.000	1.500	3.000	0.000	−3.000	−1.500	−1.000	−0.750	3
	$\Delta N^{\varepsilon} = 0$	0.000	0.000	0.000	0.000	0.000	0.000	0.000	0.000	0.000	3
	$\Delta N^{\varepsilon} = 1$	−0.750	−1.000	−1.500	−3.000	0.000	3.000	1.500	1.000	0.750	3
	$\Delta N^{\varepsilon} = 2$	−1.500	−2.000	−3.000	−6.000	0.000	6.000	3.000	2.000	1.500	3
	$\Delta N^{\varepsilon} = 3$	−2.250	−3.000	−4.500	−9.000	0.000	9.000	4.500	3.000	2.250	3
	$\Delta N^{\varepsilon} = 4$	−3.000	−4.000	−6.000	−12.000	0.000	12.000	6.000	4.000	3.000	3

(*continued*)

Table 6.2 (continued)

FDC numbers in the internal interactions between ε and γ in an SPnC crisis (III)

		$\gamma = 3$—*trans-field*									
		$\Delta N^{\gamma} = -4$	$\Delta N^{\gamma} = -3$	$\Delta N^{\gamma} = -2$	$\Delta N^{\gamma} = -1$	$\Delta N^{\gamma} = 0$	$\Delta N^{\gamma} = 1$	$\Delta N^{\gamma} = 2$	$\Delta N^{\gamma} = 3$	$\Delta N^{\gamma} = 4$	$C^{\varepsilon\gamma}$
$\varepsilon = 4$—about way of life	$\Delta N^{\varepsilon} = -4$	3.000	4.000	6.000	12.000	0.000	−12.000	−6.000	−4.000	−3.000	3
	$\Delta N^{\varepsilon} = -3$	2.250	3.000	4.500	9.000	0.000	−9.000	−4.500	−3.000	−2.250	3
	$\Delta N^{\varepsilon} = -2$	1.500	2.000	3.000	6.000	0.000	−6.000	−3.000	−2.000	−1.500	3
	$\Delta N^{\varepsilon} = -1$	0.750	1.000	1.500	3.000	0.000	−3.000	−1.500	−1.000	−0.750	3
	$\Delta N^{\varepsilon} = 0$	0.000	0.000	0.000	0.000	0.000	0.000	0.000	0.000	0.000	3
	$\Delta N^{\varepsilon} = 1$	−0.750	−1.000	−1.500	−3.000	0.000	3.000	1.500	1.000	0.750	3
	$\Delta N^{\varepsilon} = 2$	−1.500	−2.000	−3.000	−6.000	0.000	6.000	3.000	2.000	1.500	3
	$\Delta N^{\varepsilon} = 3$	−2.250	−3.000	−4.500	−9.000	0.000	9.000	4.500	3.000	2.250	3
	$\Delta N^{\varepsilon} = 4$	−3.000	−4.000	−6.000	−12.000	0.000	12.000	6.000	4.000	3.000	3

FDC numbers in the internal interactions between ε and γ in an SPnC crisis (IV)

		$\gamma = 4$—*migratory*									
		$\Delta N^{\gamma} = -4$	$\Delta N^{\gamma} = -3$	$\Delta N^{\gamma} = -2$	$\Delta N^{\gamma} = -1$	$\Delta N^{\gamma} = 0$	$\Delta N^{\gamma} = 1$	$\Delta N^{\gamma} = 2$	$\Delta N^{\gamma} = 3$	$\Delta N^{\gamma} = 4$	$C^{\varepsilon\gamma}$
$\varepsilon = 1$—about survival	$\Delta N^{\varepsilon} = -4$	3.000	4.000	6.000	12.000	0.000	−12.000	−6.000	−4.000	−3.000	3
	$\Delta N^{\varepsilon} = -3$	2.250	3.000	4.500	9.000	0.000	−9.000	−4.500	−3.000	−2.250	3
	$\Delta N^{\varepsilon} = -2$	1.500	2.000	3.000	6.000	0.000	−6.000	−3.000	−2.000	−1.500	3
	$\Delta N^{\varepsilon} = -1$	0.750	1.000	1.500	3.000	0.000	−3.000	−1.500	−1.000	−0.750	3
	$\Delta N^{\varepsilon} = 0$	0.000	0.000	0.000	0.000	0.000	0.000	0.000	0.000	0.000	3
	$\Delta N^{\varepsilon} = 1$	−0.750	−1.000	−1.500	−3.000	0.000	3.000	1.500	1.000	0.750	3
	$\Delta N^{\varepsilon} = 2$	−1.500	−2.000	−3.000	−6.000	0.000	6.000	3.000	2.000	1.500	3
	$\Delta N^{\varepsilon} = 3$	−2.250	−3.000	−4.500	−9.000	0.000	9.000	4.500	3.000	2.250	3
	$\Delta N^{\varepsilon} = 4$	−3.000	−4.000	−6.000	−12.000	0.000	12.000	6.000	4.000	3.000	3

$\varepsilon = 2$—about opportunities	$\Delta N^{\varepsilon} = -4$	3.000	4.000	6.000	12.000	0.000	−12.000	−6.000	−4.000	−3.000	3
	$\Delta N^{\varepsilon} = -3$	2.250	3.000	4.500	9.000	0.000	−9.000	−4.500	−3.000	−2.250	3
	$\Delta N^{\varepsilon} = -2$	1.500	2.000	3.000	6.000	0.000	−6.000	−3.000	−2.000	−1.500	3
	$\Delta N^{\varepsilon} = -1$	0.750	1.000	1.500	3.000	0.000	−3.000	−1.500	−1.000	−0.750	3
	$\Delta N^{\varepsilon} = 0$	0.000	0.000	0.000	0.000	0.000	0.000	0.000	0.000	0.000	3
	$\Delta N^{\varepsilon} = 1$	−0.750	−1.000	−1.500	−3.000	0.000	3.000	1.500	1.000	0.750	3
	$\Delta N^{\varepsilon} = 2$	−1.500	−2.000	−3.000	−6.000	0.000	6.000	3.000	2.000	1.500	3
	$\Delta N^{\varepsilon} = 3$	−2.250	−3.000	−4.500	−9.000	0.000	9.000	4.500	3.000	2.250	3
	$\Delta N^{\varepsilon} = 4$	−3.000	−4.000	−6.000	−12.000	0.000	12.000	6.000	4.000	3.000	3
$\varepsilon = 3$—about way of life	$\Delta N^{\varepsilon} = -4$	3.000	4.000	6.000	12.000	0.000	−12.000	−6.000	−4.000	−3.000	3
	$\Delta N^{\varepsilon} = -3$	2.250	3.000	4.500	9.000	0.000	−9.000	−4.500	−3.000	−2.250	3
	$\Delta N^{\varepsilon} = -2$	1.500	2.000	3.000	6.000	0.000	−6.000	−3.000	−2.000	−1.500	3
	$\Delta N^{\varepsilon} = -1$	0.750	1.000	1.500	3.000	0.000	−3.000	−1.500	−1.000	−0.750	3
	$\Delta N^{\varepsilon} = 0$	0.000	0.000	0.000	0.000	0.000	0.000	0.000	0.000	0.000	3
	$\Delta N^{\varepsilon} = 1$	−0.750	−1.000	−1.500	−3.000	0.000	3.000	1.500	1.000	0.750	3
	$\Delta N^{\varepsilon} = 2$	−1.500	−2.000	−3.000	−6.000	0.000	6.000	3.000	2.000	1.500	3
	$\Delta N^{\varepsilon} = 3$	−2.250	−3.000	−4.500	−9.000	0.000	9.000	4.500	3.000	2.250	3
	$\Delta N^{\varepsilon} = 4$	−3.000	−4.000	−6.000	−12.000	0.000	12.000	6.000	4.000	3.000	3

(*continued*)

Table 6.2 (continued)

FDC numbers in the internal interactions between ε and γ in an SPnC crisis (V)

		γ = 5—*synergic*									
		$\Delta N^{\gamma} = -4$	$\Delta N^{\gamma} = -3$	$\Delta N^{\gamma} = -2$	$\Delta N^{\gamma} = -1$	$\Delta N^{\gamma} = 0$	$\Delta N^{\gamma} = 1$	$\Delta N^{\gamma} = 2$	$\Delta N^{\gamma} = 3$	$\Delta N^{\gamma} = 4$	$C^{\varepsilon\gamma}$
ε = 2—about opportunities	$\Delta N^{\varepsilon} = -4$	3.000	4.000	6.000	12.000	0.000	−12.000	−6.000	−4.000	−3.000	3
	$\Delta N^{\varepsilon} = -3$	2.250	3.000	4.500	9.000	0.000	−9.000	−4.500	−3.000	−2.250	3
	$\Delta N^{\varepsilon} = -2$	1.500	2.000	3.000	6.000	0.000	−6.000	−3.000	−2.000	−1.500	3
	$\Delta N^{\varepsilon} = -1$	0.750	1.000	1.500	3.000	0.000	−3.000	−1.500	−1.000	−0.750	3
	$\Delta N^{\varepsilon} = 0$	0.000	0.000	0.000	0.000	0.000	0.000	0.000	0.000	0.000	3
	$\Delta N^{\varepsilon} = 1$	−0.750	−1.000	−1.500	−3.000	0.000	3.000	1.500	1.000	0.750	3
	$\Delta N^{\varepsilon} = 2$	−1.500	−2.000	−3.000	−6.000	0.000	6.000	3.000	2.000	1.500	3
	$\Delta N^{\varepsilon} = 3$	−2.250	−3.000	−4.500	−9.000	0.000	9.000	4.500	3.000	2.250	3
	$\Delta N^{\varepsilon} = 4$	−3.000	−4.000	−6.000	−12.000	0.000	12.000	6.000	4.000	3.000	3
ε = 4—about way of life	$\Delta N^{\varepsilon} = -4$	2.000	2.667	4.000	8.000	0.000	−8.000	−4.000	−2.667	−2.000	2
	$\Delta N^{\varepsilon} = -3$	1.500	2.000	3.000	6.000	0.000	−6.000	−3.000	−2.000	−1.500	2
	$\Delta N^{\varepsilon} = -2$	1.000	1.333	2.000	4.000	0.000	−4.000	−2.000	−1.333	−1.000	2
	$\Delta N^{\varepsilon} = -1$	0.500	0.667	1.000	2.000	0.000	−2.000	−1.000	−0.667	−0.500	2
	$\Delta N^{\varepsilon} = 0$	0.000	0.000	0.000	0.000	0.000	0.000	0.000	0.000	0.000	2
	$\Delta N^{\varepsilon} = 1$	−0.500	−0.667	−1.000	−2.000	0.000	2.000	1.000	0.667	0.500	2
	$\Delta N^{\varepsilon} = 2$	−1.000	−1.333	−2.000	−4.000	0.000	4.000	2.000	1.333	1.000	2
	$\Delta N^{\varepsilon} = 3$	−1.500	−2.000	−3.000	−6.000	0.000	6.000	3.000	2.000	1.500	2
	$\Delta N^{\varepsilon} = 4$	−2.000	−2.667	−4.000	−8.000	0.000	8.000	4.000	2.667	2.000	2

Source: author

Bold signifies the minimum value of the coefficient (i.e., 0.000)

a positive dimension means that the new version of *SPnC* has a higher relevance than before, either from ε perspective or γ perspective;

a zero dimension means that the new version of *SPnC* conserves its previous relevance, either from ε perspective or γ perspective;

– *fourthly*, the problem of "0" must be discussed:

when between two versions of an *SPnC* crisis $N^{\varepsilon} = 0$, this means that the signification is invariant or, more exactly, the replication of *SPnC* crisis does not change the signification, whatever it would be ($\varepsilon \in \{1,2,3,4,5\}$). So, $FDC = 0$, which means that, from the perspective of ε, for any N^{γ}, the *FDC* is minimum;

if *FDC* is minimum for $N^{\varepsilon} = 0$, what about $N^{\gamma} = 0$?

- algebraically, $N^{\gamma} = 0$ places us in an uncertainty, but hermeneutically, we shall consider that such a case means, like in the case $N^{\varepsilon} = 0$, that the dimension of *SPnC* crisis is zero;
- the reason consists in the fact that $N^{\gamma} = 0$ means the conservation of the relevance of *SPnC* crisis from the perspective of the chreode;
- the conservation of the relevance (either for ε or for γ or both) is the clearest signal for the fractality (i.e., self-similarity) of the *SPnC* crisis.

(b) fractal dimension of crises overlapping

To get the concept (and interpretation) of the fractal dimension of crises overlapping, the following assertions, presuppositions and assumptions can be of usefulness.

- as shown, although any crises can overlap among them (Chap. 5), not any such overlapping has fractal properties. In fact, only the crises that have non-zero numerical values for the marks ε and γ "qualify" for such an analysis;
- however, the overlapping is "permitted" for any two or more crises, under the condition they are not to be incompatible according to Table 5.2 of Chap. 5;
- here we are interested in the issue of fractal properties—more exactly, for determining the numerical values for *FDC*, in the process of crises overlapping;

- at point 6.3.4 is proposed a methodology of calculating the *FDC* (noted, for obvious reasons, $FDC^{\varepsilon\gamma}$); it will be used in those that follows.

Be two crises,[38] $C(1)^{\varepsilon\alpha\delta\beta\gamma}_{51423}$ and $C(2)^{\varepsilon\alpha\delta\beta\gamma}_{51423}$, which are compatible between them and overlap in a given space-time "point". Be the $FDC^{\varepsilon\gamma}$, respectively, $FDC^{\varepsilon\gamma}(1)$ and $FDC^{\varepsilon\gamma}(2)$, as calculated at point (a) above. We determine, now, the rapport of dominance between *C*(1) and *C*(2), according to the methodology proposed at point 5.4.3.2 in Chap. 5. Be the (normalized) dominance number between the two crises $dn(1,2) = \lambda$. We remind the three cases of qualifying the two crises overlapping, depending on *dn*: (a) if $dn(1,2) \in I^1_{dn} = [0,0.5)$, the two overlapped crises are of *IO* (*immiscible* overlapping) type; (b) if $dn(1,2) \in I^2_{dn} = [0.5,0.8)$, the two overlapped crises are of *CO* (*conservative* overlapping) type; (c) if $dn(1,2) \in I^3_{dn} = [0.8,1]$, the two overlapped crises are of *TO* (*transformative* overlapping) type.

Now, according to the numerical value of λ, we must determine the $FDC^{\varepsilon\gamma}(1,2)$. Our proposal grounds on the following reasons:

- although the $FDC^{\varepsilon\gamma}$ is based on the values of ε and γ (more precisely, the values of N^{ε} and N^{γ}), the two crises that overlap between them also have their parameters for the marks α, β and δ. These parameters confer specific profiles of the two crises, separately from the parameters of marks ε and γ;
- as a result, the parameters of the marks α, β and δ have an important impact on establishing the number of dominance between the two crises, namely *dn*(1,2);
- consequently, the fractality of the overlapped crises, which we could note them *C*(1,2), should be influenced by the dominance number; regarding the way in which such a dominance should exert, we think that:
  - the considering of the dominance, i.e. *dn* (1,2), in determining $FDC^{\varepsilon\gamma}(1,2)$ must be based on the very logic of *FDC*;
  - this means that $FDC^{\varepsilon\gamma}(1,2)$ should be divided by *dn* (1,2); indeed: as $dn\ (1,2) \in [0,1] = [0,0.5) \cup [0.5,0.8) \cup [0.8,1]$, the further to the left of the interval $[0,1]$ is situated *dn* (1,2), the more will be increased the numerical value of $FDC^{\varepsilon\gamma}(1,2)$;

so, the more will be increased the numerical value of $FDC^{\varepsilon\gamma}(1,2)$, the more will be reduced the fractality of the overlapped crises involved;

this tendency is consistent with the fact that from left to right in the interval $[0,1]$, the increased dominance increases the probability that the fractality of the dominant crisis will be imposed on the "pair" of the two crises involved in the process of overlapping—by passing from immiscibility, through conservative, till transformative overlapping.

Based on the above reasoning, we propose the "algebra" of determining $FDC^{\varepsilon\gamma}(1,2)$ be:

$$FDC^{\varepsilon\gamma}(1,2) = \frac{\overline{FDC}^{\varepsilon\gamma}(1,2)}{dn(1,2)}$$

where

$$\overline{FDC}^{\varepsilon\gamma}(1,2) = \frac{FDC^{\varepsilon\gamma}(1) + FDC^{\varepsilon\gamma}(2)}{2}$$

A stylized imagine of $FDC^{\varepsilon\gamma}(1,2)$ is presented in Fig. 6.3.

If we have more than two overlapped crises, to avoid the "problem of "n" bodies"[39] the procedure we proposed is the following:

- to consider two of the overlapped crises, $C(1)$, and $C(2)$, and calculate its $FDC^{\varepsilon\gamma}(1,2)$;
- to consider the new crisis $C(1,2)$ and a third one, $C(3)$, and calculate $FDC^{\varepsilon\gamma}(1,2;3)$;
- to repeat the procedure for the nth crisis, so calculating $FDC^{\varepsilon\gamma}(1,2,\ldots(n-1);n)$.

Of course, the fundamental key, here, is the determination of the marks of $C(1,2)$. We propose the following methodology in that matter:

Be $C(1)_{51423}^{\varepsilon\alpha\delta\beta\gamma}$ and $C(2)_{51423}^{\varepsilon\alpha\delta\beta\gamma}$. The $FDC^{\varepsilon\gamma}(1,2)$ is calculated, for each of them, based on ΔN^{ε} and ΔN^{γ}. So, the inverse problem[40] is as follows: what are the values of ε and γ, associable with the "integrated" crisis $C(1,2)$,

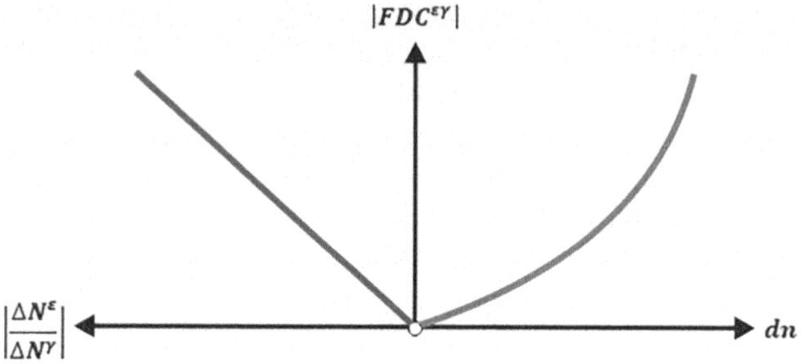

Fig. 6.3 The phenomenology of the overlapped crises fractal dimension. *Source*: author

given the $FDC^{\varepsilon\gamma}(1,2)$. The reasoning could be the following (we proceed as if it is talking about a single crisis):

- case (i): $[N(1)^{\varepsilon} < 0] \wedge [N(2)^{\varepsilon} < 0]$, then $N(1,2)^{\varepsilon} = \mathit{min}\,[|N(1)^{\varepsilon}|,|N(2)^{\varepsilon}|]$;
- case (ii): $[N(1)^{\varepsilon} > 0] \wedge [N(2)^{\varepsilon} > 0]$, then $N(1,2)^{\varepsilon} = \mathit{max}[N(1)^{\varepsilon}, N(2)^{\varepsilon}]$;
- case (iii): $[N(1)^{\varepsilon} > 0] \wedge [N(2)^{\varepsilon} \leq 0]$, then $N(1,2)^{\varepsilon} = N(1)^{\varepsilon}$;
- case (iv): $[N(1)^{\varepsilon} \leq 0] \wedge [N(2)^{\varepsilon} > 0]$, then $N(1,2)^{\varepsilon} = N(2)^{\varepsilon}$;

Nota bene: the same for γ.

Now, the question is how to get the values for $\varepsilon(1,2)$, respectively, for $\gamma(1,2)$, given the values for

$N(1,2)^{\varepsilon}$, respectively, for $N(1,2)^{\gamma}$. It seems we should choose as follows:

- case (i): $\varepsilon(1,2)$ is the ε of the crisis that "gives" the selected $N(1,2)^{\varepsilon}$—so, if $\mathit{min}[|N(1)^{\varepsilon}|,|N(2)^{\varepsilon}|] = N(1)^{\varepsilon}$, then $\varepsilon(1,2) = \varepsilon(1)$, and if $\mathit{min}[|N(1)^{\varepsilon}|,|N(2)^{\varepsilon}|] = N(2)^{\varepsilon}$, then $\varepsilon(1,2) = \varepsilon(2)$;
- case (ii): if $\mathit{max}[|N(1)^{\varepsilon}|,|N(2)^{\varepsilon}|] = N(1)^{\varepsilon}$, then $\varepsilon(1,2) = \varepsilon(1)$, and if $\mathit{max}[|N(1)^{\varepsilon}|,|N(2)^{\varepsilon}|] = N(2)^{\varepsilon}$, then $\varepsilon(1,2) = \varepsilon(2)$;
- case (iii): obviously, $\varepsilon(1,2) = \varepsilon(1)$;
- case (iv): obviously, $\varepsilon(1,2) = \varepsilon(2)$.

Nota bene: the same for γ.

To complete the marks for the integrated (overlapped) $C(1)$, and $C(2)$, we must establish the values of α, β and δ for $C(1,2)$. The best method is

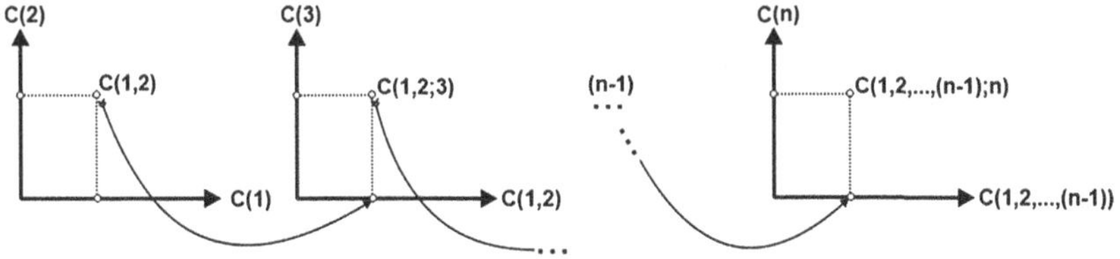

Fig. 6.4 Transforming the problem of "three bodies" into a problem of "two bodies". *Source*: author

to select, between the marks of $C(1)$, and $C(2)$, those which have the highest values. So:

$$\alpha(1,2) = \max\left[\alpha(1), \alpha(2)\right];$$

$$\beta(1,2) = \max\left[\beta(1), \beta(2)\right];$$

$$\delta(1,2) = \max\left[\delta(1), \delta(2)\right];$$

As a result, the overlapped crises, noted $C(1,2)$, will have the following marks (with $\tilde{x}$ is noted the joint mark):

$$C(1,2) = C(1,2)_{51423}^{\tilde{\varepsilon}\tilde{\alpha}\tilde{\delta}\tilde{\beta}\tilde{\gamma}}$$

The reasoning for the "three bodies" will be, now, resumed for ... two crises that overlap, namely: $C(1,2)_{51423}^{\tilde{\varepsilon}\tilde{\alpha}\tilde{\delta}\tilde{\beta}\tilde{\gamma}}$ and $C(3)_{51423}^{\varepsilon\alpha\delta\beta\gamma}$, and so on, within a recurrence procedure, until the last crisis that overlaps, as Fig. 6.4 suggests.

Notes

1. The so-called third Popper's world.
2. Karl Popper called the hypotheses through which we know (and predict) the world phenomenology ***bold hypotheses.*** We remind the readers the famous Wittgenstein aphorism in that matter: ***The limits of my language mean the limits of my world***, in Tractatus Logico-Philosophicus, 5.6.
3. In fact, we shall show that any property is the effect of a relationship—in this context, an ontological prioritization of the three possible entities (things, properties, relationships) will be proposed.

4. For example, whenever a piece of iron is heated, i.e. it comes into a relationship with a heat source, the piece of iron expands, whether or not the expansion is observed/measured by anyone.
5. The opposition is forbidden (is impossible) towards the natural necessity; this is why freedom does not exist in nature.
6. We shall see below that these scales can be of three kinds: (a) spatial/dimensional scales; (b) temporal/rhythmical scales; (c) significant/axiological scales.
7. So, rigorously, similarity is a property of a relationship. As a result, similarity is not a property on its own (likewise fractality, that is not a property on its own, too).
8. The criterion (criteria) is (are) depending on the scientific or praxeological interest, so, principled, it does not exist a criterion (or a set of criteria) *per se* in identifying the property of similarity.
9. The criterion in the case must be at least observable, although, in many cases, it should be also measurable, to facilitate and consolidate the comparison.
10. See, below, the property of symmetry for the relation of similarity—so, *a fortiori*, a relation of self-similarity is verified tautologically.
11. From a certain perspective, the possibility of self-similarity in the case of spatial displacement leads to the (general) idea of entanglement which seems to be peculiar not only to the natural sciences but also to the social sciences.
12. However, with some "benevolence", since, in fact, the fractals of Mandelbrot require both displacement in space and in time. In addition, they raise a difficult question: based on what can we consider an entity to be the same if it exhibits different scales? This issue will be resumed when we shall discuss the difference between self-similarity and fractals.
13. It is likely to exist, here, some redundancy, since the same structure is credited to unfold the same functions. However, it is, equally, possible that different structures generate the same function, so the category of self-similarity could be kept.
14. We leave aside the problem of how we could know which of the two versions of an entity is the original entity and which is the clone. A similar (less logical, however) question is raised regarding the individualization (the personalization) of two (or more) biological twins.
15. A clarification is required here. The necessity of replicating entities to make possible and relevant the discussion about similarity in time is associated only with the entities that, by their nature, are … replicable. However, in the case of entities that do not replicate by their nature but, instead, are durable (or sustainable, in the case of artefacts), the similarity can still be discussed, since we have, assigned to the different moments, two versions of the entity, although the replication did not occur and cannot occur.

16. We have self-replication in the case of living entities—either biologically living entities or logically living entities (Dinga, 2012).
17. See the life-cycle hypothesis of Franco Modigliani and Richard Brumberg, or the lifespan of an economic cycle, or the second curve hypothesis (Handy, 2016).
18. With the variants (for specific ends) as speed self-similarity, acceleration self-similarity, etc.
19. For example, Edgar E. Peters (1994) proposes such a hypothesis that "requires" that the same return of financial (more exactly, nominal, in our terminology of this study) be brought by different time horizons on which those investments are made.
20. The decreasing order of the cardinal of the sets of "individuals" of the four cases in which the similarity is posed as topic is, in our opinion: (1) case (iii); (2) case (ii); (3) case (iv); (4) case (i).
21. Inertia is a property discovered, in Mechanics, by Galileo (and taken over later in a systematic way by Newton), saying that a (mechanical) entity keeps its state (either of moving or resting) so long as an external (mechanical) force does not change that state. Today, the concept of inertia is generalized, entering the mechanical domain and the language, psychology, history, economics and social sciences (Dinga, 2012 – Chapter 17 "On the inertial phenomenon of the economic process").
22. The inertia could also be used as an explicative principle of a large class of sustainable entities (networks, systems, phenomena, processes). According to our knowledge, this association of ideas is not, now, invoked in the literature.
23. The enthusiasts of mathematics could also examine a ternary equivalence relation or, generally, a n-ary equivalence relation generated by the property of similarity.
24. This has happened because the fractals, overwhelmingly, were (and still are) viewed from a purely mathematical (topological) perspective. Even some essays—see Edgar Peters (1994) or even Benoît Mandelbrot (2008)—aspiring to bring the fractality phenomenon/process into the social field (especially in the finance sector) provide the same technical approaches inspired by the topological transforming of geometrical forms. But, as we hope our research suggests, it is needed for a qualitative and logical examination of the issue of fractals/fractality.
25. Here, exactly in the sense of the chaos theory (i.e., the theory of the non-linear dynamic systems), where a bifurcation point is a point (with the mathematical condition: $f(x) = x$, with x as the fixed point) that is either an attractor or a source, so is a bifurcation point, for the next dynamics of the system (Alligood et al., 1996).

26. The ranking of signification species seems, *prima facie*, to be non-realistic—the most dominant is the self-esteem signification, while the least dominant is the survival signification—although common sense would tell us that the rapport of dominance of signification should be exactly inverse. Properly speaking, the ranking is correct (and credible) since, in the social field, individuals live according to basic values, among which self-esteem is by far more important and relevant than simple survival. It is true, however, that in the non-human world, the survival "signification" is the most important, so the most dominant positioning and action.
27. There is, obviously, also a hetero-esteem—the esteem manifested by others regarding a given person. The coincidence between self-esteem and hetero-esteem is a *rara avis*.
28. We specify that we are referring to individual freedom.
29. Of course, between life conditions and the habits of life, there is no independence, regularly the (objective) conditions, including normativity influencing the habits. Nor is inverse causation prohibited at all.
30. Here we can appeal to the concept of revealed preferences, coined by Paul Samuelson in 1968.
31. In fact, the economic cyclicality issue itself deserves a deep logical analysis but such a task will be assumed elsewhere.
32. Honestly, Mandelbrot cited his predecessor in the matter, namely Lewis Fry Richardson, who established the logical content of the concept.
33. From this perspective, it will be especially of scientific interest to see how a given chreode (or a resulting chreode from crises overlapping) changes its fractal dimension.
34. If some readers interested in our debate decide to continue and/or develop our modest and just incipient contributions, they are, of course, welcome.
35. The reasons for keeping this denomination, although it is not talked at all about a ... fractional dimension, are (i) fractality is closely connected with self-similarity, and this property is still kept in the crisis topic; (ii) the long way of the concept of fractality in literature, so readers already own the understanding of the concept; (iii) in calculating the *FDC*, fractional numbers are, regularly, possible.
36. We recall that, in Chap. 5, Table 5.2, the numerical values of the compatibility are provided with an illustrative title only, because those values require separate reflections which are not done in this study. We give our proposal regarding the *FDC* calculus as if those separate reflections were already done.
37. Of course, the time can be replaced by space/location, without changing the reasoning.
38. The case of more crises is easy to be generalized, *mutatis mutandis*.

39. The problem has issued in Cosmology/Astrophysics, being formulated by Newton himself, for the case in which three heavenly bodies form a single gravitational system (more exactly, a network in our terminology). The solution seems to be a reduction of the case to that of two bodies, which can be easier solved. *Nota bene*: we recall that Poincaré himself messed up in providing the solution to the three-body problem.
40. The inverse problem, as evoked here, is analogous with the inverse problem in probability theory based on propensities, namely if the propensity gives the probability, how to get the propensity given the probability.

References

Alligood, K. T., Sauer, T. D., & Yorke, J. A. (1996). *Chaos: An Introduction to Dynamical Systems*. Springer.

Dinga, E. (2012). *Rebuilding Economics: A Logical, Epistemological, and Methodological Approach*. (especially Chapter 14 "On the logically living system"). Lambert Academic Publishing.

Dinga, E., Oprean-Stan, C., Tănăsescu, C. R., Brătian, V., & Ionescu, G.-M. (2022). *Financial Market Analysis and Behaviour. The Adaptive Preference Hypothesis (Annex 1)*. Routledge – Taylor and Francis Group.

Dinga, E., Tănăsescu, C. R., & Ionescu, G.-M. (2020). Social Entropy and Normative Network. *Entropy, 22*(9).

Handy, C. (2016). *The Second Curve: Thoughts on Reinventing Society*. Random House Business.

Mandelbrot, B. B. (1997). *Fractals and Scaling in Finance: Discontinuity, Concentration and Risk*, Springer (apud Alajbeg, D., Bubaš, Z., Šonje, V., The efficient market hypothesis: problems with interpretations of empirical tests. *Financial Theory and Practice*, 2012, 36(1)).

Mandelbrot, B. B. (2008). *The Misbehavior of Markets: A Fractal View of Financial Turbulence*. Profile Books.

Peters, E. E. (1994). *Fractal Market Analysis: Applying Chaos Theory to Investment and Economics*. John Wiley & Sons, Inc.

Popper, K. R. (2002). *Conjectures and Refutations. The Growth of Scientific Knowledge*. Routledge-Taylor & Francis Group.

Popper, K. R. (2005). *The Logic of Scientific Discovery*. Routledge-Taylor & Francis Group.

CHAPTER 7

Measuring of the Societal Crisis

7.1 Preamble

Principled, a societal crisis is observable from the perspective of each of the five marks of a generic crisis (α, β, γ, δ, ε), perhaps with a little bit more difficulty regarding the mark ε, because of its strong subjectivity, so idiosyncrasy. In fact, as mentioned *en passant* in Chap. 1, there is a conceptual family around observability, and we think it would be useful to review it, briefly. We have, in this matter, a quadrilateral: observability, accessibility, controllability, predictability.

7.1.1 Observability

Observability is a conscious focus[1] on an entity (thing, property, relationship as well as their combinations: even/instantiation, phenomenon, process and so on). So, observability is a relational property, or a property of a relationship, namely a property of the relationship between the observer (regularly the human being but, also, a machine as an intermediator between the entity in the case and the human observer (e.g., either in micro-cosmos or in macro-cosmos).[2] Observability has a hidden component—an area of unobservability, see Chap. 1, point 1.3.2., (1)—called a dead zone, and a "visible" component, which is exactly the observable zone. Both from a natural perspective and an intellectual one, the hidden component shrinks in time (has a historical character), in favour of the

E. Dinga, *Economic Resilience During Overlapped Crises*,
https://doi.org/10.1007/978-3-031-80224-9_7

"visible" component, due to the experience and, especially, to the development of science (and culture, in general). To be mentioned that observability, being an intentionality, has not a universal or absolute nature but a contextual one. More precisely, observability must be judged from the perspective of intentionality: we observe or do not observe only what we believe or want to observe. Observability (*O*) is the most extended space of perception we can mobilize.

7.1.2 Accessibility

Accessibility is also a relational property, like observability but it has a narrower space/area than observability (in fact, accessibility is a sub-set of the observability set). By accessibility it is understood that observability can be measured, either qualitatively (qualification) or quantitatively (quantification), no matter the more or less sophisticated level or means of such measuring. Essentially, accessibility allows somewhat a taking possession of the observability exactly by the measurement evoked. Accessibility (*A*) also has a historical character, i.e. the more the experience and science develop, the more accessibility area extends. If observability is hard to inter-personally communicate,[3] accessibility manifests especially by intermediation of such an inter-personal communication[4] (e.g., scientific theories, sociological or historical narratives, universal methodologies of knowledge such as mathematics or logic). If observability remains in the field of perception (not a simple sensation, of course), accessibility passes towards the intellect, since it proceeds to conceptualization and judgements.

7.1.3 Predictability

Both observability and accessibility are focused on the present day (or/and on the past). Predictability (*P*), as a relational property, does focus on the future. Essentially, predictability is that property of the relationship between the subject (both for observability and accessibility) and the object—any entity in the real[5] world (either objective, subjective, objectified)—that allows one to know in advance the states or the kinematics, of any kind (size, rhythm, structure, impact, signification, etc., that will occur in the future). Predictability allows both prediction (rational anticipations of the future based on theories or hypotheses) and prognoses (phenomenological extrapolations of the past into the future). While the predictions require to consider the causality, the prognoses are limited to statistical correlations, including objective (or frequential[6]) probabilities. Alongside predictions and prognoses can function on the future the Bayesian probabilities, which are simply expectations based exclusively on belief (supported, of course, by experience, too). Obviously, predictability has a sphere narrower than accessibility, which refers to only entities in the accessibility area for which there are theories or hypotheses capable of providing predictions or simple prognoses.

7.1.4 *Controllability*

Controllability (also a relational property) refers to the capacity and ability of the subject to influence the entities obeyed to predictability. By controllability (*C*) must be understood, more precisely, the possibility to exert the following categories of interventions on future events/phenomena/processes: (a) stopping or decelerating; (b) initiating or accelerating; (c) modifying.[7] Of course, controllability does not mean actual control under the three categories of interventions, since the subject could decide not to intervene at all but, as said, the possibility of exerting the control. The relationships among the four concepts discussed (*OAPC*), from the theory perspective, is the following:

$$O \supset A \supset P \supset C$$

Figure 7.1 provides a stylized image of the presumed trajectory of the four (relational) properties.

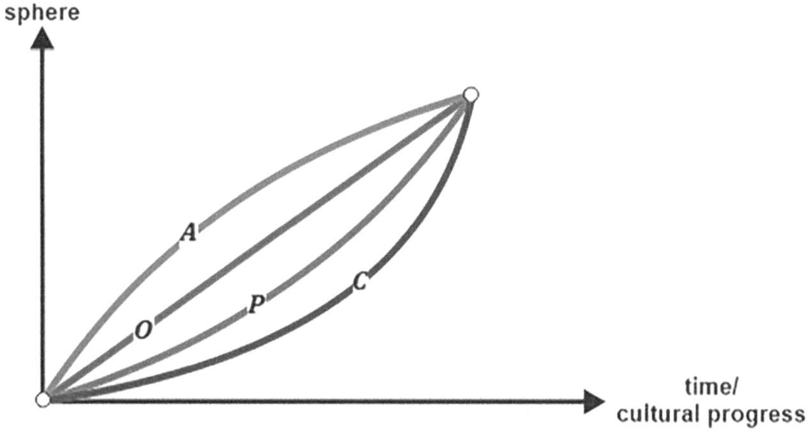

Fig. 7.1 The presumed chreodes of *OAPC*. *Source*: author

7.2 The Parameters of the Societal Crisis

First of all, it must be mentioned that the parameters of (societal) crisis are crisply different from the marks of it (*Nota bene*: we remind the marks of crisis are α—cause, β—origin, γ—chreode, δ—impact, ε—significance). In fact, the measurement of crisis addresses the mark γ—chreode only, trying to find the remarkable points (or intervals, or other parameters of interest) which characterize a generic chreode.

Secondly, the parameters of crisis are quantitative properties, while the marks are qualitative ones.

Thirdly, as shown in paragraph 7.1, measurement implies the accessibility of an entity, from the perspective of the observer—as accessibility is included in the observability, it results that the measurement implies, concomitantly, the observability and accessibility.

In such a context, the parameters of crisis aim at the crisis measurement, so they are frameable to the accessibility relational property, namely to the quantitative accessibility (while the marks of crisis are frameable to the qualitative accessibility).

7.2.1 A Typology of Parameters of Crisis

The parameters of crisis must measure/quantify two coordinates in space-time of a generic crisis: (a) the state of crisis, or the state position/positioning; (b) the kinematics of crisis, or kinematic position/positioning. In fact, the two coordinates form two classes of parameters. We note the class of state parameters with *S*, and the class of kinematic parameters with *K*.

(a) the class *S* of the parameters of crisis

Class S addresses the state of a (societal) generic crisis, that is, the quantitative dimensions that are fixed at a moment in time. All the state parameters will form the state vector of the crisis. The state vector completely describes the crisis from a static perspective, as a picture assigned to the established moment. The trajectory (the chreode) of the crisis will be the concatenation, ordered in time, of all state vectors considered. Next, we propose the components of such a state vector for a (societal) generic crisis:

(a1) (s_t^1) *cyclical position of crisis.*[8] We saw that according to γ-chreode mark, a crisis is of five kinds (synergic, migratory, trans-field, self-maintaining, and self-extinguishing). In turn, each of these species can have a punctual position, at a given time, in its unfolding. Such a (static, photographic) point we call crisisity position. The presupposition is, of course, that we (must) accept a structure of the chreode in the case, something analogous with the structure of chreode accepted for the economic (and, more generally, societal) cycle. We bring for help Fig. 7.2, which describes the generic chreode unfolding of a generic crisis:

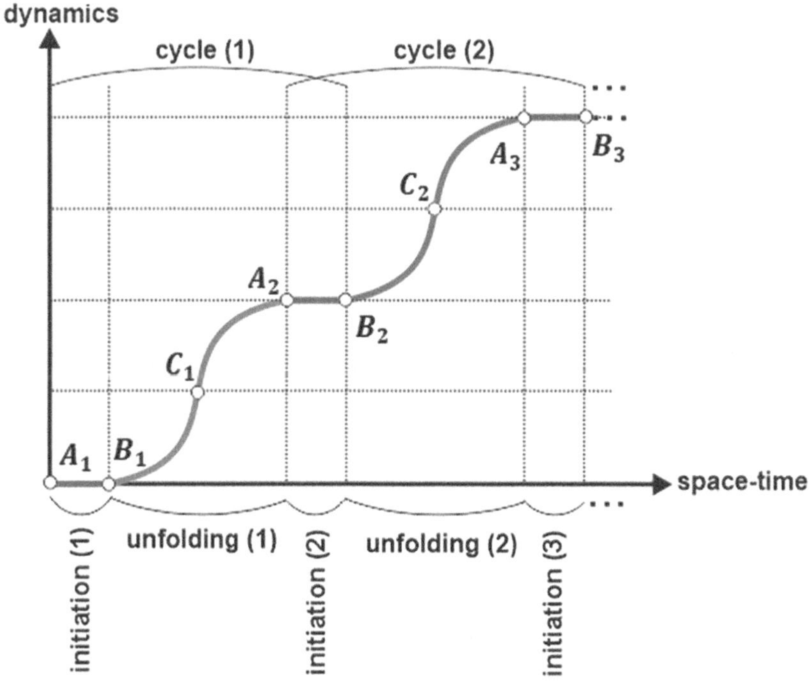

Fig. 7.2 The generic stages of crisis chreode. *Source*: author

Discussion

- the generic profile of the chreode of crisis exhibits the following basic points:
  - A_1: the point/moment when a germ of the crisis arises, in some origin (β mark) and following some cause (α mark);
  - $[A_1, B_1]$ interval: duration required for priming the crisis triggering—principled, the germ must accumulate some quantity which reaches a threshold at which the triggering of crisis is inevitable;
  - B_1: the point/moment when the crisis is actually triggered and begins its unfolding;
  - $[B_1, A_2]$ interval: duration of actual unfolding of crisis. In our opinion, the chreode of the crisis generally follows a logistic curve (the most common trajectory in the economic/social field): the process begins slowly but accelerating (duration $[B_1, C_1]$), then it continues in a decelerating way (duration $[C_1, A_2]$). This implies that during the interval $[B_1, C_1]$ the curve is convex, and during the interval $[C_1, A_2]$ the curve is concave;
  - C_1: the point/moment when the curve changes its form from convex to concave (an inflexion point);[9]
  - A_2: the point/moment when the crisis exhausts its potential and stops; of course, the impact of it (δ mark) changes the societal state and conditionalities, and generates, for the generic individual, the associated signification (ε mark);
  - with the point A_2, the crisis can (or not, after the case) manifest another version and, so, we enter the phenomenology of self-similarity and fractality, as discussed in Chap. 6;
  - the interval $[A_2, B_2]$ is a common one for the two presumed versions of the crisis—for the previous version it means the extinction of the impact and, at the same time, the assimilation of the impact in the state and conditionalities of the societal system, and for the next version it means the priming of that. In this … overlapping of the two durations consists exactly the justification of the singular character of the crisis at the societal level, as claimed before;
  - the intervals $[B_2, C_2]$, $[C_2, A_3]$, the point (of inflexion) C_2 and the interval $[A_3, B_3]$ have the same meaning as previous, *mutatis mutandis*;
  - *Nota bene*: on the ordinate is not measured anything of size/dimension/level nature but only is indicated the dynamics/kinematics of different versions of crisis.

- based on the above, the exact (or approximate) point of graph 7.2 will be identified and registered as such in the state vector for the time in the case; of course, at a given time, a single crisisity position will be registered;
- in fact, nine possible crisisity positions are available: numerical value [1] for point A; numerical value [2] for interval (A, B); numerical value [3] for point B; numerical value [4] for curve BC; numerical value [5] for point C; numerical value [6] for curve CA; numerical value [7] for (new) point A; numerical value [8] for (new) interval (A, B); numerical point [9] for (new) point B.

We have shown above that a crisis, although singular, can be repeatable (of course, not identically), and we have named this a new version of the crisis. However, for a hypostasis of a crisis to be a version of the previous one, a logical (and societal) condition must be fulfilled: the interval $[A_i, B_i]$ be common for the versions (i−1) and (i), respectively, of the same crisis. In other words, that (horizontal) interval, aimed at deleting the traces of the previous hypostasis of the crisis, should keep sufficient causality to reinitiate that crisis, of course, as its new version (something as … crisis embers). If this condition is not fulfilled, if, contingently, in the interval $[A_i, B_i]$ a new crisis is initiated, it is a new crisis, not a new version of an old crisis. The traces (that we note with ρ) address either origin (β), or cause (α) as such, but never chreode (γ), impact (δ) or signification (ε). One should not confuse the traces of a crisis (ρ) with the impact of crisis (δ), although some interferences[10] could exist here.

(a2) (s_t^2) *intensity of crisis*.[11] The issue of the intensity of crisis is complicated enough; here's why we are going to make some considerations in that matter:

- the intensity (of any nature) is a ratio number, given by the rapport between the measures (values) of two variables, one variable (N) that is distributed over a variable (n) on which the first one is distributed; in fact, an intensity (s_t^2) is a pressure of no matter what nature;

$$s_t^2 = \frac{N}{n}$$

- the bigger N, for n constant, or the smaller n, for N constant, the bigger the intensity (*Nota bene*: of course, a simultaneous increasing of N and decreasing of n accelerates the increasing of intensity, and vice-versa, a simultaneous decreasing of N and increasing of n accelerates the decreasing of intensity);
- the problem is to establish N and n, in the matter of (societal) crisis. We think that:
  - N must be a quantitative variable, more exactly, a "quantity of crisis". A quantity of crisis can be measured by measuring a combination of impact and signification;
  - we remind the general typology of impact (mark δ): $\delta = 5$: impact on meta-narrative;[12] $\delta = 4$: impact on political regime; $\delta = 3$: impact on values; $\delta = 2$: impact on rationality; $\delta = 1$: impact on structure;
  - we remind the general typology of signification (mark ε): $\varepsilon = 5$: signification of self-esteem; $\varepsilon = 4$: signification of freedom; $\varepsilon = 3$: signification of way of life; $\varepsilon = 2$: signification of the opportunities; $\varepsilon = 1$: signification of survival,
- a matrix can be formed to combine the two marks (δ and ε) to estimate the "quantity of crisis"—it is obvious enough that that quantity of crisis is estimated/evaluated rather … qualitatively, but this is sufficient for the present state of research (Table 7.1)—in order to obtain a good hierarchy, we propose to simply multiply the values of rows with the values of columns (the values in the cells are noted Q_{ij}, with $i, j \in \{1,2,3,4,5\}$):
  - since the numerical values in Table 7.1. are arbitrary (although significantly), in order to eliminate the influence of the dimension, we shall reduce all the values into the real interval $[0,1]$ as proceeded elsewhere, using the formula:

Table 7.1 Estimating the "quantity of crisis"—primary values

		ε				
		5	*4*	*3*	*2*	*1*
δ	5	25	20	15	10	5
	4	20	16	12	8	4
	3	15	12	9	6	3
	2	10	8	6	4	2
	1	5	4	3	2	1

Source: author

$$q_t = \frac{Q_{ij}^{ac} - Q_{ij}^{\min}}{Q_{ij}^{\max} - Q_{ij}^{\min}} = \frac{Q_{ij}^{ac} - 1}{24}$$

where Q_{ij}^{ac} is the current value of Q_{ij}.

Based on the normalization of the Q_{ij}, we can calculate actually the values of q_t (Table 7.2).

Nota bene: for the value 0 of the normalized intensity of crisis, it is implicitly understood that for the pair $(\delta, \varepsilon) = (1, 1)$ the intensity of crisis is situated under the minimum threshold of counting, so the intensity is perceived as null.

- if the impact is actual, then we speak about an actual quantity of crisis; if the impact is potential (anticipated, expected, desired[13]), so the quantity of crisis can be either an actual quantity ($s_t^{2.1}$) or a potential one ($s_t^{2.2}$).

Comment

One could put the problem of the weight with which each of the two marks (δ and ε) contributes to the cell values of the intensity of crisis. Indeed, this is another way to calculate the values of Q_{ij}. For example, considering a coefficient $\lambda \in [0, 1] \subset R$, we could write, for the cell (ij):

$$Q_{ij} = \lambda \cdot \delta_{ij} + (1 - \lambda) \cdot \pm \varepsilon_{ij}$$

Table 7.2 Estimating the "quantity of crisis"—normalized values

		ε				
		5	*4*	*3*	*2*	*1*
δ	5	1.000	0.792	0.583	0.375	0.167
	4	0.792	0.625	0.458	0.292	0.125
	3	0.583	0.458	0.333	0.208	0.083
	2	0.375	0.292	0.208	0.125	0.042
	1	0.167	0.125	0.083	0.042	0.000

Source: author

This is the method of a linear combination, while the first is the method of multiplying combination (we prefer the method of linear combination since it allows the introduction of the "methodological preference"). Taking $\lambda = 0.3$ (so giving more importance/relevance to the mark ε, which is harmonized with the role of significance in the economic/social/societal perception), the new Q_{ij} are the following (Table 7.3).

The formula for normalized values becomes:

$$q_t^{\lambda} = \frac{Q_{ij}^{ac} - Q_{ij}^{\min}}{Q_{ij}^{\max} - Q_{ij}^{\min}} = \frac{Q_{ij}^{ac} - 1}{4}$$

The normalized values for the new Q_{ij} are presented in Table 7.4.

In Table 7.4, the indices of the intensity of crisis by passing from the highest signification to the lowest one, and of passing from the highest impact to the lowest one,[14] are calculated in Table 7.5.

Table 7.3 Estimating the "quantity of crisis"—λ-based values

		ε				
		5	*4*	*3*	*2*	*1*
δ	5	5.0	4.3	3.6	2.9	2.2
	4	4.7	4.0	3.3	2.6	1.9
	3	4.4	3.7	3.0	2.3	1.6
	2	4.1	3.4	2.7	2.0	1.3
	1	3.8	3.1	2.4	1.7	1.0

Source: author

Table 7.4 Estimating the "quantity of crisis"—λ-based values, normalized values

		ε				
		5	*4*	*3*	*2*	*1*
δ	5	1.000	0.825	0.650	0.475	0.300
	4	0.925	0.750	0.575	0.400	0.225
	3	0.850	0.675	0.500	0.325	0.150
	2	0.775	0.600	0.425	0.250	0.075
	1	0.700	0.525	0.350	0.175	0.000

Source: author

Table 7.5 Estimating the "quantity of crisis"—λ-based normalized values

			ε								
			5	*4*	*3*	*2*	*1*	*5 → 4*	*4 → 3*	*3 → 2*	*2 → 1*
			1	*2*	*3*	*4*	*5*	*6*	*7*	*8*	*9*
δ	5	*1*	1.000	0.825	0.650	0.475	0.300	*0.825*	*0.788*	*0.731*	*0.632*
	4	*2*	0.925	0.750	0.575	0.400	0.225	*0.811*	*0.767*	*0.696*	*0.563*
	3	*3*	0.850	0.675	0.500	0.325	0.150	*0.794*	*0.741*	*0.650*	*0.462*
	2	*4*	0.775	0.600	0.425	0.250	0.075	*0.774*	*0.708*	*0.588*	*0.300*
	1	*5*	0.700	0.525	0.350	0.175	0.000	*0.750*	*0.667*	*0.500*	*0.000*
	5 → 4	*6*	*0.925*	*0.909*	*0.885*	*0.842*	*0.750*	**0.683**	**0.636**	**0.551**	**0.352**
	4 → 3	*7*	*0.919*	*0.900*	*0.870*	*0.813*	*0.667*	**0.662**	**0.616**	**0.535**	**0.347**
	3 → 2	*8*	*0.912*	*0.889*	*0.850*	*0.769*	*0.500*	**0.624**	**0.582**	**0.508**	**0.340**
	2 → 1	*9*	*0.903*	*0.875*	*0.824*	*0.700*	*0.000*	**0.530**	**0.498**	**0.443**	**0.331**

Source: author

Discussion

- quadrant I (*ij*, with $i = \overline{1,5}$, and $j = \overline{1,5}$) contains the normalized values of the intensity of crisis in the λ-based method;
- quadrant II (*ij*, with $i = \overline{1,5}$, and $j = \overline{6,9}$) contains the indices (as coefficients) of normalized values of crisis intensity, by passing the ε values from the highest value to the lowest one;
- quadrant III (*ij*, with $i = \overline{6,9}$, and $j = \overline{1,5}$) contains the indices (as coefficients) of normalized values of crisis intensity, by passing the δ values from the highest value to the lowest one;
- quadrant IV (*ij*, with $i = \overline{6,9}$, and $j = \overline{6,9}$) contains, so to speak, a ... hermeneutics of simultaneous passing among the δ mark numerical values, respectively, to among the ε mark numerical values. The way of calculus for the cell (*ij*) for $i = \overline{6,9}$ and $j = \overline{6,9}$) (with *x* is noted the value of δ passing, and with *y* is noted the value of ε passing):

$$V_{ij} = \frac{\sum_{k=1}^{5}\left(x_{ik} \cdot y_{kj}\right)}{5}$$

Example for $i = 7$ and $j = 8$:

$$V_{78} = \frac{\sum_{k=1}^{5}(x_{7k} \bullet y_{k8})}{5} = \frac{x_{71} \bullet y_{18} + x_{72} \bullet y_{28} + x_{73} \bullet y_{38} + x_{74} \bullet y_{48} + x_{75} \bullet y_{58}}{5} =$$

$$\frac{0.919 \bullet 0.731 + 0.9 \bullet 0.696 + 0,87 \bullet 0.65 + 0.813 \bullet 0.588 + 0.667 \bullet 0.5}{5} = \frac{2.675}{5} = 0.535$$

In an analogous way in which we have proceeded to identify the three basic classes of crises overlapping (see Chap. 5, point. 5.2), we can now identify from the point of view of crisis intensity. We put our attention on the following proposal:

- (class C_1^Q): for $q_t^\lambda \in [0,0.2)$—crisis with a *negligible* intensity;
- (class C_2^Q): for $q_t^\lambda \in [0.2,0.4)$—crisis with a *weak* intensity;
- (class C_3^Q): for $q_t^\lambda \in [0.4,0.6)$—crisis with a *medium* intensity;
- (class C_4^Q): for $q_t^\lambda \in [0.6,0.8)$—crisis with a *strong* intensity;
- (class C_5^Q): for $q_t^\lambda \in [0.8,1]$—crisis with a very *strong* intensity.

To be observed that, based on Table 7.4, the "population" of the classes C_k^Q, from the perspective of crisis intensity, are different, as follows: (class C_1^Q): four crises; (class C_2^Q): five crises; (class C_3^Q): six crises; (class C_4^Q): six crises; (class C_5^Q): four crises.

(a3) (s_t^3) *half-life period*. Is the time required for the crisis to reach point C (the inflection point) in Fig. 7.2. The parallel with the analogous phenomenon in Quantum Physics is supported by the following:

- during the interval $[B, C)$, the chreode of the crisis is accelerated, and after point C, during the interval $(C, A]$, the chreode is decelerated. Approximately, until point C, the crisis "consumes" half of its initial energy to penetrate the economic/social/societal and, after point C, the crisis goes, somewhat inertially, to exhaust its total energy;[15]
- of course, the state of affairs is not so linear as we said—for example, during the expansion of crisis, some new "fuel" could feed for enlarging this phase, while during the inertial period, some new obstacles could shorten that phase—our graph is just (symmetrically) stylized.

So, we can write the state vector as:

$$S_t = \begin{pmatrix} s_t^1 \\ s_t^2 \\ s_t^3 \end{pmatrix} = \begin{pmatrix} s_t^1 \\ s_t^{2.1} \\ s_t^{2.2} \\ s_t^3 \end{pmatrix}$$

(b) the class *K* of the parameters of crisis

Class *K* addresses the kinematic properties of a (societal) generic crisis, that is, the quantitative dimensions that characterize the passing of that crisis from a moment to the next one. In other words, the kinematic parameters describe the conditions in which the crisis passes from a state vector to the next state vector.[16] As the kinematic variables can have different numerical values in different moments, it is possible to construct what could be called kinematic vectors, assigned to any moment of interest. In fact, any such a moment could be assigned to two vectors: a state vector and a kinematic vector.[17] Next, we propose the components of such a kinematic vector for a (societal) generic crisis:

(b1) (k_t^1) *unfolding speed*. Addresses the speed with which the crisis goes. It is different at different points on the chreode as the last have been identified as components of *S* vector—for example, $k_t^1 = 0$ for the closed interval $[A, B]$ and has non-zero values in the rest of the chreode;

(b1) (k_t^2) *unfolding acceleration*. Addresses the acceleration ("speed of speed", or speed of order 2) which characterizes the crisis chreode at different points—for example, $k_t^2 = 0$ for the closed interval $[A, B]$, is positive on the interval (B, C), zero at point C and negative on the interval (C, A);

(b1) (k_t^3) *trans-region propensity*. This component of *K* vector indicates the probability[18] with which the crisis will pass from nominal region into the financial one $(k_t^{3.1})$, or from financial region into the real one $(k_t^{3.2})$ (see Fig. 4.13 in Chap. 4). Principled, the closer the crisis unfolding to the breaking point, the higher the probability that crisis will pass into the next region.[19]

So, we can write the kinematic vector as:

$$K_t = \begin{pmatrix} k_t^1 \\ k_t^2 \\ k_t^3 \end{pmatrix} = \begin{pmatrix} k_t^1 \\ k_t^2 \\ k_t^{3.1} \\ k_t^{3.2} \end{pmatrix}$$

Then, the matrix of the measurement of a generic crisis is:

$$M_t = (S_t \ \ K_t) = \begin{pmatrix} s_t^1 & k_t^1 \\ s_t^2 & k_t^2 \\ s_t^3 & k_t^3 \end{pmatrix} = \begin{pmatrix} s_t^1 & k_t^1 \\ s_t^{2.1} & k_t^2 \\ s_t^{2.2} & k_t^{3.1} \\ s_t^3 & k_t^{3.2} \end{pmatrix}$$

From the measurement perspective, any generic crisis, at a given moment t, is a bi-dimensional entity: $C_t = \left(s_t^p, k_t^q\right)$ with p, $q \in \{1,2,3\}$. Figure 7.3 synoptically suggests such a labelling $(t < \tau < \rho)$.

7.2.2 *Other Mentions*

Firstly, principled, a generic crisis is measurable in a bi-dimensional plan (s_t, k_t). As constructed, such a measurement provides a vector in its almost physical sense: an absolute value (s_t) and a "direction" (k_t).

Secondly, the two classes of parameters (state, and kinematic, respectively) are not completely independent from each other. For example, a given cyclical positioning of the crisis (s_t^1) is correlated, with a great probability, with a given numerical value of one (or even more) $k_t^{(\cdot)}$.

Thirdly, a potential value for the static parameters of crisis ($s_t^{2.2}$) "attracts" a certain numerical values for $k_t^{3.1}$ or $k_t^{3.2}$. The non-independence between the state variables and the kinematic ones is not a defect of the two classes of parameters but a reflection of the entanglement inside the phenomenology of (societal) crisis.

Fourthly, as Fig. 7.3. shows, at a given moment, any generic crisis is completely describable by a unique point in the plan (s_t, k_t). So, the trajectory ($T_{[0,n]}^C$) of such a generic crisis is represented, simply, by the set of pairs:

$$T_{[0,n]}^C = \left\{\left(s_0^{(\cdot)}, k_0^{(\cdot)}\right), \left(s_1^{(\cdot)}, k_1^{(\cdot)}\right), \ldots, \left(s_{n-1}^{(\cdot)}, k_{n-1}^{(\cdot)}\right), \left(s_n^{(\cdot)}, k_n^{(\cdot)}\right)\right\}$$

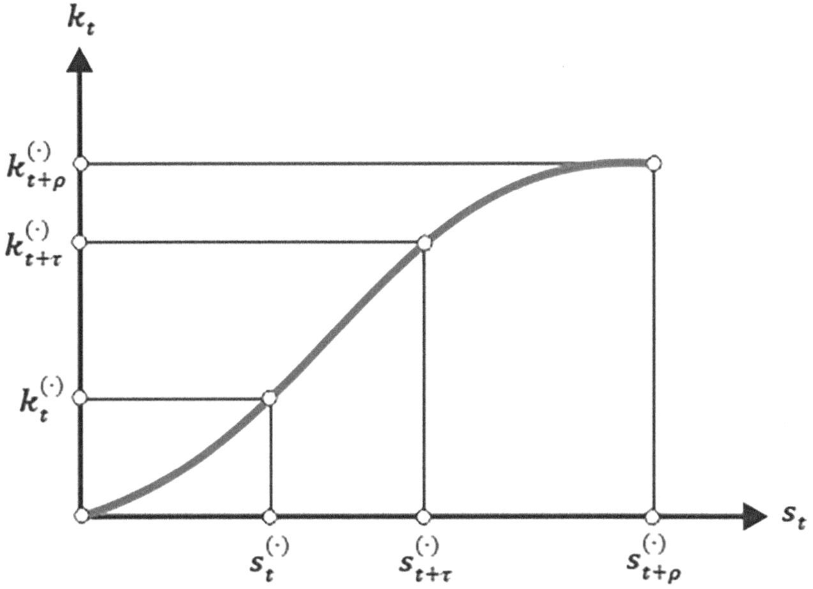

Fig. 7.3 The measures on the trajectory of a generic crisis. *Source*: author

7.3 Crises Overlapping and Crisis Measurement

We can, now, approach the issue of crisis measurement while crises overlapping occurs. First of all, of course, the problem of the way in which the crises overlapping affects the two classes of parameters regarding the measurement of the crisis must be clarified. It is what we do in the next two paragraphs.

7.3.1 *Regarding* s_t^1

Two or more crises that overlap are, generally, differently positioned in their chreode or their cycle.[20] Consequently, the "composed" crisis, generated through overlapping, will (possibly) exhibit an $\hat{s}_t^1$ measure that differs from each of the s_t^1 of the overlapped crises. The problem is how to calculate $\hat{s}_t^1$? *Nota bene*: with $\hat{s}_t^1$ is noted the s_t^1 measure of the overlapped crises. We shall develop the following reasoning:

Table 7.6 Qualitative judgement of the composed measure $\hat{s}_t^1$ (case of two crises)

C_2 / C_1	*Dominance*	$[A,B]^{21}/0^{(0)}$			$[B,C)/1$			$(C,A]/2$			$[A,B]^{22}/0^{(1)}$		
		IO	*CO*	*TO*	*IO*	*CO*	*TO*	*IO*	*CO*	*TO*	*IO*	*CO*	*TO*
$[A, B]$ (Initial	$\|C_1$	$0^{(0)}$	$0^{(0)}$	$0^{(0)}$	1	$0^{(0)}$	$0^{(0)}$	1	$0^{(0)}$	$0^{(0)}$	$0^{(0)}$	$0^{(0)}$	$0^{(0)}$
$[A, B]$.)/ $0^{(0)}$	$C_1\|$	$0^{(0)}$	$0^{(0)}$	$0^{(0)}$	1	1	1	2	2	2	$0^{(1)}$	$0^{(1)}$	$0^{(1)}$
$[B, C)$/	$\|C_1$	1	1	1	1	1	1	1	1	1	1	1	1
1	$C_1\|$	$0^{(0)}$	$0^{(0)}$	$0^{(0)}$	1	1	1	2	2	2	1	1	$0^{(1)}$
$(C, A]$/	$\|C_1$	$0^{(0)}$	$0^{(0)}$	$0^{(0)}$	1	1	1	2	2	2	2	2	2
2	$C_1\|$	$0^{(0)}$	$0^{(0)}$	$0^{(0)}$	1	1	1	2	2	2	$0^{(1)}$	2	2
$[A, B]$ (Final	$\|C_1$	$0^{(1)}$	$0^{(1)}$	$0^{(1)}$	$0^{(1)}$	1	1	1	1	1	$0^{(1)}$	$0^{(1)}$	$0^{(1)}$
$[A, B]$.)/ $0^{(1)}$	$C_1\|$	$0^{(0)}$	$0^{(0)}$	$0^{(0)}$	1	1	1	2	2	2	$0^{(1)}$	$0^{(1)}$	$0^{(1)}$

Source: author

- the composed $\hat{s}_t^1$ measure is depending on two gap-variables: (a) the gap-variable regarding the previous positioning of the overlapping crises—e.g., $s_t^1(C_1)$, $s_t^1(C_2)$, etc.; (b) the gap-variable regarding the category of crises from their natural perspective: immiscible (*IO*), conservative (*CO*), transformative (*TO*), see Chap. 5, point 5.2;
- in fact, we think the two gap-variables combined between them in a *sui generis* way, so that the composed (or mixed) measure of the overlapped crises can be judged as suggested in Table 7.6. We simplify the notations: "$|C_1$": "C_1 is affinity-based dominant, "$C_2|$": "C_2 is affinity-based dominated". We associate values of truth for the four standard positionings on the crisis chreode as follows:
  - initial $[A, B] \rightarrow 0^{(0)}$;
  - $[B, C) \rightarrow 1$;
  - $(C, A] \rightarrow 2$;
  - final $[A, B] \rightarrow 0^{(1)}$.

Discussion

- if we note with i, c, t the three alternative states in which the two overlapped crises can be (i for *IO*, c for *CO*, and t for *TO*), x_y is the punctual case of crises overlapping, where $y \in \{i, c, t\}$, then a sui generis propositional "logic" with four values of truth (tetravalent logic) could be developed. Two examples:

$$\left[|C_1(2)\wedge C_2|(1)\right]_c = 1$$

$$\left[|C_1\left(0^{(1)}\right)\wedge C_2|(1)\right]_i = 0^{(1)}$$

7.3.2 *Regarding* s_t^2

As known, s_t^2 measures the intensity of a crisis, based on a sui generis combination of the numerical values of δ and ε marks. Principled, any crisis can be associated with such a measure. Now, it is required to give a solution of measuring of two (or more) overlapped crises, e.g., $s_t^2(C_1)$, $s_t^2(C_2)$—we shall note the measure of the overlapped crises with $\hat{s}_t^2$. Starting from Table 7.5, i.e., in the λ-based evaluation, we suggest such a solution as follows:

- at a given time, two crises have, each of them, a certain value of the intensity, as calculated in quadrant I of Table 7.5—be they: $s_t^2(C_1)$, respectively $s_t^2(C_2)$;
- of course, the two crises are in affinity-based dominance relationships, either $(|C_1) \bigwedge (C_2|)$ or $(C_1|) \bigwedge (|C_2)$;
- therefore, the judgement regarding the $\hat{s}_t^2$ must consider both the values of intensity and the dominance relationship;
- in this context, we propose the following reasoning

$$(|C_1)\wedge(C_2|)\rightarrow \hat{s}_t^2 \equiv s_t^2(C_1)$$

$$(C_1|)\wedge(|C_2)\rightarrow \hat{s}_t^2 \equiv s_t^2(C_2)$$

So, we think it is not relevant to provide an algebraic calculus, whatever how justified, sophisticated and ... credible but to appeal to the perception: a crisis more intensive will be perceived as "lending" its intensity the overlapped (or composed) crises.

7.3.3 *Regarding* s_t^3

Something likewise should be, probably, did for the third state parameter, s_t^3. As was shown, this parameter refers to (or measures) the half-life

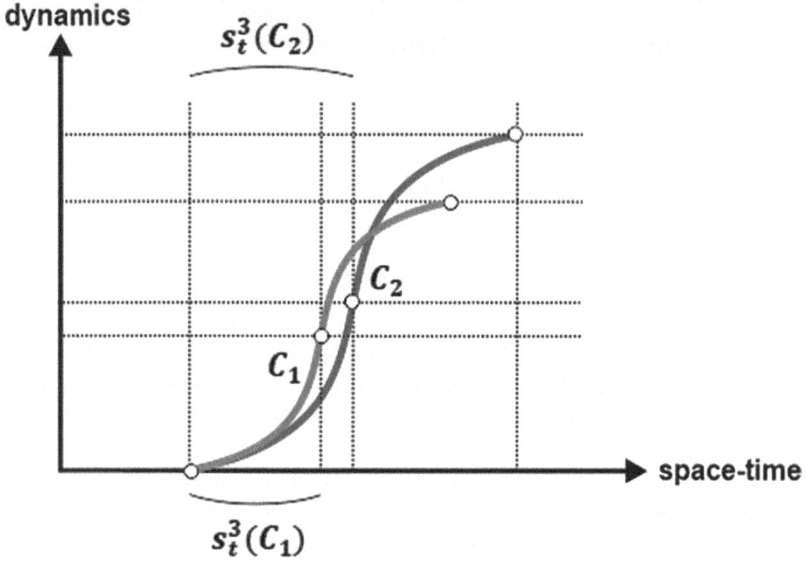

Fig. 7.4 Half-life period overlapping (case of two crises). *Source*: author

period of a crisis, i.e., the time interval until the chreode reaches the point C (inflection point). Given two crises with $s_t^3(C_1)$, respectively $s_t^3(C_2)$, it must be determined the $\hat{s}_t^3$, i.e., the half-life period of the overlapped crises. Again, we shall calibrate the reasoning based on the dominance relationship between the two given crises. Figure 7.4 illustrates the case of two overlapped crises located at different points in relation to the inflection point.

In this context, we propose the following reasoning:

$$(|C_1) \wedge (C_2|) \rightarrow \hat{s}_t^3 \equiv s_t^3(C_1)$$
$$(C_1|) \wedge (|C_2) \rightarrow \hat{s}_t^3 \equiv s_t^3(C_2)$$

7.3.4 *Regarding* k_t^1

The speed of crisis unfolding refers to the speed with which that crisis moves its position on chreode. Although this (kinematic) parameter is logically implicitly connected to the (state) parameter s_t^3, it is of relevance since the half-life period is a static parameter, in a great measure conservative as a structural property, while k_t^1 is a dynamic one. Principled, the speed of a generic crisis unfolding is calculated as a rate between the "space" travelled by a given point of that crisis on its chreode and the duration required by that travel. The "space" travelled, in the context of crisis, should be estimated by the change in the quantity of crisis, considering the generic form of the chreode curve (i.e., a logistic one). As the concept of "quantity of crisis" is already introduced at point 7.2.1, when has been calculated the crisis intensity (parameter s_t^2), it will be used here, too. Some preparations are needed, first of all:

- any moving of a crisis on its chreode, no matter the starting point or the end point, changes both the δ-value and ε-value of that crisis (so, changes the crisis intensity);
- it results that such moving on the crisis chreode must be measured by the very change of the δ-value and ε-value;
- the general effect of the δ-value and ε-value changing is already determined above (see Table 7.5) as λ-based estimations;

Consequently, we propose the following formalization in the matter:

$$k_t^1 = \frac{\Delta_{\delta\varepsilon}}{\Delta t}$$

Example 1: let us presume that a crisis pass from $\delta = 4$ to $\delta = 3$, and $\varepsilon = 2$ remains unchanged, such a process taking five time units. Then, from Table 7.5, we have:

$$k_t^1 = \frac{0.813}{5} = 0.1626$$

Example 2: let us presume that a crisis pass from $\delta = 4$ to $\delta = 3$, and from $\varepsilon = 5$ to $\varepsilon = 4$, such a process taking three time units. Then, from Table 7.5, we have:

$$k_t^1 = \frac{0.662}{3} = 0.2267$$

Example 3: let us presume that a crisis keeps $\delta = 3$ unchanged and pass from $\varepsilon = 3$ to $\varepsilon = 2$, such a process taking four time units. Then, from Table 7.5, we have:

$$k_t^1 = \frac{0.650}{4} = 0.1625$$

Nota bene: a very interesting phenomenon occurs here, namely in example 1 and example 3 is obtained the (approximated at the fourth decimal place) same result regarding the speed of crisis unfolding. This indicates us that can exist indifference curves of the speed of crisis unfolding, depending on the crisis intensity (normalized as a λ-based quantity of crisis) and on the duration within which the change of crisis intensity happens. Figure 7.5 shows a synoptic view of such a suggestion.[21]

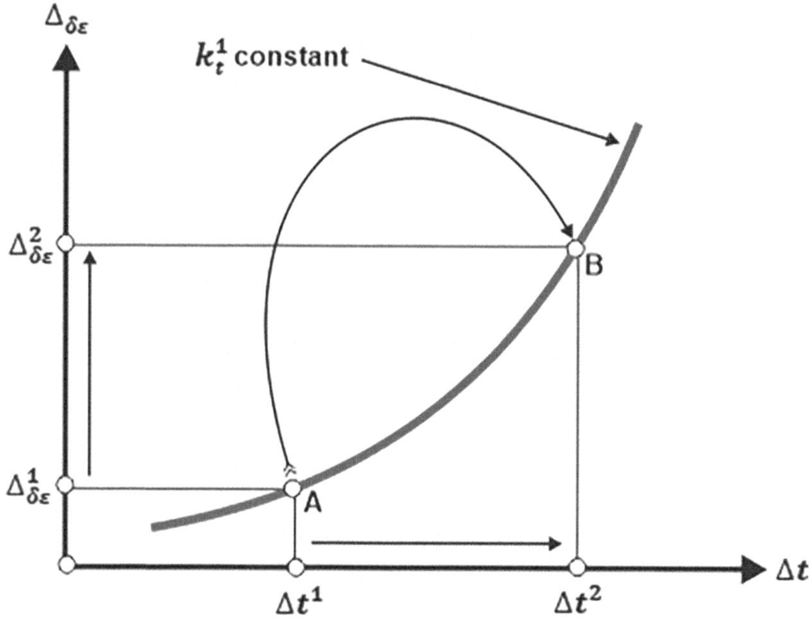

Fig. 7.5 Indifference (bi-dimensional) curves for the speed of crisis unfolding. *Source*: author

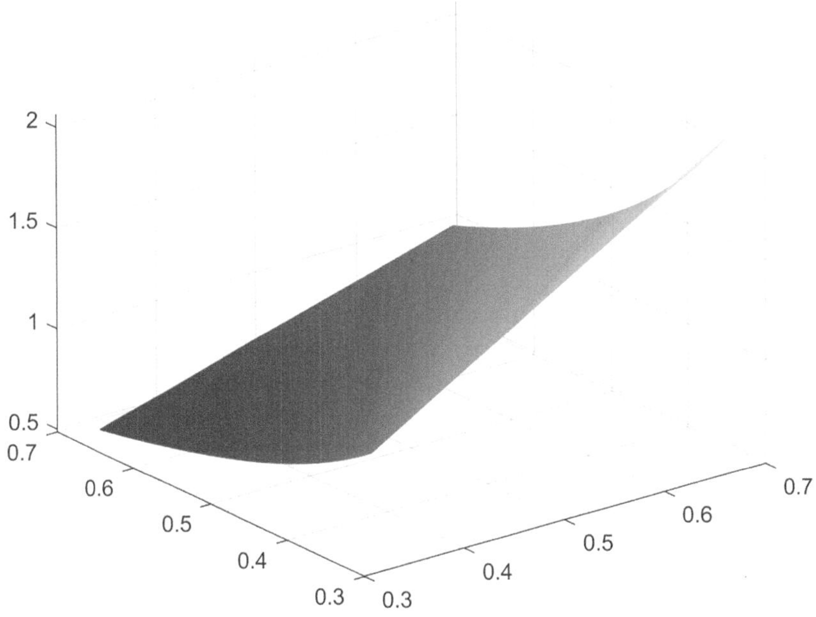

Fig. 7.6 Indifference (three-dimensional) curves for the speed of crisis unfolding. *Source*: author

Nota bene: taking the "usual" values for Δ_δ and Δ_ε, respectively, and the same for t, an illustrative picture of a three-dimensional curve would look as in Fig. 7.6.[22]

Now, we must clarify the way in which the speed of the overlapped crises must be calculated. We think the following "rules" should be considered:

- the speed perceived will be, in fact, the lowest speed among the speeds of overlapped crises; this assumption is similar to the well-known one saying: the speed of a technological process is given by the link with the lowest speed in the technological chain (i.e., by the weakest link of the chain);
- again, the affinity-based dominance appears, so that the speed of the overlapped crises (noted $\hat{k}_t^1$) will be provided by the crisis with the lowest speed of unfolding, namely:

$$(|C_1) \wedge (C_2|) \rightarrow \hat{k}_t^1 \equiv k_t^1(C_1)$$

$$(C_1|) \wedge (|C_2) \rightarrow \hat{k}_t^1 \equiv k_t^1(C_2)$$

7.3.5 Regarding k_t^2

The acceleration (or deceleration, after the case) of a crisis unfolding can, by its algebraic sign, indicate the very position of the crisis on its own chreode—namely, if the acceleration is positive, then the crisis is positioned between points *B* and *C* (see Fig. 7.2), and if the acceleration is negative (or, the same, the crisis chreode decelerates), then the crisis is positioned between points *C* and *A*. The problem is, of course, to say something about the acceleration (or deceleration) in the case of crises overlapping. Our point of view is the following:

- the acceleration (as well as the deceleration) is the variation of the speed in the time spent to get that variation, so:

$$k_i^2 = \frac{k_i^1 - k_{i-1}^1}{t_i - t_{i-1}} = \frac{\Delta\left(\frac{\Delta_{\delta\varepsilon}^i}{\Delta t_i}\right)}{\Delta t_i} = \frac{\left(\Delta_{\delta\varepsilon}^i\right)^{(2)}}{\left(\Delta t_i\right)^{(2)}}$$

where with the "exponent" written (2) is indicated the difference of order 2, i.e., the difference of the difference.[23]

- so, we have two (values of) accelerations, for two overlapped crises, namely $k_i^2(C_1)$ and $k_i^2(C_2)$, respectively;
- of course, the dominance relationship between the two crises (or more, if the case) is always present. Figure 7.7 helps us to visualize the overlapping between two crises with different accelerations;

Discussion

- the crises C_1 and C_2 overlap between them on duration *AD*. However, on duration *AB* and *CD*, respectively, the acceleration sign of the two crises is the same, namely positive on *AB*, and negative on *CD*;

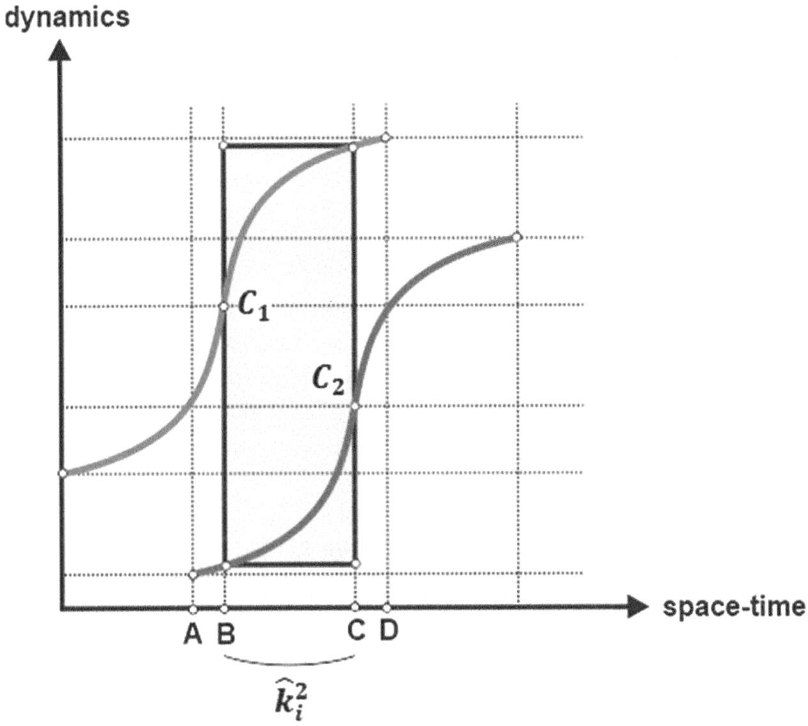

Fig. 7.7 The genesis of the overlapped crises acceleration. *Source*: author

- on the duration BC, the acceleration sign is different for the two crises: for crisis C_1, the acceleration is negative (concave branch of the chreode curve), while for crisis C_2, acceleration is positive (convex branch of the chreode curve);
- in such a context, we propose the following way to judge the acceleration (or deceleration) numerical value of the overlapped crises ($\hat{k}_i^2$), based on Fig. 7.7:

$$(IC_1)\wedge(C_2I)\rightarrow\begin{cases}\left[k_t^2(C_1)>0\right]\wedge\left[k_t^2(C_2)>0\right]\rightarrow\hat{k}_i^2\equiv k_t^2(C_1)\\ \left[k_t^2(C_1)<0\right]\wedge\left[k_t^2(C_2)<0\right]\rightarrow\hat{k}_i^2\equiv k_t^2(C_1)\\ \left[k_t^2(C_1)>0\right]\wedge\left[k_t^2(C_2)<0\right]\rightarrow\hat{k}_i^2\equiv k_t^2(C_1)-k_t^2(C_2)\\ \left[k_t^2(C_1)<0\right]\wedge\left[k_t^2(C_2)>0\right]\rightarrow\hat{k}_i^2\equiv\begin{cases}case\,IO:k_t^2(C_1)-k_t^2(C_2)\\ case\,CO:k_t^2(C_1)-k_t^2(C_2)\\ case\ TO:k_t^2(C_1)\end{cases}\end{cases}$$

$$(C_1I)\wedge(IC_2)\rightarrow\begin{cases}\left[k_t^2(C_1)>0\right]\wedge\left[k_t^2(C_2)>0\right]\rightarrow\hat{k}_i^2\equiv k_t^2(C_2)\\ \left[k_t^2(C_1)<0\right]\wedge\left[k_t^2(C_2)<0\right]\rightarrow\hat{k}_i^2\equiv k_t^2(C_2)\\ \left[k_t^2(C_1)>0\right]\wedge\left[k_t^2(C_2)<0\right]\rightarrow\hat{k}_i^2\equiv\begin{cases}case\,IO:k_t^2(C_2)-k_t^2(C_1)\\ case\,IO:k_t^2(C_2)-k_t^2(C_1)\\ case\ TO:k_t^2(C_2)\end{cases}\\ \left[k_t^2(C_1)<0\right]\wedge\left[k_t^2(C_2)>0\right]\rightarrow\hat{k}_i^2\equiv k_t^2(C_2)-k_t^2(C_1)\end{cases}$$

7.3.6 Regarding k_t^3

The parameter k_t^3 is a little bit subtler. In fact, we have to measure the propensity of a generic crisis to leave its "birthplace" (as we have shown, this is, always, the nominal field of the society) and penetrate the financial field and, possibly, even the real one. Our reasoning will be based on Fig. 4.13, in Chap. 4.

7.3.7 k_t^3 of a Single Crisis

(a) about $k_t^{3.1}$

The parameter $k_t^{3.1}$ addresses the propensity of a generic crisis to pass from its "native" place, i.e., the nominal field of the society, to the financial field.[24] As shown in Fig. 4.13 of Chap. 4, the crisis passes in the financial field when the breaking point is reached, so, we have to describe, explain and operationalize that breaking point. Our considerations in the matter are as follows:

- the road of the nominal crisis to the breaking point is not linear at all—in the phenomenology of the crisis work both positive and negative feedback, that is, both escalating and stabilizing internal forces;

- consequently, the advance of the crisis to the breaking point can be stopped, slowed down or even turned around: (a) *stopped*—if there is a punctual balance between positive feedback force and negative feedback force; (b) *slowed down*—if the negative feedback force is smaller than the positive feedback force, but not null; (c) *turned around*—if the negative feedback force is greater than the positive feedback force;
- so, to advance, rather non-linearly, as shown, to the breaking point, means, for the nominal flows, to accumulate more and more autonomy degree from the real flows. This is the qualitative phenomenon but which is the correlative quantitative one? We make a proposal:
  - an increase in the autonomy of the nominal flows from the real ones has the effect of reducing negative feedback force since the negative feedback actions exactly re-establish the real foundation of the nominal flows;
  - consequently, an increase in the gap between the positive feedback and negative feedback in favour of the positive feedback signals such an increase of the mentioned autonomy which is, in turn, a signal for approaching the crisis's chreode to the breaking point;
  - three questions must be clarified here: (i) what means, objectively, the autonomy increasing of the nominal flows from the real ones; (ii) how to measure the irreversible approaching of the autonomy of the nominal flows to the breaking point; (iii) which is the measurable criterion (parameter) of reaching (or almost reaching, or about to touch) the breaking point;

(i) by autonomy of the nominal flows from the real ones[25] must be understood a marginal variable, namely the rate of the nominal flows changes over the real (in fact, financial, as explained) flows change. If noted with V_t^{NF} the value of the nominal flows in the moment *t*, and with V_t^{RF} the value of the real (i.e., financial) flows, then the value of the autonomy degree (D_t^A) is:

$$D_t^A = \frac{V_t^{NF} - V_t^{RF}}{V_t^{RF}}$$

Nota bene: for $V_t^{NF} = V_t^{RF}$, the autonomy degree of the nominal flows is null, so the nominal flows are rigidly anchored to the real ones.[26]

(ii) as shown above, the continued approaching of the nominal flows' autonomy towards the breaking point is provided by the continued positive gap between the positive feedback and negative feedback within the "world" of nominal flows. Even in the case when, in the short term (or accidentally), the mentioned gap is negative, the so-called base effect will make that at most a slowed down to occur in the autonomy increasing, not really a turn off (reversing) of the autonomy direction. In fact, a sui generis hubbing effect happens so, despite some stumbling blocks, the grandiose and exuberant road of the nominal flows autonomy to the fatal breaking point will be, generally, not disturbed. We propose to identify the sign of reversibility of the autonomy increasing as follows: if a monotonic series of k episodes of autonomy increasing is followed by at least a monotonic series of $(k-1)$ of decreasing of the autonomy, then the reversibility is possible, even if, actually, the reversibility does not occur.[27] In the opposite case, it should be considered that it is not possible for the autonomy increase to reverse its direction;

(iii) how could we know (or predict, see paragraph 7.4) the (nearly) touching of the breaking point, i.e., the moment where the crisis passes from the nominal world into the real one? This time, we think we need a criterion/parameter of a threshold type. More exactly, we have to discuss the following issue: at what maximal threshold of D_t^A the nominal flows—better said, the network of the nominal flows—implode? In this context, the questions that have to be examined are (iii.1) what means implosion of the nominal (network of) flows; (iii.2) how a maximal threshold of the D_t^A should be established so that when it is touched this means reaching the breaking point.

(iii.1) we have seen that the nominal flows have a "natural" tendency to escalate, by a sui generis phenomenon of self-catalysing based, of course, on the profit's rationality. What are the reasons which could entitle us to presume that such a course could interrupt? The basic argument is that nominal flows self-catalyse, or equivalently, move cumulatively away from real flows, meaning that nominal flows necessarily follow a Ponzi process. Figure 7.8 tries to suggest this (self-imploding) mechanism. *Nota bene*: with ΔD_t^A is noted the variation of the autonomy degree, namely: $\Delta D_t^A = D_t^A - D_{t-1}^A$.

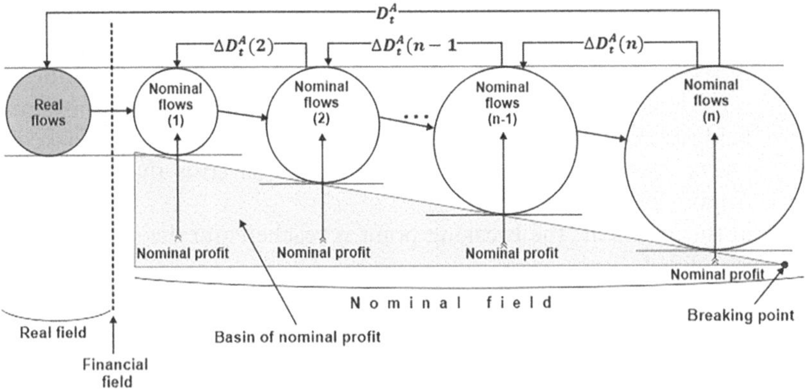

Fig. 7.8 The Ponzi process of nominal flows self-catalysing. *Source*: author

Discussion

- in the nominal field there is a basin of nominal profit, that is, the set of opportunities of different nature, especially economic ones, to fructify the nominal stocks (e.g., shares);
- initially, the nominal flows (1) are rigorously equal (in monetary terms) with the real flows, and, by nominally fructifying nominal flows (1) this increases the value till the nominal flows (2);
- this means, at the same time, a removal of the nominal flows value from that of real flows, which means, in turn, an increase of the autonomy of the nominal flows from the real ones with the value $\Delta D_t^A(2)$;
- as a result of fructifying the nominal flows (1) towards the nominal flows (2), the basin of nominal profit decreases, since the opportunities of fructifying further the nominal flows diminish (more interested agents/actors are "applying" to fructify their nominal flows by exploiting of the opportunities in that basin of nominal profit);
- the nominal flows (2) proceed similarly with the nominal flows (1) and so on, with the same consequences on the basin of nominal profit and, respectively, on the increasing of the nominal flows and on adding new gaps of the nominal flows from the real flows ($\Delta D_t^A(k)$);

- step by step, sooner or later, the nominal flows get the value "n" in Fig. 7.8, which means the basin of nominal profit cannot provide further the increase of the nominal flows—e.g., a lack of credibility regarding the solvency of the agents/actors playing in the nominal field rises or, accidentally, it is "discovered" that the "king is naked" (*Nota bene*: as happened during the financial crisis that started in August 2007 in the USA);
- in this moment, the breaking point is reached and the value of D_t^A is realized.

(iii.2) the breaking point is reached when the autonomy degree of nominal flows from the real flows passes beyond an established threshold. The issue is how such a threshold must be established? Our considerations in that matter are as follows:

- we think that to establish an absolute value of D_t^A is non-concluded, since such a value can have (and, really, has) a historical determination, more generals, a contextual determination;
- consequently, we think that such a threshold must refer not to an absolute value but to a relative one;
- the most operational such a threshold seems to us is the acceleration of the propensity to the breaking point (see the state parameter k_t^2), namely:
- if, for three consecutive periods of measurement (trimesters, semesters or years) the rhythm of D_t^A monotonically doubles, then, at the end of the three period the probability for crisis to reach the breaking point is at its maximum level;
- we shall provide some formal quantifications:
  - notations:

$$x_t = D_t^A$$

r_{x_t} : rhythm of x_t

  - definitions:

$$r_{x_t} = \frac{dx_t}{x_{t-1}} = \frac{x_t - x_{t-1}}{x_{t-1}}$$

– criterion:

$$r_{x_{t+2}} \geq 2r_{x_{t+1}} \geq 2r_{x_t}$$

Figure 7.9 suggests in a visual way the verification of the criterion to "decide" that the crisis is about to reach the breaking point and, as consequence, to pass towards the real field.

– calculus:

$r_{x_{t+n}} = 2^n \cdot r_{x_t}$, for $t = 1, 2, \ldots$

$E^{(n,2)} = \frac{r_{x_{t+n}}}{r_{x_t}} = 2^n$, i.e., the elasticity of the autonomy degree between the period n and the initial period is an exponential function with base 2.

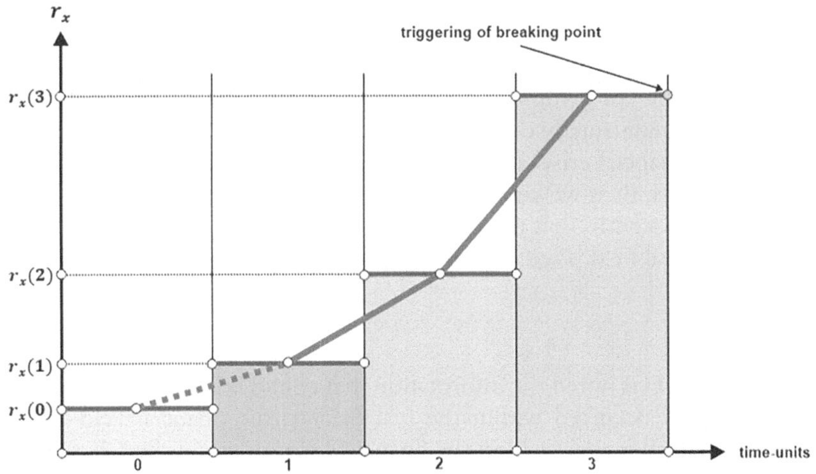

Fig. 7.9 The criterion of reaching the breaking point. *Source*: author

Nota bene: of course, doubling the rhythm of autonomy degree from one period to the next is an expert opinion, so any other opinion is valid. If the rhythm in the case is presumed to be α, then we have:
$r_{x_{t+n}} = \alpha^n \cdot r_{x_t}$, or

$$E^{(n,\alpha)} = \frac{r_{x_{t+n}}}{r_{x_t}} = \alpha^n$$

(b) about $k_t^{3.2}$

The propensity of a generic crisis to pass from the financial field into the real field is not superfluous although, from a theoretical point of view, financial flows and real flows are mutually (and equally) counterparts, monetarily expressed. We provide the following considerations here:

- although the financial flows can deviate from the real ones (e.g., as a result of inflation of prices[28]), however, generally, the adjustment between the two economic flows is (almost) automatic, by changing the rapport between the demand and the supply of the good or service in the case; in this case, the adjustment financial-real takes place within the financial-real pair, without implying the nominal field;
- consequently, a problem arises only when the financial crisis (as measured by $k_t^{3.1}$) affects the variation of the real flows, namely, has an effect on the real flows outside the internal/independent variation of them (the last being caused by the variation of the rapport between demand and supply of the real flows);
- if the financial crisis affects the real field, by externally affecting the real flows, then we say that the financial crisis passed into a real crisis or, equivalently, that the crisis of the financial field passed into a crisis of the real field. Figure 7.10 synoptically clarifies these reasonings.

Discussion

(i) with (1) is noted the information that comes from the demand and supply occurred within the real field to the financial field—as a result, the prices within the financial field are established, based on the internal causality of the real-financial field;

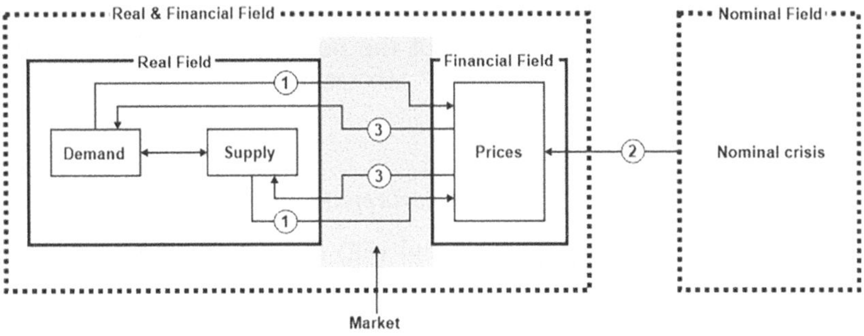

Fig. 7.10 Passing of crisis from financial field to real field. *Source*: author

(ii) with (2) is noted the information that comes from the nominal field (as a result of nominal crisis unfolding) to the prices of the financial field (namely, the $k_t^{3.1}$ action);

(iii) with (3) is noted the information that comes from the financial field to the real field, as an external push on the demand and supply (namely, the $k_t^{3.2}$ action).

- of course, it remains the question: how do we know that the financial flows' variation is the cause for the real flows' variation (i.e., there is an external push on the financial flows) and it is not the opposite case, namely, the real flows variation is the cause for the financial flows variation (i.e., there is an internal pushing on the financial flows?). About this question, we shall provide some considerations:
  - *quasi-impossibility*: this task is particularly difficult since in society the events are multi-caused and multi-conditioned; so, we cannot separate the real (or basic) causes from the causal context or causal complex in its entirety;
  - *quasi-superfluity*: on the other hand, that is, viewing from the opposite side, it is not so hard to establish, for instance, if a variation of the financial flows is or is not the direct result of a de-balanced rapport between demand and supply in the real field: (a) if yes, then we have an internal or intrinsic adjustment of the financial flows caused by the real flows, and (b) if not, then we have a transfer of the financial crisis into a real crisis;

– so, generally, the crucial parameter of a dynamic character is $k_t^{3.1}$ since the transfer of the nominal crisis into the real-financial one (see Fig. 7.10) seems to be, in fact, a single "global" event.

7.3.8 $\hat{k}_t^3$ *of Overlapped Crises*

All the above considerations must (and will) be used to discuss the two parameters of the propensity for the case of crises overlapping. The general question is if two (or more) nominal crises overlap, what about the propensity of the overlapped crises to pass from the nominal world into the financial one ($\hat{k}_t^{3.1}$), and what about the propensity of the overlapped crises to pass from the financial world into the real one ($\hat{k}_t^{3.2}$)?

(a) about $\hat{k}_t^{3.1}$

The core issue is if and how the rhythm of the autonomy degree of the nominal flows with respect to the real (or real-financial) flows should be calculated when two (or more) nominal crises overlap. Firstly, some qualitative considerations:

- the affinity-based dominance relationship between the overlapped crises maintains its determination in the case of the resulted propensity $\hat{k}_t^{3.1}$, too. We shall consider, for simplicity, two nominal crises which overlap, where C_1 dominates over C_2, so we have: $|C_1$, and $C_2|$, respectively;
- this time, the positioning of each crisis on its chreode is no longer relevant but only the autonomy degree already "gained" is relevant;
- we presume the linear additivity of the two autonomy degrees, in favour of the affinity-based dominant crisis, as proceeded in the case of s_t^2 (see point 7.2.1, a(2)), namely (we use the notations from point 7.3.6.1, (a), (iii.2), including the value for $\lambda = 0.3$):

$$\hat{x}_t = \lambda \cdot x_t(C_2|) + (1 - \lambda) \cdot x_t(|C_1)$$

The criterion of getting the breaking point by the overlapped crises remains the same, i.e.:

$$\hat{r}_{x_{t+2}} \geq 2\hat{r}_{x_{t+1}} \geq 2\hat{r}_{x_t}$$

where with $\hat{r}$ is noted the rhythm of $\hat{x}$. The entire reasoning is the same in the case of a single crisis.

(b) about $\hat{k}_t^{3.2}$

Based on $\hat{x}_t$, the reasoning about the probability of an overlapped nominal crisis to pass from the financial field into the real one remains the same as in the case of a single crisis, too.

7.4 Prediction in the Societal Crisis Phenomenology

7.4.1 *The Easy (Fast) Solution*

The prediction in crisis phenomenology is as difficult and liable to errors as in any other societal event. The difficulty comes from the presence of free will which is dominant in social/societal decision-making and action. In our opinion, at least for the current stage of the economic theory, the operational solution is as follows: replacing the prediction with prognosis, and assigning Bayesian probabilities to prognosis. We think that the same reason for which the prediction on crisis phenomenology is almost impossible (or, at least, possible only with a great value of uncertainty), namely, the presence of free will, recommends the use of the (subjective) Bayesian probabilities because these probabilities are based, by definition, on free will, more exactly, on the belief. Being subjective, the Bayesian probabilities shape, in fact, the belief of the observer (or predictor) about the behaviour of the other individuals (or groups, after the case) related to the event of interest. This is the fundamental of using the Bayesian probabilities for prediction in matters of societal crisis.

7.4.2 *Harder Solutions*

In order to recapture the prediction in the crisis phenomenology means to have or *ad hoc*-ly construct a theory based on which the prediction is formulated. As known, the logical difference between prediction and prognosis consists in the fact that prediction is formulated based on a theory (e.g., it is a lemma of a hypothesis), while the prognosis is enacted based on a phenomenological empirical pattern, i.e., on an expected replication of the past into the future.[29]

A Solution Based on the Constructal Law

The concept of constructal law was introduced into the literature by a Romanian-American researcher—Adrian Bejan (2007). Constructal law aspires to be (even) more primitive than the laws of thermodynamics,[30] (especially than the second law of thermodynamics, i.e., the law of entropy, or the law of irreversibility of exergy[31]).

The constructal law has the following wording: "for an open system, of finite dimensions, to persist over time (to survive) it must evolve in such a way as to provide easier and easier access to the flows that pass through it".[32] *Nota bene*: in constructal theory, any finite system is considered thermodynamically imperfect.

The main features of the constructal law are the following:[33]

- it is placed in the position of principle of evolution;[34]
- it targets both non-living and living nature;
- it restricts its scope to systems that are characterized by flows, more exactly, by flows that have a physical objectification[35]—both within the membrane of the system and in relation to its environment; moreover, another reduction in scope refers to the fact that the systems in question must move or live generating physical/material supports for flows,[36] the so-called dendritic tubes;[37]
- constructal evolution involves choice (either non-deliberative or deliberative, as the case may be);
- in constructal evolution, choice involves cognition;[38]
- the application of the constructal law to evolution (at least in the case of living nature) provides quantitative regularities from an allometric perspective;[39]
- constructal law rejects optimization in systems configuration;
- the constructal law is considered a law of physics but as applicable everywhere, including in the social field, engineering, innovation or psychology;
- the constructal law acts completely holistically—the evolutionary solution is formed at the level of the system which, thus, may contain subsystems that have not been regulated by the constructal law (Bejan, 2007);

- the constructal law offers a new arrow of time, compared to that provided by the second law of thermodynamics: time flows in the direction in which the access to their own life support flows of systems is greater.[40]

The way in which constructal law can be used to predict the societal crisis could be the following.

(i) *the case of a single crisis*

Any (single) crisis unfolds on a chreode (trajectory), both in space and time. Such an unfolding objectifies through the flows (nominal, financial or real—*Nota bene*: we shall examine the nominal profile of a crisis since such type is originary) that characterize that crisis. Based on the market "rationality" (in fact, of course, the rationality of individuals playing in the market), the flows will follow the profitability areas, regularly to maximize the expected profit. This is as if the flows direct themselves in space and time so that they to be "traversed" by the maximum amount of benefits (in our case, maximum amount of profit). In this perspective, it seems we are in the very phenomenology of constructal law since the crisis's flows can be considered sui generis hypostases of the dendritic tubes claimed by constructal law. As shown previously (see, especially, Chap. 4), the nominal crisis exists as long as it escalates through the self-catalysis process. So, the two elements—the flows generating the chreode and the need for self-catalysis—could constitute a logical basis to formulate a "mechanism" of prediction within the "world" of constructal law. The main considerations in the matter are as follows:

- the nominal flows will direct themselves to those opportunities that ensure an increase of their autonomy degree related to the real (or financial-real) flows;
- although the constructal law "requires" that the "flows" crossing the nominal flows be maximized, it is not always possible to maximize the increase of the autonomy degree (because the nominal investment decisions are taken based on the bounded rationality and, often, on free will which can violate the very rationality); so, a weaker condition should be accepted here, namely the nominal flows direct themselves to the available opportunities, based on the cost-benefit rationality, so that to be got the conditioned-possible increase of the autonomy degree;

- as to make a prediction means to construct an ideal theory-based arrow of autonomy that guides the process involved, we can consider that such an arrow of autonomy is just the conditioned-possible increase of the autonomy degree; consequently, the nominal flows will "search" those opportunities which verify the arrow of autonomy;
- here arises a problem: to get the opportunity (or the set of opportunities) capable of verifying the arrow of autonomy, the nominal flow (or flows) should examine all the current (or even the potential) opportunities, to find a sub-set that can provide the increase of the autonomy degree. Such an issue puts the more general problem of observability, accessibility and controllability of those opportunities (see point. 7.1—Preamble). Our position is as follows:
  - the two elements above-mentioned about the realistic decision-makers (the bounded rationality and the free will) determine the locality of searching the appropriate opportunity for the nominal flows—more precisely, the nominal flows "dendrites" will search only in a narrow neighbourhood, not across the world, the opportunity able to increase the autonomy degree;
  - such a (necessary) locality justifies the impossibility of optimization under the constructal law;[41]
- so, the nominal flows will stop searching when they find the first opportunity that verifies the arrow of autonomy. *Nota bene*: maybe the search could continue for another small number of opportunities, in the neighbourhood but not too much, and, finally, a kind of choice will be made, however, by selecting one of the opportunities found—the criterion of selection can be or cannot be related to the size of the autonomy degree, perhaps such a criterion will be linked to other idiosyncratic requirements of the decision-maker behind the nominal flows; this behaviour is similar to the river's one, when the river's flow follows the no matter how small positive gravitational gap, without searching for the largest such a gap. Again, in our opinion, the constructal law must not be required to provide optimization but only survival—the crisis's flows will feed themselves through increasing the autonomy degree, not through optimizing it or, at most, through a local optimization. In fact, this conclusion is linked to the following considerations:
  - the nominal flows of a crisis are continuous entities, and generally they "examine" the world's opportunities *from close to close*, not by jumps;

- consequently, the comparisons among the sizes of autonomy degrees are made inside a narrow neighbourhood, so it is possible that very small differences, sometimes accidentally, trigger the choice of opportunity.

(ii) *the case of overlapped crises*

Now, we must examine the way in which we could make predictions, based on constructal law, in the case of crises overlapping. Firstly, some qualitative considerations are useful:

- according to the affinity-based dominance among the overlapped crises, it seems the dominant crisis's flows will act as leading flows for the overlapped entity;
- as a result, the dominated crisis's flows are "obliged" to choose the same opportunity as the dominant crisis did, which could lead to some reducing the autonomy degree got by the dominated crisis. Consequently, the global autonomy degree reached by the overlapped crises entity is correspondingly smaller than the dominant crisis could have reached, by itself, without the overlap of the crises;
- a possible conclusion of this case could be the following: by the overlapping of crises, some internal "friction" arises among the crises involved in the overlapping process, regarding the degree of nominal flows autonomy generated inside the constructal law theoretical framework.

Nota bene 1: the very idea of internal "friction" among the overlapped crises, regarding the dynamics of the global autonomy degree course, is interesting from a technical point of view and especially useful from the perspective of the public policies aimed at handling the societal crisis phenomenology. Other scientists could take further such an idea, including determining some indicators in that matter.

Nota bene 2: one may raise the question: is it not possible, alternatively, to increase the degree of autonomy of the nominal flows of overlapping crises, in accordance with the constructal law? Our positioning is the following:

- principled, the answer is affirmative. Of course, the concrete situation is generated by the nature of the overlapped crises. Is fully possible that the affinity-based dominant crisis to choose a trajectory of its flows so that the dominated crisis's flows to be advantaged more than the last crisis could have done itself, separately. In fact both situations are almost equally possible: (a) if a negative synergy occurs as a result of overlapping, then internal *viscosity* arises—which reduces the global autonomy degree (or just the speed of global autonomy degree); (b) if a positive synergy occurs as a result of overlapping, then an internal lubrication arises—which increases the global autonomy degree (or just the speed of global autonomy degree);

- we think that to *ex ante* determine the "sign" of the synergy (either negative or positive) that will occur is rather an empirical issue than a theoretical one, since it crucially depends on the nature and characteristics of the crises overlapped.

A Solution Based on the Minimal Entropic Gradient

(i) *Preliminaries I*[42]

Suppose that in Universe 0 (the initial Universe), several dissipative systems appear simultaneously (of course, this set of dissipative systems can be constituted in a successive way, as well, not necessarily in a concomitant one, it is important that, at some point, in Universe 1 we have several such dissipative systems, both of "1α" rank and "1β" rank).[43] In this context, the notion of complementary environment becomes, so to speak, multi-relative (it was, however, relative even in the conditions of the existence of a single dissipative system, as is immediately observed, based on the use of the concept of distinction generated by membranation). This means that, given a certain dissipative system, say *A*, another dissipative system, say *B*, becomes a relatively anti-dissipative complementary environment for system *A*.[44] That being the case, we wonder how entropy will evolve in system *B*, given its certain evolution in system *A*. In other words, the question is whether we have an entropic impact of one dissipative system on another dissipative system.[45] As we realize, in order to formulate an answer, it is necessary to admit that dissipative systems "recognize", at the level of the membrane (i.e., at the level of their border), the entropic gradient between them and the complementary environment.[46] Assuming such a capacity, how do dissipative systems "choose" to achieve "entropic exchange" (i.e., to procure low entropy in exchange for high entropy, with which they "pay" for the acquisition of low entropy)? Put another way, the question is this: will a certain dissipative system "prefer" to perform the entropic exchange with other existing dissipative systems) at the maximum entropic gradient or at minimum level? Perhaps, a principle similar to that of the minimum path in physics[47] will have to be postulated here, namely, that *entropic exchange takes place at the level of the minimum entropic gradient.*[48] This principle, once accepted, generates the relativity of the complementary environment but, on the other hand, it also necessarily generates a matrix (here the term necessarily has its logical meaning) of entropic interactions. This means that if we had a "map" of the entropic gradients in Universe 1, we could tell exactly[49] what entropic interactions would take place.[50] Therefore, the complementary environment can only be defined in a multi-relative way (in fact, in a contextual way, even, as it seems to us, in a practical or empirical rather than theoretical way). The "chain" of entropic interactions based on the principle of choosing the minimum entropic gradient indicates a necessary acceleration of the global entropy of the Universe, namely, an autocatalytic entropic acceleration: the more dissipative systems, the greater the rate of global entropy. Moreover, the more evolved the dissipative systems (in the entropic sense of the term, i.e., the slower the rate of local entropy), the greater the rate of global entropy. Or, as it has been shown in the specialized literature, dissipative systems have a necessary tendency of entropic evolution. We can summarize, therefore, the following: (a) any variation of the speed of the local entropy is equivalent to an inverse and supra-proportional variation of the entropy of the complementary environment; (b) the principle of choosing the minimum entropic gradient for the entropic exchange between dissipative systems further accelerates the global entropy. The last assumption needs, however, a specific argument: suppose we are in a Universe 1 in which there are two dissipative systems, *A*, with the speed of the local entropy λ_S^A, and *B*, with the speed of the local entropy λ_S^A, so that $\lambda_S^A < \lambda_S^B$. We will note the speed of entropy in the complementary environment relative to the two dissipative systems with $\lambda_C^{A,B}$ (the notation mode means that the appearance of the two dissipative systems has led to an increase in the speed of entropy in the complementary environment—according to the proposed explanations in the present discussion—so that $\lambda_C^{A,B} > \lambda_E$). Obviously $\delta^{A,B} = \left|\lambda_S^A - \lambda_S^B\right| < \left|\lambda_S^A - \lambda_C^{A,B}\right|$ (where with δ the entropic gradient was denoted), so the entropic exchange for a further reduction of the entropy speed in the dissipative system *A* will be made between the latter and the dissipative system *B*.[51] Given the order relation between the speeds of the local entropies of the dissipative systems, the entropic exchange will consist in the taking over by system *A* of a low amount of entropy from system *B* and, conversely, the taking over of a high amount of entropy by system *B* from system *A*. Now the basic significance of the selection criterion results of the minimum entropic gradient: this selection criterion ensures a minimum transfer of low entropy from the less evolved system to the system more evolved from an entropic point of view. Indeed, it is quite obvious that in order to achieve a certain local entropy speed differential, system *A* should consume more low entropy from the complementary environment itself than it should from system *B*.[52]

Here is one last question that we would like to address: is the choice of the minimum entropic gradient to achieve the entropic exchange necessary for a dissipative system consistent or not with the Prigoginean principle of minimum entropy production? If we take the behaviour of natural systems as an argument, we should give an affirmative answer.[53]

A synoptic picture of the above considerations could be the one in Fig. 7.11 (with the notations: *G* – *CE*: general complementary environment; *CE* – *A*: complementary environment for the dissipative system *A*; *CE* – *B*: complementary medium for the dissipative system *B*; *A* – *E*: entropic interaction of the dissipative system *A* with the environment;

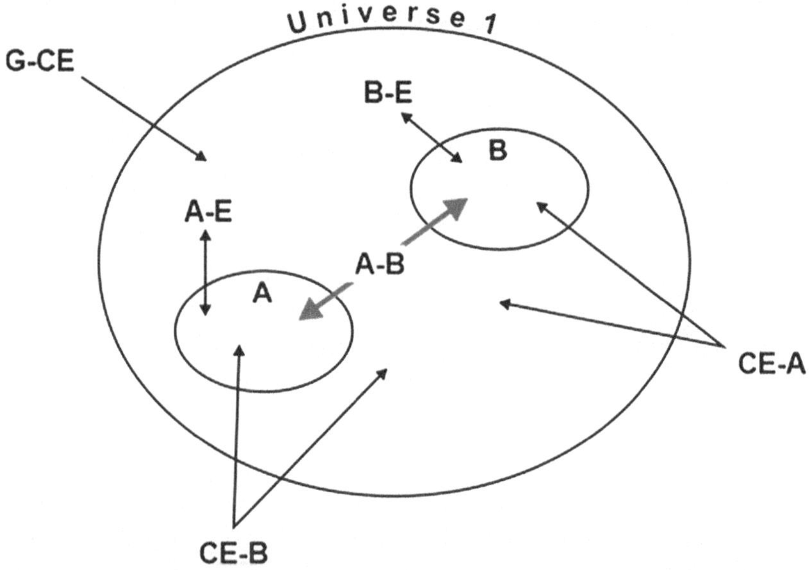

Fig. 7.11 Interactions between dissipative systems is "preferred" to interactions with the environment. *Source*: author

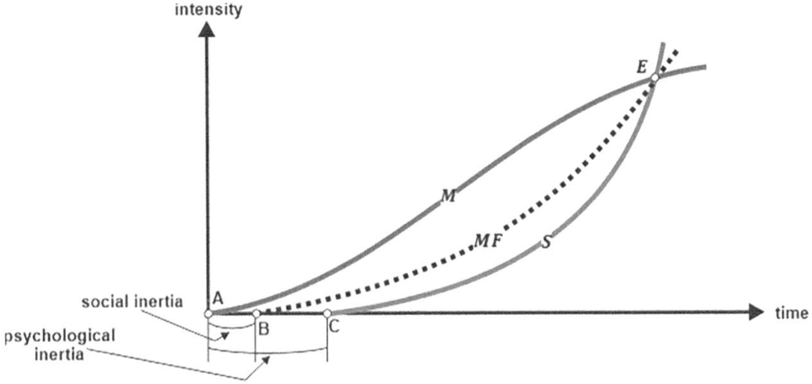

Fig. 7.12 The "physiology" of meanfication about the crisicity. *Source*: author

B – *E*: entropic interaction of the dissipative system *B* with the environment; *A* – *B*: entropic interaction between the dissipative systems *A* and *B*).

Nota bene: developed to its last consequences, this propensity to the minimal entropic interaction can be not only an explanatory model of the functioning of the financial market, but could also be a *sui generis* predictor (of behavioural type, not informational!) for the societal crisis.

(ii) *Preliminaries 2*

Let us resume the results obtained in the topic regarding the entropic aspects of the societal crisis (Chap. 3), especially the concept of societal's crisicity. The crisicity denominated a state of the (free and democratic) societal entity (as a network of systems) which can signal a crisis imminence or, equivalent, an imminent crisis. The logical and psychological basis of the crisicity is the concept of meanfication (a semantic … overlapping of meaning, i.e., explanation ontologically anchored, and signification, i.e., a comprehension gnoseologically anchored). The general relationship between meaning and signification can be represented as in Fig. 7.12 (*M* is meaning, *S* is signification, *MF* is meanfication).

Discussion

- the *M* curve (meaning curve) is a logistic one, i.e., it starts slowly to the extent of accumulating information, descriptions and explana-

tions regarding the society kinematics; after an inflexion point, the meaning is established sufficiently and irreversibly—such a state installs especially beyond the point *E*;
- the *S* curve (signification curve) is rather exponential, based on a self-catalyst phenomenon (positive feedback). The formation of signification is lagged, during the time interval AC, related to the formation of meaning (we could call this lag psychological inertia), the lag size depending on cultural traits, individual peculiarity and local conjunctures;
- the *MF* curve (meanfication curve) is a hybrid between the *M* curve and the *S* curve, so it also starts with a lag, during the time interval AB, related to the *M* curve starting (we call this lag social inertia). In its first part, the *MF* curve is slowly increasing (under the dominant influence of the *M* curve), and then, in its second part, it accelerates (under the dominant influence of the *S* curve). The "sharing" of the dominance and influence of curves *M*, respectively *S*, are, of course, rather of empirical determination than of theoretical one;
- at point *E*, the *M* curve and *S* curve intersect—from this point, the *M* curve flattens, while the *S* curve becomes more vertical. Obviously, the *MF* curve will intersect the two curves in point *E*, too.

The kinematics of the crisicity is isomorphic with the kinematics of (societal) order, in an inverse relationship—the greater crisicity, the smaller the societal order. As we already know, the smaller the societal order, the greater the societal entropy. As the crisicity can be directly assigned to the crisis, obtaining its entropic mark (*Nota bene*: the crisicity and the entropy are directly proportional) it results that, based on the crisicity, we can "observe" the entropy, and, based on the entropy, we can examine the interaction between crises and, so, it becomes possible to have a *sui generis* theory based on which some predictions (not prognoses) could be made about the societal crisis.

(iii) *The case of a single crisis*

First of all, it must be said that the inherent propensity of a generic crisis to increase the autonomy of the nominal economic flows related to the real (or/and financial) flows is maintained. In fact, this constitutes the so-called (see above) autonomy arrow, and it acts as a strong enough predictor of the direction and (sometimes) speed of the crisis phenomenology.

Now, we shall add a new arrow in the crisis behaviour, namely the arrow to the minimum entropic gradient. Let us note the autonomy degree arrow with A^{ad}, and the arrow to the minimum entropic gradient with A^{meg}. Consequently, in fact, two arrows are working in the crisis unfolding, and the (possible) predictor in such an unfolding will (must) be an … overlapping of them. About this phenomenon of overlapping the phenomenological arrows of a generic crisis, some considerations will be provided next.

- A^{ad} is a general/grounding arrow, with structural roots (so, with a permanent and continuous action), and has an embedding role regarding other (possible) factors of influence, including other arrows, in the crisis kinematics; instead, A^{meg} is a special/featuring arrow, with functional roots (so, with a discrete and discontinue action), and has a customizing role in the crisis kinematics. *Nota bene*: in a … Kantian key, and using an anthropomorphic terminology, A^{ad} is a transcendental category, providing the general possibility of prediction in the crisis kinematics, while A^{meg} is a perceptual (or transcendent) category, providing the particular possibility of prediction in the crisis kinematics;
- consequently, there is a dominance of A^{ad} over A^{meg} in objectifying the concrete, effective path of the crisis chreode and, as a result, in predicting this chreode, at least under the following considerations:
  - the mainstream of a generic crisis is directed by A^{ad};
  - in the "tunnel" established by A^{ad}, which ensures the increase of the autonomy degree of the nominal flows, occur oscillations of the crisis's chreode, caused by A^{meg}, i.e., by searching for the minimal entropic gradient of those nominal flows to fructify them;
- maybe it is the point where it is appropriate to make extra clarifications on the rationality of A^{meg}. It must be explained why a nominal flow aiming to increase its autonomy degree related to the real (or/and financial) flows (i.e., is conducted by A^{ad}) would search that interaction with an entity/a phenomenon/an event, etc., with which exhibits the minimum entropic gradient. We think of the following:
  - generally, a nominal economic flow interacts with an opportunity liable to increase the autonomy degree of that nominal flow related to the initial real economic flow (*Nota bene*: usually, the increase of the autonomy degree occurs by multiplication of the monetary value of the nominal flow compared with the monetary value of the initially real flow which generated that nominal flow);

- the functioning of the nominal flow is encapsulated in some economic order (e.g., into an investment economic model). In its turn, the opportunity envisaged is encapsulated into its order (e.g., into an exchange rate arbitrage model). Let us consider a second opportunity for the nominal flow above, e.g., purchasing bonds. The nominal flow will "calculate" the entropic gradient between its order (or, equivalent, its entropy) and the two distinct orders (or, equivalent, distinct entropies) and will choose the interaction associated with the smallest entropic gradient. Why? We think the following rationality should be accepted for such a decision:
  - the more ordered the opportunity, the less risk brought by that opportunity. As the nominal flow (*Nota bene*: of course, the human individual who handles the nominal flow in this case) has a "natural" aversion to risk, the nominal flow will choose the opportunity having the highest level of order, i.e., the smallest entropy. So, the minimum entropic gradient is preferred by the nominal flow in its path to increase its autonomy degree;
  - one could raise the question: choosing the opportunity with a smaller order, that is, with a greater entropy, that is, based on the maximum entropic gradient has more chances to bring profit, so to increase the autonomy degree. Obviously, such a phenomenon could maximize its autonomy degree but with a very small probability so we think such an event is rather accidental, not regular. As the exception strengthens the rule, our presumption seems to stay standing.

A stylized way to suggest the A^{ad} and A^{meg} functioning is provided in Fig. 7.13.

We think that the interaction based on the minimal entropic gradient is an invariant of nominal flows, and therefore of societal crises (not only in the economic sphere). Considering the general "game" between A^{ad} and A^{meg}, i.e., the "rationality" of the pair $A^{ad} - A^{meg}$, the predictions could be made on the crisis positioning on its chreode.

(iv) *The case of overlapped crises*

From the perspective of the prediction, the case of overlapped crises is a qualitatively different one compared with the case of a single crisis. The

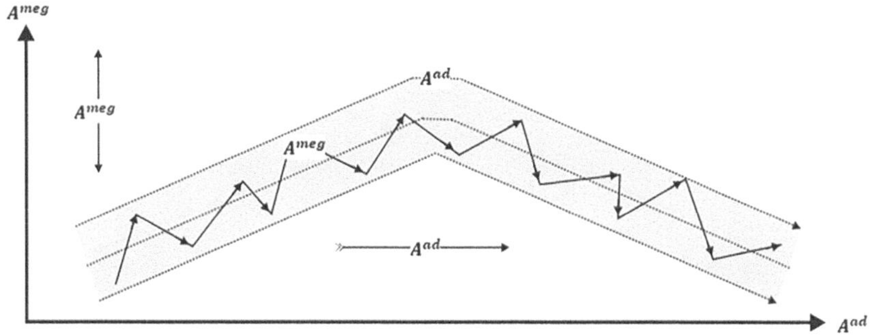

Fig. 7.13 Functioning of the two arrows in the prediction model of a single crisis. *Source*: author

phenomenology is similar to that of including a short-term crisis on a long-term crisis, as discussed in the literature regarding the calendar-based crisis, namely the ascendant stage of the short-term crisis is larger during the ascendant stage of the long-term crisis and vice-versa, its descendant stage is smaller during the ascendant stage of the long-term crisis. In our case, the main considerations in the matter are as follows:

- as shown before, in any crises overlapping a state of dominance occurs—one crisis becomes quickly affinity-based dominant over the other crisis (or other crises);
- in such a situation, the dominance relationship is transferred to the A^{ad}; be two crises that overlap $C(1)$ and $C(2)$, so that $C(1) \rtimes C(2)$. The transfer of the dominance occurs at the arrow of autonomy degree, i.e., $A_1^{ad} \rtimes A_2^{ad}$. To be mentioned that is not necessary that the speed of A_1^{ad} be greater than the speed of A_2^{ad}, any positioning of the two arrows from the perspective of speed, the A_1^{ad} will dominate A_2^{ad}. So, the arrow of autonomy degree at the overlapped crises level (noted $\tilde{A}_{1,2}^{ad}$) is more likely to function similar to rather A_1^{ad} than A_2^{ad};
- this means the tunnel of A_1^{ad} will include the tunnel of A_2^{ad}, which means the domain of variation of the arrow of entropic gradient at the overlapped crises ($\tilde{A}_{1,2}^{meg}$) will extend correspondingly;
- consequently, the prediction about the positioning of the overlapped crises on the own chreode must take into consideration the mentioned inclusions of spheres, as Fig. 7.14 indicates in a stylized way.

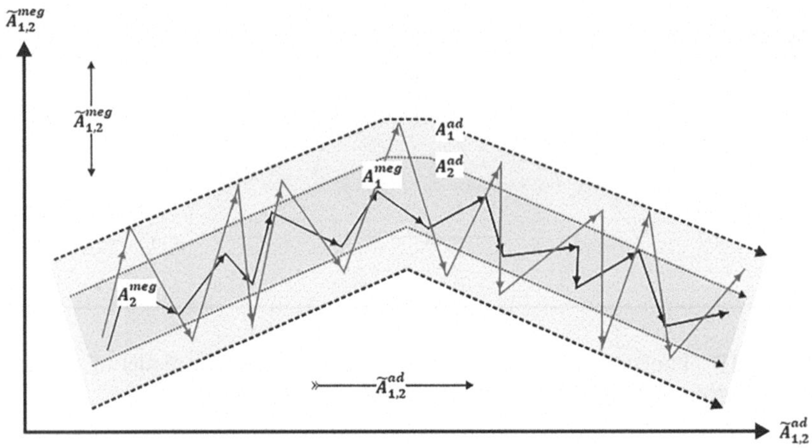

Fig. 7.14 Functioning of the two arrows in the prediction model of an overlapped crises. *Source*: author

Notes

1. Here, almost in the phenomenological perspective of intentionality.
2. The human natural senses are "operational" in the middle-cosmos only. By intermediation of machines, the human being extends both its natural senses and, especially, the intellectual senses. Such machines can be material tools (exosomatic expanding of senses) or theories (endosomatic expanding of senses).
3. However, poetry (generally, fiction literature, as well as any other branches of arts), metaphysics, religion, mythology and even politics perform such a communication easily enough.
4. For the power of communication at a social/societal level see, *inter alia*, the relatively recent works of Niklas Luhmann (about a theory of autopoietic society), or Jürgen Habermas (about the society in practical intention), or Pierre Bourdieu (about the power of language in society).
5. Less on the fantasy world, which is also a part of reality, but is not ... real.
6. Known as Kolmogorov probabilities.
7. Logically, the three interventions form the well-known concept of actualizing.
8. Or, according to previous terminology, *crisisity position*.

9. We do not mention the mathematical conditions for each point or interval since they are common and well known.
10. Or intersection/overlapping, from the perspective of the set theory.
11. One should not think that intensity is (as it seems, *prima facie*) kinetic in nature, it is in fact a static, albeit variable, property.
12. We remind the reason why the impact on meta-narrative is more important/relevant, for example, face to the impact on structure (generally, of society). The meta-narrative is the philosophical (and even, psychological) ground of observing, interpreting and handling a societal crisis, so it constitutes the "societal force" of the strongest level related to the generic crisis.
13. Quantity desired of crisis? Yes, since many times, depending on the "society competence", a crisis (including its impact of different kinds) can (or is expected to) bring benefits in many fields: economic, social, technological, environmental, etc., how and how much they affect some domains and how and how much they relax or retain constraints in those domains.
14. Only the "step by step" cases of passing are indicated but, of course, any other cases of passing (by more steps, or by passing from the lowest value to the highest one, either "step by step" or by more steps) are easy to calculate from the basic cases presented in Table 7.4.
15. The someone's temptation to introduce here the entropy as energy dissipator could be overwhelming.
16. The enthusiasts of Markov chains can find here suggestions to build up the so-called transition matrix, whose components are transition probabilities. We are not interested, for the current research, in such subtle unfolds but only want to put into evidence a system of variables (indicators) liable to describe the kinematics of a (societal) generic crisis.
17. As mentioned in note 8, for algebraic requirements, the kinematic vector should be written as an equivalent kinematic matrix having as elements exactly the transition probabilities.
18. We remind the attentive reader that propensity is the named/term usually associated with the ... possibility, internal, objective, assigned to the singular event, and undeletable of a given entity (*Nota bene*: we also remember that the propensity has been named as the probability of ... the probability or the cause of probability (Dinga et al., 2022).
19. The irreversible order of passing of the crisis from a region to another is the following: nominal region—financial region—real region, since any crisis is always originated in the nominal region (with the five "locations" suggested by mark β).
20. Of course, it is possible that the positioning of two or more crises that overlap to be similar.

21. The interested reader can, easily enough, find/build the algebra of the indifference curve in the matter: $k_t^1 = \frac{\Delta_{\delta\varepsilon}}{\Delta t}$, so $d(k_t^1) = \frac{\partial\left(\frac{\Delta_{\delta\varepsilon}}{\Delta t}\right)}{\partial \Delta_{\delta\varepsilon}} d(\Delta_{\delta\varepsilon}) + \frac{\partial\left(\frac{\Delta_{\delta\varepsilon}}{\Delta t}\right)}{\partial \Delta_t} d(\Delta_t) = 0$. From which, finally: $\frac{d(\Delta_{\delta\varepsilon})}{d(\Delta_t)} = \frac{\Delta_{\delta\varepsilon}}{\Delta_t}$, that is the marginal rate of substitution between the variation of $\Delta_{\delta\varepsilon}$ and the variation of t (in other words, the required variation of $\Delta_{\delta\varepsilon}$, when Δ_t varies with one unity, so that the speed of crisis unfolding be invariant or, the same, the crisis to unfold linearly).
22. The Matlab program used is: [x,y]=meshgrid(.331:.001:.683); z=x./y; mesh(x,y,z).
23. We remind this method is similar to that of establishing the stationarity of a time series when neither absolute data nor the first differences of the series do not conclude on its stationarity (e.g., in econometrical estimations).
24. We remind that the nominal, financial and real fields, which exhaust, in our opinion, the areas of praxeological action within the society, have the semantic content proposed in this chapter.
25. The autonomy of the financial flows from the real ones rather does not exist properly—indeed, the prices of the nominal flows, i.e., the financial flows, follow the real flows according to the market rapport between the demand and the supply, so the prices imposed by the free market are exactly the ... exact financial flows in the economy.
26. For example, this would be the case if the banking system were obliged to grant credits only as it has deposits so that the credit multiplier is null.
27. Of course, more empirical analysts could propose a number of time units after which to judge the reversibility vs. irreversibility in the case, as proceeded in the case of the so-called technical recession: three consecutive trimesters of recession.
28. The syntagma *inflation of prices* is not pleonastic, since inflation refers to the increase of any entity (e.g., prices, but not only—*Nota bene*: we remind about the inflationary ... Universe).
29. As we have frequently noted, econometricians make forecasts, although they always and ostentatiously claim to have made predictions.
30. As it is known, the laws of thermodynamics (*Nota bene*: so far, it seems that four laws of thermodynamics have been formulated) do not give any answer about the way or the rule according to which the systems are configured (i.e., acquire their shape and structure).
31. Exergy is the name for useful, available or bound energy.

32. The original formulation is *for a finite-size open system to persist in time (to survive) it must evolve in such a way that it provides easier and easier access to the currents that flow through it* (Bejan, 2007).
33. The features are taken over from Dinga et al. (2023), p.137.
34. In our opinion, the constructal law is not of the power of a principle (or a ... law of nature), as it is presented by the author, but it has the features of a mechanism (like the Darwinian theory of the evolution of life, which is a mechanism, not a principle—e.g., Darwinism cannot explain the origin of life, but only its evolution after it appeared; *Nota bene*: neither Physics can explain the singularity from the moment of the big bang, but only everything that happened later). The difference between principle/law and mechanism is as follows: principle/law answers the question "why", that is, "based on which cause", while the mechanism answers the question "how".
35. Which, obviously, detracts from the justification of its universal character.
36. But there are cases in which either there is no such material support for configuring the shape and structure to allow flows (e.g., cactus), or the movement of the systems in question is very slow (e.g., turtle) (Freire & Andrade, 2021).
37. Although the emphasis (and the examples given) refers to physical flows, it is obvious that, from a conceptual point of view, any type of flows can be accepted: informational, entropic, ideational, axiological and so on. However, such a generalization is not yet achieved, constituting, in our opinion, a challenge for researchers who consider that the constructal law is a productive direction in epistemology (*Nota bene*: we are not among these researchers, since we have our own fundamental "law" on behaviour, i.e., in a more general sense, interaction, namely, the *law of the minimum entropic gradient*—see point 7.4.2.2 in the main text).
38. It is a cognition that has an even wider scope than the one proposed by the Santiago School, because it also includes non-living (non-animated) nature.
39. Allometry (or allometrics) studies the relationships of determination between the body dimensions of living entities and the shape and dimensions of their somatic organs (either internal or external), their internal structure, functions and behaviour.
40. In addition to these two arrows of time (which are logically consistent with each other), there is also the psychological arrow of time: time increases from the point where the feelings (or lived events) in memory are less numerous to the point where those feelings are more numerous.
41. Do not forget that Nature never optimized—in essence, survival does not imply the optimization.
42. The preliminaries are adapted from our opinion provided in Dinga et al. (2023)—Chap. 3, paragraph "*Autopoieticity and minimal entropic interaction*".

43. Dissipative systems can be classified as follows (Dinga, 2012): (1) dissipative systems of rank "−1", in which the speed of entropy in the system (λ_S) is higher than the speed of entropy in the environment (λ_E), that is, $\lambda_S > \lambda_E$; (2) dissipative systems of rank "0", where $\lambda_S = \lambda_E$; (3) dissipative systems of rank "1"—in which $\lambda_S < \lambda_E$. Dissipative systems of rank "1" can, in turn, be of two types: (a) dissipative systems of rank "1α" (these are non-human type systems), provided that $0 \le \lambda_S^{1\alpha} \le \lambda_E$; (b) dissipative systems of rank "1β" (these are human type systems), provided that $0 \le \lambda_S^{1\beta} \le \lambda_S^{1\alpha} \le \lambda_E$.
44. Obviously, "*A*" and "*B*" are interchangeable without changing the reasoning, although, as we shall see, it may be necessary for the membranes of dissipative systems to be endowed with the ability to recognize the entropic gradient between the dissipative systems concerned and the complementary environment (including other dissipative systems, with different rates of local entropy).
45. We consider only the case of "contemporary" dissipative systems. The alternative case, in which the dissipative systems in entropic interaction are not contemporary, is reduced to the previous case, given that the existence of a dissipative system leaves an "entropic trace" in the complementary environment in which it "lived", a trace that will be taken into account on the occasion of the appearance of a new dissipative, non-contemporary system, in terms of the level and speed of entropy (in other words, the Universe is brought to "zero" every time).
46. Among the "functions" of the demon that replaces Maxwell's demon will obviously be that of "calculating" the entropic gradient between the dissipative system concerned and the genuine complementary environment (or between the dissipative system concerned and other dissipative systems).
47. As it is known, for example, light always follows the shortest path between two points (in general, the shortest path is the path that follows the geodesic generated by the curvature of space-time, as indicated by non-Euclidean geometries, respectively the general theory of relativity). The dissipative systems generate, in their turn, a sui generis *entropic curvature*, although in a different sense than the one referring to the physical space-time (gravitation). Specifically, dissipative systems generate "geodesics" that indicate that the entropic interaction will occur between dissipative systems with the minimum entropic gradient (the principle also works in the particular case where in Universe 1 there is only one dissipative system: indeed, in this last case, the minimum entropic gradient is just that between the dissipative system and the genuine homogeneous anti-dissipative complementary medium, so the principle is maintained).
48. The principle is suggested, moreover, by the sublunary experience (and, until proven otherwise, we should consider it valid for the whole Universe,

that is, to make a transition, under the sanction of Popper's falsifiability, from contingent to necessary) regarding, for example, the genuine food (trophic) chain: carnivorous animals at the top of the food chain do not procure low entropy directly from the plant environment, but "prefer" to do so indirectly by consuming herbivorous animals. But this only means "choosing" the entropic exchange based on the principle of the minimum entropic gradient.

49. Laplaceanism in this expression is not too difficult to recognize.
50. Of course, this deterministic enthusiasm should be substantially tempered by the fact that, instrumentally, for the moment, it is impossible for us to measure these entropic gradients. Note that, from an epistemological point of view, we have here exactly the same problem that arose in the matter of the theory of cardinal utility (in the latter case, however, we have the "solution" of recourse to the theory of ordinal utility, generating, however, in turn, so many inconsistencies between predictions and their updating). Let us note another important thing here: the entropic gradient has not only a scalar but also an algebraic sign: the entropic exchange will occur in such a way that the low entropy will "flow" from the system that has the highest entropy to the one that has the lowest entropy, never the other way around (by contrast with the case when there are not dissipative systems at all). However, this statement must be substantiated. Here is our argument: we have "established" that the finality of Universe 0 (and therefore of any possible Universe 1) is to reach the state of thermodynamic equilibrium. As the appearance of dissipative systems (systems far from equilibrium, as denominated by Prigogine) accelerates this process, it "results" that this appearance of dissipative systems is (from the "point of view" of the Universe) "rational". Now, if we were to assume that the entropic exchange, in the case of a given entropic gradient, would be done in such a way that high entropy would flow from the higher entropy system to the lower entropy system, then, as stated above, low entropy should be consumed from the higher entropy system to achieve this exchange; consequently, this would produce high entropy in the system that has just "delivered" high entropy, which would nullify, for example (or decrease, in any case), the entropic "gain" obtained by "exporting" high entropy. This result does not fall within the rationality mentioned above. Consequently, the entropic exchange will occur exactly in the opposite direction: the system with higher entropy will "pump" to the system with lower entropy—lower entropy, which will consume additional low entropy from the system with higher entropy. This time, the result is consistent with the "rationality" of the Universe in question.
51. Logically, as soon as there are at least two dissipative systems in Universe 1, there are no direct entropic exchanges with the genuine complementary

environment, but only between existing dissipative systems, based on the principle of choosing the minimum entropic gradient. It is obvious, at the same time, that the indirect entropic exchange will take place between the two dissipative systems, following that, based on the same principle of the minimum entropic gradient, the dissipative system with the entropy speed closest to that of the complementary environment will nevertheless achieve direct entropic exchange with that environment.

52. It is as if we were dealing with a kind of entropic "productivity": the amount of low entropy needed to increase by a given size the entropic differential between two dissipative systems (or between the dissipative system and the complementary environment, if in Universe 1 there is only one dissipative system). Therefore, the principle of the minimum gradient of choice of entropic interaction can also be expressed in the form, logically equivalent, of the principle of maximum productivity of variation of the entropic gradient. Here, a suggestion for economists dealing with total factors productivity might arise: perhaps, along with the Solow residue, a residue (this time with a negative sign) generated by entropic processes in economic activities should also be considered, so that we have a *global* factors productivity of the issue and not only a *total* one. But we consider the most important suggestion at this point in the discussion to be the following: there is a natural tendency for low entropy to flow spontaneously in the direction of a negative entropic gradient and high entropy to flow spontaneously in the direction of a positive entropic gradient, analogous to that heat (as a macroscopic quantity) flows spontaneously in the direction of the negative temperature gradient and "non-heat" (cold) flows spontaneously in the direction of the positive temperature gradient.
53. For example, in the case of economic systems, the emergence of specialization, based on the productive advantage (absolute or relative), which led to exchange, makes, in fact, trade relations to take place on specific "geodesics" generated by the degree of economic development. In this sense, it can be stated (but remains, of course, to be developed in a complete and coherent way) that economic flows (of goods or factors of production) follow a kind of minimum gradient of the level of economic development (the gradient may refer to either competitiveness, or productivity or opportunity, etc.). More talented analysts may find suggestions here to replace the current national specialization criteria (absolute advantage, relative advantage, competitive advantage, endowment with factors, level of average of national productivity, niches, etc.) with a more general criterion: that of ... economic geodesic. A suggestion, completely general, in this sense, is made in Dinga (2001).

References

Bejan, A. (2007). *Constructal Theory of Social Dynamics*. Springer.

Dinga, E. (2001). *The Inertial Phenomenon in the Economic Process*. Economica Publishing House. (in Romanian).

Dinga, E. (2012). *Rebuilding Economics. Logical, Methodological and Epistemological Approach*. Lambert Academic Publishing.

Dinga, E., Oprean-Stan, C., Tănăsescu, R.C., Brătian, V., Ionescu, G.-M. (2022) *Financial Market Analysis and Behaviour. The Adaptive Preference Hypothesis*, .

Dinga, E., Oprean-Stan, C., Tănăsescu, R. C., Brătian, V., & Ionescu, G.-M. (2023). *Economic and Financial Market Behaviour. The Autopoietic Market Hypothesis*. Palgrave Macmillan – Springer Nature.

Freire, L. O., & de Andrade, D. A. (2021). Novel Aspects of Constructal Law: Four Distinct and Competing Goals in Flow Channels Design. *Open Journal of Applied Sciences, 11*(6), 647–664.

CHAPTER 8

Facing Crises: Antifragility, Sustainability, Autopoieticity

8.1 Preamble

So far, we have discussed the phenomenology (anatomy and physiology) of a generic societal crisis and, especially, the process of crises overlapping—causality and phenomenology. This chapter aims to build a linkage between Chap. 1, where the concepts of antifragility, sustainability and autopoieticity were analytically enough examined, and later chapters where the "animal" called (societal) crisis was examined. As in the entire economy of the book, we shall proceed rather logically and generally, in order to provide (possible) solutions of the largest applicability. Managing the crisis (or overlapped crises) face-to-perturbation, which requires mechanisms of robustness, resilience or autopoiesis, will relate to the concept of perturbation, also discussed in Chap. 1.

8.2 Crisis as Perturbation

In Chap. 1, the concept, typology and mechanism of perturbation were extensively and intensively discussed, *per se*. Now, it is relevant to examine if the crisis phenomenon (and, correlatively, the crises overlapping phenomenon) is a kind of perturbation and, more than that, what kind of perturbation is or should be considered.

E. Dinga, *Economic Resilience During Overlapped Crises*,
https://doi.org/10.1007/978-3-031-80224-9_8

8.2.1 Remember the Definitions

The most efficacy way to examine the potential of a generic crisis to exert perturbation on the general environment where it occurs is to put the two logical definitions next to each other—of the crisis, respectively of the disturbance/perturbation.

- perturbation logical definition (from Chap. 1):

$$\mathcal{P} \leftarrow \left(PS_1^P\right) \wedge \left(PS_2^P\right) \wedge \left(PS_3^P\right)$$

where: PS_1^P—*negative meaning* for the target system (i.e., a meaning which is associated with a disadvantage of any relevant nature, either direct or indirect); PS_2^P—*significant level* for the target system (i.e., a signification which is associated with a given threshold above which the perturbation is perceived—*nota bene*: as shown previously, the meaning is rather an objective issue, claiming the explanation, so, the causality, while the signification is rather a subjective issue, claiming the comprehension, so, the intuition); PS_3^P—*mutational impact* on the target system (i.e., the potential to induce a change that, in turn, has the potential to replicate itself inside that system—*nota bene*: this means that the mutational impact addresses a structural[1] change in the target system).

- crisis logical definition (from Chap. 2):

$$C \leftarrow (CSP1) \wedge (CSP2) \wedge (CSP3) \wedge (CSP4)$$

where: *CSP*1—it is *structurally generated* (so, not simply functionally); *CSP*2—it is *functionally unexplained* (or, generally, unexplainable); *CSP*3—it is *inferentially unpredicted* (or, generally, unpredictable); *CSP*4—it is *axiologically signified* (or, generally, can take axiological significations—*nota bene*: not meanings).

8.2.2 A Short Logical Analysis

We arrange the two definitions, more exactly, the two sets of sufficiency predicates in a table with double entry (Table 8.1). The notations in the table are: ↑—high probability of crisis to cause perturbation; ↓—low probability of crisis to cause perturbation; ↔—ambiguity of the impact of crisis on perturbation.

Table 8.1 The analytical correlations between perturbation and crisis

		The crisis			
		CSP1	*CSP2*	*CSP3*	*CSP4*
The perturbation	PS_1^P	↔	↔	↑	↑
	PS_2^P	↔	↑	↑	↔
	PS_3^P	↑	↓	↑	↓

Source: Author

Discussion

- from the 12 cells in Table 8.1, 50% indicate a high probability of occurring perturbation generated by crises;
- the most susceptible sufficiency predicate of crisis to generate a perturbation is *SP*3 (*inferentially unpredictability*)—it has an impact on all three sufficiency predicates of the perturbation;
- the less susceptible sufficiency predicates of crisis to generate a perturbation are *CSP*2 (*lack of functional explanation*) and *CSP*4 (*axiological signification*)—one impact is ambiguous (on PS_2^P), and the other two are oppositely oriented from the point of view of the probability;
- PS_1^P and PS_2^P are the sufficiency predicates of perturbation the most affected by the crisis (two high probabilities and two ambiguities), while PS_3^P is, at the whole definition of a crisis, somewhat invariant—two high probabilities, and low probabilities.

The conclusion is that a (generic) societal crisis has the logical potential to generate perturbations in society, especially based on its unpredictability—one of the crisis's sufficiency predicate. Of course, as shown in Chap. 1, the first "defence line" is robustness and, after the overwhelming of this line, the second "defence line" is resilience. Only after overcoming the two "defence lines" does the third "defence line" enter into action, namely the antifragility. In this chapter, we shall consider we are before the third "defence line" and try to describe which should be the way of facing societal crises from this perspective. Figure 8.1 takes over the logic of the "defence lines" from Chap. 1 and introduces other two such "defence

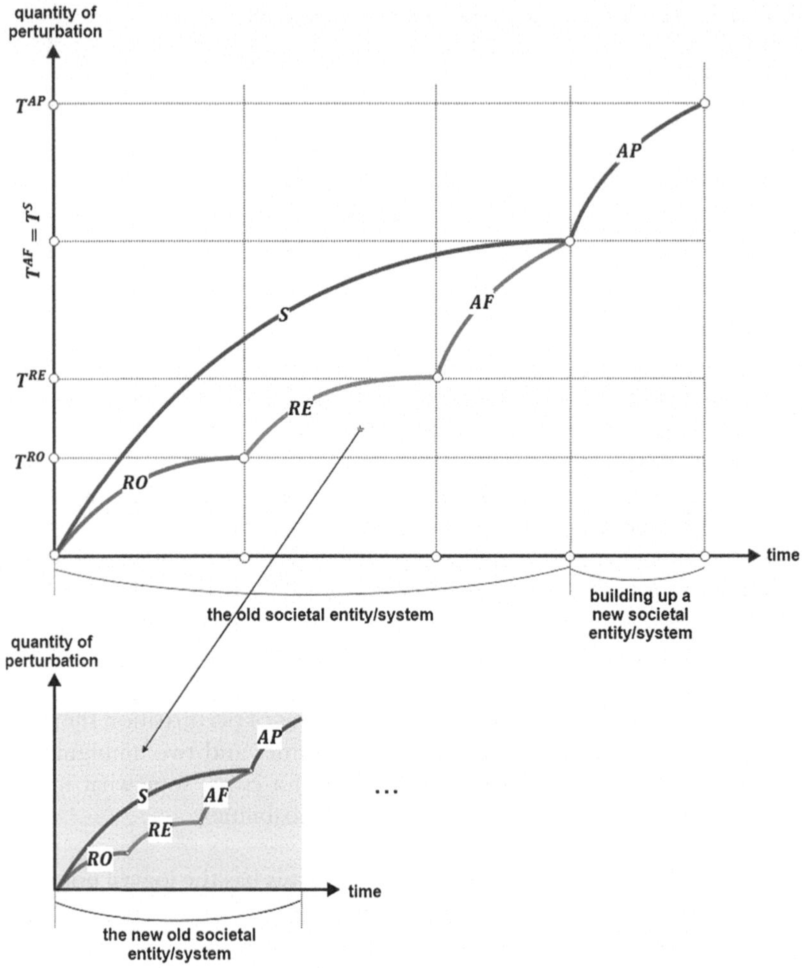

Fig. 8.1 The five "defence lines" to fight the perturbations generated by societal crises. *Source*: Author

lines" (we note: *RO*—robustness; *RE*—resilience; *AF*—antifragility; *S*—sustainability; *AP*—autopoieticity; T^{RO}—the ceiling threshold of robustness; T^{RE}—the ceiling threshold of resilience; T^{AF}—the ceiling threshold of antifragility; T^{S}—the ceiling threshold of sustainability; T^{AP}—the ceiling threshold of autopoieticity). Nota bene: $T^{AF} = T^{S}$.

Discussion

- a perturbation generated by a crisis will be avoided as long as the robustness (*RO*) property of the target entity/system does not reach its ceiling threshold (T^{RO}). The accumulation of tension/pressure exerted by the crisis until T^{RO} has no impact but, at that threshold, the perturbation in the case is objectified and changes (possibly) something in the target entity's statu quo; at this moment, the first defence line is overtaken. The accumulation of the tension/pressure is decelerated (the *RO* curve is increasingly concave), so a horizontal asymptote is formed exactly at the ceiling threshold T^{RO};
- after this point, the target entity/system tries to recover the previous state (the state before the impact of the perturbation), based on its property of resilience (*RE*). This action can be or cannot be successful—if yes, then the entity/system neutralizes the impact of perturbation (and the entity re-takes its chreode from the existing point), and if not, the ceiling threshold T^{RE} is reached when the second defence line is overtaken. The potential of the resilience capability increases concavely, too, so it goes in a decelerated way, until a new asymptote which is formed exactly at the ceiling threshold;
- at this moment, the third defence line goes into action—the antifragility (*AF*) property of target entity/system:
  - the entering into action of the property of antifragility marks the failure of the first two defence lines of the target entity/system. So the entity in this case has no other alternative than to accept the perturbation that occurred. But, a hope dawns: if there was still a disruption, let's at least get an advantage out of it;
  - consequently, the target entity starts, at point T^{RE}, to find and capture such an advantage from the perturbation. The searching is increasing, as effort (and, perhaps, as intermediate, concatenated results) and decelerated (the *AF* curve is concave);
  - because of its concavity, the *AF* curve has an asymptote, too, at the ceiling threshold $T^{AF} = T^{S}$;
  - so the *AF* curve continues to unfold until the point T^{S} or T^{AF}, that is until a new asymptote, namely the asymptote for a new curve (and defence line) called sustainability (*S*);
- sustainability is a property that integrates robustness, resilience and antifragility, being, in fact, a logical (and operational) embedder of the three properties evoked. Sustainability is an increasing and concave curve, so it has an asymptote (at the point T^{S}), where it exhausts its potential. About the functioning of this fourth defence line against

the perturbation caused by the crisis, we provide the following considerations:

- the property of sustainability is, indeed, the result of the three properties embedded and, also, of their combined (integral) effect. The robustness, resilience and antifragility contribute, each from its different perspective to objectify the sufficiency predicates that logically define the property of sustainability;
- although the impacts of *RO*, *RE* and *AF* are not algebraically additive, they combine among them so that sustainability can "manage" a greater quantity of perturbations than each of the three properties included separately; somewhat the property of sustainability is a synergic[2] effect of the three individual properties;
- inside a given societal entity/system, the property of sustainability is an increasing and concave (i.e., decelerating) curve, since the tensions accumulation towards (structural) changes as caused by the failure of robustness and resilience, respectively, press on the target entity. Even the action of antifragility to get advantages from the perturbation exhausts itself, at a moment, its potential,[3] so that the sustainability property goes to its asymptote;

• at the moment when the sustainability reaches its (horizontal) asymptote, the fifth defence line of the target entity/system comes into existence, namely the property of autopoieticity;
• as expected, the *AP* curve is an increasing and concave (i.e., decelerated) one. In fact, according to its definition (see Chap. 1), autopoieticity redesigns, resets, reorganizes, restructures and other of the same, the target entity/system, as a result of the sustainability failing. The main impact of entering into action of the property of autopoieticity is as follows:
  - another entity/system comes into existence since a new structure (so, new functions) arise as a result of the autopoieticity impact;
  - the new target entity/system enters the same "cycle" of the five defence lines as discussed above, of course, from "zero".

8.3 Facing Crises Based on Antifragility

The concept of antifragility in facing crises is relevant both in its passive understanding (that preserves the basic structure of the entity affected by perturbation—***nota bene***: here we have large interferences with the properties called robustness, or resilience) and in its active understanding (that captures advantages, of any nature, from handling the perturbation). We shall examine the latter impact of the property of antifragility, namely, extracting advantages from the perturbation caused by the crisis.

8.3.1 Preliminaries

First of all, we must revisit the logical definition of the property of antifragility (Chap. 1) and the formal description of a generic (societal) crisis (Chap. 5).

(a) the formal description of the antifragility

The typology of antifragility will be "borrowed" from Chap. 1. So, the formal description of the antifragility, which is viewed exclusively from the perspective of fructifying the impact of perturbation (i.e., of the fourth sufficiency predicate: *AF*4 *capacity of fructifying the impact of the disturbance* which personalizes the property of antifragility to the highest degree—this property can find and capture advantages from the perturbation suffered by the target entity/system), is the following:

$$AF^{mnpq}$$

where: $m \leftarrow$ *AF*4.1 (*increasing the robustness* of the target system: this mode of fructification is a species of hormesis, but it refers to the structural aspect of the system in question). More precisely, it is about the learning process—the exposure of the target system to the perturbation (actually, the impact of it) usually has or can have the effect of increasing the resistance of the target system to the perturbations. From a quantitative point of view, this effect manifests itself by increasing the threshold value up to which the system resists disturbances; $n \leftarrow$ *AF*4.2 (*increasing the resilience* of the target system): this mode of fruition is also an advantage for the target system, as it manifests itself through an increase in its elasticity to the dislocations suffered from disturbances (either state disturbances or trajectory disturbances); $p \leftarrow$ *AF*4.3 (*extending the functionality* of the target entity/system): what needs to be argued about this type of fruition or advantage obtained from the disruption is to show why the extension of functionality is beneficial to the target system; $q \leftarrow$ *AF*4.4 (*extending the behaviour* of the target entity/system): similarly, to AF4.3, this type of fructification of the impact of the disturbance refers to the extension of the relations between the target system and its environment system, i.e., those relations that transit membrane of the target system. In order to have

Table 8.2 The degrees of fructifying the impact of perturbation through antifragility

	m	n	p	q
1	Large	Large	Large	Large
2	Medium	Medium	Medium	Medium
3	Small	Small	Small	Small

Source: Author

grades in the four cases of fructifying, we propose the following (Table 8.2), so $m, n, p, q \in \{1,2,3\} \subset N$:

(b) the formal description of the generic (societal) crisis

$$C_{51423}^{\varepsilon\alpha\delta\beta\gamma}$$

where: ε means significance; α means cause; δ means impact; β means origin; γ means chreode; and $\varepsilon, \alpha, \delta, \beta, \gamma \in \{1,2,3,4,5\} \subset N$.

(c) the formal description of the generic perturbation

The typology of perturbation was also provided in Chap. 1. Here we shall make some notations to simplify the writing, so formalizing the generic perturbation. The seven criteria for classifying the perturbation are:

- the *nature*: we note this criterion with a (for a = 1: institutive perturbation; for a = 2: corrective perturbation);
- the *amplitude/*size: we note this criterion with b (for b = 1: hormetic perturbation; for b = 2: supra-hormetic perturbation);
- the *mechanism*: we note this criterion with c (for c = 1: repeatable perturbation; for c = 2: singular perturbation);
- the *origin*: we note this criterion with d (for d = 1: internal perturbation; for d = 2: external perturbation);
- the *impact*: we note this criterion with e (for e = 1: structural perturbation; for e = 2: functional perturbation);
- the *behaviour*: we note this criterion with f (for f = 1: spontaneous perturbation; for f = 2: induced perturbation);
- the *affinity*: we note this criterion with g (for g = 1: cumulative perturbation; for g = 2: isolated perturbation).

Like the case of crisis formalization, the formal perturbation will be written:

$$P^{abcdefg}$$

where: $a, b, c, d, e, f, g \in \{1,2\} \subset N$.

8.3.2 *The Phenomenology of Antifragility*

It is important to describe the (logical) way the generic crisis causes the generic perturbation and the generic perturbation is handled by the generic antifragility. Table 8.3 provides a suggestion for perturbation generated by crisis, and Table 8.4 provides a suggestion for antifragility action onto perturbation (notations in the two tables are: ↑ means with high probability;

Table 8.3 Phenomenology of generating perturbation by crisis

→			*Perturbation*													
			a		*b*		*c*		*d*		*e*		*f*		*g*	
			1	*2*	*1*	*2*	*1*	*2*	*1*	*2*	*1*	*2*	*1*	*2*	*1*	*2*
Crisis	ε	5	↑	↑		↔			↑	↔	↑	↑	↔	↑	↑	↔
		4	↔	↑		↔			↑	↔	↔	↑	↓	↑	↑	↔
		3	↓	↑		↓			↔	↓	↓	↑	↓	↑	↔	↓
		2		↑					↓			↔		↔	↓	↓
		1		↔					↓			↔		↓		↓
	α	5	↑	↔			↑	↔	↑	↔	↑	↔		↑	↔	
		4	↑	↔			↔	↓	↑	↓	↑	↔		↑	↔	
		3	↑	↔			↓		↔	↓	↑	↓		↔	↓	↔
		2	↔	↓					↓		↔	↓	↔	↓	↓	↓
		1	↔	↓					↓		↔		↓	↓		↓
	δ	5	↑	↑	↔		↔	↓	↔	↔	↑	↑		↑	↑	↔
		4	↑	↑	↔		↔	↓	↔	↓	↔	↑	↑	↑	↔	↔
		3	↔	↔	↓	↔	↓	↓	↓	↓	↓	↔	↔	↔	↔	↓
		2	↓	↓		↔	↓		↓	↓		↓	↓	↓		↓
		1	↓	↓		↓						↓				
	β	5			↑		↑	↔	↑	↑	↑	↑	↑	↑	↔	↑
		4			↔	↑	↑	↔	↑	↔	↑	↑	↔	↑	↔	↔
		3			↓	↔	↔	↓	↑	↔	↔	↑	↔	↔	↓	↓
		2				↓	↓	↓	↔	↓	↔	↔		↓	↓	↓
		1							↓	↓	↓	↓				
	γ	5			↑		↔	↔			↔	↑	↔	↑	↑	↔
		4	↑	↑	↑	↔	↔	↓	↑	↔	↔	↑	↔	↑	↑	↔
		3	↔	↑	↔	↓	↓	↓	↑	↔	↓	↔	↓	↔	↑	↓
		2	↓	↔	↓	↓	↓	↓	↔	↓	↓	↓	↓	↓	↔	↓
		1		↓			↓	↓	↓	↓		↓			↓	↓

Source: Author

Table 8.4 Phenomenology of handling perturbation by antifragility

→			*Perturbation*													
			a		*b*		*c*		*d*		*e*		*f*		*g*	
			1	*2*	*1*	*2*	*1*	*2*	*1*	*2*	*1*	*2*	*1*	*2*	*1*	*2*
Antifragility	*m*	1	↑	↑	↑	↔	↑	↔	↑	↔	↑	↑	↑	↑	↑	↑
		2	↑	↑	↑	↔	↑	↔	↑	↔	↑	↑	↑	↑	↑	↑
		3	↔	↑	↔	↓	↔	↓	↑	↔	↔	↑	↑	↔	↔	↑
	n	1	↑	↑	↑	↑	↑	↑	↔	↔	↑	↑	↑	↑	↑	↑
		2	↔	↑	↔	↑	↔	↑	↔	↓	↑	↑	↑	↑	↔	↑
		3	↔	↔	↔	↔	↔	↔	↓	↓	↔	↑	↑	↔	↓	↔
	p	1	↔	↔	↔	↔	↔	↑	↑	↔	↔	↑	↔	↑	↑	↑
		2	↔	↔	↔	↔	↔	↔	↑	↓	↓	↑	↑	↔	↔	↑
		3	↓	↓	↔	↓	↓	↓	↔	↓	↓	↔	↑	↓	↓	↔
	q	1	↔	↔	↑	↔	↔	↔	↔	↔	↔	↑	↑	↑	↑	↔
		2	↔	↔	↔	↓	↔	↓	↓	↔	↓	↔	↔	↔	↔	↔
		3	↓	↓	↔	↓	↓	↓	↓	↔	↓	↓	↓	↓	↓	↓

Source: Author

↓ means with low probability; ↔ means with medium probability). *Nota bene*: in both tables, only an indicative/exemplificative proposal (i.e., know how) is delivered, not a definitely established (i.e., know what) one.

8.3.3 About the Perturbations Overlapping

As in the case of crises, one put rise the question about overlapping of perturbations. In this paragraph, we shall provide some basically considerations in this matter.

Compatibility Among Perturbations

For two (or more) perturbations overlap, they must be compatible from a logical point of view. In Table 8.5 we indicate the cases of incompatibility, based on the general typology of perturbations evoked above ($* * *$means compatibility; $**$ means indifference; $*$ means incompatibility).

Discussion

- any "individual" of perturbation that contains an incompatibility constitutes, in turn, a (logically) impossible perturbation—for example, for the perturbation $P^{1bc2efg}$, which contains the incompati-

Table 8.5 Compatibility versus incompatibility in the relationship "perturbation–antifragility"

		Perturbation													
		a		*b*		*c*		*d*		*e*		*f*		*g*	
		1	*2*	*1*	*2*	*1*	*2*	*1*	*2*	*1*	*2*	*1*	*2*	*1*	*2*
a	1	***	*	**	*	***	**	***	*	***	***	*	***	***	**
	2	*	***	*	**	**	***	***	**	***	***	*	***	*	***
b	1	**	*	***	*	***	***	***	***	*	***	***	***	***	**
	2	*	**	*	***	*	**	***	***	***	**	**	**	*	***
c	1	***	**	***	*	***	*	***	**	***	***	*	***	***	*
	2	**	***	***	**	*	***	***	***	**	**	***	***	*	**
d	1	***	***	***	***	***	***	***	*	***	***	***	***	***	***
	2	*	**	***	***	**	***	*	***	***	***	***	***	***	***
e	1	***	***	*	***	***	**	***	***	***	*	*	**	***	*
	2	***	***	***	**	***	**	***	***	*	***	***	***	**	**
f	1	*	*	***	**	*	***	***	***	*	***	***	*	*	***
	2	***	***	***	**	***	***	***	***	**	***	*	***	***	***
g	1	***	*	***	*	***	*	***	***	***	**	*	***	***	*
	2	**	***	**	***	*	**	***	***	*	**	***	***	*	***

Source: Author

bility (a = 1; d = 2), there are 32 impossible perturbations, since five parameters are to be completed (b, c, e, f, g), each of them with two values (1 or 2), so there are 2^5 cases;

- generally, there can exist $2^7 = 128$ possible distinct "individuals" of perturbations, from which, there are 104 impossible "individuals" of perturbations (see Annex 8.1);

Annex 8.1

		ε				
		1	2	3	4	5
ε	1	$G_{(\varepsilon,\varepsilon)}(1,1)$	$G_{(\varepsilon,\varepsilon)}(1,2)$	$G_{(\varepsilon,\varepsilon)}(1,3)$	$G_{(\varepsilon,\varepsilon)}(1,4)$	$G_{(\varepsilon,\varepsilon)}(1,5)$
	2	$G_{(\varepsilon,\varepsilon)}(2,1)$	$G_{(\varepsilon,\varepsilon)}(2,2)$	$G_{(\varepsilon,\varepsilon)}(2,3)$	$G_{(\varepsilon,\varepsilon)}(2,4)$	$G_{(\varepsilon,\varepsilon)}(2,5)$
	3	$G_{(\varepsilon,\varepsilon)}(3,1)$	$G_{(\varepsilon,\varepsilon)}(3,2)$	$G_{(\varepsilon,\varepsilon)}(3,3)$	$G_{(\varepsilon,\varepsilon)}(3,4)$	$G_{(\varepsilon,\varepsilon)}(3,5)$
	4	$G_{(\varepsilon,\varepsilon)}(4,1)$	$G_{(\varepsilon,\varepsilon)}(4,2)$	$G_{(\varepsilon,\varepsilon)}(4,3)$	$G_{(\varepsilon,\varepsilon)}(4,4)$	$G_{(\varepsilon,\varepsilon)}(4,5)$
	5	$G_{(\varepsilon,\varepsilon)}(5,1)$	$G_{(\alpha,\varepsilon)}(5,2)$	$G_{(\varepsilon,\varepsilon)}(5,3)$	$G_{(\varepsilon,\varepsilon)}(5,4)$	$G_{(\varepsilon,\varepsilon)}(5,5)$
α	1	$G_{(\alpha,\varepsilon)}(1,1)$	$G_{(\alpha,\varepsilon)}(1,2)$	$G_{(\alpha,\varepsilon)}(1,3)$	$G_{(\alpha,\varepsilon)}(1,4)$	$G_{(\alpha,\varepsilon)}(1,5)$
	2	$G_{(\alpha,\varepsilon)}(2,1)$	$G_{(\alpha,\varepsilon)}(2,2)$	$G_{(\alpha,\varepsilon)}(2,3)$	$G_{(\alpha,\varepsilon)}(2,4)$	$G_{(\alpha,\varepsilon)}(2,5)$
	3	$G_{(\alpha,\varepsilon)}(3,1)$	$G_{(\alpha,\varepsilon)}(3,2)$	$G_{(\alpha,\varepsilon)}(3,3)$	$G_{(\alpha,\varepsilon)}(3,4)$	$G_{(\alpha,\varepsilon)}(3,5)$
	4	$G_{(\alpha,\varepsilon)}(4,1)$	$G_{(\alpha,\varepsilon)}(4,2)$	$G_{(\alpha,\varepsilon)}(4,3)$	$G_{(\alpha,\varepsilon)}(4,4)$	$G_{(\alpha,\varepsilon)}(4,5)$
	5	$G_{(\alpha,\varepsilon)}(5,1)$	$G_{(\alpha,\varepsilon)}(5,2)$	$G_{(\alpha,\varepsilon)}(5,3)$	$G_{(\alpha,\varepsilon)}(5,4)$	$G_{(\alpha,\varepsilon)}(5,5)$
δ	1	$G_{(\delta,\varepsilon)}(1,1)$	$G_{(\delta,\varepsilon)}(1,2)$	$G_{(\delta,\varepsilon)}(1,3)$	$G_{(\delta,\varepsilon)}(1,4)$	$G_{(\delta,\varepsilon)}(1,5)$
	2	$G_{(\delta,\varepsilon)}(2,1)$	$G_{(\delta,\varepsilon)}(2,2)$	$G_{(\delta,\varepsilon)}(2,3)$	$G_{(\delta,\varepsilon)}(2,4)$	$G_{(\delta,\varepsilon)}(2,5)$
	3	$G_{(\delta,\varepsilon)}(3,1)$	$G_{(\delta,\varepsilon)}(3,2)$	$G_{(\delta,\varepsilon)}(3,3)$	$G_{(\delta,\varepsilon)}(3,4)$	$G_{(\delta,\varepsilon)}(3,5)$
	4	$G_{(\delta,\varepsilon)}(4,1)$	$G_{(\delta,\varepsilon)}(4,2)$	$G_{(\delta,\varepsilon)}(4,3)$	$G_{(\delta,\varepsilon)}(4,4)$	$G_{(\delta,\varepsilon)}(4,5)$
	5	$G_{(\delta,\varepsilon)}(5,1)$	$G_{(\delta,\varepsilon)}(5,2)$	$G_{(\delta,\varepsilon)}(5,3)$	$G_{(\delta,\varepsilon)}(5,4)$	$G_{(\delta,\varepsilon)}(5,5)$
β	1	$G_{(\beta,\varepsilon)}(1,1)$	$G_{(\beta,\varepsilon)}(1,2)$	$G_{(\beta,\varepsilon)}(1,3)$	$G_{(\beta,\varepsilon)}(1,4)$	$G_{(\beta,\varepsilon)}(1,5)$
	2	$G_{(\beta,\varepsilon)}(2,1)$	$G_{(\beta,\varepsilon)}(2,2)$	$G_{(\beta,\varepsilon)}(2,3)$	$G_{(\beta,\varepsilon)}(2,4)$	$G_{(\beta,\varepsilon)}(2,5)$
	3	$G_{(\beta,\varepsilon)}(3,1)$	$G_{(\beta,\varepsilon)}(3,2)$	$G_{(\beta,\varepsilon)}(3,3)$	$G_{(\beta,\varepsilon)}(3,4)$	$G_{(\beta,\varepsilon)}(3,5)$
	4	$G_{(\beta,\varepsilon)}(4,1)$	$G_{(\beta,\varepsilon)}(4,2)$	$G_{(\beta,\varepsilon)}(4,3)$	$G_{(\beta,\varepsilon)}(4,4)$	$G_{(\beta,\varepsilon)}(4,5)$
	5	$G_{(\beta,\varepsilon)}(5,1)$	$G_{(\beta,\varepsilon)}(5,2)$	$G_{(\beta,\varepsilon)}(5,3)$	$G_{(\beta,\varepsilon)}(5,4)$	$G_{(\beta,\varepsilon)}(5,5)$
γ	1	$G_{(\gamma,\varepsilon)}(1,1)$	$G_{(\gamma,\varepsilon)}(1,2)$	$G_{(\gamma,\varepsilon)}(1,3)$	$G_{(\gamma,\varepsilon)}(1,4)$	$G_{(\gamma,\varepsilon)}(1,5)$
	2	$G_{(\gamma,\varepsilon)}(2,1)$	$G_{(\gamma,\varepsilon)}(2,2)$	$G_{(\gamma,\varepsilon)}(2,3)$	$G_{(\gamma,\varepsilon)}(2,4)$	$G_{(\gamma,\varepsilon)}(2,5)$
	3	$G_{(\gamma,\varepsilon)}(3,1)$	$G_{(\gamma,\varepsilon)}(3,2)$	$G_{(\gamma,\varepsilon)}(3,3)$	$G_{(\gamma,\varepsilon)}(3,4)$	$G_{(\gamma,\varepsilon)}(3,5)$
	4	$G_{(\gamma,\varepsilon)}(4,1)$	$G_{(\gamma,\varepsilon)}(4,2)$	$G_{(\gamma,\varepsilon)}(4,3)$	$G_{(\gamma,\varepsilon)}(4,4)$	$G_{(\gamma,\varepsilon)}(4,5)$
	5	$G_{(\gamma,\varepsilon)}(5,1)$	$G_{(\gamma,\varepsilon)}(5,2)$	$G_{(\gamma,\varepsilon)}(5,3)$	$G_{(\gamma,\varepsilon)}(5,4)$	$G_{(\gamma,\varepsilon)}(5,5)$

(*continued*)

Annex 8.1 continued

		α				
		1	2	3	4	5
ε	1	$G_{(\varepsilon,\alpha)}(1,1)$	$G_{(\varepsilon,\alpha)}(1,2)$	$G_{(\varepsilon,\alpha)}(1,3)$	$G_{(\varepsilon,\alpha)}(1,4)$	$G_{(\varepsilon,\alpha)}(1,5)$
	2	$G_{(\varepsilon,\alpha)}(2,1)$	$G_{(\varepsilon,\alpha)}(2,2)$	$G_{(\varepsilon,\alpha)}(2,3)$	$G_{(\varepsilon,\alpha)}(2,4)$	$G_{(\varepsilon,\alpha)}(2,5)$
	3	$G_{(\varepsilon,\alpha)}(3,1)$	$G_{(\varepsilon,\alpha)}(3,2)$	$G_{(\varepsilon,\alpha)}(3,3)$	$G_{(\varepsilon,\alpha)}(3,4)$	$G_{(\varepsilon,\alpha)}(3,5)$
	4	$G_{(\varepsilon,\alpha)}(4,1)$	$G_{(\varepsilon,\alpha)}(4,2)$	$G_{(\varepsilon,\alpha)}(4,3)$	$G_{(\varepsilon,\alpha)}(4,4)$	$G_{(\varepsilon,\alpha)}(4,5)$
	5	$G_{(\varepsilon,\alpha)}(5,1)$	$G_{(\varepsilon,\alpha)}(5,2)$	$G_{(\varepsilon,\alpha)}(5,3)$	$G_{(\varepsilon,\alpha)}(5,4)$	$G_{(\varepsilon,\alpha)}(5,5)$
α	1	$G_{(\alpha,\alpha)}(1,1)$	$G_{(\alpha,\alpha)}(1,2)$	$G_{(\alpha,\alpha)}(1,3)$	$G_{(\alpha,\alpha)}(1,4)$	$G_{(\alpha,\alpha)}(1,5)$
	2	$G_{(\alpha,\alpha)}(2,1)$	$G_{(\alpha,\alpha)}(2,2)$	$G_{(\alpha,\alpha)}(2,3)$	$G_{(\alpha,\alpha)}(2,4)$	$G_{(\alpha,\alpha)}(2,5)$
	3	$G_{(\alpha,\alpha)}(3,1)$	$G_{(\alpha,\alpha)}(3,2)$	$G_{(\alpha,\alpha)}(3,3)$	$G_{(\alpha,\alpha)}(3,4)$	$G_{(\alpha,\alpha)}(3,5)$
	4	$G_{(\alpha,\alpha)}(4,1)$	$G_{(\alpha,\alpha)}(4,2)$	$G_{(\alpha,\alpha)}(4,3)$	$G_{(\alpha,\alpha)}(4,4)$	$G_{(\alpha,\alpha)}(4,5)$
	5	$G_{(\alpha,\alpha)}(5,1)$	$G_{(\alpha,\alpha)}(5,2)$	$G_{(\alpha,\alpha)}(5,3)$	$G_{(\alpha,\alpha)}(5,4)$	$G_{(\alpha,\alpha)}(5,5)$
δ	1	$G_{(\delta,\alpha)}(1,1)$	$G_{(\delta,\alpha)}(1,2)$	$G_{(\delta,\alpha)}(1,3)$	$G_{(\delta,\alpha)}(1,4)$	$G_{(\delta,\alpha)}(1,5)$
	2	$G_{(\delta,\alpha)}(2,1)$	$G_{(\delta,\alpha)}(2,2)$	$G_{(\delta,\alpha)}(2,3)$	$G_{(\delta,\alpha)}(2,4)$	$G_{(\delta,\alpha)}(2,5)$
	3	$G_{(\delta,\alpha)}(3,1)$	$G_{(\delta,\alpha)}(3,2)$	$G_{(\delta,\alpha)}(3,3)$	$G_{(\delta,\alpha)}(3,4)$	$G_{(\delta,\alpha)}(3,5)$
	4	$G_{(\delta,\alpha)}(4,1)$	$G_{(\delta,\alpha)}(4,2)$	$G_{(\delta,\alpha)}(4,3)$	$G_{(\delta,\alpha)}(4,4)$	$G_{(\delta,\alpha)}(4,5)$
	5	$G_{(\delta,\alpha)}(5,1)$	$G_{(\delta,\alpha)}(5,2)$	$G_{(\delta,\alpha)}(5,3)$	$G_{(\delta,\alpha)}(5,4)$	$G_{(\delta,\alpha)}(5,5)$
β	1	$G_{(\beta,\alpha)}(1,1)$	$G_{(\beta,\alpha)}(1,2)$	$G_{(\beta,\alpha)}(1,3)$	$G_{(\beta,\alpha)}(1,4)$	$G_{(\beta,\alpha)}(1,5)$
	2	$G_{(\beta,\alpha)}(2,1)$	$G_{(\beta,\alpha)}(2,2)$	$G_{(\beta,\alpha)}(2,3)$	$G_{(\beta,\alpha)}(2,4)$	$G_{(\beta,\alpha)}(2,5)$
	3	$G_{(\beta,\alpha)}(3,1)$	$G_{(\beta,\alpha)}(3,2)$	$G_{(\beta,\alpha)}(3,3)$	$G_{(\beta,\alpha)}(3,4)$	$G_{(\beta,\alpha)}(3,5)$
	4	$G_{(\beta,\alpha)}(4,1)$	$G_{(\beta,\alpha)}(4,2)$	$G_{(\beta,\alpha)}(4,3)$	$G_{(\beta,\alpha)}(4,4)$	$G_{(\beta,\alpha)}(4,5)$
	5	$G_{(\beta,\alpha)}(5,1)$	$G_{(\beta,\alpha)}(5,2)$	$G_{(\beta,\alpha)}(5,3)$	$G_{(\beta,\alpha)}(5,4)$	$G_{(\beta,\alpha)}(5,5)$
γ	1	$G_{(\gamma,\alpha)}(1,1)$	$G_{(\gamma,\alpha)}(1,2)$	$G_{(\gamma,\alpha)}(1,3)$	$G_{(\gamma,\alpha)}(1,4)$	$G_{(\gamma,\alpha)}(1,5)$
	2	$G_{(\gamma,\alpha)}(2,1)$	$G_{(\gamma,\alpha)}(2,2)$	$G_{(\gamma,\alpha)}(2,3)$	$G_{(\gamma,\alpha)}(2,4)$	$G_{(\gamma,\alpha)}(2,5)$
	3	$G_{(\gamma,\alpha)}(3,1)$	$G_{(\gamma,\alpha)}(3,2)$	$G_{(\gamma,\alpha)}(3,3)$	$G_{(\gamma,\alpha)}(3,4)$	$G_{(\gamma,\alpha)}(3,5)$
	4	$G_{(\gamma,\alpha)}(4,1)$	$G_{(\gamma,\alpha)}(4,2)$	$G_{(\gamma,\alpha)}(4,3)$	$G_{(\gamma,\alpha)}(4,4)$	$G_{(\gamma,\alpha)}(4,5)$
	5	$G_{(\gamma,\alpha)}(5,1)$	$G_{(\gamma,\alpha)}(5,2)$	$G_{(\gamma,\alpha)}(5,3)$	$G_{(\gamma,\alpha)}(5,4)$	$G_{(\gamma,\alpha)}(5,5)$

		δ				
		1	2	3	4	5
ε	1	$G_{(\varepsilon,\delta)}(1,1)$	$G_{(\varepsilon,\delta)}(1,2)$	$G_{(\varepsilon,\delta)}(1,3)$	$G_{(\varepsilon,\delta)}(1,4)$	$G_{(\varepsilon,\delta)}(1,5)$
	2	$G_{(\varepsilon,\delta)}(2,1)$	$G_{(\varepsilon,\delta)}(2,2)$	$G_{(\varepsilon,\delta)}(2,3)$	$G_{(\varepsilon,\delta)}(2,4)$	$G_{(\varepsilon,\delta)}(2,5)$
	3	$G_{(\varepsilon,\delta)}(3,1)$	$G_{(\varepsilon,\delta)}(3,2)$	$G_{(\varepsilon,\delta)}(3,3)$	$G_{(\varepsilon,\delta)}(3,4)$	$G_{(\varepsilon,\delta)}(3,5)$
	4	$G_{(\varepsilon,\delta)}(4,1)$	$G_{(\varepsilon,\delta)}(4,2)$	$G_{(\varepsilon,\delta)}(4,3)$	$G_{(\varepsilon,\delta)}(4,4)$	$G_{(\varepsilon,\delta)}(4,5)$
	5	$G_{(\varepsilon,\delta)}(5,1)$	$G_{(\alpha,\delta)}(5,2)$	$G_{(\varepsilon,\delta)}(5,3)$	$G_{(\varepsilon,\delta)}(5,4)$	$G_{(\varepsilon,\delta)}(5,5)$
α	1	$G_{(\alpha,\delta)}(1,1)$	$G_{(\alpha,\delta)}(1,2)$	$G_{(\alpha,\delta)}(1,3)$	$G_{(\alpha,\delta)}(1,4)$	$G_{(\alpha,\delta)}(1,5)$
	2	$G_{(\alpha,\delta)}(2,1)$	$G_{(\alpha,\delta)}(2,2)$	$G_{(\alpha,\delta)}(2,3)$	$G_{(\alpha,\delta)}(2,4)$	$G_{(\alpha,\delta)}(2,5)$
	3	$G_{(\alpha,\delta)}(3,1)$	$G_{(\alpha,\delta)}(3,2)$	$G_{(\alpha,\delta)}(3,3)$	$G_{(\alpha,\delta)}(3,4)$	$G_{(\alpha,\delta)}(3,5)$
	4	$G_{(\alpha,\delta)}(4,1)$	$G_{(\alpha,\delta)}(4,2)$	$G_{(\alpha,\delta)}(4,3)$	$G_{(\alpha,\delta)}(4,4)$	$G_{(\alpha,\delta)}(4,5)$
	5	$G_{(\alpha,\delta)}(5,1)$	$G_{(\alpha,\delta)}(5,2)$	$G_{(\alpha,\delta)}(5,3)$	$G_{(\alpha,\delta)}(5,4)$	$G_{(\alpha,\delta)}(5,5)$

(*continued*)

Annex 8.1 (continued)

δ	1	$G_{(\delta,\delta)}(1,1)$	$G_{(\delta,\delta)}(1,2)$	$G_{(\delta,\delta)}(1,3)$	$G_{(\delta,\delta)}(1,4)$	$G_{(\delta,\delta)}(1,5)$
	2	$G_{(\delta,\delta)}(2,1)$	$G_{(\delta,\delta)}(2,2)$	$G_{(\delta,\delta)}(2,3)$	$G_{(\delta,\delta)}(2,4)$	$G_{(\delta,\delta)}(2,5)$
	3	$G_{(\delta,\delta)}(3,1)$	$G_{(\delta,\delta)}(3,2)$	$G_{(\delta,\delta)}(3,3)$	$G_{(\delta,\delta)}(3,4)$	$G_{(\delta,\delta)}(3,5)$
	4	$G_{(\delta,\delta)}(4,1)$	$G_{(\delta,\delta)}(4,2)$	$G_{(\delta,\delta)}(4,3)$	$G_{(\delta,\delta)}(4,4)$	$G_{(\delta,\delta)}(4,5)$
	5	$G_{(\delta,\delta)}(5,1)$	$G_{(\delta,\delta)}(5,2)$	$G_{(\delta,\delta)}(5,3)$	$G_{(\delta,\delta)}(5,4)$	$G_{(\delta,\delta)}(5,5)$
β	1	$G_{(\beta,\delta)}(1,1)$	$G_{(\beta,\delta)}(1,2)$	$G_{(\beta,\delta)}(1,3)$	$G_{(\beta,\delta)}(1,4)$	$G_{(\beta,\delta)}(1,5)$
	2	$G_{(\beta,\delta)}(2,1)$	$G_{(\beta,\delta)}(2,2)$	$G_{(\beta,\delta)}(2,3)$	$G_{(\beta,\delta)}(2,4)$	$G_{(\beta,\delta)}(2,5)$
	3	$G_{(\beta,\delta)}(3,1)$	$G_{(\beta,\delta)}(3,2)$	$G_{(\beta,\delta)}(3,3)$	$G_{(\beta,\delta)}(3,4)$	$G_{(\beta,\delta)}(3,5)$
	4	$G_{(\beta,\delta)}(4,1)$	$G_{(\beta,\delta)}(4,2)$	$G_{(\beta,\delta)}(4,3)$	$G_{(\beta,\delta)}(4,4)$	$G_{(\beta,\delta)}(4,5)$
	5	$G_{(\beta,\delta)}(5,1)$	$G_{(\beta,\delta)}(5,2)$	$G_{(\beta,\delta)}(5,3)$	$G_{(\beta,\delta)}(5,4)$	$G_{(\beta,\delta)}(5,5)$
γ	1	$G_{(\gamma,\delta)}(1,1)$	$G_{(\gamma,\delta)}(1,2)$	$G_{(\gamma,\delta)}(1,3)$	$G_{(\gamma,\delta)}(1,4)$	$G_{(\gamma,\delta)}(1,5)$
	2	$G_{(\gamma,\delta)}(2,1)$	$G_{(\gamma,\delta)}(2,2)$	$G_{(\gamma,\delta)}(2,3)$	$G_{(\gamma,\delta)}(2,4)$	$G_{(\gamma,\delta)}(2,5)$
	3	$G_{(\gamma,\delta)}(3,1)$	$G_{(\gamma,\delta)}(3,2)$	$G_{(\gamma,\delta)}(3,3)$	$G_{(\gamma,\delta)}(3,4)$	$G_{(\gamma,\delta)}(3,5)$
	4	$G_{(\gamma,\delta)}(4,1)$	$G_{(\gamma,\delta)}(4,2)$	$G_{(\gamma,\delta)}(4,3)$	$G_{(\gamma,\delta)}(4,4)$	$G_{(\gamma,\delta)}(4,5)$
	5	$G_{(\gamma,\delta)}(5,1)$	$G_{(\gamma,\delta)}(5,2)$	$G_{(\gamma,\delta)}(5,3)$	$G_{(\gamma,\delta)}(5,4)$	$G_{(\gamma,\delta)}(5,5)$

		β				
		1	2	3	4	5
ε	1	$G_{(\varepsilon,\beta)}(1,1)$	$G_{(\varepsilon,\beta)}(1,2)$	$G_{(\varepsilon,\beta)}(1,3)$	$G_{(\varepsilon,\beta)}(1,4)$	$G_{(\varepsilon,\beta)}(1,5)$
	2	$G_{(\varepsilon,\beta)}(2,1)$	$G_{(\varepsilon,\beta)}(2,2)$	$G_{(\varepsilon,\beta)}(2,3)$	$G_{(\varepsilon,\beta)}(2,4)$	$G_{(\varepsilon,\beta)}(2,5)$
	3	$G_{(\varepsilon,\beta)}(3,1)$	$G_{(\varepsilon,\beta)}(3,2)$	$G_{(\varepsilon,\beta)}(3,3)$	$G_{(\varepsilon,\beta)}(3,4)$	$G_{(\varepsilon,\beta)}(3,5)$
	4	$G_{(\varepsilon,\beta)}(4,1)$	$G_{(\varepsilon,\beta)}(4,2)$	$G_{(\varepsilon,\beta)}(4,3)$	$G_{(\varepsilon,\beta)}(4,4)$	$G_{(\varepsilon,\beta)}(4,5)$
	5	$G_{(\varepsilon,\beta)}(5,1)$	$G_{(\alpha,\beta)}(5,2)$	$G_{(\varepsilon,\beta)}(5,3)$	$G_{(\varepsilon,\beta)}(5,4)$	$G_{(\varepsilon,\beta)}(5,5)$
α	1	$G_{(\alpha,\beta)}(1,1)$	$G_{(\alpha,\beta)}(1,2)$	$G_{(\alpha,\beta)}(1,3)$	$G_{(\alpha,\beta)}(1,4)$	$G_{(\alpha,\beta)}(1,5)$
	2	$G_{(\alpha,\beta)}(2,1)$	$G_{(\alpha,\beta)}(2,2)$	$G_{(\alpha,\beta)}(2,3)$	$G_{(\alpha,\beta)}(2,4)$	$G_{(\alpha,\beta)}(2,5)$
	3	$G_{(\alpha,\beta)}(3,1)$	$G_{(\alpha,\beta)}(3,2)$	$G_{(\alpha,\beta)}(3,3)$	$G_{(\alpha,\beta)}(3,4)$	$G_{(\alpha,\beta)}(3,5)$
	4	$G_{(\alpha,\beta)}(4,1)$	$G_{(\alpha,\beta)}(4,2)$	$G_{(\alpha,\beta)}(4,3)$	$G_{(\alpha,\beta)}(4,4)$	$G_{(\alpha,\beta)}(4,5)$
	5	$G_{(\alpha,\beta)}(5,1)$	$G_{(\alpha,\beta)}(5,2)$	$G_{(\alpha,\beta)}(5,3)$	$G_{(\alpha,\beta)}(5,4)$	$G_{(\alpha,\beta)}(5,5)$
δ	1	$G_{(\delta,\beta)}(1,1)$	$G_{(\delta,\beta)}(1,2)$	$G_{(\delta,\beta)}(1,3)$	$G_{(\delta,\beta)}(1,4)$	$G_{(\delta,\beta)}(1,5)$
	2	$G_{(\delta,\beta)}(2,1)$	$G_{(\delta,\beta)}(2,2)$	$G_{(\delta,\beta)}(2,3)$	$G_{(\delta,\beta)}(2,4)$	$G_{(\delta,\beta)}(2,5)$
	3	$G_{(\delta,\beta)}(3,1)$	$G_{(\delta,\beta)}(3,2)$	$G_{(\delta,\beta)}(3,3)$	$G_{(\delta,\beta)}(3,4)$	$G_{(\delta,\beta)}(3,5)$
	4	$G_{(\delta,\beta)}(4,1)$	$G_{(\delta,\beta)}(4,2)$	$G_{(\delta,\beta)}(4,3)$	$G_{(\delta,\beta)}(4,4)$	$G_{(\delta,\beta)}(4,5)$
	5	$G_{(\delta,\beta)}(5,1)$	$G_{(\delta,\beta)}(5,2)$	$G_{(\delta,\beta)}(5,3)$	$G_{(\delta,\beta)}(5,4)$	$G_{(\delta,\beta)}(5,5)$
β	1	$G_{(\beta,\beta)}(1,1)$	$G_{(\beta,\beta)}(1,2)$	$G_{(\beta,\beta)}(1,3)$	$G_{(\beta,\beta)}(1,4)$	$G_{(\beta,\beta)}(1,5)$
	2	$G_{(\beta,\beta)}(2,1)$	$G_{(\beta,\beta)}(2,2)$	$G_{(\beta,\beta)}(2,3)$	$G_{(\beta,\beta)}(2,4)$	$G_{(\beta,\beta)}(2,5)$
	3	$G_{(\beta,\beta)}(3,1)$	$G_{(\beta,\beta)}(3,2)$	$G_{(\beta,\beta)}(3,3)$	$G_{(\beta,\beta)}(3,4)$	$G_{(\beta,\beta)}(3,5)$
	4	$G_{(\beta,\beta)}(4,1)$	$G_{(\beta,\beta)}(4,2)$	$G_{(\beta,\beta)}(4,3)$	$G_{(\beta,\beta)}(4,4)$	$G_{(\beta,\beta)}(4,5)$
	5	$G_{(\beta,\beta)}(5,1)$	$G_{(\beta,\beta)}(5,2)$	$G_{(\beta,\beta)}(5,3)$	$G_{(\beta,\beta)}(5,4)$	$G_{(\beta,\beta)}(5,5)$
γ	1	$G_{(\gamma,\beta)}(1,1)$	$G_{(\gamma,\beta)}(1,2)$	$G_{(\gamma,\beta)}(1,3)$	$G_{(\gamma,\beta)}(1,4)$	$G_{(\gamma,\beta)}(1,5)$
	2	$G_{(\gamma,\beta)}(2,1)$	$G_{(\gamma,\beta)}(2,2)$	$G_{(\gamma,\beta)}(2,3)$	$G_{(\gamma,\beta)}(2,4)$	$G_{(\gamma,\beta)}(2,5)$
	3	$G_{(\gamma,\beta)}(3,1)$	$G_{(\gamma,\beta)}(3,2)$	$G_{(\gamma,\beta)}(3,3)$	$G_{(\gamma,\beta)}(3,4)$	$G_{(\gamma,\beta)}(3,5)$
	4	$G_{(\gamma,\beta)}(4,1)$	$G_{(\gamma,\beta)}(4,2)$	$G_{(\gamma,\beta)}(4,3)$	$G_{(\gamma,\beta)}(4,4)$	$G_{(\gamma,\beta)}(4,5)$
	5	$G_{(\gamma,\beta)}(5,1)$	$G_{(\gamma,\beta)}(5,2)$	$G_{(\gamma,\beta)}(5,3)$	$G_{(\gamma,\beta)}(5,4)$	$G_{(\gamma,\beta)}(5,5)$

(*continued*)

Annex 8.1 (continued)

				γ		
		1	2	3	4	5
ε	1	$G_{(\varepsilon,\gamma)}(1,1)$	$G_{(\varepsilon,\gamma)}(1,2)$	$G_{(\varepsilon,\gamma)}(1,3)$	$G_{(\varepsilon, V)}(1,4)$	$G_{(\varepsilon,\gamma)}(1,5)$
	2	$G_{(\varepsilon,\gamma)}(2,1)$	$G_{(\varepsilon,\gamma)}(2,2)$	$G_{(\varepsilon,\gamma)}(2,3)$	$G_{(\varepsilon,\gamma)}(2,4)$	$G_{(\varepsilon,\gamma)}(2,5)$
	3	$G_{(\varepsilon,\gamma)}(3,1)$	$G_{(\varepsilon,\gamma)}(3,2)$	$G_{(\varepsilon,\gamma)}(3,3)$	$G_{(\varepsilon,\gamma)}(3,4)$	$G_{(\varepsilon,\gamma)}(3,5)$
	4	$G_{(\varepsilon,\gamma)}(4,1)$	$G_{(\varepsilon,\gamma)}(4,2)$	$G_{(\varepsilon,\gamma)}(4,3)$	$G_{(\varepsilon,\gamma)}(4,4)$	$G_{(\varepsilon,\gamma)}(4,5)$
	5	$G_{(\varepsilon,\gamma)}(5,1)$	$G_{(\alpha,\gamma)}(5,2)$	$G_{(\varepsilon,\gamma)}(5,3)$	$G_{(\varepsilon,\gamma)}(5,4)$	$G_{(\varepsilon,\gamma)}(5,5)$
α	1	$G_{(\alpha,\gamma)}(1,1)$	$G_{(\alpha,\gamma)}(1,2)$	$G_{(\alpha,\gamma)}(1,3)$	$G_{(\alpha,\gamma)}(1,4)$	$G_{(\alpha,\gamma)}(1,5)$
	2	$G_{(\alpha,\gamma)}(2,1)$	$G_{(\alpha,\gamma)}(2,2)$	$G_{(\alpha,\gamma)}(2,3)$	$G_{(\alpha,\gamma)}(2,4)$	$G_{(\alpha,\gamma)}(2,5)$
	3	$G_{(\alpha,\gamma)}(3,1)$	$G_{(\alpha,\gamma)}(3,2)$	$G_{(\alpha,\gamma)}(3,3)$	$G_{(\alpha,\gamma)}(3,4)$	$G_{(\alpha,\gamma)}(3,5)$
	4	$G_{(\alpha,\gamma)}(4,1)$	$G_{(\alpha,\gamma)}(4,2)$	$G_{(\alpha,\gamma)}(4,3)$	$G_{(\alpha,\gamma)}(4,4)$	$G_{(\alpha,\gamma)}(4,5)$
	5	$G_{(\alpha,\gamma)}(5,1)$	$G_{(\alpha,\gamma)}(5,2)$	$G_{(\alpha,\gamma)}(5,3)$	$G_{(\alpha,\gamma)}(5,4)$	$G_{(\alpha,\gamma)}(5,5)$
δ	1	$G_{(\delta,\gamma)}(1,1)$	$G_{(\delta,\gamma)}(1,2)$	$G_{(\delta,\gamma)}(1,3)$	$G_{(\delta,\gamma)}(1,4)$	$G_{(\delta,\gamma)}(1,5)$
	2	$G_{(\delta,\gamma)}(2,1)$	$G_{(\delta,\gamma)}(2,2)$	$G_{(\delta,\gamma)}(2,3)$	$G_{(\delta,\gamma)}(2,4)$	$G_{(\delta,\gamma)}(2,5)$
	3	$G_{(\delta,\gamma)}(3,1)$	$G_{(\delta,\gamma)}(3,2)$	$G_{(\delta,\gamma)}(3,3)$	$G_{(\delta,\gamma)}(3,4)$	$G_{(\delta,\gamma)}(3,5)$
	4	$G_{(\delta,\gamma)}(4,1)$	$G_{(\delta,\gamma)}(4,2)$	$G_{(\delta,\gamma)}(4,3)$	$G_{(\delta,\gamma)}(4,4)$	$G_{(\delta,\gamma)}(4,5)$
	5	$G_{(\delta,\gamma)}(5,1)$	$G_{(\delta,\gamma)}(5,2)$	$G_{(\delta,\gamma)}(5,3)$	$G_{(\delta,\gamma)}(5,4)$	$G_{(\delta,\gamma)}(5,5)$
β	1	$G_{(\beta,\gamma)}(1,1)$	$G_{(\beta,\gamma)}(1,2)$	$G_{(\beta,\gamma)}(1,3)$	$G_{(\beta,\gamma)}(1,4)$	$G_{(\beta,\gamma)}(1,5)$
	2	$G_{(\beta,\gamma)}(2,1)$	$G_{(\beta,\gamma)}(2,2)$	$G_{(\beta,\gamma)}(2,3)$	$G_{(\beta,\gamma)}(2,4)$	$G_{(\beta,\gamma)}(2,5)$
	3	$G_{(\beta,\gamma)}(3,1)$	$G_{(\beta,\gamma)}(3,2)$	$G_{(\beta,\gamma)}(3,3)$	$G_{(\beta,\gamma)}(3,4)$	$G_{(\beta,\gamma)}(3,5)$
	4	$G_{(\beta,\gamma)}(4,1)$	$G_{(\beta,\gamma)}(4,2)$	$G_{(\beta,\gamma)}(4,3)$	$G_{(\beta,\gamma)}(4,4)$	$G_{(\beta,\gamma)}(4,5)$
	5	$G_{(\beta,\gamma)}(5,1)$	$G_{(\beta,\gamma)}(5,2)$	$G_{(\beta,\gamma)}(5,3)$	$G_{(\beta,\gamma)}(5,4)$	$G_{(\beta,\gamma)}(5,5)$
γ	1	$G_{(\gamma,\gamma)}(1,1)$	$G_{(\gamma,\gamma)}(1,2)$	$G_{(\gamma,\gamma)}(1,3)$	$G_{(\gamma,\gamma)}(1,4)$	$G_{(\gamma,\gamma)}(1,5)$
	2	$G_{(\gamma,\gamma)}(2,1)$	$G_{(\gamma,\gamma)}(2,2)$	$G_{(\gamma,\gamma)}(2,3)$	$G_{(\gamma,\gamma)}(2,4)$	$G_{(\gamma,\gamma)}(2,5)$
	3	$G_{(\gamma,\gamma)}(3,1)$	$G_{(\gamma,\gamma)}(3,2)$	$G_{(\gamma,\gamma)}(3,3)$	$G_{(\gamma,\gamma)}(3,4)$	$G_{(\gamma,\gamma)}(3,5)$
	4	$G_{(\gamma,\gamma)}(4,1)$	$G_{(\gamma,\gamma)}(4,2)$	$G_{(\gamma,\gamma)}(4,3)$	$G_{(\gamma,\gamma)}(4,4)$	$G_{(\gamma,\gamma)}(4,5)$
	5	$G_{(\gamma,\gamma)}(5,1)$	$G_{(\gamma,\gamma)}(5,2)$	$G_{(\gamma,\gamma)}(5,3)$	$G_{(\gamma,\gamma)}(5,4)$	$G_{(\gamma,\gamma)}(5,5)$

- the "valid" overlapped perturbations are the following 24 perturbations:
  1. (no. 7): $P^{1111221}$—institutive, hormetic, repeatable, internal, functional, induced and cumulative perturbation
  2. (no. 15): $P^{1112221}$—institutive, hormetic, repeatable, external, functional, induced and cumulative perturbation
  3. (no. 16): $P^{1112222}$—institutive, hormetic, repeatable, external, functional, induced and isolated perturbation
  4. (no. 22): $P^{1121212}$—institutive, hormetic, singular, internal, functional, spontaneous and isolated perturbation
  5. (no. 24): $P^{1121222}$—institutive, hormetic, singular, internal, functional, induced and isolated perturbation

6. (no. 30): $P^{1122212}$—institutive, hormetic, singular, external, functional, spontaneous and isolated perturbation
7. (no. 32): $P^{1122222}$—institutive, hormetic, singular, external, functional, induced and isolated perturbation
8. (no. 52): $P^{1221122}$—institutive, supra-hormetic, singular, internal, structural, induced and isolated perturbation
9. (no. 54): $P^{1221212}$—institutive, supra-hormetic, singular, internal, functional, spontaneous, and isolated perturbation
10. (no. 56): $P^{1221222}$—institutive, supra-hormetic, singular, internal, functional, induced and isolated perturbation
11. (no. 60): $P^{1222122}$—institutive, supra-hormetic, singular, external, structural, induced and isolated perturbation
12. (no. 62): $P^{1222212}$—institutive, supra-hormetic, singular, external, functional, spontaneous and isolated perturbation
13. (no. 64): $P^{1222222}$—institutive, supra-hormetic, singular, external, functional, induced and isolated perturbation
14. (no. 80): $P^{2112222}$—corrective, hormetic, repeatable, external, functional, induced and isolated perturbation
15. (no. 86): $P^{2121212}$—corrective, hormetic, singular, internal, functional, spontaneous and isolated perturbation
16. (no. 88): $P^{2121222}$—corrective, hormetic, singular, internal, functional, induced and isolated perturbation
17. (no. 94): $P^{2122212}$—corrective, hormetic, singular, external, functional, spontaneous and isolated perturbation
18. (no. 96): $P^{2122222}$—corrective, hormetic, singular, external, functional, induced and isolated perturbation
19. (no. 116): $P^{2221122}$—corrective, supra-hormetic, singular, internal, structural, spontaneous and isolated perturbation
20. (no. 118): $P^{2221212}$—corrective, supra-hormetic, singular, internal, functional, spontaneous and isolated perturbation
21. (no. 120): $P^{2221222}$—corrective, supra-hormetic, singular, internal, functional, induced and isolated perturbation
22. (no. 124): $P^{2222122}$—corrective, supra-hormetic, singular, external, structural, induced and isolated perturbation
23. (no. 126): $P^{2222212}$—corrective, supra-hormetic, singular, external, functional, spontaneous and isolated perturbation
24. (no. 128): $P^{2222222}$—corrective, supra-hormetic, singular, external, functional, induced and isolated perturbation

Perturbations Overlapping: A Formal View

The overlapping of perturbations makes sense for the valid perturbations only. The "technique" to formalize an overlapping consists of the elimination of the parameters that are not coincident in the logical formula of the two (or many) perturbations. For example, if perturbation nos. 11 ($P^{1222122}$) and 19 ($P^{2221122}$), respectively, meet in the societal system at a moment *t*, the overlapped perturbation is $P(11;19)^{/22/122}$: supra-hormetic, singular, structural, induced and isolated perturbation; the parameters ***a*** and ***d*** that are non-coincident in the two individual perturbations are not accounted. All cases of overlapping perturbations are the following:

1. *Two perturbations*
   - $P(1;2)^{111/221}$; $P(1;3)^{111/22/}$; $P(1;4)^{11/12//}$; $P(1;5)^{11/122/}$; $P(1;6)^{11//2//}$; $P(1;7)^{11//22/}$; $P(1;8)^{1//1/2/}$; $P(1;9)^{1//12//}$; $P(1;10)^{1//122/}$; $P(1;11)^{1////2/}$; $P(1;12)^{1///2//}$; $P(1;13)^{1///22/}$; $P(1;14)^{/11/22/}$; $P(1;15)^{/1/12//}$; $P(1;16)^{/1/122/}$; $P(1;17)^{/1//2//}$; $P(1;18)^{/1//22/}$; $P(1;19)^{///1/2/}$; $P(1;20)^{///12//}$; $P(1;21)^{///122/}$; $P(1;22)^{/////2/}$; $P(1;23)^{////2//}$; $P(1;24)^{////22/}$;
   - $P(2;3)^{111222/}$; $P(2;4)^{11//2//}$; $P(2;5)^{11//22/}$; $P(2;6)^{11/22//}$; $P(2;7)^{11/222/}$; $P(2;8)^{1////2/}$; $P(2;9)^{1///2//}$; $P(2;10)^{1///22/}$; $P(2;11)^{1//2/2/}$; $P(2;12)^{1//22//}$; $P(2;13)^{1//222/}$; $P(2;14)^{/11222/}$; $P(2;15)^{/1//2//}$; $P(2;16)^{/1//22/}$; $P(2;17)^{/1/22//}$; $P(2;18)^{/1/222/}$; $P(2;19)^{/////2/}$;
   - ...
   - $P(23;24)^{22222/2}$.
2. *Three perturbations*
   - $P(1;2;3)^{111/22/}$; $P(1;2;4)^{11//2//}$; ...; $P(1;2;24)^{1///22/}$;
   - $P(2;3;4)^{11//2//}$; $P(2;3;4)^{11//22/}$; ...; $P(2;3;24)^{///222/}$;
   - ...
   - $P(22;23;24)^{2222//2}$.
3. *Four perturbations*
   - ...
4. *Thirteen perturbations*
   - $P(1;2;...;12;13)^{1//////}$. *Nota bene*: this is the only valid overlapped perturbation.

From 14 overlapped perturbations to 24 overlapped perturbations, including, no valid overlapped perturbations do exist.

8.3.4 *Antifragility: The Case of a Single Crisis*

The antifragility action on a perturbation is possible if and only if, from the formal point of view, that action is possible (*nota bene*: the efficacy of the antifragilizing in the case is irrelevant for our discussion). In the following, we shall examine the case in which a single crisis generates the perturbation in the case—either as a single perturbation or as an overlapped perturbation.

The Case of a Single Perturbation

Be a generic (societal) crisis—$C_{51423}^{\varepsilon\alpha\delta\beta\gamma}$—and a generic perturbation—$P^{abcdefg}$—the crisis triggers that perturbation. The possibility for the crisis to trigger the perturbation is described in Table 8.3, and we assume this possibility without other mentions and contextualization. What we must analyse is the formal possibility for the antifragility property of the society (societal system) to handle the perturbation. We remind the logical description of the antifragility: AF^{mnpq}. It results that we must see how, generally, the property of antifragility has the possibility to act on the perturbation in order to extract, from it, an advantage of any kind for the target entity/system.

The basic idea is to examine this possibility by putting together the two logical descriptions—of the perturbation and of the antifragility. We provide such an examination organized in Table 8.6. Before the analysis, some considerations are useful to be provided:

- the concrete "individual" of the crisis triggering the perturbation is not important, and will be considered as given, i.e., as an exogenous variable;
- the perturbations taken into consideration are only the 24 valid perturbations established based on Annex 8.1;
- while Table 8.3 indicates the propensity (or probability) of each parameter value of antifragility to approach each parameter value of perturbation and Table 8.5 indicates the relation of compatibility or incompatibility of each parameter value of antifragility with each parameter value of perturbation, Table 8.6 will suggest the feasibility of the relationships mentioned, i.e., a combination of the compatibility and propensity to antifragilize the perturbation.

Table 8.6 Antifragilizing the perturbation (single crisis, single perturbation)

No.	*Perturbation*	*Antifragility*			
		m (robustness increasing)	*n (resilience increasing)*	*p (functionality extending)*	*q (behaviour extending)*
1.	$p^{1111221}$	x		x	
2.	$p^{1112221}$	x			x
3.	$p^{1112222}$	x			x
4.	$p^{1121212}$	x		x	
5.	$p^{1121222}$	x		x	
6.	$p^{1122212}$	x			x
7.	$p^{1122222}$	x			x
8.	$p^{1221122}$	x		x	
9.	$p^{1221212}$	x		x	
10.	$p^{1221222}$	x		x	
11.	$p^{1222122}$	x			x
12.	$p^{1222212}$	x			x
13.	$p^{1222222}$	x			x
14.	$p^{2112222}$		x		x
15.	$p^{2121212}$		x	x	
16.	$p^{2121222}$		x	x	
17.	$p^{2122212}$		x		x
18.	$p^{2122222}$		x		x
19.	$p^{2221122}$		x	x	
20.	$p^{2221212}$		x	x	
21.	$p^{2221222}$		x		
22.	$p^{2222122}$		x		x
23.	$p^{2222212}$		x		x
24.	$p^{2222222}$		x		x

Discussion

- the institutive perturbations (no. 1…13) are liable to be antifragilized in order to increase the robustness of the target entity/system, since those perturbations add something to the target entity/system in the case;
- the corrective perturbations (no. 14…24) are liable to be antifragilized in order to increase the resilience of the target entity/system, since those perturbations delete something from or change something in the target entity/system in the case;
- the internal perturbations (no. 1,4,5,8,9,10,15,16,19,20,21) are liable to be antifragilized in order to extend the functionality inside the membrane of the target entity/system in the case;

Table 8.7 Antifragilizing the perturbation (single crisis, overlapped perturbations)

No.	*Perturbation*	*Antifragility*			
		m (robustness increasing)	*n (resilience increasing)*	*p (functionality extending)*	*q (behaviour extending)*
1.	$P(1;13)^{1///22/}$		x	x	
2.	$P(1;21)^{///122/}$	x		x	
3.	$P(1;24)^{////22/}$		x	x	
4.	$P(2;6)^{11/22//}$	x		x	x
5.	$P(2;19)^{/////2/}$	x	x		
6.	$P(1;2;4)^{11//2//}$	x		x	
7.	$P(22;23;24)^{2222//2}$		x		x
8.	$P(1;2;\ldots;12;13)^{1//////}$	x		x	

- the external perturbations (no. 2,3,6,7,11,12,13,14,17,18,22,23,24) are liable to be antifragilized in order to extend the trans-membranatical behaviour of the target entity/system in the case;
- it is to be observed that each valid perturbation can be, principled, antifragilized in two directions: the first by choosing between increasing robustness and increasing resilience, and the second by choosing between extending functionality and extending behaviour.

The Case of Overlapped Perturbations

For the case of overlapped perturbations, we must consider the list of valid overlapped perturbations found at point 8.3.3.2. We shall exemplify for (only) some of those overlapped perturbations, randomly selected, in Table 8.7.

8.3.5 *Antifragility: The Case of Overlapped Crises*

In Chap. 5, we have discussed the crises overlapping issue, based on the dominance number (*DN*)—where the dominance of a crisis over another crisis is based on the affinity relationship. The problem with the crises overlapping is, now, to find a mechanism through which the overlapped crises generate a certain class of perturbation, so as to know what type of antifragilizing will enter into action, according to Tables 8.6 and 8.7, respectively. Principled, in the case of overlapped crises, the dominant crisis will be "responsible" for generating the perturbation, since it will dominate also the perturbation that "tries" to emerge from the dominated crisis (or crises). Consequently, the way in which the antifragility will work on the perturbation is similar to the way examined in the case of a single crisis—we have here a problem of the type *as if*.[4] Of course, the main analytical effort will be transferred to the issue of establishing the dominant crisis in the overlapped group of crises.

8.4 Facing Crises Based on Sustainability

As Fig. 8.1 suggests, the property of sustainability embeds the three properties: robustness, resilience and antifragility. Consequently, the sustainability working is gradual and its logic is the following: resist, recover, fructify (*RRF*). The *RRF* mechanism is, therefore, its own mechanism of sustainability. The sustainability passes from a passive resistance (robustness) to an active recovering (resilience) and, finally, to benefitting from the state of affairs (antifragility). As mentioned before, the transition from one form to another of the sustainability working takes place only at the ceiling threshold reaching the previous specific action, namely: resilience acts when the robustness is defeated, and the antifragility acts when the resilience fails.

8.4.1 Robustness Phase

The Case of a Single Crisis

The target entity (system/network) is put under pressure to change from the perturbation generated by the (societal) crisis, because of the sufficiency predicate of robustness called *threshold sensitivity* ($RO1$). In fact, the robustness defences the targeted entity as long as it is still inside the hormesis area, that is, below the ceiling threshold (P_t^S).

What seems to be of particular interest here is the way in which the types of perturbation caused by the crisis ($P^{abcdefg}$) engage the robustness working. Our opinion is organized in Table 8.8—we advise readers to recall the meanings of the notations of how robustness works, from Chap. 1, Sect. 1.1, (ii), (c):

Discussion (Two Hypostases Randomly Selected)

- let us consider the cell ($d1$, RO_{C2}^2): we have an *internal* perturbation ($d = 1$), generated by a single crisis; from the robustness perspective, that perturbation must (or can) be countered by *decreasing* the level of the ceiling threshold of the robustness in the target entity/system (RO_{C2}^2). The justification is as follows:

Table 8.8 Robustness working against perturbations generated by a single crisis

		(C1): dead zone trend			*(C2): trend of threshold levels*			*(C3): trend of the hormesis level*		
		RO^1_{C1}	RO^2_{C1}	RO^0_{C1}	RO^1_{C2}	RO^2_{C2}	RO^0_{C2}	RO^1_{C3}	RO^2_{C3}	RO^0_{C3}
a	1		x		x					x
	2			x	x			x		
b	1	x			x				x	
	2			x			x			x
c	1			x	x				x	
	2	x				x		x		
d	1		x			x		x		
	2		x			x				x
e	1			x			x	x		
	2			x			x	x		
f	1	x					x		x	
	2		x			x		x		
g	1		x		x				x	
	2			x		x				x
Total		3	5	6	5	5	4	6	4	4

Source: Author

- being an internal perturbation, this means that the control of the target entity over the perturbation concerned is relatively high, so the robustness does not need to be too large (remember that the larger robustness, the more expensive the redundancy that must be provided by the target entity);
- let us, also, consider the cell (*g*1, RO^0_{C1}): we have a *cumulative* perturbation (*g* = 1), generated by a single crisis; from the robustness perspective must (or can) be countered by a *conservative* trend of the dead zone of the robustness in the target entity/system (RO^0_{C1}). The justification is as follows:
- being a cumulative perturbation, this means that the pressure towards change exerted on the target entity/system increases more and more. If the ceiling threshold of the robustness would be extended or narrowed, then the cumulation phenomenon would adapt to a larger or a narrower space of manifestation, so that the perturbation could escape from the control. Consequently, the moving room of reaction of the target entity/system is better to remain unchanged.

The Case of Overlapped Crises

Regarding the case of overlapped crises in counteracting the perturbation through the property of robustness, some preliminary considerations are needed:

- in the overlapped crises case, the particular perturbation initiated in the target entity/system is caused by the (affinity-based) dominant crisis in the set of overlapped crises. This means that the decision-maker in counteracting the perturbation in the case must look to the structure of the overlapped crises to identify the dominant crisis;
- the antifragilizing of the perturbation caused by the dominant crisis is very similar to the case of a single crisis;
- however, a problem could arise here: what about the recessivity of the perturbations "ready" to be initiated by the (affinity-based) dominated crises in the overlapped crises? We provide some considerations in the matter:
  - the individual crises in the overlapped set of crises have, each of them, the potential to initiate their own perturbations. As the (affinity-based) domination is an objective phenomenon, the objectification of the effective perturbation refers to the dominant crisis;
  - in such a situation, the other perturbations, belonging to the other crises in the overlapped set of crises, enter a state of recessivity;
  - but recessivity does not mean disappearing—those potential perturbations act, behind the scenes, through an invisible synergic process, namely:

    the recessive perturbations that are convergent with the dominant crisis's perturbation could strengthen the last perturbation, while the perturbations that are divergent with the dominant crisis's perturbation could weaken it;

    consequently, we can have, as a resultant, a more or less level/intensity of the dominant crisis's perturbation than the nominal, so to speak, level of it;

    of course, such a phenomenon must be under the decision-maker's attention and, if possible, should be modelled both logically and quantitatively. Perhaps, an indicator of perturbations "mass of recessivity" could be calculated, as well as synergic coefficients of perturbations in the overlapped crises sets.

Nota bene 1: in fact, such a "return" of recessivity in the case of overlapped crises happens too in the case of robustness way of counteracting the perturbation, as well as in the case of autopoieticity (see point 8.5).

Nota bene 2: it is obvious that recessivity is a general topic in societal dynamics, including the issue of societal crises—as known, in the Biology field, recessivity is well studied and understood, focused on the genes (Wilkie, 2005; Billiard et al., 2021; Bourguet, 1999). In the societal field, in Psychology (Popoveniuc, 2023), about self-reflexivity, in Philosophy of History (Florian, 1983, 1987), about the world's structure, in Logic (Lupasco, 1987), about the *hidden middle*—neither excluded nor included.

<u>Supplementary discussion: about relationships between dominance and recessivity</u>

We said above that the perturbation initiated by the dominant crisis in a set of overlapped crises usually causes the recessivity of the perturbations which, potentially, other crises under that overlapping could initiate. Here, we shall develop a little bit this idea, by combining the idea of (affinity-based) domination of the crisis over the overlapped set of crises with the general typology of perturbations, as established previously.

(i) let us consider two (societal) crises that are overlapped, and this overlapping is valid, that is, does not generate logical incompatibilities: $C_1 = C_{51423}^{35142}$, and $C_2 = C_{51423}^{31425}$. *Nota bene*: the example is taken from Chap. 5, point 5.4.1, (c);
(ii) we already know, from Chap. 5, that $G_{(12)} = 8$, so $C_1 \rtimes C_2$, that is C_1 dominates over C_2;[5]
(iii) the highest score in the dominance coefficient ($G_{(12)}$) is brought by the class of crisis parameter ε (signification), namely $\tilde{g}_1 = 16$. We can presume that the perturbation that C_1, as dominant crisis, will initiate into the target entity/system is based on the signification of the C_1;
(iv) regarding C_2, the potential perturbation it could have initiated if it was not dominated is associated with the lowest $\tilde{g}_i$ (*nota bene*: since, if C_2 would have dominated C_1, then that value would have been the highest)—this is $\tilde{g}_4 = -9$, which means the parameter α would count as the cause of the perturbation;
(v) consequently, that type of perturbation will become recessive in C_2.

Table 8.9 Intensity of recessivity of perturbations, depending on the class of parameters of crisis

		C_1				
		ε	α	δ	β	γ
C_2	ε	*	*	*	?	?
	α	**	*	*	*	?
	δ	**	**	*	*	*
	β	* * *	**	**	*	*
	γ	* * *	* * *	**	**	*

Source: Author

We shall provide now a general assessment of the recessivity in the case of overlapping crises (Table 8.9). This table functions as follows: if the effective perturbation is caused by the parameter "*x*" ($\in\{\alpha,\beta,\gamma,\delta,\varepsilon,\}$) of the dominant crisis, then one or more types of perturbations belonging to the dominated crises become recessive. *Nota bene*: the number of "stars" directly proportionally indicates the force of recessivity. Of course, the force of recessivity is directly proportional to the value of the parameter delivering the effective perturbation of the dominant crisis and inversely proportional to the value of the parameter that would have provided that effective perturbation if the dominance did not exist.

Discussion

- the degree of recessivity increases with the order of the class parameter of the generic (societal) crisis, on the one hand, and with the "positive" distance (in the order $\varepsilon\alpha\delta\beta\gamma$ of those classes, as it has been proposed previously) between the class parameters—for instance, the recessivity caused by the perturbation of a dominant crisis under the class ε on the perturbation of class β of a dominated crisis, is greater than the recessivity caused by that perturbation of the dominant crisis on the perturbation of the class α of the dominated crisis (the sign "* * *" for β, compared with the sign "**" for α);
- when the distance mentioned becomes "negative", the degree of recessivity is at the minimum level or even undetermined (the sign "?").

It could be of (at least) methodological interest and usefulness to build up something that could be called the recessivity function of the dominated perturbation. In such a matter, we propose the following considerations:

(i) notations:
- $R(x \to y)$: recessivity degree of the disturbance generated by the class parameter x of the dominant crisis on the disturbance generated by the class parameter y of the dominated crisis—absolute value;
- $r(\alpha \to \delta)$: recessivity degree – relative value

(ii) calculation:
- if we resume the two crises above mentioned ($C_1 = C_{51423}^{35142}$, and $C_2 = C_{51423}^{31425}$), then we have:
  according to class ε, "5": $\tilde{g}_5 = g_5 \cdot d_5 = 0 \cdot 5 = 0$
  according to class α, "1": $\tilde{g}_1 = g_1 \cdot d_1 = 4 \cdot 4 = 16$
  according to class δ, "4": $\tilde{g}_4 = g_4 \cdot d_4 = -3 \cdot 3 = -9$
  according to class β, "2": $\tilde{g}_2 = g_2 \cdot d_2 = 2 \cdot 2 = 4$
  according to class γ, "3": $\tilde{g}_3 = g_3 \cdot d_3 - 3 \cdot 1 = -3$
- this means that $G_{(12)} = 0 + 16 - 9 + 4 - 3 = 8$, so C_1 dominates C_1, namely the perturbation initiated by the two overlapped crises is belonging to C_1 and is of α type;
- the perturbation belonging to C_2, which enters recessivity is of δ type (the highest negative value of $\tilde{g}$ s). Nota bene: the algebraic sign must be changed to get positive value for R;
- we propose to calculate $$R(x \to y) = \frac{\tilde{g}_\alpha}{\tilde{g}_\delta}$$
- in our example: $$R(\alpha \to \delta) = \frac{\tilde{g}_\alpha}{\tilde{g}_\delta} = \frac{16}{9} = 1.78$$

(iii) interpretation:
- the absolute value of the recessivity coefficient must have a comparable (both in space and in time), so it would be useful to transform it into a value belonging to the real interval $[0, 1]$, through the numerical normalization;
- firstly, we need the maximum values for $\tilde{g}$ s; these values are:
  for ε: $M_\varepsilon = \tilde{g}_\varepsilon^{\max} \cdot d_5 = 4 \cdot 5 = 20$
  for α: $M_\alpha = \tilde{g}_\alpha^{\max} \cdot d_1 = 4 \cdot 4 = 16$
  for δ: $M_\delta = \tilde{g}_\delta^{\max} \cdot d_4 = 4 \cdot 3 = 12$
  for ε: $M_\beta = \tilde{g}_\beta^{\max} \cdot d_2 = 4 \cdot 2 = 8$

for ε: $M_\gamma = \tilde{g}_\gamma^{\max} \cdot d_3 = 4 \cdot 1 = 4$

- secondly, we need the minimum values for $\tilde{g}$ s, noted m_x; obviously, these values are 0 for all class parameters;
- thirdly, we shall normalize the values for $\tilde{g}$ s (note the normalized values with N_x), so:

$$N_x = \frac{\tilde{g}_x - m_x}{M_x - m_x}$$

- for the particular example above, we have, successively:

$$\tilde{g}_\alpha = 16$$

$$M_\alpha = 16$$

$$m_\alpha = 0$$

$$\tilde{g}_\delta = 9$$

$$M_\delta = 12$$

$$m_\alpha = 0$$

$$N_\alpha = \frac{16}{16} = 1$$

$$N_\delta = \frac{9}{12} = 0.75$$

$$r(\alpha \to \delta) = \frac{N_\alpha}{N_\delta} = \frac{1}{0.75} = 1.33$$

Extra developments

We can try to normalize to the $\tilde{g}$ s, like above, but the rapport: $\frac{\tilde{g}_x}{\tilde{g}_y}$, for $x, y \in \{\varepsilon, \alpha, \delta, \beta, \gamma\}$. For this, we need the maximum values, and the minimum values, respectively for $R(x \to y)$. Table 8.10 provides the needed information. *Nota bene*: for algebraic reasons (more exactly, to avoid the value 0 for the minimum values of $\tilde{g}$ s, we introduce a change, namely:

$\tilde{g} = g \cdot (d+1)$. Consequently, we have: $M_\varepsilon = 25$, $M_\alpha = 20$, $M_\delta = 15$, $M_\beta = 10$, $M_\gamma = 5$, respectively: $m_\varepsilon = 5$, $m_\alpha = 4$, $m_\delta = 3$, $m_\beta = 2$, $m_\gamma = 1$).

In Table 8.11 are determined the difference $R_{max}(x \to y) - R_{min}(x \to y)$

- if we note $\bar{r}(\alpha \to \delta)$ the normalized value of $r(\alpha \to \delta)$, it results, for the example taken above, that $\bar{r}(\alpha \to \delta) = \frac{N_\alpha^r}{N_\delta^r}$;
- as $N_{(\alpha \to \delta)}^r = \frac{R(\alpha \to \delta) - R_{\min}(\alpha \to \delta)}{R_{\max}(\alpha \to \delta) - R_{\min}(\alpha \to \delta)} = \frac{1.78 - 0.27}{6.67 - 0.27} = 0.236$, so the intensity with which the perturbation of type δ that would have been produced by C_2 in the absence of C_1 domination becomes recessive is relatively small, it is at circa 23.6% from the origin of the unitary real interval.

The issue of recessivity of the "best qualified" perturbation in the dominated crises when a crisis overlapping happens is of great importance for prediction at the societal level. Of course, the predictability regarding the recessivity, i.e., regarding the benign character of the perturbation concerned, is inversely proportional to the value of $N_{(x \to y)}^r$. This way, the overlapped crises could be better handled and, as one of the (possible) results, the antifragility could better work.

8.4.2 *Resilience Phase*

The resilience defence line enters into action when the ceiling threshold of robustness is reached. If robustness is, so to speak, a plastic property, resilience is an elastic one. This means that, when the ceiling threshold of robustness is reached, the target entity/system registers a structural change. Then, the resilience, which is a conservative force, tries to move back the target entity/system to its state existing before the robustness failure. The resilience, resilient property and resilientor device were described in Chap. 1, point 1.2, and those ideas will not be repeated here—the reader is invited to refresh them from Chap. 1.

Table 8.10 Data regarding maximum and minimum values of $R(x \to y)$

	ε	α	δ	β	γ
ε	$R_{max}(\varepsilon \to \varepsilon) = 5$	$R_{max}(\varepsilon \to \alpha) = 6.25$	$R_{max}(\varepsilon \to \delta) = 8.3$	$R_{max}(\varepsilon \to \beta) = 12.5$	$R_{max}(\varepsilon \to \gamma) = 25$
	$R_{min}(\varepsilon \to \varepsilon) = 0.2$	$R_{min}(\varepsilon \to \alpha) = 0.25$	$R_{min}(\varepsilon \to \delta) = 0.33$	$R_{min}(\varepsilon \to \beta) = 0.5$	$R_{min}(\varepsilon \to \gamma) = 1$
α	$R_{max}(\alpha \to \varepsilon) = 4$	$R_{max}(\alpha \to \alpha) = 5$	$R_{max}(\alpha \to \delta) = 6.67$	$R_{max}(\alpha \to \beta) = 10$	$R_{max}(\alpha \to \gamma) = 20$
	$R_{min}(\alpha \to \varepsilon) = 0.16$	$R_{min}(\alpha \to \alpha) = 0.8$	$R_{min}(\alpha \to \delta) = 0.27$	$R_{min}(\alpha \to \beta)=0.4$	$R_{min}(\alpha \to \gamma) = 0.8$
δ	$R_{max}(\delta \to \varepsilon) = 3$	$R_{max}(\delta \to \alpha) = 3.75$	$R_{max}(\delta \to \delta) = 5$	$R_{max}(\delta \to \beta) = 7.5$	$R_{max}(\delta \to \gamma) = 15$
	$R_{min}(\delta \to \varepsilon) = 0.12$	$R_{min}(\delta \to \alpha) = 0.15$	$R_{min}(\delta \to \delta) = 0.2$	$R_{min}(\delta \to \beta) = 0.3$	$R_{min}(\delta \to \gamma) = 0.6$
β	$R_{max}(\beta \to \varepsilon) = 2$	$R_{max}(\beta \to \alpha) = 2.5$	$R_{max}(\beta \to \delta) = 3.33$	$R_{max}(\beta \to \beta) = 5$	$R_{max}(\beta \to \gamma) = 10$
	$R_{min}(\beta \to \varepsilon) = 0.08$	$R_{min}(\beta \to \alpha) = 0.1$	$R_{min}(\beta \to \delta) = 1.13$	$R_{min}(\beta \to \beta) = 0.2$	$R_{min}(\beta \to \gamma) = 0.4$
γ	$R_{max}(\gamma \to \varepsilon) = 1$	$R_{max}(\gamma \to \alpha) = 1.25$	$R_{max}(\gamma \to \delta) = 1.67$	$R_{max}(\gamma \to \beta) = 1.67$	$R_{max}(\gamma \to \gamma) = 5$
	$R_{min}(\gamma \to \varepsilon) = 0.04$	$R_{min}(\gamma \to \alpha) = 0.05$	$R_{min}(\gamma \to \delta) = 0.07$	$R_{min}(\gamma \to \beta) = 0.07$	$R_{min}(\gamma \to \gamma) = 0.02$

Source: Author

Table 8.11 Data regarding $\Delta_{(x \to y)} = R_{max}(x \to y) - R_{min}(x \to y)$

	ε	α	δ	β	γ
ε	$\Delta_{(\varepsilon \to \varepsilon)} = 4.8$	$\Delta_{(\varepsilon \to \alpha)} = 6$	$\Delta_{(\varepsilon \to \delta)} = 7.97$	$\Delta_{(\varepsilon \to \beta)} = 12$	$\Delta_{(\varepsilon \to \gamma)} = 24$
α	$\Delta_{(\alpha \to \varepsilon)} = 3.84$	$\Delta_{(\alpha \to \alpha)} = 4.2$	$\Delta_{(\alpha \to \delta)} = 6.4$	$\Delta_{(\alpha \to \beta)} = 9.6$	$\Delta_{(\alpha \to \gamma)} = 19.2$
δ	$\Delta_{(\delta \to \varepsilon)} = 2.88$	$\Delta_{(\delta \to \alpha)} = 3.6$	$\Delta_{(\delta \to \delta)} = 4.8$	$\Delta_{(\delta \to \beta)} = 7.2$	$\Delta_{(\delta \to \gamma)} = 14.4$
β	$\Delta_{(\beta \to \varepsilon)} = 1.92$	$\Delta_{(\beta \to \alpha)} = 2.4$	$\Delta_{(\beta \to \delta)} = 2.2$	$\Delta_{(\beta \to \beta)} = 4.8$	$\Delta_{(\beta \to \gamma)} = 9.6$
γ	$\Delta_{(\gamma \to \varepsilon)} = 0.96$	$\Delta_{(\gamma \to \alpha)} = 1.2$	$\Delta_{(\gamma \to \delta)} = 1.6$	$\Delta_{(\gamma \to \beta)} = 1.6$	$\Delta_{(\gamma \to \gamma)} = 4.98$

Source: Author

8.4.3 *Antifragility Phase*

This phase was already discussed at point 8.3. Of course, the antifragilizing process enters into action if and when the resilience action fails.

8.5 Facing Crises Based on Autopoieticity

As shown in Chap. 1, the autopoieticity is a self-organizing property of a system (or network, after the case) aimed at transforming the system/network so that its previous cycle finishes and a new cycle begins—it is as if that system/network would be reset. About this resetting some considerations could be of usefulness.

- autopoieticity is characterized by the four sufficiency predicates established in Chap. 1: namely (AP_1): structural replicability;[6] (AP_2): operational closure; (AP_3): relational openness; (AP_4): procedural closure. It is to be observed that, from the four attributes, three are "hosted" by the entity itself (AP_1, AP_2, and AP_4), being of a closure nature;
- coming into existence of the autopoieticity has the following features and "reasons":
  - the action of autopoieticity is triggered if and when the sustainability exhausts its potential and, as a result, the target entity/system becomes or is on the point of becoming unstable. Therefore, in our model, as provided in this book, the *sharp identity* of the target entity/system is preserved throughout the four (concatenated defence lines: robustness–resilience–antifragility–sustainability). By sharp identity we understand the following characteristics:

the structure of the target entity/system is maintained almost punctually, only with inherent oscillations inside the minimal threshold of structural breaking;

consequently, the functions of the target entity/system keep their predictability based on invariant structure;

the state vectors of the target entity/system are similar during the action of the *RRAS* (robustness–resilience–antifragility–sustainability) pattern;

- the "sign" that the target entity/system is on the point to lose its sustainability is delivered by a too-large (beyond a pre-accepted threshold) failure in predictions (so, in predictability) of the functions/effects associated with the target entity/system functioning;

- the way in which the autopoieticity works can be described as follows:
  - since the autopoieticity enters into action when the unsustainability exhibits its first signals, it is needed to identify the exact perturbation that has provoked such a situation—in fact, the perturbation in the case has infringed all the four defence lines of *RRAS*, so it is about a perturbation very "performant";
  - this means that, in the structural statu quo of the target entity/system, is (perhaps, repeatably) possible that a perturbation to infringe the *RRAS* defence device;
  - in conclusion, something must be modified in the target entity structure so that the probability that a future perturbation to penetrate the *RRAS* device be considerably mitigated or at limit eliminated;
  - the solution is a self-reparation of the structure, or a self-restructuring, namely, exactly the logical content of the autopoiesis;[7]
  - the process of autopoiesis is based on the four sufficiency predicates above mentioned of the property of autopoieticity.

8.5.1 Distinguishing Between the Two Kinds of Unpredictability

We have seen above that the triggering moment of the autopoieticity is indicated by the entering of the target entity/system into a state of unpredictability, since the sustainability provides a large area of predictability. Generally, the unpredictability of an entity/system/network is based on its complexity. By complexity, we understand a property that is provided exclusively by the presence of free will. Free will is encapsulated in cultural beings only, and cultural beings are those beings capable of representations—that is, of perception without the *in actu* presence of the perceived object. In such a conceptual framework, any entity/system/network in which humans exist is, *eo ipso*, unpredictable. The question is: if this is the state of affairs, it means that an entity "endowed" with humans is always unpredictable (at least to some degree), so it is not required at all to exhaust the RRAS procedure to trigger the action of autopoieticity. We comment on this issue:

- free will is a property that provides the possibility (not the necessity) to oppose artefactual (not natural) constraints.[8] The representation capacity allows at least two capabilities: (a) *ex-ante* factual imagination and (2) *ex-post* counterfactual testing;
- so, we have to distinguish between the unpredictability triggered by free will (let us call it: *immanent unpredictability*) and the unpredictability triggered by sustainability exhaustion, as shown before (let us call it: *transcendent unpredictability*);
- while the immanent unpredictability is a necessary unpredictability, the transcendent one is contingent, i.e., possible and non-necessary;
- in such a… structure of the unpredictability property, how could we distinguish between the two species of unpredictability? We advance the following proposal:
  - properly speaking, it is difficult enough to *ex-ante* distinguish between immanent unpredictability and transcendent unpredictability, since the unsustainability arising could happen at the same time as the manifestation of free will. In fact, here the following aspects should be highlighted:

    the immanent unpredictability can exist without any connection (either causal or conditional) to the transcendent unpredictability, namely even inside the "tunnel" of *RRAS* device;

    instead, the transcendent unpredictability cannot happen else than by intermediation of the immanent unpredictability, since all predictions are made by human beings, so the transcendent unpredictability takes the coat of the immanent unpredictability;

    this is the crucial reason based on which the two kinds of unpredictability cannot, principled, be ex-ante distinguished;

- however, *ex-post*, the two kinds of unpredictability should be distinguished, in order to know if the moment of autopoiesis has come or not yet—the autopoieticity's time to enter into action is signalled by the transcendent unpredictability. We think as follows:
  - the transcendent unpredictability is based on a (theoretical) rationality model, namely, the predictions issued are based on predictors with a structural nature;
  - as unsustainability signifies a structural change in the target entity/system (else, the sustainability would have continued), it results that it is needed for a new structure, or a sufficient change of the existent structure, so to reconstruct the required structural predictors;
  - in conclusion, the basic criterion to distinguish between immanent unpredictability and transcendent unpredictability is either the lack or the significant deterioration of the structural predictors in the target entity/system.[9]

8.5.2 *About the Identity Threshold*

So, if the signal of the unsustainability of the target entity/system arises,[10] then the autopoieticity enters into action. The "task" of autopoieticity, as said before, is to repair, reconstruct or even invent a structural basis of the target entity so that the cycle of the fight against the perturbations generated by the societal crisis (or the set of overlapped crises) be resumed inside the *RRAS* process. The question is: after autopoieticity action, does the target entity/system remain the same, in other words, should the autopoieticity preserve the identity of the target entity? We develop our positioning in the following:

- principled, the autopoieticity action is not required to preserve the identity of the target entity, it should implement all the changes needed (at a logically sufficient level) in order to restore its sustainability;
- as shown before, both sustainability and unsustainability are effects of the structure of the target entity; if unsustainability can be eradicated only by such a structural change so that the identity of the target entity is compromised, that compromising is not "illegal" from our point of view in the matter, so it must be done;

- as the entity/system identity is provided by the very structure of that entity/system, it results that:
  - related to the system identity, we think the proposition of Imre Lakatos[11] regarding the concept of paradigm (Kuhn, 1970) in the knowledge field (Lakatos, 1970) is valid;
  - the identity of a system is done by its role in the environment into which it is "sunken". The role is, of course, accomplished by the system's functions which, in turn, are the result of the system's structure;
  - however, not all functions are directly involved in role objectifying, but only a few of them are decisive/crucial in this matter. We would call this set of functions hard-core functions, and they are responsible for generating and preserving the very identity of the system concerned;
  - following Lakatos's suggestion, and *mutatis mutandis*, the system's functions that are not decisive/crucial for the role accomplishing will be called auxiliary functions. While the hard-core functions are necessary, the auxiliary functions are contingent;
  - to conclude, the immanent unpredictability exists even in the case in which the hard-core functions are unchanged, i.e., the corresponding hard-core structure of the system is preserved, while the transcendent unpredictability exists if and only if the hard-core functions are changed, i.e., the hard-core structure of the system is not preserved;
  - this means it can be accepted (at least theoretically) that there is a threshold that marks the point at which the autopoieticity entered into action initiates another system—it could be called the *identity threshold*;
  - in fact, autopoieticity cannot act any other way than altering the identity of the system, while the entire path *RRAS* had preserved that identity.

Nota bene: one could ask how we know that the two systems—the system before the autopoieticity action and that after the autopoieticity action—are somewhat connected or, more, if the second is the heritage of the first. Although not always such a question has significance, it raises, however, the issue of the continuity in the dynamics of systems hit by the societal crisis (either singular or embedded in an overlapped set of crises). Our opinion is formulated next:

- for different reasons, an assessment regarding the continuity of a chain of systems affected by the autopoiesis triggered by a societal crisis could be significant, for both theoretical and practical (i.e., from the public policies side) requirements;
- like in the case of the person's identity fate under the changes that happen during his/her life, there is a "connection line" which is the witness of the system's heritage: the history. In fact, there are two historical witnesses: (a) internal history; (b) external (environmental) history;
  - in the case of a person, the internal history is the very psychological memory of that person and the external history is constituted by the social registrations (including the psychological memories of other contemporary persons) of actions and other forms of manifestations of the person in the case;
  - in the general case of (any) system, the internal memory is held by the system itself—remember that both the resilience property and antifragility property require a memory device in order to know all time the state that must be recovered, respectively the state that could be improved by fructifying the perturbation generated by the crisis; as for the external memory, it is, like in the case of a person, constituted by the registrations held by the other systems in the environment of the system concerned.

Generally, autopoieticity action has as one of the main secondary objectives (the primary one is, of course, to restore sustainability or, equivalently, transcendent predictability), namely that of preserving the role of the system concerned. If that role cannot be preserved by modifying the hard-core structure, i.e., by altering the identity of the initial system, then either the role is changed (in a more complex process of rearranging the roles in the society) or the hard-core functions are (re)designed so that they can accomplish the (approximate) same role.

8.5.3 *Autopoieticity Working: The Case of a Single Crisis*

In the case of a single crisis ($C_{51423}^{\varepsilon\alpha\delta\beta\gamma}$) becomes important to identify the most probable[12] perturbation that could trigger the autopoiesis action in the target entity/system, related to the generic perturbation $P^{abcdefg}()$.

Firstly, we must identify the parameter of the generic (societal) crisis that is most probable to generate a perturbation capable of modifying the hard-core of the structure inside the target entity. It seems to be the δ parameter, that is, the impact of the crisis. Regarding the species of this parameter that could be credited with the potential to affect the hard-core part of the structure so that the new state of the target entity generates unpredictability (from the transcendent unpredictability side), we think they are either the species $\delta = 1$, i.e., the impact is exerted directly on the structure, or $\delta = 2$, i.e., the impact is exerted on the rationality which is valid/accepted within the target entity/system. So, the crisis-agent of the perturbation is: $C_{51423}^{--\delta--}$, with the individuals: (a) C_{51423}^{--1--}; respectively (b) C_{51423}^{--2--}.

Secondly, we must identify the species of perturbation which is (again) the most probable[13] to be generated by the two individuals of the crisis. In this matter, we make the following considerations:

- the Bayesian probabilities can be allocated to the two values of the crisis's parameter δ so the generating processes of perturbations in the target entity/system are the following (Table 8.12)—the notations have the meanings: "1" means high Bayesian probability; "0" means medium Bayesian probability; "−1" means low Bayesian probability.

Table 8.12 Qualitative Bayesian probabilities allocation from crisis to perturbation

		δ	
		1	*2*
a	1	1	0
	2	0	0
b	1	−1	0
	2	0	1
c	1	−1	−1
	2	0	0
d	1	−1	0
	2	0	1
e	1	1	0
	2	0	0
f	1	0	−1
	2	0	1
g	1	0	1
	2	−1	0

Source: Author

Discussion

- for $\delta = 1$, the perturbation that is the most probably to be generated by the singular crisis is $P(\delta = 1)^{1---1--}$, namely, a perturbation structurally caused, of institutive character and structural manifestation;
- for $\delta = 2$, the perturbation that is the most probably to be generated by the singular crisis is $P(\delta = 2)^{-2-221}$, namely, a perturbation rationally caused, in the supra-hormetic area, from external origin, with induced character, and cumulative behaviour;
- of course, from another crisis's parameter perspective, other "individuals" of perturbations will be generated. In this context, a hierarchical scheme could be designed, to form a *sui generis* database to use when the events happen;
- analogously with the case of crisis dominance in a set of overlapped crises, we can calculate the dominance relationship between the two active (by contrast with recessive) perturbations. So, we have (with $D_P^{\delta(1\to2)}$ we note the dominance relationship between $P(\delta = 1)^{1---1--}$ and $P(\delta = 2)^{-2-221}$, compared in this order):

$$D_P^{\delta(1\to2)} = (1-0)\cdot7 + (0-2)\cdot6 + (0-0)\cdot5 + (0-2)\cdot4 + (1-2)\cdot3 \\ + (0-2)\cdot2 + (0-1)\cdot1 = 7-12-8-3-4-1 = -21$$

- it results that the perturbation $P(\delta = 2)^{-2-221}$ is dominant over the perturbation $P(\delta = 1)^{1---1--}$, so autopoieticity will try to modify the hard-core of the target entity structure from the perspective of $P(\delta = 2)^{-2-221}$, namely regarding the model of rationality based on which the target entity functions.

8.5.4 *Autopoieticity Working: The Case of Overlapped Crises*

In the case of overlapped crises, what happens additionally compared to the case of a single crisis is the issue of the recessive perturbation (or perturbations) of the dominated crisis (or crises, after the case). In this matter, we provide the following considerations:

(i) analogously with the case of sustainability (point 8.4), the recessive perturbation/s in a set of overlapped crises is/are identified based on the opposite marks of Bayesian probabilities in Table 8.12 (for taking further the particular case at point 8.5.3);

(ii) consequently, we have two recessive perturbations: (a) one generated by $\delta = 1$; (b) one generated by $\delta = 2$, namely:
- for $\delta = 1$: $P_r(\delta = 1)^{abcdefg} \rightarrow P_r(\delta = 1)^{-111--2}$, that is, a perturbation structurally caused, hormetic, repeatable, internal and isolated;
- for $\delta = 2$: $P_r(\delta = 2)^{abcdefg} \rightarrow P_r(\delta = 2)^{--1--1-}$, that is, a perturbation rationally caused, repeatable and spontaneous;

(iii) let us calculate the dominance relationship between the two recessive perturbations in the set of overlapped crises; we have:

$$D_{P_r}^{\delta(1\rightarrow 2)} = (0-0)\cdot 7 + (1-0)\cdot 6 + (1-1)\cdot 5 + (1-0)\cdot 4 + (0-0)\cdot 3 + (0-1)\cdot 2 + (2-0)\cdot 1 = 6 + 4 - 2 + 2 = 10$$

(iv) so, the recessive perturbation $P_r(\delta = 1)^{-111--2}$ dominates the recessive perturbation $P_r(\delta = 2)^{--1--1-}$;

(v) consequently, the property of autopoieticity would try to modify the hard-core structure of the target entity/system, if this perturbation had not been recessive.

Notes

1. However, it can be accepted also functional perturbations (see Chap. 1) but, for the discussion in this chapter, we shall "select" only the perturbations with the potential to change the (basic) structure of the target system.
2. It is to be observed that the synergy is not in space but in time: resilience takes over the results of the "work" of robustness, while antifragility fructifies the results of the "work" of both robustness and resilience.
3. Getting advantages from the perturbation is not unlimited, since the conservation of the entity/system involved could be overtaken by those changes associated with the advantages (based on this reason, the *AF* curve is concave in Fig. 8.1). Consequently, the sustainability is, principled, "undermined" from the inside—above the ceiling threshold T^S, the entity becomes unsustainable.

4. See the (epistemologically) decisive book in the matter of Hans Vaihinger, *The Philosophy of "As If"*—germ. *Die Philosophie des Als Ob* –, Routledge, 2021.
5. We remind the numerical determination: according to class "5": $\tilde{g}_5 = g_5 \cdot d_5 = 0 \cdot 5 = 0$; according to class "1": $\tilde{g}_1 = g_1 \cdot d_1 = 4 \cdot 4 = 16$; according to class "4": $\tilde{g}_4 = g_4 \cdot d_4 = -3 \cdot 3 = -9$; according to class "2": $\tilde{g}_2 = g_2 \cdot d_2 = 2 \cdot 2 = 4$; according to class "3": $\tilde{g}_3 = g_3 \cdot d_3 - 3 \cdot 1 = -3$. The dominance between C_1 and C_2, ($G_{(12)} = \sum_{i=1}^{5} \tilde{g}_i$), is calculated as follows: $G_{(12)} = 0 + 16 - 9 + 4 - 3 = 8$.
6. As will be mentioned below, the structural replicability in the case of autopoieticity is understood under the constraint of preserving the role of the system concerned, not of preserving the very functions—this is a crucial difference from the property of sustainability, which ensures the replicability under the constraint of preserving the functions as such. Of course, how a new set of functions could provide the same role is a question in itself, for example, here arises the issue of the classes of equivalence of those functions, under the criterion of the role identity.
7. Autopoiesis is the process of objectifying the property of autopoieticity.
8. The most common example of such an opposition is that regarding the opposition to the social norms, i.e., to the normative framework of the society. What matters is the very nominal opposition as such, neither the reasons nor the penalties paid for the opposition (violation) of those norms.
9. Of course, free will does not need predictors to make predictions, so sustainability or unsustainability is indistinguishable from the free will perspective.
10. Such an event has an objective character; it does not matter if that event is or is not observed by an observer or actor in the societal framework.
11. Lakatos tried to make compatible Popper's theory of falsifiability and Kuhn's theory of the paradigm, by introducing the concepts of hard core, respectively auxiliary hypotheses, based on which his concept of the research programme is edified.
12. The syntagma "most probable" has a logical (not Kolmogorovian) meaning, namely, it means *most plausible*.
13. Some extra considerations in the matter are, probably, needed here. The most qualified type of probability for the topic under discussion is, of course, the Bayesian one, based both on the objective propensities, as they are known at that time, and on the subjective propensities, associated with the human individual who must take the decision required.

References

Billiard, S., Castric, V., & Llaurens, V. (2021). The Integrative Biology of Genetic Dominance. *Biological Review, 96.*

Bourguet, D. (1999). The Evolution of Dominance. *Heredity, 83.*

Florian, M. (1983, 1987). *Recessivity as a structure of the world.* Eminescu Publishing House (issued in Romanian: "Recesivitatea ca structură a lumii").

Kuhn, T. S. (1970). *The Structure of Scientific Revolutions* (2nd ed.). The University of Chicago.

Lakatos, I. (1970). Falsification and Methodology of Scientific Research Programmes. In I. Lakatos & A. Musgrave (Eds.), *Criticism and the Growth of Knowledge.*

Lupasco, S. (1987). *Le principe d'antagonisme et la logique de l'énergie* (2nd ed.). Éditions Hermann.

Popoveniuc, B. (2023). Self-reflexivity, Recessivity and the Evolution of Psychology. *Brain. Broad Research in Artificial Intelligence and Neuroscience, 14*(4).

Wilkie, A. O. M. (2005). Dominance and Recessivity. In *Encyclopedia of Life Sciences.* John Wiley & Sons, Ltd.

CHAPTER 9

The Crisis Triad: Destabilizing–Redesigning–Restabilizing

9.1 An Introduction

9.1.1 Preamble

We want to advance here a general conjecture on the unfolding of the generic crisis, namely that the stability of the society is exactly the society's neg-entropic state. The "natural" tendency (or propensity) of the society is towards an increase of what must be called social entropy or, more exactly, societal entropy (see Chap. 3 for a detailed examination of this concept). As known, stabilization in the natural world means, essentially, homogenization of the structure (e.g., the thermodynamic death). It is required to clarify this issue regarding the society case. Our position in this matter is as follows:

- any functioning[1] implies an exchange, of a certain kind, between the entities that interact. More than that, no interaction happens if no exchange is possible between involved entities;
- the possibility of an exchange or, in other words, for an exchange to happen, it is required that a disequilibrium between the entities interacting subsist, regarding the exchange object;

E. Dinga, *Economic Resilience During Overlapped Crises*,
https://doi.org/10.1007/978-3-031-80224-9_9

- let us consider the economic interaction between seller and buyer: the seller has many goods but a little money, and the buyer has a lot of money but a few goods (in this example, we have, in fact, a double disequilibrium between seller and buyer). As a result, both entities try to reduce or annihilate those disequilibrium(s), in the market: the buyer gives some money to the seller, and the seller gives some goods to the buyer (as known, the rate of the exchange is called transaction price). So, an exchange happens between those entities, caused by the disequilibrium between them. If the seller had sufficient money, and the buyer had sufficient goods, no exchange would have place;
- the typical economic exchange is a *quid pro quo* phenomenon—someone gives x for receiving y, where $x \neq y$ in nature, although $x \equiv y$ in signification, that is, x is equivalent to y (or can be so, or is presumed to be so);

- the genus of exchange (of which the *quid pro quo* exchange is a species) is the exchange of entropy. The entropy acts in the general interaction like the price in the economic interaction, that is, as a reductionist principle of the exchange;
- consequently, anywhere and anytime an entropic gap happens between two entities (things, properties, relationships), there and then an exchange between the involved entities happens;
- but how the exchange of entropy could happen between two entities with different entropy? We make the following considerations in this matter:
  - *firstly*, we shall talk about the social entropy only, not about thermodynamic or informational entropy;
  - *secondly*, the entropic difference between two entities can be represented either by the entropy or by the neg-entropy;
  - *thirdly*, this means to consider a "law" of the arrow of entropy.[2] The arrow of entropy means that between two interacting systems, if not one of them is of a dissipative type, the entropy spontaneously moves from the system with a (relatively) higher entropy to the system with a (relatively) lower entropy—something analogous with the heat moving law, which is the base of the second principle of Thermodynamics. Let us find the (logical) reasons for which such an arrow of entropy should be accepted:

according to the second law of Thermodynamics, the global entropy in a closed system always tends to increase. Of course, this is an axiom, since it is established inductively (more exactly, based on abduction);

methodologically, we can construct however many closed systems, locally. Even if they are not exactly really closed systems, ideally (i.e., as mental experiments), we can conceive such "pure" closed systems;

so, locally, the second principle of Thermodynamics can whenever work. Consequently, the arrow of entropy seems to be a principle of *causa sui* type;

- a problem that can be raised regards the essence (eidos) of the entropy. Generally, the entropy is a property of a system (no matter it is closed or open) to exhibit a certain degree of order—*Nota bene*: it is about a structural order, of course. But, especially in the societal field, some conceptual difficulties come:
  - the concept (and term) of order versus disorder are, we think, bearer of value, that is, it is axiological, so too anthropomorphic. Maybe, the concept of heterogeneity versus homogeneity could be more appropriate;
  - the reason for such a replacing is very simple: the order is always identified by comparing the actual (structural) state of the system with a pre-existent list of ... known (structural) orders which the observer has, so the qualification of the order/disorder is ambiguous under two perspectives: (a) has a historical nature (the list of orders becomes richer in time, depending on the experience); (b) has an idiosyncratic nature (the list of orders is depending on the scientific [or other] interest of the observer—*Nota bene*: as known, we see only what we already know, that is, there is a theoretical closure of the observational competence);
  - instead, the heterogeneity is much more objectively donated to (any) observer—exactly in the phenomenological view of the donation (of things, properties or relationships) based on intentionality;
  - of course, the heterogeneity is of a structural nature, not of a simple functionality one, so it is measurable (e.g., in Boltzmann's way regarding the Statistical Mechanics). So, the entropy should be viewed as a measure of the heterogeneity (or, better, as a rapport between heterogeneity and homogeneity—perhaps an ingenuous

scientist could bring this rapport inside the real interval [0,1], by numerical normalization) so making it generally comparable in time and space;

- the problem is, now: any heterogeneity can be associated with the entropy? More precisely, the simple increase of the (structural) heterogeneity means, automatically, a decrease of the entropy (and vice-versa)? Some considerations in the matter are done below:
- firstly, it must be accepted that the greater the structural homogeneity, the lower the functionality of a given system. Somewhat, it must be accepted as a "mystic" hypothesis, according to which the functionality is fed by the tension (i.e., disequilibrium, imbalance) between two components/elements of that system (see, e.g., the well-known case of the electrical current which does not circulate inside a conductor material if between the ends of that conductor is not a difference of electrical tension);
- consequently, we must introduce a criterion to identify the "good" (structural) heterogeneity and to dissociate it from the "bad" or "neutral" (structural) heterogeneity. The danger here is to introduce, on the back door, the ... order. To avoid such a danger, we provide the following mentions:
  - the observer (or analyst) does not need to have a list with the known orders associated to any system in the word, where s/he should search an analogy with the observed order in the immediate reality;
  - instead, the observer must either know or desire the role that a given system must play (*Nota bene*: not the functions, but the role[3]);
  - so, an increase in the (structural) heterogeneity of a system is expected to lead to a better accomplishment of the system's role.[4] Although, the introduction of the role seems to take us back to the concept of order, the state of affairs is not quite like that, since:
    - in the society (societal system), any entity is an artefact, so is "endowed" with a role to be accomplished aiming at objectifying the purpose for which that entity has been built;
    - consequently, the role of a given system is known by the human beings involved in observing or working with (or inside) the system in the case;
    - this time, it is not needed to observe (examine) the internal order of a system, but just to compare the role that system

actually accomplishes with the programmed (already known) one;

so, our proposal considerably reduces the difficulties engaged by the issue of identifying the entropy in an entity of artefactual nature; however, the subjective evaluation is not (and cannot be) eliminated;

- to conclude on this issue: the entropy decreases when an increase in the (structural) heterogeneity of a given system happens if and only if the role of that system is preserved or, presumably, augmented; of course, this criterion does not forbid change in the hard-core itself of the system's structure, again, with the condition of preserving (or augmenting) the established or expected role in the case;
- this means that autopoiesis—the only process likely to change the role of a target entity/system by changing its heterogeneity—must "spread" its action until a threshold marking the loss of the target entity/system's identity.

9.1.2 *Identity and Change*

The *first* question that arises in relation to the concept of change is that which concerns the primitiveness of this concept. Is the concept of change a primitive concept, that is, a concept that does not need another concept to logically precede and ground it? The answer is obviously negative. The concept of change needs a foundational concept different from itself, and that is the concept of *identity*. Although the concept of identity is even more problematic than that of change, *hic et nunc* we will proceed axiomatically and consider that it is self-founding, so it is a primitive concept (perhaps on another occasion we will develop, in a separate discussion, the concept of identity). So, starting from the concept of identity we will introduce a concept-vehicle that will "transport" us to the concept of change: this concept-vehicle is that of *alterity*. In the phenomenology of philosophy (i.e., in its logical history), alterity has been considered mostly in a transcendent way (e.g., the *alter ego* has a transcendent nature). For the purposes of the discussion we provoke here, we will consider the more general case of otherness, that is, that case in which it, otherness, can be both transcendent (e.g., for most people God's posing or being is transcendent) and transcendental (e.g., Leo Tolstoy's or Gustav Jung's religious conception calls for a hypostasis or a transcendental being of God).

I would like to make it clear right away that, in our discussion, the concept of transcendental does not necessarily have the meaning introduced by Kant—namely, *a priori*—but it does, however, have the meaning of necessary in a logical sense, that is, non-contingent. In other words, although identity is a primitive (self-grounded) concept, it needs to be truly itself, a "mirror" (the mirror, as a conceptual metaphor, does not entirely preserve the mirrored entity, i.e., it replaces, reciprocally, left to right). The mirrored identity is the very alterity. Let us specify, in a short parenthesis, that the logical necessity of the mirror results, among other things, from the Hegelian considerations regarding the progress of the being of the spirit. It follows, therefore, that identity necessarily generates alterity, that is, the conceptual "vehicle" that, as we see things, will lead to the concept of change and, by a specification to which we will refer at the end of our report, to that of metamorphosis.

The *second* question refers to the very change. Alterity, therefore, distorts identity through mirroring. In other words, identity is necessarily altered (there remains still an insufficiently discussed hypothesis of the disappearance of alterity in the case of reaching the maximum level of entropy in the Universe; in this hypothesis, we will arrive at an identity that is Heideggerian thrown alone into the world, unable to find itself in the absence of otherness. In other words, identity will exist in itself, but it will not exist for itself. This loneliness of identity as the end point of the Universe is, of course, an anguish that itself deserves a separate metaphysics). Altered identity must be considered, from a conceptual point of view, change. At this point in the discussion we will find it useful to accept, previously proposed, the more general case of alterity, namely both as transcendent alterity and as transcendental alterity. Transcendent alterity would mean that the mirror responsible for the "self" of the identity is external to the identity itself (what, in layman's language, we call the benchmark or reference—note, here the term reference does not have its meaning in semiotics, but in physics), while transcendental otherness means that the mirror is internal to identity itself. For example (we will return to this at length in the next paragraph), spatial displacement (which is a species of change) represents a transcendent alteration of identity, since a reference external to identity itself is needed to ascertain spatial displacement, whereas transformation (which, in turn, is a species of change) needs only an inner reference to ascertain that transformation (by the way, in the latter case an outer reference is of no use for ascertaining the transformation, it not being visible from the transcendent). The transcendental alterity is crucial to internalize the signification of change (as the signification of crisis, as shown above).

9.1.3 Change Typology

To arrive at change as transcendental otherness, we will set forth a conceptual scheme that fixes all possible species of change in the Universe, thus:

(1) *Modification*: quantitative alteration of identity, with two sub-species:
   (1.1) *Movement*: change that alters spatial identity;
   (1.2) *Growth*: change that alters dimensional identity;
(2) *Evolution*: qualitative alteration of identity (by qualitative alteration we mean alteration of structure):
(3) *Development*: evolution caused by growth:
(4) *Transformation*: evolution caused by ends (Aristotelian final causes);
(5) *Progress*: evolution caused by values.

A first remark may refer to the fact that modification (with its two subspecies) is a species of change that requires transcendent alterity, in the sense discussed above, while the next four species of change require transcendental alterity. A second remark may refer to the fact that, with regard to species of change that demand a transcendental alterity, evolution and development represent species of change of a general character, that is, species of change not conditioned by the nature of the subject involved (cultural or non-cultural. *Nota bene*: by cultural subject we understand the subject capable of formulating final causes—goals), while transformation and progress represent species of change with a local character (they take place only where we have cultural subjects). Well, in our opinion, it is precisely these last two species of change that are relevant to change as transcendental alterity. We will make three brief comments on this:

(i) since there can be values not associated with a goal (i.e., there can be values without an intention to objectify them through the achievement of a goal), progress and transformation are not confused. Although the idea of a value producing a change without being "embedded" in a goal seems too metaphysical, it is acceptable because, for example, attitude is an externalization of a value not necessarily assigned to a goal but the attitude can produce change;[5]

(ii) neither the concept of transformation nor that of progress should receive any binary connotation: good–bad, desirable–undesirable etc. Change that is evaluated as progress by one subject-observer may be qualified as "regression" by another subject-observer, if the two subject-observers have different (or even opposite) axiological matrices. What is important here is only the fact that the change is generated by values. The concept of transformation must also be viewed in the same way: different subjects who have different goals (e.g., expectations) may qualify a certain goal-generated change as transformation (if their goal has actualized) or as stagnation (if their goal has not actualized) but, however, if that change was caused by the update of a goal, then we are dealing with a transformation;

(iii) neither transformation nor progress need a transcendent reference; they can "self-ascertain" by comparing the two chronologically different versions (of course, an immanent memory is needed here, but this matter will be ignored in the current point), that is, the reference (the "mirror") has a transcendental nature. So, by change as transcendental alterity we will understand only two species of change, as introduced above: transformation (caused by purpose), respectively progress (caused by values). Of course, a deep discussion could be caused by the question: are there really transformations, that is, changes caused by goals but without underlying values? But we ignore here these conceptual developments.

Nota bene: we want to very shortly introduce the concept of *metamorphosis*. Metamorphosis is a species of change that involves neither goals nor values, but involves qualitative alterations. Our feeling is that metamorphosis is a term used to designate, in fact, the concept of development, that is, it refers to an evolution caused by growth. In other words, the pressure of growth will generate qualitative alterations of identity (hence evolution). We find this content of the concept, as such, both in nature and in culture. If, on the other hand, we want to assign purposes or values to metamorphosis (e.g., in the cultural world), then we must be ready to give up the term metamorphosis, since for the concepts of these species of change we already have other naming terms.

9.1.4 Two Problems

(1) The criterion for the system's identity

By now, our belief regarding the preserving of the identity of an entity/system/network was the following: identity preserving is (logically) equivalent to hard-core preserving. This time we must, however, be more rigorous and say that the identity preserving of an entity/system/network is (logically) equivalent to preserving that hard-core structure that conserves or augments the role of that entity/system/network. Of course, this implies we know and can measure that role. It is to be observed that this criterion is a pragmatic one, in line with William James's pragmatism, although this time we do not relate to the utility, but to the role's conservativeness.

(2) Two systems—the same role

What can one say about the situation in which two systems, so having different hard-core structures, achieve the same role? We must dissociate this question into two species: (2.1) the two systems with the same role co-exist; (2.2) the second system derives from the first one by changing the hard-core structure, for instance, through an autopoietic process.

(2.1) Same role—different hard-core structures

This case seems to be possible. Such a possibility is, however, in turn, of two sorts: (a) of ontological sort; (b) of significance sort.

(a) The ontological possibility

The ontological possibility of co-existing of the same role generated by two (or more) different hard-core structures appeals to the issue of what we can call *objectifying equivalence of function sets*. So, we have two different sets of functions, S_F^1, and S_F^2, respectively, so that S_F^1 is generated by a hard-core structure HC^1, and S_F^2 is generated by a hard-core structure HC^2, or: $S_F^1 = f\left(HC^1\right)$, and $S_F^2 = g\left(HC^2\right)$. Principled, the two hard-core structures can be identical among them or different from each other. The key here are the functions *f* and *g*, respectively, that is, the combinations of the structural elements of the two hard-core structures. We shall advance some considerations in this matter.

- the same functions can be combined in different ways, so that every combination can objectify its own role (*Nota bene*: somewhat, the relationships among functions—i.e., the functionality of an entity/ system—manifest as an ontological outcome—i.e., as behaviour). This causal and conditional relationship between functionality and behaviour is not something new in the theory of systems;
- it must be noted that, obviously, we ca write:

$$\left(HC^1 \neq HC^2\right) \rightarrow \begin{cases} f\left(HC^1\right) \neq f\left(HC^2\right) \\ g\left(HC^1\right) \neq g\left(HC^2\right) \end{cases}$$

- in fact, we are searching the condition in which $f(HC^1) \equiv g(HC^2)$
- the way in which different combinations of the functions assigned to a given hard-core structure could objectify the same role (as behavioural manifestation) can be represented, principled as in Fig. 9.1—in fact, there is an indifference curve that describes those combinations of functions that have, as an outcome, the same role (with R^x is noted the role x, with C_R^1 is noted the curve of the potential roles generated by S_F^1, with C_R^2 is noted the curve of the potential roles generated by S_F^2).

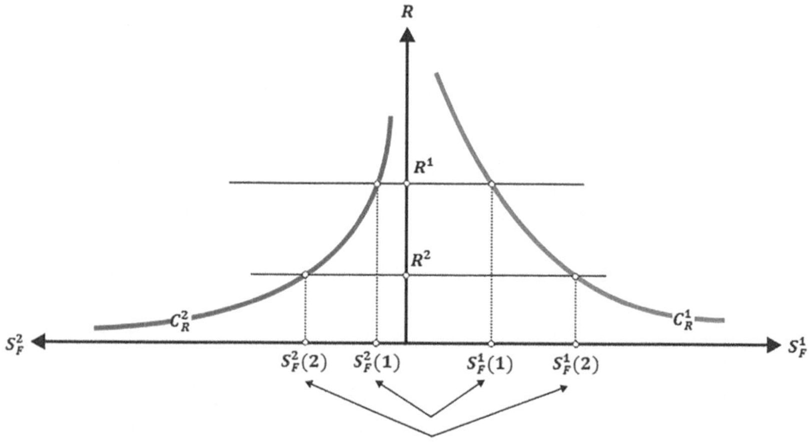

Fig. 9.1 The same role provided by different hard-core structures. *Source*: author

Discussion

- suppose (arbitrary enough, but this arbitrariness does not compromise the reasoning) that the two curves describing the roles that potentially can be achieved by different combinations of functions derived from the two hard-core structures are convex and decreasingly. Note that on the ordinate the roles are "measured" qualitatively, not quantitatively, and on abscissas, the values for S_F^1 and S_F^2 are, also, measured qualitatively, not quantitatively;
- so, for the sets of functions S_F^1, generated by the hard-core structure HC^1, and S_F^2, generated by the hard-core structure HC^2, the same role is reached, namely R^1 (a similar reasoning is valid for the role R^2). This means that the combinations of the functions are more important or more relevant than the sets of functions as such. Of course, the role is depending from two variables: (a) the set of functions that are generated by the hard-core of structure; (b) the way in which those functions are combined to obtain the outcome—that is, the operators noted *f* or *g*;
- the fact that two different causes (namely, two different hard-core structures) can generate the same effect, by two different ways of combining the two different sets of functions that emerged from the two hard-core different structures, is of great importance in managing the systems phenomenology from an ontological perspective.

(b) The significance possibility

The significance possibility that two different hard-core structures generate the same role of the systems involved is more comprehensible, since, as shown in the crisis logical formula, the significance is the parameter of the highest level of determination (ε parameter). We have to do here, in fact, with a hermeneutics, which assigns to the two perceived (e.g., measured) roles the same signification, no matter their ontological differences among them.

(2.2) Other role by autopoieticity

Now, it remains to be discussed the case of a hard-core structure generated by the autopoieticity action, so we have, in fact, a kinematics from an initial structural hard-core to a final structural hard-core, without the condition of preserving the role.[6] A solution can be that of considering the former case—see (2.1)—namely that when the two successive structural hard-cores are assigned to two different systems. In other words, we can, logically, transform the problem of succession into one of co-existence. But we are interested here in considering the phenomenon of succession. In such a context, the following considerations could be of usefulness:

- the succession of a system from itself can be "proved" by comparing the two roles of the two systems: if the role is the same,[7] then the two systems has the same identity; if not, the two systems are different to each other;
- if the succession is not needed as a result of perturbation caused by a crisis, because the perturbation is rejected as such—we are in the presence of robustness;
- if succession is not needed as a result of perturbation caused by a crisis, because the change induced by the perturbation is restored "*in integrum*"—we are in the presence of resilience;
- if succession is not needed as a result of perturbation caused by a crisis, because the perturbation is, in fact, beneficial to the target system—we are in the presence of antifragility;
- if succession is needed inside the same role, although the hard-core can be changed—we are in the presence of sustainability;
- if succession is needed as a result of perturbation caused by a crisis but the hard-core changing lead to the change in the role—we are in the presence of autopoieticity.

Figure 9.2 illustrates synoptically this "in cascade" reasoning.

The autopoieticity action is aimed at passing beyond the sustainability border, which conserved the role of the target entity/system although changed the hard-core structure. When the sustainability of the system cannot be maintained, the only solution is to change the very role of the target entity/system through the property of autopoieticity. In our opinion, the autopoieticity changes the identity of the target entity/system and, so, the (new) target entity/system takes the pentagonal path of robustness–resilience–antifragility–sustainability–autopoieticity (the *RRASA* path) from the beginning, from the perspective of the new role conferred by autopoieticity.

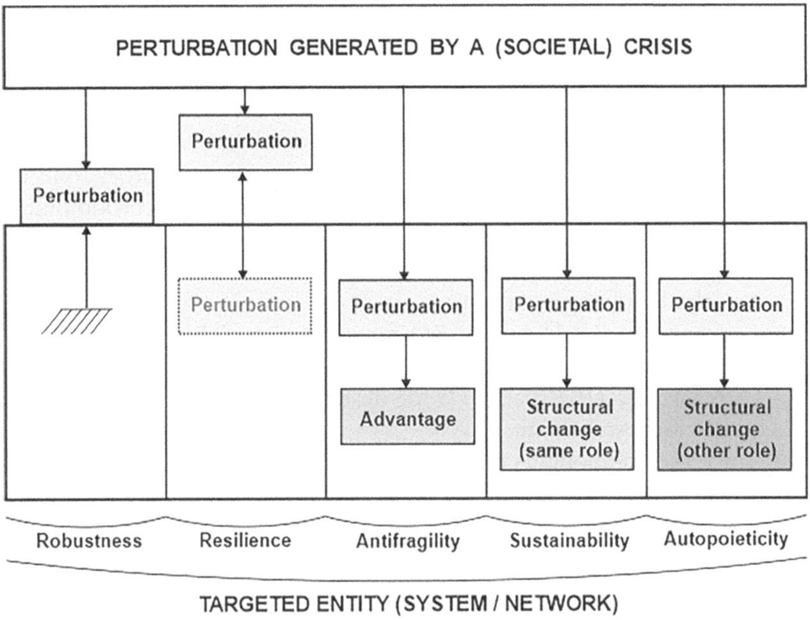

Fig. 9.2 The general "map" of the *RRASA* phenomenology. *Source*: author

9.2 The General Rational of the Crisis's Path

In Chap. 4, we have proposed a rational(ity) of the crisis path in society—its nominal origin, and the necessity of extending from nominal flows to real flows, passing through financial flows. This rational(ity) is, so to speak, a geodesic[8] rational(ity); the crisis cannot avoid following that path. But we need here to develop a more analytical and more comprehensive model of the crisis expansion.

We shall develop a trinomic model of a crisis unfolding, namely a *DRR* (destabilizing–redesigning–restabilizing) model of the society involved.

What we have to clarify is, in fact, to establish a logical (and, if possible, chronological) relationship between the two ways/paths of unfolding of the (societal) generic crisis, including the case of overlapped crises: (a) the *RRASA* path; (b) the *DRR* path. Some preliminary considerations are very adequate here:

- the *RRASA* path is a logical one, as shown and argued previously, while the *DRR* path is an ontological one;
- the concatenation of *RRASA* components is triggered if and as the conditions established are verified, so they are mandatory both in nominal and in chronological order;
- the concatenation of *DRR* components is not mandatory, one or more of them can lack, although, if they appear, the chronological order of that appearance is mandatory too;
- to discern, in writing between the two paths, we shall use, from here on, the following notations:
  - regarding *RRASA* path: *RO*: for robustness; *RE* for resilience; *AF* for antifragility; *S* for sustainability; *AP* for autopoiesis;
  - regarding *DRR* path: *DS* for destabilizing; *RD* for redesigning; *RS* for restabilizing;
- since the components of the *RRASA* path have been explained and interpreted by now, we shall do some considerations on the components of *DRR*, as follows:
  - (*DS*) component of ***destabilizing***: the destabilizing process of *DRR* phenomenology starts, in fact, with the antifragility action. One could observe that the antifragilizing of the target entity/system does not yet mean the identitary change of it, since the role is still preserved, although the structure (even the hard-core structure) could be changed to some extent exactly to integrate/assimilate the advantage provided by antifragilizing. Although we think that the stability of the system (by ensuring the sustainability, as shown before) is not really threatened until the autopoieticity enters in action, that is, until the role is changed or, at least, gains the potential to be changed, however the effect of antifragilizing is or could be that of… fragilizing the target entity/system stability.[9] Essentially, the stage of destabilizing in a target entity/system chreode means the creation of a vulnerability regarding the possibility of changing the role of that entity/system[10]—we think that vulnerability is a necessary companion (or a ***quid pro quo***) of the antifragilizing process. It must be mentioned that the destabilizing stage is an ***operational*** one;
  - (*RD*) component of ***redesigning***: the redesigning stage of *DRR* phenomenology could unfold either triggered by the destabilizing stage or it can be an ordinary (or, even, a planned) action or activity inside the target entity/system. As triggered by the destabiliz-

ing stage, the redesigning stage is mapped on the particular effects generated by the perturbation the crisis is throwing on the societal system, that is, it constitutes a *reaction*, with the adequate reaction norms. As triggered within a plan of adapting the target entity/system to future challenges[11] (including the … predictable crises), the redesigning stage implies an *action*, usually under the logic of the second curve (Handy, 2016). It must be mentioned that the redesigning stage is, however, a *non-operational* one;

- (*RS*) component of *restabilizing*: the restabilizing stage of *DRR* phenomenology addresses the implementation of the outcomes of redesigning stage, especially the outcomes focused on the hard-core structure of the target entity/system. The restabilizing stage is a completely deliberative process (*Nota bene*: as mentioned above, often it is even planned, i.e., is predictable) and, from a logical point of view, it constitutes a hypothesis subject to factual falsifiability—the stability can be or can be not recovered in the future. Of course, the restabilizing stage, at least as intentionality, is unfolded under the aegis of autopoiesis, as this property has been described previously. It must be mentioned that the destabilizing stage is an *operational* one.

In fact, the *DRR* process unfolds in a spiral chreode (Fig. 9.3).

Figure 9.4 tries to suggest, in an overall synoptics, the inter-acting between *RRASA* and *DRR* paths.

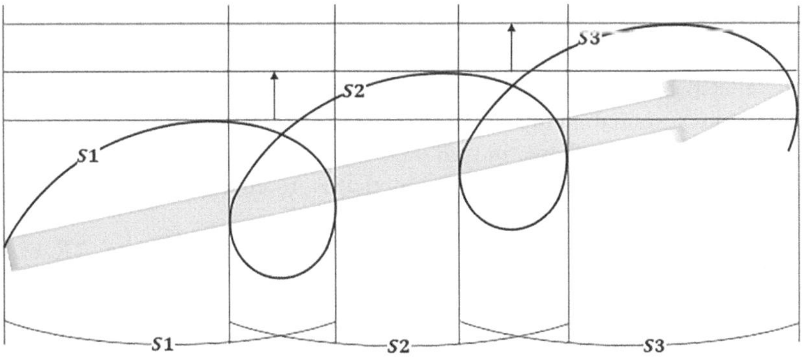

Fig. 9.3 The spirally unfolding of *DRR* concatenation. *Source*: author

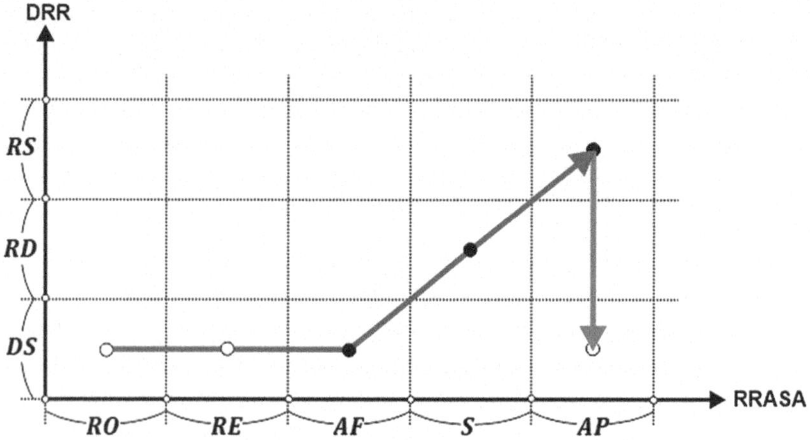

Fig. 9.4 *RRASA — DRR* entangled phenomenology. *Source*: author

Discussion

- the empty circles signify a potential (i.e., not yet actualized) of destabilizing the target entity/system, while the filled circles signify the three stages of the *DRR* logic already actualized;
- inside the robustness and resilience phases of *RRASA* logic the destabilizing of the target entity/system is not possible for the known reasons, while once the antifragility enters into action, the possibility of destabilizing arises;
- the phase of sustainability action (that encapsulates the robustness, resilience and antifragility), in the *RRASA* logic, is compatible with the stage of redesigning from the *DRR* logic;
- when sustainabilizing action fails, the target entity/system enters the autopoieticity phase, in *RRASA* logic, which corresponds to the restabilizing stage in *DRR* logic, that is, to change the hard-core of the structure in the target entity/system;
- once the autopoieticity phase is implemented within the *RRASA* logic, it changes the very role of the target entity/system (i.e., alters its identity), the spiral of the target entity/system chreode take its cycle from the beginning, that is, from the phase of destabilizing within the *DRR* logic.

9.3 The Destabilizing Impact of the Societal Crisis

9.3.1 An Abstract Typology

To examine the destabilizing impact of the societal crisis, we must return to the generic formula of such a crisis, namely $C_{12345}^{\alpha\beta\gamma\delta\varepsilon}$, where: (1) the cause of crisis; (2) the origin of crisis; (3) the chreode of crisis; (4) the impact of crisis; (5) the significance of crisis. According to the relevance for both the observer and actor, the formula becomes $C_{51423}^{\varepsilon\alpha\delta\beta\gamma}$, where each of the five parameters is given five numerical values with a precise meaning, as previously discussed (see Chap. 5).

Obviously, the most "qualified" parameter to provide signals for a possible destabilizing of the target entity/system is δ that addresses exactly the impact. As shown before, the meanings of the numerical values assigned to this parameter are $\delta = 1$—the impact of perturbation generated by the crisis is exerted on the structure, including the hard-core structure; $\delta = 3$—the impact is exerted on the values in the society; $\delta = 2$—the impact is exerted on the rationality beyond the general perception of the crisis and its perturbation; $\delta = 4$—the impact is exerted on the political regime of the society in the case; $\delta = 5$—the impact is exerted on the meta-narrative (i.e., the founding "myth") of the society. *Nota bene*: the order in which the numerical values are listed is exactly the decreasing order of the gravity of the perturbation action on the society as a whole.

We think that another parameter of the generic crisis can also provide "signals" related to the destabilizing impact of the perturbation, namely the parameter ε, that addresses the signification for the observer/actor. The meanings of the numerical values assigned to this parameter are $\varepsilon = 1$—the signification of perturbation generated by the crisis is about survival; $\varepsilon = 4$—the signification is about freedom; $\varepsilon = 2$—the signification is about opportunities; $\varepsilon = 5$—the signification is about self-esteem; $\varepsilon = 3$—the signification is about way of life. *Nota bene*: the order in which the numerical values are listed is exactly the decreasing order of the intensity of signification with which the perturbation does act on the observer/actor.

We think that by combining the two parameters—the very objective impact and the signification of the impact—the true impact of the destabilizing "function" of the generic crisis at the societal level is obtained. More than that, we can identify a typology[12] of the destabilizing impact based

Table 9.1 A typology of the destabilizing impact of the generical crisis

		ε				
		$\varepsilon = 1$	$\varepsilon = 4$	$\varepsilon = 2$	$\varepsilon = 5$	$\varepsilon = 3$
δ	$\delta = 1$	DS_{11}	DS_{14}	DS_{12}	DS_{15}	DS_{13}
	$\delta = 3$	~~DS_{31}~~	DS_{34}	DS_{32}	DS_{35}	DS_{33}
	$\delta = 2$	DS_{21}	DS_{24}	~~DS_{22}~~	DS_{25}	DS_{23}
	$\delta = 4$	DS_{41}	DS_{44}	DS_{42}	DS_{45}	DS_{43}
	$\delta = 5$	~~DS_{51}~~	DS_{54}	~~DS_{52}~~	DS_{55}	DS_{53}

Source: author

exactly on the mentioned combination (Table 9.1.)—$DS_{(\delta\varepsilon)}$ means destabilizing impact of the pair $(\delta\varepsilon)$.

So, 25 theoretical categories of destabilizing impact can exist.

Discussion

- the (four) cancelled cells seem do not work, that is, it seems there is incompatibility between the numerical values of the two parameters;
- the type of destabilizing impact of the generic crisis directly results from the indexes $(\delta\varepsilon)$. For example:
  - DS_{24} means: destabilizing impact exerted on the rationality which the society is based on, perceived as having the signification of reducing/limiting freedom;
  - DS_{15} means: destabilizing impact exerted on the structure of the society, perceived as having the signification of affecting the self-esteem of individuals within that society;
  - DS_{43} means: destabilizing impact exerted on the political regime of the society, perceived as having the signification of affecting the way of life of individuals within that society;
  - the destabilizing impact always manifests in the combined manner only, as Table 9.1. suggests;
  - the (combined) impact strength of the destabilizing stage decreases along the first diagonal in Table 9.1, that is, from DS_{11}—the strongest impact—to DS_{53}—the weakest impact. A synoptic image of such a variation of the degree of impact is suggested in Fig. 9.5, which contains the information of Table 9.1.

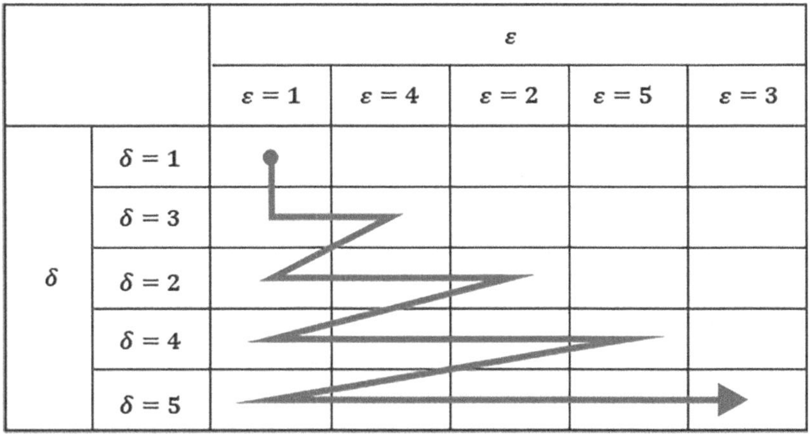

Fig. 9.5 The decreasing "curve" of the impact force of destabilizing stage of a crisis. *Source*: author

9.3.2 *On the Background of the Destabilizing Stage*

As we have seen (especially) in Chap. 4, the generic (societal) crisis has a necessary character—it necessarily occurs in the nominal economy, and necessarily "migrates" towards the real economy. In this paragraph, we shall discuss the ontology of the destabilizing stage (within the *DDR* logic) of the crisis. The following issues seem to be of scientific interest: (i) is the destabilizing stage of the crisis within the *DDR* logic necessary? (ii) is there an own kinematics of the destabilizing stage? (iii) the causal structure of the destabilizing stage.

(i) Necessity versus contingency in the destabilizing stage

The question if the destabilizing stage of the crisis in *DRR* logic is necessary or contingent is not superfluous at all. Indeed, a crisis could be a response (from either the market or the state side) to a former crisis (either just finished or in course). In the hypothesis that the former or current crisis already generated a destabilization (according to the pair ($\delta\varepsilon$) above), then it seems to be inappropriate to speak about a destabilizing stage of the concerned crisis—in fact, it is about rather a restabilizing stage. In this point, we must discuss a very important issue, namely about proper versus improper crises.

A crisis is proper when it holds all the three stages in the *DRR* logic: destabilizing, redesigning, restabilizing. If one or two of the three stages lack, we must speak about an improper crisis. We could speak about: (a) *proper* crisis—crisis holding all the three stages; (b) *improper* reactive crisis of *type 1*—crisis holding the redesigning and restabilizing stages; (c) *improper* reactive crisis of *type 2*—crisis holding the restabilizing stage only. About the last two types of improper crises, we provide the following comments:

- the improper reactive crisis of type 1:
  - it is not so rare case when a perturbation caused by a crisis is "solved" by using another crisis that causes a perturbation that can neutralize the former perturbation. But, of course, it is neither a too-usual procedure, since the deliberatively triggered crisis could cause collateral perturbation which must be, in turn, neutralized, so initiating a regression *ad infinitum*;
  - if it is possible to "construct" a crisis aimed at neutralizing the undesirable impact of a former crisis, then, perhaps, it, to some extent, is possible to restore the target entity/system without using a new … crisis (Costa Lima et al., 2014);
  - one could ask if the improper reactive crisis of type 1 is always a deliberative (discretionary) action or could be also an automatic one. Our opinion in this matter is as follows:

    it must be deliberative/discretionary only, since, as shown previously, the automatic stabilizers—which anticipate the perturbations and treat them when occur—are placed before the phase of antifragility, which is credited as the point when the perturbation has its first chance to happen; more exactly, usually, it is placed inside the phase of resilience;

    of course, conceptually we can speak about the designing of a respondent-crisis into the target entity/system, but methodologically, we cannot speak about that.

Nota bene: here arises a conceptual question: a perturbation is not necessarily an effect of a crisis, although a crisis leads necessarily the target entity/system into a perturbation.

- the improper reactive crisis of type 2:
  - this type could be understood as a particular case of type 1, namely by using a redesigning held in a library of solutions to disturbances generated by societal generic crises; such a library can be completed according to the history of the crises that occurred;
  - like the type 1, this type of improper reactive crisis has a deliberative/discretionary character.

In conclusion, we think the destabilizing stage of a crisis according to the *DRR* logic is a necessary one (Grinin & Kototayev, 2023), else we would have a simple smooth adjustment of the target entity/system, without affecting the structure (a fortiori without affecting the hard-core structure) but, at most, the peripherical functionalities of that system.

(ii) Linearity versus non-linearity in the destabilizing stage

The linearity versus non-linearity of the chreode of the destabilizing stage of a crisis must be examined from the perspective of the presence of free will in the very process of interpretation, decision-making and action. In the societal system, the free will is ubiquitous and it is the main cause of the non-predictability of the societal events. We shall propose a link between the free will presence in societal events and the non-linearities that characterize those events, including, of course, the phenomenology of the crises.

- free will means that the individual can decide to oppose the rationality of artefacts. Somewhat, that individual ignores (or deliberatively chooses to ignore) the known logic of the artefacts' functioning, based on different reasons (including an alternative and idiosyncratic rationality);
- the most frequent entering into action of free will occurs when the individual anticipates some path of the concerned artefact's functioning—such anticipation can be triggered, for example, by an

announcement of someone or through observing the behaviour (decision or/and action) of the other participants to the societal game;
- this behaviour is logically equivalent to the change of initial conditions regarding the concerned artefact's functioning;
- but, the (high) sensibility to the (change of) initial conditions is the very predicate of the non-linear dynamic systems;[13] at least in the financial phenomenology, the chaotism is present enough (Asano & Yokoo, 2019);
- consequently, anywhere and whenever the free will is present, the probability that the system concerned to behave chaotic, that is, non-linearly, is very high or, at least, high.

Based on the above reasoning, we think that the destabilizing stage of the crisis, in *DRR* logic, has a non-linear phenomenology. Of course, the non-linearity is not equivalent to the non-predictability,[14] although free will necessarily causes the non-predictability.[15]

(iii) Cause versus effect in the destabilizing stage

The destabilizing stage in the chreode of a generic societal crisis has a double nature from the causality perspective: it is a cause of the redesigning stage and is an effect of the perturbation generated by the concerned crisis. The necessary character of this stage confers to the generic societal crisis of a general function of (factual) testing. Any crisis acts like an earthquake: rearranges the structures, so reconfigures the functions and, in the gravest cases, even replaces the role of the target entity/system (by autopoiesis). The necessary character, together with the double causality (back and forward), assigns to the destabilizing stage the possibility to be modelled using Bayesian probabilities or, better, the propensities (as discussed before).

9.4 The Redesigning Vehicle of the Societal Crisis

The redesigning stage of the crisis in its *DRR* logic is a contingent one—that is, it is possible but not necessary. The possibility results from the fact that the destabilizing stage highlights the vulnerabilities of the target entity/system in relation to the perturbations generated by crises. Once the vulnerabilities were identified, we have, in fact, the "place" of the changes which, if made, could save us, in the future, from the vulnerabilities in the case. The non-necessity results from the following reasons: (a) the vulnerabilities put into evidence are not so serious or have a peripherical location and impact; (b) in fact, the vulnerabilities are locally autopoietic and do not require dedicated changes; (c) the vulnerabilities are liable to be "adjudicated" by the antifragility property of the target entity/system, so they could be ignored, or even "protected", till they are fructified as such.

In the most cases, however, the destabilizing stage leads to the stage of redesigning of the target entity/system, in order to regulate the structure, the role and the functions which are desired and useful. The stage of redesigning is, *par excellence*, a stage of innovation, of all sorts, in the margin of the destabilizing stage.

9.4.1 The Innovative Vocation of the Destabilizing Stage

The destabilizing stage highlights on the vulnerabilities of the target entity/system, leading to the redesigning stage and, further, to the restabilizing of the system concerned. This is exactly the content of the innovation[16]—something new compared with the *statu quo*, aimed at either solving a current (or anticipated, as the case could be) problem or avoiding, for the future, the concerned problem occurring. Although the destabilizing stage of the crisis can also activate the invention, generally, it activates the innovation. Although the term "innovation" evokes, massively, the technical/technological sort of innovation, in fact, the most important innovations in the society are the social (or societal) innovations. The social/societal innovations subsume the praxeological and the practical categories of innovations.[17] Of course, the innovations also could destabilize the target entity/system. This is possible because innovation can modify the hard-core structure of the system concerned—in fact, such an innovation, which we can call disruptive innovation, acts like a crisis. There are many examples in history when innovations, especially operational ones, as financial innovations are or can be (Hashimoto et al., 2022), have triggered perturbations labelled as destabilizing phenomena. Since this type of effect (or crisis) is so common in the societal praxis, some extra considerations could be of usefulness.

- an innovation, no matter its type or category, can come out of the blue or can be the very effect of a current crisis. *Nota bene*: some analysts call the last type a destabilizer of a stable crisis—in our opinion, it should be spoken about a (logical) negation of a destabilizer, but the term is not so important if the concept is clear;
- the innovation is a necessary phenomenon only if it is a response (see point 9.5.) to a destabilizing phenomenon, else it has a contingent nature;
- however, an innovation is not, *per se*, a destabilizing event. The logical conditions in which an innovation is (or might be) a destabilizer are, as we believe, the following alternative (disjunctive) conditions:
  - it has not a neutralizing purpose regarding a destabilized state of the target entity/system, so it occurs independently from an existing efficient cause;[18]
  - it has a neutralizing purpose regarding a destabilized state of affairs within the target entity/system, but that purpose exceeds the destabilization that must be neutralized—as usually said, it "jump over the horse". In fact, it is about adverse effects that accompany the intentioned effect. Those adverse effects must be of such intensity or size that replace the neutralized destabilization with another one, perhaps of other type or category, which, in turn, requires a new innovation and so on.

Nota bene: what about the creative destruction?[19] The syntagma is not too proper, in our opinion, because, generally, the novelty either does not destroy anything—acting by addition or completion—or incorporates the old items by generalization. We do not reject the cases in which some old items (ideas, devices, procedures, values etc.) are replaced "in integrum" but we do not believe that the creation in the innovation field is always destructive related to the old state of affairs. For example, the infinitesimal calculus of Leibniz/Newton did not destroy the common algebra, the trivalent (or polyvalent) logic did not destroy the bivalent logic, the Quantum Theory did not destroy the General Theory of Relativity and so on.

9.4.2 *About a General Physiology of the Redesigning Stage*

The need for redesigning the structure (especially the hard-core structure) of the target entity/system is directly proportional to the "left-up" location of the perturbation that caused the destabilizing (see Fig. 9.5). More than that, the more left-up-ed location of the perturbation the higher the probability that the redesigning be done. Figure 9.6 provides a general scheme of the redesigning phenomenology.

Discussion

(1) the destabilizing impact is the very starting point in the process of redesigning the target entity/system, since it is observable, by contrast to the perturbation itself which is, generally, unobservable as such (*Nota bene*: we have here a kind of the "revealed preference" of Samuelson—to the observer the destabilization is the observable fact, but this is the effect of a hidden event, namely the perturbation brought by the crisis);

(2) the perturbation that caused the destabilization of the target entity/system is, in fact, logically inferred from the observed destabilization. The inference implies, of course, a theory that provides a specific hermeneutics able to get the perturbation-cause from the destabilization-effect (*Nota bene*: we have here a kind of the black-box-ism copiously used by behaviourism in the economic and social modelling, namely the input inferring from the observed output);

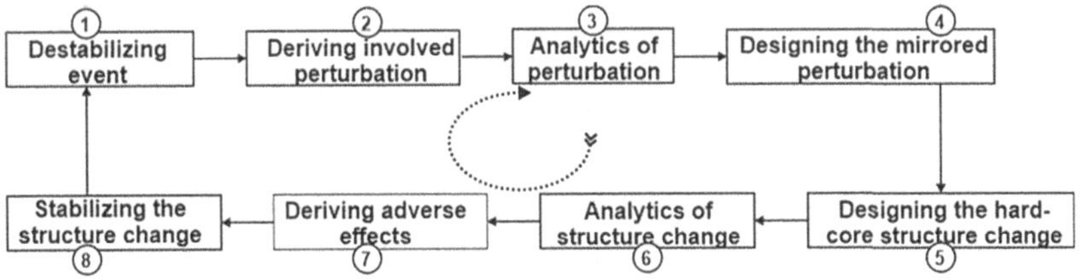

Fig. 9.6 The general phenomenology of the redesigning stage. *Source*: author

(3) this step is dedicated to a detailed, multifaceted and interdisciplinary analysis of the inferred perturbation, in order to identify its structure, mechanism, thresholds and so on, that characterize the perturbation concerned. The theory involved in step (2) is also used now to deliver a (desirably) complete description of the perturbation. It is expected that this step will provide a true logical (or/and) mathematical model of the perturbation in the case, so it can be computationally manipulated to learn as much as possible about its anatomy and physiology, and, especially, to make possible the performance of step (4);
(4) the first three steps constitute rather the (logical) infrastructure for step (4). The true content of the redesigning stage is, however, this step (Ferraro, 2020; Ranucci & Wang, 2024). Its basic coordinates are as follows:
   - the redesigning of the (hard-core) structure of the target entity/system is of autopoietic nature. Indeed, it cannot be of a resilience nature, since, as said before, the perturbation that is taken into consideration is, earliest, that occurred under the antifragilizing of the target entity/system but only if the antifragilizing process (no matter is or is not successful) signals the failure of the sustainability property of the concerned system. If such a signal is issued, then the autopoiesis process (i.e., the autopoieticity property) enters into action;
   - the redesigning of the (hard-core) structure of the target entity/system can be, however, focused on all the five phases of that system, within the *RRASA* logic:
      on *robustness*: to increase the ceiling threshold beyond which the robustness is defeated;
      on *resilience*: either to increase the ceiling threshold beyond which the resilience does not work anymore or to increase the "elasticity" of the target entity/system;
      on *antifragility*: to increase the spectrum[20] of perturbation that could be fructified after they exert the impact on the target entity/system;
      on *sustainability*: to better combine and dynamically correlate the three components of sustainability—robustness, resilience, antifragility;

on *autopoieticity*: to change the role (i.e., the structural identity) of the target entity/system, in order to avoid the destabilizing impact of future perturbations;

- regarding the re-setting of the target entity/system within the autopoieticity action, that causes such a change in the hard-core so that the role of the system concerned is changed, the following mentions could be of usefulness:

  two objectives, well chronologically ordered, must be taken into consideration:

- initiating a mirrored perturbation that should act as a (logical) negation of the perturbation identified as the cause of the destabilizing event—this initiation is better to be done through hard-core structure change, in order to avoid the reversibility of that negation;
- hard-core structure changing so that the destabilizing does not occur in the future, either by blocking the perturbation concerned or by sterilizing that perturbation regarding its potential to produce destabilizing;

  some comments on the concept of sterilizing the perturbation against destabilizing impact are as follows:

- to sterilize something is to block, in one way or another, the capacity of that something to generate its main outcome (if possible, it is desirable to block all potential outcomes). For example, in biological life, to sterilize means to block the capacity of an individual to reproduce itself, while in the financial field, to sterilize the monetary supply means to reduce that supply till the point when the inflation is not triggered anymore;[21]
- to sterilize a perturbation generated by a crisis should mean blocking that perturbation in producing destabilization of the target entity/system. The basic ideas here could be:
  (i) to block the potential of perturbation to change the hard-core structure of the target entity/system so that the system will be unable to achieve its role;
  (ii) the standard way to do that blocking could be either designing a counter-process inside the perturbation involved aimed at neutralizing the tendency of changing the hard-core or endowing the hard-core structure with some internal principles of reversibility of a change beyond an established threshold;[22]

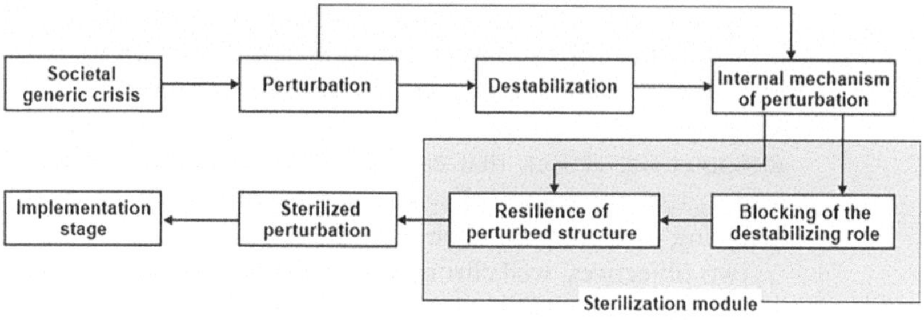

Fig. 9.7 Perturbation sterilization in the redesigning stage. *Source*: author

(iii) redesigning the target entity/system could be made having the purpose of implementing the property of self-sterilization. The property of self-sterilization could be implemented, of course, by intermediation of the automatic devices of self-sterilization (*ADSSs*). The balance between discretionary devices of sterilization (*DDSs*) and *ADSSs* is one of the highest challenges in the redesigning stage following the crisis impact.

Figure 9.7 provides a synoptic image of the perturbation sterilization in the redesigning stage.

(5) this step consolidates, formally and institutionally, the details regarding the changes required in the hard-core structure of the target entity/system, so that the future perturbations brought by the societal generic crises are neutralized or avoided;
(6) now, a simulation (an *ex-ante* testing) of the structural change (especially in the hard-core structure) of the target entity/system is performed, in order to identify the (possible) adverse effects accompanying that change;
(7) the identified adverse effects are analysed, catalogued and eliminated or prevented, after the case, by the final "profile" of the structural change which is established;
(8) now all the results obtained along the chain (1)–(7) are synthesized, and, in a sense, the change in the hard-core structure of the target entity/system is stabilized or "approved". So, the third stage in the *DRR* logic of the impact of the crisis is open.

9.5 The Restabilising Finality After Crisis

The role of the societal system is best accomplished in a stable dynamics of the system in the case. Consequently, a destabilizing episode must be managed so that the stability is either restored or redesigned.

9.5.1 Restoring the Stability

Restoring the stability means restoring the whole context of the target entity/system so that the "old" role (as the concept of role has been introduced above) of the system continues to be accomplished. Of course, the role does not necessarily be performed in a punctual way but rather inside a pre-accepted interval of variation—this detail is of no importance now. Consequently, to restore the stability of the system means to neutralize the perturbation that has distorted the current stability. As shown above, some cases and, correspondingly, some ways (solutions) to this problem can exist:[23]

(a) The case in which the antifragilizing action does not restore the previous role

This case signifies a complete remanence of the perturbation generated by the crisis. The solution towards restoring the stability, that is, towards restoring the effectiveness of the previous role of the target entity/system, is to build up a neg-perturbation—a "mirrored" perturbation as a negation of the initial one—so that the neg-perturbation can annihilate/neutralize the initial one, of course in a period that could be estimated. Consequently, in this case, the autopoieticity achieves its highest function, that of designing the complete neg-perturbation and implementing it. But what does the term "neg-perturbation" mean? We shortly provide below some consideration in that matter.

- a disturbance is a disturbance only related to a benchmark; it does not exist as such. The benchmark we established in this matter is the role that the target entity/system must accomplish. So, the disturbance is defined as an event/phenomenon that blocks the performance of the established/expected role;
- to block the role accomplishment presupposes causing a change in the hard-core structure of the target entity/system that makes the role accomplishment impossible;

- so, what must be done is to reverse the change in the hard-core structure. This reversion implies a new perturbation of an opposite "sign" (or in mirror/mirrored);
- as a result, a neg-perturbation is always a bound-perturbation (*BP*) related to a free-perturbation (*FP*), so that the bound-perturbation has the potential to reverse the change caused by the free-perturbation in the hard-core structure of the target entity/system;
- metaphorically speaking, a neg-perturbation is a ... vaccine (*BP*) administered to the *FP*;[24]
- from a logical perspective in designing the *BP*s, the phenomenon of hysteresis must be considered—this means that the reverse trajectory of the change in the hard-core structure (as conducted by *BP*) does not perfectly overlap the trajectory of the change operated by *FP*, that is, it will go on a different "road". This peculiarity is not ... distorting since what is relevant is just the final point (the final reverse change in the hard-core structure).

Figure 9.8 illustrates the neg-perturbation working.

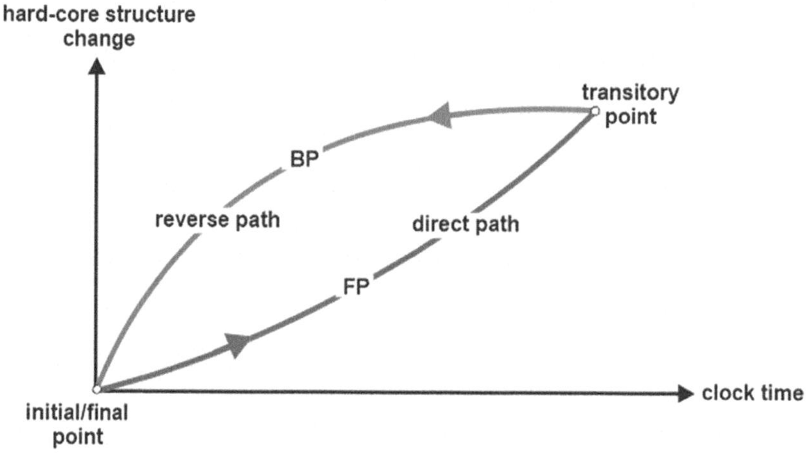

Fig. 9.8 The neg-perturbation phenomenology in the autopoietic process. *Source*: author

Discussion

Regarding the neg-perturbation, an issue could be raised: does the same role imply the same structure? Although, implicitly or explicitly, such an issue has been also approached before, here we provide some extra considerations in that matter:

- restoring the role of the target entity/system could mean either restoring the initial hard-core structure, through the neg-perturbation, or setting a new hard-core structure that generates that initial role;
- it seems the neg-perturbation is of two kinds: (a) neg-perturbation structurally oriented—*BPSO*; (b) neg-perturbation finally oriented—*BPFO*;
- regarding the *BPSO*, the autopoiesis must restore simply the hard-core configuration of the target entity/system, based on the principle that the same structure generates the same role. This principle is not invulnerable, since a given structure generates an expected role if the context (the environment) of the system in the case stays, in turn, unchanged;
- regarding the *BPFO*, the autopoiesis must modify both the hard-core of the target entity/system and the context (environment) of that system, so that the new role coincides with the old one, although it is speaking about a different hard-core structure;
- somewhat, we have to do with the invariance of the role, based on a concomitant and harmonized variation of both the hard-core structure of the target entity/system and the environment;
- but how to change the environment structure, if we are speaking about autopoiesis, which is an internal operator (since one of the sufficiency predicates of autopoiesis is called the procedural closure, S_4—see Chap. 1). In this question, we think as follows:
  - the role of the target entity/system means, especially, a behavioural attribute, that is, an impact of the system on its environment;[25]
  - consequently, when the hard-core structure is changed by the autopoiesis process, that change is made so that, considering the environment's structure, the role of the system is feasible;
  - as a result, even when the initial hard-core structure is restored as such, that restoring is made by considering the environment's

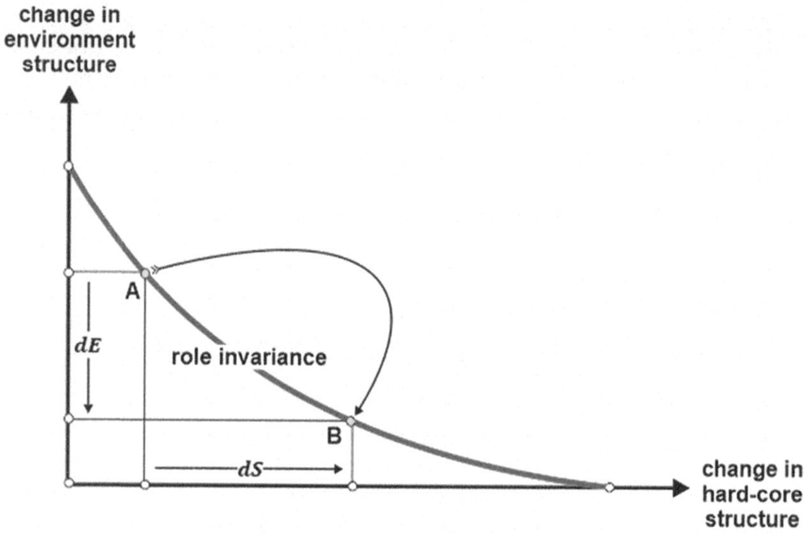

Fig. 9.9 The invariance between change in hard-core structure and in environment structure. *Source*: author

structure; so, it is correct to say that the binomial: the hard-core structure of the system—environment structure is restored;[26]

- in this context, the difference between restoring the initial hard-core structure and changing the hard-core structure is not so radical but it is rather logically equivalent.

Figure 9.9 indicates such an invariance (*dE* is the environment structure change; *dS* is the system structure change).

(b) The case in which the antifragilizing action does restore the previous role without "rest"

This case is introduced here from a logical reason only, since if the antifragilizing process restores completely the previous role of the target entity/system, in fact, we do not have to do anymore with an autopoietic task to restabilize the stability concerned. The case addresses the capability of the target entity/system to reverse the hard-core change, so that the initial hard-core structure is re-put in place. The way in which such a phenomenon is performed consists in implementing the neg-perturbation in its entirety.

(c) The case in which the antifragilizing action does partially restore the previous role

This case implies a combination between maintaining the initial role of the target entity/system and redesigning the hard-core structure to maintain that role. The case is more difficult than both (a) case, that is, failing to restore the initial role, and (b) case, that is, completely restoring off the initial role, since it must accommodate the two ways of solving the problem. In our opinion, case (c) is the most probable phenomenon to occur in practice.

(d) The case in which the antifragilizing action does restore the previous role, but with some new necessary distortions

This case is a new "animal". It means that, although the initial role of the target entity/system has been restored, some adverse effects accompany this result.[27] The adverse effects, in turn, must be solved. We shall discuss the following issues of this case: (d1) what refers to the adverse effects? (d2) what is the nature of those adverse effects? (d3) how could the adverse effects be solved?

(d1) What refers to the adverse effects?

Since the purpose of autopoiesis is to eliminate the perturbation that has changed the role of the target entity/system, the adverse effects act to compromise or, at least, vulnerabilize the achievement of that role. In other words, although the adverse effects do not block the performance of the role, they either diminish the standards at which the role is accomplished or lateralize the impact of the role. In conclusion, the adverse effects of restoring the role in the case consist of some distortions of the role compared with its initial performing;

(d2) What is the nature of those adverse effects?

Essentially, the adverse effects are generated by the phenomenon of hysteresis (see Fig. 9.8). Since the recession of the perturbation[28] follows a different path compared with the path of emergence of perturbation, it is possible to produce new (unpredictable) structural damages in the hard-core, which act as sui generis perturbation—this time, an internally originated perturbation. In fact, this is the content of the so-called internal crisis as a solver of an external crisis. Of course, a solver-crisis can be initiated either non-deliberatively—as the case here discussed—or deliberatively, within the autopoiesis process.

(d3) How could the adverse effects be handled?

Logically, the adverse effects of restoring the role of the target entity/system constitute the opportunity cost of choosing to restore that role, so the choice is obeying the standard criteria of optimizing under the concept of opportunity cost. Since the role of the target entity/system may oscillate inside a pre-accepted tunnel of variation, if the perturbed role by the adverse effects does not lead the system outside that tunnel, the adverse effects could be ignored. Else, the adverse effects must be treated as a new perturbation (internally originated) and the reasoning must be re-taken from the beginning, as shown above.

9.5.2 *Towards a New Stability*

The restabilizing stage moves the target entity/system to a new pattern of stability. This moving affects all the phases of the *RRASA* logic, usually by improving them and, in critical cases, the role of target entity/system (i.e., the identity of that system) is changed. Of course, it is presupposed that the new role is compatible and serves the purpose/goal of the target entity/system. It is, therefore, well understood that a purpose/goal can be accomplished through many roles, as a role can be accomplished through many functions, as a function can be accomplished through many hard-core structures.[29] Consequently, the target entity/system inside which an autopoietic action is unfolding, generally reaches a new stability around a new role—so that, the whole phenomenology of the two inter-related logics, *DDR* and *RRASA*, respectively, takes everything from the beginning. Some mentions regarding the relationships among purpose, role, function and hard-core structure could be of usefulness:

(i) *firstly*, for a purpose to be supported by a role, the last must have as its main outcome, the purpose's *eidos*. The eidos—which means the essence, quiddity—cannot be other than the *significance* of the purpose. So, we can build an equivalence class of the roles assigned to a given purpose, namely based on the same significance of the involved roles for the observer (or actor, after the case). Of course, if a group is involved instead of an individual, then we need a significance accepted by that community (an example could be a normative purpose for whose implementation many more roles are "equally" qualified, since a normative purpose is opposable to all individuals within the community in the case);

(ii) *secondly*, referring to the functions required to accomplish a given role, the specific eidos is not anymore the significance but the *performance*.[30] The performance is a measure of the degree of accomplishment of the role. In this context, we can build an equivalence class of the functions assigned to a given role, so that the role in the case is, approximately, accomplished at the same degree by any of the functions entering the class of equivalence;[31]

(iii) *thirdly*, when discussing different hard-core structures capable of generating the same function (better said, the same "composed individuals" of functions), we must speak about *adequacy*. Adequacy is understood as a certain logical convergence between the expectation (i.e., the desired function) and the capability (i.e., the hard-core structure). This way we can, also, build an equivalency class of the hard-core structures that equally have the capability (i.e., sufficient adequacy) to generate the function/s in the case.

A suggestion of the logical "cascade" about which is discussed above if provided by Fig. 9.10—with *R* is noted the role, *F* the function (either as singular or as a composed one) and *S* the hard-core structure.

If none of the possibilities shown in Fig. 9.10 are objectified, then the process of autopoiesis simply replaces the old role. The question is, of course, if by replacing the role of the target entity/system, the purpose is preserved. As Fig. 9.10 indicates, such a case is met if the interest of the people involved in the target entity/system is, in turn, conserved, at least in its basic features. Some comments seem to be required here:

(i) the interest is incapsulated into the purpose, while the significance/signification is incapsulated into the role. So, the

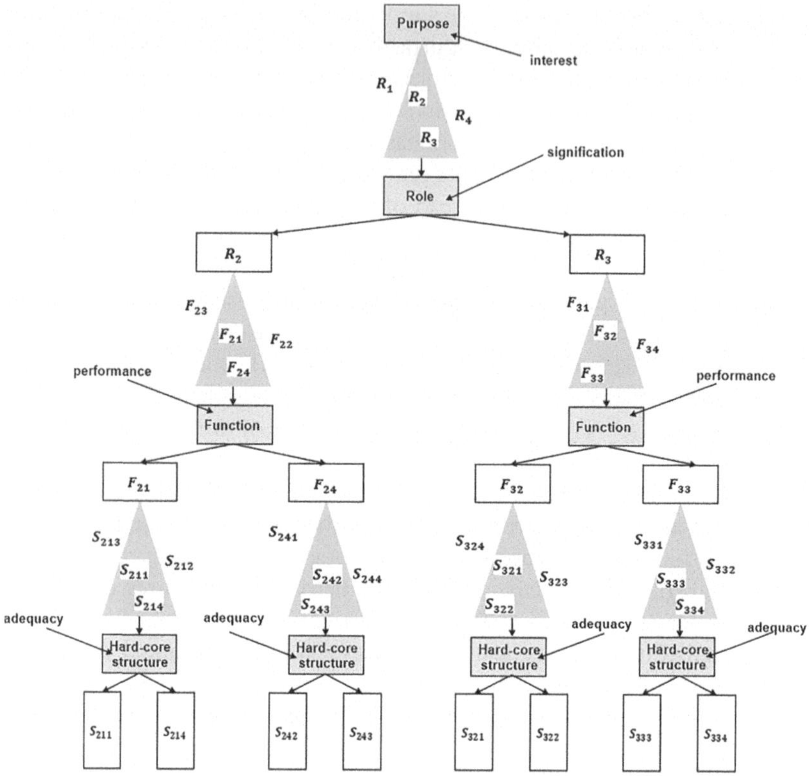

Fig. 9.10 The logical system "hard-core–function–role–purpose". *Source*: author

question is about the possibility that two different roles could deserve the same interest;

(ii) *prima facie*, it seems a bijective relation exists between interest and role, which means that always we have the situation: "a role—an interest" or vice versa: "an interest—a role";

(iii) consequently, to preserve an interest means finding two roles having the same significance;

(iv) an interest could be quantitative or qualitative—in the former case the signification can be calculated and compared for two concurrent roles but in the latter case the signification has a hermeneutic "raiment" and the comparison is more difficult.

We think the question is, in fact, the following: is there an area in which the changing of the role, by autopoiesis, could preserve the interest that defines a purpose? Theoretically, this is not impossible but praxeologically the probability that things unfold this way is small, if not purely accidental. So, once autopoiesis has changed the role of the target entity/system, the purpose of that system almost necessarily changes—we have simply another target entity/system. This is the reason for which, in Fig. 9.4, the autopoieticity brings the target entity/system at a new start point.

Notes

1. We speak about functioning/functionality in a more general sense, which includes the behaviour.
2. Do not confuse with the arrow of time, provided by the entropy dynamics in a closed system (e.g., our known Universe).
3. The difference between the role and the functions is as follows: the functions are aimed at objectifying the role or, equivalently, the role is the aggregate (sometimes synergic) effect of working of the functions.
4. Remember that role is associated with the (structural) hard-core of a system, while the function is associated with the peripheral structure of that system (see Chap. 8).
5. Analogously with how Austin's perlocutionary sentence can produce change.
6. In fact, our reasoning led us from the idea that sustainability is fundamentally defined by the structure replicating to the idea that sustainability must be defined by the replicating of the role, which allows (as what was just shown in the main text) the structural change, including the change of the hard-core structure. This is a theoretical advance of the highest relevance and importance, in our opinion, regarding the concept of sustainability.
7. Of course, we can consider a sameness in a punctual way or (better) in an interval way. These analytics are left at the reader's latitude.
8. A geodesic is, in the societal field, like in Cosmology, a mandatory path, that is, without alternative, through which a phenomenon must pass. The most important feature of a geodesic is the following: it does not allow the choice (or, in an anthropological terminology, it does not allow the freedom, i.e., the free will).
9. This ambivalence of the effect of antifragilizing process (antifragilizing could cause … fragility) is interesting enough—since, in its attempt to gain

an advantage from perturbation, the target entity/system must modify, to some extent, its (hard-core) structure. But any change in the hard-core structure is liable to move the target entity/system in a bifurcation point (mathematically, a fixed point, i.e., a solution of the equation $f(x) = x$). As known, the bifurcation point is, generally, undecidable, that is, has the potential to generate instability.

10. It is a notorious idea that a crisis is an occasion for improvement of the "weak link" through which the crisis entered the system concerned. This idea observes something fundamental but it does not observe that the "weak link" might be generated by the target entity/system itself, just by the antifragilizing process above evoked.
11. It must be observed that such a plan has no relationship with the property of antifragility—the plan to redesign the target entity/system is punctual (e.g., has a list of future identified and expected challenges), instead the property of antifragility is "blind" related to what perturbations follow to be off-set.
12. We remember that a typology is obtained through logical reasoning, while a taxonomy is obtained by empirical (factual) reasoning.
13. Those systems are called, also, chaotic systems.
14. For example, the bifurcation points (mathematically: fixed points) in the chaotic systems are perfectly calculable and predictable.
15. Conceptually, nothing happens outside of causation, only that there are three categories of causes assigned to three categories of events: (i) *deterministic* events (perfectly predictable—e.g., the natural events); (ii) *stochastic* events (probabilistically predictable); (iii) *random* events (non-predictable—e.g., events "endowed" with humans, i.e., with free will).
16. The conceptual family around innovation is larger. Firstly, we must discern between invention and discovery—the discovery is something existent but non-observed yet (the discoveries are possible through the lens of science only), while the invention is something that does not exist and is proposed based on either the sciences or the free intuition. Both discovery and invention are conceptual "animals". Instead, innovation is a methodological issue—it is an improvement, of a different nature or degree of either a discovery or an invention, from four disjunctive perspectives: (a) technical/technological; (b) praxeological (especially economical); (c) practical (including ethical); (d) artistical.
17. Unfortunately, the main pushing, firstly financial, across the world (including the European Union) is exerted on technical/technological innovation. The current crises (and, especially, the anticipated crises) regarding climate change, inter-cultural migration, gender issues, hyper-liberalism

(e.g., culture cancelling, conservatism rejection, nations' "caducity") etc. will highlight the mandatory primordiality of the social (societal) innovation.

18. Obviously, it cannot arise outside causality—since the causality is ubiquitous—but that cause is not of efficient type (better said, of efficacy type) but, usually, of final type.
19. Even if the syntagma is assigned to Schumpeter, the respective concept was used first time by Marx, while the term was first used by Werner Sombart (germ: *schöpferische Zerstörung—creative destruction*).
20. We remember (see Chap. 1) that antifragility is "blind" related to the possible perturbations to come, else we would speak about antifragility but, simply, about ... predictability.
21. See the ingenious curve LM (liquidity—money) in Macroeconomics, as suggested by Keynes and formalized by Hicks.
22. From a logical point of view, this means to endow the hard-core structure with an own resilience, separated from the resilience assigned to the target entity/system as a whole.
23. Do not forget that we are in a post-antifragile "era", which means the neutralizing of the perturbation is not possible anymore by fructifying it.
24. Of course, a ... library of such vaccines can be built, following a list of the most probable free perturbations, for different fields in the societal system, based on which some automatic stabilizers could be pre-designed and implemented, so avoiding the discretionary (possibly disturbing) interventions in administering the vaccines.
25. Of course, the role implies also the functionality of that system, that is, the relationships among the system's components.
26. This observation constitutes the very background for the evolutionist paradigm of the crisis emergence and unfolding, which will be examined in this chapter.
27. Here is the very seed of our proposal for a tetravalent logic for the economic (more general, social) field (see Annex 4.1 in Chap. 4).
28. More exactly, the reconstruction of the hard-core structure.
29. Logically, we have here a case in which the same effect can be generated, alternatively (so, substitutably) by more causes.
30. Both the purpose and the role are non-ontological entities. Instead, the functions (and, as we shall see, the hard-core structures) are ontological entities. It results that the eidos as significance can be assigned only to purposes and roles, while for the functions and/or hard-core structures we must "invent" something else, for example, the performance.
31. Of course, the class of equivalence can contain groups of functions, as "composed individuals", not singular functions. For example, a role cannot be accomplished else than by a group of functions. In this case, we

must form those "composed individuals" so that the equivalence class under discussion is constituted by them, not by individual functions. The "composed individuals" of the equivalence class are formed based on both complementarity and substitutability among the individual functions entering a given "composed individual".

References

Asano, T., & Yokoo, M. (2019). Chaotic Dynamics of a Piecewise Linear Model of Credit Cycles. *Journal of Mathematical Economics, 80.*

Costa Lima, B., Grasseli, M. R., Wang, X.-S., & Wu, J. (2014). Destabilizing a Stable Crisis: Employment Persistence and Government Intervention in Macroeconomics. *Structural Change and Economic Dynamics, 30.*

Ferraro, G. (2020). After the Crisis: The Role of Resilience in Coming Back Stronger. *Connections: The Quarterly Journal,* (4).

Grinin, L. E., & Kototayev, A. V. (2023). Introduction. Destabilization as a Phenomenon of Social Dynamics. In *History and Mathematics: Entropy and Destabilization.* 'Uchitel' Publishing House.

Handy, C. (2016). *The Second Curve. Thoughts on Reinventing Society.* Random House.

Hashimoto, K., Im, R., Kunieda, T., & Shibata, A. (2022). Financial Destabilization. *Journal of Mathematical Economics, 13.*

Ranucci, R., & Wang, S. (2024). Resilience in Top Management Teams: Responding to Crisis by Focusing on the Future. *Long Range Planning, 57*(1).

CHAPTER 10

On the (Co)Evolution of Crises

10.1 Preamble

The societal crisis is, of course, a symbolic species, since it is an artefact generated by the very behaviour of individuals or social groups. Consequently, the crisis is a mix between necessity and contingency, that is, between determinism and free will. The human being is, in turn, a mix between biological determinism and cultural determinism, while each of these determinisms is, also, a mix between necessity and contingency. Here is to be observed that the (often inextricably) combination between necessity and contingency is exactly the background (substrate) of the concept of evolution. Indeed, the mutation in an entity could be, generally, random (i.e., obeys contingency), but the selection of that mutation is, generally, pre-known (i.e., obeys necessity).

10.1.1 Social Necessity

We must carefully distinguish between natural necessity and social necessity. While the natural necessity (*NN*) is necessarily generated, the social necessity[1] (*SN*) is contingently generated. In other words (as said in previous chapters), the *NN* is an intra-necessity necessity, and the *SN* is an intra-contingency necessity. Another distinction between *NN* and *SN* is the following: *NN* is homo-poietic (or autopoietic), while *SN* is

E. Dinga, *Economic Resilience During Overlapped Crises*,
https://doi.org/10.1007/978-3-031-80224-9_10

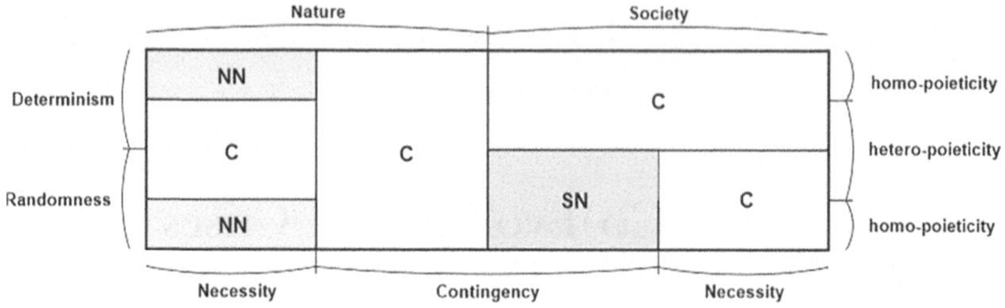

Fig. 10.1 Social necessity. *Source*: author

hetero-poietic. This means that *NN* is its own effect (something like a causa sui), while *SN* is an effect of an external cause. The question arising here is the following: could exist an internal process of symbolic species, as a societal crisis, so that the (social) necessity is "prepared" for a change (even if that change will be effectively caused from outside)? It is obvious that, again, we have here the very content of the concept of evolution: an internal factor that "signalizes" a required change (mutation).[2] Figure 10.1 suggests the logical place and signification of *SN*, which will be operationalized further (with *C* is noted the contradiction, i.e., the logical impossibility).

So, the main predicates of the social necessity (SN) are:

- it is a necessity inside the contingency;
- its emergence is non-deterministic, i.e., obeys randomness;[3]
- the social necessity is reversible, by contrast with the (irreversible) natural necessity;
- the social necessity is a contingent effect that generates a necessary cause;[4]
- the social necessity allows the free will, while the natural necessity does not;
- the social necessity encapsulates the natural necessity as invariants—in other words, the social necessity contains a background (substrate) of invariants that constitutes the very natural necessity;

10.1.2 Social Discretionarity

Any social entity is an artefact, so it is discretionarily[5] intentioned, designed, and objectified (implemented). It is not, however, mandatory that a system of such artefacts to be the object of a strategy or program, although in contemporary (very politized) societies, the strategies/programs are more and more used. Social discretionarity is understood as the liberty for people to initiate artefacts, of any kind, inside which they will function. The constraints for those artefacts are, on the one hand, the invariants of the natural necessity, and, on the other hand, the own restrictions of different sorts: resources, values (including ethical ones), and, of course, the sustainability of the artefact concerned. The causality of such social kinematics is one of the most difficult issues of the social philosophy or of the philosophy of history, and, as it is obvious, this issue is much outside of the modest goals of this book.[6] Consequently, we shall list the most significant predicates of the social discretionarity:

- social discretionarity is objectified through the normative framework of the society. In fact, the normative framework is exactly the practical[7] content of the social necessity;
- the normative framework cannot be contradictory with the natural necessity, although, of course, neither can norm the natural necessity, as shown above;
- so, social discretionarity expresses what humans can make (if they want) within the natural necessity;
- one of the things (better said, one of the processes) humans make inside their society is exactly the (societal) crisis.

10.2 The Concept of Symbolic Species

10.2.1 Preamble

The concept of species comes from biology and refers to a certain degree of semantic aggregation (conceptual system) but also ontological aggregation (real system) of individuals within a given population. The species contains those individuals that check certain predetermined criteria/traits and that are not found in other individuals (which possibly belong to another species/species, by the same aggregation mechanism). The concept of species has not only the role of systematizing the structure of populations, but has a fundamental meaning: evolution (biological, in the case just discussed) occurs exclusively at the level of the species. Strictly speaking, therefore, we speak of evolution only as the evolution of the species, while, relative to the individuals composing the species, we speak of development. *Nota bene*: the process (or duration) of development extends from the moment the individual is born until the moment the individual in question reaches maturity, usually from a reproductive point of view (in the case of humans, the cultural side of development requires that, outside the criterion of reproducibility, the criterion of discernment, education, sometimes even instruction, etc., also function). The concept of species has "migrated" from biology to other fields of knowledge or practice, so that it is found, in an abstracted form, from mathematics and logic to cosmology. This caused this concept to gradually acquire symbolic denotations, that is, to form what can be called a symbolic species. In this chapter, the concept of the symbolic species will be examined in close relation with the concepts of evolution and co-evolution of the symbolic species—because the role of the species as a "container" of evolution/co-evolution is also preserved in the case of species symbolic.

10.2.2 The Concept of Species and Co-species

Regarding the (punctual) identification of the species, three definitions are proposed in the literature (Kratochwil & Schwabe, 2002):

(a) *Morphological* definition: individuals having the same structural characteristics;
(b) *Genetic* definition: individuals who are reproductively isolated;[8]
(c) *Ecological* definition: syntopic and synchronous species cannot form the same species.[9]

The process by which a species arises is called *speciation*. There are two distinct categories of speciation:[10]

(i) *Allopatric* speciation: due to the isolation of a species following the appearance of an obstacle of physical (geographical) separation—a river, a mountain, etc. In allopatric speciation, two steps are required:
   - step 1: geographical *separation*;
   - step 2: development of *isolation* mechanisms (*Nota bene*: there are two types of isolation: (a) meta-gametic isolation: mating incompatibility; (b) pro-gametic isolation: prevention of mating—the latter is also called cyclical or seasonal isolation);[11]

(ii) *Sympatric* speciation: it is due to competition, or the emergence of particular traits, between individuals (of a species) living in the same physical and temporal area. The concept of co-species is quite controversial, both logically and epistemologically. Logically, a species is related (inter-action) to every other species in the environment of that species, so for a given (fixed) species, a co-species should refer to only one species (chosen, in turn) from the environment, with which the fixed species is "credited" to interact exclusively or predominantly. This is a rather pronounced abstraction, so logically speaking, identifying a co-species means operating a segmentation of the analysis space (of course, there may be cases where such a segmentation is justified either theoretically, methodologically, or instrumentally). Epistemologically, the term co-species should separate between two entities that can only be defined relative to each other—a co-species exists only in relation to (or associated with) a fixed species, so there is no co-species in general, but only in relation to the fixed species. This means that each species has (or, more generally, has only) one co-species, namely from the perspective of a particular interest in knowledge or action.

There arises, of course, in connection with the co-species, the problem of the environment in relation to a fixed species. As we know, the evolution of a species (e.g., of a biological type) is the result of a selection, of a cumulative (gradual[12]) type, that the environment of a fixed species makes on the mutations undergone by the fixed species, in the direction of increasing the fitness[13] of that fixed species. In this context, logically, a species' environment should be considered to be co-species relative to the fixed species (and vice versa, of course). In certain contexts, such a perspective will be operated, with strict methodological precautions.

10.2.3 The Concept of Symbolic Species—Narrative Level

The concept of symbolic species will be examined from the perspective of several predicates that it necessarily implies:

- the symbolic species exists (appears, maintains, evolves and disappears) exclusively in the cultural world. By cultural world we mean only the world "endowed" with people, i.e., with beings capable of having representations;[14]
- accordingly, the symbolic species is an artefact, regardless of whether this artefact is objective in its nature, e.g., a stock (a product) or flow (a service), subjective in its nature, e.g., a belief or a preference,[15] or it is objectified[16] in its nature, e.g., a scientific theory or a political regime, or a myth;

- in principle, a symbolic species is the result of a combination between ontology and gnoseology (or, in some cases, between ontology and epistemology). For example, public policy is an artefact of an institutional nature that, as a species, includes individuals such as: monetary policy, fiscal policy, income policy, social policy, etc., so it is a symbolic species. The symbolic species, however, has both an ontological status—it exists as real, more precisely it has a reality objectified by inter-subjective agreement, as shown above—and a gnoseological (or, at least, epistemological) status—it is an effect or a result of knowledge activity;
- the symbolic species can also be an imaginary species (which has no real character)—for example, fairy tales or myths, literary species, utopias (including dystopias) of any kind, heterotopias and the like constitute symbolic species (being, obviously, artefacts), even if they do not find a correspondent in the reality opposite to all (that is, in the objective reality).

In the syntagma symbolic species, there is nothing new, compared to biology, about the term species. By species is meant a population group of individuals that have a significant, relatively invariant pool of common traits (e.g., genes), especially with regard to the replication/reproduction of the individuals in question. Relative, however, to the term symbolic, there are notable and, in most cases, decisive differences (from a conceptual and methodological point of view) between the biological[17] domain and the, let's say, artefactual domain (i.e., the society). In this sense, we believe that the following considerations can bring some clarification to the term symbolic in the phrase syntagma species:

- the term symbolic has nothing to do, in the phrase symbolic species, with the symbolic term from semiotics. In semiotics, the symbol is a species of sign with some iconic characteristics in common with the referent (denoted or signified), while, in the case discussed in this chapter, the predicate of symbolic refers exclusively to the fact that the species in question is an artefact. We specify that an artefact is not necessarily a result of a deliberative action/activity, it can also appear accidentally or in a necessary but not deliberative/aware way;
- although, in the just mentioned meaning of the symbolic predicate, it seems that the appearance (construction) of a symbolic individual is much more frequent than a symbolic species, from a taxonomic

point of view, in the matter of symbolic species, we can have species that contain a single individual;[18]

- of course, a species containing only one individual raises some problems from the perspective of evolution:
  - question: since at the level of the individual we cannot talk about evolution, but only about development (as we have shown before), then how can the concept of evolution be introduced in the case of a symbolic species that contains a single individual?
  - answer: unlike the biological case, in the case of symbolic species, it is not necessary for a certain trait (such as a mutation) to become dominant in the individuals of that species to declare that an evolutionary step has taken place in the sense of that mutation. The explanation of such a possibility lies in the fact that, in the case of symbolic species, the main (i.e., predominant) type of evolution is Lamarckian, not Darwinian. Moreover, since we are discussing artefacts, it follows that the rate of occurrence of symbolic[19] mutations is considerably higher than in the biological case. We must also specify the fact, fundamentally, that in the case of symbolic species, mutations lose, for the most part, the random character they have in the biological case. In fact, mutations within a symbolic species can be part of a deliberative, sometimes long-term, program to modify the characteristics of the symbolic species according to the purpose for which that symbolic species was created (*Nota bene*: we remember that, in the biological case, there is no purpose in evolution, although there is a directed finality of improving fitness);
  - also based on the "quality" of the artefact, a symbolic species having a single individual can replicate itself by replicating that individual, either without any change (mutation) compared to the previous version or with changes (Lamarckian mutations);
  - the decentralization/deconcentration that works in the case of institutional symbolic species makes the taxonomy allopatric speciation/sympatric speciation (encountered in the biological case) superfluous because the basic traits of the individuals of the decentralized/deconcentrated symbolic species are established on a normative basis and are, during the validity period of the norm, invariants;
  - on the basis of what has just been mentioned, on the one hand, the statement regarding the absence of the random character of

the mutations occurring in the genome of the individuals of the symbolic species is strengthened, and, on the other hand, it becomes possible to anticipate (as a rule, programmatically) the mutations that they will "intervene" in the future;

- in the case of the symbolic species, the following aspect appears: regardless of the space in which a certain individual of that species "lives"/functions and, to a certain extent, regardless of the time considered, the individual in question is identical to itself. Logically, it is therefore possible for there to be clones in the domain of symbolic species, which in biology is impossible;[20]
- according to the above, we can say that, in the case of symbolic species, such a species can contain identical individuals (clones), in numbers however large or small, so there is no need for these individuals to be different from each other, so as it happens in the case of biological species;[21]
- symbolic species have been identified in various fields—thus, in the field of humanities, the brain and language are considered symbolic species that co-evolve (Deacon, 2007), in the field of finance, more precisely the financial market, information and price are considered symbolic species in co-evolutionary relationships (Dinga et al., 2023), at the level of the corporation (microeconomics) (Nelson & Winter, 1982), the routine and its environment are considered in co-evolutionary relationship.

10.2.4 The Concept of Symbolic Species—Sufficiency Predicates

Having described the content of a symbolic species, we can now proceed to try defining this concept more rigorously. We will do this by identifying the minimal set of sufficiency predicates that, once verified by a given species, earns the "right" to be called a symbolic species. In our opinion, these sufficiency predicates are as follows:

(i) (**SSP1**) is an *artefact*[22]—either physical, intellectual (institutional, epistemological, logical, theological, artistic, etc.), or social (political, religious, etc.).

Discussion

This sufficiency predicate is fundamental to the identification/extraction of a symbolic species. Logically, all the other three sufficiency predicates (which follows) are impossible in the absence of predicate (SP1).

Although there are authors who believe that there can be symbolic species that are not artefacts (Deacon, 2007), for example the brain or language (which are analysed from a co-evolutionary point of view), in our opinion we are dealing, in the mentioned cases, with an abuse of language or with a conceptual lack of clarity.[23] In this regard, our opinion is as follows:

- it is about a confusion between language, as a system of symbolic representation, and a … symbolic species. In the terminology we use here, the symbolic predicate does not refer to a form of representation (for example, a form of expression, possibly also used in communication, etc.) but to the fact that it excludes the natural predicate;
- the same confusion also occurs in relation to the "symbolic" brain species—the brain is obviously a natural-social mix evolutionary product, and it functions, from the point of view of representation, at most as a "device" for thinking (the formation of perceptions, concepts, judgements and reasonings—to follow exactly the logic of thinking). Although it is true that thinking, especially in terms of judgements and reasonings, proceeds symbolically (with or without the mediation of language in some cases—Lohmar, 2012), the radical conclusion that the brain is a symbolic species cannot be drawn from this;
- we assume that the author discussed here has in mind a characteristic (shared by both language and the brain), namely that the "species" in question are not autonomous in relation to a material body, hence cannot replicate/reproduce through own principles, and this evolutionary infirmity is considered sufficient to call the two entities as symbolic species, in the sense that they are not "real" species. We reject such nomenclature;

(ii) (**SSP2**) mutations are predominantly *non-random* and *Lamarckian*—as is known, mutations in biological species (i.e., natural species) are random but in symbolic species mutations are predominantly non-random. At the same time, mutations in the case of symbolic species no longer follow Darwinian but Lamarckian logic.

Discussion

First of all, the expression *predominantly non-random* is requested to be made explicit. This means that, most of time and in most cases, the mutations that intervene on the genome are deliberative and often programmatic. Of course, it is not excluded that some mutations occur non-deliberatively, i.e., randomly. So, in the case of symbolic species, we will accept a mix of the character of genetic mutations—between the random, minority character and the deliberative, majority character.

Secondly, the *Lamarckian* expression is requested to be made explicit. As is well known, Darwinism, which was developed exclusively on the basis of biological (natural) species, correctly assumes the random nature of genetic mutation. This means that the transmission of the new characteristics of the ancestors (generated by mutations) to the descendants is done if and only if these random mutations occur in the genome of the ancestors before their replication. In the case of symbolic species, the offspring can acquire new features of their functions without the mediation of genetic mutations (random or deliberate). Somehow, if in the case of Darwinism, structure creates function (where structure means the genome), in the case of Lamarckism, function creates structure—in the sense that the necessity of a function will lead to the related (logically and causally compatible) genetic mutation. So, this reversal of the causal arrow is peculiar to the symbolic species and, by extension, peculiar to social evolution or, more broadly, societal evolution.

Third, it must be stated that there is no correlation of consistency or compatibility between the predominant non-random character of genetic mutation and the Lamarckian character of selection (and evolution) in the case of symbolic species. The two characteristics of this sufficiency predicate are complementary to each other. An overview of the considerations regarding this sufficiency predicate is given in Fig. 10.2.

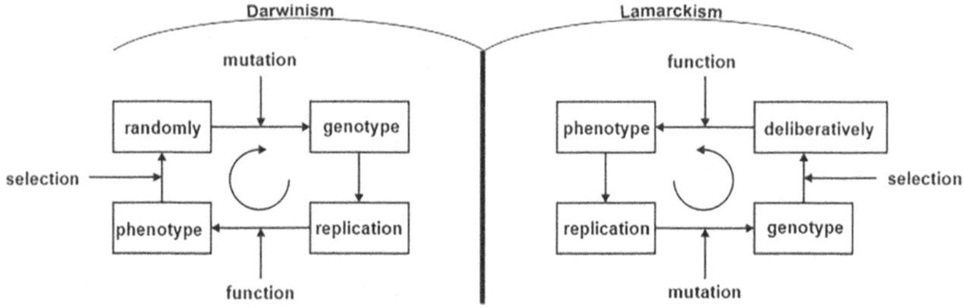

Fig. 10.2 Darwinism vs. Lamarckism. *Source*: author

(iii) (**SSP3**) selection is predominantly *saltationist*—saltationism in the evolutionary selection of symbolic species (artefacts) is explained by the predominance of deliberativeness in the very genesis of the artefacts in question. Thus, they are designed teleologically (according to a pre-existing or pre-established purpose), and this way of appearance of the artefact gives it a certain stability—either objective or subjective, the latter generated by the subject's attachment to the artefact. This causes the pressures of gradual change, including small random mutations, to be ignored until they accumulate a critical mass of such a nature as to call into question the very stability in question, at which (threshold) moment they are accepted or challenged, also in deliberative selection of that accumulated pressure, thus resulting in saltationist selection.

Discussion

As the content of the sufficiency predicate (SSP3) also says, saltationist selection of symbolic species is predominant in the integral process of evolutionary selection, but not unique. Mutations (or pressures to change) may occur which are gradually selected—especially in a free and democratic society, for example, by the invisible hand of the market. The gradual, cumulative selection in the case of symbolic species takes place mainly at the functional level (the level of functions) not at the structural level (of "organs"). For example, some refinements at the administrative level or at the level of organizational culture, etc., can take place in the form of a gradual cumulative selection.

(iv) (**SSP4**) has *inauthentic genotype* – the in-authenticity of the genotype of the symbolic species consists in the fact that it is not structurally located in the phenotype but, in fact, is located in the human subject. Mutational pressure will therefore be exerted on the human subject, albeit through or stimulated by the phenotype of the symbolic species in question. At the level of the phenotype of the symbolic species, there will be a "false" genotype. Based on the above, it can be said that, logically, a symbolic species is a deliberative construct (Berger & Luckmann, 2008) that meets the four predicates of sufficiency. If we denote the symbolic species with *SS*, then it can be written:

$$SS \leftarrow (SP1) \wedge (SP2) \wedge (SP3) \wedge (SP4)$$

10.2.5 *The Social Significance of Symbolic Species*

By being artefacts (see sufficiency predicate SP1) symbolic species represent individuals of Popper's third world (objectifications of subjective thought contents). For these objectifications to take place, there must be some agreement, bordering on consensus, among the contemporary members of society, at the time of the objectification in question, as to the desirability, appropriateness, and utility of that objectification. There is the question of the type of agreement/consensus required by the construction of symbolic species. In our opinion, this agreement/consensus must be, simultaneously, of three species: (a) epistemic agreement; (b) practical agreement; (c) praxeological agreement.

(a) Epistemic Agreement

Epistemic agreement refers to the relational categories *true/false*. For example, a scientific theory or ideology (including a religious or mystical kind) must concern the categories of truth/false with respect to the symbolic species in question. To take an example from the history of the natural sciences, the quantum physics theory has sparked (and still sparks) extremely heated controversies between members of the vision who claim that this theory truly expresses objective reality and supporters of the vision who claim that the theory in question is a bit incomplete (*Nota bene*: historically, the most famous representative of the first vision was Niels Bohr, and of the second vision was Albert Einstein). Let us take an example from economic theory : (a) the vision of inductivists—with the representatives of the marginalist and statistical school: Jevons, Menger, Edgeworth, German Historical School; (b) the vision of the deductivists—with the representatives of introspection, such as John Stuart Mill, respectively, of psychologism, where Keynes also "fits in", partially (Maas, 2014). Epistemic agreement, therefore, involves an agreement, at the level of the community of interest—such as a scientific community, a political community, a theological community, or an artistic community—that a certain objectification can be accepted as true. In other words, the truth is approved by "voting" at the level of the community concerned. Of course, there are also cases where this consent must be given by the society as a whole—for example, the establishment of a certain political regime in that society. Epistemic agreement is generally of two types: (a) distributive epistemic agreement; (b) collective epistemic agreement (Schmid, 2012).

Distributive epistemic agreement implies the agreement of each member of the "voters", pointwise identically, while collective epistemic agreement implies the agreement of the "voters" as a group, identically though not pointwise identically. Epistemic agreement implies a certain degree of *epistemological discernment* among the population of the society in question.

(b) Practical Agreement

Practical agreement refers to the ethical categories of *acceptable/unacceptable*. This is because, as is known, following Kant, practical action aims at inter-subjective relations—for example, political or religious action is of a practical type. Practical agreement means that the members of the community (at the limit, society as a whole) must admit that a certain symbolic species verifies, with a general and permanent character, a minimal set of maxims of behaviour between individuals, within the symbolic species in question (*Nota bene*: so, each time the public debate intended to lead to practical agreement is carried on in relation to the symbolic species in view). Of course, informal agreement on a given symbolic species can be accompanied/reinforced by a corresponding codification in the normative framework of society, which transforms the ethical/moral into normative (positive law). This doubling of the informal practical agreement is not mandatory, but from the point of view of increasing the likelihood that the informal agreement will be respected, normative codification may represent a good solution. Practical agreement implies a certain degree of *ethical discernment* among the population of the society in question.

(c) Praxeological Agreement

Praxeological agreement refers to the *rational/irrational* action categories, which, in fact, implies agreement on a model of rationality to be implemented at the level of society (or a narrower community, as the case may be). A model of rationality, in a simplified definition, is a logical model that causally and functionally correlates the purpose of an action and the means of achieving that action. In this sense, an action (or decision, which is logically prior to the action) is rational if it derives, inferentially validly, from the axioms or theorems of the model of rationality in question, and an action (or decision) is irrational if it is inferred invalidly from a given model of rationality. So, rationality or irrationality is always assigned to a model of rationality, there is no such thing as rational action relative to any model of rationality, and the same must be said of irrational action. In other words, an action can be rational (in the sense described above) in relation to one model of rationality, and, concomitantly, it can be irrational in relation to another model of rationality. The same can be said of irrational action. As for a-rational action, it is that action (or decision) that cannot be assigned to an inference (either valid or invalid) from a fixed model of rationality. Praxeological agreement implies a certain degree of *logical discernment* among the population of the society in question.

10.2.6 The Concept of Symbolic Species—Necessary New Predicates

Logically, any predicate of sufficiency, once the entity in question has been epistemologically generated by the set of predicates of sufficiency, becomes, *eo ipso*, a predicate of necessity. However, after the emergence of that entity, it is possible for it to generate new necessity predicates (SNNPs) which, this time, are no longer sufficiency predicates. For the generic case of a symbolic species generated by the meeting of sufficiency predicates, we consider the following two new necessity predicates to be assumed:

(i) (**SNNP1**) the individuals of the symbolic species are, in some cases, *predominantly clones*—this new (admittedly polemical) predicate of necessity "requires" that the design of the individuals of a symbolic species be done in a unitary, homogeneous way, which justifies the use, here, of the term clone. The reason this new predicate of necessity should be retained is that, most of the time, a symbolic species is required to function unitarily/homogenously over large spaces or time horizons.

Discussion

And here the use of the adverb "predominantly" covers the (possible) situations where a symbolic species may contain individuals that are not exactly clones of, say, a representative individual (or, as a rule, of the species itself). It is the case of the deconcentration/decentralization of some public institutions, in which the territorial specificity can induce some (non-essential, i.e., purely functional) differentiations between the individuals of the species in question. For example, the process called "best practices" can also lead to some surface (not substrate) differentiation between the individuals of a symbolic species, by assimilating some practices—that is, some particular ways of functioning—that have been proven by utility in some such individuals. On the other hand, it may also be the case that the *ab initio* design of some individuals of the symbolic species is intentionally/programmatically made different, in order to maximize the impact of the functioning of the individuals in question in different social environments with irreducible characteristics. It should be noted that clone-individuals are specific to certain symbolic species—we will call them codified institutional symbolic species. So those symbolic species that are not institutionally codified, although they may still be institutional—e.g., moral rules—are not "required" to contain clone-individuals. For example, the symbolic species related to scientific theories contains individuals who often have fundamentally/axiomatically opposite configurations and function differently as individuals both within the species and in relation to their environment. The logical causality of SNNP1 is as follows:

$$SNNP1 \leftarrow (SSP2) \wedge (SSP3)$$

Although, as we have shown, clone-individuals occur only in the case of the category of symbolic species called the coded institutional symbolic species, we have thought it appropriate to specify this possibility as a new predicate of necessity, with the precautions already taken earlier, because the general, common case is that individuals of a species (including symbolic ones) have different traits from each other, i.e., they are non-clones, precisely to allow environmental selection (understood in the widest possible referential sense).

(ii) (**SNNP2**) the emergence (speciation) of the symbolic species is a *contingent* fact, not a necessary one.

Discussion

Contingency (like necessity, for that matter) is, firstly, not completely isolated from necessity, and secondly, it can enter into a hypercycle with necessity. In this sense, we can have contingency intra-necessity, and, necessity intra-contingency. Intra-necessity contingency is an episode of contingency in a longer chain of necessity, and intra-contingency necessity is an episode of necessity in a longer chain of contingency. Especially in the field of symbolic species, these oscillations between necessity and contingency are, in our opinion, characteristic. Of course, the question of necessity in the cultural field is one of the thorniest, because it not only refers to the idea of determinism, but—what is more "serious"—suggests the absence of free will in the decisions that are made by individuals or groups of individuals in the category humans. In addition, the question of necessity calls for the discussion of so-called historical laws (which are assumed to have a necessary character, analogously to the laws of nature). In relation to the last problem associated with the idea of necessity, three approaches are remarkable: (a) the Marxist approach to dialectical materialism, in the footsteps of Hegel's "general" dialectic; (b) the structuralist approach (initiated by phonology—Saussure, Jacobson, Greimas, Hjelmslev, etc., and developed by Claude Levi-Strauss in anthropology/ethnology, but which also permeated literature (Propp, Barthes); (c) the psychoanalytic approach, initiated by Freud and taken over (also from a structuralist perspective, by the way) by Lacan (Dosse, 1997). The logical causality of SNNP2 is as follows:

$$SNNP2 \leftarrow (SSP1)$$

10.2.7 Speciation of Symbolic Species

We have previously shown that speciation—that is, the appearance, the emergence of species—is of two types: (a) sympatric speciation; (b) allopatric speciation. We will examine the possibility of these categories of speciation in the case of the symbolic species and, based on the results obtained, we will ask the question whether there can be (and what exactly are) speciation categories specific to symbolic species, considering their sufficiency predicates.

(a) Examination of General Types of Speciation

As we have shown, sympatric speciation is the effect of competition or the appearance of particular traits between individuals (of a species) that live/function in the same physical and temporal area (they are co-existing and contemporaneous), while allopatric speciation is the effect of the isolation of a species following the appearance of an obstacle of physical (geographical) separation—a river, a mountain, etc. or, one might add, of temporal separation. In this paragraph, we will examine whether and under what conditions these "classical" types of speciation are also maintained in symbolic species.

(a1) Regarding sympatric speciation in the symbolic case

The content of sympatric speciation in the standard case (of the biological species) is space-referenced (and, logically, also time-referenced, since individuals of a species in the same space must also be contemporaneous for the environment to make selection at the phenotype level). In the case of the symbolic species, both space and time, that is, both coexistence and contemporaneity are relevant (*Nota bene*: perhaps even, as it seems to us, with a stronger emphasis on the community of time, that is, contemporaneity). For example, regarding space, in the case of the symbolic species we call science, the directions that some approaches registered on the European continent were different (or even opposite) to those registered in Great Britain or the Americas. The same can be said about approaches to the symbolic species called politics or society (free and democratic societies in Western Europe, closed and authoritarian societies in Asia). In relation to sympatric speciation generated by contemporaneity, things are a bit more complicated. Some symbolic species have more to do with contemporary individuals—for example, symbolic species in the domain of social organization and functioning—while other symbolic species have as much to do with contemporary individuals as with noncontemporary individuals. For example, in the case of the symbolic species called science, many (if not most) individuals in an era relate, either from a critique/delineation perspective or from a compatibility/takeover perspective, to individuals who have lived (more precisely, worked) in past, sometimes very distant ages (as is the case with philosophy, especially metaphysics/ontology). So, in the case of sympatric speciation that applies to symbolic species, both the spatial component (coexistence) and the temporal component (contemporaneity), although present, are much diminished, in the sense that sympatric speciation of symbolic species has a much greater degree of freedom than sympatric speciation of natural (biological) species.

(a2) Regarding allopatric speciation in the symbolic case

It is obvious, based on the conclusion drawn from the examination of sympatric speciation of symbolic species, that allopatric speciation of these species is moot. Specifically, the fact that symbolic species have an essential informational component in their very existential structure (for example, theoretical science is almost exclusively information/knowledge), the inter-spatial and inter-temporal dialogue is obstructed by almost nothing (except some problems raised by translation into other languages). We therefore conclude that, from the perspective of the standard categories (associated with natural/biological species) of speciation, symbolic species retain an adjusted sympatric speciation—which allowed standard allopatric speciation to be subsumed into this adjusted sympatric speciation. For the purposes of the present study, we will refer to this adapted sympatric speciation associated with symbolic species as non-standard speciation.

(b) Other speciation categories specific to symbolic species

In this paragraph, we will examine the possibility of the existence of some categories of speciation that are exclusively working in the case of symbolic species, by virtue of the sufficiency predicates, respectively, the newly established predicates of necessity.

(b1) Preliminary considerations

The types of speciation characterizing only the symbolic species will be referred to hereafter as symbolic speciation (*Nota bene*: as we have shown above, non-standard speciation is common, at its core, to biological species and symbolic species). It is clear that symbolic speciation is an exclusively cultural phenomenon (while non-standard speciation also maintains a natural component in what we call its core, i.e., in terms of the biological and social/symbolic common elements of speciation). Being an exclusively cultural phenomenon, the causality of symbolic speciation must be sought in the cultural matrix (axiological, ethical/moral, praxeological, practical/pragmatic, etc.) of society, i.e., in the commandments of the social construction and functioning of the individual. Accordingly, the "rules" or criteria that will be considered, in the following, regarding the identification of categories (classes) of symbolic speciation are the following:

- symbolic speciation is the effect of categories (classes) of human activity—theoretically, there are as many categories (classes) of this type of speciation as relevant categories (classes) of human activity (under a structural, not historical aspect) can be identified, in turn;
- symbolic speciation verifies the sufficiency predicates established for the concept of symbolic species;

- the symbolic species is, effectively, a creative act of man/society (exactly in the sense in which, from a mystical point of view, the biological species is considered to be a creative act of a divine entity);
- the stability of the symbolic species only arises as a result of its codification through the normative framework of society. This is a direct (and unavoidable) effect of the sufficiency predicate of the symbolic species denoted above by SSP1;
- the evolution of the symbolic species is, to the greatest extent, a hetero-evolution (that is, an evolution decided and directed from the outside—human society), unlike the evolution of the biological species which is almost entirely a self-evolution.

(b2) The Speciation Categories of Symbolic Species

(b2.1) *Firstly*, there is a need to establish the criteria for identifying categories of symbolic speciation. According to the above, we consider that the following such criteria exist (or may exist as such) overlapping the distinct and relevant categories of human activity from a logical and structural perspective:

(i) The *theoretical/epistemological* criterion: generated by the theoretical activity of society. Theoretical activity refers to the cognitive activity carried out by the subject regarding the general relationships between objects. Examples of theoretical activity: knowledge from the natural sciences, knowledge that ignores the institutional role of the subject in the humanities, knowledge from the social sciences, where individuals are treated passively, as simple invariant nodes of inter-action, knowledge from the field of philosophy, knowledge in the field of general theoretical methodology (mathematics, logic);

(ii) The *practical/inter-actional* criterion: generated by the practical activity of society. Practical activity refers to the activity of inter-relationship (from any point of view) of individuals, that is, to the activity that is carried out with regard to the general relations between subjects. Examples of practical activity: religion (not as doctrine, but as social application of doctrine), ethics/morality, anthropology, politics (also, not as doctrine, but as social application of doctrine) and the like;

(iii) The *praxeological/transformational* criterion: generated by the praxeological activity of society. Praxeological activity refers to the inter-action activity between subject and object, from the perspective of entropic exchange, respectively from that of maintaining or decreasing social entropy (implicitly the economic one) at the societal level. The representative example of praxeological activity is economic activity, but, of course, other relationships between subject and object can have the purpose/goal of reducing or at least maintaining entropy at the societal level;

(iv) The *artistic/mythical* criterion: generated by the artistic activity, which includes a mix of inter-actions between subjects, between subject and object, as well as between objects, intended not for knowledge, but for the reconstruction of the world, on an ideational level, in accordance with the turmoil human regarding the most general relationships between the individual and the world. Examples of artistic activity: fiction, music, painting, sculpture, architecture, mythology and others, characterized by the transfiguration of reality from the perspective of values that we call artistic-mythical values;

(v) The *institutional/normative* criterion: generated by the institutional activity of the society. Institutional activity refers to what is also called the social construction/re-construction of reality (Berger & Luckmann, 2008), i.e., the establishment of norms, institutions and organizations intended to ensure the imperative framework for the organization and functioning of society (and societal system).

Discussion

It is easy to see that, through the five categories/classes of human actions, at the individual level or at the group/society level, the entire spectrum of possible activities (or, at least, manifested, so far, from the point of view of historical view) within human society is caught. Criterion four (artistic/mythical) brings together the artistic and the mythical on the basis of an obvious affinity between the domains (worlds) of the manifestation of the human spirit. Indeed, the mythic—the creator of mythology—is at least as productive, in terms of prolificacy and complexity, as the artistic one. This is without mentioning the inevitable transition from the artistic to the mythical and vice versa—for example, the current post-structuralist and post-modernist trends illustrate in the most eloquent way this inevitable entanglement between the artistic and the mythical. It is no longer necessary (due to the aforementioned) to explain the distinction (not without some interferences, however) between praxeological and practical, to show that each of the two fields deserves to have its own theoretical "citizenship".

(b2.2) *Secondly*, and based on the chosen criteria (logical, i.e., an-historical), we propose to consider, for what follows, the following categories of symbolic speciation (*Nota bene*: all the speciations mentioned above are characterized here only by their proximate or predominant causality, which is always subjective. At the same time, since it is of the nature of artefacts, the result of the speciations in question is always objective).

1. *Cognitive* speciation: it is carried out based on the theoretical/gnoseological criterion, resulting in scientific theories in any field, i.e., theories that refer to object-object relations, regardless of the nature of those objects;
2. *Ethical* speciation: it is carried out on the basis of the practical/interactional criterion, resulting in ethical (moral), political, religious and similar systems, that is, systems that refer to subject-subject relations;
3. *Objective* speciation: it is carried out on the basis of the praxeological/transformational criterion, resulting in systems of interaction between the subject and the object, in the direction of the transformation of the object in accordance with the purposes of the subject. This includes economic systems and other action systems that, within society, aim to reduce (or at least maintain) social entropy;
4. *Constructive* speciation: it is carried out on the basis of the artistic/mythical criterion, resulting in the creation of imaginary worlds (alternatives to the real world described by the species generated by cognitive speciation), in the form of artistic (aesthetic) works or in the form of founding or functional myths, as the case may be;
5. *Normative* speciation: it is carried out based on the normative institutional criterion, resulting in objectified constructs through intersubjective agreement in relation to all areas of society's existence and functioning. This mainly includes the positive normative framework (positive legislation—fundamental, primary, secondary, tertiary and quaternary).

Discussion

Although we have kept the name speciation, the concept that was developed above is that of generation—in the sense that it is a process by which not species are created but ... genera. A genus is an integrator comprising several species, just as a species is an integrator comprising several individuals. The result is that each speciation (which should therefore be called a generation) actually contains several species which, in turn, contain several individuals. For example, in the case of cognitive speciation, we can have the species of natural sciences (with related individuals like: physics, chemistry, biology), the species of social sciences (with related individuals like: sociology, political science), the species of human sciences/humanities (with related individuals like: anthropology, linguistics). Likewise, in the case of constructive speciation, we can have the species of literature (with related individuals such as poetry, novel, theatre), the species of music (with related individuals such as symphony, sonata, pop, blues), the species of painting (with related individuals such as monumental painting, decorative painting, easel painting). Normative speciation will be of particular interest to us in this chapter. And it, as a generation, contains distinct species such as institutional norms (which create "institutional individuals"), regulative norms (which create "regulative individuals") and so on. From another perspective, normative speciation targets species in zones or areas of social activity such as fiscal norms, monetary norms, moral norms, political norms and so on.

10.2.8 The Concept of Evolution of the Generic Symbolic Species

(a) Background items

As is well known, one can only talk about evolution properly in relation to the species—in relation to the individuals that make up the species, the appropriate term for changes over time is developmental (for example, in the biological case, from birth to adulthood, where adulthood means the level of development of the individual at which it is capable of viable reproduction/replication within the species). In this paragraph we will discuss the concept of evolution in the case of the symbolic species, as it was previously introduced—of course, for the moment, only the generic symbolic species is considered, without a particularization of it.

First of all, it must be said that the evolution of a symbolic species is not an independent fact, but one dependent on the creator of that species, that is, on the generic human subject, respectively on human society as a whole.

Secondly, the evolution of the symbolic species is purpose-directed. As is known, the evolution of the biological species is not governed by purpose, but by finality. In the case of the symbolic species, the finality of evolution takes the form of the purpose of evolution.

Thirdly, the purpose of evolution in the case of the symbolic species is an externalized one. This means that that purpose is not peculiar to the symbolic species in question, but, by virtue of the non-independence of evolution of the symbolic species, belongs to the creator of that species. More specifically, it should be said that the symbolic species evolves in accordance with an externalized purpose that is logically a means to the realization of the purpose of the creator of the species. This finding is very important for the evolutionary process of the symbolic species; therefore, we will offer some analytical developments in the matter:

- the ultimate goal of the individual (and, by aggregation, of society) is survival. This is explained by the fact that the human subject, in terms of his animal component, is endowed with the instinct of survival, either through cooperation (in most cases) or through competition;
- survival is an effect of practical/instrumental rationality, although the human subject (and therefore society) also has a theoretical rationality—beliefs, preferences, etc.;
- practical rationality requires the choice and use of means (adequate from the perspective of efficiency—the effect-effort ratio) to achieve the goal;
- one of the means on which we will focus in this chapter is the generic symbolic species;
- therefore, the goal belongs to the human subject (by logical extension, to society), it cannot belong to the means itself, i.e., to the symbolic species; more precisely, the goal is projected from the outside onto the symbolic species, therefore it appears as externalized in relation to the symbolic species in question.

(b) The Evolutionary Mechanism of the Symbolic Species

Based on what was stated in point (a) of this paragraph, we will present, below, an outline of the evolutionary mechanism of the generic symbolic species. We will use a synoptic representation (Fig. 10.3).

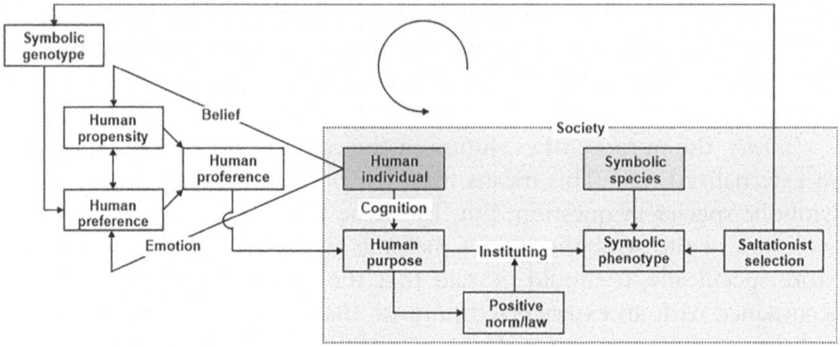

Fig. 10.3 The evolutionary mechanism of the generic symbolic species (stylization I). *Source*: author

Discussion

It is noted that while the phenotype of the symbolic species is within the society, the genotype is outside the symbolic species (including its phenotype)—as shown above, the genotype is formed within the proference (Dinga et al., 2022), which is a logical-functional combination of propensity and preference (*Nota bene*: the name of proference is a terminological mix made up of the two names—propensity and preference). Human propensity is generated at the level of belief, which constitutes the most solid foundation of human behaviour, including principles, values, traditions of the greatest importance and significance for the individual concerned. Human preference is generated, predominantly, by emotion/affectivity which, on the one hand, originates in the biological evolution of the individual and, on the other hand, is constituted on the basis of life experience. Some emotions (such as fear) are formed and become persistent sometimes after a single episode of individual experience; others need repetition of the episodes in question. On the basis of the proference, which is anchored, for the most part, in the unconscious, the human subject formulates its purpose (for which the symbolic species becomes the means), by intermediation of cognition, that is, of rational models compatible with belief (and sometimes even with affectivity). This purpose, once established by means of the legal norm (positive law), becomes the very phenotype of the symbolic species in question. It should be mentioned a crucial difference between the establishment of the phenotype in the biological case and its establishment in the symbolic case: thus, in the biological case, the phenotype is not generated as such, it undergoes a process of growth/development, at the end of which the phenotype itself appears (in most cases, it is about reaching the adult state of the individual, i.e., about acquiring the biological capacity for viable reproduction), while, in the symbolic case, the phenotype is generated as such, all of a sudden, without the need for a period of growth/development. As previously shown, selection occurs on the phenotype, from the environment in which that symbolic species functions, namely in a saltational, non-gradual (or non-cumulative) manner. As in the biological case, selection is also driven by fitness maximization, except that social (or symbolic) fitness is different from biological fitness. As we will show later, the maximization of fitness in the case of the symbolic species refers to the adequacy of the functioning of that species to the intended goal—from the instrumental point of view, it is about the adequacy of this functioning to the content of the institutional norm (positive institutional laws).

(c) The Concept of Autonomous Evolution of the Symbolic Species

As follows from point (b) above, although it is not excluded that the environment in which the individuals of a symbolic species function may generate mutations in the functioning of those individuals, mutations which, then, will be taken into account by the creator/user of the symbolic species concerned, these external influences (which are overwhelmingly in the case of biological species) are rare, of minor intensity, and generally target superficial aspects of the functioning of the individuals concerned. Almost all impulses of change (i.e., mutations) that occur in the evolution of a symbolic species originate in the decision of the creator of the symbolic species itself. We develop below, briefly, the basic mechanism that justifies, in our opinion, the idea that, in the case of the symbolic species, it is an autonomous or quasi-autonomous evolution in relation to the environment in which it functions. Evolutionary autonomy/quasi-autonomy with respect to the environment is equivalent to total or quasi-total evolutionary dependence with respect to the creator/user (individual or society, as the case may be) of the symbolic species.

- the occurrence of the symbolic species is a cultural fact—it is created deliberatively, either by intellectual decision (a theory, a myth) or by legal decision, by means of regulation (an institutional structure);

- as a cultural fact, the creation of a symbolic species can even be programmatic—that is, it can be part of a program or a strategy assumed by the individual, group or social structure that intends to create that symbolic species;
- whatever the reason for which a symbolic species is created, it serves a predetermined purpose, functioning as a means to achieve that purpose;
- as a means to an end external to itself, the symbolic species is susceptible above all to adjustments/modifications/mutations coming from its creator, based on his/her model of rationality—a model of rationality, especially a model of practical rationality, is a logical model that associates, more or less optimally, but at least adequately, a means to an end;
- especially if the symbolic species considered has a programmatic character (e.g., it is part of a medium or long-term program or strategy), the modifications/mutations likely to be implemented in its structure and operation originate in the creator of that symbolic species;
- therefore, dominantly (overwhelmingly), the evolution of the symbolic species is causally external to it, although, as we have already said, some influences may also come from the environment in which it operates, but even these influences pass through the filter and depend on the decision of the creator of the symbolic species;
- the evolutionary autonomy of the symbolic species is probably (along with and as a result of the fact that it is an artefact, i.e., a social construct) the most important characteristic of this category of species. This characteristic will, moreover, be the basis of the entire co-evolutionary model that will be developed in the present chapter, regarding the (societal) crisis.

(d) Other Remarks on the Evolution of the Symbolic Species

We present, next, some useful observations, which result from the examination (made above) of the evolution of a generic symbolic species:

- non-functioning of the population (statistical) criterion in the evolution of a symbolic species:
  - it is not possible for a certain individual mutation to acquire, by means of selection, a dominant weight in a symbolic species, because a mutation, which always occurs in the genotype con-

tained in the human subject with respect to that symbolic species, is applied, by the saltationist (and, as a rule, normative-imperative) decision of the human subject, of all individuals of the species in question—so the evolution of the symbolic species is of a non-population type, because the share of a given mutation suddenly becomes common to all individuals of the species;
  - the impossibility of the population dominance of a mutation in the symbolic species is accompanied, from a logical point of view, by the non-necessity of such dominance, because the reproduction of the individuals of the symbolic species is ensured, according to the mutation occurred, with certainty, being operated by the human subject, not by the proper individuals of that symbolic species;
- a mutation occurs with respect to all individuals of a symbolic species, not just one or a certain number of such individuals, because, once the mutation appears in the genotype, it is incorporated, by the human subject, in all individuals of the symbolic species in question;
  - here the predicate of necessity of the symbolic species NNP1 works, in the sense that, as a rule and overwhelmingly, the individuals of a symbolic species are clones;
- it is, however, necessary for a mutation to register a critical mass, but this happens not at the population level of the symbolic species, but at the decisional level of the human subject—either based on the internal, programmatic logic of a symbolic species or as result of some signals coming from the environment in which that symbolic species functions; the human subject will "wait" until s/he considers that the operation of the mutation on the individuals of the species is required and then s/he will implement that mutation simultaneously at the level of all the phenotypes in question in operation;
- the extensive or restricted reproduction, as appropriate, of individuals of a symbolic species is also at the discretion of the creator human subject of a given symbolic species;
- there is the possibility for the human subject to design, for a given symbolic species, mechanisms for incorporating some mutations coming from the operating environment of the corresponding individuals automatically (through automatic stabilizers); even in this case, the taking over of the mutation is done saltationally and in a generalized way—with respect to all individuals of the species—as in the discretionary case of taking over the mutation;

- in accordance with the NNP2 necessity predicate, the following considerations are useful:
  - a mutation (coming either from the human subject or from the environment in which a given symbolic species functions) may or may not be applied (*Nota bene*: unless it is automatically taken over); here appears the possibility of a certain cumulativeness of selection, analogous to the case of the biological species;
  - the mentioned cumulativeness has a passive character, in the sense that the mutation (or mutational pressure) in question has not yet been taken over, but "waits" either for a confirmation or for a strengthening or for a disappearance, as the case may be, before a decision is made of takeover in phenotype;
  - as we said above, here there is "room" for conceptual developments from the perspective of the Kuhnian paradigm, by introducing the mutational anomaly, so to speak: a verification/testing occurs (for example, from the perspective of meaning or that of persistence of the mutation in question) before making the decision to select that mutation.

10.2.9 The Concept of Generic Symbolic Species Co-evolution

Logically, there is no such thing as co-evolution, since any evolution is co-evolution, because evolution involves selection, and selection is operated by an "agent" external to the individuals that make up the species in question. This statement is absolute in relation to the biological species. The question arises as to whether and to what extent it is also valid for the symbolic species, as it has been described and examined previously.

(a) Background Items

The analysis of co-evolution involves the operation of a separation (Spencer-Brown, 1972) between the analysed species (which we can call the target species) and the environment in which that species functions. The environment of a species contains two distinct components, in turn: (i) the undifferentiated environment (either non-anthropic or anthropic); (ii) other species (either natural or symbolic). It follows that a target species will simultaneously be under the selection force of both components of its environment. In this context, to talk about co-evolution means to consider, alternatively, two situations: (1) to consider the environment as a species, without differentiating it into the two mentioned components, which means that the environment, as such and in its entirety, is considered a co-species for the target species; (2) to extract, from the environment, a certain species, which alone will be considered a co-species for the target species. Although there are certain methodological differences between them, the two options are equivalent from a logical-conceptual point of view, and the choice of one or the other of the options is at the discretion of the researcher, depending on the purpose and objectives of the research. On this general basis of co-evolution, we will make some particular considerations relating to symbolic species:

- being artefacts (see sufficiency predicate SP1), symbolic species function, overwhelmingly, in an environment also populated by symbolic species. Thus, one could speak of symbolic environment functioning, either as a whole or through a given symbolic species and which is contained in the symbolic environment, as a co-species for the target species;
- between co-evolution and co-adaptation, the differences are nuanced, because, ultimately, the adaptation of a species to another species (or to the environment of the first species) resides in the selection of a mutation that appeared in the first species, a selection made by the second species, and reciprocally, i.e., they reside in a chain of co-adaptations. Therefore, the chain of co-adaptations (mutual adaptations) between the two co-species has the ultimate meaning of co-evolution, which means that, conceptually, co-adaptation is an intermediate (stage) form of co- evolution;
- even if the impulse/mutation that is addressed to a symbolic species comes from the non-symbolic component of the environment in which that symbolic species (target species) functions—for example, it comes from the human subject—the selection of the mutation in question must be carried out by the co-symbolic species or, at the limit, by the symbolic component (symbolic environment) of the "total" environment in which the target species functions. It could be said that mutations or non-symbolic mutational pressure are only cues or signals for the symbolic mutation to be integrated by the selection process;
- unlike the case of biological species, in that of symbolic species automatic (non-discretionary) selection devices are in the minority, although, as will be shown below, they are not excluded and have

their role and functions in co-evolution of symbolic species. The explanation for this state of affairs lies in the fact that, in the case of symbolic species, the cultural factor (first, values and, second, political, taken in the broadest sense) is decisive in the selection process. Of course, this arises the question of the programmatic character of mutations/selection specific to symbolic species—one could say that this programmatic character is equivalent, i.e., has the same functions, to the automatic character of mutation/selection (which works, for example, in an automatic stabilizer). With the mention that a programmatic character of the evolution/co-evolution of a symbolic species is indeed of the nature of the automatism of mutation/selection, we will say that, however, here we do not have the necessity that subsists, for example, in a model of rationality, but we have, in fact, an intra-necessity contingency.

(b) The Symbolic Co-evolutionary Mechanism

Both evolution and co-evolution are, in fact, planned by the human subject. This is a logical consequence of the fact that the symbolic species is an artefact, and one of the new predicates of necessity is the one that requires the contingency of the symbolic species (NNP2), thus of its evolution. The conscious, deliberate and, as we stated before, even programmatic character of the creation and evolution of the symbolic species makes its evolution and co-evolution in the nature of a social project (in some cases, in the nature of an intellectual project). Since co-evolution involves two symbolic species, it follows that this process is itself already designed into the norms of organization and functioning of the two symbolic species involved. In fact, it should be said that, at the level of society as a whole, the entire set of symbolic species functioning at any given time are engaged in a *sui generis* co-evolution. *Nota bene*: moreover, not even in nature (at the level of the set of contemporary biological species) does it happen otherwise—the evolution or co-evolution, as the case may be, of any biological species or of any pair of biological species that interact more or less directly, occurs in such a way that all species influence all species. Of course, some influences are stronger than others, or more relevant to the human subject (or to society as a whole) than others but, essentially, there is a general entanglement between species. From an analytical point of view, we will always consider only two species (either biological or symbolic), but we will not forget that each of them takes on all the influences in which it is involved in the general evolutionary process in society. Based

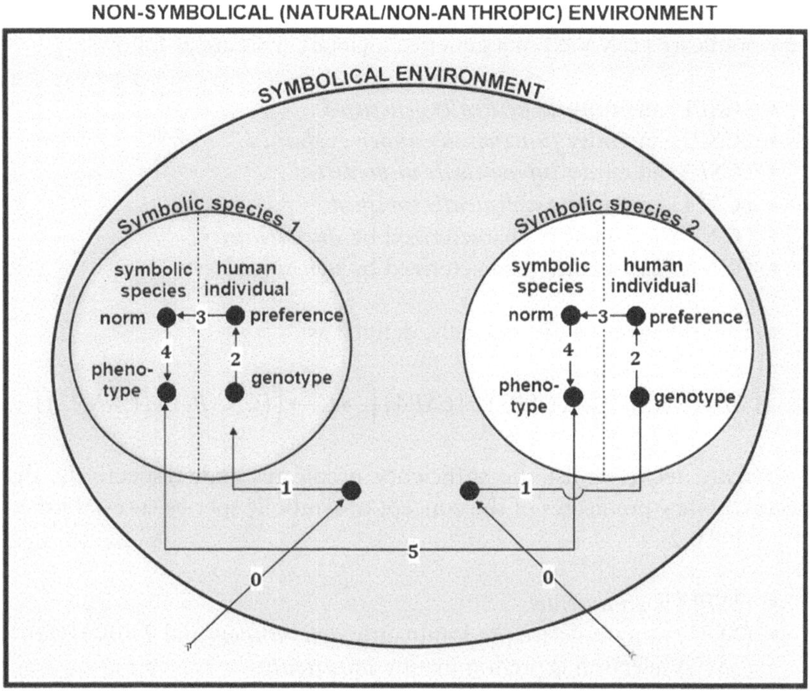

Fig. 10.4 The evolutionary mechanism of the generic symbolic species (stylization II). *Source*: author

on these general considerations, we can represent the symbolic co-evolutionary mechanism (involving symbolic species) as in Fig. 10.4.

10.3 Societal Crisis as Symbolic Species

In this paragraph, we shall examine the possibility that the (societal) crisis is a symbolic species, as this concept has been analysed above. Let us remember the sufficiency predicates that were found for the concept of generic crisis (Chap. 2).

Firstly, we have two views from which a crisis is perceived: (a) the ontological view—called ω-perspective—that provides the rationality model (RM) of the crisis; (b) the epistemological view—called ε-perspective—that provides the comprehension model (CM) of the crisis. To ω-perspective is assigned the meaning of the crisis, while to ε-perspective is assigned the signification (significance) of the crisis.

Secondly, the sufficiency predicates (*CSPs*), respectively, the necessary new predicate (*CNNPs*) of a generic (societal) crisis are as follows:

- (*CSP1*) an entity *structurally generated*
- (*CSP2*) an entity *functionally under-explained*
- (*CSP3*) an entity *inferentially unpredicted*
- (*CSP4*) an entity *axiologically signified*
- (*CNNP1*) an entity characterized by *discontinuity*
- (*CNNP2*) an entity characterized by *non-singularity*

so that the crisis (*C*) is, logically, defined as:

$$\left[(CSP1)\wedge(CSP2)\wedge(CSP3)\wedge(CSP4)\right]\rightarrow C\rightarrow\left[(CNNP1)\wedge(CNNP2)\right]$$

Thirdly, let us re-list the sufficiency predicates and, respectively, the necessary new predicates of the concept of symbolic species, as established at point 10.2.

- (*SSP1*) is an *artefact*
- (*SSP2*) mutations are predominantly *non-random* and *Lamarckian*
- (*SSP3*) selection is predominantly *saltationist*
- (*SSP4*) has *inauthentic genotype*
- (*SNNP1*) the individuals of the symbolic species are, in some cases, *predominantly clones*
- (*SNNP2*) the emergence (speciation) of the symbolic species is a *contingent* fact

So that the symbolic species (*SS*) is, logically, defined as:

$$\left[(SSP1)\wedge(SSP2)\wedge(SSP3)\wedge(SSP4)\right]\rightarrow SS\rightarrow\left[(SNNP1)\wedge(SNNP2)\right]$$

Fourthly, we must verify, based on the two sets of sufficiency predicates, and, of course, on the two sets of necessary new predicates—one for the concept of symbolic species, and one for the concept of generic (societal) crisis—if the crisis is an individual of the class of symbolic species.

As known, for an entity to be included in another entity, the sufficiency predicates of the first entity (in our case: the crisis) must verify the sufficiency predicates of the second entity (in our case: the symbolic species).

Table 10.1 Analysis based on the sufficiency predicates

↲↑	*SSP1*	*SSP2*	*SSP3*	*SSP4*
CSP1		↑		↑
CSP2	↑		→	
CSP3		↑		→
CSP4	↑		↑	

Source: author

Table 10.2 Analysis based on the necessary new predicates

↲↑	*SNNP1*	*SNNP2*
CNNP1	↑	→
CNNP2	↑	→

Source: author

We shall proceed to such an analysis, based on Table 10.1, respectively, on Table 10.2. *Nota bene*: the notations in the two tables are: ↑ necessarily implies; → probably implies.

The same for the necessary new predicates (Table 10.2).

As we have said many times before, the most rigorous comparison between two concepts is performed by comparing their sufficiency predicates two by two (often is relevant to compare in the same way the necessary new predicates too). It is obvious that from such a comparison results that the generic (societal) crisis should be considered a symbolic species in the societal phenomenology, since its sufficiency predicates imply, in a great extent (two predicates from four), the sufficiency predicates of symbolic species. In addition, the necessary new predicates of crisis imply, also, the necessary new predicates of symbolic species.

10.4 On the Genotype of Societal Crisis

The evolutionist paradigm implies identifying the evolutionary "ingredients" for the entity considered as being an evolutionist one. Such a crucial "ingredient" is, of course, the genotype of crisis. To identify it, we resume the analytical formula of a generic crisis (see Chap. 3), i.e., $C_{12345}^{\alpha\beta\gamma\delta\varepsilon}$. We remind the meaning of the five parameters: α: crises' cause/s; β: crises' origin; γ: crises' chreode (trajectory); δ: crises' impact/s; ε: crises' significance.[24] The "headquarter" of the genotype[25] is located in the human individual who is "responsible" with the generic (societal) crises, and addresses the significance, i.e., the parameter ε.

The authentic genotype resides in the consciousness/consciousness of the human subject. The structure of the authentic genotype seems to be the following (*Nota bene*: *CG*x denoted the x structural component of the authentic genotype of the crisis):

- (*CG*1) a *propensity* associated with phenomenon of the societal crisis. This can consist of beliefs or convictions, traditions, experiences and the like, which do not necessarily crystallize into models of rationality, being, rather, an implicit "secretion" of the unconscious;
- (*CG*2) an *ideology* (theory) in the field of societal crisis, which is at the conscious level, and has the explicit form of a model of theoretical rationality;
- (*CG*3) a *pragmatics*, located at the conscious level, and which has the explicit form of a model of practical rationality.

The genuine genotype of the crisis must possess a set of properties/characteristics that allow it to perform its functions (see below) within the co-evolutionary mechanism of the crisis (*Nota bene*: with *PG*x was denoted the property x of the genuine genotype of the crisis):

- (*PG*1) *high sensitivity*: this property is required in order that the genotype to function as a genotype, that is, as a recipient of changing pressures from the environment with crisis. Of course, we are talking here about an intellectual sensitivity, not a sensory one;
- (*PG*2) *activation thresholds*: the sensitivity property must not, however, have a continuous character, i.e., it is not admissible that any change pressure, coming from the environment with crisis, regardless of its nature, intensity or duration, be "perceived" by crisis genotype. If so, it would simply mean that the crisis would be so volatile (admittedly discretionary, not automatic) that it would not allow for any kind of predictability in the matter. As a result, the genotype will integrate/internalize change pressures only after their amount (intensity multiplied by exercise duration) exceeds a certain threshold called the *threshold of significance* (see the parameter ε above). The significance is of a cultural nature. At the same time, the thresh-

olds in question depend on the nature of the pressure to change. It follows that there will be a system of thresholds, classified by the nature of the change pressure, that will regulate the operation of the sensitivity of the crisis's genotype. The second reason for the existence of thresholds in the sensitivity of the crisis's genotype (the first being the avoidance of excessive volatility of the crisis, which leads to the decrease of predictability in the matter) is that of avoiding the internalization of conjunctural, seasonal or accidental change pressures. Indeed, some signals in the direction of changing the action related to the crisis may have a non-structural or, at least, non-systematic character or, in many cases, may manifest themselves in the short or very short term, after which they cease. The "certainty" of the pressure to change increases as it is allowed to manifest itself for a certain period of time in which it does not deny itself, or this is ensured precisely by establishing thresholds of significance;

- (*PG*3) *discretionary reversibility*: this property is very important because it avoids introducing an "arrow" in the genotype change, for example, a permanent increase, or a permanent decrease, or a permanent stationarity of crisis pressure. It should be noted that reversibility, as a property, has nothing to do with reversibility as an intrinsic process of the pressure of conjunctural change that was discussed in the previous property of the crisis's genotype. The reversibility has exactly the same "physiology" as the initial change, except that it occurs in the opposite direction, by approximately the same amount.[26] The discretionary character of reversibility refers, of course, to the fact that any change in the (genuine) crisis's genotype can only be performed through the medium of the human subject.

Based on the structure of the genuine crisis's genotype, as well as its properties, we can now highlight the possible functions for this genotype, within the general evolutionary mechanism of the crisis—environment binomial (*Nota bene*: with *FG*x it was noted function x of the genuine crisis's genotype).

- (*FG*1) *recording*: of course, the first function of the genuine crisis's genotype must be to record, to "take notice" of (here, in the proper sense of the phrase, since it is about the human subject) the pressure of change that comes from the environment with crisis. The genotype simply compiles a list of changes as suggested by the change pressure in question—this is a primary list of genotype recording (*PLG*) within an episode of genotype impressment.

- (*FG2*) *filtering*: this function clearly distinguishes the personality of the (genuine) crisis's genotype from the genotype of the biological species—while the genotype of the biological species has a passive character, of simple impressionability (in the sense that the pressure to change is taken over *tale quale* and transmitted in the phenotype, following that it will be subject to selection, of course), the genotype of the symbolic species, in this case the genotype of the crisis, has an active character. The pressure to change belongs to the human individual, so it must be subject to an examination—either on intuitive grounds or on rational grounds but, obviously, mostly on rational grounds—that leads to a sui-generis selection of the very elements of the pressure to change that will be effective when taken into the genotype. From a theoretical point of view, we have, here, a selection, *avant la lettre*, carried out, this time, on the environment. This situation is not at all mysterious—indeed, the standard selection, i.e., the selection made by the environment on the phenotype called crisis, still falls to the human subject (as we shall see below), so, by this *sui generis* selection, the subject the human only anticipates his/her own position that s/he will manifest when s/he makes the "true" selection. Conceptually, it is obvious that filtering is a species of selection, so we will call it *a priori* selection, while the selection performed on the genotype will be called *a posteriori* selection. Of course, the human subject may err in making the *a priori* selection, but this error will be picked up by the next change pressure, or sometimes even corrected by the *a posteriori* selection. From a kinematic point of view, the pair *a priori* selection – *a posteriori* selection (which signifies the introduction of the prominent role of the propensity, i.e., of the model of theoretical rationality) can lead, if the *a priori* selection is performed "correctly", to the reduction of the stabilization time of the crisis, in the sense of reducing the interval in which change pressures continue to occur on the crisis's genotype. From the perspective of (cybernetic) systems theory, the *a priori* selection generated by the crisis's genotype filtering function is a feed-forward—as is known, feed-forward reduces the need or intensity of feedback. *A priori* selection leads to obtaining the secondary list (*SLG*) of genotype changes within the genotype imprinting episode.

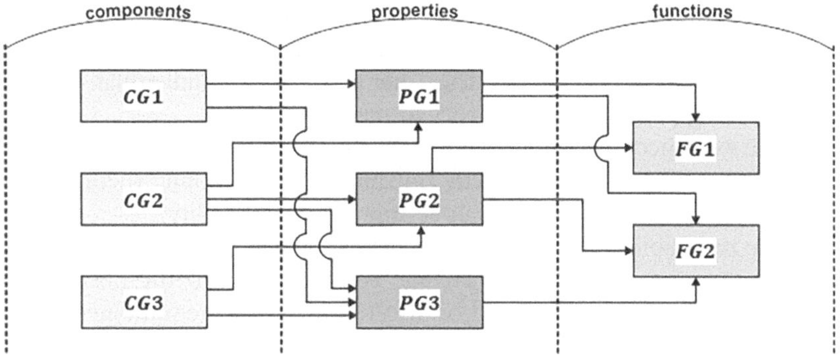

Fig. 10.5 Functioning of the authentic crisis's genotype. *Source*: author

Nota bene: the question arises, namely, why *SLG* formation does not exhaust the phenotype change? In other words, why is there still a need for the transcription and translation (see below) into the phenotype of the changes made in the genotype? The explanation is as follows:

- the modifications contained in *SLG* are modifications accepted by the human subject outside of their factual testing, namely, they are accepted on the basis of one's own propensity or, in a broader sense, on logical grounds; also, here the belief and experience of the human subject in question (in a word, his/her model of rationality) comes into play;
- however, the appropriateness of the changes in question (their "truth") must be a factual judgement. Such a factual judgement can only occur with respect to the phenotype, thus with respect to the empirical functioning of the changes present in *SLG*. The "physiology" of the genuine crisis's genotype is represented in Fig. 10.5.

Discussion

- the logic of the causal generation between the components, properties and functions of the authentic crisis's genotype is as follows: (a) the properties are generated by the components; (b) functions are generated by properties;

- the genuine genotype sensitivity of the crisis is generated, on the one hand, by the propensity (belief, model of theoretical rationality) of the human subject, and on the other hand, by that individual's ideology (e.g., the economic theory in mind);
- the existence of thresholds is guaranteed both by the ideology of the human subject (based exactly on the agreed economic theory) and by its pragmatics, i.e., its model of practical rationality;
- the reversibility of changes in the crisis's genotype (reversibility that occurs after the genotype change is translated into the phenotype configuration) is generated or affected by all the genuine genotype components of the crisis;
- the recording function is generated by the properties of sensitivity and the existence of thresholds: indeed, sensitivity allows the observation of change pressures, while the existence of thresholds allows recording only when the threshold of accumulation of that change pressure is reached;
- the filter function (the one that generates the secondary list (*SLG*) of changes in the genotype) is generated by all three properties of the genuine genotype.

So, based on the above, we can now describe the genuine crisis's genotype as:

(1) the authentic genotype of the crisis consists of the two lists, primary (*PLG*) and secondary (*SLG*), susceptible to being influenced—the first, by pressures to change coming from the environment "endowed" with crisis, the second, by *a priori* selection made by the human subject deciding on the content of the primary list;

(2) it can be considered that a *sui generis* testability (in the sense of Popperian falsifiability) is operating here, which could be described as follows:
   - a third list is drawn up—which we can call the testability control list, abbreviated *TCL*—which contains the elements from the primary list that are not found in the secondary list;
   - in the next cycle of drawing up the primary list, it is checked whether, in the new suggestions that the environment makes regarding the change imposed by the crisis, there appear components that were excluded by applying the filter in the previous cycle (that is, they were excluded as a result of the *a priori*

selection from the previous cycle)—we call these wit the syntagma *recursive components*;
- if such components appear (called recursive), it means that the a priori selection from the previous cycle was, in fact, an adverse selection—the solution is: those components to be selected for the preparation of the secondary list in the current cycle;

(3) regarding the recursive components, methodological measures must, of course, be taken to ensure that it is speaking of the same components that were rejected in the previous cycle, only in this way the procedure approaches or has (roughly) the significance of a falsifiability type of testing—it is as if we would have hypothesized that those rejected components are not relevant and their reappearance would have disproved this hypothesis.

Additional Discussion

The secondary list of crisis's genotype changes contains two categories of information or two components/classes: (a) the class of changes selected *a priori* from the primary list (*PLG*)—let's call it the *class of internalized exogenous changes*; (b) the class of changes proposed autonomously (or, more precisely, endogenously) by the human subject that forms the secondary list of changes (*SLG*)—let's call it the *class of endogenous changes*. The two classes of crisis's genotype changes do not have to exist in the secondary list—only changes from the first class, or only from the second class, or a mix of both classes of changes can occur in that list.

10.5 On the Phenotype of Societal Crisis

10.5.1 Generalities

As is known (here the analogy with the mechanism operating at the level of biological species is justified *omnia in omnibus*) the phenotype is the entity that is subject to selection on the basis of its fitness. We recall that, in the case of symbolic species, the phenotype does not undergo growth processes, but only evolution—forcing the analogy with the biological case, the phenotype of the symbolic species is capable of "reproduction" from the very moment it is "born" (the equivalent of adulthood in the case biological). The phenotype represents, therefore, the version of the entity of interest that faces its environment, in the evolutionary process. In this sense, the phenotype is the very individual of the symbolic species in question, functioning according to the structure conferred upon it. Thus, in a given symbolic species, each spatial, temporal or (sometimes) even functional hypostatization represents an individual of that species, that is, it represents a particularization of the species' phenotype. Do not confuse concretization with particularization: concretization refers to the effective hypostatization of the species—the species, *per se*, does not exist[27] (and this is also valid for the biological species); it is an epistemological[28] abstraction, so the transition from the species to the individual, i.e., in the aforementioned hypostasis, it is done through concretization—while particularization refers, so to speak, to the concretization in time and space (*hic et nunc*), of a given phenotype. Since we are considering the phenotype of the symbolic species, we will that the phenotype of symbolic species represents an actualized version (*Nota bene*: here the term actualization has its Aristotelian meaning) of its possibility. This possibility can subsist from the most different perspectives that can be constituted as artefacts, which allows us to propose the following typology of the phenotype of the symbolic species:

- *Substantial*[29] symbolic phenotype: this phenotype has the "texture" of what you call, typically, a thing (as different from relation or property)—a building, an industrial product;
- *Intellectual* symbolic phenotype: this phenotype has informational "texture", no matter in which way it presents itself and, obviously, regardless of the cultural field to which it belongs: science, religion, mythology, art—all intellectual creations, including intellectual meta-creations, enter this symbolic phenotype category;
- *Social*[30] symbolic phenotype: this phenotype is represented by social constructs, either deliberate or emergent[31]—administrative organization, wars, politics, etc.;[32]
- *Institutional* symbolic phenotype: this phenotype refers to the cases in which it is produced (and reproduced) once its "template" has been elaborated and activated. For example, a property rule will produce the phenotype called property[33] as long as the constitutive conditions for the activation of that rule are met. It should be noted that this feature is not found in any of the symbolic phenotype categories already mentioned.

Comment

Of course, mixed forms of symbolic phenotype are not only not prohibited but, on the contrary, are the majority—for example, a scientific theory (which is an intellectual phenotype) is presented in the form of a written text (a book) which is a substantial phenotype. Considering the fact that there are, in general, three categories of flows: substantial, energetic and informational, the question arises: why is there not (or why can't) a category of energetic symbolic phenotype also be conceived? The answer is the following: the possible symbolic energetic phenotypes necessarily take on the "appearance" of one of the other four categories mentioned. Furthermore, given the concept of entropy—both as thermodynamic entropy, and as social entropy (Dinga et al., 2020)—any of the four symbolic phenotype categories requires low entropy consumption (i.e., available or bound energy) to be created or manifest according to its nature.

10.5.2 *On the Phenotype of the Societal Crisis*

Let us return to the formal mark a generic (societal) crisis: $C_{12345}^{\alpha\beta\gamma\delta\varepsilon}$ (with: α: crises' cause/s; β: crises' origin; γ: crises' chreode (trajectory); δ: crises' impact/s; ε: crises' significance). If we have located the genotype in the parameter ε, now, we think the phenotype of the crisis should be "captured" from the parameter δ—the impact of the crisis. The justification for such a choice consists in:

- the phenotype is the "adult" of a symbolic species, so that it is capable of viable reproduction/replication; indeed, for both observer and actor, the societal crisis is replicating itself at the very level of its impact, i.e., of the objectification of its effects on the society as a whole, even if the cause, origin, chreode or signification are different;
- what is, in fact, directly visible for the observer is just the impact of the societal crisis—not the other four parameter characterizing the generic crisis;
- the most important argument here is, of course, the following: the selection of the mutation/s in the crisis's genotype (after the mutation/s is/are integrated into the phenotype) is operated on the objectified effect of the crisis phenomenology, that is, on the impact.

Consequently, in what follows, the phenotype of the societal crisis will be considered the impact, of course, taking into consideration the five hypostases of the impact. Regarding the type of the impact, we think it is of the mix social-institutional. Although any institutional is social too, the social share of the mentioned mix can differ in different cases, and the same can be said about the institutional share in that mix.

10.6 On the "Map" Genotype—Phenotype of Societal Crisis

By now, we have talked the genotype and phenotype, respectively, in a rather abstract way, that is, by referring the parameters of the formal crisis in which they originate. As each of the two parameters can take five "values", it is of interest to analyse this development from the perspective of identifying the "pairs" genotype—phenotype (noted G_xP_y) there are, theoretically possible. This analysis is organized in Table 10.3.

Discussion

- The forbidden ("cut") combinations between *G* and *P* seem to have too little "viability" from a logical point of view;
- The combinations held have, in turn, a possibility (not probability!) mark which depends from the lower indices; we shall call the hierarchy so instituted: order (hierarchy) of sensibility;
- From Table 10.3, we have the following order of sensibility (in a decreasing order) by combining genotype and phenotype of the societal crisis: (1) G_1P_1; (2) G_1P_2; (3) G_2P_1; (4) G_2P_2; (5) G_3P_2; (6) G_3P_3; (7) G_3P_4; (8) G_4P_3; (9) G_4P_4; (10) G_5P_2; (11) G_5P_3; (12) G_5P_5;
- We could call the five values of genotype and of phenotype, respectively, regions of actualizations (*RA*s), so, we have regions of actualizations for the genotype (RA_x^G), respectively, regions of actualizations for phenotype (RA_x^P)
- This means that, once a mutation occurred in a RA_x^G , only the phenotypes that enters the above list of order of sensibility (i.e., only the RA_x^P) will be affected in its fitness;

Table 10.3 Possibility and viability of the GP combinations

ε (genotype) / *δ (phenotype)*	(T_5^1) *survival*	(T_5^2) *opportunities*	(T_5^3) *way of life*	(T_5^4) *freedom*	$T_5^5)$ *self-esteem*
(T_4^1) *structure*	G_1P_1	G_2P_1	~~G_3P_1~~	~~G_4P_1~~	~~G_5P_1~~
(T_4^2) *rationality model*	G_1P_2	G_2P_2	G_3P_2	~~G_4P_2~~	G_5P_2
(T_4^3) *values matrix*	~~G_1P_3~~	~~G_2P_3~~	G_3P_3	G_4P_3	G_5P_3
(T_4^4) *political regime*	~~G_1P_4~~	~~G_2P_4~~	G_3P_4	G_4P_4	~~G_5P_4~~
(T_4^5) *meta-narrative*	~~G_1P_5~~	~~G_2P_5~~	~~G_3P_5~~	~~G_4P_5~~	G_5P_5

Source: author

- Such a rationality allows a *sui generis* predictability both from genotype to phenotype and from phenotype to genotype;
- Exactly in that presumptive predictability, it is interesting to analyse if a given mutation (i.e., a given ε-region: RA_x^G) could affect more δ-regions: RA_x^P ., and vice-versa. We provide some considerations in this topic:

1. *one* RA_x^G *– more* RA_x^P *s*
    - no matter of the origin of the mutation occurred into the genotype (either the primary list or the secondary list), it is possible that a mutation in a RA_x^G could be objectified in changes in more RA_x^P ;
    - such a possibility is based on a kind of dominance (rather of ontological nature) of some regions of the phenotypes over other regions of the phenotypes;
    - we think such an order of (ontological) dominance is given by :
        - the very "natural" order of $T_4^{(\cdot)}$, is: $T_4^1 \rtimes T_4^2 \rtimes T_4^3 \rtimes T_4^4 \rtimes T_4^5$, so the dominance within the RA_x^P is from left to right;
        - consequently, if a RA_x^G is focused on a RA_x^P, then it is possible (not probable!) to be also focused on the dominated RA_x^P ; for example, if there is s mutation in the RA_4^G (freedom), then it is possible to have an objectifying of it on the RA_3^P (value matrix) but, also, on the RA_4^P (political regime);
        - of course, in the case of more phenotypes affected by the same mutation in the genotype, a certain idiosyncrasy in objectifying the change occurring in the phenotypes must be taken into consideration in one way or another;
2. *one* RA_x^P *– more* RA_x^G *s*
    - this case is "operational" only from the perspective of the primary list of potential mutations (*Nota bene*: as we have seen, some of them could be deleted in the secondary list);
    - again, the possibility (not probability!) that a change pressure to come from the environment (i.e., from the particular phenotype of the societal crisis) and generate mutations in more RA_x^G is governed by the dominance order, this time regarding the RA_x^G, namely: $T_5^1 \rtimes T_5^2 \rtimes T_5^3 \rtimes T_5^4 \rtimes T_5^5$;
    - for example, the RA_1^P (structure) could be influenced both by RA_1^G (survival) and by RA_2^G (opportunities).

Nota bene: the greater number of RA_x^P influenced by a single RA_x^G is three: (a) RA_2^P, RA_3^P and RA_4^P, under the influence of RA_3^G (way of life); (b) RA_2^P, RA_3^P and RA_5^P, under the influence of RA_5^G (self-esteem). Reciprocally, the greater number of RA_x^G influencing a single RA_x^P is four, namely RA_2^P (rationality model), under the influence of: RA_1^G, RA_2^G, RA_3^G and RA_5^G.

Of course, the logic of mutual relationships between RA_x^G and RA_x^P could be brought further by building some chains of (co)evolutive phenomenology.

10.7 Fitness in the Crisis Phenomenology

10.7.1 The Concept of Fitness in the Evolutionary Process

An evolutionary process always has an arrow, called an *evolutionary arrow*. This arrow is represented by fitness. Fitness is understood as such a state of an entity (thing, property, relationship) that is validated by its environment, that is, a sufficient[34] degree of harmonizing between the entity and its environment. A question arises here, namely if fitness is a primitive (primary) concept in the evolutionary process or a derivative (secondary) one. We provide a short reasoning in the matter:

- we can ask two questions here: (i) why does the environment validate that fitness? (ii) how does the environment validate that fitness?

(i) why the validation of fitness is performed?

Any entity sunken into its environment necessarily interacts with it through the well-known flows: substantial, energetic and informational,[35] generally by exchanging entropies. The universal tendency in any interaction is to minimize (at limit, to cancel) the entropic gap between the entity concerned and its environment.[36] To this end, the entity and its environment reciprocally adapt to each other—so, in a (co) evolutionary process, to reduce the entropic gap between them (*Nota bene*: an exception from the principle of the minimum entropic gradient of interaction is the dissipative entity/system, that increases or, at least, do not decreases that entropic gradient).

(ii) How the validation of fitness is performed?

The validation of fitness is made by the entity concerned itself during its functioning within its environment. If fitness does not react with foetal reaction norms to the environment's actions or, equivalently, does not direct foetal action norms to the environment, the harmony between the entity and its environment deteriorates. Consequently, how the fitness is validated by the environment is the calibration of the reaction norm, from both sides: the entity concerned and its environment. We have, especially on a (co)evolutionary process, a mutual fitness validation: the environment validates the fitness of the entity, and, reciprocally, the entity validates the fitness of environment.

- Based on the above-mentioned, it seems that the fitness is not (cannot be) a primitive concept in the (co)evolutionary process—rather such a primitive concept seems to be the minimal entropic gradient in performing any interaction. Such way, the fitness remains, however, the most general effect of the principle of minimal entropic gradient;
- We can say, in other words, that the primitive concept, i.e., the minimal entropic gradient, is, ontologically, at the micro(scopic) level of reality, while the fitness is, ontologically, at the macro(scopic) level of reality.[37]

10.7.2 What Is the Fitness of Symbolic Species

Now, let us find the *eidos* of fitness in the case of symbolic species. As the symbolic species is, definitionally, an artefact, it is designed and implemented in a Lamarckian way, namely, by accommodating the structure to the purpose, where the last is the primary and primordial element established in the artefactual construction. Of course, these allegations are valid for the deliberative instituting of artefacts but, as we have seen before, artefacts can be built also in a non-deliberative way, by the "laws of the market", namely by unintended finalities of the myriad of interactions within the society. No matter the channel through which the symbolic species comes into existence (either deliberative or non-deliberative), its fitness is "hosted" by the phenotype, which is changed by the intermediation of mutations. Consequently, the fitness of symbolic species is exactly the degree in which the mutations in the respective phenotype are in harmony with its general environment. More exactly, it is about the degree to which the new version of phenotype verifies the general framework (i.e., the macro-artefact) of the society functioning: positive norms, ethical rules, traditions, expectations, idiosyncrasies, and others of the same. The concept of harmony, used above, seems, *prima facie*, to be vague enough, so we provide some extra considerations:

- it is a concept much more general than other concepts as concordance, fetality, convergence, non-consistency, etc.;
- it targets, concomitantly, the structural compatibility, and functional performativity;
- it acts not as a state but as a kinematic: more exactly, the harmony is instituted step by step, by improving the previous degree of harmony.

Nota bene: We find here, too, the famous Quine-Duhem thesis in epistemology, according to which a rejection of a prediction (in Popperian factual falsifiability) cannot, principled, reject the hypothesis (or theory) based on which the prediction is the case was formulated. Similarly, the fitness of symbolic species which does not improve harmony with its environment is not rejected,[38] so the next episode of changing the fitness has the chance to improve the harmony in the case. The threshold issue in this matter follows to be examined elsewhere, namely after how many non-improvements of harmony the fitness acquired is rejected? For the moment, we think the non-decreasing of the harmony degree should not lead us to reject the fitness.[39]

10.7.3 What Is the Fitness of Societal Crisis

Starting from the general considerations on the fitness in the case of symbolic species, we can, now, particularize those considerations to the concept of generic societal crisis. As we have seen, the phenotype of the crisis is its impact. So, the mutations that occurred in the authentic genotype of crisis, located in the mind of the human being "responsible" for monitoring and managing the societal crisicity, modified the crisis's chreode and, consequently, modified the crisis's impact, i.e., the phenotype. The new phenotype (that is, the new impact configuration) is verified by the societal environment from the harmonization point of view, and (see below) consequently, the selection process is, in turn, configurated.

10.7.4 Other Mentions on Fitness in the Societal System

In the end of this paragraph, we shall provide some short considerations on the "probabilities" (better said, possibilities) with which the harmony improvement between crisis's phenotype and its environment occurs.

- The difficulty of transcribing and translating the mutation arrived in the genotype of the crisis increases with the transition of the categories of crisis's impact from T_4^1 to T_4^5 (see Table 10.3). So, from the perspective of the human being (regularly, an institution like the Government or Parliament) responsible for societal crises, a mutation required into the structure is easier to design and implement into the crisis's phenotype than a mutation required into the meta-narrative of the society as a whole;
- More realistic, the difficulty to transcribe and translate the mutation into the phenotype follows the order of the (decreasing) sensibility as this concept was introduced at point 10.6, by considering also the signification of the mutation and, correspondingly, of the phenotype change, namely (1) G_1P_1; (2) G_1P_2; (3) G_2P_1; (4) G_2P_2; (5) G_3P_2; (6) G_3P_3; (7) G_3P_4; (8) G_4P_3; (9) G_4P_4; (10) G_5P_2; (11) G_5P_3; (12) G_5P_5;
- Some "equilibria" between the 12 cases of sensibility, respectively, difficulty of transferring the mutation into the phenotype could be examined, especially for the "symmetries" of lower indices, namely the pairs: G_1P_2 vs. G_2P_1, and G_3P_4 vs. G_4P_3.

10.8 Selection in Societal Crises Co-evolution

10.8.1 What Is the Selection?

First of all, it must be established some "technicalities" in the selection process. There are, in some papers, confusions or, at least, ambiguities regarding the object of selection: in fact, what exactly is selected by the (environmental) selector, the mutation or the fitness reached by the phenotype by integrating that mutation?

In our opinion, for the selector,[40] is "visible" only the fitness (*Nota bene*: in the case of societal generic crisis, the fitness was called above harmony degree with the… selector), not the mutation as such. Consequently, we can discuss the issue of multi-determination of the fitness, namely of a multi-causality in generating a given fitness/harmony degree:

- a mutation (a cause) that has occurred in the (authentic) genotype of crisis, "announces" a change in the phenotype (i.e., in the impact) of that crisis—of course, that mutation must be objectified in the phenotype concerned (for example, through a normative dedicated change);
- the change implemented into the phenotype is expected to increase the harmony degree of the crisis's impact with the general (global) environment inside which the crisis concerned acts;
- but (see Chap. 9) a role can be determined by different functions or, more generally, by different sets of functions, likewise how a function can be determined by different hard-core structures or, more generally, by different sets of hard-core structures configured in one way or another. Consequently, following the general principle here evoked, a change in crisis's impact can be caused by different mutations or, more generally, by different combinations of mutations;
- so, the selector (for example, the environment inside which the crisis unfolds) is not "interested" in the mutation (or set of mutations) that occurred inside the genotype but only by the very effect of it (or them) on the presumed impact of the crisis in the case;
- the crisis's impact modification, i.e., the crisis's fitness changing is the only object of the selection act performed by the crisis's environment—somewhat, the new fitness forgets its cause and appears before the selector as an autonomous fact or state of the world.

So, the selection is simply a validation of the harmony degree between the entity selected and the entity selector (the environment of the entity selected). As said before, any evolution is a co-evolution. Even in the most generical case, i.e., in which the environment (the selector) is considered, conceptually, as the second species that faces the first one (the selected species), we still have a co-evolution. Especially in the case of symbolic species, it seems the co-evolution has not only a conceptual background but, also, an ontological one.

- A symbolic species, as artefact, does not appear by itself, but it is designed and implemented by the action of the subject (human being);
- Being an artefact, a symbolic species has two operational properties:
  - is, from the beginning, designed so that to harmonize with its future environment;

- the environment itself is prepared, before designing the symbolic species, to ensure (at the limit, to maximize) its harmony with the future symbolic species to come. Nota bene: in extreme cases, the needed harmonizable environment is, simply, designed, in turn, as required by the intentioned symbolic species;

- So, the limit case in the matter of symbolic species is that in which both the intentioned symbolic species and its environment are concomitantly designed and implemented in the societal structure.[41]

10.8.2 Selection Mechanism in the Societal Crisis Phenomenology

The mutation regarding the crisis's phenotype (i.e., the crisis's impact) occurs in the (authentic) genotype hosted by the human being, as either an actor in the crisis's environment or regulator for societal crises. More precisely, as shown before, the genotype elaborates on three lists of mutations before transcribing and translating them. Based on the third list of mutations, the human being involved as a "host" of the crisis's genotype proceeds to the transcription of mutations. This operation consists in actualizing his/her models of rationality (both theoretical and practical), i.e., in preparing the institutional, legal (and, if needed, of legitimacy) conditions so that the mutations selected to be translated into norms that will modify the behaviour[42] towards reducing or annihilating the negative components of crisis's impact. Here happens a significant difference compared with the case of biological species, namely the following: the translation of mutation must not wait for the phenotype that has integrated the mutation to replicate and, then, the new fitness be selected (or rejected, after the case), since the mutation is introduced in the current phenotype (that is, regarding the same generation of crises) and the new phenotype's fitness is selected (or not) on the go, so to say.

Figure 10.6 shows the stylized way in which the mechanism of selection works in the case of societal generic crisis.

10.8.3 Emphasizing on Co-evolution in Crisis Phenomenology

(a) Preliminaries

As suggested above, in the case of symbolic species, regularly, the species and its environment are designed and implemented concomitantly.

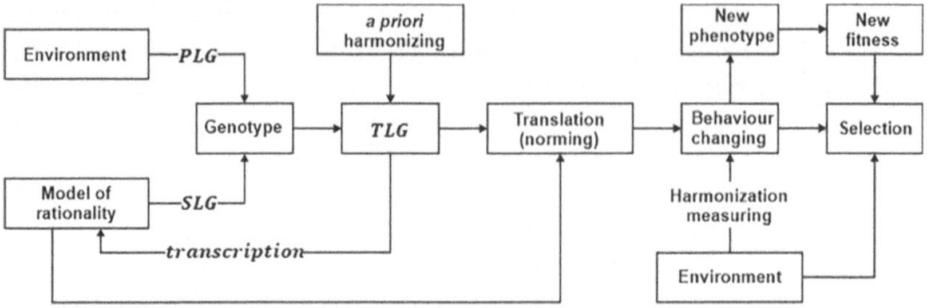

Fig. 10.6 Selection mechanism in societal crisis phenomenology. *Source*: author

The reason is that, in an overwhelming proportion,[43] the environment of any symbolic species is a symbolic species, too. Consequently, the harmonization between the symbolic species and its environment is, somewhat, anticipated, based on the model of rationality for both the symbolic species and its environment. Such a state of affairs leads to the conclusion that still from the beginning, the symbolic species and its environment are designed as co-evolutive species.

(b) Co-evolution in the Societal Crisis Phenomenology

(b1) Crisis's Environment Phenotype

First of all, we must mention that both the genotype of crisis and the crisis's environment are hosted by the same human individual (either as a physical person or as an organization/institution). The question is, which is the phenotype of the crisis's environment, knowing that the crisis's phenotype is the crisis's impact? Regarding the phenotype of the crisis's environment, we provide the following considerations:

- the sought phenotype must have the capability, of one kind or another, to recognize the crisis's phenotype. As the crisis's phenotype is the crisis's impact, it results that the environment's phenotype must be capable of recognizing the crisis's impact. *Nota bene*: we note for what follows: CP – crisis's phenotype, i.e., crisis's impact; CEP – crisis's environment phenotype;
- since the CF is recognized in the process of social activity (behaviour) and that behaviour is ruled trough the normative framework of the society (societal system), it seems to us that exactly the normative framework should be the very phenotype of the crisis's environment (CEP);

- as the CP (i.e., the crisis's impact) affects the general behaviour, which is ruled through the general normative framework, it results that not only the part of normative framework addressing the topic of societal crises must constitute CEP but the entire normative framework in force at the moment of interest.

In the hypothesis that the entire normative framework[44] of the society constitutes CEP, it is useful to examine the fundamental hypostases in which that normative framework (NF) is concretized in the vivid life of the society. Our opinion is that there are five such hypostases, as follows:

(i) (*I*) *institutive* norms: norms aimed at designing and implementing institutions required by the desired functioning of the society;
(ii) (*R*) *regulative* norms: norms aimed at establishing the rules (positive law) according to which the institutive norms must work;
(iii) (*E*) *evaluative* norms: norms aimed at assessing, either permanently or in critical situations (*Nota bene*: for example when a societal crisis occurs), the adequacy and efficacy of institutive norms functioning;
(iv) (*C*) *corrective* norms: norms aimed at adjusting, inside the basic regulative norms, the institutive norms so that some anomalies are removed;
(v) (*P*) *predictive* norms: norms aimed at formulating anticipations (not expectations!) regarding the adequacy and/or efficacy of institutive norms working.

(b2) Dendrites

Starting from the basic hypostases of the two phenotypes—of crisis and of crisis's environment, respectively—we can introduce the concept of dendrites to describe the concrete way in which the two phenotypes interact and reciprocally select themselves.

- <u>CP dendrites:</u> we choose only the first (in the order of sensibility, as established in Table 10.3) pair GP (impact – signification),[45] so we have five dendrites emanated by the phenotype of the societal crisis: (1) G_1P_1; (2) G_1P_2; (3) G_3P_3; (4) G_3P_4; (5) G_5P_5;
- <u>CEP dendrites</u> – (1) (*I*); (2) (*R*); (3) (*E*) ; (4) (*C*) ; (5) (*P*).

The two symbolic species enter a co-evolutionary process that has as essence the reciprocal selection at the level of the phenotype, namely the selector (environment) of CP is CEP and, symmetrically, the selector (environment) of CEP is CP.

We advance the conjecture that the selection, i.e., the verification of the fitness to be of a sufficient (acceptable) degree of harmony with the corresponding environment taking place at the level of dendrites. Somewhat, the dendrites examine reciprocally and decide on the selection in the case. We develop some details of such a mechanism of selection in a process of co-evolution.

(b3) A (Stylized) Mechanism of Dendritically Co-selection in Crisis Phenomenology

We shall examine now the above-advanced conjecture according to which the "crisis–normative framework" pair of symbolic species co-evolves. Table 10.4 indicates the cases in which the dendritical interactions are or are not performative (with *F* are noted the foetal interactions, and with *N* are noted lack of interactions).

Discussion

- About half of the possible dendritic connections between the two phenotypes (crisis and normative framework, respectively) are not working;
- The most dendritic foetal connections from the normative framework part are gathered by the institutive hypostasis of the normative framework (4 connections), followed by evaluative hypostasis (three connections), and the others (2 connections each);
- The most dendritic foetal connections from the crisis part are collected (3 connections each) by G_1P_1—impact of crisis on structure with survival signification, G_3P_4—impact of crisis on political regime with way of life signification, and G_5P_5—impact of crisis on meta-narrative with self-esteem signification, followed by the others (with 2 connections each).

The dendritic connections in Table 10.4 could be used to build up a graph (network) of relationships between the two phenotypes aimed at analytically examining the co-evolution of the pair "crisis–normative

Table 10.4 Viable or non-viable dendritic interactions between phenotypes

	I	*R*	*E*	*C*	*P*
G_1P_1	*F*	N	N	*F*	*F*
G_1P_2	N	*F*	*F*	N	N
G_3P_3	*F*	N	*F*	N	N
G_3P_4	*F*	*F*	N	*F*	N
G_5P_5	*F*	N	*F*	N	*F*

Source: author

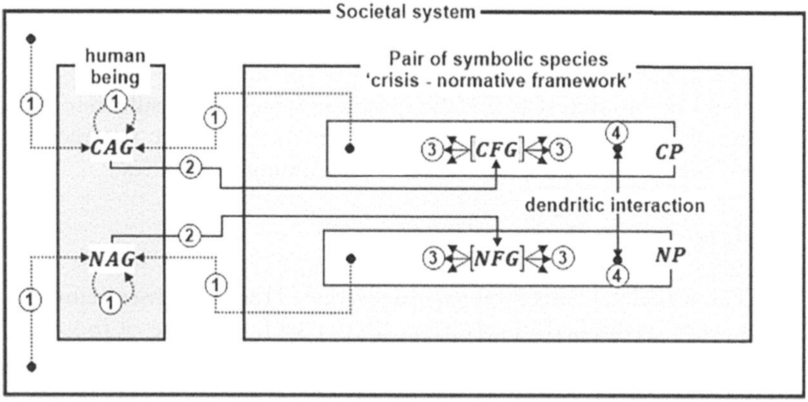

Fig. 10.7 The "physiology" of the dendritic co-evolution of pair "crisis – normative framework". *Source*: author

framework" of symbolic species, including, where is possible, quantitative indicators calculation (e.g., regarding the intensities or durations of those dendritic interactions). Nota bene: the phenotypical hypostases will be the nodes of the graph (network), and the connections between them will be the arcs. We leave to the curiosity and interest of the reader to develop in this direction our stylized considerations above.

Based on the above, we can now describe the abstract mechanism of co-evolution of the pair of symbolic species "crisis–normative framework" (Fig. 10.7). The notations are *CAG*—crisis's authentic genotype; *CFG*—crisis's false genotype; *NAG*—normative framework's authentic genotype; *NFG*—normative framework's false genotype; *CP*—crisis's phenotype; *NP*—normative framework's phenotype.

Discussion

1. Expresses forming of the three lists of mutations that press on the authentic genotype hosted by the human being;
2. The mutations in the third list are transcript into the false (inauthentic) genotypes hosted by the phenotypes;
3. The transcriptions of mutations are translated into the normative framework;
4. The dendritic interactions between the two phenotypes (i.e., the coevolution processes) begin

(b4) About the Dendritic Phenomenology

It could be of interest to ask the question: which is the substrate (i.e., ontological background) based on which the dendritic interactions between the two phenotypes arise? Our positioning is as follows:

- *Regarding the Dendritic Unfolding*

A generic societal crisis exhibits, usually, one of the five classes of impact, as they were established in this paper. Better said, only one of those five classes of impact is both visible and registered as such (through the effects that the impact throws on the societal system). Some issues should (even if shortly enough) be discussed in this matter: (i) Is there a reason according to which a certain class of impact is more probable than other/s? (ii) Once a class of impact[46] comes into existence, is it possible (and how) that it generates other classes of impact (that is, other dendrites)? (iii) Is there a "theory" of unfolding the dendrites based on which a societal generic crisis objectifies itself?

(i) The Reason

The question is reducible to the following one: can we (at least, approximately) predict the class of crisis's impact, by knowing the values (the concrete individuals) of the other four parameters of a generic societal crisis? Let us resume the general formula of a crisis: $C_{12345}^{\alpha\beta\gamma\delta\varepsilon}$ (where the meaning of the parameters is: α: crises' cause/s; β: crises' origin; γ: crises' chreode (trajectory); δ: crises' impact/s; ε: crises' significance). If Chap. 5 examined the affinity in the case of overlapping crises, now the concept of affinity will be applied to a singular crisis to find some internal causal determination between the parameters α, β, γ and ε, on the one part, and the parameter δ on the other part. To this end, we try to form some ***inside causality chains*** for the impact of a singular crisis. *Nota bene*: of course, this result can be used then in the case of overlapping crises to "predict" the aggregated impact of the set of overlapped crises by combining the inside causality chains for each crisis in that set. Let us resume a part from Table 5.2 of Chap. 5, namely Table 10.5.

Table 10.5 Inside causality chains in a singular crisis

		δ - impact				
		1. on structure	*2. on rationality*	*3. on value*	*4. on political regime*	*5. on meta-narrative*
α - cause	1. by insularization	0	2	2	3	1
	2. by friction	2	1	1	2	1
	3. by insemination	0	0	0	2	2
	4. by exhaustion	4	2	3	3	2
	5. by futurization	0	0	4	4	3
β - origin	1. theoretical	0	5	0	0	4
	2. praxeological	3	4	0	0	3
	3. practical	2	3	5	4	3
	4. political	3	0	0	5	2
	5. natural	0	2	2	0	0
γ - chreode	1. self-extinguishing	0	3	2	4	3
	2. self-maintaining	1	0	0	0	3
	3. trans-field	2	2	0	0	3
	4. migratory	0	2	3	2	3
	5. synergic	3	2	0	3	4
ε - significance	1. to survival	3	3	0	1	0
	2. to opportunities	3	3	0	2	0
	3. to way of life	0	3	3	0	2
	4. to freedom	4	0	4	5	3
	5. to self-esteem	0	0	5	0	3

Source: author

Discussion

- we use the numerical values of compatibility as they were established in Chap. 5. More exactly, we combine the highest compatibility numbers of all the four parameters vs. δ-parameter;
- the "nodes" of the possible inside causality chains are the following nine ones: $\alpha_4\delta_1$; $\alpha_5\delta_3$; $\alpha_5\delta_4$; $\beta_4\delta_2$; $\beta_3\delta_3$; $\gamma_1\delta_4$; $\gamma_5\delta_5$; $\varepsilon_4\delta_4$; $\varepsilon_4\delta_3$;
- the order based on the logical formula of a generic societal crisis ($C_{51423}^{\varepsilon\alpha\delta\beta\gamma}$) is the following: $\varepsilon_4\delta_4$; $\varepsilon_4\delta_3$; $\alpha_5\delta_4$; $\alpha_5\delta_3$; $\alpha_4\delta_1$; $\beta_4\delta_2$; $\beta_3\delta_3$; $\gamma_5\delta_5$; $\gamma_1\delta_4$;
- a crisis triggered by the parameter ε, namely ε_4 (i.e., having the signification of freedom), will generate the impact δ_4 (i.e., on the political regime of the society) but, the same parameter ε_4 will generate also the impact δ_3 (i.e., on the values). So, we can say that we have *two impact-dendrites*—δ_4 and δ_3—under the signification of crisis;
- a crisis triggered by the parameter α (i.e., referring the cause of crisis): α_5 (i.e., cause based on a vision on the future) will generate the impact δ_4 (i.e., on the political regime of the society), but the same parameter α_5 will generate also the impact δ_3 (i.e., on the values), and α_4 (i.e., having as cause exhaustion) will generate the impact δ_3 (i.e., on the values). So, we can say that we have *three*[A7] *impact-dendrites*—δ_4 and δ_3—under the causation of crisis;
- a crisis triggered by the parameter β (i.e. referring the origin of crisis): β_4 (i.e., a political origin of crisis) will generate the impact δ_2 (i.e., on the rationality model of the society), and β_3 (i.e., a practical origin of crisis) will generate the impact δ_3 (i.e., on the values). So, we can say that we have *two impact-dendrites*—δ_4 and δ_3—under the origin of crisis;
- a crisis triggered by the parameter γ (i.e., referring to crisis's chreode): γ_5 (i.e., a self-esteem chreode) will generate the impact δ_5 (i.e., on meta-narrative of the society), and γ_1 (i.e., a self-extinguishing chreode) will generate the impact δ_4 (i.e., on political regime). So, we can say that we have *two impact-dendrites*—δ_5 and δ_4—under the chreode of crisis.

(ii) The General Causality

The dendrites are generated by the own causality of the crisis, better said, by the master-dendrite—i.e., the dendrite that dominates the general impact of the crisis concerned. This means that, as related to a given crisis, we have a *causa sui*, i.e., an inherent unfolding of a set of dendrites inside the δ parameter of crisis, without any external determination or conditioning.

(iii) The "theory"

Based on the *causa sui* paradigm of generating the dendrites of the crisis impact, we should formulate a "theory" that grounds such a generation. For the moment we shall appeal to the general suggestion of the *constructal law* (Bejan, 2007). This proposal generally claims the following: an entity, either natural or cultural (i.e., artefact), unfolds in those directions and in those forms (dimensional, spatial, temporal), including dendrites, that satisfy a maximization criterion assigned to that entity—*Nota bene*: the original proposal also suggested such a criterion: the needed flows (e.g., aimed at surviving). Starting from this point, we shall develop our proposal for a theoretical ground of generating the impact dendrites in a societal generic crisis phenomenology (we would name such a "theory": the *saturation principle* or *the saturation law*): *SL*.

- some generalities
  - the saturation principle/law addresses exactly the criterion according to which the dendrites arise—this criterion replaces that proposed by the original constructal law abovementioned;
  - the saturation principle/law requires that a crisis, once initiated, seek to exhaust all internal (see *causa sui*) possibilities to impact society;
  - the saturation principle/law is guided by a minimization[48] criterion (by contrast with the maximization one in the original constructal law), namely: the dendrite that accompanies the master-dendrite is always one (or ones) that are placed in the greatest proximity, from the sensibility point of view—as this concept was developed in the present paper—of the master-dendrite; if more than one dendrite is causally entitled, than the third such dendrite verify the next minimum greatest proximity of the mater-dendrite, and so on;
- the content/working
  - the dendrites of a given societal crisis arise in the number and category that the logical formula of that crisis allows, so it is

not needed for a stopping criterion (by the way, a maximum of five dendrites can be unfolded, in the theoretical framework of the present study);

the advantage (for the human being—generally, a governmental institution—"responsible" for managing the societal crisis) of this working of the dendrites unfolding constitutes both a predictor and a suggestion for state intervention measures/actions (either acts or abstentions) in preventing, counter-acting, and, in some lucky cases, antifragilizing those crisis's impacts.

- *Regarding the Connection Choice and Working*

  i. The Reason

As shown before, the co-evolution of the pair "crisis–normative framework" implies the connections between the dendrites of the two symbolic species in the case. The explanation (reason) for this proposal of interactions consists in the following:

- the mutual selection cannot be done than at the level of phenotype—the two phenotypes in co-evolution are exactly the crisis's impact, on the one hand, and the norms liable to regulate the crisis's impact, on the other hand;
- the signals that come from the environment to the authentic genotype (hosted by the human being) to generate the corresponding mutations come, in fact, for each genotype from the phenotype of the other symbolic species, so that, there is a mutual roads from a phenotype's signal to the paired genotype of the other phenotype;
- all the above implies the direct and permanent contact between the two phenotypes' dendrites;
- this is a general choice, namely the choice according to which the phenotypes' dendrites of the two symbolic species must be connected and must stay permanently in connection;

  ii. The General Causality

The causality that conducts the inter-dendrites connections is an internal one, too, with the difference that the "insideness" is, this time, related to the pair of the two symbolic species, not only to each separated species. So, we have here, too, a *causa sui*, but viewed at the level of the set of the two symbolic species.

iii. The "theory"
   - some generalities
   - like the case of dendritic unfolding, where was functioning the principle/law of saturation, we need too a principle/law in the case of the inter-dendritic connection choice; we propose such a principle/law called: the *minimum entropic gradient* (see Chap. 7): *MEG*;
   - consequently, the crisis's dendrite will connect itself with the normative framework's dendrite with which has the minimum entropic gradient;
   - here, by the minimum entropic gradient is understood the minimum adjustment needed in the norm in the case to translate the described mutation in the respective genotype;
   - the principle of the minimum entropic gradient between the two dendrites connected—one from the crisis's impact, and the other from the normative framework—is a kind of (universal) principle of minimization applied in the field of artefacts, more precisely, in the field of symbolic species;
   - the content/working
   - by the inter-dendritic connection, an informational exchange (of course, intermediate by a human being) takes place between the two phenotypes, in trying to reciprocally adapt one to other;
   - this trying, somewhat (in principle, based on a procedure) the entropic gradients between the crisis's dendrites and the normative framework's dendrites are calculated and ordered, so establishing the minimum values of the entropic gradients that choose, then, the dendritic connections between the dendrites of the two symbolic species.

A (pure) illustrative picture (Fig. 10.8) suggests the way in which the dendritic interaction takes place in the logical model of co-evolution in the pair "crisis–normative framework".

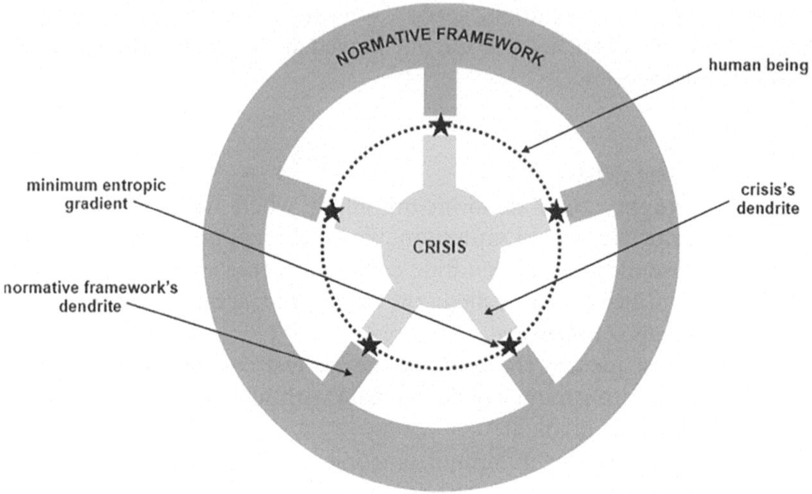

Fig. 10.8 The dendritic interaction in the pair "crisis–normative framework". *Source*: author

Notes

1. We remember, for instance, that the free will is defined as the (possible) opposition to or negation of the social rules, not of the natural rules.
2. We do not resume the features of the symbolic species, since they have been exposed previously—however, at point 10.2, these features will be particularized related to the (societal) crisis.
3. Of course, it does not obey stochasticity, since this property contains a certain "determinism", the so-called statistical determinism, which is, logically, a dynamical determinism of the ... average of the population concerned.
4. Here a problem arises: what means *necessary cause* in the context of social necessity? In fact, we must discern between the cause of the natural necessity (*NNC*) and the cause of the social necessity (*SNC*). We shall say that *NNC* is inherent, i.e., inevitable, while *SNC* is optional. In the context of *SN*, the necessity can be avoided, through free will (of course by paying the corresponding price—the sanction stipulated by the norm that has instituted the *SN* in the case), while, in the context of the *NN* the sanction is, usually, the survival losing.
5. Discretionarily does not mean arbitrarily but explicitly and (most often) formally. Likewise, being discretionary means being conscious, explicit and (most often) formal in decision-taking or acting.

6. Probably, three perspectives are the most relevant in this matter: (a) the *historical laws*—for example, the Marxian historical materialism; (b) the *structuralism*—for example, the initial one in France; (c) the serial succession—for example, Xenopol or Conta.
7. We remember that the qualifier *practical* addresses the relationships subject-subject.
8. Reproductive isolation refers to the fact that the individuals in question can only reproduce in a viable way (i.e., provided that the offspring can, in turn, reproduce) only among themselves (*Nota bene*: the most "popular" case is that of the mule—mating between a horse and a donkey—the mule cannot have viable biological offspring).
9. Syntopic species: species that occupy the same physical area; synchronous species: species that occupy the same time "area".
10. Here only a general characterization is given, and later, namely, in connection with the crisis individual and species, particular considerations will be developed.
11. If, after the first geographical separation, there is still the possibility that the two species resulting from allopatric speciation have areas of contact (including for reproductive relations) then we speak of *parapatric speciation*, i.e., species resulting from sibling hybridization (Brener's, Encyclopedia of Genetics—Second edition, 2013, pp. 222–224), (Maloy & Huges, 2013).
12. There is, as is well known, saltationist (or catastrophic) selection, as opposed to cumulative/gradual selection (Gould & Eldredge, 1977).
13. The fitness of a species (or, sometimes, individuals of that species) means the degree of functional adaptation of the species (or individuals) to its/their environment.
14. A representation is a perception that does not need the presence *in actu* of the perceived object.
15. See our concept of propensity, formed on the basis of the concepts of propensity (an analog of belief, usually a-rational), respectively of preference (Dinga et al., 2022).
16. By objectification we mean a non-problematic agreement of an intersubjective nature. It is easy to see that the three categories of artefacts overlap Popper's three worlds in exactly the order presented.
17. There are author who consider the discipline/theory of economics to be a discipline/theory of the type of biology (as can be said of any other social discipline/theory)—see, in this sense, Alex Rosenberg, in Chap. 3 (Is economics a science, what kind of science is it?) from *The Oxford Handbook of Philosophy of Economics* (editors: Harold Kincaid and Don Ross), Oxford University Press, 2009. Moreover, the current stream of evolutionary economics borrows, by adaptation, many of the evolutionary mechanisms known in the case of biology.

18. This is a crucial difference from the biological case, where a species cannot contain a single individual but at least two individuals, namely a male and a female, to ensure the replication/reproduction within that species.
19. By symbolic mutation we simply mean the mutation that occurs within a symbolic species, so we go beyond the purely semiotic meaning of the expression in question.
20. We ignore, as not relevant, the cases in which, lately, in the biological world, clones at the individual level are introduced, even if experimentally.
21. Here arises the problem of Lebniz: how to discern among identicals? The answer is: through the space-time locality of the identicals.
22. Either contingent or necessary (e.g., economics as a social activity is a necessary artefact—given the dissipative system nature of the human subject and consequently of society as a system).
23. Probably, the fact that language is the tool for the symbolic vocation of the brain led the author to consider the two entities as symbolic species.
24. We remind the readers that significance is very different from meaning.
25. Do not forget that, in the case of symbolic species, the genotype inside the phenotype is always an inauthentic one (the authentic genotype is located into the human being involved).
26. The existence of an equality of impact between changing the tax rate in one direction and changing it in the opposite direction is not strict from a theoretical point of view—it is important that reversibility in the variation of the tax rate is allowed.
27. Here we meet the issue of the "battle" of universals, or, from another perspective, the relationship between nominalism and realism—more precisely, that the general does not exist as such but only by its particularisations (individuals).
28. Just as, for example, number does not exist per se, but exclusively in the form of concrete numbers: 2; 3.14, etc.
29. The term substantial has a meaning of its own, here (as opposed to its common/"civilian" meaning), namely that it refers to those phenotypes that take the perceptible form of substance, in its physical sense.
30. That take the perceptible form of substance, in its physical sense. We draw attention to the possibility (justified, from the semantic point of view) to consider that this type (this category) of symbolic phenotype is redundant (so superfluous) since any symbolic phenotype is obtained and obtainable exclusively in a social setting (cases of individualism such as Robinson Crusoe are not relevant here). Although this observation is correct, we propose to accept this distinct category, of social phenotype, from the perspective that the impact of such phenotypes is so extensive and profound that it affects the entire society, even over several generations.

31. An emergent phenomenon is that phenomenon that is not the result of a plan/goal of an individual or a collective (including the whole society). An example from economics is the so-called invisible hand (a concept proposed, although not named as such, by Adam Smith in The Theory of Moral Sentiments): microeconomic equilibrium occurs without anyone watching or intending it.
32. It should be noted that the very concept of symbol (as, for that matter, the entire semiotic theory) is a symbolic phenotype. We make this observation precisely to draw attention to the fact that the expression "symbolic phenotype" has nothing to do with the symbolic character (in the semiotic sense) of that phenotype.
33. Here the term property has its economic/legal meaning, not the logical one.
34. By the qualifier *sufficient* is understood something rather empirical (contextual) than theoretical. From a logical point of view, fitness is a way through which can be operated the falsifiability in Popper's sense.
35. The term *informational* is to some extent, anthropomorphised here, since there are entities that are not endowed with awareness, consequently, do not perceive information but only data or signals.
36. Here we find again our principle of minimal entropic gradient of any interaction.
37. Approximately, in the same sense in which the molecules' speed in a gas is the microscopic sub-strate of the temperature, while temperature is the macroscopic supra-strate of the molecules' speed.
38. But, of course, it is rejected if the degree of harmony decreases.
39. Here, by contrast with Popper's epistemological positioning, we think that each non-improving (and non-dis-improving) of the harmony degree between the new fitness and the environment of the phenotype increases the probability that the next "test" records an improving of that harmony degree. Of course, here is "room" for developing some probabilistic considerations, including matrices of transition probabilities, etc.
40. This allegation is valid not only for the societal crisis (or for symbolic species) but also for all evolutionary selection processes in Nature and society. *Nota bene*: there are, of course, selection processes that are non-evolutionary—for example, decision theory but we address here the evolutionary selection processes only.
41. Obviously, such a possibility is ensured by the normative framework. In some cases (for example, if it is about political symbolic species), the population is prepared to accept the future symbolic species—this preparation has the sense of creating the environment for that future symbolic species.
42. As shown before, the crisis is an artefact, so it is generated (and, symmetrically, is managed) by the very behaviour of individuals. Consequently, to

modify the symbolic phenotype it is required (and, generally sufficient) to adequately modify that behaviour only.

43. In a small proportion, however, some non-artefactual environment's components subsist for any symbolic species coming into existence.
44. The normative framework, in its general and abstract understanding, constitutes what is called, in social theory (especially, in the social justice theory) the basic structure of society. *Nota bene*: the "headquarter" of the basic structure of society is the Constitution.
45. The reason for which we do not consider simply the five categories of impact is already known by the reader: the impact is a "true" impact on the individual (either actor or observer) only if it is "coloured" by its signification.
46. It must be well understood that, factually, not a class of impact becomes visible but a concrete individual of that class—do not forget that neither genus nor species have concrete existence but only their hypostatization *hic et nunc*.
47. Here we have an interesting phenomenon, namely two different categories of the parameter α (α_5 and α_4,) generate the same impact δ_3.
48. It is interesting to observe that, generally, Nature rather minimizes than maximizes, while Culture (i.e., the society or societal system) rather maximizes than minimizes—see, here, the capitalist ideology and social system functioning.

References

Bejan, A. (2007). *Constructal Theory of Social Dynamics*. Springer.
Berger, P. L., & Luckmann, T. (2008). *Construirea socială a realității*. Editura Art.
Deacon, T. (2007). *The Symbolic Species: The Co-evolution of Language and the Brain*. W. W. Norton & Company.
Dinga, E., Oprean-Stan, C., Tănăsescu, R.-C., Brătian, V., & Ionescu, G.-M. (2020). Social Entropy and Normative Framework. *Entropy, 22*(9). https://doi.org/10.3390/e22091051
Dinga, E., Oprean-Stan, C., Tănăsescu, R.-C., Brătian, V., & Ionescu, G.-M. (2022). *Financial Market Analysis and Behaviour. The Adaptive Preference Hypothesis*. Routledge – Group Taylor & Francis.
Dinga, E., Oprean-Stan, C., Tănăsescu, R.-C., Brătian, V., & Ionescu, G.-M. (2023). *Co-Evolution of Symbolic Species in the Financial Market – A Framework for Economic and Political Decision-Making*. Palgrave Macmillan – Springer.
Dosse, F. (1997). *History of Structuralism* (Vol. 1). University of Minnesota Press.
Gould, S. J., & Eldredge, N. (1977). Punctuated Equilibria: The Tempo and Mode of Evolution Reconsidered. *Paleobiology, 3*(2), 115–151.

Kratochwil, A., & Schwabe, A. (2002). Evolution, Coevolution, and Biodiversity. In E. Box & S. Pignatti (Eds.), *Frontiers of Life, Vol. Four: The Living World-Discovery and Spoliation of the Biosphere (Part Two)* (Vol. IV, 1st ed., p. 806). Academic Press.

Lohmar, D. (2012). Language and Non-linguistic Thinking. In D. Zahavi (Ed.), *The Oxford Handbook of Contemporary Phenomenology*. Oxford University Press.

Maas, H. (2014). *Economic Methodology. A Historical Introduction*. Routledge, Taylor & Francis Group.

Maloy, S., & Huges, K. (Eds.). (2013). *Brenner's Encyclopedia of Genetics*. Academic Press.

Nelson, R. R., & Winter, S. G. (1982). *An Evolutionary Theory of Economie Change*. Belknap Press of Harvard University Press.

Schmid, H. B. (2012). Sharing the Truth: Phenomenology of Epistemic Commonality. In D. Zahavi (Ed.), *The Oxford Handbook of Contemporary Phenomenology*. Oxford University Press.

Spencer-Brown, G. (1972). *Laws of Form*. The Julian Press.

Index[1]

[1] Note: Page numbers followed by 'n' refer to notes.

E. Dinga, *Economic Resilience During Overlapped Crises*,
https://doi.org/10.1007/978-3-031-80224-9

D

E

P

Q

R

S

The manufacturer's authorised representative in the EU is Springer Nature Customer Service Centre GmbH, Europaplatz 3, 69115 Heidelberg, Germany. If you have any concerns regarding our products, please contact ProductSafety@springernature.com

Printed and bound by CPI Group (UK) Ltd, Croydon, CR0 4YY

01/10/2026

02225954-0011